Mediascape

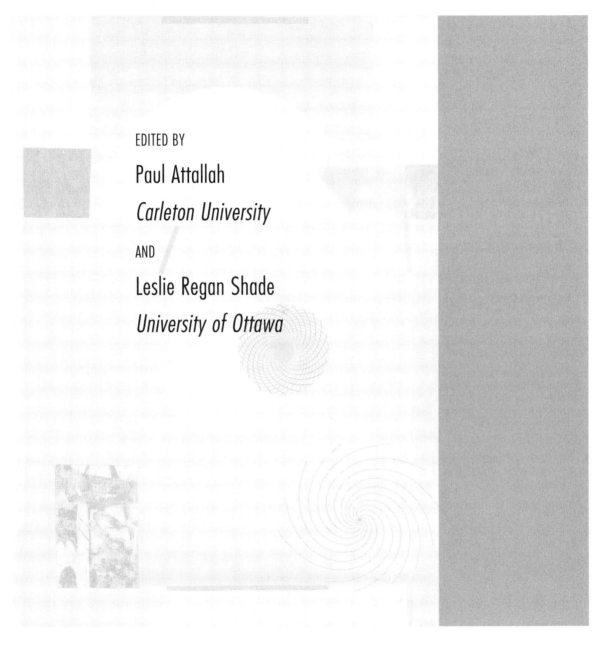

Mediascapes
New Patterns in Canadian Communication

EDITED BY

Paul Attallah

Carleton University

AND

Leslie Regan Shade

University of Ottawa

THOMSON

NELSON

Australia   Canada   Mexico   Singapore   Spain   United Kingdom   United States

THOMSON
★
NELSON

Mediascapes: New Patterns in
Canadian Communication

Edited by Paul Attallah and
Leslie Regan Shade

Editorial Director and Publisher:
Evelyn Veitch

Acquisitions Editor:
Anne Williams

Marketing Manager:
Murray Moman

Developmental Editor:
Joanne Sutherland

Production Editor:
Bob Kohlmeier

Production Coordinator:
Helen Jager Locsin

Copy Editor:
Sarah Robertson

Creative Director:
Angela Cluer

Proofreader:
Gilda Mekler

Interior Design:
Katherine Strain

Cover Design:
Katherine Strain

Cover Image:
Detail: *Elemental-al* series, by
Judith Welbourn

Compositor:
Brenda Prangley

Indexer:
Dennis Mills

Printer:
Transcontinental Printing Inc.

**National Library of Canada
Cataloguing in Publication Data**

Main entry under title:

Mediascapes : new patterns in
Canadian communication

Includes bibliographical references
and index.
ISBN 0-17-604203-2

1. Mass media—Canada. 2. Mass
media—Study and teaching
(Higher)—Canada. 3. Mass media
policy—Canada. I. Attallah, Paul
1954– II. Shade, Leslie Regan,
1957–

P92.C3M46 2002   302.23'0971
C2001-903232-3

C O N T E N T S

Preface
Paul Attallah and Leslie Regan Shade   vii

Part I: The Institutional Context

Introduction   1
Paul Attallah

1 Considering Critical Communication Studies in Canada   4
Sheryl N. Hamilton, McGill University

2 A Not-So-British Invasion: Cultural Studies in Canada   27
Anne-Marie Kinahan, Carleton University

3 Knowledge Matters: The Institutionalization of Communication Studies in Canada   46
Michael Dorland, Carleton University

4 Coming of Age: Communication Studies in Quebec   65
Roger de la Garde, Université Laval, and François Yelle, Université de Montréal

Part II: Audiences

Introduction   87
Paul Attallah

5 The Audience   90
Paul Attallah, Carleton University

6 Sipping Starbucks: (Re)Considering Communicative Media   107
Charlene Elliott, Carleton University

7 Empirical Approaches to the Audience   120
Gord Lucke, University of Ottawa

8 Good Kids/Bad Kids: What's a Culture to Do?   136
Eileen Saunders, Carleton University

Part III: Communication Industries

Introduction   159
Leslie Regan Shade

9 The Canadian Radio Industry   161
Pierre C. Bélanger, University of Ottawa

10 Canadian Film 179
Gary Evans, University of Ottawa

11 A Brief History of the Recording Industry 197
Don Wallace, Carleton University

12 Television in Canada 216
Paul Attallah and Derek Foster, Carleton University

13 Computers and the Internet 235
Susan Bryant, University of Windsor, and Richard Smith, Simon Fraser University

14 On-line Journalism 252
Mike Gasher, Concordia University

Part IV: Social and Policy Issues

Introduction 271
Leslie Regan Shade

15 Globalization, Communication, and Diaspora 272
Karim H. Karim, Carleton University

16 First Peoples' Television in Canada's North: A Case Study of the Aboriginal Peoples Television Network 295
Lorna Roth, Concordia University

17 Convergence 311
Matthew Fraser, Ryerson University

18 Lost in Cyberspace 325
Dwayne Winseck, Carleton University

19 Intellectual Property and Copyright Issues in the Global Economy 343
Daniel M. Downes, University of New Brunswick, St. John

20 Privacy and New Media 360
Valerie Steeves, Carleton University

21 Media and Politics 380
Anne McGrath, University of Calgary

22 O Canada: What Happens When the Mouse Meets the Mounties? 397
Leslie Regan Shade, University of Ottawa

Contributors 411

Copyright Acknowledgments 415

Index 417

PREFACE

The future of communication in Canada does not look like its past. There are three main reasons for this fact. The first has to do with the rate and nature of technological change. Anyone who has observed technology even superficially in the past decade will realize that the rise of digitization and the Internet has profoundly altered the way in which media content is produced, distributed, and consumed. Formerly separate technologies such as the telephone, publishing, and music are now converging around a common technological infrastructure. Furthermore, the technological convergence is driving business or corporate convergence as companies merge or form alliances and partnerships. The world in which telephones were regulated separately from music distribution has been challenged by convergence and mergers.

The second main reason for our new communication future is related to what is very broadly called "globalization." The flow of capital, people, and knowledge around the world has both accelerated and altered our expectations about which types of information, entertainment, and knowledge should be available, and to whom. The worldwide reach of the Internet, for example, has severely challenged the ability of governments and corporations to control information for their own advantage. It has also underlined the necessity for forms of regulation or law that are not simply national but international as well. The same is true of satellite-delivered news and entertainment. As a new global culture emerges, new trade regimes and trade organizations such as NAFTA, the European Union, and the World Trade Organization have also come into existence. So, too, have new expectations about appropriate and desirable communication.

The third main force driving our new communication future is the changing public or audience for media. Canadian society is becoming increasingly multicultural in its demographic composition. The old world in which everyone was united around a single culture or cultural representation no longer exists. Technology has made us more open to diverse cultures, interests, and tastes. This openness has been accompanied by an increasing sophistication on the part of audiences. Nowadays, no one consumes the media innocently. As we become increasingly skilled in decoding their messages and meanings, we demand media content as sophisticated as we are.

We now experience the media not as a national phenomenon, but as a global phenomenon. Consequently, this is a book about media *in* Canada, not specifically about Canadian media. The old world in which we used media to protect ourselves against the world is being replaced by a new future in which access to global media makes up the world. This book is concerned with that future.

Features of the Text

Each of the four major parts of the book opens with an introduction that identifies salient themes addressed in the chapters. Each chapter concludes with *questions* that reinforce the main ideas presented in the chapter; a list of relevant *Web sites*; and a *references* list, a *selected bibliography*, and/or a *further reading* list. Some chapters also include end-of-chapter *notes*.

Acknowledgments

We thank the reviewers who commented on draft versions, among them Doug Brent, University of Calgary; Bert Deyell, University of Calgary; Gordon Gow, Simon Fraser University; Laurie Harnick, University of Western Ontario; Dawn Johnston, University of Calgary; Pascal Michelucci, University of Toronto (Erindale); Catherine Murray, Simon Fraser University; Michael Nolan, University of Western Ontario; Alexandre Sévigny, McMaster University; and Rebecca Sullivan, University of Calgary. We also thank the following people for their contributions to the preparation of this book: Charlene Elliott, who assisted us with the long and difficult task of editing and proofreading; our editors at Nelson Thomson Learning—Anne Williams, Joanne Sutherland, and Bob Kohlmeier; and our eagle-eyed copy editor, Sarah Robertson. We owe a special thanks to our contributors for their respective talents and dedication to the project.

Part I
The Institutional Context

Introduction

It is easy to assume that "communication" has always been with us, since people have always "communicated." While it is true that people have always used language and other symbols to create meaning, what they have understood as "communication" has, unfortunately, never been simple or straightforward.

For example, if we consider two people talking—for many observers the most fundamental communication situation—we immediately run up against some rather daunting difficulties. How do the two people manage to agree that their words will mean the same thing for both of them? Wouldn't that agreement depend on the context in which the words are spoken rather than the content of the words themselves? In order to attach the same meanings to words, the two people would have to share not only the same language but also an entire universe of cultural and other assumptions about which words to use and when to use them, about who speaks and in which order, about the proper way to demonstrate sincerity or convey the truth of one's statements, and so on. Indeed, the two people could share all of these assumptions and still manage to misunderstand one another.

As a result, if I wish to say something that you will understand, I have to imagine what you are likely to understand even before I speak. I have to try to imagine the world from your point of view in order to say something that will seem reasonable to you. On closer examination, then, even the most fundamental communication situation proves to be no simple matter.

Of course, most of the time we aren't concerned just with two people talking. This is because even in so basic a situation we have to take account of the *context* in which communication occurs. The context gives us many of the cues that tell us how to interpret meanings, when to use meanings, and when meanings are appropriate and inappropriate. Consequently, we tend to examine *communication in context*. This is one of the important meanings of the term *mass communication*. It means not just that communication affects lots of people or that it occurs on a grand scale but also that the *context* in which it happens—the nature of our society—has a determining influence on the nature of communication.

The chapters that follow are concerned precisely with trying to understand the relationship between communication and the context in which it occurs. At the most basic level, the chapters ask questions about that relationship. Is Canada like or unlike the United States or other modern countries? Is communication defined the same way here as in other places? Is it carried out in the same manner or style?

Is it organized by various players—the media, government, individuals—in the same way?

It is fair to say that communication has been regarded as a *problem* worthy of study only within the last 200 years or so. Before then, people did not consider communication as something outside themselves that merited attention. It was just part and parcel of everyday culture, an assumed aspect of daily life. With the rise of *modernity*, however, communication became a problem. Modernity refers to that state of affairs, beginning roughly around the time of the democratic revolutions—American Revolution (1776), French Revolution (1789), European Revolutions (1830–44)—when people suddenly had to take responsibility for the organization of society. The ancient monarchies were overthrown and along with them their social structures and modes of thought. Indeed, even where the monarchies were not overthrown, as in Britain, new deliberative bodies—parliament, congress, national assembly—that represented the will of the people gained in prominence and authority.

As a result, virtually nobody today believes that rulers are chosen by God or that they rule by divine right, the dominant social belief prior to modernity. With modernity has come the general view that rulers are chosen, however imperfectly, by the people and that the laws they enact, for better or worse, are ultimately the responsibility of the people. Modernity marks that moment when people come together and use reason to determine consensually the rules of social organization and collective behaviour.

And that is precisely why communication has become such a problem in modern society. To determine the rules by which society should be organized, we've had to communicate with each other, share ideas, engage in debate, exchange models, reach consensus, and the like. But in order to do these things, we've had to reflect long and hard on communication. What ideas are appropriate to express to others? How should they be expressed? Is everyone who speaks equal to everyone else? How do we know when a true idea has been expressed? How can we ensure that everyone has access to the ideas and a chance to participate in the general debate?

To all these questions we have found answers that, while not perfect, are at least serviceable and reasonable. To guarantee that everyone can speak, we have instituted such notions as freedom of speech and have even enshrined these notions in institutions like parliament. To facilitate participation in the debate, we have created elections, referendums, and other means by which people can express themselves and assume responsibility for social organization. Finally, to ensure that knowledge and information are widely shared and easily accessible, we have created the media. This is why arguments over such issues as freedom of the press, concentration of ownership, and privacy are so fierce and so indispensable: they go directly to the heart of the type of society we wish to make.

Modernity, then, led to the creation of institutions of communication: free speech, elections, parliament, the media. But the mere existence of the institutions does not mean that everything said in them will be transparently true, morally uplifting, or intellectually enlightening. It is easy to use the institutions poorly.

Furthermore, the institutions have generated new sets of unanticipated problems. For example, while their original function was to widen the sphere of public debate by making information widely available, the mass media have acquired unexpected characteristics. They tend to be industries with their own internal requirements for profit generation and operational efficiency. Indeed, their autonomous development often means that it is in their best interest to shape or handle information in ways that will enhance their own operations. A central question, therefore, is the extent to which our institutions of communication actually widen the sphere of public debate or merely manipulate information in order to shape public opinion.

Communication in Canada has been institutionalized in significantly different ways from communication in the United States. Not only is the organization of our media significantly different, but so too are our cultural and political traditions. Indeed, the central fact of public life—the existence of two dominant language groups with their own cultural perspectives—has itself resulted in a different range of questions about communication. In the United States, communication has been generally understood *instrumentally*, as a means to convey content. This has resulted in questions about the effectiveness of the conveyance and the impact of the content. In Canada, attention has been devoted less to the means of conveyance than to the ways in which the very existence of the means may have shaped public life. Canadian research has therefore tended to identify communication with culture—with a whole way of life—and to examine such questions as how culture embodies values, shapes long-term views, or excludes possibilities as well as including them.

Whether this identification of communication with culture has resulted in greater truth is itself one of the questions within the Canadian tradition. Although we are unlikely to arrive at a single, definitive answer, we can seek to understand the strands that make up the tradition and so place ourselves in a position to offer our own views on it.

1

Considering Critical Communication Studies in Canada

Sheryl N. Hamilton[1]
McGill University

The claim is often made that Canadian communication studies is *critical* whereas American studies is merely *administrative*. Canadians apparently question what exists; Americans seek merely to profit from it. Therefore, we look with patronizing bemusement on American studies and the way it seems to promote corporate media interests and advertisers. We chuckle knowingly at the repeated folly of seeking to understand the effects of media messages on individuals. In contrast, we look fondly on Harold Innis, George Grant, Northrop Frye, and Marshall McLuhan, noting that they were politically committed and interested in exploring answers to "the big questions" for the greater social good.

The claim that Canadian communication studies is unique because it is critical may contain a kernel of truth, but it also produces blind spots. It might even assume more than it explains. If we want to argue that Canadian communication studies is critical, we must first define the term. In Canada, the claim to being critical is usually advanced as a good and desirable thing. However, the meanings associated with the word "critical" are frequently as unfavourable as favourable. As Halloran (1983) notes, "critical" when used to describe research has variously functioned as a synonym for "unscientific," "philosophical," "qualitative," and "politically motivated" (p. 270). Carey (1982) would add that "critical" has served to distinguish humanities from the sciences, interpretation from analysis, subjective from objective, and romanticism from rationalism.

CRITICAL VERSUS ADMINISTRATIVE: TWO COMMUNICATIONS EVENTS

The notion of critical communication research forms an assumed perspective in much Canadian scholarship but is rarely defined. Any attempt to define it inherits the initial troubled distinction between administrative and critical communication research from the United States. Although there is no agreed-on definition of critical communication studies, it remains nonetheless possible to recognize a set of ontological, epistemological, and methodological commitments shared by scholars who identify themselves as critical communication researchers—commitments that can inform discussions in both the United States and Canada.

The distinction between critical and administrative research has functioned as one of communication's "principal fault lines" (Mosco, 1996, p. 247). Despite its inaccuracy and oversimplicity, the distinction continues to be one of the central underlying frames through which scholars have aligned, organizations have developed, and the history of the field is taught and understood. How did we come to divide the field into these two camps? There are two American communications events that establish the distinction between critical and administrative. The first is Paul Lazarsfeld's 1941 article, "Remarks on Administrative and Critical Communication Research," which first named the distinction and, while calling for a rapprochement, ensured the primacy of administrative over critical research approaches. The second event is the special issue of the *Journal of Communication*, published in 1983, that exposed tensions within the field, created the frames in which subsequent debate would take place, and demonstrated—counter to its stated purpose—that there could be no coming together of administrative and critical communication studies. These two events worked together to map the terrain on which all subsequent discussions of critical research have taken place.

Naming the Distinction

Paul Lazarsfeld is considered to be one of the "founding fathers" of communication studies. His research, along with that of such researchers as Harold Lasswell, Elihu Katz, Kurt Lewin, and Wilbur Schramm, produced some of the first communication theories in the United States. The research of these early scholars was generally funded through alliances between philanthropic foundations, universities, and interested corporations. Their primary concern was to explore the effects of different media on behaviour with the ultimate goal of using media more effectively.

In pursuing their research, the early scholars used quantitative research, focusing on large-scale surveys and statistical analysis. In the late 1930s, this approach was challenged by a group of émigré Jewish scholars who fled Nazi Germany to settle in the United States and came to be known as the Frankfurt School. Trained in European schools of thought, heavily influenced by Marxism, and deeply concerned about what they saw as the industrialization of culture, scholars such as Max Horkheimer, Theodor Adorno, and Herbert Marcuse both enriched and came into conflict with the quantitative and industry-driven approach to communication being taken up in the United States at that time.

The impetus for Lazarsfeld's article came out of a particular set of circumstances involving himself and Theodor Adorno, perhaps the leading figure of the Frankfurt School. In 1937, the Rockefeller Foundation provided funds to establish the Office of Radio Research at Columbia University. The directors of the Office, Hadley Cantril (Princeton) and Frank Stanton (CBS), hired Lazarsfeld as its research director. The following year, Lazarsfeld, with the collaboration of Max Horkheimer, invited Adorno to the United States to direct the music component of the Office of Radio Research. What followed was a very difficult year for both

Lazarsfeld and Adorno as their very different research agendas and epistemological approaches came into conflict. That clash is what produced the distinction between administrative (Lazarsfeld) and critical (Adorno) research or, more broadly, American scholarship and the Frankfurt School. Lazarsfeld tried to persuade Adorno, whose ideas and prose style were strongly influenced by classical philosophy, to express his theoretical ideas in a manner that could be measured using quantitative methods. As it happened, "The actual course of events was quite different from those expectations (Lazarsfeld, 1969, p. 323).

In 1939, the Rockefeller Foundation refused to renew the music project because it was not producing useful results. Much discussion of these events has subsequently taken place (Fleming and Bailyn, 1969; Gitlin, 1981; Slack and Allor, 1983), but it was Lazarsfeld's 1941 article that created a distinction that would organize professional and intellectual practice in North American communication studies for at least the next 50 years. In the article, which was published in the Frankfurt School's journal, *Studies in Philosophy and Social Science*, Lazarsfeld grapples with the different approaches he (and his American colleagues) and the Frankfurt scholars brought to research. He characterizes the two styles of research as *administrative* and *critical*.

Administrative research is "carried through in the service of some kind of administrative agency of public or private character" (Lazarsfeld, 1941, p. 8). Viewing media as useful tools, administrative researchers pose such questions as "Who are the people exposed to the different media? What are their specific preferences? What are the effects of different methods of presentation?" (Lazarsfeld, 1941, p. 3). Lazarsfeld (1941) recognizes the limitations of administrative research approaches, noting that they may not take full account of history and that "they solve little problems, generally of a basic character, when the same methods could be used to improve the life of the community if only they were applied to forward-looking projects related to the pressing economic and social problems of our time" (p. 8).

In contrast, critical research assumes that "prior and in addition to whatever special purpose is to be served, the general role of our media of communication in the present social system should be studied" (Lazarsfeld, 1941, p. 9). It therefore differs from administrative research in two respects: "it develops a theory of the prevailing social trends in our times, general trends which yet require consideration in any concrete research problem; and it seems to imply ideas of basic human values according to which all actual or desired effects should be appraised" (Lazarsfeld, 1941, p. 9). Thus, critical research begins with social theory, contains normative values, and places communication in the larger social context.

Lazarsfeld (1941) suggests that critical scholars are always conscious that "what we need most is to do and think what we consider true and not to adjust ourselves to the seemingly inescapable" (p. 10). The concern of critical research with threats to human dignity and values is evident in the research questions it raises: "How are these media organized and controlled? How, in their institutional set-up, is the trend toward centralization, standardization and promotional pressure expressed?

In what form, however disguised, are they threatening human values?" (Lazarsfeld, 1941, p. 10).

Lazarsfeld is suggesting that the purpose and methodologies of the research, the moral commitment of the scholar, the relationship between theory and empirical reality, and the place of values in research are crucial lines of distinction between critical and administrative research. In his view, critical research assumes the task of revealing how media function in order to reproduce dominant ideology in their given social context. Furthermore, he recognizes that such an approach is essentially theoretical because it makes certain assumptions (e.g., about the power of media, the susceptibility of audiences, the nature of the media–audience contact) that are not always empirically verifiable. It is this embrace of theory without concern as to its "prove-ability" that Lazarsfeld sees as the primary weakness of critical approaches (Lazarsfeld, 1941, pp. 12–13).

Lazarsfeld's short article has had a lasting impact in three ways. First, it named a distinction—between critical and administrative research—that has organized the discipline ever since. Second, it brought to the attention of communication studies the work of the Frankfurt School scholars. Third, it articulated the conditions for the ongoing domination of the administrative approach within the American context. Lazarsfeld concluded the article by expressing a desire for a convergence of European theory and American empiricism. Ultimately, his goal was not to challenge or change the underlying characteristics of research; rather, he sought to enhance administrative research by incorporating into it some of the theoretical richness of critical approaches. The debate did not end there, however.

Framing the Debate

Although the "dominant paradigm" in American communication studies continued to be administrative research until at least the 1980s, tensions between critical and administrative approaches also continued to simmer. They were spurred on by the translation of the work of European Marxist thinkers such as Antonio Gramsci and Louis Althusser, the development of cultural studies, and radical shifts in the social, economic, and cultural context of the mass media and their study in the United States.

The 1983 publication of a special issue of *Journal of Communication*, titled *Ferment in the Field*, marked another watershed event in the dialogue—and potential rapprochement—between critical and administrative research. The editor, George Gerbner, gathered together 35 original articles from 41 international scholars from both traditions to reflect on the distinction that Lazarsfeld had advanced 42 years earlier. As Gerbner (1983a) wrote in his introduction, "This volume represents the first time that so many internationally prominent scholars have examined and commented upon communications as a field of study in one publication" (p. 4).

Ferment in the Field remains one of the most significant reflections on the state of the field in the history of communication studies—in Gerbner's words, a "coming of age." Throughout the volume, the distinction between critical and administrative is accepted rather than challenged and the result is a much more detailed exposition of its parameters and implications than had been offered by Lazarsfeld. *Ferment in the Field* further entrenches the distinction between critical and administrative research and recognizes the conflicts and tensions at work in professional circles throughout the United States.

DEFINING CRITICAL COMMUNICATION STUDIES

In the late 1980s, Sholle (1988) noted that "[a] number of attempts to define the field of critical communication research have been [undertaken], but there is no widely accepted definition of the field" (p. 38). The same holds true today. What can be said about critical communication studies is that it is not a single entity. It includes approaches from political economy, cultural studies, Marxist sociology, semiotic analysis, institution studies, dependency theory, international communications, and more. What it offers is a range of different ways to study communication—all of which are in opposition to administrative research (Slack and Allor, 1983, p. 208).

Discussions of the distinction between critical and administrative research have been hindered by a number of trends present in both sides of the debate. First, there is a tendency to reduce the other position to a homogeneous straw man, rendering administrative research as simple-minded empiricism and critical research as ideological polemic. Second, there has been a lack of self-reflexivity, which shows up in the inability to recognize that one's own position may have weaknesses as well as strengths. Third, and especially within the critical tradition, debates sometimes serve not as a means of achieving genuine understanding, but rather as a forum for theoretical posturing. (The best example of such posturing may be the ongoing war between political economy and cultural studies.[2]) Finally, the very fact that the tension between the two approaches has been framed as a debate has led to an either/or attitude that hardly does justice to the range of research and analysis within communication studies.

A number of scholars have attempted to step outside of these limits. Schiller (1983) suggests that the *shared characteristics* of critical research include a focus on production rather than individual consumption; an examination of the sources and exercise of power; and an assumption of continuous change in social processes and institutions. According to Smythe and Van Dinh (1983), critical research sets as its problem how to reshape or create institutions to better serve the needs of a greater number of people; uses historical, materialist research techniques; and is ideological in the sense that it links critical problems and tools "with interpretations that involve radical changes in the established order" (p. 118) (see also Rogers, 1982; Slack and Allor, 1983). Commonalities identified by Carey (1983) include a less positivist approach to research; diverse methods; a sceptical view of the media; the occasional influence of pragmatism or symbolic interactionism; the inevitable influence of Marxism; and an interest in questions of culture and politics as they relate to communications and mass media.

The following sections examine the shared characteristics of critical communication research in the following categories: research problem, understanding of social power, methodology, researcher orientation, theoretical influences, and knowledge claims. These categories reflect beliefs about the nature of reality and the way we can know that reality. They set the limits as to what a critical approach to communication can offer.

The Research Problem

How does critical communication studies define its research problem? Critical communications scholars have generally focused on the relations between communication and social power. This focus has been variously framed as a question of (1) social control and power (Halloran, 1983); (2) concern with structures of power (Gerbner, 1983b); or (3) an investigation into domination, contradiction, and struggle (Mosco, 1983). The central unit of knowledge is society rather than the individual, and communication practices are considered within their various social contexts.

Simply stated, critical communication research takes on the larger questions. As Rogers (1982) notes, "Critical scholars believe that a theory of communication is impossible without a theory of society, so their scope of analysis is much wider than that of empirical scholars" (p. 125). Therefore, critical researchers ask such questions as: Who controls the media? How can media be used by a greater diversity of people? How do we negotiate our roles within and between social groups through practices of communication? How do communication structures work with other social, economic, and cultural structures to order society?

Generally, this focus has meant a shift in emphasis from the effects of media on individuals to analyses that are more historically grounded and socially situated. Critical work has concentrated on ownership and control of media systems, the linking of media structures to other larger social structures, and analyses of the institutional aspects of communication. When considering individuals, critical scholars view them as members of groups—groups already partly determined by social power arrangements—and explore their resistance and domination. As Slack and Allor (1983) note,

> The communication process . . . is no longer defined in terms of the effects of messages on individuals but on the effectivity (or social role) of communication (as both institutional structures and symbolic constructions) in maintaining, enhancing, or disrupting the social formation (the existing interrelationship of politics, economics, and culture). (p. 214)

Understanding Social Power

Clearly, critical researchers ask the questions they do because they hold a different understanding of the relationship between communication and power. Bailie (1997) suggests that "[c]ritical communication scholarship is rooted in the assumption that social institutions and human relations are relations of history, power and struggle" (p. 33). Critical scholars therefore view social power as unequally distributed and generally subscribe to a conflict-based model of social relations that focuses on struggle and difference rather than on agreement and consensus. Indeed, critical communication studies rejects the *linear model of causality* at work in administrative research and replaces it with more *complex forms of social determination*. Consequently, whereas administrative research is content to study, for example, the impact that radio advertising might have on listeners, critical research wants to investigate the historical origin of radio advertising, the type of interest that tends to use radio advertising, the ways in which the advertising binds listeners to the capitalist system, and so on. Furthermore, it is precisely because the study of complex forms of social determination can lead in so many directions that distinctions— between cultural and economic determinism, for example—among critical scholars have emerged. Notwithstanding the specific areas to which critical scholars may direct their interest, all share an opposition to the *liberal pluralist notion* of social power, which sees power as potentially equally shared and as neutral.

In advancing a more diverse and less idealistic understanding of social power and how it intersects with communication structures and practices in society, critical scholars have been criticized for assuming rather than demonstrating that social power really works as they claim. The theory is powerful and seductive but not always easy to demonstrate. Furthermore, *postmodernist* and *poststructuralist* conceptions of power pose a challenge to the critical understanding. This is important because assumptions about the nature of social power and its organization—Does it always operate from the top down (i.e., from an elite to a mass)? Is it always coercive or can it also be productive? Are there opportunities for resistance?—are at the heart of the often unstated norms and values that critical communication research espouses. Indeed, depending on one's definition of power, one will also draw different conclusions about what types of actions to take, what types of outcomes are appropriate, how power should be wielded, and who should wield it.

Methodology and Methods

As a result of the two preceding assumptions—(1) the appropriate object of study is the relation between power and communication, and (2) social power is unequally distributed—critical communication scholars use different methodologies and methods than administrative researchers. Indeed, it is because critical research defines its object of study differently and because it views social power as being unequally distributed that it *logically* uses methods that will reveal those facts.

Much of the debate between the critical and administrative approaches is concerned with distinctions in methodology. In fact, the administrative approach is sometimes called the *empirical* approach because it studies immediately observable phenomena using "scientific" methods. In contrast, critical research is often seen as methodologically unrigorous because it rejects empirical approaches to knowledge and is not concerned with demonstrating its theoretical claims through scientifically verifiable data. As a result, critical research is sometimes accused of producing ideological claims rather than scientific knowledge: "We can recognize that data without adequate theory are intellectually sterile, but we must also acknowledge that theory, unless subjected to rigorous and wide-ranging empirical test, is polemic" (Stevenson, 1983, p. 269).

Critical researchers have pointed out, however, that critical research frequently uses empirical methods (Mosco, 1983). As well, a number of scholars have observed that critical research is compatible with empirical methods (Allen, 1999; Elasmar, 1999; Gerbner, 1964; Halloran, 1983; Rogers, 1982). Whether or not critical scholars deploy empirical research methods, their epistemology—that is, their explanation of the process of knowing or knowledge construction—is very different from that of administrative or empirical scholars. Critical scholarship is not primarily interested in making scientifically verifiable knowledge claims.

The framing of the debate between critical and administrative approaches, as between qualitative and quantitative research methods or between science and the humanities, has resulted in three unproductive lines of discussion. First, it has led to claims of moral superiority by both sides of the debate. For critical scholars, the moral superiority derives from a sense of the importance of the work being done; according to Halloran (1983), "[W]e have to accept that it is more important to be important than to be impeccable" (p. 278). For administrative scholars, claims to moral superiority are grounded in science and "pure" knowledge untainted by ideology.

The second unproductive debate results from the fact that no distinction is being made between *empirical* and *positivist*. Empirical methods seek to describe, through the application of established procedures, an aspect of material reality; positivist methods emerge out of a belief that objective truth can be rendered through the scientific method. Although the methods employed by critical researchers can certainly produce empirical results, critical researchers make no claim to produce positivist (i.e., objective) results. On the contrary, they would argue that the claim to objectivity or *value neutrality* is itself a thoroughly ideological claim.

Third, debates about methodology have led to attempts to find a "middle ground," a strategy that often favours the empirical perspective. According to Rosengren (1983), "Those who ask the most provocative questions often cannot provide sound empirical answers; those who can, often fail to ask the right questions" (p. 185). The search for a compromise and the ultimate favouring of the empirical approach are tendencies that are doomed to fail because the debate is not about *methods* (everyone can use the same methods), but about differing ontologies and epistemologies (what does the world consist of and how can we know it?).

When the middle-ground strategy is applied, larger questions, debates, and positions are ultimately reduced to a debate about methods.

This reduction has imposed certain limitations on critical communication studies. Because issues of methodology have been aligned with positivism, questions of methodology and method often stop there. Interrogations of how nonpositivist methods can usefully inform and develop critical communication questions is an issue that requires more attention. Administrative researchers have been correct in pointing out that critical communication researchers have tended to devote insufficient attention to methodology and methods; however, the solution is not to be found in a turn to positivist or quantitative methods, but rather in a more sustained exploration of the relationship between theory and our ability to describe lived social reality.

Researcher Orientation

The first three assumptions of critical research are: (1) the appropriate object of study is the relationship between communication and power; (2) social power is unequally distributed; and (3) theory is more important than methods. Following from these is the fourth assumption advanced by critical researchers, which addresses the relationship between researcher and researched—in other words, the orientation of the researcher to his or her work. This debate has taken place on the field of ideology and interrogates what it means to do ideological research. Interestingly, both proponents and critics of the critical approach to communication research have labelled critical approaches "ideological." For critics, this label means that critical research is unscientific, polemical, and simply reflective of the beliefs of the researcher. One scholar offers a classic formulation of the criticism when he suggests that critical scholars often "mistake ideology for sociology" (Lang, 1979, p. 92).

For its proponents, however, the term "ideological" is a way to show that research not only *analyzes* ideology as an object (i.e., it demonstrates the symbolic traces of social power) (Sholle, 1988), but it is *also* political in itself because it is committed to the disruption of the status quo (Blumler, 1983; Mosco, 1983, 1996; Smythe and Van Dinh, 1983). Both sides of the debate therefore agree that critical communication research is not value-free (i.e., it is guided by its values in its selection and treatment of research questions). Critical researchers feel that applying values is an inevitable part—and, indeed, a positive aspect—of doing research. Administrative scholars, on the other hand, feel that values corrupt the objectivity of research. A critical approach argues, of course, that even if the administrative/empirical school of thought does not acknowledges its values (objectivity, truth, science, utility, pluralism), those values are still reflected in the choice of research questions and methods.

While critical scholars have been willing to acknowledge the existence of values in their research, they have become increasingly circumspect about what those values are. It is often assumed that critical researchers are on the "left" in political terms, but this orientation is not often defined (see, for example, Slack and Semati, 1997). Hence, critical research can affirm certain ideological and political norms even without intentionally articulating, considering, and discussing them.

Theoretical Influences

A fifth basis on which to understand critical communication research is to ask what are its theoretical influences. The theoretical legacies of critical communication research that are acknowledged within the field include European critical theory, American pragmatism and the Chicago School, and Marxist thought.

One of the distinguishing aspects of critical approaches is their recognition of the influence of European critical theory—specifically, the Frankfurt School (Hardt, 1992; Grosswiler, 1996; Jansen, 1983; Schramm, 1983; Sholle, 1988; Stevenson, 1983). European critical theory includes the work of first-generation Frankfurt School members such as Adorno, Horkheimer, and Marcuse, as well as second-generation thinkers such as Jürgen Habermas. The influence of European critical theory has been to frame critical communication research in relation to larger critiques of modernism, to explore the specificity of commodity culture, and to offer a stinging critique of the industrialization of the cultural domain, with hope for greater democratization of the means of communication and their divorce from industrial production.

The theoretical influence of American pragmatism and Chicago School symbolic interactionism comes from the work of John Dewey, Kenneth Burke, George Herbert Mead, and Herbert Blumer (Hardt, 1992; Carey, 1982, 1983). Emerging from this work is a concern with the practice of communication in relation to progressive social change and a shift from one-way models of communication to interactive models of meaning-making and identity formation.

The third major theoretical influence is Marxist theory. The development of this influence can be mapped through the shifting theorization of ideology and culture from more simple deterministic models to approaches from Althusser and Gramsci. As a result, critical communication attaches great importance to ideology, to debates about questions of determination and the related question of where to locate culture, and to a shared recognition that one cannot consider communication messages and practices outside of their socioeconomic contexts.

All three theoretical influences have obviously enriched the field of communication studies, particularly in relation to more administrative or liberal pluralist approaches. However, critical communication scholars have been slow to recognize the value of other critical approaches not growing out of a Marxist, class-based analysis or narrowly political economic analysis. For example, both feminism and postcolonialism have produced deeply interesting theory that could enrich the field of critical communication studies as a whole. While this work has been accepted within the field, its applicability has tended to be seen as specific to gender, race, and ethnicity, as opposed to offering rich resources for critical communication studies more broadly.

Knowledge Claims

The sixth shared assumption answers the question, What kinds of knowledge claims can—and do—critical communication researchers make? Critical communication seeks both to engage critically with existing social relations and to change those relations. Critical communication scholars work to produce "research that both advances criticism of the existing world system and promotes the 'critical state' that would transform it" (Mosco, 1983, pp. 245–246). Research should therefore offer resources to effect positive social change (Halloran, 1983). Slack and Allor (1983) suggest that

> [i]t is not possible to characterize approaches as "critical" based solely on their conceptions of causality. The epistemological consideration of the question of causality must necessarily be linked to the political consideration of the exercise of social power before discriminatory judgement is possible. (pp. 213–214)

Whether seen as creating conditions for free (or freer) communication, social democracy, or unfettered expressions of self, critical research sets as one of its central objectives the production of intellectual and political resources for social transformation and individual and collective emancipation (Bailie, 1997; Gerbner, 1964; Haight, 1983; Halloran, 1983; Jansen, 1983). Consequently, not only must communication be thought about more critically, but so too must the place of the researcher and his or her work in society. However, it must be underlined again that the normative standard that is implicitly at work in these claims is rarely articulated expressly. Who is to determine what counts as *positive change* and whose vision of emancipation is at work are questions that merit further reflection by critical communication scholars.

From the foregoing discussion of critical communication studies arising out of debates primarily within the American context, a set of elements emerges, shared ontological and epistemological assumptions through which we can begin to distinguish what constitutes a critical approach to communication studies. Critical communication studies (1) takes as its primary question the relationship between communication and social power; (2) understands social power as a dynamic structuring force and recognizes that power is unequally distributed within society; (3) privileges theory over method and is more concerned to produce social critique than objective knowledge; (4) embraces the role that values play in producing knowledge; (5) has its theoretical roots in American and European radical thought; and (6) seeks to produce knowledge that will effect positive social change.

CANADIAN CRITICAL COMMUNICATION STUDIES

The story of what constitutes critical communication studies in North America has primarily been defined as an American encounter with European theory, framed as an ongoing conflict between critical and administrative approaches. This section considers where Canada fits into this narrative. In a sense, Canada has functioned as a structuring absence in the debates, in part because of its instrumental marginality to American communication scholarship (as argued by Carey, 1975), but more significantly because Canadian communication studies sees itself as always, already critical. It sees itself as beginning where the American debates end.

The status of Canadian communication studies as critical does not arise from "ferment in the field," but from its very history. In this sense, "critical" is an underlying and often uninterrogated *assumption* in Canadian communication studies. In Canada, the question has not been whether or not Canadian communication studies is critical, but rather in what ways communication studies in Canada is distinctly Canadian.

The Ghost of Innis: Critical-ness Assumed

Babe (2000a), who has written that "Canada has a rich heritage of communication thought" (p. 19), traces the foundations of Canadian communication thought through the work of ten scholars: Graham Spry, Harold Innis, John Grierson, Dallas Smythe, C.B. Macpherson, Irene Spry, George Grant, Gertrude Robinson, Northrop Frye, and Marshall McLuhan. At its very foundations, Babe argues, Canadian communication thought is dialectical, holistic, ontological, oriented to political economy, and concerned with mediation; most significantly for our purposes, it is critical.

Babe sees Canadian communication thought as operating fundamentally within the critical tradition, in opposition to administrative or pluralist approaches. More specifically, by critical research he means "evaluative research, presuming enduring criteria for enduring goals towards which we should strive judging policies, activities, events, human relations, institutions and so forth" (Babe, 2000a, p. 16). It is this ability to evaluate critically that marks Canadian scholars as critical in the American sense of the term. Indeed, there is general agreement that, in its historical origins, Canadian communication thought is critical (Acland and Buxton, 1999; Carey, 1975; Kroker, 1984; Robinson and Theall, 1975). Theall (1975) suggests that Innis, through the "process of criticizing North American history by rewriting it, developed a 'critical' approach to communication studies" (p. 21). American scholars such as Carey (1975, 1983), Hardt (1992), and Grosswiler (1996) have lent American authority to the claims that Canadian communication thought is a priori critical. Carey (in Salter, 1981a) suggests that "[Innis's] work was critical in the contemporary sense that he was not proposing some natural value free study, but a standpoint from which to critique society and theories of it in light of humane and civilized values" (p. 80).

What has been the legacy of these foundational thinkers in terms of understanding what critical communication studies means in Canada? According to the few scholars considering it, the question, like its American counterpart, takes as its central concern larger questions about the ways in which power and communication intersect. As Babe (2000a) notes, "Power considerations figure prominently in Canadian communication thought" (p. 310). Power in this context is understood with an attention to history and the interplay of historical forces (Kroker, 1984, Theall, 1975; Tremblay, 1981). It shares assumptions with other critical communication approaches about the nonlinear nature of social power, but theorizes that power in a specifically dialectical model (Babe, 2000a; Kroker, 1984; Theall, 1975). In other words, history is produced through the encounter of contradictory social forces. Furthermore, the historical legacy of foundational communication thought has offered some significant attempts to think through the place of technologies of communication (rather than only mass media) in processes of modernization (Carey, 1983; Kroker, 1984). As well, it has placed at the forefront values having to do with human emancipation and exploring the conditions of a better life (Babe, 2000a; Kroker, 1984).

Interestingly, a majority of the foundational thinkers identified as pivotal to Canadian communication thought were developing their communication ideas before the institutionalization of the field of communication studies in Canada. While most observers would agree that they were critical thinkers who contributed to the foundation of Canadian communication thought, it is less clear how their ideas have played out in communication studies as a discipline in Canada since the 1960s. According to Robinson (2000), "While the general outlines of Innis' and McLuhan's work are known, whether they have inspired a unique kind of Canadian scholarship is much more difficult to determine" (p. 122). In examining what critical communication studies might mean in Canada, can we escape the ghost of Harold Innis? Is the discipline of communication studies still critical?

Hurdles to Delimiting the Field

Any appraisal of Canadian communication scholarship as a discipline, or at least as a field with certain shared problematics, is hindered by the striking lack of a well-detailed and readily apparent map of the field. Robinson (1987) lamented that "[m]uch remains to be done in providing a detailed account of communication studies in Canada" (p. 4). Unfortunately, the need continues.

When and how did communication studies become institutionalized in Canada within the university? When were the first professional associations established and with what effect? What journals serve this academic community? How can one characterize the work done in the field? Can we identify generational patterns? Is there a canon that emerges after Innis, McLuhan, et al.?

The first hurdle in answering these questions is the diffuse nature of Canadian communication scholarship. In the early 1980s, Salter (1981b) noted that much work in communication studies was appearing in the journals of other disciplines or was being published in communication journals in the United States or Europe. More than two decades later, and notwithstanding the 25-year history of the *Canadian Journal of Communication* (*CJC*)—the only English-language academic journal in Canada devoted to communication studies—Salter's claim remains true. The editor of the *CJC* himself regrets that we cannot look to *CJC* to map the history, development, and trends of communication studies in Canada; Canadian communication scholars, Lorimer (2000a) recognizes, continue to publish in international journals or in contexts outside of the discipline altogether, and many do not identify strongly with Canadian communication studies.

In addition to the diffuse nature of Canadian communication scholarship, another hurdle in delimiting the field is the lack of a comprehensive and accepted historical account of its development. Such an account might be found in a single work, and yet none exists. Lorimer had hoped the special issue of *CJC* published in 2000 might accomplish this. Instead, individual scholars offered reflections on the institutionalization of the discipline in their particular university (Tate, Osler, Fouts, and Segal, 2000). As well, one might look to undergraduate communication textbooks in Canada for such an overarching narrative. Yet a review of current undergraduate texts (e.g., Biagi and McKie, 1999; Holmes and Taras, 1992; Lorimer and Gasher, 2001; Lorimer and McNulty, 1996; McKie and Singer, 2001; Szuchewycz and Sloniowski, 1999; Vivian and Maurin, 2000) comes up empty, a fact recognized by others (Tate et al., 2000).

In terms of addressing these gaps in Canadian communication scholarship, the present collection is a welcome and significant contribution to the field. In the chapters by Michael Dorland, Roger de la Garde and François Yelle, Anne-Marie Kinahan, and others, students will gain a familiarity with the institutional, professional, and intellectual history of the field in English Canada and Quebec. Yet, without a recorded history, myths of origin are weak. Perhaps it has been this lack of well-established, historical myths and narratives that has structured the attempts to define Canadian communication studies into the predictable identity crisis of whether or not it is uniquely Canadian. It is in and through this issue that the critical elements of Canadian communication studies have been negotiated, articulated, and ultimately limited.

Uniquely Canadian

The debate about Canadian national identity, which is at the heart of so much substantive Canadian communication research, also plays itself out in the consideration of the discipline as a whole. In some ways, this is not surprising. The third goal of Babe's (2000a) book is "to discern whether there exists a mode of communication inquiry that might be termed 'quintessentially Canadian'" (p. 4). He has not been alone in this pursuit. Kroker (1984) attempts to map a distinctly "Canadian mind," while Robinson and Theall (1975) suggest that Canada can claim a "unique communications philosophy" (p. 1).

Claims to a specific Canadian approach to communication studies rest on two central arguments. First, Canadian communication studies is unique because it is critical. Critical functions as a largely undefined marker of distinction from the American administrative approach. It also casts Canadian communication studies research as morally superior to its American counterpart. Second, Canadian communication studies is framed as unique because of its distinctive epistemological position—one of in-betweenness or marginality—and it is this epistemological position that produces the specifically Canadian critical stance.

On his return to Simon Fraser University in the mid-1970s, Dallas Smythe, disheartened by his experience in communication studies in the United States, called for Canadian communication thought to distinguish itself from American approaches through its critical stance. He clearly hoped that Canadian communication research would not reproduce what he considered to be the errors of many American scholars. This notion of defining Canadian uniqueness through criticalness took hold in the field. Babe (2000a) argues that it is the values of Canadian scholarship that make it critical: "the fact that most of these theorists are able to contemplate a superior human nature, that is, to compare things as they should be with things as they are, qualifies them as critical theorists in the tradition acknowledged by Lazarsfeld" (p. 316). He recognizes the role of religion in foundational Canadian communication thought and suggests that it may be responsible for the "high moral standard" of these thinkers (Babe, 2000a, p. 308). The overtones of moral superiority or a location outside of ideology are also present in Kroker's (1984) claims that "the Canadian discipline ... represents a courageous, and creative struggle to think outside of and against the closed horizons of technological society" (p. 13).

In these kinds of claims, which abound in Canadian communication conferences, analyses, and classrooms, the chain of reasoning proceeds as follows. Canadian communication thought is unique (i.e., non-American) because it is critical. It is critical now (in the present) because it was critical then (when Innis was writing). And because it is critical, ultimately it is better than communication studies in the United States.

Unfortunately, these assumptions can have unanticipated consequences for knowledge. First, there is a lack of considered attention to what critical might mean now, as opposed to when Innis was writing. The claim is simply made rather than demonstrated. Second, it sets as the standard the distinction between critical and administrative research articulated by Lazarsfeld, rather than the longer history of debates within American communication studies. Therefore, it does not engage with a more sophisticated understanding of what critical communication studies might be. Finally, it reduces the important question of what critical might mean to the less interesting question of how we are different from our American counterparts. A notable example of this third consequence appears in Babe (2000a); after offering what, despite its shortcomings, is an arguably seminal treatment of the foundations of Canadian communication thought, he concludes his book with the following paragraph:

> [I]t is worth remarking that a quite different field of questions is raised by the seminal and foundational Canadian communication theorists than by those often taken to be the founders of American communication thought (Lazarsfeld, Lasswell, Lewin, Hovland, Schramm). It is likely more than merely coincidental that raising important ontological questions, adopting a critical stance, and employing holistic modes of analysis detract from the lustre both of technological achievement and of the free flow of information—mainstays of American thought and policy. (p. 319)

There is a sense of superiority operating here that discourages ongoing self-scrutiny. Canadian communication studies research is assumed to be *already* within a critical paradigm, and the paradigm itself is assumed to be necessarily and essentially political economic. Unfortunately, such assumptions do not do justice to the diversity of work being produced under the name "critical," including policy studies, institutional analyses, feminist research, industry analysis, and technology studies. Indeed, an examination of the graduate communication theses deposited in Canadian universities quickly shows that the field is both broader and more vital than is imagined or promoted even by its proponents.

The second major defining characteristic of Canadian communication studies that has been identified is in its in-betweenness and marginality. Canadian political, social, geographic, and economic marginality (mostly in relation to the United States) is seen as producing an epistemology of the margins. A number of scholars identify Canadian communication scholarship as unique in that it draws on both European and American traditions. Hence, while it is concerned with social rather than individual effects and is theoretical like European approaches, it is also more grounded like American approaches (Salter, 1981a). Kroker (1984) sees Canadian communication thought as an oppositional mode between European and American perspectives; he feels it is characterized by its location "in-between," which he defines as "a restless oscillation between the pragmatic will to live at all costs of the American and a searing lament for that which has been suppressed by the modern, technical order" (p. 7). From this position of in-between, Canadians offer a unique, critical perspective.

Some scholars go further than in-betweenness and claim that a defining characteristic of Canadian communication thought—and, indeed, of all Canadian intellectual and cultural development—is its marginality (Babe, 2000a, 2000b; Carey, 1975; Robinson and Theall, 1975; Theall, 1975). The belief that a critical stance emerges from a sense of marginality is echoed in claims made by

American and British critical scholars (Carey, 1982; Garnham, 1983; Hardt, 1992; Smythe and Van Dinh, 1983). According to Robinson and Theall (1975), "Canada's geopolitical marginality on the fringe of the North American continent seems to have given rise to two distinct outlooks: a particular perception of this country's cultural mission and a unique communication studies philosophy" (p. 3). Babe (2000a) argues that "[p]eople at the margins can see things differently, that is, dialectically: unable to escape exposure to dominant discourses, they nonetheless understand that these discourses are not their own" (p. 23).

Yet what are the limits of this epistemological positioning on the margins? The claim to criticality through marginality rests on the examples of the canonical Canadian communication thinkers: Harold Innis, Marshall McLuhan, George Grant, and Northrop Frye. But how pertinent is the sense of geographical marginality expressed by a few great thinkers to our definition of "the margins" today? How does marginality play itself out in relation to the globalizing context of the early 21st century? Furthermore, how can marginality function as a self-conscious characteristic? Theall (1975) claims that "[t]his phenomenon of marginality provides a natural negative perspective" (p. 20), but how can a phenomenon that has been thus articulated be considered natural? He goes on to suggest that marginality must be explicitly recognized as a strength in intellectual criticism (Theall, 1975, p. 23). Perhaps, as Canadian musician Bruce Cockburn suggests, the trouble with normal is it always gets worse.

The Trouble with Normal

What can be seen from the foregoing discussion is that the critical-ness of Canadian communication studies has been mapped onto discourses of the ongoing search for a unique Canadian national identity. Indeed, the search for Canadian uniqueness has derailed a sustained interrogation of what a critical approach to communication might entail and whether or not it is even present in the Canadian field. In short, the criticism is that the field has not been critical enough. Lorimer (2000b) criticizes generations of communication scholars in Canada for not moving past Smythe's limited "political economy" understanding of critical communications; he suggests, as have others, that as the discipline has matured, its critical edge has dulled (see also Salter, 1987). De la Garde (1987) asks:

> [H]ave we embarked on a sea of intellectual calm following the rise of the Innis empire within the scientific community and are we falling prey to the "commodification of knowledge" with its monopolistic discourse or are we on the eve of renewing our problematic, even if it means living through a period of "disturbances," of vigorous debates—and of democracy? (p. 20)

In short, de la Garde is asking, has there been enough ferment in our field?

The mapping of a critical disciplinary identity onto a national identity has also produced certain blind spots. As Meisel (1987) notes, "[T]he questions asked by researchers—and the questions not asked—are greatly conditioned by their societal and national setting" (p. 57). The cultural nationalist position, for example, has always accepted a strong, legitimate state presence. Yet is approval of an interventionist state consistent with an approach that defines itself as critical and therefore as being in opposition to the normalizing power of any state? Although communication studies in Canada did not become institutionalized in the university system as a result of a close relationship with media industries (as in the United Sates), it might be that it has done so in a close relationship with government. In fact, a significant number of scholars attribute the rise of communication studies in Canada to the needs of royal commissions studying media (Robinson, 2000; Salter, 1987; Tate et al., 2000). Tate et al. (2000) regard this as a positive development:

> What tends to be invisible in the equation is precisely the important role which royal commissions and other government-created study groups and task forces have tended to play in our scholarly life. Focused stimulus, funding, and collegiality are generated that tend to give structure to new and emerging areas of organized scholarship. Arguably, it is not coincidental that the CCA [Canadian Communication Association] and the *CJC* (in its evolved form as a peer-reviewed scholarly journal) were established in the wake of the LaMarsh Commission. (p. 86)

Lorimer (2000b) calls for more such research: "We . . . must maintain the role of collecting information and providing analyses of those industries so that government has a sound foundation on which to act" (p. 14).

Yet one of the hallmarks of critical research, even as Lazarsfeld framed it, was its intellectual independence. Gerbner (1983b) reminds us that "[c]ritical inquiry is the distinguishing feature of a discipline and the hallmark of independent scholarship" (p. 355). Others have urged more caution regarding this close relationship with the government's research agenda (de la Garde, 1987). Salter (1987) suggests that "[t]he influence of government funding on the research programs of a discipline should never be underestimated" (p. 35); she goes on to remark that "there are some dangers in relying upon the needs of government to create the research foci within a discipline" (p. 41). If we are to follow Gerbner's call for critical inquiry, it would seem that this relationship with the interests and agenda of the Canadian state requires more scrutiny—a scrutiny that will not take place if we do not recognize our institutional history and if we do not abandon the assumption that we are *already* critical.

Not Enough Ferment in the Field

Critical communication studies in Canada situates itself in relation to debates within American communication studies, and specifically the distinction between critical and administrative approaches. Critical communication studies in the United States can be described through a series of commitments to the question of the intersection of communication and power in society, to a nonlinear under-standing of social power, to nonquantitative methods, to an epistemological posi-tion that recognizes the place of values in research, to theoretical roots in radical thought, and to the production of knowledge that contributes to a broader project of human emancipation.

When Canadian scholars have directed their minds to their own discipline, they have tended to focus on questions of national identity, assuming that Canadian communication studies is critical (as defined above) and mobilizing as their evidence the work of foundational thinkers such as Harold Innis, Marshall McLuhan, and Northrop Frye. Insufficient attention has been paid to writing, understanding, and engaging critically with the history of the field since the foundational thinkers. Current claims about critical-ness rest on the relationship of many scholars to political economy or critical cultural studies approaches, or generally to a leftist/humanist/cultural nationalist orientation. If a critical approach is going to mean something, and not be just a normal—and normal-izing—label, then we need to think about the ways in which our work is truly critical. One way to do this would be to map out a broader critical approach to communication studies—an approach that draws on, rather than smugly ignores, the American experience and at the same time incorporates the specific Canadian contributions of a focus on history, a dialectical approach to power, a concern with technology and culture, an awareness of nondominant epistemo-logical positions, and the inclusion of specific values. Arguably, in an era of attacks on universities, the erasure of the political left, a general anti-intellectual malaise, and economic and social globalization, critical communication research is as necessary as it has ever been.

Bailie (1997) suggests that "critical communication studies are intricately linked to a project that promotes a critical imaginary: the ability to think beyond present social, political, and economic conditions to participate in the construction of alter-native futures" (p. 33). Carey, too, uses the language of imagination when he argues that "a critical theory of communication must affirm what is before our eyes and transcend it by imagining, at the very least, a world more desirable" (1982, p. 33). To echo and paraphrase C. Wright Mills, who was addressing the discipline of sociology in the 1950s, perhaps what we need in Canada is a more active critical communications imagination—the kind that might be sparked through both honouring our ghosts and encouraging more ferment in the field.

QUESTIONS

1. What are the major differences between administrative and critical research as defined by American communication studies?

2. What are the six shared assumptions of critical communication research?
3. Why is it difficult to determine if Canadian communication studies is critical?
4. How does Canadian communication studies define itself as unique (i.e., distinct from U.S. communication studies)?
5. Discuss the ways in which Canadian communication studies is and is not critical.
6. Select a current communications phenomenon. How would you analyze it as a critical communication scholar? What kinds of questions would you ask?

WEB SITES

Journal of Communication: **http://joc.oupjournals.org/**
Journal of Communication Inquiry: **http://www.sagepub.co.uk/frame.html**
   http://www.sagepub.co.uk/journals/details/j0239.html
University of Iowa Department of Communication Studies, Links to Resources:
   http://www.uiowa.edu/~commstud/resources/

NOTES

1. The author wishes to thank Jessica Wurster for her invaluable research assistance and McGill University for its support of this research.
2. See the *Colloquium in Critical Studies in Mass Communication*, 1995 (special issue of the journal *Critical Studies in Mass Communication*).

REFERENCES

Acland, Charles R., and William J. Buxton. (1999). *Harold Innis in the new century: Reflections and refractions*. Montreal and Kingston: McGill-Queen's University Press.

Allen, Mike. (1999). The role of meta-analysis for connecting critical and scientific approaches: The need to develop a sense of collaboration. *Critical Studies in Mass Communication, 16*, 373–379.

Babe, Robert E. (2000a). *Canadian communication thought: Ten foundational writers*. Toronto: University of Toronto Press.

———. (2000b). Foundations of Canadian communication thought. *Canadian Journal of Communication, 26*, 19–37.

Bailie, Mashoed. (1997). Critical communication pedagogy: Teaching and learning for democratic life in democratizing communication? In M. Bailie and D. Winseck (Eds.), *Democratizing communication? Comparative perspectives on information and power* (pp. 33–56). Creskill, NJ: Hampton Press.

Biagi, Shirley, and Craig McKie. (1999). *Media impact: An introduction to mass media*. Toronto: ITP Nelson.

Blumler, Jay G. (1983). Communication and democracy: The crisis beyond and the ferment within. *Journal of Communication, 33*(3), 166–173.

Carey, James. (1975). Canadian communication theory: Extensions and interpretations of Harold Innis. In G.J. Robinson and D. F. Theall (Eds.), *Studies in Canadian communications* (pp. 27–60). Montreal: Graduate Program in Communications.

———. (1982). The mass media and critical theory: An American view. In Michael Burgoon (Ed.), *Communication Yearbook 6* (pp. 18–34). Beverly Hills: Sage.

———. (1983). The origins of the radical discourse on cultural studies in the United States. *Journal of Communication, 33*(3), 311–313.

de la Garde, Roger. (1987, Winter). The 1987 Southam lecture: Mr. Innis, is there life after the 'American Empire'? *Canadian Journal of Communication,* 7–21.

Elasmar, Michael G. (1999). Opportunities and challenges of using meta-analysis in the field of international communication in critical studies. *Mass Communication, 16,* 379–384.

Fleming, D., and B. Bailyn (Eds.). (1969). *The Intellectual migration: Europe and America, 1930–1960.* Cambridge, MA: Harvard University Press.

Garnham, Nicholas. (1983). Toward a theory of cultural materialism. *Journal of Communication, 33*(3), 314-329.

Gerbner, George. (1964). On content analysis and critical research in mass communication. In Lewis Anthony Dexter and David Manning White (Eds.), *People, society and mass communication* (pp. 476–500). New York: Free Press.

———. (1983a). Introduction. *Journal of Communication 33*(3),1–4.

———. (1983b). The importance of being critical—In one's own fashion. *Journal of Communication, 33*(3), 355–362.

Gitlin, Todd. (1981). Media sociology: The dominant paradigm. In G. Cleveland Wilhoit and Harold E. Bock (Eds.), *Mass communication review yearbook, 12* (pp. 73–121). Beverly Hills: Sage.

Grosswiler, Paul. (1996). The dialectical methods of Marshall McLuhan, Marxism, and critical theory. *Canadian Journal of Communication, 21*(1), 95–124.

Haight, Timothy R. (1983). The critical researcher's dilemma. *Journal of Communication, 33*(3), 226–236.

Halloran, James D. (1983). A case for critical eclecticism. *Journal of Communication, 33*(3), 270–278.

Hardt, Hanno. (1992). *Critical communication studies: Communication, history & theory in America.* London and New York: Routledge.

Holmes, Helen, and David Taras (Eds.). (1992). *Seeing ourselves: Media power and policy in Canada.* Toronto: Harcourt Brace Jovanovich Canada.

Jansen, Sue Curry. (1983). Power and knowledge: Toward a new critical synthesis. *Journal of Communication, 33*(3), 342–354.

Kroker, Arthur. (1984). *Technology and the Canadian mind: Innis/McLuhan/Grant.* Montreal: New World Perspectives.

Lang, Kurt. (1979). The critical functions of empirical communication research: Observations on German-American influences. *Media, Culture and Society, 1*, 83–96.

Lazarsfeld, Paul Felix. (1941). Remarks on administrative and critical communication research. *Studies in Philosophy and Social Science, 9*(1), 2–16.

———. (1969). An episode in the history of social research: A memoir. In D. Fleming and B. Bailyn (Eds.), *The intellectual migration: Europe and America, 1930–1960* (pp. 270–337). Cambridge, MA: Harvard University Press.

Lorimer, Rowland. (2000a). Editorial: The genesis of this issue—Twenty-five years of the *CJC. Canadian Journal of Communication, 25*, 3–7.

———. (2000b). Introduction: Communications teaching and research—Looking forward from 2000. *Canadian Journal of Communication, 25*, 9–17.

Lorimer, Rowland, and Mike Gasher. (2001). *Mass communication in Canada.* Don Mills, ON: Oxford University Press.

Lorimer, Rowland, and Jean McNulty. (1996). *Mass communication in Canada.* Toronto: Oxford University Press.

McKie, Craig, and Benjamin D. Singer. (2001). Communications in Canadian society (5th ed.). Toronto: Thompson Educational Publishing.

Meisel, John. (1987, Winter). Some Canadian perspectives on communication research. *Canadian Journal of Communication*, 55–63.

Mosco, Vincent. (1983). Critical research and the role of labour. *Journal of Communication, 33*(3), 237–248.

———. (1996). *The political economy of communication.* Thousand Oaks, CA: Sage.

Robinson, Gertrude J. (1987, Winter). Prologue: Canadian communication studies: A discipline in transition? *Canadian Journal of Communication*, 1–5.

———. (2000). Remembering our past: Reconstructing the field of Canadian communication studies. *Canadian Journal of Communication, 25*, 105–125.

Robinson, Gertrude Joch, and Donald F. Theall (Eds.). (1975). *Introduction in studies in Canadian communications* (pp. 1–6). Montreal: Graduate Program in Communications.

Rogers, Everett M. (1982). The empirical and critical schools of communication research. In M. Burgoon (Ed.), *Communication Yearbook 5* (pp. 125–144). New Brunswick, NJ: Transaction Books.

Rosengren, Karl Erik. (1983). Communication research: One paradigm or four? *Journal of Communication, 33*(3), 185–207.

Salter, Liora (Ed.). (1981a). *Communication studies in Canada/Études Canadiennes en communication.* Toronto: Butterworths.

———. (1981b). Editor's introduction. In L. Salter (Ed.), *Communication studies in Canada/Études Canadiennes en communication* (pp. xi–xxii). Toronto: Butterworths.

———. (1987, Winter). Taking stock: Communication studies in 1987. *Canadian Journal of Communication*, 23–45.

Schiller, Herbert I. (1983). Critical research in the information age. *Journal of Communication, 33*(3), 249–257.

Schramm, Wilbur. (1983). The unique perspective of communication: A retrospective view. *Journal of Communication, 33*(3), 6–17.

Sholle, David J. (1988). Critical studies: From the theory of ideology to power/knowledge. *Critical Studies in Mass Communication, 5*, 16–41.

Slack, Jennifer Daryl, and Martin Allor. (1983). The political and epistemological constituents of critical communication research. *Journal of Communication, 33*(3), 208–218.

Slack, Jennifer Daryl, and M. Mehdi Semati. (1997). Intellectual and political hygiene: The 'Sokal' affair. *Critical Studies in Mass Communication, 14*(3), 201–227.

Smythe, Dallas W., and Tran Van Dinh. (1983). On critical and administrative research: A new critical analysis. *Journal of Communication, 33*(3), 117–127.

Stevenson, Robert L. (1983). A critical look at critical analysis. *Journal of Communication, 33*(3), 262–267.

Szuchewycz, Bohdan, and Jeannette Sloniowski (Eds.). (1999). *Canadian communications: Issues in contemporary media and culture*. Scarborough, ON: Prentice Hall/Allyn and Bacon Canada.

Tate, Eugene D., Andrew Osler, Gregory Fouts, and Arthur Segal. (2000). The beginnings of communication studies in Canada: Remembering and narrating the Past. *Canadian Journal of Communication, 25*, 61–103.

Theall, Donald F. (1975). Communication theory and the marginal culture: The socio-aesthetic dimensions of communication study. In G.J. Robinson and D.F. Theall (Eds.), *Studies in Canadian communications* (pp. 7–26). Montreal: Graduate Program in Communications.

Tremblay, Gaétan. (1981). Préface. In L. Salter (Ed.), *Communication studies in Canada/ Études Canadiennes en communication* (pp. vii–x). Toronto: Butterworths.

Vivian, John, and Peter J. Maurin. (2000). *The media of mass communication* (2nd ed.). Scarborough, ON: Allyn and Bacon Canada.

2

A Not-So-British Invasion: Cultural Studies in Canada

Anne-Marie Kinahan[1]
Carleton University

Talking about culture in Canada is something of a national pastime. Whether the topic of discussion is nationalism, the popularity of American programming, or government support of the CBC, everyone has something to say about Canadian culture. But talking about culture also means talking about communication. Canadian culture, communication, and mass media are fundamentally linked, for in talking about Canadian culture, we are engaged in a process of defining ourselves and our relationship to the world.

Cultural studies developed as an attempt to assess, understand, and explore the role of culture in everyday life. Arguing that the notion of culture must be expanded to include aspects of popular culture such as magazines, newspapers, and other products of media industries, cultural studies analyzes the ways in which meaning is constructed in these artifacts or "texts," how audiences engage with the products of popular culture, and the role media play in society as a whole. These questions may be especially pertinent in Canada given the proximity of the United States and the strong presence of American popular culture.

Cultural studies first took shape in Britain. However, there are important differences between the concerns that motivated the original British researchers and the types of questions posed by the Canadian situation. These differences are reflected in the positions and theoretical arguments of both.

DEFINING THE TRADITION: BRITISH CULTURAL STUDIES

In the late 1950s and early 1960s, a new critical approach to the study of mass media and culture began to emerge in Britain. Growing out of the work of such scholars as Raymond Williams, Richard Hoggart, and E.P. Thompson, this new approach analyzes the emergence of mass-mediated popular culture and interrogates the connection between culture and society. This work stood in sharp contrast to the then-dominant approach to the study of culture, which was concerned with "high" culture and the maintenance of a strong cultural tradition, and which feared that mass-mediated culture would "level the playing field" and render any discussion of quality and value irrelevant.

Into this context came Hoggart's *The Uses of Literacy* (1958), Williams's *Culture and Society, 1780–1950* (1958) and *The Long Revolution* (1961), and Thompson's *The Making of the English Working Class* (1963). Collectively, these books signal the emergence of cultural studies and an approach to cultural inquiry that engages with popular culture critically and thoughtfully. While none of the books aimed specifically to create a cultural studies tradition, they all attempted to understand the connection between culture and society in a way that did not reproduce the dominant assumptions but rather questioned them.

Hoggart (1958), for example, chronicles the existence—and eventual demise—of a strong British working-class culture in the early 20th century. Placing himself within his narrative, he describes his childhood in a working-class neighbourhood. For Hoggart, as for Williams and Thompson, the personal experience of working-class culture was at odds with the scholarly tradition of Britain that devalued and marginalized such cultures. They approach the study of culture not as elite productions intended for affluent, well-educated audiences but rather as a *whole way of life*, as lived experience and patterned interaction among individuals, their communities, and society at large. What further characterizes this new approach is its *critical* assessment of the role of culture. Concerned with reclaiming working-class cultures from intellectual obscurity, Hoggart, Williams, and Thompson also seek to explain how culture participates in the maintenance and reproduction of social norms, codes, and traditions.

In his investigation of the connections between culture and society, Williams (1992) finds that the traditional approach to culture, which advocates a division between "high" and "low" culture and the creation of cultural canons, serves to negate the possibility of working-class culture entirely. Aesthetic judgments as to what constitutes "good" and "bad" create hierarchical relationships between the culture of the affluent and the culture of the working classes. In addition to recovering and discussing the culture of the working classes, Williams explains the process by which culture serves to reinforce hierarchical relationships within society. To that end, he provides a historical examination of the meaning of the word "popular." To a certain extent, "popular" means "that which belongs to the people," but Williams (1992) shows that the term "popular culture" also conveys an aesthetic and cultural judgment:

> Popular culture was not identified by the people but by others,
> and it still carries two older senses: inferior kinds of work . . .
> and work deliberately setting out to win favour . . . as well as the
> more modern sense of well-liked by many people. (pp. 231–232)

So, while culture is seen as an important way in which individuals participate in their community, it is also critically regarded as a means by which unequal, hierarchical, and inegalitarian social relations are continually reinforced.

Cultural studies, therefore, poses questions that are specifically concerned with the means by which society reinforces and maintains itself and its social norms, the role of culture (and specifically mass media) in this process, and the ways in which individuals receive, consume, and engage with mass-mediated culture. The Centre for Contemporary Cultural Studies at the University of Birmingham was the primary institutional locus for cultural studies in Britain. Created in 1964, with Hoggart as its director, the Centre sought to examine the lived experience and cultures of different classes. In 1980, Stuart Hall replaced Hoggart as director. Under his guidance, the Centre investigated the operation of power and ideology in mass media. As a result, cultural studies researchers began to foreground the study of ideology within popular culture. The study of ideology provides them with an entry point into a discussion of media texts, meaning construction, audience reception, and the reproduction of social norms, attitudes, and traditions. Central concerns revolve around the process by which cultural texts create meaning, how audiences decipher the produced messages and make them meaningful, and how this process of communication relates to society as a whole.

MARXISM, IDEOLOGY, AND THE STUDY OF CULTURE

> The ideas of the ruling class are in every epoch the ruling ideas: i.e., the class which is the ruling material force of society is at the same time its ruling intellectual force. The class which has the means of material production at its disposal consequently also controls the means of mental production, so that the ideas of those who lack the means of mental production are on the whole subject to it. (Marx and Engels, 1846/1992)

The work undertaken within the cultural studies tradition is explicitly engaged with a Marxist assessment of British society in the late 20th century. Hall, Williams, Hoggart, Thompson, and others all engage with Marxist social and political theory. However, they also break with traditional Marxism in its treatment of culture.

Traditionally, Marxism views culture as the result of economic processes and the products of culture as unworthy of serious academic study since they merely act out more fundamental forces. Within cultural studies, however, culture is seen as a "relatively autonomous" realm and its products are subject to critical examination. Cultural studies, therefore, challenges the tendency of traditional Marxism to view culture and cultural products as solely determined by the economic function of the market; instead, it views culture as a complex process that cannot be reduced to purely economic functions or relations (Turner, 1990, p. 24).

Bennett (1981) notes that the *economistic* focus of traditional Marxism has resulted in a neglect of how culture "actively influences and has consequences for economic and political relationships rather than simply being passively influenced by them" (p. 7). Consequently, the traditional Marxist focus on economic factors ignores the role of language in interpreting and understanding the material world (Turner, 1990, p. 25). In contrast, cultural studies employs a critical Marxism that seeks to elucidate the connections and interrelations between culture, economy, and society.

IDEOLOGY

Traditional Marxism sees capitalism as an ideology that casts a veil over the eyes of the working classes, causing them to suffer from a "false consciousness" that prevents them from realizing or understanding their own oppression. In contrast, Louis Althusser argues that ideology is a *web of relationships*, a *conceptual framework* through which we interpret, understand, and participate in the world (Althusser in Turner, 1990, pp. 25–26).

Althusser, whose views are part of the theoretical challenge to Marxism, argues that the economy is not the only mechanism that influences society. He sees society as consisting of *ideological state apparatuses* (ISAs). These include—but are not limited to—the legal system, the family, the educational system, and the political system. Essentially, ISAs bring together various forces, systems, and structures that demand specific actions and performances from individuals. They *situate* individuals according to their position within various social, cultural, legal, and political institutions. For example, an individual's identity and position within society is never limited to that of worker or owner; rather, all individuals are also parents, members of religious communities, students, and so on. These different *locations* require different actions and performances, and in fulfilling the roles required of them as parents, believers, workers, or students, individuals participate in the ideological reproduction of society. ISAs are thus deeply engaged in the cultural transmission of ideas, values, beliefs, and traditions. As such, they are inherently concerned with the establishment and reproduction of social norms and values.

The ISA approach is important because it shows that ideology is reproduced through various institutions and structures, rather than being simply a veil of false consciousness, and that relations of dominance and subordination are not solely enacted through the market. In addition, Althusser's interest in the structural functioning of ideology gives us a way to focus on the role of the mass media in constructing, reinforcing, and reproducing social norms and values. Bennett (1981) and Hall (1973/1980, 1982) are among those scholars who use Althusser's theory of ideological state apparatuses as a way of initiating discussion about the operation of ideology in media texts, news reporting, and popular culture.

MASS MEDIA, POPULAR CULTURE, AND HEGEMONY

In the 1980s, cultural studies became concerned specifically with the study of ideology and power in mass media and popular culture. It draws upon a number of approaches in order to assess mass media and popular culture critically, combining the theoretical studies of literature, sociology, semiotics, and history with social critique. Cultural studies, then, is not merely a celebration of the popular. Rather, it is a critical assessment of popular forms of culture, the ways in which audiences participate in them, and the process by which they engender political beliefs, social norms, and traditions.

Its interest in the study of the mass media also reflects the extent to which cultural studies sees value in the lived experience of everyday life. Specifically, cultural studies claims that the "signifying practices" operating within the mass media—that is, the way in which news stories and journalistic practices construct "social issues"—reflect the role of mass media in creating and maintaining social hierarchy. For example, Hall, Critcher, Jefferson, Clark, and Roberts (1978) argue that news coverage of muggings in Britain was constructed according to specific social, cultural, and racial codes. The issue of mugging, they maintain, was made intelligible to the "general public" through the social category of race. Similarly, Watney (1987) argues that media coverage of the AIDS crisis depended on the construction of homosexuality as a threat to society at large. However, rather than arguing that news coverage is part of a conspiracy to ensure the dominance of one point of view over others, these studies show how certain codes, symbols, and meanings are created through the very construction and use of language in everyday life. Institutional practices such as editorial decisions, while seemingly objective, reflect the extent to which language itself is a cultural construction.

Drawing on linguistic theory and semiotics, cultural studies analyzes language as a medium through which we construct, understand, and render intelligible the "reality" of the material world. Mass media such as newspapers do not, and cannot, merely "report" reality; they tell news stories in specific ways in order to ensure that readers will interpret and understand them accordingly. As Hall (1973/1980) notes, "Reality exists outside language, but it is constantly mediated by and through language: and what we can know and say has to be produced in and through discourse" (p. 131). The role of the audience in decoding and understanding the content of mass-mediated messages is an essential aspect of the study of media in society.

ENCODING, DECODING: THE ROLE OF THE AUDIENCE

In his influential article "Encoding/Decoding," Hall (1973/1980) argues that the primary weakness of mass communication research in the United States is that it theorizes the communication process as a "circulation circuit or loop" (p. 128). This unidirectional sender/message/receiver model overlooks the extent to which the communication process also depends on the activity of the audience in receiving, decoding, and understanding messages. In contrast to scholars who focus on the media's perceived ability to influence behaviour, Hall contends that the communication process is a "complex structure in dominance" (p. 128). Hence, we should focus on the ways in which messages are *encoded* at their source and *decoded* at their destination.

What is important about this approach is the way in which Hall analyzes the communication process as a relationship of dominance and subordination. The dominant position is that which controls the means of communication; the subordinate position is the one that receives and interprets those messages. For Hall, the media-effects research predominant in the United States is misguided because it fails to analyze the ways in which messages are constructed and encoded in order to produce a dominant or appropriate interpretation. Indeed, the media-effects tradition assumes that messages are *naturally* the way they are. Hall argues, therefore, that a semiotic approach to media study—an approach that shows how, from all the possible ways of making or reading a message, one in particular emerges—must operate at both ends of the communicative process. A semiotic approach assesses how mass-mediated messages are encoded and constructed in order to be meaningful to their audiences and how audiences draw on available social norms, knowledge, symbols, and meanings in order to decode messages.

This semiotic approach is based on the linguistic theory of Ferdinand de Saussure (1857–1913), who saw language as a "sign system" or "signifying practice." As a "sign system," language is a way to order, interpret, and comprehend external "reality." The linguistic signs that make up the system always consist of a *signifier* and a *signified*. The signifier refers to the physical form of the sign (the arrangement of letters or sounds that describe a physical object); the signified is the object referred to by the signifier (Turner, 1990, p. 18). The meaning of any sign is created through the relationship between the signifier and the signified. In order for meaning to accrue to the object, there must be a strong level of correlation between the object and the sign. However, this correlation is culturally constructed. The meaning of any sign is dependent on its relation to the larger signifying system of language, symbols, and meanings. Language therefore does not merely describe physical reality but is itself a process of constructing meaning and organizing reality (Turner, 1990, p. 13). It conveys meaning because it is part and parcel of a larger repertoire of images, symbols, and meanings that are operational within any social system. Language is not a natural given, but rather a cultural and social construction, a system of words and images that renders the material world intelligible. It is one of the primary means by which individuals comprehend and make sense of their world.

The important contribution of semiotics is that it provides an entry point for studying the way meaning is constructed in various texts, from novels to newspaper articles to television shows. Semiotics provides a terminology through which popular culture can be analyzed, deciphered, and critiqued. This approach to the cultural construction of meaning in texts is an essential element in the cultural studies tradition (Turner, 1990, p. 22). But cultural studies does not merely import theoretical models and approaches from other disciplines. Rather, it critically engages with semiotic theory, expanding its focus from the text to the *text within society*. The attempt to determine the ways in which meaning is constructed leads to an assessment of the function of the text (understood as a variety of cultural expressions and products) within society as a whole.

For Hall, the study of mass media, and of news coverage of social issues in particular, is predicated on an engagement with Marxist theory and attention to the construction of meaning. Together, these allow us to see how texts reproduce social norms and values. The key moment in the analysis occurs when we examine the *encoding* of the text and its *decoding* by audiences:

> In speaking of *dominant meanings*, . . . we are not talking about a one-sided process which governs how all events will be signified. It consists of the "work" required to enforce, win plausibility for and command as legitimate a decoding of the event within the limits of dominant definitions in which it has been connotatively signified. (Hall, 1973/1980, p. 134)

When Hall refers to communication as a "complex structure in dominance," he is referring to the process by which the encoding of texts successfully defines the terms by which it can be decoded and understood by its audience:

> Unless they are wildly aberrant, encoding will have the effect of constructing some of the limits and parameters within which decoding will operate. If there were no limits, audiences could simply read whatever they liked into any message. No doubt some total misunderstandings of this kind do exist. But the vast range must contain some degree of reciprocity between encoding and decoding moments, otherwise we would not speak of effective communication exchange at all. (Hall, 1973/1980, p. 135)

Cultural studies argues that the ideological role of the media is not reflected in a process of personal influence, as American media studies claimed, but rather in the ways in which the media contribute to the maintenance of the social and political system through a combination of coercion and consent:

> The movement—towards the winning of a universal validity and legitimacy for accounts of the world which are partial and particular, and towards the grounding of these particular constructions in the taken-for-grantedness of "the real"—is indeed the characteristic defining mechanism of "the ideological." (Hall, 1982, p. 65)

Ideology is thus defined as the representation of particularistic and partial views of the world as universal and valid for all of society. Cultural studies, then, is inherently concerned with the unmasking of ideology within popular culture texts.

FROM IDEOLOGY TO HEGEMONY

Cultural studies also draws on Antonio Gramsci's (1891–1937) theory of hegemony as a refinement of the analysis of ideology in mass media. Gramsci demonstrates the extent to which the political, economic, and cultural domination, or hegemony, of the ruling class is predicated on the consent of the governed:

> Hegemony implied that the dominance of certain formations was secured, not by ideological compulsion, but by cultural leadership. . . . The critical point about this conception of "leadership" . . . is that hegemony is understood as accomplished, not without the due measure of legal and legitimate compulsion, but principally by means of winning the active consent of those classes and groups who were subordinated within it. (cited in Hall, 1982, p. 85)

Certain rights, privileges, and advantages are provided to the subordinated classes in order to ensure the continued reproduction of dominant ideology. Hegemony, understood as the means by which the interests and perspectives of the ruling class are presented as common sense, is a process that is constantly under negotiation. In formally democratic societies such as Britain, the United States, and Canada, the dominance of a ruling class is buttressed by the continual support and consent of those governed. What contemporary cultural and social theory seeks to explain is the process by which this consent is continually reinforced and secured. Hence, the study of mass media investigates the extent to which media are not merely reflections of social reality, as well as the ways in which media actively participate in the construction of social reality.

In its approach to ideology, hegemony, and power in the media, cultural studies launches a critique of Marxism and Marxist critical theory while expanding their relevance for contemporary study. Marxist theory tends to be burdened with class analysis and economic determinism. But a number of scholars (e.g., Hall, 1973/1980, 1982; Hebdige, 1979; McRobbie, 1992; Willis, 1977) demonstrate the extent to which the ideological function of mass media also operates at the level of the lived experiences of race, class, gender, ethnicity, and sexual orientation.

SUBCULTURE STUDIES

The work of Dick Hebdige and Angela McRobbie is especially interesting for the way in which it engages with subcultures and focuses on individual agency and resistance to strategies of containment. By examining fashion, language, gender, consumption, and style as "signifying practices," they show how culture is an important element in the way individuals participate in their larger community.

Expanding the study of popular culture to consider everyday practices of schooling, shopping, and fashion, as well as media consumption, subculture theorists approach culture as a field of play, as the expression of personal and individual identity, and as a marker of membership in different subcultural communities. In *Subculture: The Meaning of Style* (1979), Hebdige demonstrates the ways in which punks actively cultivated and reinforced a marginalized identity. He shows how punks took the words and images used to marginalize and demonize them and turned them into a social identity for expressing their resistance to mainstream culture.

The study of culture, media, identity, and society—what McRobbie (1992) calls "identity-in-culture" (p. 730)—suggests that communication is culture. The intersection between communication and culture has repercussions not only for the functioning of the market and the delivery of content to audiences, but also for the ways in which we understand our world, our sense of ourselves, and our place within society. Arguing that the study of mass media is larger than the study of its effects on consumer decisions, personal attitudes, and individual behaviour, cultural studies approaches media and communication as social processes. In the process of transmitting content, mass media also transmit attitudes, ideologies, and beliefs that obscure the operation of power in everyday life. In addition to transmitting entertainment, sports, and information, mass media transmit a view of the world: they order social life, categorize social groups, define issues of concern, and reassert a normative view of the world.

CROSSING OCEANS AND DISCIPLINES IN A SINGLE BOUND: BROADENING CULTURAL STUDIES

So far, we have focused on the British tradition of cultural studies, specifically its institutional locus, theoretical concerns, and relationship to Marxism. But the political, cultural, and historical factors that shaped cultural studies in Britain are highly specific to that country and that time. We would do well to remember this when examining the relevance of cultural studies to other countries and other contexts.

In the 1950s, Britain experienced the emergence of a postindustrial, consumer-based, and supposedly classless society. At the same time, it witnessed the rise of mass media, mass culture, and mass audiences that introduced American popular culture to British audiences. British cultural studies, then, focuses on the analysis of power, ideology, and domination in media. It also focuses on the cultures of working-class men, as well as on subcultures as sites of resistance and agency. Most important, British cultural studies is concerned with an analysis of culture as everyday life and lived experience. Not limited to the study, condemnation, or celebration of popular forms of culture, cultural studies seeks to understand the means by which individuals and groups participate in society, how they make sense of their lives, and how culture informs a sense of belonging to or dislocation from contemporary life. These intellectual and cultural investigations are part and parcel of an engagement with the legacy of Marxism and its relevance for contemporary society.

The work of British cultural studies is connected to a left-wing intellectual and political project that not only seeks to explain the operation of power and domination in contemporary social life but also looks for strategies for intervention and an improvement in social relations.

FROM COMMUNICATION AS CULTURE TO CULTURE AS COMMUNICATION: CULTURAL STUDIES IN CANADA

While British cultural studies was shaped by historically specific forces, it bequeathed a variety of theoretical and methodological approaches, social and political concerns, and analytical methods that influence cultural studies work in such countries as the United States, Australia, and Canada. The attempt to define or explain the practice of cultural studies in Canada—a testament to the increasing influence of such scholarly approaches to culture, media, and society—can be represented in two distinct ways.

The first way can be called simply "cultural studies in Canada." This refers to the intellectual tradition that originates in Britain, travels across the Atlantic, and is being continued and expanded in North American universities. Hence, while British cultural studies is specifically concerned with the study of British popular culture and social life, its theoretical approaches are applicable to the study of culture and society in other countries. This movement suggests the importance of cultural studies in providing a useful and nuanced analysis of the role and function of culture in everyday life. The arrival of this British import in North America indicates not only the adoption of these theoretical frameworks by Canadian scholars but also the articulation of specifically Canadian concerns within this context. Hence, the second meaning of cultural studies in Canada is the deployment of these theoretical models in order to assess, criticize, and analyze the various questions related to culture in Canada.

Regardless of its specific geographical or institutional location, cultural studies aims to unmask and critique the operation of power in everyday life. It is, therefore, also an inherently political project that aims to transform social relations. Within a Canadian context, this political focus is not as explicitly concerned with working-class culture, as in Britain, but examines instead the varieties of cultural expression and experience in Canadian life. Blundell, Shepherd, and Taylor (1993) suggest that

> the problem goes further than that of identifying "culture"
> and "society" and attempting to understand the relationship
> between them. It lies rather in trying to grasp what it feels
> like to live within particular cultural and social circumstances,
> and how that feeling or "structure of feeling" (as Williams
> referred to it) is embedded within and acts upon wider social
> practices. (p. 3)

Admittedly, the attempt to explain how it feels to live in a given place, at a specific historical, cultural, and political moment, is a vast project. We might legitimately ask, What are the means by which we make sense of culture and society? What methods, theories, or arguments are best suited to launching such an analysis? One of the defining characteristics of cultural studies stemming from these questions is that it is not limited to any particular discipline. It draws on disciplines as varied as communication, history, sociology, film studies, art history, and English literature.

Straw (1993) observes that this inter- and multidisciplinary approach has prevented cultural studies from becoming a specialized practice. Indeed, while cultural studies in Canada is an intellectual pursuit, it is not solely limited to academic disciplines. Publications such as *CinéACTION* and *Border/Lines* represent an attempt to move beyond academic audiences to wider publics. Through these scholarly publications, and others such as *Theory Rules* (Berland, Straw, and Tomas, 1996), academics, critics, visual artists, and authors seek to explore the interrelation between critical and cultural theory and artistic practice. This refusal to locate the practice of cultural studies within a specific discipline or institution means that cultural studies in Canada is understood less as a specific academic discipline and more as an informed, critical, and engaged perspective that offers insights into the lived experience of everyday life.

Within the context of communication, cultural studies provides the means by which we can assess the specificities of culture and communication in Canadian life. The fact that cultural studies straddles both the social sciences and the humanities means that it lends itself well to an assessment of communication and media studies, which have been similarly situated in the gap between these two areas. Cultural studies was framed by two developments in the study of media and society: (1) the advent of media policy studies, which is concerned with "economic dependence and government complicity in the development of Canadian broadcasting and cultural industries"; and (2) the increasing academic interest in questions of identity, subjectivity, critical social theory, and Marxism (Straw, 1993, pp. 94, 95).

The value and promise of the cultural studies approach in Canada was that it had the potential to bridge the gap between these two perspectives (Straw, 1993, p. 95). The explicitly political project of cultural studies—the attempt to transform social relations—gave intellectuals a specific role in the policymaking process. Armed with an appreciation of the role of popular culture in everyday life, they would be able to make informed interventions into the official realm of cultural policy. The attempt to understand the connection between "culture as policy" and "culture as a whole way of life" is one of the central problems in discussions about culture in Canada. The variety of approaches suggested by cultural studies, then, provides an opportunity to assess the complexities of culture in Canada. Applied to the Canadian context, cultural studies is able to critically assess not only governmental attempts to construct Canadian culture through specific practices and policies but also the ways in which individuals participate in the creation and consumption of culture and media.

THE 'PROBLEM' OF CULTURE IN CANADA

Cultural studies in Canada emerged from sets of questions, issues, and problematics entirely different from those that characterized British society in the second half of the 20th century. Generally speaking, Canadian culture is the product of a variety of cultural, historical, and political forces. Historically, Canada became a colony of Britain and represented the extension of the British Empire into the "New World." But the two "founding" nations, Britain and France, are representative of two different cultures, languages, and political traditions. The tension between British and French cultures is still a prevalent concern, one articulated in debates about Quebec sovereignty and the recognition of Quebec as a "distinct society." Canadian culture is also marked by the legacy of the displacement of Aboriginal peoples. Questions about the "place" of Aboriginal culture in Canadian society are paramount concerns in discussions of Canadian politics, history, and culture (Valaskakis, 1988).

The attempt to construct a strong and unified sense of Canadian culture is further problematized by the regional and multicultural characteristics of the Canadian nation. A defining characteristic of Canada is the extent to which it has attempted to construct a unity out of its diversity. Often described as a "cultural mosaic," Canada is seen as a nation that allows for the expression of regional and localized cultures as well as a variety of ethnic and national heritages. The attempt to define what it means to be Canadian often invokes the ways in which Canada is understood as a compilation of diverse, multiple, and different cultures.

The internal problematics of Canadian culture—English–French dualism, the treatment of Aboriginal peoples, the regionalism of the nation, and the commitment to multiculturalism—are not necessarily barriers to the construction of a unified national identity. Rather, they are historical, cultural, economic, and social factors that characterize and define Canada. Any attempt to promote and foster a national identity must contend with these diverse, and often competing, cultural practices and traditions. Also to be considered is the external influence presented by the proximity of the United States. Questions about the creation and maintenance of a Canadian culture and identity are necessarily concerned with the influence of American culture.

The purposes of Canadian culture, then, are twofold: (1) to provide imagery, symbols, and materials to unify a culturally diverse and spatially dispersed population; and (2) to protect our culture from the impact and influence of American culture (Blundell, Shepherd, and Taylor, 1993, p. 11). One of the most striking characteristics of Canadian society is its reliance on government to ensure the continuance of Canadian culture through cultural policy, government subsidies, and the creation of cultural industries.

CONSTRUCTING CANADIAN CULTURE

Canadian culture has a complicated, problematic, and political history. As Manning (1993) argues, the central problematic of Canadian culture is that it is perceived as constantly under threat from American culture. The political characteristics of Canadian culture stem from the necessity of fending off this perceived threat through the provision of protectionist or promotional policies (Manning, 1993, p. 5). Hence, the dominant approach to culture in Canada is administrative and political and defines culture as a necessary element in the attempt to ward off the detrimental effects of American popular culture.

Official (i.e., government) approaches to culture in Canada have been explicitly concerned with nation-building, which involves forging a strong nationalism in order to ward off continentalism. The forces of American influence through culture and economy must be mitigated through the provision of outlets (both cultural and economic) for Canadian artistic expression. This approach gives Canadian culture a defensive and protectionist role. While Canadian culture is acknowledged as the expression of Canadian identity and experience, it is not seen as the organic, spontaneous expression of a community. Rather, it is created and enabled through government support of cultural industries. In this sense, culture in Canada becomes a political construct, a means through which Canadian identity is created and maintained.

In many ways, Canadian culture represents and embodies the transmission and ritual views of communication suggested by Carey (1989). On the one hand, mass communication is concerned with the transmission of messages, programs, and advertisements to audiences. On the other hand, mass communication is also a ritual that communicates traditions and values and can contribute to a sense of community. Within the Canadian context, the media of mass communication are by and large involved with the transmission of American content to Canadian audiences. This reality breeds the fear that American values and traditions are also being transmitted, threatening both the expression of Canadian identity and the formation of a Canadian community.

It is for these reasons that Canadian culture, supported by the government and enabled by cultural industries, is viewed as an essential element in the expression and maintenance of Canadian identity. In a historical context, the media of mass communication provide the technological and the cultural material that serves to unify the country. In the current context, Canadian culture must provide a voice for the expression of Canadian experience. Attempts to support Canadian culture aim to ensure markets for Canadian products and a Canadian audience for home-grown cultural expression.

CANADIAN CULTURE IN A GLOBAL CONTEXT

Contemporary research devoted to the discussion of Canadian communication technology and mass media reflects considerable concern over the position of

Canadian culture in North America. In discussing the emergence of Canadian communication media, Babe (1988) rejects the common perception that Canadian mass media have served to offset the detrimental effects of American culture:

> . . . [I]n Canada, techniques, systems and industries specializing in the diffusion of messages have most generally resided, even from the outset, under American control, and have been deployed consistently rather to further Canadian political, economic and cultural absorption into the U.S.A., to such an extent that it can be said with confidence that Canada persists despite, not because of, media of communication. (p. 59)

The study of mass communication evinces a strong concern about Canada's cultural industries and government support of these industries, about the arts in general, and about the globalization of American culture. Underlying these concerns are the assumptions that culture is a reflection of society and a means by which we express a national identity, and that the prevalence of American popular culture in Canada poses a serious threat to our cultural sovereignty, identity, and traditions. These perspectives are essential to a study of the increasing role played by economics in the cultural realm. Furthermore, institutionally focused analyses of the industrial structures of media institutions, the dependency on American cultural output, and the impact of international trade agreements on Canadian cultural industries attest to the global reach of American culture. These analyses suggest the importance of preserving indigenous cultural expression in the face of the increasing reach and influence of American culture.

POPULAR CULTURE IN THE CANADIAN CONTEXT

While discussions of Canadian culture in a global context provide an interesting perspective on the presence of American culture in Canada, they tend to overlook the role of Canadian audiences in receiving and consuming American popular culture. Too often, studies of the problems, failings, and potential promises of cultural policy assume that Canadians are passive receivers of American media content. While such studies point to the difficulties of protecting national cultures, attention must also be paid to the ways in which Canadians receive, consume, challenge, or resist the messages conveyed in American popular culture. Furthermore, such studies also assume that Canadian culture has always been deprived of any means of expression.

In contrast, Martin Laba argues that popular, folklore, and regional cultures provide the best means of expressing the Canadian experience. Indeed, Laba argues that regional and local cultures in Canada have been continually silenced and marginalized by attempts to construct a national identity. He describes local and popular culture as "the articulation of popular sentiment and social identity within limited contexts (region, community, class, for example), through the expressive, symbolic, and popular processes of culture" (Laba, 1988, p. 83). Such an approach underlines the potential for the expression of the various and diverse regions that constitute Canada. However, the drive to assert and maintain a strong national culture actually threatens the existence of these regional cultures. This relationship of "containment-resistance" has characterized Canadian regional development and remains the issue at the heart of Canadian cultural identity (pp. 83–84).

Culture within the Canadian context is subject to various strategies of containment and domination. In response to the omnipresence of American popular culture, its popularity with Canadian audiences, and the perceived threat to Canadian cultural identity, the federal government has made a concerted effort to ensure the maintenance of official Canadian culture. The creation of the CBC, for example, has afforded a strong, centralized, Canadian presence on radio and television. In addition, the establishment of the Canadian Radio-television and Telecommunications Commission (CRTC) reinforced the attempt to secure the expression and articulation of Canadian issues, concerns, sentiments, and traditions. However, as Laba (1988, pp. 83–84) argues, the increasing centralization of the CBC and the drive to express a "national" identity necessarily entails the marginalization of distinctive, regional, and local cultures.

The attempt to investigate and understand the position of Canadian culture within these strategies of domination and containment reveals the extent to which Canadian culture can be understood as a site of resistance and struggle. These struggles are multiple and further complicate the field of cultural studies in Canada. A fundamental struggle is the struggle to defend against the cultural homogenization of the United States. This struggle has entailed strong government support for cultural industries in Canada and is concomitant with the assertion that culture is a political necessity. In addition, there is the struggle within Canada to forge a sense of nationality within a context of thriving regional, local, and limited popular cultures.

NEGOTIATION AND RESISTANCE: CULTURE AND CANADIAN AUDIENCES

Research into Canadian popular, regional, and folklore culture has begun to investigate the ways in which culture expresses the Canadian experience. Such research also seeks to demonstrate the ways in which Canadians participate in, resist, challenge, and engage with popular culture in their everyday lives. In discussing the place of Canadian culture in an American media landscape, Manning (1993) characterizes Canadian popular culture as indicative of "reversible resistance." Arguing that Canadian audiences knowingly and ironically negotiate American popular culture, Manning asserts that scholars and academics must pay attention to the complex ways in which meaning is constructed and negotiated in media texts. In addition to the tradition of research that assesses the corporate ownership of media industries, there exists a field of research that investigates the "broader subject of Canada's popular culture and the means through which it is communicated and performed" (Manning, 1993, pp. 3–4). While such an approach still addresses the prevalence of American culture in Canada, it also focuses on the "response of the Canadian audience to that enormous influence, along with the significance of that response in the creation of Canadian popular culture" (p. 4). Increasingly, the argument is made that, despite our avid consumption of American popular culture, we still manage to retain a sense of ourselves as Canadian. Indeed, a central characteristic of Canadian popular culture is its engagement with, and resistance to, American cultural forms.

In discussing the characteristics and forms of Canadian popular culture, Walton (1993) suggests that Canadians employ strategies of resistance, irony, and parody in their engagement with American popular culture. While the construction of a Canadian identity is necessarily dependent on our proximity to the United States, this proximity also serves to define our difference. The engagement with Canadian culture almost necessarily demands a discussion of the impact and influence of American culture, but scholars such as Walton and Manning assert that such engagement is often ironic, playing on the assumption of Canada's supposed cultural inferiority. Furthermore, the success of Canadian actors and comedians in the United States, as well as the popularity of such films as *Wayne's World*, suggests that cultural influence is not a one-way street:

> The construction of Stan Mikita's doughnut shop in *Wayne's World* (a parodic play on Tim Horton's and a play that I would venture to suggest most Canadians "got" and most Americans missed) . . . [is] just as representative of Canada as National Film Board documentaries. (Walton, 1993, p. xii)

This attention to the ways in which popular culture expresses and reflects distinctly Canadian sensibilities is an important contribution to the interrogation of culture in Canadian society. Cultural studies research in Canada represents a significant movement away from perspectives that assume the detrimental effects of our proximity to the United States. The adoption of a cultural approach to the study of communication in Canada foregrounds discussion of culture as a social process—a negotiation between a text and its audience, between theory and practice, between policy and cultural consumption. A cultural studies perspective aims to continually interrogate the process by which artists, producers, critics, and audiences actively engage with a variety of cultural forms.

THE RELEVANCE OF CULTURAL STUDIES IN CANADA

The study of popular culture in Canada is far-reaching and cannot be limited to one theoretical approach. This is perhaps the most useful contribution that a cultural studies approach can make to the study of Canadian culture. Cultural studies provides fruitful avenues for the investigation of Canadian culture by drawing on a critical assessment of hegemony, ideology, and power; by analyzing the ways in which texts connote meaning; and by acknowledging the agency of the audience and its potential for resistance. A cultural studies approach to the ways in which Canadian culture reflects and expresses Canadian identity and experience will certainly provide us with a provocative and germane field of inquiry.

QUESTIONS

1. Why is culture such an object of concern and debate in Canada?
2. What is the connection between cultural studies and communication studies? In what ways are they different?
3. How does cultural studies challenge and expand the study of mass media?
4. In what ways can a cultural studies approach enhance our understanding of the relationship between culture and Canadian society?
5. What objects, activities, and practices define Canadian culture?

WEB SITES

Bad Subjects: Political Education for Everyday Life (webzine): **http://eserver.org/bs/**
Critical Mass (webzine of communications issues):
   http://hoshi.cic.sfu.ca/~cm/index.html
Media and Communication Studies (links to journals, newsletters, and archives):
   http://www.aber.ac.uk/media/Sections/journ01.html
Popular Culture (tutorial):
   http://www.ucalgary.ca/applied_history/tutor/popculture/
Theory.org.uk (popular culture and media theory site): **http://www.theory.org.uk**

NOTE

1. The author wishes to thank Paul Attallah and Leslie Regan Shade, as well as several anonymous reviewers, for their instructive comments on an earlier draft of this paper. Anne-Marie Kinahan was supported by a fellowship from the Social Sciences and Humanities Research Council of Canada in the completion of this research.

REFERENCES

Babe, Robert. (1988). Emergence and development of Canadian communication: Dispelling the myths. In Rowland M. Lorimer and Donald C. Wilson (Eds.), *Communication Canada: Issues in broadcasting and new technologies* (pp. 58–79). Toronto: Kagan and Woo.

Bennett, Tony. (1981). *Popular culture: Themes and issues*. Milton Keynes: Open University Press.

Berland, Jody, Will Straw, and David Tomas (Eds.). (1996). *Theory rules: Art as theory/theory and art*. Toronto: University of Toronto Press and YYZ Books.

Blundell, Valda, John Shepherd, and Ian Taylor. (1993). Editors' introduction. In Valda Blundell, John Shepherd, and Ian Taylor (Eds.), *Relocating cultural studies: Developments in theory and research* (pp. 1–17). London: Routledge.

Carey, James. (1989). *Communication as culture: Essays on media and society*. Boston: Unwin Hyman.

Easthope, Anthony, and Kate McGowan (Eds.). (1992). *A critical and cultural theory reader*. Toronto: University of Toronto Press.

Hall, Stuart. (1973/1980). Encoding/decoding. In Centre for Contemporary Cultural Studies (Ed.), *Culture, media, language: Working papers in cultural studies, 1972–79* (pp. 128–138). London: Hutchinson.

———. (1982). The rediscovery of 'ideology': The return of the repressed in media studies. In Michael Gurevitch, Tony Bennett, James Curran, and Janet Woollacott (Eds.), *Culture, society and the media* (pp. 56–90). London: Routledge.

Hall, Stuart, Chas Critcher, Tony Jefferson, John Clark, and Brian Roberts. (1978). *Policing the crisis: 'Mugging', the state and law and order*. London: Macmillan.

Hebdige, Dick. (1979). *Subculture: The meaning of style*. London: Methuen.

Hoggart, Richard. (1958). *The uses of literacy*. London: Penguin.

Laba, Martin. (1988). Popular culture as local culture: Regions, limits and Canadianism. In Rowland M. Lorimer and Donald C. Wilson (Eds.), *Communication Canada: Issues in broadcasting and new technologies* (pp. 82–101). Toronto: Kagan and Woo.

Manning, Frank. (1993). Reversible resistance: Canadian popular culture and the American other. In David H. Flaherty and Frank E. Manning (Eds.), *The beaver bites back?: American popular culture in Canada* (pp. 3–28). Montreal and Kingston: McGill-Queen's University Press.

Marx, Karl and Frederick Engels. (1846/1992). The German ideology. In Anthony Easthope and Kate McGowan (Eds.), *A critical and cultural theory reader* (pp. 47–49). Toronto: University of Toronto Press.

McRobbie, Angela. (1991). *Feminism and youth culture: From "Jackie" to "Just Seventeen."* London: Macmillan.

———. (1992). Post-Marxism and cultural studies: A postscript. In Lawrence Grossberg, Cary Nelson, and Paula Treichler (Eds.), *Cultural studies* (pp. 719–730). London: Routledge.

Straw, Will. (1993). Shifting boundaries, lines of descent: Cultural studies and institutional realignments. In Valda Blundell, John Shepherd, and Ian Taylor (Eds.), *Relocating cultural studies: Developments in theory and research* (pp. 86–102). London: Routledge.

Thompson, E.P. (1963). *The making of the English working class*. London: Penguin.

Turner, Graeme. (1990). *British cultural studies: An introduction*. London: Routledge.

Valaskakis, Gail. (1988). Television and cultural integration: Implications for Native communities in the Canadian North. In Rowland M. Lorimer and Donald C. Wilson (Eds.), *Communication Canada: Issues in broadcasting and new technologies* (pp. 124–138). Toronto: Kagan and Woo.

Walton, Priscilla L. (1993). Introduction. In Lynne Van Luven and Priscilla L. Walton (Eds.), *Pop can: Popular culture in Canada* (pp. ix–xii). Scarborough, ON: Prentice-Hall.

Watney, Simon. (1987). *Policing desire: Pornography, AIDS and the media*. Minneapolis: University of Minnesota Press.

Williams, Raymond. (1958). *Culture and society, 1780–1950*. London: Penguin.

———. (1961). *The long revolution*. London: Penguin.

———. (1992). Popular. In Anthony Easthope and Kate McGowan (Eds.), *A critical and cultural theory reader* (pp. 231–232). Toronto: University of Toronto Press.

Willis, Paul. (1977). *Learning to labour: How working class kids get working class jobs*. London: Saxon House.

3

Knowledge Matters: The Institutionalization of Communication Studies in Canada

Michael Dorland
Carleton University

KNOWLEDGE MATTERS

Knowledge does not fall from the sky. It is the product of individuals and their connections to others (teachers, colleagues, students, and the like); institutions (especially universities and governments) and their policy preoccupations; and media industries with their differing patterns of development. In this sense, knowledge is socially constructed.

Given the pre-eminence of U.S. institutions, it is hardly surprising that the study of communication in Canada was for a long time seen as a minor subset of American communication studies. Indeed, the very status of the field in Canada seemed to depend on the way in which American scholars constructed it. Generally, they constructed it through the key figures of Marshall McLuhan and Harold Innis. In the late 1960s and 1970s, James W. Carey, at the University of Illinois, wrote some influential pieces on both Innis and McLuhan (Carey, 1967, 1970, 1975). In the early 1980s, Daniel J. Czitrom's *Media and the American Mind* named Innis and McLuhan as the two "most radical and elaborate" of America's media theorists (Czitrom, 1982, p. 147). That Innis and McLuhan happened to be Canadian was noted but not elaborated on. From the American perspective, Canadian communication studies had provided the two most provocative minds in *American* communication studies, but it remained little more than a rivulet in the broader American mainstream.

The situation started to change in the mid-1980s when serious academic discussion began to investigate the history of the field itself. The discussion, which began in the United States, opened the way for a reconsideration of communication studies outside the United States. In her contribution to the discussion, Gertrude Robinson, then at McGill University, took as one of her central metaphors the old maps of the 15th and 16th centuries on which unknown and unexplored lands were simply identified with the phrase "Here Be Dragons." Canada was the Dragonland, but Canadian academics constructed the field differently than their counterparts in the United States. American scholars knew

McLuhan much better than Innis, but in Canada McLuhan was deemed unworthy of serious consideration and drummed out of the academy's worldview. This was largely because McLuhan's work was popular and could be interpreted as presenting an apologetic view of American media.

Attention solidified instead around the figure of Harold Innis (see especially Melody, Salter, and Heyer, 1981). Innis's work on staple products (the fur trade, lumber exports, etc.) meshed easily with the idea of economic and/or cultural "dependency." Significantly, from the 1970s on, *dependency* was an idea highly favoured by left-leaning Canadian academics because it seemed to offer an explanation for two facts of Canadian life: (1) the peculiarities of Canada's economic development (specifically, its export-driven economy and lack of an internal and independent manufacturing sector); and (2) the overwhelming presence of U.S. media products in film, television, books, and magazines—an influence that had preoccupied public intellectuals and government officials since at least the 1920s.

The concept of dependency also coincided with a broader social shift. The 1960s and 1970s witnessed an upsurge of public concern over Canada's economy and culture. This upsurge had direct consequences for the field of communication in Canada and, specifically, for *what* was to be studied. In short, Canadian communication studies came of age when nationalism was reasserting itself and it consequently defined itself in relationship to nationalism. Thus, whereas American university communication programs were more closely linked to the growth of American media industries, university programs in Canada were more closely linked to the growth of the public policy agenda. In the first case, communication study was, loosely speaking, market-driven; in the second case, it was politically and institutionally driven, especially by the state.

The political and institutional objectives that drove Canadian communication studies had other noteworthy roots. In this connection, it may seem surprising to focus on McLuhan's Catholicism, but it was meaningful on two levels. First, it was obviously central to where he taught (always at Catholic universities and at St. Michael's College, University of Toronto, which had a strong association with Catholicism). Second, it informed the more utopian aspects of his teaching (the idea that media had a potential for re-creating a global village was borrowed from the Christian ideal of the Second Coming), many of which were themselves taken up by the state and other institutions.

Hence, while McLuhan's theology may have alienated his more left-leaning colleagues, the Catholic "connection"—its interest in the message and the best way to deliver it—proved key to the creation of Canada's first university department of communication studies. In 1965, John J. O'Brien, a Jesuit scholar at Montreal's Loyola College, established the first college-level department devoted to the academic study of communication. O'Brien went on to become head of communications for the Vatican, while Loyola's communication department became part of Concordia University (which itself resulted from the fusion in 1975 of Sir George Williams University and Loyola). Needless to say, Catholicism itself was an "institution" with its own public policy concerns. And it is institutions and their research needs that shaped the emergence of Canadian communication scholarship.

From this tangle of influences, it is possible to identify three main forces that shaped communication studies in Canada. The first was the need of the state, at both the federal and provincial levels, to acquire policy-related information through royal commissions and special task forces struck to examine media-related problems.[1] The second force, located more strictly within the academy, was the use of economics, and especially political economy, to address economic and cultural "imperialism" (see Clement and Drache, 1978; Smythe, 1977). The third force, one that had given rise to the study of sociology in Quebec universities, was 20th-century Catholic social thought. These three forces did not always mesh perfectly, but they did have some important overlaps. Most significantly, perhaps, is the fact that all laid claim to "social redemption" by proposing strategies for a better world. All three also expressed a concern with culture, broadly conceived, and with the quality of community and social exchange.

It is within this roughly triangular structure that the institutionalization of communications in Canada took shape. The public agenda was set by the dominant pole of state-sponsored (or "administrative") research. A second pole criticized the first in the form of "critical" (largely political economy) research and claimed to achieve the goals that the first could not. The third pole criticized the first two and claimed a greater concern with culture; it later became "cultural studies."

INSTITUTIONS MATTER

In the United States, doctoral-level communication programs began to develop as the Second World War ended. Today, in the United States alone, there are some 2000 schools and departments of communication awarding 50,000 B.A. degrees and 250 doctoral degrees annually (Rogers and Chaffee, 1993, p. 367). In Canada, it was not until the 1970s that master's-level programs began to be established, particularly in Quebec. Doctorate programs in communication were established at McGill University and Simon Fraser University in 1976 and 1983 respectively; in 1987, a Joint Ph.D. in Communication was established by Concordia, the Université de Montréal, and Université du Québec à Montréal (UQAM). Among the 13 graduate-level communication programs currently available in Canada, six offer (or are about to offer) Ph.D. programs (see Table 3.1). As Table 3.1 makes clear, Canadian graduate communication programs vary widely by faculty and subject area, although all deal with aspects of communicative forms and practices.

TABLE 3.1 Major Canadian Communication Programs[1]

University	Faculty	Degrees Offered	Home School	Area of Focus
Alberta	Extension	M.A.		Communication and technology
Brock[2]	Social Sciences	B.A.	Department of Communications, Popular Culture and Film	Business; media and culture; policy; information technology
Calgary[3]	Communication and Culture	B.A., M.A.	Communication Studies	Cultural industries; interpersonal; intercultural; organizational law
Carleton	Public Affairs and Management	B.A., B.J., M.A., M.J., Ph.D.	School of Journalism and Communication	History; political economy; technology and impact of communication; journalism
Concordia	Arts and Science	B.A., B.J., Graduate Diploma, M.A., Ph.D.[4]	Department of Communication Studies	Mass media; media practice; broad communication application
Laval	Lettres	B.A., M.A., Graduate Diploma	Département d'information et communication	Cultural industries; media; public communication; journalism
McGill	Arts	B.A., M.A., Ph.D.	Department of Art History and Communication Studies	Visual culture; new media; image technology; social semiotics; social context ualization; culture
Montréal	Arts et Sciences	B.A., B.Sc., M.Sc., Ph.D.	Département de communication	Médias de masse/nouvelles technologies; aspects sociaux, culturels, juridiques et institution-nels des médias; organisationnel
Ottawa	Arts	B.A.	Department of Communication	Organizational; communication and media studies
Ryerson	School of Graduate Studies	B.J., M.A., Ph.D.[5]	Program in Communication and Culture	Media and culture; politics and policy; technology in practice; applied perspectives
Simon Fraser	Applied Science	B.A., M.A., Graduate Diploma, Ph.D.	School of Communication	Media; social communication; journalism; political economy; technology; cultural industries
Toronto	Graduate Studies – Faculty of Information Studies	M.I.S., Ph.D. (in Information Studies)	McLuhan Program in Culture and Technology	Media; culture; technology
UQAM[6]	Lettres, langues et communications	B.A., B.J., M.A., Ph.D.	Département de communication	Media; culture; group communication; sociopolitique; psychosociologique; sémiotique; anthropologique; ergonomie cognitive pour la nouvelle concentration en multimédia interactif
UWO[7]	Information and Media Studies	B.A.[8]	Media Information and Technoculture/ Journalism	Critical; institutions, practices, and cultural meanings associated with technologies of communication, information, knowledge, learning, and entertainment
Wilfid Laurier University	Arts	BA, BA Hons.	Dept. of Communication Studies	General overview of communications in Canada, with attention to specific media of communication such as film
Windsor	Arts and Social Sciences	B.A.	Department of Communication Studies	Media practices; theory and criticism; policy and systems
York	Arts	Diploma, B.A., M.A., Ph.D.	Division of Social Sciences– Communication Program	Traditional forms of mass communication (print, radio, film, television); emerging interactive telecommunications networks and computer systems; new media

1 This table presents an overview of major communication programs. In the Maritimes, the University of King's College offers a program in journalism; the University College of Cape Breton has a Department of Communication; the University of New Brunswick (Fredericton) has a multimedia studies program in its Faculty of Arts; and UNB (St. John) offers a B.A. in Information and Communication Studies.

2 Brock began offering an Interdisciplinary M.A. Program in Popular Culture in September 2001.

3 The University of Calgary's Graduate Program in Communication, as part of the new Faculty of Communication and Culture, began offering a Ph.D. in September 2001.

4 Joint Ph.D. in Communication offered by Concordia, Université du Québec à Montréal, and Université du Montréal.

5 The M.A. and Ph.D. are offered jointly with York.

6 UQAM = Université du Québec à Montréal.

7 UWO = University of Western Ontario.

8 UWO offers a Ph.D. in Library Science and Information Science.

In the late 1970s and early 1980s, Canadian academic researchers (I include Quebec researchers here, and will continue to do so, although the broader question of communication studies in Quebec is the subject of Chapter 4) begin to offer up some initial reflections on the Canadian field. These initial thoughts (Proulx, 1979; Tremblay, 1981; and Salter, 1981) are sometimes internally contradictory, but seem also to indicate five common themes that outline a process of institutionalization.

The first theme is the relative ease of distinguishing "Canadian" communications from the American variety. The second theme is the acute awareness that the establishment of the field in Canada is a struggle for the recognition of certain key features of knowledge in contemporary media societies. The third theme, which follows from the second, is the recognition that research funding is highly dependent on government and industry sources. The fourth theme is the conviction that a "science" of communication exists, though it is not clear just how scientific it really is. The fifth (and for our purposes most important) theme is the insistence on the intimate relationship among the changing characteristics of contemporary social organization and, as a result, the emergence of a body of knowledge that emphasizes communication. This framework is not without paradoxes and the themes are rarely presented in convenient, easily separable ways.

CONTEMPORARY SOCIAL ORGANIZATION AND THE EMERGENCE OF COMMUNICATION STUDIES

Gaétan Tremblay, the first president of the Canadian Communication Association, argued that the development of the science(s) of communication bears a strong correlation to the changing technological bases of modern societies (Tremblay, 1981). The problems of coordination and control stemming from increasingly complex forms of social organization led, he claimed, to identifiable problems in social communication. For example, political campaigns modelled themselves increasingly on advertising and marketing campaigns in order to control voter outcomes, while opinion polls played an ever more important, and unsuspected, role in the exercise of power. In response, both individuals and collectivities were demanding a greater degree of control over the definition of their own social identities and futures. For Tremblay (1981), the development of the study of communication "was [profoundly] linked to the increased complexification of relations of production and of social structure in contemporary societies" (p. ix).

Whatever the specifics of Tremblay's view, it is important to note that he argued for the existence of a "science of communication":

> A science of communication exists, although it still lacks both a history and an epistemology. It will only be through the critical development of its own postulates and methods that it will be able to become a scientific discipline and *not an instrument of political disciplining* [italics added]. (Tremblay, 1981, p. x)

It was one of the tasks of the new Canadian Communication Association, created in 1980, to promote that development.

Tremblay's (1981) essay points to the self-consciousness associated with being part of a newly emerging field of study—an awareness that social organization and knowledge were intertwined in a process of transformation with broad but uncertain implications for both. Accompanying this awareness is the suggestion that the emerging science of communication might represent a powerful mutation of a "knowledge formation," a new form of knowledge about knowledge, a "knowing" knowledge or superscience that can do one of two things: (1) align itself with existing forms of intellectual domination and so reinforce the arsenal of instruments of political disciplining; or (2) truly become a "new science" by developing its own self-understanding. These contradictory goals are reflected in the tension between the increasing numbers of students who are "seduced" by—and wish to reproduce—the highly visible communicative practices of their society (radio, television, public relations, advertising, etc.) and their professors, who evince a professional desire to contribute to a new field of "critical" or self-reflexive knowledge (Proulx, 1979, pp. 116–117).

EPISTEMOLOGICAL CONVICTIONS AND HISTORIOGRAPHICAL PROBLEMS

The 1980s

According to Tremblay (1981), a science of communication definitely existed by the early 1980s, in Canada and elsewhere, although it had neither much of a history nor an epistemology. Nonetheless, Serge Proulx, writing in 1979 about the Quebec university context, argued that "a new academic domain"—communication—had emerged in the 1970s as a result of institutional pressures: the creation of new programs of study at the B.A., M.A., and doctoral levels; rising demand from students; increased infrastructure for often costly equipment; larger government subsidies for teaching and research; and an "important number" of new professorial positions in the new field (Proulx, 1979, p. 103). These infrastructural changes had, in turn, brought together "the minimal internal conditions" for the development of a new domain of scientific knowledge: (1) an accumulation of specialized investigation, (2) the emergence of a scientific community, and (3) mechanisms for the transmission of a specific and homogenous corpus of knowledge (Proulx, 1979, pp. 103–104). Note that conditions 1 and 3 are intellectual, while condition 2 is their socioprofessional consequence (e.g., a learned society, an academic journal, and so on).

According to Proulx (1979), the mass media's rising social predominance meant that the communications media would become the concern of governments and social groups. Thus, the creation of university communication programs resulted "*first of all* [italics added]" from the needs of state and industry, and second, from the demands of social groups (Proulx, 1979, p. 104). As a result, academic researchers were both *linked and opposed to* (1) government and industry needs; (2) the uncertainties of university planning, as well as the ways in which they understood contemporary social reality and their relationship to social movements; (3) their own strategies of self-promotion as individuals and as professionals; and (4) their personal research interests. Epistemological issues relating to the emerging field were thus nestled within a complex interlocking set of social issues, state policy priorities, and questions of professional advancement.

For Liora Salter, as editor of a 1981 collection intended to reflect the diversity of Canadian communication research, the immediate task was to extract common themes from the "seemingly diverse articles" contained in her book (Salter, 1981, p. xii). To her mind, these themes revealed themselves first of all as sets of tensions "between the social dimensions of experience and technology, between the centre and the periphery ... between advertisement and expression, and between region-alism and centralization" (pp. xii–xiii). The Canadian approach differed both from the U.S. attempt to isolate the effects of a communication process and from the European tendency to pure theory. For Salter, "Canadian studies look at the media system rather than its specific content, at regulatory problems rather media effects" (p. xiv). Its focus is on "systems," "consciousness," and "culture."

While all of these terms suggest phenomena of considerable generality, Salter insists that in the Canadian context they mean something specific and historical. For example, she suggests that "communication studies in Canada seldom focuses on communication process in the abstract" (Salter, 1981, p. xviii). Thus, an emphasis on "system" translates into a concern with either the problems posed by proximity to the United States or the problems of state intervention in broadcasting and in the economy. "Consciousness" becomes "how Canadian consciousness is shaped by current political debates" (p. xiv). As for "culture," Salter has this to say: "To put the point in its simplest terms: communication studies in Canada takes culture itself as the problematic" (p. xviii).

Unfortunately, Salter's meaning is not clear. On the one hand, she seems to suggest that "culture" is the object that results "[o]nce the elements of political economy, epistemology, experience and technological form are seen as intrinsically related" (Salter, 1981, p. xviii). On the other hand, she also raises the issue of "the unique status of culture in the Canadian context":

> [Here] the answer is likely to be troubled . . . a non-answer . . .
> [because] culture in the Canadian case cannot be assumed . . .
> [or] used . . . as a basis for comparison or as a starting point . . .
> More significantly, in the general Canadian context, culture
> does not seem to be clearly identifiable. (p. xviii)

In Salter's view, it is precisely the difficulty of identifying Canadian culture that makes of it a central communication problematic: "*Culture becomes linked to communication studies when it can neither be identified nor assumed* [italics added]"

(p. xix). She goes on to state that, when such a sense of culture becomes the problematic of communication studies, the process of communication itself can no longer be understood as a model of transmission (the American approach) because it ceases to be a question of either what is being transmitted or how. Instead, for Salter, "Cultural experience is at the centre of what is being studied, not a variable in a process of encoding and decoding messages" (p. xix).

What Salter is driving at is that "culture" is *constitutive* of both consciousness and systems. She is attempting to put into words what would later be referred to as "the cultural turn" in the humanities and social sciences—a turn that began with the rise of structural linguistics and semiotics and the resulting displacement of the object of study to the "language games" or changing technological bases Tremblay had already referred to. What is interesting about Salter's 1981 analysis is its attempt to put into words a set of problems that would not be better identified until later in the decade.

Such statements were not, of course, restricted to the field of communication, but given its interdisciplinary porousness, it acted as a repository of the substantial transformations and rearticulations that swept across many existing disciplines such as literary criticism and history. In the process, existing disciplines were profoundly transformed while at the same time there emerged new interdisciplinary sites (film studies, gender studies, etc.) that were rearranging the structures of knowledge.

The 1990s

In 1987, Salter reviewed the issues raised in her 1981 introduction. The most striking difference in her 1987 paper—a paper unfortunately limited in its discussion to English Canada—is her conviction that the field of communication had in the intervening years solidified as a discipline with a specific object of study and with greater agreement as to how to study it. The object now was "information," understood not as bytes or data streams, but as what Salter had termed "culture" in her 1981 paper.

In the 1987 paper, information includes both signifying components and the directly observable features of a given environment; it is always something characterized by overabundance (of meanings, for instance) or supplementarity. For this reason, the study of communication had become "the process of selection and organization that [makes] this overabundance of information manageable" (Salter, 1987, p. 3).[2] Since 1981, information technologies—the so-called new communication technologies (NCTs)—had further altered "both the production and the interpretation of information" (p. 4), as had changes in public policy and industry structures. The emphasis on NCTs was significant not only because communication technologies were gaining ever-greater prominence and use, but because they themselves "'biased' the type of development that would [continue to] occur" (p. 7).

In her 1981 paper, Salter had argued that culture was communication's particular problematic. By 1987, it was more evident that the problematic was, in fact, a preoccupation with *cultural policy*. By 1997–98, communication studies in Canada had become centrally concerned with (1) information; (2) the management of information by individuals, social groups, and corporate entities; (3) the effects of new information technologies on processes of information management; and (4) cultural policy issues.

Between 1981 and 1987, Canadian communication studies became a discipline. In its earlier incarnation, communications had been more interdisciplinary (and therefore more radical in its critiques of other existing disciplines), but it had occupied only a marginal position in the university community—a marginality that some attempted to celebrate (see Theall, 1975). In the mid-1980s, a time of fiscal cutbacks in universities, coming-into-disciplinarity represented "the end result of a positioning of work within a field to achieve its institutional recognition and position of dominance" (Salter, 1987, p. 11). For Salter, "the establishment of new departments and programs in Communication in various [universities] and the increased interest by governments is a testament to the organizational and entrepreneurial skills of their participants" (p. 12). Hence, the *entrepreneurship* of Canadian communication scholars paid dividends in the form of institutional recognition.

Institutional recognition also translated into a claim to expertise with regard to the concept of information, a claim that other disciplines could not encompass. Indeed, as it evolved, the field of communication developed "a specialized language" of its own (Salter, 1987, p. 13). Moreover, government funding of highly pragmatic policy studies "raise[d] the profile of media studies within the field . . . [and] also . . . shift[ed] the balance between theoretical and applied work toward applied or policy research" (p. 14). Another aspect of the emergence of communication as a discipline was a focus on "the relationship between the technical organization of society . . . and how that society is organized and understood" (p. 15).

While communication may have become a discipline, it may also have lost some of its initial promise. Salter finds "troubling" some post-1981 developments in the field, but she concludes that we should not "criticize Communication for having solidified its status as a discipline"; rather, we should search for more systematic and rigorous ways to study the relationships between "text and context, media and culture, and technology and society" (Salter, 1987, pp. 17, 18).

For Tate (2000), Salter's 1981 paper was "a 'Central Canadian' history of Canadian Communication Studies" (p. 70) in its preoccupation with how, in Ontario and Quebec, communication studies had become dependent on state policy. Indeed, one can argue that communication studies in Central Canada had always entertained suspect relations with the state apparatus and with nationalist ideologies. As early as the mid-1980s, Collins (1986) noted that the enthusiasm of intellectuals in Canada (and Quebec) for the metaphor of dependency bespoke a decided intellectual "bias" that fetishized the central state as the means of achieving cultural autonomy. Indeed, one the key arguments used to justify the creation of a Joint Ph.D. in Communication involving Concordia, the Université de Montréal, and Université du Québec à Montréal was precisely the perception of Quebec's "high degree of dependency" vis-à-vis Canada and the United States with respect to higher education, scientific research, and, most dramatically, communication studies (see Comité interuniversitaire, 1984). In short, a centralized authority could end the dependency and dependency justified the actions of the centralized authority.

It would require several more years before the problematic relations of Canadian intellectuality and the state became the object of critical analysis. (To the credit of communication studies, these critiques developed from within the field itself.) In the intervening years, there were only occasional stabs at thinking further about the characteristics of the field in Canada. In 1989, for example, McLuhan's contribution to communication thought was belatedly recognized in a special issue of the *Canadian Journal of Communication* marking the 25th anniversary of the publication of *Understanding Media* (1964). In that special issue, a number of claims were made for the existence of a "Toronto School of Communication" that had ostensibly emerged in the 1940s when Innis, McLuhan, and Eric Havelock were teaching at the University of Toronto. This sort of historical reconstruction, however, seems to be little more than intellectual self-congratulation, a suspicion bolstered by de Kerckhove's (1989) claim that the Toronto School proffered "a radical new ideology . . . [that] may soon be seen to compete with Marxist and Freudian models . . . [of] a deep structure of human behaviour" (p. 78).

The early 1990s witnessed the publication in Canada of three books that were highly critical of the orientations of state policy in broadcasting and film development policies (see Magder, 1993; Pendakur, 1990; Raboy, 1990). Significantly, all three books were derived from their authors' doctoral dissertations in Canadian graduate programs. It was not until the late 1990s that a senior Canadian scholar tried once more to envisage the development of the Canadian field as a whole. Gertrude J. Robinson, invited in 1999 by the Canadian Communication Association to give the Southam Lecture at its annual conference, struck a cautionary note: "[W]e have only an incomplete understanding of the ways in which different 'schools' in different Canadian universities began their programs and how their departments developed the unique idea structures and disciplinary perspectives which make up the field today" (Robinson, 1999/2000, p. 8).[3]

Robinson adapted Roger de la Garde's (1987) periodization of the emergence of communication studies—beginning with a "prephase" of what he terms the communicative "echo chambers," which in the Quebec context sounded the rumblings that became the Quiet Revolution. The period beginning in the 1960s was marked by truly massive federal government intervention in communications policy debates and industry regulation (an intervention followed by the Quebec, Ontario, Alberta, and B.C. governments) in communications policy debates and industry regulation. By specifically identifying the legislation, Crown corporations, royal commissions, task forces, white papers, and diverse funds created to support this or that cultural industry, Robinson gives a face to what Dorland (1996) had rather too generally termed "the symbolic environment" in which Canadian communication studies underwent institutionalization. In such a context, as Tremblay feared in 1981 and Salter confirmed in 1987, the disciplinary solidification of communication had been purchased at the price of becoming "an instrument of political disciplining" (Tremblay, 1981), an intellectual resource primarily at the service of state policy, whether at the federal or provincial level.

None of these developments, it should be stressed, are inconsistent with the general patterns of institutionalization of the social sciences.[4] The rise of the research university as of the mid-19th century had placed powerful forms of knowledge at the disposal of heavy industry in the natural sciences and sophisticated new forms of social control in the hands of the state. That the social sciences, from economics to sociology, had earlier had more dramatic agendas for social betterment (from vastly improving industrial working conditions to solving the problems of urban poverty) is almost unnecessary to recall. Social knowledge, as we've mentioned, is both socially constructed and socially constrained.

In the Canadian context, if the institutionalization of the field primarily mirrored state priorities and secondarily university and ministries of education politics, that process would in turn also reproduce the major political divisions of the Canadian public sphere. In the 1970s and 1980s, this meant principally the failure of the belated attempt at creating a meaningfully bilingual society and, through this, the often bitter divergences between Ottawa and Quebec over control of communications and communications policy. More strongly put, what this amounts to is the acceptance by the intellectual class of a de facto version of linguistic and cultural division as a precondition of their intellectual labour and the funding of their research.

This is a topic Robinson approaches in her 1999 Southam Lecture with extreme caution. Gingerly, she raises the question of what she terms "the English/French divide in the ways in which communication studies" have been defined and studied in the academy (Robinson, 1999/2000, p. 16). She goes on to remark that not enough research has been done on the differences in the professional formation of English- and French-speaking faculty—or on how these differences might have affected professorial research agendas. Drawing on de la Garde's 1987 Southam Lecture, she reiterates his argument that Quebec's modernization agenda unduly and prematurely narrowed Quebec researchers' scholarly concerns, short-circuited historically based studies, and overemphasized questions of Quebec national identity while ignoring research initiatives in the rest of Canada (p. 16). She also adds, with startling naiveté, that it "is presently unknown" whether there were similar processes at work in English Canada.

Nonetheless, Robinson does at least raise the linguistic/cultural question, which surely constitutes a crucial defining characteristic of the institutionalization of communication studies in the Canadian context—indeed, a characteristic as significant as the role of the state in setting research priorities and establishing graduate programs. The "linguistic divide," therefore, reinforces the highly fragmented nature of communication studies in Canada, a fragmentation already encouraged by the various disciplines from which different programs emerged and by their regional location.

KNOWLEDGE IN CONTEMPORARY MEDIA SOCIETIES

All of the analyses we have looked at thus far explicitly or implicitly make claims relating to fundamental changes with respect to knowledge and the production of knowledge in contemporary societies. At their most sweeping, these claims range from a metahistory that develops a framework of epochal divisions linked to a dominant mode of communication and the resulting monopolies and biases of historically articulated knowledge forms, to, more narrowly, what one might term the "cultural" biases caused by information machines or new communication technologies.

There is a paradox in such a broad range: the communication of knowledge is vitally important to social organization, but, as a result, knowledge is also increasingly socialized and therefore that much more monopolizable by social institutions and social actors. This paradox creates a tremendous problem in explaining not so much how "new" knowledge is created as how it can possibly gain purchase on existing, institutionalized forms of knowledge. Consequently, new knowledge is highly vulnerable to institutional influence. That is why recognition by the state becomes the institutional secret of all the emerging social and human sciences, from political economy to psychoanalysis. That is also why, reverting to Proulx (1979) and Salter (1981), there was such a high degree of awareness that communication studies would be—and risked remaining—utterly dependent on state or industry for research funding. The other side of the coin, raised defensively by Salter (1987) but also more directly by de la Garde (1987) and implicitly by Robinson (1999/2000), is whether or not the costs, in terms of intellectual integrity and freedom of inquiry, were too high.

The short answer would be no, in part because Canadian communication scholars were making a unique contribution to (national) scholarship (or so they claimed), but also because they were saying something important about the changed characteristics of knowledge in mass-media societies. In other words, securing institutionalization involved two important moves: (1) an *external* move to differentiate communication from similar bodies of knowledge by emphasizing its "Canadianness"; and (2) an *internal* move to differentiate communication from other, existing disciplines by emphasizing its differences.

THE 'CANADIANNESS' OF CANADIAN COMMUNICATION STUDIES AND DISCIPLINARY DIFFERENCES

Whereas Robinson remained agnostic on the Canadianness of Canadian communication studies, Babe (2000) is firmly convinced of the distinctiveness of Canadian communication thought (or at least of *English-Canadian* communication thought, as he is largely silent on French-language communication research beyond a nod to "linguistic duality") (p. 30). In effect, he views Canadian communication thought as a reworking of the larger Anglo-American traditions or, as he puts it more sweepingly, "[as] but a small part of a much larger field of study dating back at least to the early Greeks" (Babe, 2000, p. 5).

Babe proposes a fourfold typology of the larger field along a horizontal humanities/social sciences axis and a vertical critical/administrative (or pluralist) axis; thus, for instance, the critical pole could comprise cultural studies along the arts–humanities axis, rivalling with political economy along the same axis. To the critical antinomy he juxtaposes administrative research (polling, market surveys, audience ratings, etc.), adding to this a "pluralist" dimension or the presumption that there are few institutional or other (class, gender, etc.) impediments "to people making their way" (Babe, 2000, p. 16) through the density of social relations.

Babe's description of the general characteristics of the Canadian imaginative context repeats many familiar clichés: it is nonrevolutionary, collectivist, or communitarian; is made up of garrison mentalities; and has been marked by a harsh and barren landscape with a shared emphasis in English and in French on survival. More interesting are Babe's claims that Canadian thought, and communication thought in particular, distinguishes itself (from *American* thought especially) by its emphasis on dialectics, ontology, a critical theory and humanities tradition that includes both cultural studies and political economy, and a notion of social totality in which "the irreducible unit of analysis is *the relation*, not the thing [italics added]" (Babe, 2000, p. 28). What characterizes Canadian communication thought for Babe is its focus on media or *mediation*, in which experience is seldom direct and relations among people are "mediated by institutions, by technologies, by philosophies[,] . . . stories or myths, by property, by mass media, and so forth" (p. 32). He goes on to note that understanding such factors as who controls the means of mediation "goes a long way towards neutralizing . . . power and perhaps encouraging resistance" (p. 32).

Does Babe's framework amount to a convincing typology of "Canadian" distinctiveness? One way of putting his claims to the test in a less vague framework would be to look more specifically at the predominant disciplines that imprinted on Canadian communication studies as it took form within specific university programs. In this light, we can say that the institutional context for the development of communications in Canada was roughly triangular (influence of the state, critique of the state by political economy, and critique of both state and political economy by the cultural "sciences"), and that there was an equivalent triangulation of disciplinary formations. Thus, in more or less chronological order, the first corner of the disciplinary triangle emerged from the shift in English studies from literary texts to the analysis of other kinds of "texts" (film, advertising, and so on, along the model of Barthes' *Mythologies*). The second corner derived from sociology and its extensions across the social sciences (social psychology, sociology of mass communication, political economy, etc). The third corner arose out of the analysis of the problematics of public speech, notably through the prisms of journalism studies, speech communication, and rhetoric.

If we apply this triangulation to specific departmental programs (allowing for historical change as graduate programs are added to undergraduate ones), we find in the literary or textual analysis corner of the triangle Loyola/Concordia, McGill, Windsor, and Brock. Occupying the sociological corner are Simon Fraser, UQAM, York, and Carleton, while emerging from the analysis of public speech we find Carleton (on its journalism side, but also in regard to some of its communication concerns), Western, Laval, Ottawa, Calgary, and King's (in journalism). In this perspective, the predominant set of problematics of Canadian communications turn out to be, by a slim margin, those concerned with "free speech and public discourse (rhetoric, clarity, persuasion, etc.) It [thus] conceived of the 'mass' not as an alienated public but rather as one of the conditions of a functional democracy" (Paul Attallah, personal communication, December 14, 2000).

It makes a great deal of sense that the core preoccupations of communications in the Canadian context are those concerned with the articulations of and (in)articulateness of public speech, due largely to the fragmented nature of public speech in this country (a fragmentation stemming from the language divide and the diasporic cultural effects of enormous spaces and small communities). In an important rejoinder to Salter (1981), Tate (2000) makes a case for the study of rhetoric in the Canadian context. Rhetorical training played a central role not only in the curricula of Upper and Lower Canadian colleges in the 19th century, but also in speech communication programs offered in the Maritime and the Western provinces in the 20th century. In the Maritimes, speech communication programs became Departments of Educational Communication within colleges of education; in the West, these programs were found in many community colleges in Alberta and British Columbia. In a cross-Canada survey of the 1960s, Lew Wilson found that speech communication programs were strongest in Maritime and Western universities—this at a time when, in Central Canada, McGill and Concordia were just beginning to set up their own programs in communication (Tate, 2000, p. 70).

CONCLUSION

The line of inquiry suggested by Tate must for the time being remain a research hypothesis in need of further investigation. One of its possible consequences could be to weaken the "Canadian distinctiveness" thesis by aligning communication in Canada to a greater degree with the rhetorical tradition of the Scottish Enlightenment, with its focus on the rhetorical training of citizens in emerging commercial societies (see Hubert, 1994), and also with the transformations of the 19th-century elocutionary movement in the United States and the problems of democratic eloquence (see Cmiel, 1990; Gronbeck, 1998). The lack of research with respect to the linguistic divide, microhistories of specific departments and programs, and both the research agendas and professional formation of faculty members means that much remains to be done in order to reach a better understanding of communication studies in Canada.

For these reasons, it is important to stress the important role played by *ambivalence* in the institutionalization processes of communications in Canada, with respect to both the emerging discipline and the institutional actors within universities and beyond. In 1969–71, a period when communication programs were being institutionalized at McGill, Loyola, and the Université de Montréal, as well as within the Quebec Ministry of Education, ambivalence was rife (Jim Taylor, personal communication, December 27, 2000). Loyola was "still a pretty Catholic shop," while McGill's English department under Donald Theall was "highly eccentric" and "became a (very) loose interdisciplinary effort." At Université de Montréal, departments and faculties waged a fierce competition over communication between departments as well as faculties; "psychology got it because it wanted it the least, and the university wanted to avoid choosing between the two other powerful faculties."

Taylor repeatedly makes the point that ambivalence was key to discussions of program models. (For example, programs at both McGill and Loyola resembled the Annenberg program at the University of Pennsylvania *before* George Gerbner brought to it an aura of scientificity; it then became the model for Université de Montréal.) He stresses the extent to which Université de Montréal suffered from "a split personality" resulting from "open conflict" within the social sciences. Finally, he emphasizes his own "personal ambivalence" (he received his doctorate, in literature, in Britain), which he feels was reflected in deliberately ambiguous hiring decisions.

In 1972, Diana Crane published *Invisible Colleges*, a pathbreaking study on the diffusion of knowledge in scientific communities. In the book, she looked at how "variations in communication patterns among scientists actually affect the development of knowledge" (Crane, 1972, p. 11). She found enormous variations within research areas, a high degree of epistemological uncertainty, and rapid obsolescence of knowledge. In this highly fluid situation, the role of personal communication between researchers in informal communication networks (invisible colleges) becomes central. As Crane puts it, scientific communication can be understood as the interaction between a volatile research front (from which new knowledge emerges) and a stable, much less flexible formal communication system that evaluates and disseminates new knowledge beyond the boundaries of the research area that produced it. With the research front continually changing, it becomes increasingly difficult for researchers to keep abreast of new findings by relying solely on the formal communication system.

The enormous growth in new knowledge necessitates both effective informal communication networks and greater flexibility in the formal communication system. Crane (1972) elaborates:

Progress in manipulating this system may come about as a result of increased understanding of the ways in which scientists use ideas and of the types of ideas that are most useful to them. The full range of innovations in the formal communication system has yet to be explored. (p. 128)

Crane reminds us that knowledge—and in particular the communication of knowledge—matters. And knowledge, as she notes, is the product of "a complex network of groups of interacting individuals" (p. 142) about whose membership and patterns of communication we have much yet to discover.

QUESTIONS

1.   How does knowledge come about? Identify some of the key factors involved, and the kinds of formal and informal communication networks that result.
2.   What do you know about Marshall McLuhan's main ideas? What does the phrase "the medium is the message" suggest to you?
3.   What were the five major defining differences between Canadian communication thought and American communication studies?
4.   Explain in your own words Liora Salter's observation that "culture is constitutive."
5.   What are the main characteristics of public speech in Canada?

WEB SITES

Canadian Journal of Communication: **http://www.cjc-online.ca/**
Carleton School of Journalism and Communication, First Annual Kesterton
     Lecture: **http://www.carleton.ca/jmc/news/events/starowicz.html**
Media Awareness Network: **http://www.media-awareness.ca/eng/**
University of Iowa Department of Communication Studies, Links to Resources:
     http://www.uiowa.edu/~commstud/resources/

NOTES

1.   A partial list of royal or special commissions since 1951 would include the 1957 Royal Commission on Broadcasting, the 1960 Royal Commission on Publications, the 1965 Committee on Broadcasting, the 1970 Special Senate Committee on Mass Media, the 1972 Royal Commission on Book Publishing, the 1976 Royal Commission on Violence in the Communications Industry, the 1981 Royal Commission on Newspapers, the 1982 Federal Cultural Policy Review Committee, and the 1986 Taskforce on Broadcast Policy. Each

commission's work was backed by research studies on various topics undertaken by communication scholars and academics in related fields. For example, Dallas Smythe—the "founding father" of Canadian political economy of communications (after Innis, of course)—was the primary author of the report of the 1957 Royal Commission on Broadcasting (see, for example, Raboy, 1990; Robinson, 1999/2000).

2. Page numbers in parenthetical citations for Salter (1987) refer to a typescript of the article. For bibliographic details of the published version, see Salter (1987) in the references list.

3. Page numbers in parenthetical citations for Robinson (1999/2000) refer to a typescript of her lecture. For bibliographic details of the published version, see Robinson (1999/2000) in the references list.

4. On the institutionalization of the social sciences, see the still-prophetic *The Coming Crisis of Western Sociology* (Gouldner, 1970) and the more recent *Unthinking Social Science* (Wallerstein, 1991).

REFERENCES

Babe, Robert E. (2000). *Canadian communication thought: Ten foundational writers.* Toronto: University of Toronto Press.

Carey, James W. (1967, Spring). Harold Adams Innis and Marshall McLuhan. *Antioch Review, 27,* 5–39.

———. (1970). Marshall McLuhan. *World Book Encyclopedia.*

———. (1975). Canadian communication theory: Extensions and interpretations of Harold Innis. In G.J. Robinson and Donald F. Theall (Eds.), *Studies in Canadian communications* (pp. 27–59). Montreal: McGill University Program in Communications.

Collins, Richard. (1986, Winter). The metaphor of dependency and Canadian communications: The legacy of Harold Innis. *Canadian Journal of Communication, 12*(1), 1–19.

Comité interuniversitaire Concordia University, Université de Montréal, UQAM. (1984, July). Dossier pour la création d'un doctorat conjoint en communication, Rapport. Unpublished document.

Clement, Wallace, and Daniel Drache. (1978). *A practical guide to Canadian political economy.* Toronto: Lorimer.

Cmiel, Kenneth. (1990). *Democratic eloquence: The fight over popular speech in nineteenth-century America.* New York: William Morrow.

Crane, Diana. (1972). *Invisible colleges: Diffusion of knowledge in scientific communication.* Chicago: University of Chicago Press.

Czitrom, Daniel J. (1982). *Media and the American mind: From Morse to McLuhan.* Chapel Hill: University of North Carolina Press.

de Kerckhove, Derek. (1989, Fall). McLuhan and the "Toronto School of Communication." *Canadian Journal of Communication*, 73–79.

de la Garde, Roger. (1987, Winter). Mr. Innis, is there life after the 'American Empire'? (The 1987 Southam Lecture). *Canadian Journal of Communication*, 7–21.

Dorland, Michael. (1996). Introduction. In M. Dorland (Ed.), *The cultural industries in Canada: Problems, policies and prospects* (pp. ix–xiii). Toronto: Lorimer.

Gouldner, A.W. (1970). *The coming crisis of western sociology*. New York: Basic Books.

Gronbeck, Bruce E. (1998). *Paradigms of speech communication studies: Looking back toward the future*. Boston: Allyn and Bacon.

Hubert, Henry A. (1994). *Harmonious perfection: The development of English studies in nineteenth-century Anglo-Canadian colleges*. East Lansing: Michigan State University Press.

Magder, Ted. (1993). *Canada's Hollywood: The Canadian state and feature films*. Toronto: University of Toronto Press.

Melody, William H., Liora Salter, and Paul Heyer (Eds.). (1981). *Culture, communication and dependency: The tradition of Harold Innis*. Norwood, NJ: Ablex.

Pendakur, Manjunath. (1990). *Canadian dreams and American control: The political economy of the Canadian feature film industry*. Toronto: Garamond.

Proulx, Serge. (1979, janvier-avril). Les communications: Vers un nouveau savoir savant? *Recherches sociographiques, XX*(1), 103–117.

Raboy, Marc. (1990). *Missed opportunities: The story of Canada's broadcasting policy*. Montreal and Kingston: McGill-Queen's University Press.

Robinson, Gertrude J. (1999/2000). Remembering our past: Reconstructing the field of Canadian communication studies. (The 1999 Southam Lecture). Typescript, 28 pp. Published under the same title in *Canadian Journal of Communication, 25*(1), 105–126.

Rogers, Everett M., and Steven H. Chaffee. (1993). The past and the future of communication study: Convergence or Divergence? In Mark R. Levy and Michael Gurevitch (Eds.), *Defining media studies: Reflections on the future of the field* (pp. 367–373). New York: Oxford University Press.

Salter, Liora. (1981). Editor's introduction. In Liora Salter (Ed.), *Communication studies in Canada* (pp. xi–xxii). Toronto: Butterworths.

———. (1987). Communication studies in Canada: The emergence of a discipline. Typescript, 18pp. Published under the title "Taking Stock: Communication Studies in 1987" in *Canadian Journal of Communication*, Winter 1987, 23–45.

Smythe, Dallas. (1977, Fall). Communications: Blindspot of western Marxism. *Canadian Journal of Political and Social Theory, 1*(3), 1–27.

Tate, Eugene D. (2000). Introduction to the beginnings of communication studies in Canada: Remembering and narrating the past. Special dossier in *Canadian Journal of Communication, 25*(1), 62–70.

Theall, Donald F. (1975). Communication theory and the marginal culture: The socio-aesthetic dimensions of communication study. In G.J. Robinson and Donald F. Theall (Eds.), *Studies in Canadian communications* (pp. 7–26). Montreal: McGill University Program in Communications.

Tremblay, Gaétan. (1981). Préface. In Liora Salter (Ed.), *Communication studies in Canada* (pp. vii–x). Toronto: Butterworths.

Wallerstein, Immanuel. (1991). *Unthinking social science: The limits of nineteenth-century paradigms.* Cambridge, U.K.: Polity Press.

4

Coming of Age: Communication Studies in Quebec

Roger de la Garde   and   *François Yelle*
Université Laval   *Université de Montréal*

This chapter deals with the history and main characteristics of French-language university research as conducted principally within Quebec.[1] Our task is greatly aided by two articles, written by Lacroix and Lévesque (1985a, 1985b), that examine the emergence of communication studies in Quebec.

1848–1950

The earliest period is usually associated with the conservatism of the regime of Premier Maurice Duplessis (1936–39, 1944–59). However, not all of society—and especially not civil society, the realm of social relations not governed by the state—could simply be labelled "traditional." The dominant discourse of this period, while heavily influenced by organized religion and the state and strongly favouring such values "as the family, Christian morality, respect for order and submission to duty" (Paquette, 2001, p. 112), perhaps surprisingly *also* promoted a progressive state.

Indeed, progress within a context of stability appears to have been the main theme of the period. The state, contrary to the usual view, actually promoted "the emancipatory principles of modernity such as law, liberty and progress" (Paquette, 2001, p. 113), as well as economic development and social welfare. In addition, other institutions (the family and the Church) helped promote a lay ethic that inculcated deference to authority and individual responsibility toward collective life from which grew "an image of living together" (Paquette, 2001, p. 117). The lay ethic, with its sense of collective responsibility, eventually became a notion of the public good.

The period 1848–1950, therefore, is one in which Quebec society, like the rest of North America, emerges from its traditional roots and enters modernity. It brings with it certain inheritances—most notably the transfer of traditional modes of "living together" into the modern notion of the public good—but it is also resolutely modern. It is against this background that we can distinguish two phases in the "structuration of the communication research apparatus" (Lacroix and Lévesque, 1985a). The "research apparatus," of course, refers to the whole range of institutions, techniques, and strategies involved in the study of communication.

This "apparatus" is established over two periods: an emergence phase (1957–67) and an institutionalization phase (1968–85) (Lacroix and Lévesque, 1985a).

The origins of the emergence phase actually stretch back to the period between the two world wars (1919–39). Nonetheless, this phase was characterized by "major transformations in Quebec society" and by the appearance of the first specialized research forums. However, research at this time was mainly concerned with the mass media and their "effects" and was for the most part conducted not by "public" institutions, but by "private" institutions such as the Church:

> Before 1957, there did not exist in Quebec any institutions devoted to communication research. . . . It is quite clear that the situation undergoes rapid transformation from the mid-50s onwards. Between 1957 and 1967, the National Catholic Centre, the research arm of Radio-Canada, the ICEA (Canadian Institute for Adult Education) and CROP (Centre de recherche sur l'opinion publique) became the leading institutional agents of research on social communication. And yet, they did not exhaust the field. (Lacroix and Lévesque, 1985a, p. 7)

The period before 1957 is characterized by dramatically contradictory impulses (de la Garde, 1991). On the one hand, there were modernizing, emancipatory, progressive, and open-minded impulses, as evidenced by the pervasiveness of new technologies (daily press, tabloids, magazines, comic books, film, vaudeville, radio, advertising) and cultural products produced locally and imported from the United States and France. On the other hand, there were conservative, moralistic, disciplinary, and patriarchal impulses that were reflected in the objective content of the "media" themselves, ranging from the most traditional (e.g., regular radio broadcasts of the Sunday sermon) to the most modern (as expressed, for example, in scholarly publications).

Indeed, the fact is that the mass media had occupied an important place in Quebec society for about a century (Linteau, Durocher, and Robert, p. 1979). Their popularity only *seemed* sudden but it nevertheless raised the question of modernity within French-Canadian society and indicated a fracturing of traditional beliefs. The consumption of mass cultural products was also concomitant with the rise of industrial labour, urban life, secular thought, democratic life, and the formation of social movements. Intellectuals naturally tried to understand the mass media by drawing on these same dominant themes (industrialization, urbanization, secularization, nationalism, language, religion, and the family).

1960–1980

While the period 1960–80 has often been hailed as marking Quebec's belated entry into modernity, as well as the birth of Quebec nationalism (and the concomitant decline of French-Canadian nationalism), it should be clear from the above that Quebec's modernization actually began at the end of the 19th century (Lamonde, 2000). Consequently, the 1960s can more adequately be understood as the period of emergence of the welfare state:

> If the Quiet Revolution is to be understood as an event or rupture to be celebrated, it has nothing to do with the "arrival of modernity" within Quebec but with the entry into the Welfare state and the affirmation of a new set of values. . . . [S]tate institutions were restructured so that the public sphere could take control of domains such as social services, health and education, which had previously and mainly been left to institutions of the private sphere. (Paquette, 2001, pp. 121–122)

The 1960s witnessed the creation of new ministries of education, health, and cultural affairs; most important for our purposes was the creation of the Quebec Ministry of Communication in 1969. Not only were these new ministries entirely characteristic of the rise of the welfare state but the state extended its interest elsewhere as well. For example, Lacroix and Lévesque (1985b) state that from 1965 onward, communication studies in general, and those concerned with television in particular, increasingly showed signs of the state's intervention. They note that the state was "not only one of the main producers of communication research" but also "one of the main forces behind the emergence of both private applied social research firms and university departments of communication" (Lacroix and Lévesque, 1985b, p. 191). (In Chapter 3, Michael Dorland also mentions the theme of state intervention in reference to the emergence of communication studies in Canada.) Below is a chronology of the foundation of communication departments and communication programs in Quebec:

> 1965: Loyola College (now Concordia University), B.A. in Communication Arts
>
> 1968: Université Laval, B.A. in Journalism
>
> 1969: Université de Montréal, communication stream, Department of Psychology
>
> 1973: McGill University, M.A. in Communications
>
> 1973: Université du Québec à Montréal (UQAM), B.A. in Communication
>
> 1974: Université de Montréal, M.A. in Communication
>
> 1976: McGill University, Ph.D. in Communications
>
> 1981–82: UQAM, M.A. in Communication

1983: Concordia University, M.A. in Communication

1986: Université Laval, MA. in Public Communication

1987: Concordia University, UQAM, Université de Montréal, Joint Ph.D. in Communication

1997: Université du Québec à Trois-Rivières (UQTR), B.A. in Social Communication

2001: Université de Sherbrooke, B.A. in Communication, Multimedia and Writing

Coinciding with the increasing role of the state was an increasing awareness of market forces and the ways in which communication could be used to navigate through them. All communication research, whether governmental, private, or university-based, was increasingly subject to market imperatives. Not surprisingly, then, within communication departments where "all types of research are undertaken" and where various schools of thought (functionalism, Marxism, behaviourism, semiology, systems theory) met, "the main thrust of research [was] taken up with content studies" (Lacroix and Lévesque, 1985b, p. 192). Content studies, inasmuch as they were concerned with television, both promoted the state's agenda of using communication for identity-building purposes and crossed over into the study of audiences and the market success of different content types. Under these conditions, socioeconomic studies on new technologies played second fiddle to content studies; similarly, critical approaches and studies of information or alternative uses of the media, while attractive, remained a minority undertaking.

Lacroix and Lévesque (1985a) sum up the beginnings of communication research as follows:

> The emergence of a specific field of communication studies is linked in Quebec to the creation of an interventionist state and occurs in a period of dramatic social change during which the media and applied social research played an increasingly important role. It was at this precise moment that the first institutions specializing in communication research appeared. (p. 8)

The early core of university and administrative research, with its focus on "cultural industries" and more specifically on television, grew up during this period. It was characterized by the predominance of a double approach: a political economic orientation growing out of the alliance between state and industry and a "culturalist" analysis focused largely on French-language soap opera (*téléromans*) (Bouchard, 2000).

Interestingly, in the early 1990s, a pan-Canadian and multidisciplinary group of researchers was called on to "conduct a literature review [of the years 1973–92] and analyze the impact of the globalization of open economies on Canada's cultural development." In their report, the two Quebec researchers (de la Garde and

Tremblay, 1993, 1994) identified five main themes or problematics associated with communication research: (1) cultural identity fed into (2) state intervention; both (1) and (2) were subject to the vagaries of (3) technological advances and (4) economic globalization; and all these themes revolved around (5) an examination of the ways in which television and broadcasting (radio, TV, cable) were used by citizens, which accounted for 46 percent of all research undertaken in that time period.

1980 AND BEYOND

By the mid-1970s, the welfare state in Quebec and elsewhere had entered a crisis phase. The causes of the crisis, as characterized by Paquette (2001), were not only financial and economic but also societal and cultural:

> [It is] no longer clear why the state should continue to substitute itself for welfare (legitimacy crisis), the bases and meaning of social relationships are no longer clear, there's no longer any consensus on how best to represent "collective life." (p. 129)

It was against this background of "crisis" in the welfare state that, roughly after 1975, the second phase of the "structuration of the communication research apparatus in Quebec" occurred; communication research within the various university departments was now driven less by state intervention and more by the "commodification of culture" and the imperatives of social control (Lacroix and Lévesque, 1985a).

Significantly, it was precisely at this moment of realignment from state sponsorship to market sponsorship that communication studies began to explode in Quebec:

> The increase in the number of [communication] teaching programs is accompanied by an increase in student clienteles, a progressive improvement of costly infrastructural equipment, an increase in teaching and research budgets, and the posting of a large number of university teaching positions (24 in all) in this new field. (Proulx, 1979, p. 103)

The new field was doubly profitable because it both drew in a growing student population—to the detriment of the more traditional social sciences such as sociology and political science—and linked "simultaneously and contradictorily [its own research interests] to the needs of the state and of industry" (Proulx, 1979, p. 104). Furthermore, Proulx underlines a "strange paradox":

> The great popularity of these programs is linked partly to the seduction of the media themselves to which students are drawn and about which they want to know more; however, the teaching staff consists mostly of academic researchers more drawn to criticism of media practices. (pp. 116–117)

This "strange paradox" merged into an articulation that now seems neither strange nor paradoxical. Today the situation described by Proulx—the split between student "demand" (an interest in and seduction by the practical aspects of the media) and teachers' offerings (an interest in formal communication theories)—is less problematic or at least less thought about.

However, the practical and the formal had to be articulated. With respect to teaching, the articulation took the fairly clear shape of a range of programs offering everything from professional training (Université Laval) to the formal education of experts (Université de Montréal). As for research, the articulation between applied approaches and fundamental or formal research is clearly weighted in favour of the former. Indeed, the application of specialized knowledge to information and "image" industries (public relations and advertising), as well as to the telecommunications sector and to organizational communication, hugely outstrips the critical sociology of the media and the cultural industries.

KEY TURNING POINTS

The years 1969 and 1987 are key turning points because they represent, in the first instance, the *institutionalization* of a new field of university-level teaching and research, and, in the second instance, its *legitimation*. Indeed, the creation in 1969 of the Quebec Ministry of Communication signalled not only the state's awareness of the "commodification" of culture and the consolidation of the cultural industries but also its willingness to occupy this domain that was rapidly becoming the focus of the struggle for national identity. The creation of communication programs and departments, between 1965 and 1973, in the five largest Quebec universities is best understood within this context.

The legitimation of the field occurred with the creation in 1987 of the Joint Ph.D. in Communication, which signalled the desire on the part of the Quebec research community to place itself on the Canadian, North American, and international scenes. This desire for presence was itself part of an irresistible movement toward the "Montrealization" of Quebec's cultural industries. Montreal was rapidly becoming

- a major centre for mass media production, including newspapers, magazines, publishing houses, film production, sound recording studios, advertising agencies, theatres, festivals, public and private radio and television networks;
- a centre for the development of new technologies (from cable television to computer systems);
- a major artistic colony; and
- a university centre of excellence and an "incubator" for scientific research.

The "institutionalization phase," which began in 1968 and occurred "under the sign of commodification and in the name of national identity" (de la Garde, 1988, p. 18), appears to have been accomplished. But this fact has led to a rather dramatic change in how the field understands itself. A focus on cultural industries was once deemed essential because it corresponded to a concern with identity and markets. The centre of interest has clearly shifted. Today identity is seen as less important than markets. Whereas communication technologies were once discussed only in utopian terms—in terms of what they could do for society—they are now discussed exclusively in practical and economic terms.

OVERVIEW OF UNIVERSITY ACTIVITY

We turn now to a consideration of the current situation of communication as a discipline within French-language Quebec universities. This section summarizes the various teaching programs, with particular emphasis on their objectives and orientations. It also takes note of their immense popularity with students, as well as of the diversity of the fields and objects of research.

Communication Programs

As we saw earlier, the six Quebec university communication departments[2] are relatively young compared to departments of psychology, anthropology, or sociology. While many establishments offered communication programs in the early 1970s, it was not until the 1980s and 1990s that the programs were extended to cover all three degree levels, from B.A. to Ph.D. Currently, ten Quebec universities (including Télé-université[3]) offer more than 53 programs that range from a certificate in technical writing to a doctorate, and that include specialized or multidisciplinary B.A. programs and minors in journalism or public relations.

As a result of the diversity of university communication programs, and a constant growth in student registration over the past few years, the discipline has become one of the most popular of the humanities in Quebec. In Fall 1996, more than 4700 students, to which can be added 800 new admissions, were registered across all the programs, including certificates. Since 1997, roughly 6000 new admission requests across all three degree levels are received each year.

B.A. Programs

The six communication departments offer a wide range of diversified programs. Several factors account for the diversity, not the least of which is the fact that universities must demonstrate to the Ministry of Education that each new program meets a distinct market "demand." Universities are subject not only to quality control but also to a highly competitive marketplace as they attempt to attract and retain students. To these factors must be added the traditions developed within each university that are reflected in their research and teaching orientations. Finally, the professors hired by the departments play a key role in the evolution of the programs both through their areas of expertise and their own university backgrounds.

The programs, while diverse, are also complementary:

> As regards complementarity, the universities of Quebec offer programs which can be located on a continuum that ranges between one pole where theoretical content, study and reflection on communication phenomena predominate and another pole where professional training oriented towards media crafts is the main objective. Whichever pole constitutes its home, every program provides an introduction to the main debates and the key questions in the communication field as well as a basic introduction to the media. (Commission des études sur les programmes, 1997)

Beyond the basic similarities that are both necessary and normal in any discipline, the B.A. programs in communication can be distinguished by their various objectives. The programs at Université Laval and UQAM are specialized; Laval's programs are aimed at communication practitioners (journalism, public relations, social advertising), while UQAM's programs are professional and oriented toward the same crafts, to which can be added a multimedia specialization. The recent restructuring of the B.A.[4] at Université de Sherbrooke allows that program to maintain its goal of training writing specialists while devoting more time to multimedia. UQTR's B.A. in Social Communication focuses on "the understanding of processes of social interaction" and is aimed at training social intervenors who will possess an articulated critical vision and who will work in various organizations related to the field of communication (Université du Québec à Trois-Rivières, 1997). Aimed at a more general education, Télé-université's "distance" B.A. is focused on "basic knowledge" and theoretical/ disciplinary questions, and has an interest in organizational communication (Télé-université, 1990). The two B.A. programs offered by Université de Montréal, whose basic training is based largely on theory and research methods, focuses on "training people to analyze, design, plan and organize communication strategies" (Département de communication, 1997).

Alongside the basic courses offered by these institutions (communication/ media theory, media institutions, organizational communication), one finds the expected repertory of courses on advertising, public relations, journalism, new technologies, and multimedia. There are also pedagogical innovations in the form of (1) Web-based courses involving pedagogical follow-up and discussion via on-line forums, and (2) increasingly direct contact with the world of work (e.g., long-term work placements at Université de Sherbrooke, the student advertising agency Préambule Communication at Université Laval, and the partnership between cooperation projects and community-based organizations at UQTR).

The newness of the field of communication studies has meant that there is a relative scarcity of books and articles devoted to it. Until the end of the 1980s, Quebec students drew on their knowledge of English, which was fortunately reasonably good, in order to gain access to the broader disciplinary debates. Of course, certain extracts from classic American texts of the 1940s, 1950s, and 1960s had been translated into French by European researchers, mostly in the early 1970s (Balle and Padioleau, 1973). In addition, Marshall McLuhan's books were available in French almost immediately following their publication in English.

Nonetheless, Quebec teachers did not have access to pedagogical works comparable in quality to the American "classics." The first Quebec publications, which did not appear until the 1980s (see, for example, Attallah, 1989, 1991; Charron, 1989; Finlay-Pelinski, 1983; Grenier and Brunet, 1991; Laramée, 1989a, 1989b; Schiele and Bélisle, 1984), demonstrated the long-term contributions of Télé-université and the scholarly journal *Communication* to the field of communication studies.[5] In the 1990s, the publishing arms of Université de Montréal and especially of Université Laval contributed greatly to the development of the field, as did the publishing house Boréal after it issued Philippe Breton and Serge Proulx's *L'explosion de la communication*. This seminal overview of the main currents in communication research opens with a history of media before the 20th century, provides a synthesis of 20th-century communication theory, and concludes with an analysis of the "modern ideology of communication" (Breton and Proulx, 1989).

As French-speaking European researchers became increasingly interested in communication studies, there was a growth in the number of specialized periodicals and general studies. On this side of the Atlantic, major scholarly journals of the field are linked to university departments, particularly *Communication*[6] at Université Laval; *Loisirs et société* at UQTR, and *TIS: Technologie de l'information et de la société* at UQAM; co-edited with the Université de Liège (France). Students and professors in the new millennium, then, have access to a range of French-language books, articles, and periodicals that could only be dreamt of 20 years ago.

Graduate Studies

Université de Montréal and UQAM have offered an M.A. in Communication for approximately 25 and 20 years respectively. In 1987, they created, in collaboration with Concordia University, a Joint Ph.D. Program in Communication. Université Laval established its own M.A. in Public Communication in 1986, while Université de Sherbrooke has offered a selection of M.A. courses in communication and writing since 1994. In Fall 1996, 287 students—of whom 123 were new admissions—were registered in these various programs. The rate of completion and graduation increased from 42 graduates in 1990 to 75 graduates in 1996.[7]

Université de Montréal's M.A. in Communication offers two main options (media studies and organizational communication), while UQAM's M.A. in Communication offers specialization in media, organizational communication, international communication, and interactive multimedia. Université Laval, within the framework of an M.A. in Public Communication, steers students toward professional practices, political communication, media and culture, and communication and social intervention.

Since 1974, 302 students have graduated from Université de Montréal's Department of Communication (Département de communication, 2001). At Université Laval, 57 theses and 83 research essays have been deposited in the information and communication department since 1989 (Département d'information et communication, 2000). UQAM's Department of Communication has a much larger teaching staff and is therefore able to direct a large number of M.A. students.[8] As a result, between 1982 and 1999, it granted no fewer than 372 MAs.

It is impossible in the space provided to give a full account of the diversity of objects, problematics, sectors, and domains of study represented by more than 700 M.A. theses. The diversity and originality of the objects of study, which range from theoretical models to interactive computer installations, demonstrate clearly the dispersal of communication studies as well as the interdisciplinarity that the founders of departments in the 1970s had wanted to foster (Faculté des études supérieures, 1972). The following M.A. thesis titles drawn from those deposited at Université de Montréal's communication department in 1999 and 2000 illustrate the claim:

- *A Study of the Influence of Haptic Guidance in Exploring the Functionality of a Hypermedia Environment*
- *The Constitution of Space in the Architectural Photography of the Bauhaus*
- *American Critical Discourse on Popular Music. The Case of French Music between 1965 and 1975*
- *Psychotropes and Governmentality: An Analysis of Discursive Practices*
- *Adolescents' Appropriation of "Chat" and "Talk" Groups in a Domestic Context*
- *The Practices of Organizational Development Consultants and Communication within Workgroups*
- *Artistic Use and Creation of Holographs*

The Joint Ph.D. in Communication is the only bilingual communication doctorate in North America. Since this program was established in 1987, Université de Montréal and UQAM have granted 18 and 34 doctorates respectively. The theses deposited with the graduate faculties clearly reflect the joint program's four major research emphases: information technologies, mediated discourses, organizational communication, and development communication. We should also note the growing contribution of international students from Asia and the French-speaking countries of Africa (Tunisia, Morocco, Algeria, Zaire, Burundi, Ivory Coast,

Cameroun). Indeed, their research projects, often related to their countries of origin, have both favoured and justified the fourth emphasis (development communication), as 14 of the 52 theses are directly related to it.

UNIVERSITY-LEVEL COMMUNICATION RESEARCH

While we should expect the general orientation of graduate teaching to reflect the research interests of professors, it would be naive to assume that the teaching that can be observed from the B.A. to the Ph.D. exhausts the types of research conducted in the various departments. There were 134 professors across all the Quebec-based communication departments (including those at McGill and Concordia) in 1997, compared with only 24 in 1979. In February 2001, there were 104 teaching positions in the French-language departments.[9] The professors who held these positions contributed to a vast array of centres, groups, and research laboratories that provided opportunities for numerous graduate students, as well as to the endowment of chairs such as the UNESCO-BELL Chair (UQAM), the Chair in Ethical Studies (Concordia-UQAM), and the Chair in Science Journalism (Laval).

The annual average for research grants and contracts held by the French-language departments between 1993 and 1996 was $1,312,740, or 82 percent of the total amount gained by all communication departments in Quebec[10]; 40 percent of the research funds come from recognized granting agencies, 35 percent from research contracts, and 25 percent from various other funding sources. It is not possible to determine the part played by the private sector in the granting of research contracts.

Between 1993 and 1996, the professors of French-language departments delivered 536 scholarly papers and published 73 books, 151 book chapters, 466 journal publications, and 115 research reports. The existence of the various centres, groups, and research laboratories clearly promotes collaboration among professors within their home departments and among all the departments (both French- and English-speaking). As the projects undertaken jointly with private enterprise, ministries, and various public and parapublic institutions (hospitals, schools, nongovernmental organizations, public broadcasters, etc.) demonstrate, the collaborative efforts referred to above frequently reach well beyond the confines of the discipline and of the university. Finally, researchers have also developed pan-Canadian and international research networks that tend to be focused on Europe rather than the United States.

CULTURAL INDUSTRIES

So far, this overview of communication studies and its current organization suggests a double articulation. At the turn of the 20th century, and under the impact of emergent popular culture and the new delivery vehicles (radio, advertising, movies, etc.) that made it widely available, intellectuals first began to think of communication phenomena within a scientific and rational framework. Such attempts at social analysis are observable in both Canada and the United States.

It's easy to imagine the shock that must have been produced when the liberal ideas of our southern neighbours (especially those from New York) concerning industrialization, urbanization, geographical mobility, public education, technology, and news and entertainment were brought north. The emergence of tabloid newspapers, comic strips, silent film, advertising, and jazz not only highlighted modernity's visibility but also made its implicit threat more menacing.

That the public loved the new media can be gauged by the increasing number of venues for the diffusion of popular culture (newspapers, magazines, movie theatres, radio stations, vaudeville houses, etc.), especially in Montreal but also in other urban areas. Clothing and musical styles also changed. Of course, the opposition did not wait long to manifest itself. From the circles of official culture (the clergy as well as writers, educators, and editors of the "quality press") emanated a condemnation of modernity that, while not absolute, nonetheless constituted a serious warning to the public.

As mentioned above, the first attempts at social analysis, growing out of the writings of certain French intellectuals and organized around the condemnation of "American materialism," had begun to take shape at the beginning of the 20th century. This strand of social thought reached its high point in 1957 when the Semaines sociales du Canada (1957) devoted its 34th annual conference to the theme of "The Influence of the Press, Film, Radio and Television." The conference proceedings, published in that same year, make a surprisingly media-centred argument. On the one hand, new technology is praised to the extent that it represents progress. On the other hand, it is conceived as something that has to be restricted to "proper uses," including the promotion of "good" values: the family, morality, individual responsibility, and the public good. It would be easy to dismiss these writings as merely conservative and accusatory. In fact, they grew out of American studies that themselves claimed to expose the alienating effects of the modern media, especially when they fell into "the wrong hands."

The social discourse that focused on the media and their effects received a boost in the 1950s with the arrival of television. Television's impact was without precedent and social discourse on this new technology fastened on four main factors:

1. *Its rapid social diffusion.* In the years 1952–59, almost 90 percent of Quebec homes acquired a television set.

2. *Its ease of use.* Television was the first truly "mass" medium. It required no special learning, such as reading and writing, beyond the ability to understand speech and to see.

3. *Its location in the home.* As a household technology, television promoted common activities (group watching) and allowed family members to "participate" in social life through news, games, and stories without ever leaving the private comfort of home.

4. *Its relationship to the state*. For the state, television was the ideal vehicle for the consolidation of national identity. The user-friendliness of television, and the fact that U.S. networks were increasingly available in English Canada and Quebec, made both the federal and the provincial governments even more determined than they had been in the case of publishing, radio, or film to help build a national broadcasting infrastructure and to finance content production (hence public television devoted to the promotion of a national culture).

The impulses of the Quebec government and the liberal nature of American mass media in the 1960s and 1970s coincided with the development of two research traditions: (1) a relatively new tradition of media-centred analysis and (2) a relatively mature tradition of effects-based studies. Both traditions took as their first object of study the cultural industries. Hence, television could be examined both as a medium with its own formal characteristics (the media-centric tradition) *and* as a medium with potentially dire social and cultural effects (effects-based studies). The nascent university research tradition in Quebec, whose first object of study was the cultural industries, can therefore be characterized as a confluence of youth and maturity, dispersal and consensus, isolation and networks of convergence.

However, this initial intellectual moment also contained certain contradictions that would lead to its abandonment. Chief among these were (1) the mismatch between the available analytical models (the two research traditions mentioned above) and the complexity of reality that endlessly seemed to escape the models; (2) the distance between university research oriented toward theory and pure knowledge and governmental research oriented toward control and the economy; (3) the financial dependence of the earliest researchers on the industries they wished to study (there were no independent sources of funding); (4) economic reductionism (the view that even cultural events can be explained in purely economic terms); and (5) "the dramatic lack of data on cultural activities" (reliable empirical studies on which to base anything had yet to be undertaken) (de la Garde and Tremblay, 1993, p. 45).

In the new millennium, the cultural industries are no longer the major driver of university communication research. Over the past 20 years, private consultancies have mushroomed; they conduct specialized research that is perfectly adapted to the needs of ministries, industry, and lobby groups. The reports commissioned by the Quebec Ministry of Culture and Communication draw less and less on university researchers and more and more on private organizations. Furthermore, those who commission the reports are just as likely to hire M.A. and Ph.D. students as to hire tenured professors.

Finally, those researchers who still prefer to study the cultural industries are usually those who have been ensconced in their departments for at least 15 years. As a result, the new generation of professors is usually hired as a function of academic complementarity. Indeed, in order to avoid reproducing the expertise of existing faculty, new faculty tend to specialize in the so-called subfields of the discipline, which include organizational communication (from functionalism to language theory), new technologies (from cognitivism to multimedia production to the sociology of science), and international communication (from ethnography to international law). Hence, university researchers still interested in the cultural industries constitute a distinct minority within communication departments.

SOCIOTECHNOLOGICAL ORIENTATION

Over the last 15 years, two new subfields have emerged to engage the interest of growing numbers of M.A. and Ph.D. students. The two subfields—organizational communication and NCITs (new communication and information technologies)—have led to a gradual rearticulation of the formerly media-centric discipline.

For a long time, organizational communication was associated with the internal and external communicative strategies of industry. Today, though, it is one of the leading research thrusts within Quebec. There has been a steady increase in the number of professors working in this area and organizational problems are popular among M.A. and Ph.D. students. Indeed, the reputation of Quebec-based communication research extends into the United States where the expression "Montreal School" is sometimes used to describe the work of James Taylor (Université de Montréal) and his former students.

Nonetheless, NCITs are definitely the new motor driving communication departments. This is due to their hybrid character. On the one hand, they draw on a multiplicity of approaches, methods, and research streams. On the other hand, they are global in the sense that they directly affect virtually all social spheres and are found virtually everywhere internationally. As an illustration, in the "Communication" section of the annual conference of ACFAS (Association canadienne-française pour l'avancement des sciences) only 3 of the 48 papers presented in 1996 dealt with NCITs. In 2001, however, 42 of the 60 papers presented dealt directly with NCITs. Significantly, these papers demonstrated that while there is an emerging consensus on computer-mediated communication (CMC), the researchers engaged in this study are bound together less by their departments than by their location within interuniversity (and often international) research networks (George and Totsching, 2001).

The earliest evidence of research on communication and information technologies in French-speaking Quebec dates back to the early 1980s. The first M.A. thesis on computer communication was deposited in 1979 (Leduc, 1979). However, the interest of students and professors in the area is confirmed only as of 1985. Indeed, since that date, there has been an increasing number of scholarly publications dealing with the uses of microcomputers (Caron, Giroux, and Douzou, 1987; Proulx, 1988), the Alex and Videoway systems (Bélanger, 1991), and the work of the GRICIS groups at UQAM on cable television (Tremblay and Lacroix, 1991).

The earliest studies on microcomputers often approached the subject from the point of view of effects, uses, content, and political economy (Trudel et al., 1983). More current research on NCITs and CMC covers a much broader range of domains (organizational, international, media, interpersonal) and approaches (constructivism, interactionism, cognitivism, functionalism, cultural studies, postmodernism, neo-Marxism, philosophy, semiology, historiography). A good example is provided by Bardini and Proulx (2000).

EPILOGUE

The communication subfields that have multiplied and diversified in Quebec over the last 15 years point to a surprising transdisciplinarity, as well as to centripetal rather than centripetal tendencies. The rise of transdisciplinarity could be a predictable result of the long-term intellectual and cultural effects of Montreal's Joint Ph.D. Program in Communication. It could also be a consequence of the normal evolution of the interdisciplinarity that the founders of communication departments had called for in the early 1970s. Whatever the case, transdisciplinarity is clearly one of the major characteristics of French-language communication research in Quebec; it is a characteristic that demarcates this research from U.S. research traditions preoccupied with their disciplinary status and the search for a unified theory (*Journal of Communication*, 1993).

Throughout this chapter, we have attempted to identify some of the factors that shaped the face of communication departments and their course offerings during the 1980s. These factors are summarized below:

- the rise of neoliberalism and the stagnation of education budgets;
- the rise of new technologies and the proliferation of discourses that hailed their revolutionary character;
- the growing popularity of communication studies among undergraduates and the establishment of new graduate programs at both the M.A. and the Ph.D. levels;
- the creation of Montreal's Joint Ph.D. Program in Communication and its opening to the theoretical preoccupations of the English-speaking academic milieu;
- the first signs of exhaustion within community groups interested in the media and the growing privatization of media production and distribution processes;
- the publication of specialized pedagogical communication texts in Quebec and an increasing interest in international English-language academic activity; and

- the establishment of a Quebec and international research network and the steady success of grant applications.

The predictions of the 1970s have come true. Indeed, the economic and social importance of NCITs, which were originally linked both to the national question and to the withering of democracy, are now regularly invoked as a justification for the establishment of communication departments. Nowadays, both as research objects and drivers of the new economy, NCITs are the best possible guarantee for the continued existence of departments that have grown with the province and have now entered adulthood as their populations steadily increase and their professors emerge as the experts on technological and social transformation.

The process of institutionalization has attained a certain maturity. Communication departments appear to have reached the stage of contemporary university excellence as measured by the sustained popularity of student demand, the high rate of graduation, the scholarly productivity of professors and researchers, the grant-application success rate, and reputation and influence. In an age when many social and human science departments are undergoing a decline, communication departments appear to be a model of success in the eyes of university administrators.

But all may not be well. According to some well-informed observers, university communication researchers are no longer as involved politically and socially as they were 15 years ago. They appear to have become prisoners of their ivory towers and professional obligations. One is tempted to respond that those very same researchers now have twice the workload they had 15 years ago and that if academic careers are increasingly driven by a defensive ethic, this is itself the result of years of draconian budget cuts. One could even add that the same relative social and political disengagement is hardly specific to this discipline and can be observed virtually everywhere.

Nonetheless, the occasional voice does rise up to denounce the slow disappearance of the critical attitude necessary for the full development of a research discipline that claims to be progressive:

> [I]f communication theorists wish to participate in the effort to understand society as a whole and the transformations traversing it, they will truly have to come to grips with its complexity and propose something other than a determinist vision centred only on technology and its effects. (Tremblay, 1995, p. 480)

Tremblay's observation underscores a very real characteristic of Quebec-based communication departments today—namely, their discretion vis-à-vis social and political matters.

Another type of discretion is that concerned with the political and epistemological dimensions of communication studies in Quebec. Until recently, few researchers have bothered to ask questions about the history of their epistemological orientation and its ties to politics or society. Those who did ask such questions did so mostly in the late 1970s and early 1980s. This is the period in which

- Serge Proulx conducted his survey of communication professors (1979);
- the Canadian Communication Association was founded (Halifax and Montreal);
- the *Canadian Journal of Communication* (1981) published its special issue on Canadian communication studies;
- the first book on Quebec television studies was published under the editorship of Annie Méar (Méar 1980);
- UQAM and McGill University undertook a joint study of the 1980 referendum (Robinson, 1998);
- *Communication* devoted a special issue to theory under the editorship of Marike Finlay-Pelinski (1983); and
- Lacroix and Lévesque (1985a and 1985b) published the results of their study.

Since those days, the French-speaking community appears to contribute less than the English-speaking community to studies dealing with the history and epistemology of its own disciplinary work (*Canadian Journal of Communication*, 2001). It would be premature, however, to attribute this silence to a loss of interest in such questions. It may be reasonable to conclude with the observation that while the French-language communication research community in Quebec has achieved a level of maturity as a disciplinary field, it has not yet attained the maturity, or the distance, that would allow it to conduct its own self-critique.

—Translated by Paul Attallah

QUESTIONS

1. How does the evolution of communication studies in Quebec compare with the evolution of communication studies in the rest of Canada?
2. What are the main turning points, and their consequences, in the history of communication research as recorded in the French-language universities of Quebec?
3. Would you say that the study of NCIT (new communication and information technologies) is more or less important than the study of cultural industries (television, film, radio)? Give reasons for your answer
4. Is it accurate to say of your own department or experience that there is a split between what draws students to communication and what professors want to teach? How would you characterize that split? Is it a good thing or a bad thing?

5. What are the main communication trends that most interest you? How are they connected to present-day social issues?

WEB SITES

Centre d'études sur les médias (Université Laval):
  http://www.cem.ulaval.ca/MotsCadre.html
Commposite (scholarly publication for new researchers): **http://commposite.uqam.ca/**
CREPUQ (universities in Quebec): **http://www.crepuq.qc.ca/Univ/univ2.htm**
Joint Ph.D. Program in Communication:
  http://concordia.umontreal.uqam.ca/phdcom/
La toile du Québec (main Quebec portal): **http://www.toile.qc.ca/**
Ministère de la culture et des communications du Québec (reports, studies, statistics, cultural industries, etc.): **http://www.mcc.gouv.qc.ca/index.html**
Québec audiovisuel (film and television):
  http://www.quebec.audiovisuel.com/fran/core.asp
Réseaux (French journal of communication): **http://www.enssib.fr/autres-sites/reseaux-cnet/**

NOTES

1. Of course, French-language communication research also occurs outside of Quebec (at universities in Ontario and New Brunswick, for example), but this chapter confines itself to the situation in Quebec. The question of what should or should not count as French-language research, even within Quebec, can be quite complex. For example, many French-speaking professors teach and conduct research in English-language institutions such as McGill University and Concordia University. In addition, the Joint Ph.D. in Communication, which brings together the communication departments of Université de Montréal, UQAM, and Concordia, offers courses in both French and English and constitutes an excellent example of Montreal's bilingual reality as well as providing a unique forum for exchange among researchers (students and professors). Finally, many French-speaking professors who teach in French-language institutions have conducted their own studies in English in Montreal, elsewhere in Canada, or in the United States.

2. These departments are located in the following universities: Université de Montréal, UQAM, Université Laval, Université de Sherbrooke, UQTR and Télé-université. Four universities have no departments but offer short programs or certifications: Université du Québec à Chicoutimi (UQAC), Université du Québec à Hull (UQAH), Université du Québec à Rimouski (UQAR), and Université du Québec en Abitibi-Témiscamingue.

3. Télé-université is the world's second-oldest "distance education" university. Its student population consists principally of adults studying part-time for a diploma (certificate or BA). Télé-université's structure is not based on departments but on teaching units. Its particular centre of interest is the Humanities, Literature and Communication unit. While Télé-université differs from more conventional institutions in a number of respects, the Humanities, Literature and Communication unit meets many of the criteria for a department, especially since in January 1990 Télé-université was obliged to submit for approval, as would any other university, its proposal for the creation of a B.A. in Communication to the CREPUQ (Conférence des Recteurs et des Principaux des Universités du Québec).

4. The Université de Sherbrooke's B.A. in Communication, Writing and Multimedia grew out of the recent restructuring of the Department of Literature and Communication. The new B.A. admitted its first students in September 2001.

5. Since 1989, Télé-université (in collaboration with the Presses de l'Université du Québec) has published 19 books concerned directly with communication studies.

6. This scholarly publication, founded in 1975 by Roger de la Garde (editor-in-chief) and Line Ross (sub-editor), has become an important touchstone in the evolution of communication research in Quebec, Canada, and the French-speaking world.

7. Although the traditional thesis-based M.A. remains the most popular program, universities are now also offering shorter programs (graduate studies diploma) and new options (work/study M.A.).

8. UQAM's Department of Communication is by far the largest in Quebec, with 44 professors and 156 registered M.A. students in 1996.

9. The breakdown of professors by French-language department is: Laval (26), Montréal (14), UQAM (42), Sherbrooke (3), Télé-université (11), UQTR (8).

10. The total average amount was $1,607,520 (Commission des études sur les programmes, 1997, p. 4).

REFERENCES

Attallah, Paul. (1989). *Théories de la communication: Histoire, contexte, pouvoir.* Ste-Foy, QC: Presses de l'Université du Québec.

———. (1991). *Théories de la communication: Sens, sujets, savoirs.* Ste-Foy, QC: Presses de l'Université du Québec.

Balle, F., and J. Padioleau. (1973). *Sociologie de l'information: Textes fondamentaux.* Paris: Larousse.

Bardini, Thierry, and Serge Proulx. (2000). Les promesses du cyberespace. Méditations, pratiques et pouvoirs à l'heure de la communication électronique. *Sociologie et sociétés, XXXII* (2).

Bélanger, Pierre. (1991) *Le système Vidéoway: Modalités d'adoption d'un système interactif de télévision*. (Doctoral dissertation, Université de Montréal).

Bouchard, Nathalie N. (2000). À la recherche des téléromans. *Communication*, 20 (1), 217–248.

Breton, Philippe, and Serge Proulx. (1989). *L'explosion de la communication: La naissance d'une nouvelle idéologie*. Paris/Montréal: La découverte/Boréal.

Canadian Journal of Communication, 8(1). (1981). Special issue on Canadian communication studies.

Canadian Journal of Communication, 25(1). (1997). Special Millennium Issue.

Caron, André H., Luc Giroux, and Sylvie Douzou. (1987). L'appropriation du "virage technologique": Le micro-ordinateur domestique. *Cahiers de recherche en communication*. Université de Montréal.

Charron, Danièle. (1989). *Une introduction à la communication*. Ste-Foy, QC: Presses de l'Université du Québec.

Commission des études sur les programmes (CUP). (1997). Communication. *Enseignement et recherche: complémentarité et concertation*. Rapport no. 2. Montréal: CREPUQ.

de la Garde, R. (1988). Le déclin de l'Empire, monsieur Innis? *Communication*, 9(2), 11–29.

———. (1991). Y a-t-il un public dans la salle? In Michel Beauchamp (Ed.), *Communication publique et société* (pp. 246–284). Montreal: Gaetan Morin.

de la Garde, Roger, and Gaétan Tremblay. (1994). Cultural development: State of the question and prospects for Québec. *Canadian Journal of Communication, 19* (3/4), 447–475.

de la Garde, Roger, and Gaétan Tremblay (with Michael Dorland and Denise Paré). (1993). Le développement culturel dans une économie ouverte: État de la question. In Stuart McFadyen, Colin Hoskins, and Adam Finn (Eds.), *State of the art review of research on cultural development in an open economy*. Ottawa: SSHRC.

Département de communication. (1997). *Rapport: Projet de modification de programme*. Université de Montréal.

———. (2001). *Liste des thèses et des mémoires (Bibliographie)*. Université de Montréal.

Département d'information et communication. (2000). *Guide de l'étudiant 2000–2001*. Université Laval.

Faculté des études supérieures. (1972). *Nouveau programme de maîtrise Ès-Sciences (communication) présenté au Comité des programmes du Conseil des universités*. Université de Montréal.

Finlay-Pelinski, Marike (Ed.). (1983). Il était une fois la théorie. *Communication*, 5(2/3).

George, Éric and Michael Totsching. (2001). Vingt ans de CMO: Dialogue sur l'histoire d'un concept et d'un champ de recherche. Communication présentée au colloque "La communication médiatisée par ordinateur: Un carrefour de problématiques," Congrès de l'ACFAS, 15 mai.

Grenier, Line, and Manon Brunet (Eds.). (1991). Explorations. *Communication,* *12*(1).

Journal of Communication, 43(3/4). (1993). The future of the field.

Lacroix, Jean-Guy, and Benoît Lévesque. (1985a). L'émergence et l'institutionnalisation de la recherche en communication au Québec. *Communication,* 7(2), 7–31.

———. (1985b). Principaux thèmes et courants théoriques dans la littérature scientifique en communication au Québec. *Communication,* 7(3), 153–212.

Lamonde, Yvan. (2000). *Histoire sociale des idées au Québec, 1760–1896* (Vol. 1). Montréal: Fides.

Laramée, Alain. (1989a). *La communication mass-médiatique au Canada et au Québec: Un cadre socio-politique.* Ste-Foy, QC: Presses de l'Université du Québec.

———. (1989b). *La communication dans les organisations: Une introduction théorique et pragmatique.* Ste- Foy, QC: Presses de l'Université du Québec.

Leduc, Nicole. (1979). *La communication médiatisée par ordinateur: Une nouvelle définition du dialogue de groupe.* (M.A. thesis, Université de Montréal).

Linteau, Paul-André, René Durocher, and Jean-Claude Robert. (1979). *Histoire du Québec contemporain. De la Confédération à la crise, 1867–1929.* Montréal: Boréal Express.

Méar, Annie (Ed.). (1980). *Recherches québécoises sur la télévision.* Montréal: Éditions Saint-Martin.

Paquette, Martine. (2001). *Production de l'espace public médiatique et formes de la régulation politique: Le cas du Québec de 1945 à 1999.* Manuscript.

Proulx, Serge. (1979). Les communications: Vers un nouveau savoir savant? *Recherches Sociographiques, XX*(1), 103–118.

Proulx, Serge (Ed.). (1988). *Vivre avec l'ordinateur: Les usagers de la micro-informatique.* Montréal: Éditions G. Vermette.

Robinson, Gertrude J. (1998). *Constructing the Quebec referendum: French and English media voices.* Toronto: University of Toronto Press.

Schiele, Bernard, and Claire Bélisle (Eds.). (1984). Les représentations. *Communication,* 6(1/2).

Semaines sociales du Canada. (1957). Influence de la presse, du cinéma, de la radio, de la télévision. Compte rendu des Cours et Conférences. Montréal: Secrétariat des Semaines sociales du Canada.

Télé-université. (1990). *Baccalauréat en communication: Dossier de programme.* Ste-Foy, QC: Université du Québec.

Tremblay, Gaétan. (1995). The information society: From Fordism to Gatesism. *Canadian Journal of Communication, 20,* 461–482.

Tremblay, Gaétan, and Jean-Guy Lacroix (with Marc Ménard and Marie-Josée Régnier). (1991). *Télévision: Deuxième dynastie.* Québec: Presses de l'Université du Québec.

Trudel. Lina, et al. (Eds.). (1983). *Négocier le virage technologique, Actes du colloque sur la télématique*. Montréal/Ste-Foy: Institut Canadien de l'Éducation aux Adultes/Centrale des Enseignants du Québec.

Université du Québec à Trois-Rivières. (1997). *Rapport du projet de modification du programme de baccalauréat en génagogie*. Département des sciences du loisir.

Part II
Audiences

Introduction

One of the most interesting aspects of audience studies is the way in which they upset commonly held assumptions about how communication and the media work. It is often assumed that we are passive in our response to the media, absorbing more or less uncritically the content they deliver. However, this largely pessimistic view, while undoubtedly true in some instances, is very often contradicted by actual audience observation.

For example, studies of television audiences—the most frequently studied audience—have revealed a staggering array of factors that contradict the theory of passive absorption. Television, like radio, is rarely a "discrete" activity. Very often people are doing all sorts of other things while watching television: eating, reading, talking to friends on the telephone, channel surfing, using the computer, and so on. Consequently, the basic conditions for its imperious takeover of the human mind are rarely united.

Studies of how audiences *interpret* the content of television have likewise revealed some rather striking inconsistencies. Researchers around the world have examined how audiences interpret public-affairs programs and prime-time drama. Their results could hardly be more disorienting—it was as if individual audience members hadn't even watched the same show. Of course, we cannot conclude from this that every audience member sees something different and that no single content ever means the same thing for two or more people. The simple fact is that many books, movies, news reports, television programs, and so on do indeed result in broadly shared agreement as to their meaning, value, or impact. We are rarely faced with a situation of total breakdown in which the *intended meaning* of a media message is always or necessarily or systematically misunderstood, evaded, or ignored. On the contrary, we are very often faced with situations in which there is at least *some* agreement as to the meaning of messages.

It seems likely that those who construct messages—politicians, entertainers, religious leaders, advertisers, and so on—try to construct them in such a way that their intended audience will have *no choice* but to interpret them as intended or at least *want* to interpret them as intended. They make their messages transparent, seductive, fun, engaging, and the like. They try to focus our interest, draw us away from other messages, and make us forget alternatives.

While some of these strategies are effective (at least some of the time), there's no gainsaying the fact that audiences can be notoriously recalcitrant. It is a standard joke in the advertising business—a business overwhelmingly interested in audiences—that half of every advertising budget is wasted (unfortunately, nobody knows which half). Advertising and other forms of communication (news and entertainment programming, public-service messages, etc.) are routinely treated "ironically," subjected to jokes, dismissal, parody, contradiction, and so on. All but the youngest of children approach communication with a certain amount of savviness and cynicism. Communication nowadays is as likely to be rejected as it is to be accepted.

This is a huge problem for anyone who wants to reach an audience. One way to make a message acceptable to its intended audience is to *build into it* audience cynicism, distrust, or irony. A common strategy is to flatter the audience by casting actors who can function as idealized versions of the people for whom the message is intended. Almost every rock video features hip young people—idealized versions of the audience producers suppose is watching. The same technique is reflected in the casting of models in advertising and roles in movies and television sitcoms.

Another strategy is to disarm criticism by making the message funny; here the makers of the message signal to the audience that they know the message shouldn't be treated seriously. Producers also try to embed in the message the cultural codes of their intended audience. They deliberately incorporate their audience's perceived attitudes into their visual style and narrative structure. They shock or amuse not for the sake of shocking or amusing but as a strategy to reach a target audience. Extremely common in advertising, this strategy is also employed by the producers of such shows as *South Park* or *Conan O'Brien*.

Of course, even the best-laid plans don't always work, and the relationship between message-makers and audiences remains fraught with difficulty and contradiction. Indeed, it raises the intractable question, Where does meaning lie? More specifically, is meaning to be found in the intentions of those who make the messages or in the interpretations of the audiences who receive and use the messages?

It is often assumed that meaning lies with the producers of the messages. This is why there is so much agitation over "media impacts" and "media effects." The assumption is that the meaning is contained within the message, which therefore has the ability to impose itself on all audiences everywhere. This approach views meaning as being highly stable (it is in the message and does not change) and already decided (there is no debate as to what the received message really means). However, this type of message imposition rarely happens.

If meaning lies with audiences, it becomes undecidable and open to debate. The makers of a message *might have intended* a certain meaning, but there's no guarantee that the audience will accept that meaning. The implication here is that every message acquires a new meaning as it is received by new audiences. The process is endless because there are always new audiences and meaning is therefore never stable. However, that rarely happens either.

It is much more likely that meaning is the result of an encounter between the intentions of producers and the interpretations of audiences. In other words, it results from what producers imagine audiences to know and from what audiences already know about how producers try to reach them. No producer reaches audiences innocently and no audience is innocent in its reception of messages. Both have histories. The audience in particular has a history of the media—an understanding of how they operate and try to reach them, of how others have reacted to the media, of how they should act now in order to mark their individuality over and against messages. Every message, then, is a theory of the audience and every audience is an instruction on how to produce messages.

5

The Audience

Paul Attallah
Carleton University

The audience is an indispensable though often misunderstood element of communication thought. Every medium of communication represents an attempt or strategy to reach an audience, and every theory of communication contains within it a view of the audience. What, then, is an audience?

It is often said that we live in a mass society, in very large agglomerations of several million people—Toronto, New York City, Hong Kong—and find this arrangement quite normal. (Our ancestors, of course, mostly lived in much smaller groupings. The phenomenon of large cities is fairly recent, beginning with the industrial revolution in the late 1700s and early 1800s.) Just as we tend to live in large cities, we tend to work in large private- or public-sector institutions alongside large groups of fellow employees. We even shop in places that bring together very large numbers of people (malls, big box stores, shopping centres, department stores, etc.). For us, it is normal to gather in large numbers in order to consume goods, exchange information, and so on.

Organizations such as trade unions also bring together very large numbers of people; indeed, the effectiveness of a union is often considered a function of the number of people it brings together. Our political institutions similarly depend on the participation of large numbers of people. The democratic system of most modern countries depends crucially on its ability to reach huge numbers of citizens and derives its legitimacy from the fact that these citizens express their opinions on the issues of the day. However imperfect, our political system reflects the fact of agglomeration.

All of the above forms of agglomeration are themselves reflected in the fact that our culture, our methods of communication, our forms of public or collective life are also mass phenomena. We do not live in a culture created by isolated individuals for the benefit of other isolated individuals. Rather, we live in an age of mass culture, of industrially or mass-produced phenomena intended for the consumption of masses of people.

TWO VIEWS OF MODERN SOCIETY

The media constitute a central focus in modern society. Not only are they constant and pervasive but they are an extremely effective way of reaching very large numbers of people. The media and the content they provide constitute ways not only of reaching audiences but also of constructing and influencing them.

Two main theories have emerged to account for the relationship between media and audiences. The first theory derives from *behaviourism* and is called *stimulus-response* (SR) theory; the second theory derives from *media sociology* and is called *functionalism.* Both theories contain a view of the audience and therefore a view of society and of the media themselves. SR theory sees the audience as essentially fragile and in need of protection and guidance. It condemns mass society for creating and promoting the fragility of individuals and proposes strict controls on media use and content. Functionalism, on the other hand, sees the audience as essentially vigorous and able to choose its own course freely. It sees mass society as pluralistic or democratic to the extent that it draws in more and more people. It is therefore relatively permissive in its view of media use and content.

Stimulus-response theory grew out of the work of the Russian scientist Ivan Pavlov (1926/1960). In a series of now-legendary experiments, Pavlov found that through repetition he could elicit certain specific responses in animals. In his most famous experiment, he isolated a dog and gave it food. Whenever the dog saw the food, it began to salivate. Pavlov then proceeded to associate a noise with the presence of the food: whenever he fed the dog, he also turned on a metronome. As before, the dog salivated and ate the food. Eventually, Pavlov found that it was sufficient to turn on the metronome—without any food—in order to make the dog salivate.

Pavlov had demonstrated that a *conditioned reflex* could be created in animals through repetition or *habituation*. He had also demonstrated that behaviour could be modelled, shaped, or stimulated by an outside agency. In other words, if one could control the outside stimulus, one would also control the response or behaviour. Pavlov's theory thus became known as stimulus-response theory.

Many people seized on Pavlov's experiments to express their fears of modern society. If conditioned reflexes could be instilled in animals, could not the same be done to people? The process would likely be more complex, but the outcome would be the same. It would be possible to control stimuli in order to control human behaviour. Indeed, some feared that given the nature of mass society, such an outcome was almost inevitable.

In modern mass society, people *do* tend to live relatively isolated or anonymous lives. The point is not that they have no friends or acquaintances but that society promotes isolation. As a result, it can be quite common for people not to know their next-door neighbours. It is also true that city life confers a certain anonymity on urban dwellers. It is quite possible to go out into the city in order to lose oneself in the crowd. In addition, the anonymity of the modern world makes it difficult for people to share a common culture. It is very difficult for us all to come together around a common event or spectacle or happening. As a result, we tend to form smaller and disarticulated groups that might share nothing at all.

Under the conditions of mass anonymity and isolation, people will naturally feel a need for contact. They will seek out others with whom they can share their time, their lives, and their interests. They will automatically turn to a strong voice that can provide the communal links that are lacking in modern society. Modern mass society thus creates the conditions under which a single, powerful, centralized voice or medium can coordinate the activities of millions of people.

The perceived nature of group life in mass society led to a concern among theorists with the media. The SR theorists pointed to two new phenomena of the early 1920s: propaganda and advertising. The memory of World War I still fresh in their minds, people wondered how it had been possible to visit such destruction on the world. The SR theorists believed that propaganda had made it possible to persuade so many millions to risk their lives. Propaganda had indeed proven highly effective in World War I. The warring armies and the countries that supported them had been shaped into enthusiastic support for slaughter on a scale never before seen. Propaganda demonstrated how in mass society millions of anonymous individuals could be stimulated into collective behaviour. It showed how, by controlling external stimuli—the content, frequency, vividness of messages—it was possible to bring about desired behaviour on a mass scale.

Here, then, was a fully formed—though fully unflattering—theory of the audience, one that brought together the nature of the message, the means for its control and delivery, and the intended outcome.[1] It can be represented as follows:

$$\text{Message (stimulus)} \Rightarrow \text{Behaviour (response)}$$

In this model, the power of the message to shape behaviour is much stronger than the power of the individual to resist. In SR theory, the media are powerful and humans are weak. The mind is understood to be highly malleable and easily manipulable, just like Pavlov's dogs.

The SR theorists added that what was true of propaganda was also true of advertising and of virtually all modern media. Indeed, how else could we explain the rise of a mass consumer society if it were not for the controlling power of advertising? Advertising was a message system that, very much like propaganda, controlled and coordinated stimuli in order to produce appropriate outcomes in large numbers of people. How else can we explain why quite suddenly in the 1920s millions of people began to want new products of whose existence they had only recently become aware?

The ability to shape behaviour was implicit in all modern media because the media are communication systems that operate in a one-way fashion, from the centre to the periphery. People, located at the periphery, can usually only listen or watch. This creates the conditions under which the media can instill beliefs and attitudes, as well as behaviours and actions. It is precisely this unflattering view of modern society that made many people suspicious of new forms of communication. The movies, for example, brought large numbers of people together in a darkened room and subjected them to images and emotions that were larger than life. Under such conditions, who knew that might happen? Indeed, much of the fear expressed around any new medium of communication results from the strong media/weak minds theory. This theory, commonly called the "hypodermic needle" or "magic bullet" theory, sees the media as instruments capable of injecting attitudes, values, beliefs, and behaviours into susceptible audiences. Almost all media have fallen under some form of suspicion.[2] Novels and comic books were at various times suspected of corrupting the morals of vulnerable readers. Television is perennially suspected of inducing laziness and stupidity. And the Internet is often accused of diverting users from normal social activities and serving as a breeding ground for offensive and illegal content.

The oft-repeated concern over television violence descends directly from the SR view of society. A medium (television) circulates content (violent representations) that the audience cannot resist. In mass society, which actually contributes to the weakness of the individual, users of a medium are likely to run off and do dangerous things. As a result, regulators should subject both the content and the medium to control or scrutiny. To do so is in the best interest of society.

The stimulus-response view of communication, which prevailed in North America from the 1920s to roughly the 1950s, remains powerful (although it is no longer the only view). To sum up, its basic elements are: (1) powerful media and powerful messages (stimuli) (2) operate in a mass society (3) composed of individuals who are weak and unable to resist external stimuli, (4) which produce direct effects observable in the behaviour (response) of the weakened individuals, and (5) necessitate media and audience controls.

Beginning in the 1940s, SR theory was challenged by another view of modern society. This second view, known as functionalism, is most closely associated with the work of Paul Lazarsfeld. In the 1940s, Lazarsfeld and his associates studied U.S. presidential elections in order to understand what influenced voters (Lazarsfeld, Berelson, and Gaudet, 1948). Since most newspapers in their day supported the Republican Party, they expected the presidential election of 1940 to follow a predictable path. The incumbent president, Franklin Delano Roosevelt, was a Democrat. Lazarsfeld therefore expected that voters subjected to newspaper messages favouring the Republican Party would abandon the Democrat Roosevelt and vote for his Republican opponent. That did not happen. Roosevelt was re-elected and proved to be an extraordinarily popular president. Why had media stimuli not been effective? Lazarsfeld found his answer in the nature of modern society.

Stimulus-response theorists assumed that mass society was composed of isolated, anonymous individuals and that their isolation drove them to seek forms of contact and guidance, which they found in the media. Their dependence on the media therefore made the media powerful and enabled them to deliver stimuli that shaped the behaviour of audiences. Lazarsfeld found something quite different. When he asked his survey sample who or what had influenced their vote, he was surprised to discover that most respondents said they had been influenced not by the media but by other people. On further investigation, Lazarsfeld discovered that his respondents—and by extension all members of society—did not live in isolation but actually enjoyed a rich associative life. In fact, they lived in *membership groups*—small groups of friends, family, co-workers, fellow students, and so on who spend time together (Katz and Lazarsfeld, 1955). By definition, the members of a group tend to share similar attitudes and opinions; if they did not, they would not be members of the same group.

Lazarsfeld also found that members of groups tended to pay only secondary attention to most media. Indeed, he specifically found that although the media produced lots of messages, the membership groups paid attention only to those messages that *already agreed* with their predispositions and interests. Jazz lovers, for example, tended not to pay much attention to the views of those who disparaged jazz. Membership groups, then, exhibited only *selective exposure* to media messages.

Within each membership group there was one person called an *opinion leader*. The opinion leader was the member of the group most interested in a particular topic (film, fashion, politics, etc.). The opinion leader followed the media more closely than the other members on that particular topic and it was through the opinion leader that media messages found their way into the group. The opinion leader thus *filtered* media messages, reporting mostly or only those messages that agreed with the group's attitudes and beliefs.

Lazarsfeld called this process the *two-step flow* of information (Katz and Lazarsfeld, 1955). It can be represented as follows:

Media (messages) ➡ Opinion leaders (filters) ➡ Membership groups

In step 1, messages flow from the media to the opinion leader. In step 2, they flow from the opinion leader to the membership group. However, the opinion leader filters the messages in a manner consistent with pre-existing group opinion. Membership groups and opinion leaders therefore constituted filters or barriers to the flow of messages. They did not *obey* media messages, they *resisted* them.

Furthermore, each of us lives in several membership groups that form complex interlocking networks. In order to reach membership groups, the media were forced to tailor their message to what they believed to be the pre-existing interests of the groups. Far from transmitting powerful stimuli, the media had to try to discover what people liked; they had to try "to give the people what they wanted." If they made a mistake, people would cease consuming their messages, and the media would die. This was exactly the opposite of SR theory, which had suggested that the media did things *to* people. Functionalism indicated that people did things *with* the media. Instead of an anonymous and alienated mass society, Lazarsfeld found complex sets of interlocking membership groups. Instead of powerful media, he found weak media. Instead of weak individuals subject to the power of the media, he found strong individuals (opinion leaders) immersed in their membership groups and able to filter and reject media messages. As a result, there was little need to worry about the potential effects of the media. Media and audience controls would serve little purpose beyond meddling in private affairs.

Functionalism gained prominence (especially after the 1950s) and remains influential to this day. To sum up, its principal elements are: (1) powerful individuals (opinion leaders) living within (2) complex sets of interlocking membership groups (3) select only the messages with which they agree, (4) forcing the media to try to meet prior audience interests and expectations, and (5) thereby making media and audience controls neither necessary nor desirable.

MEDIA AND AUDIENCES

All mass media want an audience. However they may be organized and whatever their specific content, their goal is to reach an audience. Indeed, without an audience, there's no real point to their efforts. The audience thus confers meaning on the activities of the media. We can often measure the success, relevance, or importance of a particular medium by examining the type or composition and size of its audience. For example, media are often judged to be successful when they attract large audiences. Hence the film *Titanic* or the television show *Survivor* are both judged successful largely because of the enormous audiences they were able to generate.

But audience size is not the only criterion of success. Sometimes we scorn a large audience. For example, although musical acts such as Britney Spears or the Backstreet Boys generate extremely large audiences, they tend not to receive much critical praise or respect. The important element here is not the size of the audience but rather its composition. We assume that some audiences, no matter how large, are less sophisticated or more easily pleased and are therefore not worth much attention. Consider the audience for daytime soap operas. Although soap operas typically attract large and fanatically loyal audiences, they and their audiences generally have a low status. We can see the same phenomenon at work with newspapers. If a newspaper is little read, we might first conclude that it is not very important. However, if its small readership consists of all the leading decision-makers, then we are likely to conclude that, despite its small circulation, it may in fact be a very important newspaper. Again, the important criterion in our judgment is the *composition* of the audience.

Statistical and empirical methods are excellent ways of learning about the size and composition of audiences. They can give us extremely helpful insights into their demographic makeup. For example, it is tempting to assume that all viewers of a television program or film share certain characteristics. This may be a flawed assumption and statistical methods can show us exactly who makes up an audience. On the basis of that knowledge, we can then ask even more refined questions about why diverse groups come together around a particular cultural event or experience, what the event means to them, how they would want to change or repeat it, and so on. Indeed, such methods (the subject of Chapter 7) can be extremely helpful in explaining why audiences are fragmented and in identifying the conditions under which they can be unified.

Beyond audience size and composition—two common ways of determining the success and importance of a medium—is another factor that can be called *audience competence*. Some media seek to address not large audiences but very specific and specialized audiences. Consider specialist forms such as science fiction, horror comics, or jazz. People who do not appreciate these forms often make harsh judgments about those who do, dismissing them as nerds, poseurs, wannabes, and so on. Whether these judgments are valid or not is not our concern. More significant is the fact that, whether we belong to a specialized audience or not, we all recognize that the cultural form involved addresses not a mass but a specialist audience. Consequently, in order to enjoy the specialized form fully, the audience members must develop an expertise or *competence* that allows them to make fine distinctions within the form.

Audience competence is obvious in specialized forms such as jazz or experimental film, but in fact *all* audiences tend to develop competence.[3] Indeed, the more time they spend with a particular cultural or media form, the more sophisticated audiences become. The process of increasing competence and sophistication can be illustrated by the VCR. Before the mid-1980s, VCRs were not very common; today almost every household in Canada has one. Most people use their VCRs primarily to watch movies. Responding to the demand, Hollywood releases to video not just its recent films but its entire back catalogue. As a result, even casual viewers become acquainted with the history and particularities of film in general or of a particular genre in which they are most interested. Through their VCRs, moviegoers develop the same sort of background competence that voracious novel readers already possess. This process, which was never planned but simply happened, will undoubtedly be repeated with DVD and whatever new technology comes after that.

The new sophistication of film audiences feeds back into the types of films Hollywood makes. It is becoming increasingly difficult to end films with classic "happy endings" precisely because audiences know that this is the classic way to end a film. The knowledge that such an ending is a cliché impels Hollywood to look for new ways of bringing films to a close, or for novel types of motivations so that even a "happy ending" might seem fresh and innovative. Similarly, every new blockbuster needs bigger effects, more spectacular action, something fresher and newer precisely because audiences know all about the predecessors.

The process of increasing sophistication is even more evident with television because the production cycle is so much faster than with film. A program such as *The Simpsons* depends crucially on a high degree of audience sophistication just to get the jokes. A viewer unfamiliar with the history of television itself, with other TV programs, or with popular attitudes toward television is unlikely to find *The Simpsons* very funny. *South Park* can similarly be understood as a highly self-conscious, though sophomoric, gesture toward the sophistication of the audience. It is a deliberate parody of our expectations about "good" animation, proper moral tone, socially acceptable behaviour, and so on.

One of the most striking examples of audience sophistication is to be found in so-called *fan fiction*, stories written by fans but based on characters and situations provided by the media. Jenkins (1992) has called this form of writing "textual poaching." Among the earliest examples of fan fiction were the K/S stories written by fans of the original *Star Trek*. These stories involved the characters of Kirk and Spock (hence K/S, pronounced "K slash S") and developed what the fans believed were the unspoken sexual tensions between them. Since then, numerous television programs and movies have given rise to fan fiction; the only audience for this form of writing is other fans.

Finally, a technology such as Napster also demands from its users a good deal of background musical knowledge. To know which songs you want and how you want to mix them up with other songs—in what order, with what mood, and so on—is to possess considerable background knowledge about what songs are available, a fairly articulate set of aesthetic judgments (what's good and what's bad), an insight into the impact the music will or should have (what order to give the songs), and so on. This is not to say that all Napster users are musical sophisticates but that for such a technology to work and be valuable to its users, those users must possess a degree of musical sophistication.

MASS VERSUS FRAGMENTED AUDIENCE

The very fact of audience competence raises another question. It is often assumed that the modern audience, simply by virtue of the nature of society, is a mass audience. The view of the audience as an undistinguished mass, in which everyone enjoys the same content and draws the same meanings from that content, is closely related to the mass-society hypothesis and to the stimulus-response view of modern society.

More recently, however, the view has emerged that audiences are in fact highly fragmented. The view that they are multiple, interlocking, and driven by highly differentiated interests and desires is itself very close to the functionalist view of society. The fact of the matter is that a permanent tension exists between the functionalist and stimulus-response poles and that we can find examples of both types of audience. Indeed, it may be the case that each type depends on the other for its very existence.

Television is a clear example of a formerly mass medium confronting the *fragmentation* of its audience. This fragmentation, which has occurred over the past 20 years, is reflected in the organization of the television industry. Where once there were only a few channels, there are now hundreds. The major networks that used to dominate audience ratings have seen their shares decline precipitously. Having discovered that it does not have an audience but rather *multiple audiences*, television is moving toward the model of book publishing, magazines, and newspapers. In these media, numerous offerings are common and it is easy for a reader of one type of content to know little or nothing about other types of content. This is the same transformation that confronted radio 50 years ago when television was first introduced.

At the same time, some media—including television—are still capable of generating large audiences. Every summer, blockbuster films attract massive audiences, and certain television programs or events (the O.J. Simpson verdict, *Who Wants to Be a Millionaire*, *Survivor*, etc.) are still capable of attracting remarkably large audiences. A best-selling novel or popular song can have the same effect. It seems that while audiences like to consume private pleasures in small, fragmented groups, they also measure the quality and desirability of those pleasures against a common cultural standard. For example, while some people may greatly enjoy the all-romance or all-wrestling channel, their ability to *know* that this is their preferred content depends on their ability to locate that content within a broad range of other content types. After all, if we only ever know one thing—country music or green clothes—then we can never know whether we like those things a lot or only a little. To know what we like demands that we know what others like too. It is only in that confrontation with the tastes of others that we can actually come to understand something about our own tastes.

Specialized interests, then, can emerge only after exposure to generalized interests or in relationship to them, even if that relationship consists in denigrating and avoiding those other interests. As audiences, we clearly tend to fluctuate between the two states of mass and fragmentation. For example, many millions of people will see a blockbuster film but from that common *mass* experience different audience *fragments* will develop an increased liking for specific elements of the film (lead actor, special effects, plot, etc.). Common experiences can spin off into specialized interests and specialized interests are shaped in relation to common experiences.

Finally, there are certain events which seem to *demand* that we come together as a mass audience. These are often events of significant public life such as a general election (on election night we constitute a mass audience around television), the death of a public figure (the funerals of Pierre Trudeau and Princess Diana generated mass audiences), a big sporting event (the Olympic Games, hockey playoffs, the World Cup), unusual events (high-profile televised trials), or acts of war (the Gulf War) or terrorism (the destruction of the World Trade Center). All of these events call us together as a *mass* audience and usually assume that we all draw the same meanings from them. They can also be the basis for us spinning off into specialized or fragmented audiences. Thus, while we may prefer to be with our fragmented groups most of the time, it may be the case that we have to be together at least some of the time.

AUDIENCE ADDRESS AND BEHAVIOUR

Different media address the audience in different ways. Hence, while we might be fans of a specific television show, prefer certain types of movies, and enjoy particular types of music, all of these media address us as audiences in quite different ways (see Marshall, 1997). Film, for example, has traditionally been a special event, requiring us to leave the home, pay money for the privilege of watching the film, and sit in a darkened theatre with a group of other people we have never met. The situation is sufficiently strange that, if we did not enjoy the experience, we might never go to another movie. To encourage us to repeat the experience, film promotes its various elements as "special." Film stars are presented as larger than life, distant, and mysterious, and moviegoers, typically left wanting to know more about them, turn to gossip columns and fan magazines to satisfy their curiosity. Film budgets are regularly touted as an indicator of just how "special" the event is. So are the box office grosses, the advertising campaigns, the promotional tie-ins, and the like.

If film attempts to instill the sense of a special experience by maintaining a distance between itself and the audience, television does the opposite. Because television is typically consumed in the home and is available virtually all the time, it tends not to be a special event. Television stars are not as big, as distant, or as mysterious as movie stars. On the contrary, they offer themselves almost as family members. Accordingly, we tend to know almost everything about them. For example, Oprah Winfrey, a huge television star, has revealed to her audience everything from her weight problems to her literary preferences. In order to make us want more, television strives not to be a special event that we crave but rather a friend whose company we expect. Whereas films maintain distance and promote themselves as special, television closes the gap and presents itself as friendly and familiar.

The music industry addresses us in yet another way. It tends to be directed more at emotions and at setting moods. It is therefore commonplace for people to associate particular songs with particular events in their lives (hence the saying, "They're playing our song"). People tend not to remember television programs or movies with the same degree of intensity or emotional attachment. Music tends to evoke not just strong feelings in the present but also strong feelings about the past, and about attitudes and attachments. Consequently, music stars tend to have a charismatic authority. The audience they attract is interested not so much in their appearance or personal life but in the whole set of emotions and values they represent.

It is, of course, possible to be a fan—to be a part of the audience—of film, television, *and* music despite their different modes of address. Indeed, it is quite common for our tastes to be relatively *coherent* across media. Part of our maturing as adults consists in constructing a coherent attitude and set of judgments across a multitude of media events and experiences. The judgments we form of these events are closely tied to the life cycle. Very young children have typically "childish" tastes. Young adults consume a tremendous range of cultural and media artifacts and tend to invest strongly in a small cross-section of them. Old people seem to have a more restricted range of preferences, often dating back to when they were themselves young. It is also likely that people's media menu evolves with age as well, with television being highly consumed by both the young and old, and music and film being heavily favoured by young adults. These are not hard-and-fast rules to which no exceptions may be found. Rather, they are indicators of the broad and strangely shifting contours of the audience.

We have seen that film tends to cultivate an aura of specialness, while television and music promote a sense of familiarity and charisma respectively. As a result of these differences, these three media also tend to produce different types of responses in their audiences. In the music industry, stage concerts that bring together in a single location very large numbers of people are commonplace. During a concert, the audience typically celebrates the physical presence of all its members and affirms the symbolic values it believes the music represents. (Concerts also share with sporting events the potential for danger that exists whenever large groups of people gather.) An extreme example of this phenomenon is provided by the "Deadheads," the hardcore fans of the Grateful Dead who virtually toured with the band and developed their own subculture; the music, in this instance, was linked to a set of beliefs that translated itself into a lifestyle. A less extreme expression of the same phenomenon can be observed in raves. People come together for a good time but also to affirm the values they believe the music represents and to translate those values into collective behaviour. Indeed, clothing styles—a visible marker of one's values—are much more closely linked to music than to television or to movies. Music, then, is associated with intensity, the physical presence of audience members, and the collective affirmation of values.

The responses of television audiences are quite different. A television audience is rarely roused to action. Its members are by definition dispersed and are usually represented only as ratings statistics. Because it is not presented with the opportunity to celebrate the physical presence of its members, a television audience is unlikely to translate its shared values into a visible behaviour pattern. What television does instead is cultivate a sense of familiarity. This is reflected not just in talk shows like *Oprah Winfrey* but in a wide range of television programming. Situation comedies are typically set in ordinary, everyday locations. Soap opera takes as its subject matter the most banal of daily occurrences. Much prime-time drama is filmed in real locations.

The fact that so much of television is ordinary and everyday generates among its audience the belief that the ordinary and everyday *deserve* to be on television. Television thus tends to establish an equivalence between its spectacle and reality. It is easy to assume that *because* television stars are familiar and friendly, then friendly and familiar people can themselves become television stars. This assumption is what drives viewers to become contestants on game shows or guests who reveal their most intimate secrets on talk shows. Rather than affirming collective values, television is aimed at making the famous ordinary and the ordinary famous.

Whereas music rouses people to action and television cultivates a desire for self-exposure, film tends to propose models of individual behaviour. The movie star's physical beauty, lavish lifestyle, and personal pursuits and hobbies are set forth as examples of highly desirable behaviour and, in many cases, become cultural ideals. The fixation with youth and corresponding enthusiasm for plastic surgery among the general population is derived from behaviour patterns associated with the glamour of the movie star. Of course, it is precisely because stars are unavailable, and because the film industry constructs itself as a distant yet special event, that the behaviour of stars becomes such an object of fascination.

AUDIENCE SWAPPING

As mentioned above, whatever the particular mode of address, it is quite possible for audiences to be coherent *across* media. Because of the relative coherence of audience tastes, the various media frequently undertake to swap audiences back and forth among themselves and to use audience success in one medium in order to build it in another. For example, *The X-Files* was sufficiently popular on television to be made into a movie. The hope was that its television audience would follow the characters into film and that, conversely, film audiences that were first introduced to the program through the film would be inspired to become a part of the *X-Files* television audience.

Crossovers between television and film are hardly new. The best-known example is probably the *Star Trek* films and television shows, all produced by Paramount Pictures with the specific intention of increasing profits by building audiences in both media. There are also, of course, crossovers between music and other media. Elvis Presley became a movie star and innumerable musical groups have appeared in films. The tradition has continued down to Will Smith who began his career as a rapper, had a hit television show (*Fresh Prince of Bel Air*), then became a movie star who also recorded the hit songs based on his movies. Judy Garland is an example of a film star who launched a successful music career. There have been crossovers between almost any other combination of media one cares to imagine. Michael Jordan even managed to cross over from sports to film (*Space Jam*). Perhaps the most enduring form of crossover is that between a novel and the film based on it.

A strategy movie studios commonly use to capitalize on existing audiences and to bring new people into the audience is the cross-media tie-in. Such promotions include novelizations and soundtracks, toys and games given away at fast-food restaurants, and merchandise bearing the logo of the movie. It is not uncommon for children to learn about the existence of a movie, and to be persuaded into wanting to watch it, from seeing colouring books featuring the characters or from receiving a free toy based on the movie. The same principle of persuasion applies to movie sequels and prequels.

The greatest danger of the strategy of swapping audiences back and forth is that the product will become overexposed and audiences will tire of it. After initial success, John Travolta made a number of bad and unmemorable films. (Performers are often accused of "selling out" or "betraying their audience" when this happens.) There was a long dry spell before *Pulp Fiction* revived Travolta's flagging career and gave him the opportunity to reconnect with his audience. A second and more insidious danger media industries face is that they will reach the wrong audience, thereby alienating their original audience. When a book is made into a movie, fans of the book are often disappointed because the movie somehow fails to match what they had imagined. Many fans of the comic book *Batman* were displeased with the 1989 *Batman* movie, for example.

MASS, PUBLIC, AUDIENCE

We have already seen that a particular audience member's tastes can be coherent across media, despite different modes of address and behaviour. A larger question we can ask is, What constitutes an audience in the first place? There are many types of groups, and not all of them qualify as audiences. A group of people walking downtown is not an audience even though its members share the same physical space and can be in very large numbers.

To be an audience, a group of people must not be random like the group walking downtown. Instead, it must be united for a particular purpose or around a common goal. But what about those groups of people who come together for the specific purposes of protesting against the government, raising a barn, or praying for the dead? Such groups of *purpose-oriented* individuals do not qualify as audiences. The mere fact of having a purpose does not make a group an audience.

An audience must be a nonrandom group and the purpose guiding its formation must be of a particular type. The purposes driving the groups mentioned above—protesting, barn raising, prayer—are the wrong type of purpose. The purpose that unites audiences is an *experience*. Audiences come together not to *do* something but to *experience* something. This is one of the main differences between political rallies and, say, movies or television. The purpose of political rallies is not to make those who attend them feel good; it is, rather, to encourage attendees to work toward the achievement of a particular goal that is political in nature. By contrast, movies and television usually seek not to bring about action but to provide an *experience* they hope the audience will enjoy enough to want to repeat. For an experience-seeking audience, a good experience is one that can be repeated. This is not the case with action-driven groups. If the goal of a political rally is achieved, there is no need to hold another rally that has the same purpose. For this reason, meetings of action-driven groups can be one-time affairs.

The type of experience most frequently sought by audiences, then, is an *entertainment experience*. The examples of protesting, barn raising, and prayer are clearly not entertainment experiences. They are goal-oriented activities whose duration can be quite limited. Indeed, the groups that engage in these activities can cease to exist once their goal has been achieved. An audience, however, will tend to be an ongoing phenomenon. Each particular experience will be valuable in itself but will also instill the desire for a repetition of the experience. In this respect, the process of forming an audience is never complete. The audience can always be re-formed—and frequently *wants* to be re-formed—around another experience, at another time, in another place.

Furthermore, audiences need not occupy the same physical space. The audiences for film and television, as noted above, are typically highly dispersed in time and space. The members of an audience for a sporting event *can* be concentrated in a particular location at a specific time to witness the event, but that audience can be supplemented by other more distant audiences following the event on television or radio, reading about the event in the newspaper the next day, or re-creating the event as part of a computer game.

The fact that audiences are usually associated with entertainment experiences often leads to a devaluation or dismissal of their activity, and to the conclusion that what they do is unimportant. While this conclusion may sometimes be accurate, it may also be an overstatement. A concern with entertainment experiences is not necessarily incompatible with rational judgment or behaviour. On the contrary, as we noted in our discussion of *audience competence*, there can be a high degree of rationality and sophistication involved in the act of being an audience member.

Nonetheless, the audience is usually compared unfavourably to the *public*. Whereas the audience is an entertainment or consumer concept, the public is held to be a political concept. Whereas the audience is associated with preferences and enjoyment, the public is associated with reason and judgment. Whereas the audience can be dismissed as fickle and ephemeral, the public is usually seen as growing out of principles that it expresses with constancy. The audience, then, is often treated as a degraded form of the public. It is often said to involve consumerism, whereas the public involves citizenship. Indeed, the media are often condemned specifically for treating people as *consumers* rather than as *citizens*, for doling out entertainment instead of information, and for transforming information *into* entertainment.

The reality of audience competence may require that we temper such judgments. There are, in fact, similarities between the audience and the public. Both are nonrandom groups and both are oriented toward a goal. The fundamental distinction between the two groups concerns the nature of the goal (experience vs. action), with action being judged the superior goal. However, both also require the use of rationality, though in different ways. The public uses its reason to determine the nature of social life and the limits of personal behaviour. The audience uses reason to determine the nature and quality of its experience. Neither group is more nor less rational than the other though they clearly use their reason to achieve different ends.

An important distinction separating the two groups is that, while both are nonrandom, their internal coherence springs from different sources. The members of an audience come together because they share a common experience or a common judgment on the nature, value, and desirability of the experience. In short, audiences come together on the basis of *elective affinities* (i.e., self-chosen reasons for coming together). A public *can* come together on the basis of elective affinities but its goal is not to prolong the pleasure of the experience or to repeat it. Its goal is to establish an external norm—a law, rules, methods of procedure—that would itself set the parameters under which people can come together. It seeks to institute a state of affairs that indicates appropriate and inappropriate activity or behaviour. Thus, whereas a public seeks to prescribe limits on behaviour, an audience does not. Whereas a public sees individual behaviour as a problem to be controlled, an audience sees individual preference as the precondition of its existence.

These distinctions and similarities may be brought into even sharper focus by comparing both the audience and the public with yet another type of group—the *mass*. Like the public and the audience, the mass is a nonrandom group of people oriented toward a purpose. The main characteristics of the mass are (1) its purpose is usually externally given (members of a mass do not assemble on the basis of elective affinities), and (2) it tends not to exercise reason in achieving its purpose. The members of a mass do not originally come together with the intention of forming a mass. Usually, a mass occurs suddenly when a large group of people has assembled for some other reason. An unexpected incident occurs and the group turns into a mass. Events such as riots, for example, are rarely planned. They tend to be spontaneous events whose origins are difficult to explain, and whose course and conclusion is almost impossible to foresee. Furthermore, the members of a mass typically set aside their conscious judgment and allow themselves to be guided by the spirit or mood of the crowd. That is why members of a mass find themselves engaging in behaviour—often of a violent or destructive nature—they would never engage in on their own. Conscious judgment is replaced by a group mind.[4] To sum up, the mass is a type of nonrandom group that is oriented toward a goal that is not self-chosen, and that accomplishes the goal through actions based on emotion rather than reason.

It would be wrong to claim that the three modes of being that human groups can assume—the mass, the public, and the audience—are completely separate and distinct states. In fact, they form a fluid continuum in which one state can easily morph into another. The Nazi movement, for example, was a political party and therefore a nonrandom group organized around a goal. At the same time, the actions of Nazi members at mass rallies and other gatherings exhibited all the traits of mass behaviour; individual judgment was replaced by a group mind. Similarly, entertainment can be merely an enjoyable experience but it can also instill beliefs and values. Many a book has been written with the specific purpose of teaching moral lessons; many a movie has been made that deals with complex issues and situations, and that invites audience members to respond by coming away with a greater tolerance for the point of view of others. The mass—the sheer fact of people coming together in large numbers and being able to undertake action—is probably the basis of both the audience and the public. At times, mass behaviour results in outcomes we applaud (defeat of tyranny at the hands of the oppressed, etc.). The mass, then, should not be condemned out of hand. As communication scholars, our role is first to understand the shifting and fluid relationships among mass, public, and audience, and always to resist quick and easy judgments about any of them.

QUESTIONS

1. How is an audience different from a mass?
2. Describe a group that is capable of morphing into an audience, a mass, and a public.
3. Can audiences undertake "political" action? Explain your answer.
4. How is an audience different from a public?
5. What are the basic elements of (a) stimulus-response theory, and (b) functionalism?
6. Describe the respective modes of address the film, television, and music industries use to attract an audience.

WEB SITES

Fan Fiction on the Net: **http://members.aol.com/ksnicholas/fanfic/**
Media Jargon Dictionary: **http://www.carat_na.com/facts/dictionary/a.html**
Rethinking Audiences for Cultural Industries (on-line article):
   http://media.ankara.edu.tr/~erdogan/jeffrey.html

NOTES

1. One of the best examples of this view at work can be found in George Creel, *How We Advertised America* (New York: Harper, 1920). Creel had been head of U.S. propaganda during World War I and his book was a proud report of his efforts. An unanticipated consequence of his account of the effectiveness of propaganda was to make people suspicious of advertising.
2. Perhaps the most legendary book on the topic of media influence is Frederic J. Wertham's *Seduction of the Innocent* (New York: Rinehart, 1954), which purports to show how crime comics can lead young people into a criminal life. An excellent overview of the debates, and evidence produced in their support, can be found in Willard D. Rowland, *The Politics of TV Violence* (Beverly Hills: Sage, 1983).
3. An excellent analysis of how audiences for a specific literary form—romance novels—develop a highly sophisticated competence that allows them to make extremely fine judgments is found in Janice Radway, *Reading the Romance* (Chapel Hill: University of North Carolina Press, 1984).
4. For a compelling account of the psychology of British soccer fans, see Bill Buford, *Among the Thugs* (London: Secker, 1991). The author, an American living in London, went underground by posing as a soccer "hooligan." The resulting book offers fascinating insights into the nature of crowd behaviour.

REFERENCES

Jenkins, Henry. (1992). *Textual poachers, television fans and participatory culture*. New York: Routledge.

Katz, Elihu, and Paul F. Lazarsfeld. (1955). *Personal influence*. New York: Free Press.

Lazarsfeld, Paul F., Bernard Berelson, and Hazel Gaudet. (1948). *The people's choice*. New York: Columbia University Press.

Marshall, P. David. (1997). *Celebrity and power*. Minneapolis/London: University of Minnesota Press.

Pavlov, Ivan. (1926/1960). *Conditioned reflexes: An investigation of the physiological activity of the cerebral cortex*. New York: Dover Publications.

FURTHER READING

Ang, Ien. (1991). *Desperately seeking the audience*. London: Routledge.

Canetti, Elias. (1973). *Crowds and power*. London: Penguin.

Freud, Sigmund. (1959). *Group psychology and the analysis of the Ego* (Rev. ed.). (Trans. of *Massenpsychologie und ich-analyse*.) London: Hogarth Press.

Jowett, Garth. (1999). *Propaganda and persuasion* (3rd ed.). Thousand Oaks, CA: Sage.

Le Bon, Gustave. (1963). *La psychologie des foules* (Nouv. ed.). Paris: Presses universitaires de France.

Liebes, Tamar and Elihu Katz. (1993). *Export of meaning: Cross-cultural readings of "Dallas"* (2nd ed.). Cambridge: Cambridge University Press.

Lindlof, Thomas. (1988). Mass audiences as interpretative communities. In *Communication Yearbook: Vol. 11* (pp. 81–107).

Modleski, Tania. (1986). *Studies in entertainment*. Bloomington: University of Indiana Press.

Morley, David (1989). Changing paradigms in audience studies. In E. Seiter (Ed.), *Remote control: Television, audiences, and cultural power*. New York: Routledge.

———. (1996). Populism, Revision and the "New" Audience Research. In James Curran (Ed.), *Cultural studies and communications*. London: Arnold.

Neuman, W. Russell. (1991). *The future of the mass audience*. Cambridge, U.K.: University Press.

6

Sipping Starbucks: (Re)Considering Communicative Media

Charlene Elliott
Carleton University

Colour, objects, scent, sound, and taste are vibrant communicators in cultural life, signifying a dizzying array of meanings. Yet in a culture preoccupied with new technologies and mass media forms, these "communicators" often become relegated to the background. At best, they are overlooked; at worst, they are considered unworthy of analysis.

This is unfortunate, for communication is more than media, and the communication field is far richer when viewed through a panoramic lens. Regarding communication solely as *mass* communication is reductionist, and some scholars have lamented the field's current confined "mediacentric perspective" (Mattelart, 1996, p. x) and its "unduly limited dialogues of media research" (Golding and Harris, 1997, p. 9). We are wise to heed these concerns and, as a result, to consider communication that might be less "wired," but of equal importance.

Take, for instance, the communicator of colour. In 2000, Sears decided to brighten Canada's landscape by making "aubergine" the hue of its ubiquitous, if bizarre, marketing campaign geared to reinvent Eatons, which reopened on November 25th, 2000, in six cities across Canada. The campaign's goal was not to associate a colour with a brand, but to make the colour *the* brand. And so, huge 150-kilogram aubergine objects—a giant three-dimensional lipstick, a martini glass, and a shoe—were hoisted and affixed onto superboards; images of aubergine pearls and watches sprang up on transit posters; and what Sears has generously identified as "the catchy melody of the aubergine theme song" blared on the radio.

It is the ubiquity of the brand in today's world that prompts marketers to seek new ways to grasp attention. The Eatons stores were located in major urban centres where clutter and fragmentation would make it difficult for the aubergine campaign to stand out. Aubergine, as unique as it was, allowed for a measure of high visibility. But what proves shocking to many about the branding of colour is that its signification increasingly is being codified and granted legitimacy by our legal regimes. Sears has filed a trademark application for the *word* "aubergine," and it is also exploring the possibility of trademarking the *colour* alone (Eatons, personal communication, Case 90462, March 12, 2001).

Given the recent developments in trademark law, there is a real possibility Sears will succeed in its quest. In March 1995, the U.S. Supreme Court sent shockwaves through legal circles by granting, for the first time, a trademark to colour alone or colour *per se*. Australia followed suit the following year, and in March 1999 Germany's Supreme Court also ruled that colour *per se* could be owned. Although Canada's Supreme Court has yet to rule on this issue, the basis for a similar decision is certainly in place, for the Canadian Trademark Act is worded such that there is no reason in *law* why colour trademarking should not be possible.

The implications of owning colour are far-reaching. But why should this matter to communication students? It matters because it reveals that communication is brighter and louder, more flavourful and smelly—and also more subtle—than often realized. And it matters because marketers are increasingly recognizing the power of these unique communicators to influence an audience. Hence we have efforts to own a colour, a shape, a scent, or a sound. For instance, Coca-Cola's bottle and Morton-Norwich's cleanser container have been trademarked, as have NBC's three "signature" chimes, ABC's characteristic musical notes, and the fragrance of plumeria blossoms on sewing thread (Carraway, 1995, p. 246ff; James, 1996, p. 422ff). In Germany, the Flensburger Pils brewery even tried to trade mark the sound of a beer bottle opening! ("Germany Overturns," 1999, p. 6). Since we are not only surrounded but also *influenced* by these communicators, it proves necessary to explore how they are being used to target, build, and persuade an "audience."

FLAVOURFUL BRANDS: ATTRACTING THE AUDIENCE

Other chapters of this book discuss the ways in which media such as film, television, newspapers, and Web sites relate to the vast numbers of people who make up the audience. However, audiences exist in several forms. Not merely moviegoers and music fans or viewers of reality TV, an audience comprises the grocery shoppers choosing *President's Choice* cookies over Nabisco *Chips Ahoy!*, and the coffee drinkers sipping Starbucks in trendy corner cafés.

If colour, scent, tastes, and objects are communicative media, then the channelling of their meanings (often at the hands of marketers) is done with the audience in mind. As such, the mass media concerns of audience composition and competence, diversity and fragmentation also play out in these less overtly *media*-ted forms. Marketers of fragrance, food, and drink—and aubergine—all begin with ideas about the audience and theories of what will be persuasive. *How* these symbolic forms of communication are marketed proves particularly fascinating, and the following case study illustrates how something as simple as a coffee bean can be transformed into something symbolically exciting in order to attract an audience of coffee drinkers whose experience is based in the consumption experience itself.

STARBUCKS AND HAUTE-CAFFEINE: CREATING THE COFFEE SNOB [1]

Coffee is one of the most valuable commodities in world trade and a key export product for developing countries. Accounting for over 70 percent of foreign exchange earnings for some of the least-developed countries (ICO, 2000), coffee has clear economic and political import. But coffee is also the preferred beverage of Canadians and Americans (second only to water), and its sociocultural significance is equally remarkable. Sixty-two percent of Canadians and 52 percent of Americans drink coffee daily (Cherney, 1998, p. A6) and specialty coffeehouses adorn the urban landscape like bright confetti. Starbucks Coffee Company, the ubiquitous purveyor of specialty coffees, has retail stores throughout North America, the United Kingdom, the Pacific Rim, and the Middle East. It competes with a host of other popular specialty retailers—including even the McDonald's Corporation, which recently joined the brouhaha with a $24-million (U.S.) chain of coffee bars in Britain (Stanley, 1999, p. B3). Jamaican coffee producers also entered the retail market in January 1999, opening the "first of a planned 2,000 strong chain of coffee stores across the globe" ("Jamaica Boosts Coffee," 1999, p. C14).

Clearly, coffee is big business. Yet it is also symbolic business, dealing with the production, packaging, and consumption of meaning—a meaning repeatedly ingested by Starbucks' patrons. The cultural "text" of coffee is particularly interesting, for it is multilayered; meaning resides in the form itself (i.e., the "artifact" of the bean/beverage) and in the discourses surrounding that form (i.e., in its packaging and marketing). These discourses "blend" within the cup and are literally and figuratively consumed.

Furthermore, coffee is a unique artifact for analysis because the commodity flow is from south to north. While coffee has from the onset been stamped with a European thumbprint, there is no question that this ancient, foreign beverage has radically reshaped the social relations and complexion of both work and leisure within the consuming countries. Historically, coffeehouses served as forums for political discussion and learning (Naiman, 1995, p. 52; Pendergrast, 1999, pp. 7–15); they have transformed over the years into "retail theatres" used primarily for socializing (MacLeod, 1997, p. B4). The beverage itself has become integral to working and professional culture: it is simultaneously a pick-me-up that provides greater productivity and a pause (in the form of the coffee break). Arguably, coffee has transformed Western society through a kind of tempered coffee colonialism, in which an imported commodity has been wholly embraced to become a fixture of Western consumer society and a marker of (Western) identity.

Consuming caffeine, then, entails more than brewing or buying. "Going for coffee" has social and global implications. Coffee beans, physically removed from their place of origin, have been conceptually repackaged, and the resulting discourse operating both through and about coffee targets a particular audience interested in a cosmopolitan, sophisticated, and distinctive consumption experience.

While it is possible to explore coffee's packaging and marketing from various perspectives, this chapter follows Arjun Appadurai's lead in focusing on the commodity itself—the "thing that is exchanged" (Appadurai, 1986, p. 3)—and how it relates to the consumer audience. Since an audience (on a fundamental level) comes together to *experience* something, often *repeatedly*, it is crucial to note how the coffee bean is transformed into a distinct social experience. As Starbucks illustrates, identical commodities do not necessarily brew into identical products; because of this, the audience of Tim Hortons is far different from the patrons of Starbucks' specialty coffees.

THE WORLD OF STARBUCKS

Starbucks is the world's largest retailer, roaster, and brand of specialty coffee. With over 3300 stores operating in 15 international venues (Starbucks, 2000a, 2000b), Starbucks' coffee discourse circulates widely and is quaffed copiously. Consequently, it provides a meaningful illustration of how one simple commodity has been costumed for Western consumption. Starbucks' messages are steeped in the beverage itself, the names of the coffee blends, and the labelling of the beans. This construction, packaging, and presentation of coffee works to create and appeal to a particular audience, where the "entertainment" experience is literally consumed and where Starbucks' patrons are distinguished from "regular" coffee drinkers. But first, it is important to explore how the coffee bean itself has come to acquire this meaning.

In their extensive study on the social role of advertising, communication scholars William Leiss, Stephen Kline, and Sut Jhally reiterate the Marxist perspective on commodity fetishism, a process whereby all traces of production are erased from the object produced. "Goods reveal or 'show' to our senses their capacities to be satisfiers," they affirm, while "draw[ing] a veil across their own origins" (Leiss, Kline, and Jhally, 1990, p. 324). Since goods "do not bear the signatures of their makers" (p. 325), only the most astute shoppers realize the components of things and who made them. Jameson's (1991) analysis of postmodernity voices similar concerns, in which "the point" of consumerism, arguably, is to

> forget about all those innumerable others for awhile; you don't
> want to have to think about Third World women every time you
> pull yourself up to your word processor or all the other lower
> class people with their lower class lives when you decide to use
> or consume your other luxury products. (p. 315)

Traditional coffee marketing does not belie these ideas. Starting from the 1920s, when coffee became a major consumer product, national corporations like Standard Brands and General Foods advertised the stimulant as a regular part of the workaday world. By 1950, coffee was the favourite beverage of the American middle class (Pendergrast, 1999, p. xviii), and in the decade that followed consumers could select from an array of coffees that masked their origins completely. Maxwell

House, Folgers, Nestlé, Sanka, and the inaptly named Chock Full o' Nuts certainly did little to connote their source or those producing the beans.[2] Origins were insignificant. As an American roaster of the 1960s claimed, U.S. consumers simply wanted "normal" coffee in paper cups and "diluted to the tastes of the time, along with a hamburger and fries" (cited in Pendergrast, 1999, p. 271).

Arguments for commodity fetishism prove less convincing in 2002, a time when fairly traded coffee and "environmentally friendly" coffee (such as shade grown and organic) are readily available—for an added price, of course. The Transfair and Quality Mark labels highlight attempts in the producing countries to raise—and acknowledge—public awareness; both labels guarantee interested consumers that coffee producers have received fair prices and a stable market for their crop. Shade-grown and organic coffee marketing, in contrast, focus on the ecological impact of coffee harvesting, emphasizing either the alternatives to pesticides or water and soil conservation initiatives. Thus, rather than veiling the wearisome information on where and how coffee is produced, fair trade, organic, and shade-grown products foreground such considerations. Shoppers know the coffee bean's "history" and can deliberately choose the coffee "experience" of labels they support.

In the case of Starbucks, the interplay between global/local and producer/product is much more intricate—and ironic. While Starbucks introduced organic coffee into its product line on April 20, 1999 (to commemorate Earth Day) and shade-grown coffee in August (Starbucks, 1999c, 1999a), it is not a Transfair member company. And when Starbucks entered the Beijing market in January 1999 (Starbucks, 1999b), it chose to serve imported coffee even though China's southwestern province of Yunnan produces thousands of tons of dried coffee beans annually (Virant, 1999).

Moreover, Starbucks' promotional brochure, *The World of Coffee*, highlights the role of the purveyor, not the producer, when it declares that the company's goals are "to do whatever it takes" to provide "a great cup of coffee." Giving its audience this exceptional taste experience involves not only "finding and purchasing the best green beans in the world" but also "listening and responding to the coffee and helping it reach its highest flavor potential" (Starbucks, 1998). Here Appadurai's (1986) notion that "commodities have social lives" (p. 3) gains added significance in that Starbucks personifies the bean as something to be "listened to" and conversed with before being ground up and sold to consumers. All told, these elements suggest that the *audience*, not the source (i.e., producers/origin), is of primary concern—a suggestion confirmed by the maxim typed on every Starbucks package: "Whether this Starbucks came from Africa, Arabia, Indonesia or Latin America, its destination is your cup."

CAFFEINATED CARTOGRAPHY

Although Starbucks proudly serves its coffee around the world, the company's sense of geography is refracted through a commodified Western lens—a lens meant to appeal to a mass audience. Reflecting on his Starbucks experience, one journalist carped that unsuspecting Starbucks consumers must choose from "beans from countries that college graduates cannot find on a map" (cited in Pendergrast, 1999, p. 371).

Indeed, Starbucks' coffees embrace a range of growing locations, from Mexico, Guatemala, Colombia, Indonesia, and New Guinea to Kenya, Ethiopia, and Yemen. That consumers are not *expected* to find these places, but merely to consume them symbolically, is reflected in the way which the brand creates and deals with the audience. While a particular type of audience might come to Starbucks for a taste experience, it is important to emphasize that the *experience* outranks the taste. Consumers may have little knowledge of the coffee bean's birthplace, yet this is insignificant. What matters (to Starbucks, at least) is the appeal that comes from labelling coffee *differently*, for it makes the buying experience that much more entertaining. Furthermore, Starbucks recognizes that its "audience" is not a monolith and caters to its consumers' diversity of tastes accordingly.

Proof of both the *symbolic role of place* and the *acknowledgment of taste* is found in Starbucks' Coffee Categories, which arrange the beans according to flavour, not origin. In this categorization, Lively Impressions subsume the "flavorful, bright and inviting" (Starbucks, 1998) coffees from Costa Rica, Papua New Guinea, and East Africa under one sprightly heading. Rich Traditions, in contrast, offers "well-rounded and balanced" flavours from sources as diverse as Kenya, Java, and Guatemala. Finally, Bold Expressions—"assertive," "exotic," and "intense" coffees—stem from Arabia, Indonesia, and Ethiopia. These "categories" speak to the consumers' desire for a particular taste and utterly discount the reality of the world's spaces. And while Starbucks' cartography of coffee may initially appear to substantiate Harvey's (1992) view that global culture makes people "much more sensitized to what the world's spaces contain" (p. 294), the sensitivity is wholly superficial. "Sensitivity," in this case, is an awareness that the "world's spaces" of Java, Sulawesi, New Guinea, or Guatemala "contain" one thing of import: the Starbucks coffee bean.

Starbucks' cartography of coffee is further problematized by its array of trademarked blends. Shoppers curious about a blend's origin can learn, through Starbucks' edifying brochures, that the company's "master roasters" create these flavourful brews by combining various coffee beans to attain a desired "tasteprint." In this way, Starbucks seeks to create a level of *audience competence*—a specialized audience that will appreciate the finer details of the coffee "experience" and consequently return to experience it again and again. But how is this done and *what does it mean*? Starbucks' brochure explains that a commodity of Yemen is ground with a commodity of Indonesia to "create" Arabian Mocha Java, while the beans of East Africa mix with those of Latin America to become Siren's Note Blend. In this way, the world's coffees are "relocated" just like the other non-Western commodities imported into North American society—just like the Costa Rican bananas, Indonesian sweet potatoes, and Chilean grapes housed in the local supermarket.

Starbucks' relocation, however, has greater symbolic power. The commodity, identified by its location, has been fused with another; the country of Indonesia is symbolically annexed with Yemen. Even this is beguiling, for the marketing literature fails to identify Yemen as a source. Rather, it refers to the geographically vague Arabia, a place with no defined borders. Moreover, Starbucks' blends are commonly packaged under vague or misleading names. Yukon Blend, for example, is actually composed of Indonesian and Latin American coffees. Caffe Verona has the same distant ingredients, only in different proportions. And Italian Roast has nothing to do with the lovely red, white, and green label that evokes Italy's flag.

Starbucks' "master roasters" thus function as modern *bricoleurs*, playing with commodity pieces to construct a tasty—and trademarked—text for consumption. Symbolically, the play is highly charged in that the beans identified by their origins are more than pieces—they index places. The *audience competence* encouraged by Starbucks is based, then, not on a reality but on a brand image. This image captivates audiences and creates the Starbucks "experience." Moreover, as an audience participates in Starbucks' "culture" by gaining coffee competence and developing personal tastes, Starbucks' image too becomes part of their own identity.

PLAYING WITH THE MAP

Geographic recombination also occurs within Starbucks' menu and in its store, where language, country, and commodity all provide symbolic grist for the Starbucks mill and where Starbucks' retail theatre promises a worldly experience for its audience. Customers do not purchase from servers, they order from baristas. Cup sizes do not come in small, medium, or large, but in the equally Italian short, grande, and venti. Popular espresso-based drinks such as cappuccino and café latte can be ordered con panna or as macchiatos. Consumers with a certain competence are thus encouraged to display their expertise. For those *without* the knowledge, Starbucks readily provides the information necessary to participate. In this way, the Starbucks audience continually expands as the coffee novice, with little effort, transforms into a coffee aficionado.

As Starbucks' customers sip their grande café au laits in a Seattle-based coffee-house, they also partake in a cultural experience: they imbibe a style of coffee (espresso) that was invented in France, perfected in Italy, and sourced from Latin America and Indonesia. Tellingly, Starbucks chooses not to identify the bean "origins" of Espresso Roast™, the blend used in every espresso drink on the menu. Espresso Roast™ is described simply as the "heart and soul of Starbucks ... caramelly, smooth, great balance" (Starbucks, 1988), suggesting that the essence of Starbucks could only have a corporate origin. This is also true of Starbucks' signature and most popular coffee, Starbucks House Blend, which is described solely as a "wonderful, round, balanced, straightforward cup of coffee" (1988). Here the cloaking of origins is deliberate and supports the "veiling process" Leiss, Kline, and Jhally (1990) deem as characteristic of Western advertising. With this kind of naming and marketing, Starbucks reveals that "space" or "place" is merely a style to be utilized for semantic purposes and discarded when not wanted.

As consumers of Starbucks and participants in the coffee experience, we must ask *why* the marketing masks certain countries of origin and articulates others; only by answering this question will we have true "audience competence" when sipping our lattes and coffee blends. The question is difficult, and must be answered from a more theoretical perspective. Studies in anthropology and advertising theory prove very helpful, for the evocation of difference has both a strong cultural function and marketing value. Anthropologist Sidney Mintz (1985) reveals that today's "commonplace" imported commodities have shifted in meaning over time. Sugar, for instance, was first introduced to European society as a luxury item and coveted precisely *because* of its distant origins. This is also true of tea and chocolate, which only gradually became integrated (through increased use and availability) into wider society (Mintz, 1985).

These foreign goods ultimately transformed into staples and markers of both European and Western cultures; the physically deterritorialized commodities became conceptually reterritorialized into the realms of the familiar and the local. Thus for years consumers jump-started their mornings with the trusted, quotidian brands of Maxwell House, Folgers, or Nescafé. But the rise of specialty coffee worked to refresh this common staple, to make the banal better, and to add what marketing guru Rosser Reeves calls a "Unique Selling Proposition" (cited in Macrae, 1991, p. 36)—the special perk that the competitors do not offer. Hence the evocation of the exotic. Foreign beans, made common, are traced back to their roots to heighten coffee's consumer appeal. As Howes (1996) notes, "[I]n general, the only time when the foreign nature of an imported product is emphasized in the West by its marketers . . . is when part of its appeal to Westerners lies in its exotic nature" (p. 186).

"Foreignness" within the specialty coffee market allows consumers to conceptually partake of exotic locales. Coffee aficionados use geography to illustrate their knowledge and taste preferences by ordering Brazil Ipanema Bourbon™, Kenya, Sumatra, Kona, New Guinea Peaberry, or Colombia Narino Supremo™. In short, they order a place in a cup. And since the coffee beans' origins are only a "spice" within Starbucks' marketing, they can be tinkered with. Kenya, the country, is a coffee name, but so is Kona, a region in western Hawaii. Ethiopia Sidamo, which Starbucks offers as a beverage, is both a place and a people: Sidamo refers to the Cushitic-speaking inhabitants of southwestern Ethiopia. Starbucks' Guatemala Antigua coffee is an inversion of the capital and country of Antigua, Guatemala.

Finally, as merely a "spice," coffee's exotic origins can be omitted from the marketing at will. Reference to the foreign is used to make products appealing rather than threatening (Howes, 1996, p. 187), and marketers strive to ensure that their products (even those positioned as exotic) maintain a strong pull of familiarity so that they appeal to consumer lifestyles or lifestyle aspirations (Leiss, Kline, and Jhally, 1990). This explains why Starbucks' packaging, marketing, and menu remain silent about the beans in the company's House Blend and Espresso Roast™. There is the practical reason of wanting to appeal to the largest-possible audience by offering both exotic and familiar fare—but the logic extends deeper. Starbucks has established itself as an upscale, worldly, but pointedly American chain. Accuracy with regards to global details (such as geographical and source identification, or coffee names) proves secondary to Starbucks' marketing and image. As Starbucks' promotional flyer affirms: "Starbucks works backwards from a cup of coffee. It proudly considers the product first."

THE RHETORIC OF STARBUCKS; OR, 'SPEAKING OF COFFEE . . .'

Starbucks' "world of coffee" reaches beyond naming the beans. Coffee descriptors used in the company's marketing literature reveal Starbucks to be more than geographically challenged: it is steeped in an ethnicized rhetoric that the audience, perhaps unwittingly, participates in while supporting the brand. As noted earlier, the Starbucks blends that target the widest possible audience—Espresso Roast™ and House Blend—are described in positive and nonthreatening terms. They are "wonderful," "balanced," "straightforward." and "smooth"; they are the "heart and soul of Starbucks"; they are "bright" and "mild." Coffees with designed or entirely created names, such as Yukon Blend™, Caffe Verona™, Gold Coast Blend™, or Italian Roast present equally laudatory descriptors: Yukon Blend™ is "bright" and "brisk" and "well rounded"; Caffe Verona™ is "classic" and "versatile"; Gold Coast Blend™ is "sophisticated, 'big city'," a "courageous cup of coffee"; and Italian Roast, with its "sturdy, assertive flavor," is a coffee for connoisseurs.

Contrast these descriptors with those of the "exotic" coffees, which have laudatory but loaded terms. Sulawesi is "exotic but approachable," Kenya is "intense" but "refreshing," and Arabian Mocha Java is "exotic" and "wild." As consumers, we would do well to recognize that many of these words and phrases are consistent with what Said (1978, pp. 1–4) would classify as Orientalist discourse—the ethnocentric and stereotypic means of viewing, describing, restructuring, and ultimately dominating Muslim lands in Africa and Asia. Orientalism pivots on the notion of the "mysterious East" (Said, 1993, p. x) and often portrays the foreign as primitive. Starbucks' exotic coffee descriptors convey those very categories. Coffees are "magical," "intriguing," "fleeting," "elusive," "nearly indescribable" (i.e., mysterious), and "wild" and "earthy" (i.e., primitive). As with Orientalism, these descriptors exist to be observed and consumed by the West. Thus Guatemala Antigua coffee may seem "simple at the beginning," but to the persistent connoisseur it promises "many levels of discovery."

Arabian Mocha Sanani's description brings together many of these threads, combining Starbucks' sense of the exotic and its Western gaze with the mysterious and primitive to create a coffee profile with multiple meanings—one that consequently appeals to more than one type of audience:

> Arabian Mocha Sanani—A wild and wonderful coffee with an intense berry flavor and hints of spice, rum and cocoa. Sanani's layers of exotic flavor appeal to the coffee adventurer as well as the sophisticated coffee connoisseur. (Starbucks, 1998)

Orientalism also emerges in the sexually charged terminology Starbucks uses to define its "exotic" coffees. Taste descriptors refer to the body or female sexuality: coffees are "full-bodied," "well-rounded," and "soft," with "luxurious texture"; they are also "smooth and satisfying." It is meaningful to contrast these descriptors with those of Starbucks House Blend, Espresso Roast™, Caffe Verona™, Italian Roast, and French Roast—none of which make reference to the body.

Starbucks accentuates its ethnicized rhetoric by presenting, for those who seek adventure in their coffee experience, the "wild side" of coffee. Said (1978) notes that "a principal dogma" of Orientalism is that the East is unpredictable, savage even, and "something to be feared" (p. 301). These random and savage elements emerge in the three Starbucks coffees labelled "Arabian"—they are the only Starbucks coffees deemed "wild." Arabian Mocha Java is "wild," "spicy," and "intense," while Arabian Mocha Sanani is all these things and "unpredictable" besides. "You never know how it's going to taste," declares Starbucks' promotional brochure.

To keep these elements under control, Starbucks offers on its Web site The Coffee Taster—a service that acknowledges that particular tastes exist in the wider coffee audience, and that helps consumers find their niche within Starbucks' universe. Customers who answer the following seven questions can receive a personal-taste profile and a list of matching Starbucks coffees.

1. What does coffee do for you?
2. What taste characteristics do you seek?
3. What flavors do you enjoy?
4. How do you describe yourself as a coffee drinker?
5. How do you drink your coffee?
6. How do you like your coffee brewed?
7. What do you generally order in a restaurant?

The answers, from a semantic perspective, are complex. Again, Starbucks subordinates the commodity to personal taste in order to foreground the audience, but even its taste profiles are symbolically charged. If consumers identify themselves as coffee-nervous or coffee-novice by answering in preference of mild flavours, consistent tastes, and coffee with added cream and/or sugar, then The Coffee Taster affirms that Starbucks House Blend, Siren's Note Blend, or French Roast—in short, the nonexotic coffees—are a "sure thing." For these consumers, it would be "adventurous" to try Colombia Narino Supremo or Guatemala Antigua, and "daring" to try Arabian Mocha Java. For those consumers who identify themselves as coffee risk-takers, and who enjoy experimenting, "extremes," and the "wild," The Coffee Taster recommends Arabian Mocha Java and other exotic coffees. Regardless of the answers given, Starbucks' signature and "non-exotic" coffees never appear under the "daring" category; Starbucks House Blend is listed either as a "sure thing" or not at all.

CONSUMING CAFFEINE

To truly experience the richness of communication, we need to understand communication as something that is fully sensorial (i.e., full of tastes, colours, sounds, and smells). We also need to understand that "audience" extends beyond moviegoers and television viewers. The audience—defined as a group of people who seek, and hope to repeat, an experience (often an entertainment experience)—can equally be found in coffeehouses, sipping their "communication" while sharing it with others.

In the case of Starbucks, the audience is targeted with *reference* to representations that, while global in part, are predominantly local. Coffee beans, distanced from their origins, have been relocated in an American chain, and while Starbucks seemingly respects the imported commodity, it refashions it completely to appeal to an audience desiring sophistication and the signs of worldly taste. While coffee may be commonplace, specialty-coffee purveyors have reintroduced its global dimension and transformed the banal bean into something symbolically exciting.

The resulting issues of the palate are not confined within a bowl of Starbucks cappuccino or a mug of Starbucks House Blend. While Starbucks offers the audience a "unique" and distinctive coffee experience, it accomplishes this experience by remapping world geography and appropriating Third World spaces. Kenya and Estate Java coffees *claim* to substantiate Africa and Indonesia respectively, but what Starbucks is actually substantiating is the audience's taste for the exotic. Coffee's commodity form has been made and remade in Western society, and while Starbucks' current marketing blends within its semantic coffeepot the exotic and familiar, as well as the local and global, the resulting brew is poured from a Western perspective. Despite Starbucks' marketing of global culture to attract sophisticated consumers, what the audience *really* consumes are local and stereotyped representations. This fact is confirmed, albeit unintentionally, by Starbucks' key slogan: "Starbucks—The World of Coffee." Indeed, it is Starbucks' world of coffee—and not the world's coffees—that is being packaged for consumption.

QUESTIONS

1. What types of audiences can we study other than media audiences?
2. How does Starbucks construct audiences?
3. What does Orientalism refer to?

4. How does Starbucks remap world geography to create its products?
5. Should "colour" or any other artifact be trademarked? Give reasons for your answer.

WEB SITES

No Logo (interactive site inspired by Naomi Klein's *No Logo: Taking Aim at the Brand Bullies*): **http://www.nologo.org/**
Starbucks: **http://www.starbucks.com**

NOTES

1. Portions of this analysis are drawn from Elliott (2001).
2. The exception is Juan Valdez, the mule-escorted, sombrero-wearing coffee grower invented by the National Federation of Coffee Growers of Colombia in the 1960s to laud Colombian coffee. This highly successful advertising campaign focused on Colombia's rich growing conditions and its hand-harvesting methods, which ensured consumers a better-tasting coffee (Pendergrast, 1999, p. 284).

REFERENCES

Appadurai, Arjun. (1986). *The social life of things*. Cambridge: University of Pennsylvania.

Carraway, C. (1995). Color as a trademark under the Lanham Act: Confusion in the circuits and the need for uniformity. *Law and Contemporary Problems*, *57*(4), 243–279.

Cherney, Elena. (1998, November 9). Trends. *National Post*, p. A6.

Germany overturns colour practices. (1999, July/August). *Managing Intellectual Property*, *91*, 6.

Elliott, Charlene. (2001). Consuming caffeine: The discourse of Starbucks and coffee. *Consumption, Markets and Culture*, *4*(4).

Golding, Peter, and Phil Harris (Eds.). (1997). *Beyond cultural imperialism*. London: Sage.

Harvey, David. (1992). *The condition of postmodernity*. Cambridge: Blackwell.

Howes, David (Ed.). (1996). *Cross-cultural consumption: Global markets, local realities*. New York: Routledge.

ICO (International Coffee Organization). (2000, September 9). *The story of coffee: Market information*. Retrieved from http://www.icoffee.com/MainFrame.asp

Jamaica boosts coffee industry with chain of shops. (1999, January 8). *National Post*, p. C14.

James, R. (1996). Trademark Law—Lanham trademark act of 1946. *Duquesne Law Review, 34*(2), 419–434.

Jameson, Frederic. (1991). *Postmodernism; or, the cultural logic of late capitalism*. Durham, NC: Duke University Press.

Leiss, William, Stephen Kline, and Sut Jhally. (1990). *Social communication in advertising*. Scarborough, ON: Nelson.

MacLeod, Ian. (1997, May 7). Beans with a premium: Rich exotica of specialty coffees sweeps continent. *Hamilton Spectator*, p. B4.

Macrae, Chris. (1991). *World class brands*. England: Addison-Wesley.

Mattelart, A. (1996). *The invention of communication*. Minneapolis: University of Minnesota Press.

Mintz, Sidney. (1985). *Sweetness and power*. New York: Viking.

McCracken, Grant. (1988). *Culture and consumption*. Bloomington: Indiana University Press.

Naiman, Sandy. (1995, February 26). Spilling the beans. *Toronto Sun*, p. 52.

Pendergrast, Mark. (1999). *Uncommon grounds*. New York: Basic Books.

Said, Edward. (1978). *Orientalism*. New York: Vintage.

———. (1993). *Culture and imperialism*. New York: Vintage.

Stanley, Bruce. (1999, March 27). Coffee conquers British tastes. *Hamilton Spectator*, p. B3.

Starbucks Coffee Company. (1998). *The world of coffee* [Brochure].

———. (1999a, August 2). *Coffee that's made in the shade* [Press release]. Retrieved from http://www.starbucks.com/company/archive

———. (1999b, January 10). *Starbucks coffee company opens first store in Beijing, China* [Press release]. Retrieved from http://www.starbucks.com/company/archive

———. (1999c, April 20). *Starbucks offers a new line of organic coffee* [Press release]. Retrieved from http://www.starbucks.com/company/archive

———. (1999d, December 2). *Starbucks reports November revenues* [Business wire 0348]. Retrieved from http://www.businesswire.com/cnn/sbux.htm

———. (2000a). *Starbucks coffee company opens first stores in Hong Kong and Shanghai* [Business wire 0012]. Retrieved from http://www.businesswire.com/cnn/sbux.htm

———. (2000b). *Starbucks reports August revenues* [Business wire 2506]. Retrieved from http://www.businesswire.com/cnn/sbux.htm

Virant, Christiaan. (1999, January 12). Starbucks pours first coffee in China: 7 more outlets planned. *National Post*, p. C12.

7

Empirical Approaches to the Audience

Gord Lucke
University of Ottawa

INTRODUCTION

We are bombarded daily with the results of research. Breakthroughs in medicine, the latest public-opinion poll, companies advertising claims about the quality of their product—each is reporting findings based on research. However, many of the claims being made may well contain inherent bias. In this chapter, we explore some of the research results, the methodologies supporting them, and the lessons that may be learned.

There are two questions that readers need to ask in order to begin appraising research critically. The first question is, What methodologies were used to gather the information? Assuming that questionnaires were developed and people were surveyed, were the questions worded in a relatively unbiased fashion? How were people selected for the study? Who was selected? How many were selected, and why? Once we understand the methodology, there is a second—and equally important—question to address: have the results been analyzed and interpreted fairly and accurately?

This chapter applies these questions to three case studies. It first examines the results of a public-opinion poll that asked respondents if they supported the idea of a tax increase in order to keep Canada's six National Hockey League (NHL) teams in Canada. (The results of that study were sponsored by, and published in, the *Ottawa Citizen*.) The chapter then looks at some of the methodologies and interpretations used in television audience research. Finally, it examines issues relating to the strong claims made about Internet use and reviews the difficulties inherent in making claims in this area.

THE CASE FOR KEEPING CANADIAN NHL TEAMS IN CANADA

As most hockey fans are aware, the hockey world—like an increasing number of professional sports—is divided into "large-market" and "small-market" teams. These definitions typically refer to a population size in the local market coupled with the team's ability to generate advertising revenue, gate receipts, and merchandise sales. Cities such as New York, Chicago, and Detroit are large hockey markets in the United States (as their player payroll budgets attest!). With the exception of the Toronto Maple Leafs and possibly the Montreal Canadiens, the four other NHL teams in Canada—Vancouver, Calgary, Edmonton, and Ottawa—are referred to as "small-market teams." These cities simply do not have the capacity to generate the revenues of the large-markets teams.

In 1999, Ottawa Senators majority owner Rod Bryden began publicly lobbying the federal, provincial, and local governments. Bryden noted that, compared to U.S. owners, Canadian ownership groups do not receive the same tax concessions due to existing tax laws in Canada. His position was simple: if Canadian teams are to compete financially against their American counterparts, then a comparable tax structure should be in place in both Canada and the United States. If some changes were not made, Bryden would sell the team and it would be moved to the United States—a fate similar to that experienced in recent years when the Quebec Nordiques relocated to Colorado and the Winnipeg Jets moved to Phoenix. There was often talk, from numerous commentators in the media, about the importance of hockey to Canada's national identity. There was concern that if the Senators went, Calgary, Edmonton, and Vancouver would not be far behind. Surely fans would be willing, the argument went, to have their tax dollars help Canada's hockey teams stay in Canada. But would they? Nobody knew for certain.

When faced with such a situation, private companies, governments, and other types of organizations often hire social researchers to find out what their audiences think about a particular topic. These social researchers are also known as market researchers, pollsters, or public-opinion companies, but at the end of the day they each provide largely the same service: providing clients with timely information on attitudes, perceptions, beliefs, and behaviours of audiences with respect to various topics. Over the past several decades, this research has been conducted over the telephone. You, or someone you know, may have received a call inviting you to participate in a telephone survey or questionnaire.

Although thousands of Canadians participate in these studies every year, the bulk of this research is not made public. The large majority of paying clients, such as various departments in federal, provincial, and municipal government, political parties, lobby groups, and corporations, rarely share the results or findings from their research. They want it kept secret so that competitors do not share whatever they learn about their audiences/customers. The media, on the other hand, usually share the results of research they sponsor. The results often make for interesting, easily understandable stories on current affairs. For example, during election campaigns various media outlets often cosponsor polls in order to keep readers informed as to the popularity of competing candidates and their respective parties. Sometimes marketing and polling companies that conduct research carry out studies without a paying client, often with the intent of giving the results to various media outlets in order to advertise their service.

On October 24, 1999, the *Ottawa Citizen* published the results of a poll it had sponsored concerning attitudes toward the tax issue and professional hockey. The article's front-page headline—"Give Senators Tax Money to Stay: Poll"—was followed by the byline: "More than half of Ottawa-Carleton residents prepared to bear costs." These were very interesting and important findings, particularly in light of Rod Bryden's public relations campaign. But there are two questions that a critical reader should ask: (1) How was this research conducted? and (2) How were the results analyzed and interpreted?

How Was the Research Conducted?

When researchers undertake marketing or public-opinion research, all sorts of methodological concerns emerge. How will we reach people to participate in our study? Which people should participate, and how many? What questions will we ask them? To whom can we generalize the results?

To begin with, it is critical to distinguish between sampling a population and conducting a census. If the aim is to contact literally everybody in the population, that would be a census. The Government of Canada conducts a census every five years, asking for age, address, number of residents, sex, and so on, in order to understand growth and aging trends in the population and to plan for future services. But this is an exceptionally costly and time-consuming endeavour. Statistics Canada, the government department responsible for the collection of this information, hires thousands of part-time representatives in communities across Canada to help it conduct its research. Nearly all (99%+) Canadians fill out and return their census questionnaires.

By contrast, marketing and public-opinion research relies on sampling members of the population in question. That is, rather than attempt to contact every resident in a population, the researcher will speak to only a tiny portion of that group. Typically, polls range between several hundred and a few thousand participants, while actual populations can range from several thousand to several million people. For example, though the population of Canada is over 30 million, polls often sample only about 1000 respondents. Amazingly, the results are frequently reflective of the population in question.

How can surveying only a few hundred people reflect the opinions of millions? There are sampling procedures available that assist researchers in selecting who should participate in the research. The first requirement for successfully employing these procedures is to determine whether background information is available for the population in question. What if we were interested in polling Canadians on the taxation/hockey issue? Who would we select? Well, we know from previous census data—the ideal listing of background information on Canada's population, and that most relied on by market researchers and pollsters—the percentage of Canadians who live in the various provinces; the percentage who live in the various cities within each province; the percentage who speak French, English, or another language as their mother tongue, and their sex and age. Consequently, if approximately 10 million Canadians live in Ontario, and if Canada's population as a whole is over 30 million, it is clear that about one-third of Canadians (33%) live in Ontario. Researchers make similar calculations for each of the other regions across Canada.

The second requirement in properly using these sampling methods is to ensure that the background information used is representative of the Canadian population. Continuing from the above example, this means that if we were to conduct a national poll today, 33% of our sample would reside in Ontario. So, if we decided at the outset to make our sample size equal to 1000 Canadians (which quite often happens), then that means about 333 (or so) people in our sample would have to be living in Ontario. Precisely the same logic applies to the other background characteristics. If the census showed that 51% of Ontario residents are women and 49% are men, then, of the 333 Ontario residents in the national sample, 170 would be women and 163 would be men. If the census showed that 24% of our population spoke French as a first language, we would aim to ensure that 24% of our sample (about 240 of the 1000 respondents) spoke French, and so forth. But how many background characteristics should be adopted in a study?

There are some tricks of the trade that help us out. Pollsters and market researchers have used region (Atlantic Canada, Quebec, Ontario, Prairies, and British Columbia), whether a person resides in an urban or a rural setting, sex, mother tongue, and age in developing representative national samples. Employing all five of these characteristics is usually reserved for larger samples, which involve the participation of several thousand Canadians. Most often, ensuring that region and sex are properly represented is sufficient for samples involving around 1000 people. As well, researchers tend to oversample smaller (less-populated) regions such as Atlantic Canada and the Prairies. Why would they do that, after going to all the effort to ensure that the percentage of people sampled reflects that of the entire population? The reason is that doing so increases the accuracy of the data captured at the regional level.

All polls include something known as the *margin of error*. We need not be concerned with its statistical details or the calculations behind it. But there is one point to remember: after the population size reaches several thousand people (let us say 10,000, just to be on the safe side), the margin of error decreases as the sample size increases. Unless the researchers are conducting a census—and very few, apart from those at Statistics Canada, can afford to—they must rely on a sample. According to probability theory, sampling always involves some level of error. Consider this: as the sample size increases, the range in which the true population value exists narrows; the true population value is what we would discover if we conducted a census rather than relying on a sample.

The best way to understand this is through concrete examples. Suppose that we had sampled 300 people in our national study. Providing our total population size is over 10,000 people, our margin of error would be about +/–6% (this is a statistical law—how and why is beyond the scope of this chapter). What does this mean?

We can confidently predict that the true population results are located somewhere within the margin of error, based on the fact that we are sampling only 300 people out of the entire Canadian population. The statistical law known as the margin of error *does not* mean that we must sample 300 people out of a total population of 10,000. It means that *so long as* our total population *is greater than 10,000* (and the population of Canada at 30 millions qualifies), then a sample size of 300 people will always produce a margin of error of +/–6%.

In addition, a range of *plus or minus* 6% actually means that the final result can vary by 12% (the range from –6 to +6 being 12). If our results showed that 60% of Canadians support using tax dollars to aid Canadian hockey teams, then, with a sample size of 300, the real population value could be as low as 54% (60%–6%) or as high as 66% (60%+6%). Unfortunately, because our sample is so small, we have to live with a rather large range of probably true results. The true population value could lie anywhere from 54% to 66%—this is the impact of the margin of error on our results.

Let's assume, now, that we conducted the same study but increased our sample size from 300 to 1110 participants. And, for simplicity's sake, let's say that again we found that 60% of Canadians support helping the hockey teams with tax dollars. In this instance, our margin of error would drop to about +/–3%. In other words, the range of probably true percentages would get smaller as our sample size got bigger. Including 800 more respondents in our sample (300+800=1100) produces a margin of error ranging from 57% (60%–3%) to 63% (60%+3%). Thus, the range of probably true responses decreased from 12% (i.e., from 54% to 66% in the sample of 300 people) to 6% (i.e., from 57% to 63% in the sample of 1100). Since the margin of error tolerated by most pollsters and their clients is about +/–3%, most polls use a sample size somewhere in the neighbourhood of 1000–1200 people.

There is one aspect of all this that many students find mind-boggling. As noted earlier, the margin of error can be calculated as long as the total population from which the sample is drawn is greater than 10,000 people. Consequently, is the margin of error affected if the population being sampled is, say, Canada's (at 30 million people) rather than that of the United States (at about 280 million people)? The answer is *no*. The same margins of error apply in both countries. If you sample 300 people from either Canada or the United States, you will always obtain a margin of error of about +/–6%; if you sample 1100 people from either country, you will always obtain a margin of error of about +/–3%. You could replace the population in question with that of any other country and always end up with exactly the same margins of error. The important thing is not the total population of a country, but simply the fact that the population from which the sample is drawn is greater than 10,000 people. If you can appreciate this mathematical law, you can begin to understand the power of what are known as *probability-based sampling procedures*: the idea is that everyone in the population has an equal and known chance of being selected.

How does all of this apply to our earlier comment about the common practice of oversampling in less-populated regions? Well, you now know that if you design a national study with 1000 people, about 333 people in your sample will be from Ontario given that 33% of Canadians live in that province. A sample (or, in this case, subsample) of this size will result in a margin of error, as noted earlier, of about +/–6%. But the population of the four Atlantic provinces might represent only about 15% of Canada's total population. To ensure representativeness, the result would be 150 people in our national sample of 1000. But a sample size of 150 would lead to a huge margin of error—in the neighbourhood of +/–11%. This sample size is simply too small to detect any meaningful regional trends, so researchers will oversample the region in order to lower the margin of error. There are techniques for ensuring that, in spite of the oversampling, the actual results are not over weighted compared to the population at large.

The general sampling guidelines outlined in this section have three main benefits:

1. When researchers have access to background data on the population (comparable to that provided by a census), as well as telephone books, directories, and computers that generate telephone numbers to dial, then the conditions are in place for ensuring that a *representative and random* sample is taken from the population.

2. When researchers have access to background data on the population (comparable to that provided by a census), as well as telephone books, directories, and computers that generate telephone numbers to dial, then the conditions are in place for ensuring that a *representative and random* sample is taken from the population.

3. Researchers who follow the guidelines can generalize their results to the entire population in question. So, based on a sample of 1100 Canadians, we can say with a great deal of confidence that (in light of our ongoing example) 60% of Canadians (+/–3% of that total) would support the use of tax dollars to keep professional hockey in Canada.

What type of sampling procedure did the *Ottawa Citizen* study use? It was clearly a probability-based sampling procedure. As the newspaper reported, the survey

> [was] administered to a representative sample from 11 municipalities of the Ottawa-Carleton region. A total of 301 people were interviewed Oct. 22, 1999. Samples of this size are considered to be accurate to within 5.8 percentage points, 19 times out of 20. ("Give Senators," p. 1)

In terms of the benefits outlined above, this statement means the following:

1. The researchers probably used the relative population weighting in each municipality and sex as background characteristics to ensure representativeness. In other words, if one of the municipalities represented 20% of the total Ottawa-Carleton population, then about 20% of the 301 people sampled would also be from that municipality.

2. Since the area has a population of nearly 800,000 (well above the 10,000 threshold), the margin-of-error rules discussed above are applicable. As noted in the article, the smaller sample size (n=301) results in a margin of error greater than most researchers are willing to live with (+/−5.8%).

3. The population, for this study, was Ottawa-Carleton. Since probability-based sampling was used, the results emerging from the study could be extrapolated to the entire Ottawa-Carleton region.

How Were the Results Analyzed and Interpreted?

As a reminder, the *Ottawa Citizen* headline/byline read: "Give Senators Tax Money to Stay: Poll / More than half of Ottawa-Carleton residents prepared to bear costs." Among the survey questions leading to this claim was the following: "*Generally speaking, should governments move part way toward reducing some of the tax disadvantage of Canadian teams competing with American teams?*" This question resulted in the following percentages: definitely (41%); probably (27%); probably not (13%); definitely not (17%); do not know (3%).

With respect to the wording of the question, it is unclear what "move part way" would entail. Does it refer to decreasing corporate, entertainment, and related taxes levied against NHL franchises? Or does it mean increasing taxes for individual Canadians in order to subsidize teams? Realizing the potential for confusion, the researchers had prepared a follow-up question to further probe those respondents agreeing that the government should "definitely" or "probably" act. It is very important to note that this probe question would be posed to only 68% of the sample (or 205 out of 301 people), which is the sum of the "definitely" (41%) and the "probably" (27%) respondents from the previous question.

The probe question is more direct and specific: "*If this meant a moderate tax increase for you personally, would you still think governments should reduce the tax disadvantage of Canadian teams?*" The results: definitely (23%); probably (37%); probably not (17%); definitely not (22%). Remember, these results are the responses from only 68% of the sample; 30% had already rejected the idea of government action posed in the previous question. In assessing the responses to the probe question, let's focus on those respondents who "definitely" (23%) and "probably" (37%)

support the idea of a moderate tax increase. If we multiply this total (23%+37%= 60%) by the proportion of the sample who actually answered the probe question (68%), we arrive at a figure of 40.8%.

Let's take our analysis a step further. A large number of respondents (37%) said they would "probably" support the idea of tax increases; in reality, however, this group could waver. The group least likely to change its mind—probably the biggest hockey fans—consists of those who "definitely" support" the idea of a moderate tax increase. If we isolate the "definitely" group (23%) and eliminate the "probably" group, we arrive at a figure of 15.6% (23 multiplied by 0.68, the proportion partic-ipating from the entire sample). Thus, only about 16% of the sample would "defi-nitely" support moderate personal tax increases to help Canadian teams.

According to a senior partner in the polling firm that conducted this research, these results are a "call for action." But are they? Overall, about 123 out of 301 people, or about 41% of those sampled in this study, say they would "definitely" or "probably" favour moderate personal tax increases to ensure the Senators' survival in Ottawa. But this was not reported in the *Ottawa Citizen* article. What was reported were the results highlighting the apparent majorities from each question; there was no accounting for the results of the entire sample. Moreover, in a sample of this size, with a margin of error of nearly +/–6%, those results could range as high as about 47% (41%+5.8%) or as low as about 35% (41%–6%). Most impor-tant, this analysis reveals that the results are contrary to the byline's declaration, "More than half of Ottawa-Carleton residents prepared to bear costs."

The senior partner also stated in the article that "what the survey is clearly saying is that hockey is important to Canadians." Although this statement may be true, it cannot be said to reflect the results of this particular survey. The sample included only people from the Ottawa-Carleton region. It might have been possible to conclude that "hockey is important to the people of Ottawa-Carleton," but it is not at all possible to draw the same conclusion regarding the views of all Canadians. Indeed, it would be interesting to compare the results of the Ottawa sample to those of other small-market teams, or perhaps to the views of people who live in communities that do not have easy access to NHL teams. How many people in rural Saskatchewan, or on Cape Breton Island, would support the idea of using their tax dollars to support NHL teams?

Moreover, to better understand the level of "importance" someone may attach to an issue, researchers often ask participants to compare their feelings on a variety of issues. In the poll sponsored by the *Ottawa Citizen*, respondents were asked the following question:

> Right now, six of the 28 teams in the NHL are in Canada. In the past few years, two Canadian cities—Quebec City and Winnipeg—saw their teams move to the United States. In your opinion, how important is it that Canada have more than just the Toronto Maple Leafs and the Montreal Canadiens in the NHL? ("Give Senators," 1999, p. 1)

The response to this question was "very important" (52%) and "moderately important" (25%). The potential bias in the wording of this question notwithstanding, there is a larger concern here. A substantial number of respondents felt that it is important that Canada have more than two teams in the NHL—but important compared to what? The overall health of the economy? Health care and education spending? What about the environment and the quality of our drinking water? The people sampled might find it important that Canada have more than two hockey teams in the NHL, but what the study does not ask is how important this issue is compared to all sorts of other concerns. As a result, the fact that a majority claim that the NHL issue is "important" is not particularly meaningful.

What does all this mean? We began by highlighting two important questions that communications students should ask in order to become critical readers of research: (1) What methodologies were used to gather the information? and (2) Have the results been analyzed and interpreted fairly and accurately? Generally speaking, the methodology employed in the *Ottawa Citizen* study was acceptable. A probability-based sampling procedure was obviously used. Although this procedure allows analysts to generalize their findings to the population in question, the smaller sample size used in this poll meant that a larger margin of error would have to be tolerated. Sometimes the way in which a question is worded can skew the results of a poll; the failure of the *Ottawa Citizen* pollsters to provide a context for the word "important" is a case in point. One is always led to wonder if the purpose of such polls—and specifically the interpretation of the results accompanying them—is an attempt to create momentum in public opinion.

In early 2000, the federal government announced that it would offer tax breaks to the six NHL teams, conditional on offers from their respective provincial and municipal governments. Two days later, in response to a firestorm of national protest, then Industry Minister John Manley announced that the government was reversing its decision. If the government had conducted an analysis of poll results comparable to the one conducted in this section, it would have understood that public support for such initiatives was more tenuous than some analysts and commentators would suggest. After the government's reversal, Senators owner Rod Bryden adopted another approach: rather than sell the team and move it to the United States, he increased ticket prices and embarked on a successful season-ticket selling drive.

AUDIENCE RESEARCH IN JOURNALISM AND THE BROADCAST MEDIA

Audience research is critical to the survival of companies in the Canadian television, radio, newspaper, and magazine industries. The principal benefit of audience research is the light it sheds on market share. In the print media, for example, exposure to newspapers and magazines is measured primarily through circulation. Figures generated by newspapers and magazines are based on print runs and copies sold. As well, third-party independent bodies, such as the Audit Bureau of Circulations, measure print-audience sizes. In the broadcast media, ACNielsen Canada and the BBM Bureau of Measurement provide objective television-audience data, while only BBM measures radio. Data describing market share, in turn, are linked to advertising revenues. The latest information concerning relative audience size allows companies to price and sell their advertising space based on their market share. Companies with a higher audience market share are generally able to sell their advertising spaces at a higher price, while a shrinking market share usually results in declining advertising revenues. Market share and the possibility of charging more money for advertising spots is key to the viability of most media companies (the publicly owned CBC being the primary exception). Since the broadcast media (particularly television) attract the lion's share of advertising dollars in Canada, the following discussion will focus on how these audiences are measured.

There are a number of noteworthy similarities between audience research and public-opinion polling. When it comes to gathering participants, both polling and audience research rely on sampling and then projecting those results to the population in question. In the past, television-audience measurement in Canada relied heavily on the *viewing diary*, a method still used by the BBM Bureau of Measurement. A random and representative sample of Canadians are contacted and asked to participate. Those who accept are asked to record in a diary the station and time they watch television over a one-week period (typically broken down into 15-minute time slots between 6 a.m. and 2 a.m.). Seasonal "sweeps," conducted during November and March, are intensive multi-week periods of measurement. Although consecutive weeks are surveyed, each week is measured using an entirely different set of respondents. Sweep samples are comparatively large, encompassing about 60,000 total participants, or 20,000 people per week, over a three-week period. The large number of people sampled reflects an effort to make local/regional data meaningful and reliable.

Unfortunately, diary-based surveys have numerous shortcomings, most of which relate to the inadvertent errors made by participants. For example, since the large majority of households have a minimum of 30 channels to choose from, it is easy for a participant to misidentify the station watched (especially when a Canadian station is substituting an American program on its channel). As well, rather than faithfully record the shows they watch at the exact time of their broadcast, many participants complete their diaries well after the fact, such as on the weekend when they have free time. This practice often leads to reporting errors, since people typically recall popular shows more readily than they do less prominent shows. Another concern is the layout of the diary. Although viewers often surf channels regularly, the diary allows only one entry for each 15-minute time slot. Finally, the proliferation of specialty stations means that people are more likely to be occasional viewers. A television diary that extends over only a one-week period can lead to underreporting of viewing of specialty stations, because viewing behaviour might be occasional but reported as nonexistent.

In response to these substantive concerns, ACNielsen Canada introduced the *people meter* in September 1989. This device is attached to a television set and automatically monitors when the television is turned on or off and which station is tuned at any given time. To indicate their presence, family members are required to press a number or letter on the remote control. Each number or letter has already precoded the background characteristics associated with a particular family member. At the end of the viewing day, meters automatically upload the day's tabulations to the host computer at the offices of the measurement service. Whereas it takes weeks for television-diary data to be mailed back to the main office, entered into a database, and then analyzed, the people meter reduces turnaround time to days.

The people meter is attached to a household television for a period of two years. Tracking the behaviour of the same participants over an extended period such as this is referred to as the *panel study method*. In spite of the obvious benefits of not having to rely on one-week intervals (as with the television-diary method), the people meter is not problem-free. Motivation is one issue: do all family participants consistently push the proper buttons indicating individual watching behaviour over the two-year period? Another drawback of the people meter is that the sample size remains relatively constant; there is no large-scale increase in participation for the three-week period during sweeps in order to gather sufficient local-level data in measuring viewership.

More generally, while audience research measures what people listen to or watch, it does not report on the interest level of viewers or listeners, their depth of feeling, or their level of involvement. The drawback faced with the data gathered is that it is only quantitative in nature. What is lacking is an in-depth understanding of how programming affects the viewer on an emotional, intellectual, or other level. New measurement systems integrating elements of artificial intelligence will begin to address some of these overlooked human elements. The "passive people meter" will use visual imaging and image-recognition systems to scan the room containing the television. With the built-in ability to identify household members, participants will no longer face the burden of logging themselves in and out; the scanner will take care of that in real time by "recognizing" participants as they enter and leave the television viewing room. As the technology improves, it will be possible to detect facial expressions and listen to comments made by people as they watch. While the new technology will greatly assist in the gathering of qualitative information largely lacking in audience research thus far, it raises a series of privacy issues that may curtail its progress and acceptance.

MEASUREMENT ISSUES AND THE INTERNET

In many ways, surfing the Internet is comparable to channel surfing on television (although the Internet offers a far wider range of options). The comparison also holds true when applied to the perspective of researchers trying to measure and determine Internet behaviour—many of the same measurement problems that arise during the tracking of television viewing behaviour also emerge with regard to the Internet. If you are a marketing executive trying to determine where best to invest your company's advertising, you will be faced with some data that makes important claims about Internet use; your position will require you to determine how reliable and meaningful the available information really is.

Just as there is plenty of data that describes when and which Canadians typically watch television, there is comparably reliable data on Canadian Internet usage. Statistics Canada regularly tracks and publishes the results of research examining Internet usage among Canadians. A survey of 25,090 Canadians aged 15 and over that was conducted by Statistics Canada in 2000 reveals some interesting patterns of Internet use. For example, the *gender gap* has closed substantially in recent years. In 1994, 22% of men used the Internet, compared to 14% of women. In 2000, 49.6% of women and 56.1% of men reported using the Internet. (Men remain more intensive users, using e-mail and chat groups more often, and playing more on-line games.) Overall, 56.3% of Canadians were on-line in 2000, up from 18% in 1994.

More striking differences emerged with respect to *age*. Of those aged 15–24 years, 84.5% reported using the Internet in 2000, a percentage that decreases with every older age group, up to those aged 55 and over (18.7%). A similar pattern emerges with respect to *education* (30.9% of those with less than a high-school degree are Internet users, compared to 79.3% of those with a university degree) and *household income* (32.8% of households with less than $30,000 annual income are Web users, compared to 80.5% of those households earning more than $80,000 annually). Overall, there is a division between young, well-educated, high-earning households—where Web use is widespread—and older, less-educated, and low-income households. Some observers are concerned that Internet access, or lack of it, reinforces economic and social differences among Canadians.

Far more daunting than understanding the background characteristics of Internet users and television watchers is the task of measuring the reactions, questions and concerns, and the information a Web surfer takes away from each advertisement seen. Anyone who has surfed the Web, either looking for specific information or casually browsing, knows that it is easy to lose track of the sites visited. But consider the questions advertisers want answers for: How long did you stay at each Web site or page? What did you read on each page? Did you notice any banners or advertisements? If so, did they entice you to click on them? If you're a company advertising manager, you will use the answers to these and other questions to make decisions about where precisely you should advertise. Is your company's Web site a sufficient advertising space, or your should company purchase advertising elsewhere on the Internet?

Attempting to answer such questions has led to the evolution of a Web site visitation tracking industry. Media Metrix, Nielsen/NetRatings, and PC Data are considered the current leaders in this emerging area. Typically, they are hired by other companies to count and describe the people who visit Web sites. Media Metrix measures visits over a 30-day period using what it calls its "Unique Visitor" rankings. For example, it found that Walmart.com, with 7.07 million unique visitors in December 2000, was the sixth most-visited retail site during that month. In other words, those 7.07 million people had never been to the Walmart Web site prior to that month. Media Metrix conducts its research using a panel of between 55,000 and 60,000 Americans who allow the company's software to follow them around the Internet. To ensure that its panel-member demographics mirror the U.S. Internet population, Media Metrix conducts a monthly telephone survey and changes the composition of panel members in response to any shifts in usership.

The Media Metrix approach is not without its critics. Perhaps the biggest concern is that Media Metrix tracks only American users even though global access is a mainstay of the Internet. Many companies contend that Media Metrix undercounts their traffic because it does not include international workplace users at all in its sampling. Others claim that the number of people at work and school is not sufficiently represented, in spite of evidence suggesting that numerous sites get their highest number of visitors during work and school hours. The number of times you've visited a U.S. Web site in the past year is likely to be quite high. If Media Metrix is not adequately representing your usership in its data collection and rankings, then these criticisms have merit. Another charge levelled against Media Metrix is that its panel composition may not change quickly and frequently enough to reflect the continual shifts in the demographics of the Internet user. Media Metrix, for its part, claims that its sampling and panel updating procedures are adequate.

Whereas Media Metrix attempts to measure Internet usage both at work and at home, Nielsen/NetRatings collects information only on activity in the home on the grounds that it is not possible to access an appropriate workplace sample. Results from the two different sampling procedures suggest that Internet use from home and from work are very distinct from each other. For example, Media Metrix found that approximately 53,373,000 unique visitors had visited AOL sites in October 1999, while Nielsen/NetRatings claimed that number was about 40,391,000 over the same period. Although AOL sites were ranked number one by both companies, the difference in the number of unique visitors was almost 13 million. With large sums of advertising dollars and potential revenues at stake, it is likely that the Internet industry will develop measurement standards designed to keep discrepancies to a minimum.

Compared to television audience research, Internet research, like the Web itself, is in its infancy. It has been shown that traditional probability-based sampling techniques (e.g., people meters, mail-in questionnaires, telephone surveys) can be relatively effective in determining how many people use a television or access the World Wide Web, and when they do so. The difficulties begin when researchers try to determine precisely who it is that is watching which show or visiting which

Web site. Questions about Internet usage are comparable to those that have long been posed with respect to television audience research. Who went to which Web site and when? While there, did the surfer notice the advertisements? If so, how did he or she respond to them? What measures would establish if surfers did or did not notice and respond? Are Web site traffic and the estimated amount of unique visits sufficient indicators, or would the actual sale of a product or service be a more adequate measure? It is likely that the people selling advertising space would rather have "visits" serve as the most important measure, while the companies purchasing spots would rather see their advertising costs more directly linked to "revenues" generated. On the larger questions of researching advertisement effectiveness, the Internet still has a long way to go.

Open-access on-line surveys that ask questions about the effectiveness of advertisements are generally not meaningful. Part of the problem with the large majority of these surveys is *self-selection bias*: open-access on-line surveys cannot control the characteristics of the person filling out the survey the way probability-based sampling procedures can. You may recall that the key to probability-based sampling is having a list of background characteristics on the population in question and then requiring that the researcher sample individuals who reflect the population's statistical distribution. People who volunteer to participate in a study on-line (or anywhere for that matter) without the researcher's prior knowledge of their demographic information are selecting themselves to participate. Radio phone-in shows are not representative for the same reason—those who call in select themselves rather than being selected by researchers.

From a survey methodology perspective, it would make sense to develop a list of all Internet users and then sample a number of them, asking which sites they visit and for how long, how useful they find the sites and why, and so on. But this approach runs into problems similar to those associated with the television diary. How would people be able to specify which site they visited (perhaps by chance), say, 12 days ago? Recall, motivation, and accuracy would be substantive concerns. Another problem relates to the interpretation of survey results. As we saw earlier, these results are not generalizable to the larger Internet user population in question unless the participating sample reflects that population along a host of continually shifting demographic characteristics.

SUMMARY

This chapter began with the premise that an important skill set for critical communication studies is the ability to appraise research critically. There are two questions worthy of consideration: (1) What research methods are used to gather information and (2) Are the results interpreted fairly and accurately?

Lessons Learned from the Research Methods Used

1. Whether you are analyzing a newspaper poll or television/Internet audience research, you should first look for evidence of probability-based sampling. If a margin of error can be calculated and displayed, then you know probability-based sampling was used. Remember, if the total population being measured is greater than 10,000 people, the margin of error changes only in relation to sample size: as the sample size increases, the margin of error decreases. Thus, a sample size of 1000 people has the same margin of error whether the sample is drawn from Saskatchewan or from all of China.

2. The majority of on-line surveys are not probability-based samples. If you volunteer to participate in a survey, you have self-selected. Even if several thousand volunteers participate, there is no way of guaranteeing that they reflect the population in question. What if the questions you are answering are relevant to someone who does not have access to the Internet, who chooses not to participate, or who simply has not seen the survey? Without the researcher monitoring and controlling who participates, the data cannot be generalized meaningfully to the population at large (notwithstanding the claims of those who conduct such research).

3. Probability-based sampling is used in audience research measuring television viewing and Internet surfing. However, this research lags behind other types of measurements when it comes to questions about feelings, responses toward what is seen, and advertising effectiveness in particular.

4. There is a large discrepancy in the number of "unique visitors" reported by two leading companies that track Web site visits. Part of the discrepancy has to do with the fact that Media Metrix measures Internet usage both at work and at home, whereas Nielsen/NetRatings collects information only on activity in the home.

Lessons Learned from the Interpretation of Results

1. Although they purport that their surveys are neutral and unbiased, pollsters are in business to help their clients, whether to make money or to affect public opinion. For example, the *Ottawa Citizen* poll made a reference to the importance "Canadians" place on hockey, yet only people in the Ottawa-Carleton region were surveyed.

2. The way in which key terms are defined can have an impact on the interpretation of results. For example, the *Ottawa Citizen* pollsters emphasized the importance of hockey within Canada. But, as we saw, the concept of "importance" is relative. How important is the survival of NHL hockey compared to other issues, such as the economy, health care, and the environment? The key to defining "importance" is to ensure that respondents have the opportunity to express what they mean by the concept.

3. How will advertising "success" on the Internet be defined? Which measure is the most meaningful: Web traffic (estimating the number of unique visitors to a site) or actual revenues generated from products sold? The answer to this question will depend largely on whether you are a buyer or a seller of advertising in cyberspace.

4. Overall, the methodology and data interpretation concerns that are at the heart of research being carried out on the Internet are largely the same as those faced in the more traditional television audience and public-opinion polling research. In short, the media may change, but the issues remain largely the same.

QUESTIONS

1. What two questions should we ask when critically assessing research?
2. What is the difference between sampling a population and conducting a census?
3. What does margin of error refer to?
4. Why is audience research important for the media industry?
5. What are some criticisms of Media Matrix's measurement of Internet usage?
6. How can empirical measurements inform an understanding of audience competence?

WEB SITES

ACNielsenCanada: **http://www.acnielsen.ca**
Audit Bureau sa: **http://www.statcan.ca/**

REFERENCE

Give Senators tax money to stay: Poll. (1999, October 24). *Ottawa Citizen*, p. 1.

FURTHER READING

Couper, Mick. (2000). Web surveys: A review of issues and approaches. *Public Opinion Quarterly, 64,* 464–494.

Kaye, Barbara, and Norman Medoff. (2001). *Just a click away: Advertising on the Internet.* Toronto: Allyn and Bacon.

Withers, Edward, and Robert Brown. (1995). The broadcast audience: A sociological perspective. In Benjamin Singer (Ed.), *Communications in Canadian society* (4th ed.). Toronto: Nelson Canada.

8

Good Kids/Bad Kids: What's a Culture to Do?

Eileen Saunders
Carleton University

Contemporary culture is characterized by a strong ambivalence toward children. On the one hand, as cultural theorist David Buckingham (2000) notes, "children are increasingly seen as threatened and endangered" (p. 3). We find evidence of this in Canada recently, whether in sensationalist press coverage of the release of a pedophile or in provincial inquiries into cases in which the social services system failed to protect children at risk. What underlies this perception is generally an image of the child as innocent, vulnerable, uncontaminated, and, most important, in need of adult protection. Indeed, the child represents the archetypal innocent and the archetypal victim.

On the other hand, "children are also increasingly perceived as a threat to the rest of us as violent, anti-social and sexually precocious" (Buckingham 2000, p. 3). In Canada, there have been public calls for tougher measures to curb crime by young people and for more punitive approaches to dealing with young offenders:

> Whether Canadians like to admit it or not, Canada's war on crime is increasingly becoming a war against youth. From varying proposals to reintroduce the death penalty for young killers to the implementation of boot camps for all young offenders, Canadian society is embarking on a crusade to increase punishment for children. (Schissel 1997, p. 9)[1]

This second construction is accompanied by an underlying image of the uncontrollable, uncivilized child—the child who lacks internal discipline, feelings, or empathy and therefore requires intensive external controls. Such a perception is fuelled by events like the 1999 Columbine massacre, in which two teenagers killed 12 classmates and a teacher in their Littleton, Colorado, high school before taking their own lives. In response to the Columbine massacre and the copycat killings that followed it,[2] we have become increasingly fearful of the "terror of adolescence" (Schissel, 1997, p. 11).

Interestingly, as Oswell (1998) points out, we shift our language depending on the particular "construction" of the child we are employing:

> Whereas those in danger are constituted as "children," those
> deemed dangerous are quite clearly constituted as "youth." The
> category of "youth" is deployed when young people are seen to
> no longer perform the proper modes of conduct of "childhood."
> (p. 38)

In a similar fashion, children are also constructed as either "victims" or "threats." Oswell cites the infamous and tragic 1993 murder, in Britain, of a toddler named James Bulger at the hands of two 10-year-old boys. Press coverage of the case at the time consistently referred to the boys as "youths," despite their relatively young age. One might compare this with the outcry against Calvin Klein Inc. in 1995, when the company launched a controversial ad campaign for CK jeans that featured scantily clad young adults in a sexually provocative context. A storm of criticism ensued, and the company was eventually forced to withdraw the $6-million campaign. As Tucker (1996) has shown in an analysis of media coverage of the event, the frame used to "define" the controversy was that of child pornography or "kiddie porn"; the ads were framed as being exploitative of innocent victims, despite the fact that the models used in the campaign were all over 18.

So, youth become children or children become youth not based on any firm or fast biological definition of childhood or adolescence, or because of any fixed cultural meaning of either concept. There is a broader set of interests and concerns at play. As Buckingham (2000) notes:

> The meaning of "childhood" is subject to a constant process of
> struggle and negotiation, both in public discourse (for example,
> in the media, in the academy or in social policy) and in inter-
> personal relationships, among peers and in the family. (p. 6)

The "constructionist" understanding of the categories of childhood and youth stands in opposition to earlier "naturalistic" understandings that relied on markers such as biological age or were linked to stages of physical and cognitive development. This approach posited a universal model of childhood. Ariès (1962) and other historians laid the foundation for questioning such a model by demonstrating that the "idea" of childhood did not emerge in Europe until after the 15th century—a claim that challenged both the biological understandings of childhood and the cross-cultural implications of naturalistic models. Ariès also argued that the idea of adolescence begins to appear even later. It was only during the 18th century that we begin to detect a period of transition between childhood and adulthood. As Valentine, Skelton, and Chambers (1998) point out:

> Throughout the nineteenth century this transitional stage
> became prolonged and young people became more separated
> from the adult world, as the middle classes became increasingly
> preoccupied with the need to control "working class" youth as
> well as their own offspring. (p. 4)

If we start to think of childhood or adolescence as something "constructed," inevitable questions arise: Constructed how? By whom? Where? The notion of construction is quite simple. At different times and in different contexts, we think about and speak about children and youth in different ways. These ways then connect to how we respond to children as individuals, how we codify our understanding of them in law and in social policy, and how we represent them in public imagery. These ideas are found in different places in society. We could identify, for example, psychology as one location within which ideas about childhood emerge, and from which they are circulated through media such as academic journals, advice books for parents, and even daytime talk shows. The family is another location; how parents think about children or teens might differ quite dramatically from what a child psychologist would say, and we might find considerable differences in families across different class, racial, or ethnic communities. The psychologists might argue that their set of ideas is grounded in scientific knowledge, while the parent relies on personal experience, but the fact is that each offers a constructed form of knowledge about childhood and adolescence.

It is important to recognize that the different discourses circulating in society about childhood and adolescence are not independent of one another. Academic or scholarly discourses exist alongside and interconnect with other public discourses. For example, there has been much media attention given of late to the increase in childhood obesity and the decrease in the amount of time young people devote to physical activity. Worried parents, teachers, public health officials, and even daytime talk-show hosts point with escalating alarm to the signs of a generation gone to fat. In such "media-enhanced social 'crises,' educators and parents, governments, the public, and advocacy groups look to scientific research to explain and solve social problems" (Luke, 1990, p. 1). Medical practitioners are called on by the media to provide "expert" advice to worried parents; sociologists are asked to describe the effect of decreased "family time" on children's physical activity; and communication researchers are sought out to provide the link between television viewing or video-game usage and decreased physical activity. Each offers an outline of the problem and a solution to the "crisis" (e.g., reducing high-fat snacks or setting time limits on television viewing).

KIDS AND MEDIA: CONTEXTUALIZING DISCOURSES

The idea of linking popular culture to widespread concern about children is hardly new. It has become commonplace to point out that 2400 years ago, the Greek philosopher Plato cited the threat posed to vulnerable young people by poets.[3] Many researchers have noted the tendency to treat each new technology and each emergent cultural innovation with alarm, and to predict dire consequences for the young and for society. In an interesting historical investigation, Springhall (1998) details the public outcry in Victorian England against penny theatre (a form of cheap, unlicensed entertainment for working children usually held in empty ware-houses or workshops) and the association drawn between this form of entertain-ment and juvenile crime (pp. 11–37). In the early part of the 20th century, social concerns focused on the "movie problem"—the perception that children were spending too much time at daytime cinema (see Luke, 1990, pp. 31–44). Educators worried about the effect on academic performance, while parents were anxious about the "moral health" of their children. This concern was followed in subsequent decades by a succession of "scares" linked to radio, comic books, television, music videos, video games, Internet chat rooms, action animation series—the list could go on. While each scare has its own unique characteristics and its own predictions of dire consequences for the youthful audience, all of them share a strong moralistic argument about how popular culture threatens the moral fibre of the young.

However, as Springhall (1998) pointedly suggests, "Media or moral panics often tell us a great deal more about adult anxieties, fear of the future, of technolog-ical change and the erosion of moral absolutes than about the nature of juvenile mis-behaviour" (pp. 160–161). The current panic about raves illustrates this point well. Although raves emerged in Britain and North America in the 1980s, it was not until the 1990s that these all-night dances in clubs, outdoor venues, and vacant ware-houses began to attract widespread public concern. For baby-boomer parents who grew up with Elvis, the Beatles, and the Rolling Stones, the profusion of musical subgenres associated with electronic dance music is bewildering to say the least:

> There's music for the clubs: sophisticated, adult-oriented sounds like house, garage, and the more purist, Detroit-affiliated forms of techno. There are hardcore sounds designed for one-shot raves and for clubs that cater to rave-style bacchanalia as opposed to more "mature" nightclub behavior: jungle, gabba, trance, happy hardcore. And finally, there's music for the home: album-oriented ambient techno and atmospheric electronica. (Reynolds, 1998, p. 8)

Layered on top of this generational divide over musical tastes is the association of rave culture with drug use, in particular the drug Ecstasy.[4] Parents might recog-nize many similarities between rave culture and the disco culture of the 1970s.[5] Yet, despite the theme of "peace, love, unity and respect" attached to rave culture from its origins, press coverage is framed primarily in reference to rampant drug use and the potential for violence. This "panic," especially following the 1999 death of a "raver" in Toronto, has led to calls for stricter policing of raves and a tougher stance by municipal authorities. Witness a random sampling of recent headlines: "Police Seek Man in Rave Shooting" (*Ottawa Citizen*, April 16, 2001); "Jury Recommends Licensed Venues for Raves after Toronto Inquest" (Canadian Press, June 1, 2000); "Drugs Cause Crackdown on Raves" (Canadian Press, April 6, 2000); "Search Ravers: Mayor" (*Toronto Sun*, June 2, 2000). As is generally the case with media panics about young people, analyses of the "problem" are usually accompanied by calls for stricter control, and are usually heavily influenced by those individuals and groups with an interest in exerting more control over the young.

The intersecting and shifting discourses of the "child in danger" and the "dangerous child" are reflected across a range of popular culture forms, from film and television news to talk shows and raves. These two opposing constructions of the child as both innocent and dangerous can be understood in greater detail by examining two specific communication debates. The first concerns advertising and children; the second is about media violence and children.

THE CONSUMING CHILD

Picture this typical scene. Six-year-old Sarah exits her school bus at the end of a busy school week. Happy that the weekend lies ahead, she pauses to straighten her Lion King sweatshirt, then picks up her Teletubbies lunch box in one hand and her Harry Potter knapsack in the other. As she heads up her front steps, she spots her bright pink Barbie skipping rope and Sailor Moon sidewalk chalk on the driveway. Once inside she heads upstairs to her Tigger-wallpapered room with the Winnie-the-Pooh duvet. Later she and her mother head out to their local theatre to see the Disney hit, *Hunchback of Notre Dame*. They stop for supper on the way at McDonald's, where Sarah is delighted to find a plastic Esmeralda along with her hamburger.

What's the problem with this seemingly innocent scenario? For critics of such scenes, the problem comes down to one simple charge: the commercial exploitation of children in their role as consumers. The idea of children as consumers, and the active targeting of them by advertisers who see them as a potential audience, is relatively recent. As Kapur (1999) notes, "The most significant change in the cultural notion of childhood in the last decades of the twentieth century has been the construction of children as consumers" (p. 124). This is not to suggest that children did not constitute a market prior to this period; rather, "they were not sold to directly. Instead they were imagined as untainted receivers of gifts" (Kapur, 1999, p. 125). Their value to advertisers and product manufacturers was in the influence they brought to bear on parents and extended family members in purchase decisions. They constituted, in other words, an important "market of influence," possessing what Buckingham (2000) calls "pester power" (p. 147).

While this aspect of children as a market continues, there has also been a shift toward targeting children directly as consumers. Several factors were involved in the recognition of children as an important "primary market" of consumption (see McNeal, 1992, pp. 22–36). The economic and demographic expansion of the postwar 1950s gave teenagers real spending power. The identification of a preteen market came soon after, and by the late 1960s trade publications began to identify children as a separate market (McNeal, 1992, p. 5). The first ad agency to specialize in targeting children, Helitzer, Waring and Wayne, opened in the United States in 1963 (Pecora, 1998, p. 17). Other sociological changes contributed to a new appreciation of the child consumer. Fewer children per family, an increase in discretionary incomes, the emergence of dual-income families, and more single-parent families have all increased the influence of children in consumer decisions (McNeal, 1992, p. 7). Finally, technological innovations ranging from television to the Internet have increased the access of advertisers to the child audience.

POLITICAL ECONOMY AND THE CHILD CONSUMER

Despite the fact that advertisers had discovered the importance of children to product manufacturers long before, little attention was given to this area by communication researchers until the 1970s: "although there were over 300 studies on children and the media, prior to 1970, virtually no academic research was conducted on children's advertising" (Pecora, 1998, pp. 17–18). When communication research did turn its attention to this issue, it was largely framed within the context of the effects tradition.[6] In this approach, then dominant within North American social science, the research conducted was primarily concerned with television advertising. The short-term effects of the media–child audience relation was the focus, with research conducted on such issues as patterns of attention, capacity for comprehension, and behavioural and attitudinal influences.

In addition, such research characterized children as being more vulnerable than adults to the effects of advertising. As Alexander and Morrison (1995) note:

> [A] deficit model has dominated research on children: children cannot distinguish selling intent, children have trouble distinguishing advertisements from programming, children are easily misled by what they see on the screen. The same assumptions are not made about adults who are consciously savvy in their consumption behavior. (p. 345)

Political economic discourse has thus framed the "child as consumer" debate in a light that tends to view the child as victim.

Political economic analyses generally begin with an attempt to understand popular culture as an industry that is driven by broad economic forces and that has important consequences for how we think about the world around us. The key, then, is to locate media industries within the broader context of the forces and relations of capitalist production, and to understand media "messages" in the context of ideological meaning. Analysis of advertising and children is framed in terms of understanding the particular economic forces that shape the relations of children to consumption, with a view to determining the economic and cultural causes and consequences of this relation. Some political economic work in this field is focused more on the institutional and economic forces that structure children's culture (see, for example, Englehardt, 1986; Pecora, 1998), while other work (notably Kline, 1993) focuses on the cultural consequences.

One of the first arguments made by critics who adopt a political economic approach is that children and their spending power have become an increasingly important force in the market. When combined with influence spending (the "pester" effect), the direct purchasing power of children adds up to considerable profit. According to researched conducted by Leonhardt and Kerwin in the United States, the preteen market in 1998 accounted for $20 billion (U.S.) in direct spending and another $200 billion in "influence spending" by their parents (cited in Kapur, 1999, p. 125). One the most recent niche markets to emerge and capture the eye of advertisers is the "tween" market (children aged 9–14), who number over 2.4 million in Canada alone; according to research conducted by YTV, "today's tweens represent almost $1.4 billion worth of spending power" and "[their] financial clout will continue to grow" (Steinberg, 1998, p. 60). In addition to profiting from the consumer choices made by this group, advertisers are keen to develop their brand loyalty and secure them as future consumers as well. Successful companies are those that can "capture" the consumer as early as possible: Baby Gap grows into GapKids and, once a teen, graduates to The Gap. The challenge for advertisers is to target the child audience in a manner that transforms market potential into consumer spending.

A second argument links the role of children as consumers to two key industries: toys and television.[7] Briefly, the argument is that transformations in the marketing of toys to children go hand in hand with transformations in the nature of television programming for children—and both are subject to economic imperatives of the marketplace. As Pecora (1998) succinctly notes:

> Over time these two industries have come together in a symbiotic relationship that blurs the lines between program and product. On television, programs offer the toy-industry advertisements for characters and the toys present the entertainment industry with readily identifiable characters. (p. 40)

Most critics agree that the factors involved in this shift are both economic and political in nature. The increased competitiveness of the television industry in the United States, brought about by the emergence of cable networks and independent stations alongside the major networks, meant more competition for children's audiences, programming, and advertising dollars. In Canada, this increased competition developed toward the end of the 1980s when Shaw Cablesystems Inc. was given a licence to develop YTV, a new cable channel that styled itself on the U.S. cable channel Nickelodeon and was to enjoy future success. "By the mid-1990s, YTV was often winning the ratings war in the 2–14 age group, and established broadcasters (especially Global) were playing catch-up, imitating the station's look and style in their kid-vid time slots" ("TV Advertising," 1996, p. C2).

In the early 1980s, there was an effective deregulation of children's advertising and programming by the U.S. Federal Communications Commission (FCC). The relaxation of earlier restrictions on the amount of ad time on children's television and the use of promotional toys for product tie-ins made children's television a much more attractive site for advertisers. Canadian regulators, however, kept such restrictions in place for Canadian networks. According to Kline (1993), "Canadian policy makers blithely ignored what was happening, overlooking the new infra-structure (satellite, cable, video) which transformed the distribution of children's culture in Canada" (p. 272).

In the same period, the toy industry was shifting in a number of ways. Toy man-ufacturing, through mergers and acquisitions, became increasingly consolidated in the hands of a small number of large, multinational corporations. In 1980, three manufacturers—Hasbro, Mattel, and Coleco—controlled only 20 percent of the market; by 1992, the market was effectively controlled by five or six companies (Pecora, 1998, p. 48). At the same time, there were changes in the way toys were marketed. Toy buying became "deseasonalized" in the sense that "toy purchases became a weekly or monthly occurrence rather than a twice-a-year event occurring at Christmas and birthdays" (Seiter, 1993, pp. 196–197). Pecora (1998) adds that the emergence of large transnational retail outlets like Toys "R" Us aids this con-stant cycle of toy consumption by providing a stable outlet for year-round pur-chasing; annual revenues went from $200 million (U.S.) in 1975 to $7.2 billion in 1992 (p. 50). Finally, as part of a strategy to increase sales, the toy industry adopted "line extensions." According to Seiter (1993), line extensions offer a simple and effective way of building on children's established taste preferences:

> The toy industry surrounds its successful characters each year with new companions, adversaries, locations, and older or younger versions of the original toys. . . . Girls' mass-market line extensions involve the addition of siblings or peers, rather than adversaries, and the expansion of domestic space. . . . The line extensions for boy's action figures involve an infinitely expand-able array of villains and monsters—each sold separately, on a bubble card. (p. 203)

The crucial link between shifts in the children's television industry and those in the toy industry is found in the development of character licensing, a technique Englehardt (1986) has dubbed "the strawberry shortcake strategy." The deregula-tion of the television industry, in conjunction with a search for ever-increasing expansion in the toy market, created an environment ripe for changes in marketing techniques aimed at children.[8] The Strawberry Shortcake doll, first produced in 1980, was merely one of the early products introduced to take advantage of this new marketing environment. The parent company behind the doll's introduction, American Greeting Cards Ltd., created for the doll and its companions a marketing plan that involved everything from the actual dolls, to bedsheets and clothes, to (most important of all) a series of animated televisions programs that in effect served as 30-minute commercials for the range of licensed goods available for pur-chase (Englehardt, 1986). Imitators quickly followed, and children's television was flooded with program-length commercials for a wide range of toys, including My

Little Pony, the Care Bears, Teenage Mutant Ninja Turtles, and She-Ra. The annual revenues raised through licensing royalties skyrocketed from $9.9 billion (U.S.) in 1980 to about $70 billion in 1990 (Pecora, 1998, pp. 56–57).

The licensing of popular characters from children's popular culture is not a new phenomenon. From Raggedy Ann to Shirley Temple to Davey Crockett, there has been a history of successful "characters" (and, indeed, Walt Disney was a master at licensing his own characters). What is new is both the extent to which children's culture is dominated by licensed characters/toys—from books, to movies, to video games—and the manner in which they are introduced. As Kline (1989) notes, "This combination of television and playthings in a comprehensive and integrated market gambit reversed the time-honored marketing approaches of spin-offs and changed the way kids' cultural products are developed" (p. 307). Toys are now introduced at the same time as or before the television series and movies on which they are based. Before the latest kid's movie is released, the toys, clothing, and books based on the movie are already on store shelves.

One effect of this new marketing approach is the squeezing of nonlicensed toys from the market. As Leonhardt and Kerwin show, in 1997 about 50 percent of all toys sold were licensed products from film or television (cited in Kapur, 1999, p. 128). Consider as well the licensed-toy sales projections in 1995 for three U.S. "characters": $300 million (U.S.) for Power Rangers toys, $130 million for Batman merchandise, and $100 million for products related to the Disney film *Pocahontas*. The difference between those figures and the projected $50 million in sales for the most popular nonlicensed toy that year—the flying doll, Sky Dancer—demonstrates the profits at stake for toy companies and the entertainment industry (Pereira and Bannon, 1995). It should come as no surprise, then, that toy companies have come to exert more control over the production of children's popular culture, whether through commissioning animated television series directly or through influencing the kinds of characters developed. Here is an example:

> A Disney animator says one scene in *Pocahontas*—when the raccoon Meeko briefly braids the star's hair—was created after a suggestion from Mattel, which wanted to be able to make Braided Beauty Pocahontas dolls.... For *Batman Forever*, Kenner got Warner Bros. to put the Riddler in tights because baggy pants don't look good on action figures, said Rick Watkins, a former Kenner toy-development manager. (Pereira and Bannon, 1995, p. A21)

SELLING INNOCENCE?

One might ask, where is the harm? According to political economists of communication, the problem lies in the colonization of children's play and children's imaginations

(Kline, 1993). Toy culture and entertainment industries are dominated by large megacorporations that seek to lower risk and enhance profit margins. The result is that the shaping of children's popular culture—from story lines, to personality characteristics, to production quality—is at the mercy of business interests. According to Pecora (1998):

> One of the consequences of the arrangements between the leisure and entertainment industries has been economic stability for the industries and a material culture for children. Mutually beneficial arrangements bring about a culture of play driven by characters available at Toys "R" Us, not creative imagination. (p. 60)

Children's play, Kline argues, is shaped by marketing factors that lead to a highly "ritualized" form of play and a prepackaged set of scripts; both what children play with and how they play is a consequence of market forces. In the end, this arrangement threatens the very innocence of childhood:

> [G]iven the enormous promotional apparatus directed at influencing parents and children's preferences in the market, I ... find it difficult to maintain that contemporary children's culture expresses children's autonomous choices and preserves their innocence. . . . Indeed, autonomy and innocence seem antithetical to the current practices of our cultural industries as they struggle ceaselessly to increase their hold over our children's imaginations. (Kline, 1993, p. 19)

The view of the child as innocent prey and the market as an all-powerful and manipulative corrupter of children translates into a policy position that seeks to restrict access of commercial interests to children. Political economy suggests a discourse of protection, a call to adults to shield their young from the commercial market:

> Short of revolution, it would appear there is little we can do. However, it is our responsibility as adults to see that children are not discouraged from the true magic of the world but that we recognize storytelling has become a business. (Pecora, 1998, p. 158)

The self-regulatory codes already in place in the industry[9] are seen as largely ineffective and easily circumvented. While policy alternatives are seldom directly detailed, there is a generalized call for radical change in favour of noncommercial arrangements—what Kline labels "a new framework for the culture industries" (1993, p. 350).

At first glance, such initiatives appear persuasive. But they depend on some problematic assumptions about the *child* and about *children's culture*. Regarding the child, political economic analyses imply a passive and vulnerable viewer who has no cognitive defences against the powerful tactics of advertisers. Also implicit in this model is a more traditional, behaviourist view of how children react to advertising. The vulnerable child is exposed to the powerful machinery of toy marketing in conjunction with popular culture industries and the unmediated effect is found in a spiral of escalating consumerism and diminished childhoods.

Yet the evidence is not conclusive. We know from developmental research that even very young children can distinguish ad content from program content and understand the persuasive intent of an ad (see John, 1999). Also, as Buckingham (2000) points out, the available research does not support the link between exposure to advertising and cultivation of "consumerist" values; one's family and friends appear to have more influence in that respect (p. 151). Finally, as Seiter (1993) notes from her work with children, children are more active than we give then credit for in the way they interact with cultural objects; they do not simply *react* but instead "create their own meanings from the stories and symbols of consumer culture" (p. 10).

Regarding the conception of children's culture, an underlying theme of political economic work is a moral condemnation of mass culture for children. Kline (1993), for example, suggests that "[t]he marketplace will never inspire children with high ideals or positive images of the personality, provide stories which help them adjust to life's tribulations or promote play activities that are most help to their maturation (p. 350). But, as Seiter (1993) notes of such arguments, "intellectuals tend to exclude the categories of "quality" toys and "creative" play, that is, the kinds of goods and services targeted at their own children" (p. 194). In other words, there is a line drawn between "good" toys sold in independent specialty toy shops (think Playmobil sets) and "bad" toys sold in retail chains like Toys "R" Us (think Barbie). In fact, Seiter (1993) argues, they are simply different segments of the same market, reflecting class differences rather than consequences for creativity and imagination: "The fear that children's creativity and individuality are somehow under assault is probably unfounded. That fear stems more from the aspirations of middle-class parents than from any observation of children's behavior" (pp. 225–226).

Finally, in conjunction with the assumption of the child as vulnerable and the market as corrupting, the policy discourse of restricting children from the marketplace seems shortsighted at best. As Buckingham (2000) notes:

> Attempting to create a "safe space" for children, in which they will remain uncontaminated by commercial influences as is the case in current moves to ban advertising from children's television is to retreat into an unreal fantasy world. Rather than seeking to protect children from the marketplace, we need to find ways of preparing them to deal with it. (pp. 166–167)

In Buckingham's view, children can be so prepared through a combination of education and media literacy as well as safeguarding their "rights" as consumers. This view represents a shift in conceptions of the child, from hapless victim to active participant in popular culture. With the change in conceptions of the child, the solution shifts from tougher controls on cultural producers to education of the child consumer, or, more specifically, providing the tools he or she needs to be a critical consumer.

THE VIOLENT CHILD

Headlines on youth and violence over the past decade have had the same under-tones of menace. To cite but a few examples: "The Columbine Effect" (*Time*, March 19, 2001); "Kids Who Kill" (*Maclean's*, August 1994); "The Dark Side of Teen Culture" (*Chatelaine*, May 1993); "Our Violent Kids" (*Time*, June 1989). The man-ifestations of increased violence among the young appear to be everywhere.

Yet, there is considerable debate over the issue of whether contemporary youth are, in reality, more or less violent than their predecessors. On the one hand, the official crime statistics reveal a steady drop in youth crime and violence over the past decade. On the other hand, some might argue that the official crime rate fails to register many incidents, either because victims are too scared to report them to authorities or because they are handled through informal channels. Whatever one's position on the facts, it is clear that the *perception* of greater youth violence is growing, and that the media have an important role to play in this outcome. The result is that, at some point, the appearance of youth violence is linked to media vio-lence, and a public outcry for the media to "clean up their act" soon follows. Commissions of inquiry are formed, public hearings are held, and the entertain-ment industry is pitted against regulators and parents in a battle to define the "youth problem."

In the 1990s, the public outcry against media violence gathered steam in both the United States and Canada. In Canada, a crystallizing moment came in November 1992 when a petition against television violence was submitted to the House of Commons. Virginie Larivière, a Quebec teen whose younger sister had been murdered, was convinced that television violence was a key factor in this tragedy, and she collected over 1.3 million signatures on a petition calling for tougher government legislation. Such public calls to action are usually followed by government promises to get tough on media violence and by threats to impose new codes of conduct for media.[10] Overwhelmingly, the relationship between media violence and violent children has been approached through a single model, the effects tradition, which proposes that "bad media = bad kids."

Behaviourism, Learning, and Violent Kids

The debate about the effects of media violence on children can be traced to some of the earliest research in communication studies. Writing in 1923, for example, psychologist Joseph Geiger concluded that children learned both amoral messages and antisocial behaviour from movies (cited in Luke, 1990, p. 33). This link was further explored in the Payne Fund Studies, 12 volumes of research (published in

1933) on the effects of cinema on the child viewer. One of the more widely popularized studies attempted to link viewing violent movie content to increased acts of juvenile delinquency and crime, while another focused on general erosion of moral standards (Lowery and Defleur, 1995, pp. 37–39). The link between media violence and real violence among the young became firmly established in communication studies and was resurrected often over the decades, receiving even more support with the appearance of each new medium. It is not an exaggeration to suggest that more work has been published on this question than any other single issue in media research (over 3000 studies on television violence have been published since the 1950s), and that questions about media/youth violence have been the subject of more government commissions of investigation than any other area.

The approach to the media/youth violence question was established early on in the research. Indeed, the Payne Fund Studies were important in cementing the kinds of questions that were asked, or not asked, about children and media violence. This research "articulated particular concerns, conceptualized effects and produced a construct of the child" (Luke, 1990, p. 36), and in so doing established the parameters for later research. What is interesting about the Payne Fund Studies is that while questions were asked about such things as frequency of movie attendance, violent content, perception and retention, and emotional and behavioural response, nothing was asked about the economic structures of film or the social and historical context of the period. Rather, the research agenda is reflective of the more general effects tradition, in which media content is conceived of as "stimuli" and children are "measured" for their behavioural or attitudinal responses. As noted earlier, the effects tradition has been the dominant paradigm of most media research in North America throughout a good part of the last 75 years.

It is important to situate the central assumptions of an effects model of media violence and establish the types of evidence used to make the case. An effects model of media violence generally begins with the assumption that one can isolate and measure behavioural, attitudinal, and emotional variables and link them in a causal or correlative way to messages carried by media content. In other words, it offers some variation or refinement of the stimulus-response model, or *behaviourist* approach, in which media offer stimuli to which children respond. Over the years, the crude notion of *direct* or unmediated effects of media, which characterized much of the early work, was overtaken by concern with *indirect* or mediated effects.

A direct-effects approach (famously labelled the hypodermic needle model by Harold Lasswell) reflects the "classic" behaviourist approach that dominated North American psychology in the prewar period. Violent media messages were seen to serve as dangerous stimuli that had the same effect on all children who might be exposed.[11] This crude behaviourism was gradually replaced by social behaviourism, an approach that sought mediating variables between the media and the receiver. Research in this area focuses on the factors that might qualify the power of the media over the individuals, the kinds of individuals who are more susceptible to violent images, and the social categories (class, race, gender, etc.) that are more likely to become violent after media exposure. The object of research is to isolate these mediating variables so that one might predict the kinds of media situations and the types of children in which violence was likely to be found. Nevertheless, the originating media message is still seen as the key factor in explaining why a child thinks, reacts, or behaves in a violent manner.

Various models have emerged over the years, under the general rubric of an effects tradition, to explain the process by which violent children emerge out of contact with violent media. All retain a focus on human experience as something that can be measured, quantified, predicted, and ultimately controlled if the right external factors are put in place. The details of the models are less important here than the general conclusions they offer about the impact of media in fuelling violence. The effects tradition continues to have a hold on the field of communication and on public discourse about violence and children. Some research has focused on the "aggressive cues" model. Pioneered by Berkowitz and his colleagues, this model seeks to find various factors, including cognitive skill differences among children, that stimulate children to acts of violence (see, for example, Berkowitz and Green, 1966). Other work adopts a "social learning" model, based on the early work of Bandura (1973), and attempts to isolate the variables that enhance or minimize the probability that a child will imitate or model aggressive behaviour seen in media. "Reinforcement" models analyze the extent to which violent media can strengthen existing predispositions to aggressive behaviour among certain types of children (see, for example, Josephson, 1987).

Some of the most widely known research is that of George Gerbner and his colleagues at the University of Pennsylvania. They propose a "cultivation" approach that attempts to link the quantity of violence on television to particular cultural attitudes toward violence. The gist of the argument is that a steady diet of media violence has consequences for how different groups think about violence; that is, television "cultivates" feelings and attitudes about violence in terms of who commits it, when it is legitimate, who the likely victims are, and so on. (See, for example, Gerbner, Gross, Morgan, and Signorielli, 1986.) To demonstrate the volume of violence children receive, Gerbner and his associates developed a "violence index" that tabulates the frequency of violent acts on television; the index is used annually to evaluate media performance in the United States. Though not a behaviourist explanation in the manner of the other models (Gerbner does not argue, for example, that media violence will fuel individual violence), this work does share an emphasis on the empirical measurement of both violence in the media and cultural attitudes.

Another factor to consider is the kind of evidence used by effects research to substantiate claims about media producing violent children. Two broad bodies of evidence are usually offered as "proof." The first type of evidence concerns the content of media, while the second type concerns the behaviour and attitudes of children. Content research generally focuses on establishing the volume and degree of violence found in different media sectors. This work is linked to audience research on the time children spend consuming media. The shock value of the statistics means they are regularly reported in the media: for example, we are told the average child will witness 8000 murders and 100,000 violent acts on television alone, before leaving elementary school (Hamburg, cited in Bok, 1997, p. 188).

Evidence of children's behaviour and attitudes is gathered either through controlled laboratory experiments, which measure immediate short-term effects of violent stimuli under controlled conditions, or through field studies, which measure such things as viewing patterns and responses in more "natural" environments such as the home, daycare centres, and schools. Listed below are some of the key arguments made in the research: [12]

- Children are exposed to heavy doses of media violence, and exposure increases with age.

- High exposure to violence is correlated with higher levels of violent behaviour and higher acceptance of violence as a legitimate response.

- The probability of imitating television violence increases when the violent role model is not punished.

- The probability of imitating violence increases when the child identifies with the violent hero.

- Heavy viewing of violence among young children is associated with a range of antisocial behaviour at later ages.

- Adolescent boys are more likely than adolescent girls to be affected by media violence.

- Some groups of children have been identified as more susceptible to the effects of media violence (in particular, visible-minority and immigrant children, low-income children, emotionally disturbed children, and abused children).

The link between public and academic discourses is particularly close in the case of media violence. Public-opinion polls regularly report parental concern over the amount of violence in media, and the public's belief that it contributes to violence in society.[13] The effects research tradition has been closely aligned with calls for stricter controls on violent content. In almost all the various commissions of inquiry established in the United States and Canada over the decades, effects research provided the "expert" evidence to support government action.[14] In general, the policy positions aligned with an effects approach involve attempts to curb violence in children *by restricting their access* to violent media content, with the parent serving as the primary "enforcer" of controls. Among the policy measures aligned with this research are industry codes of conduct (which are stricter in Canada than in the United States); ratings systems that evaluate violent content and display ratings through on-screen icons, package warnings, and viewer advisories; and technological devices designed to block access (V-chips installed in television sets, software blockers for computers, etc.). Whether these measures are actually effective is another matter. For example, a 1999 survey conducted in the United States found that parental supervision of television viewing has declined since 1997, and that only 38 percent of parents use television ratings to guide the selection of appropriate program material for their children.

Fuelling Violence?

The linking of bad kids with bad media has been repeated so often over the years—whether in government reports, press coverage, or talk shows—that it has almost achieved the status of "common sense." Yet, the assumptions on which this link is based are problematic. First, there are methodological problems in the research, including an overemphasis on short-term effects (which may not last over the long term), the artificial and hence unrealistic nature of the laboratory as a setting to predict violence in real life, and the confusion of correlation with causation.[15]

Second, this research tradition adopts a view of the child as "passive" and open to suggestion and manipulation in the face of the enormous power of the media. As Buckingham (1993) notes, "The media are seen to have an extraordinary power to penetrate the thin veneer of civilisation and release the anarchic, anti-social forces that lie beneath" (p. 4). This passive view stands in contradiction to the view of the child, held in cultural studies, as an active participant in interpreting media and constructing meaning. Meaning is not simply reducible to messages; it is not something "transmitted directly into the mind and thence the behaviour of the viewer" (Buckingham, 1993, p. 7). Rather, the child engages in a series of interpretive processes through which he or she constructs meaning (rather than just receiving messages) about the violence on the screen. Most important, children do not construct this meaning in some universal, predictable fashion.

A third key weakness is found in the way violent representations are selected for measurement, and with the relative lack of attention to the contexts in which they appear (Kinder, 1999, p. 3). The idea that one can simply extract a violent act from the overall text and assume it is equivalent to other violent acts is seriously flawed. As Martinez (1992) notes in summarizing various critiques of Gerbner's "violence index":

> Violent acts, detached from their social and moral context, are added together (for example, a violent act perpetrated by a brutal, sadistic character has the same value as a violent act in the "Road Runner" cartoon), which serves to inflate or conceal the true nature of television violence. (p. 9)

One cannot, in other words, easily identify violence as a simple and quantifiable attribute of a media message.

Perhaps the most damning critique is that, despite decades of research and repeated government commissions of inquiry, the evidence is neither definitive nor conclusive. The most we can really say is that violent media is one risk factor among many others for violent young people, that the relationship to influencing aggressive behaviour is "positive, though weak," and that the link cannot be upheld cross-culturally (Martinez, 1992, p. 47). As Buckingham (2000) succinctly points out:

> [T]his research in fact fails to prove its central hypothesis: that media violence makes people more aggressive *than they otherwise would have been*, or that it causes them to commit violent acts *they would not otherwise have* committed. . . . In this context, to seek evidence of "the effects of media violence" is to persist in asking simplistic questions about complicated social issues. (p. 130)

CONCLUSION

There are two opposing constructions of the child in cultural discourse: one sees the child as pure, innocent, vulnerable, and in need of adult protection; the other sees the child as threatening, potentially violent, open to manipulation, and in need of adult control. These constructions are manifested across a range of debates in the communications studies field and can be illustrated by looking at two different theoretical perspectives: (1) the political economic approach, and (2) the effects approach. Political economic work has focused on the corrupting influences of the market and their impact on childhood innocence, while effects research has detailed the ways in which violence in the media can unleash real violence by the young. One approach posits the child as victim, the other as threat. Each demonstrates the point that a theoretical position frames the way we look at any social issue; it leads us to make certain assumptions about individuals and audience behaviour, about causality and evidence, and about social policy.

There is overlapping ground between the political economic and effects constructions. Each begins with the assumption that there is something different about children and young people. In the case of political economy, children lack the cognitive skills or defences available to adults that would protect them from the effects of consumerism. In the case of violence effects research, there is something about media power over the young audience that makes them especially susceptible to violent "cues." Buckingham (2000) would argue that both views reflect a "*pre-social*" definition of children (p. 14); in other words, the child is not yet fully formed or civilized. Furthermore, thinking of children as presocial "effectively prevents any consideration of them as social beings, or indeed as citizens" (Buckingham, 2000, p. 15). This view is linked as well to a conception of the child as a passive receptor. According to this conception—a conception political economy and effects research share—children and young people are reactors rather than actors in popular culture.

It is interesting that both these approaches to communication research lead to policy positions that require exerting more control over children and youth. Through mechanisms that restrict access to cultural products or programming deemed offensive and/or exploitative, we attempt to limit the choices available to children and youth. Control is both centrally located in institutions of regulation (censor boards, licensing bodies, watchdog agencies, etc.) and dispersed in the form of parental controls (software blockers, V-chip, etc.).

Finally, we need to recognize that discourses about "children as innocent" and "children as threat" need to be connected also to questions of class, race, and gender. Media studies scholar Henry Jenkins characterizes the "innocent child" as follows:

> In our culture, the most persistent image of the innocent child
> is that of a white, blond-haired, blue-eyed boy and the markers
> of middleclassness, whiteness, and masculinity are read as
> standing for all children. (cited in Giroux, 2000, p. 5)

When we consider the "dangerous child," however, the markers of race, class, and gender work differently. As Giroux argues, "the notion of innocence does not apply to certain children and is being renegotiated for others" (2000, p. 8). In other words, the myths of innocence and danger that pervade our culture are not equally distributed across all sectors of childhood. This in itself is perhaps the best evidence for the argument that childhood as a separate developmental stage is a social concept that is constantly being constructed and reconstructed.

QUESTIONS

1. Identify recent examples of media-induced "social crises" about children and youth other than those cited in the chapter.
2. How do advertisers employ the "innocent child" construction in ad campaigns?
3. If you were writing a code of ethics for television children's programming, what would it entail and why?
4. How might a political economist of communication describe the relation between real violence and media violence?
5. Find examples in a newspaper that reflect the "dangerous child" construction.
6. According to many critics, the global marketing of toys and popular culture by corporations like Toys "R" Us and Disney results in the disappearance of national cultures and a homogenization of children's play around the world. Do you agree or disagree? Give reasons for your answer.
7. How do advertisers target boys and girls differently?

WEB SITES

Annenberg Public Policy Center: **http://www.appcpenn.org/**
Children Now: **http://www.childrennow.org/media/**
KidScreen: **http://www.kidscreen.com/**
Media Awareness Network: **http://www.media-awareness.ca/**
V-Chip Canada: **http://www.vchipcanada.ca/**

NOTES

1. In his book *Blaming Children*, Bernard Schissel goes so far as to title the first chapter "The Study of the Hatred of Children."
2. In a cover story titled "The Columbine Effect," *Time* magazine refers to the way in which this tragedy has entered the vocabulary of the young. Students who flirt with the idea of bringing weapons to school are now asked by friends whether they are going to "do a Columbine" (*Time*, March 19, 2001, p. 18).
3. For an interesting discussion of Plato's position, see Buckingham (1993, pp. 1–6).
4. Useful sources on the history of rave culture can be found in Reynolds (1998) and Thornton (1996).
5. For an interesting analysis of the similarities and differences, see Lori Tomlinson, "This Ain't No Disco—Or Is It? Youth Culture and the Rave Phenomenon," in Jonathan S. Epstein (Ed.), *Youth Culture: Identity in a Postmodern World* (Malden, MA: Blackwell Publishers, 1998).
6. The next section considers this approach in communication in terms of its framing of the media violence debate.
7. The following discussion refers to commercial television, not public television for children. However, as Pecora (1998) demonstrates, while public broadcasting for children has traditionally set higher standards than commercial television, it too is increasingly using the "product-oriented shows of commercial television" (p. 110).
8. Besides character licensing, marketing techniques used to reach children include more sophisticated test marketing of toys, more consumer research on children, and more money spent on packaging design and shelf placement. A useful source of information on these techniques is McNeal (1992).
9. In English Canada, television advertising is governed by the voluntary Broadcast Code for Advertising to Children. In 1980, Quebec imposed tighter restrictions by banning, under the Consumer Protection Act, all advertisements directed at children under 13. Cable and satellite distribution, of course, undermine this type of measure.
10. In the wake of the Larivière petition, for example, the Canadian broadcasting industry was pressured by the Canadian Radio-television and Telecom-

munications Commission (CRTC) into adopting a new self-regulatory code to curb violence in programming.

11. An example of this type of research can be found even in the postwar period. Frederic Wertham's *Seduction of the Innocent* (1954) argued that comic book violence stimulated violent acts and attitudes in children who read them. A useful review of his arguments can be found in Lowery and Defleur (1995).

12. More extensive summaries of the key research are can be found in Josephson (1995), Martinez (1992), and Reiss and Roth (1993).

13. One U.S. poll reported that 80 percent of Americans think television violence is harmful to society, while in Canada four out of five women think television fuels more violence in society (cited in Media Awareness Network, Statistics and Public Opinion, at: http://www.media-awareness.ca).

14. See Rowland (1983) for an interesting discussion of the politics behind the use of social science in government commissions on media violence in the United States.

15. In other words, proving that aggressive kids also consume heavy doses of violent media tells us nothing about the *cause* of their aggression.

REFERENCES

Alexander, Alison, and Margaret Morrison. (1995). Electric toyland and the structure of power: An analysis of critical studies on children as consumers. *Critical Studies in Mass Communication, 12*, 344–353.

Ariès, Philippe. (1962). *Centuries of childhood: A social history of family life*. New York: Knopf.

Bandura, A. (1973). *Aggression: A social learning analysis*. Englewood Cliffs, NJ: Prentice-Hall.

Berkowitz, L., and R.G. Green. (1966). Film violence and the cue properties of available targets. *Journal of Personality and Social Psychology, 3*, 525–530.

Bok, Sissela. (1997). TV violence, children and the press. In Pippa Norris (Ed.), *Politics and the press* (pp. 185–216). London: Lynne Rienner Publishers.

Buckingham, David (Ed.). (1993). *Reading audiences: Young people and the media*. Manchester, U.K.: Manchester University Press.

——— (2000). *After the death of childhood*. Cambridge, U.K.: Polity Press.

Englehardt, Tom. (1986). The strawberry shortcake strategy. In Todd Gitlin (Ed.), *Watching television* (pp. 68–110). New York: Pantheon Books.

Gerbner, George, Larry Gross, Michael Morgan, and Nancy Signorielli. (1986). Living with television: The dynamics of the cultivation process. In J. Bryant and D. Zillman (Eds.), *Perspectives on media effects* (pp. 17–39). Hillsdale, NJ: Lawrence Erlbaum.

Giroux, Henry A. (2000). *Stealing innocence: Youth, corporate power and the politics of culture*. New York: St. Martin's Press.

John, Deborah Roedder. (1999). Through the eyes of a child: Children's knowledge and understanding of advertising. In C. Macklin and Les Carlson (Eds.), *Advertising to children: Concepts and controversies* (pp. 3–36). London: Sage.

Josephson, W. (1987). Television violence and children's aggression: Testing the priming, social script and disinhibition predictions. *Journal of Personality and Social Psychology, 53*, 882–890.

———. (1995). *Television violence: A review of the effects on children of different ages*. Ottawa: Department of Canadian Heritage.

Kapur, Jyotsna. (1999). Out of control: Television and the transformation of childhood in late capitalism. In Marsha Kinder (Ed.), *Kids' media culture* (pp. 122–136). Durham, NC: Duke University Press.

Kinder, Marsha (Ed). (1999). *Kids' media culture*. Durham, NC: Duke University Press.

Kline, Stephen. (1989). Limits to the imagination: Marketing and children's culture. In Ian Angus and Sut Jhally (Eds.), *Cultural politics in contemporary America* (pp. 299–316). London: Routledge.

———. (1993). *Out of the garden*. Toronto: Garamond Press.

Lowery, S., and M. Defleur. (1995). *Milestones in mass communication research* (3rd ed.). White Plains, NY: Longman.

Luke, Carmen. (1990). *Constructing the child viewer*. New York: Praeger.

Martinez, Andrea. (1992). *Scientific knowledge about television violence*. Ottawa: Canadian Radio-television and Telecommunications Commission.

McNeal, James U. (1992). *Kids as customers*. New York: Lexington Books.

Oswell, David. (1998). A question of belonging: Television, youth and the domestic. In Tracy Skelton and Gill Valentine (Eds.), *Cool places: Geographies of youth cultures* (pp. 35–49). London: Routledge.

Pecora, Norma. (1998). *The business of children's entertainment*. New York: Guilford Publications.

Pereira, Joseph, and Lisa Bannon. (1995, September 12). Hollywood is major source of inspiration for new lines of toys. *Globe and Mail*, p. A21.

Reiss, Albert Jr., and Jeffrey Roth (Eds.). (1993). *Understanding and preventing violence*. Washington: National Academy Press.

Reynolds, Simon. (1998). *Generation Ecstasy*. New York: Little, Brown and Company.

Rowland, W. (1983). *The politics of TV violence: Policy uses of communication research*. Beverly Hills: Sage.

Schissel, Bernard. (1997). *Blaming children: Youth crime, moral panic and the politics of hate*. Halifax: Fernwood.

Seiter, Ellen. (1993). *Sold separately*. New Brunswick, NJ: Rutgers University Press.

Springhall, John. (1998). *Youth, popular culture and moral panics*. New York: St. Martin's Press.

Steinberg, Shawna. (1998, May 13). Have allowance; will transform economy. *Canadian Business*, 60.

Thornton, Sarah. (1996). *Club cultures: Music, media and subcultural capital*. Hanover, NH: University Press of New England.

Tucker, Lauren R. (1996). Calvin Klein jeans advertising: Kiddie porn or media ado about nothing? In Murray Pomerance and John Sakeris (Eds.), *Pictures of a generation on hold: Selected papers* (pp. 195–204). Toronto: Media Studies Working Group.

TV advertising for kids is like shooting fish in a barrel. (1996, December 7). *Globe and Mail*, p. C2.

Valentine, Gill, Tracy Skelton, and Deborah Chambers. (1998). Cool places: An introduction to youth and youth cultures. In Tracy Skelton and Gill Valentine (Eds.), *Cool places: geographies of youth cultures* (pp. 1–34). London: Routledge.

Part III
Communication Industries

Introduction

The chapters in this section examine the social diffusion of six communication technologies: radio, film, sound recordings, television, computers and the Internet, and on-line journalism. Each chapter provides a brief technological and social history of the communication technology in question; describes key Canadian highlights in policy and regulation around the technology; illustrates the main social uses of the technology (including unintended uses by various groups); considers ethical issues arising from the technology; and identifies technical and social trends in the technology's development.

It is important when we look at contemporary uses of communication technologies to consider previous uses of other communication technologies. Doing so often makes us aware that current hype about the potential of technologies is nothing new. Consider what was said about the radio when it first emerged at the turn of the last century. Douglas (1987) has recounted how journalistic accounts influenced attitudes toward radio culture, as well as ideas about who should control and use the new technology: "this was primarily a white, middle-class, male construction, a process from which most women and minorities were excluded" (p. xxix). For instance, the press and popular magazines of the day reported extensively on early amateur radio operators and inventor-heroes. Amateur (or "ham") radio operators were a distinct subculture of men who found, through their tinkering and technical mastery of the new technology, a way to cope with (and subvert) the pressures of modern bureaucratic conformity. Douglas documents in detail the way in which popular culture fawned over the ideal of the boy inventor-hero:

> Everything could be achieved through technical mastery. Playing with technology was, more than ever, glorified as a young man's game.... Few inventions were more accessible to the young man than the latest marvel, wireless telegraphy. Just as articles giving instructions on "Building Your Own Wireless Set" began appearing with increasing frequency, so did stories and books that celebrated boy wireless experimenters. (p. 191)

How is this significantly different from media reports that extolled the heroics of young Internet entrepreneurs in the months preceding the onset of the dot-com crash in March 2000? In the United States and Canada, the media celebrated the tireless work and entrepreneurial zeal of teenaged Internet innovators. Rather than looking critically at the role of the Internet in daily life, the media became a relentless cheerleader for industry and government.

Several important themes emerge in the following chapters. One theme is the crucial role that communication technologies have assumed, in Canadian life, in forging and promoting a Canadian identity. Forms of cultural protectionism, such as the Canadian content rules that govern radio and television broadcasting, are a subject of hot debate in Canada, and they are being considered in conjunction with the Internet.

Tensions between public and private broadcasting is a second theme. As several of the chapters show, the CBC has assumed a vital role in stitching the Canadian fabric together; in contrast with the situation south of the border, public broadcasting has the support of the Canadian public. Yet, as we begin to enter the world of cross-media convergence, many of the regulatory measures that would develop and distribute Canadian-made cultural fare are not in place.

A third theme is the ways in which communication technologies are being transformed through technological innovations such as digitization. Innovation results in diverse and often novel social uses of the technology, from the informal communication facilitated by Internet chat rooms to use of Web-based technology in education.

Finally, there is the question of the fate of Canadian media in our globalized environment. As the chapters in this section highlight, Canadian cultural industries are supported by legislative mechanisms, but they are often not widely known beyond our borders. Should we care about this? Or will the Internet erase these geographic borders and allow for a proliferation of content irrespective of national boundaries?

REFERENCE

Douglas, Susan J. (1987). *Inventing American broadcasting, 1899–1922*. Baltimore, MD: Johns Hopkins University Press.

9

The Canadian Radio Industry

Pierre C. Bélanger[1]
University of Ottawa

The history of the radio industry in Canada covers virtually all of the last century. Indeed, the euphoria surrounding wireless communication in the late 1800s and early 1900s was entirely similar to modern enthusiasm for the information highway. In 1895, the Italian physicist Guglielmo Marconi became the first person to transmit electrical signals *without wires* over a distance of approximately one kilometre. This achievement was extended in 1901 when, standing on Signal Hill in Newfoundland, Marconi received the Morse code signal for the letter "S," transmitted by a collaborator sitting across the Atlantic in Cornwall, England. That widely covered event definitively thrust Marconi into the history books.

From a Canadian perspective, a name that may merit wider exposure is Reginald Fessenden, who competed with Marconi for funding and, more important, for recognition of his scientific contribution. While Marconi could transmit Morse code, Fessenden was the first person to broadcast music and the sound of the human voice. The broadcast, which occurred on Christmas Eve, 1906, was heard by startled radio operators on ships at sea. Unfortunately, Fessenden was overshadowed by Marconi and never came close to having his work properly recognized.

Events moved rapidly. The Marconi Wireless Telegraph Company of Canada conducted many successful experiments in its laboratory. Convinced that it had the "next big thing," the Marconi Company became the first enterprise ever to hold a *broadcasting* or *radio* licence, albeit an experimental one. The licence was granted in 1918 by the Department of Naval Service, which had acquired responsibility for wireless. The station, XWA in Montreal, later changed its call letters to CFCF. It began broadcasting sporadic programming in 1919. In 1922, CKAC Montreal became the first French-language station to go to air. No longer just wishful thinking, radio was becoming, like the piano and the phonograph, a household utility and means to bring music wirelessly into the home.

From then on, the developments within the industry spread like wildfire. The technology became so popular that the newly formed Canadian National Railway (CNR) installed special *radio cars* on some of its trains. Passengers travelling from Ottawa to Toronto were treated to highbrow musical programming consisting of opera, orchestras, and drama. By 1932, the CNR had a national and regional network comprising some 20 radio stations constructed alongside its tracks.

A TIME OF FIRSTS

No other event underlined the information poignancy of radio quite so powerfully as the sinking of the *Titanic* in 1912. Major newspapers were dependent on radio news for details of the catastrophe. The coverage that newspapers inevitably gave radio significantly heightened its legitimacy and usefulness in the public eye and acted as a strong catalyst to convince people of the advantages of obtaining their own receiver.

Shortly thereafter, some Canadians began to complain that radio was simply becoming a jukebox, playing nothing but dance music and jazz. A demand grew for more serious, socially elevating, and nation-building content. In retrospect, the early state of affairs is hardly surprising. The history of technological and communication innovations shows time and again that new media typically borrow their content from the old media they allegedly replace. Radio borrowed its musical content from the phonograph. Gradually, though, it started to develop a personality of its own. In 1921, the first Canadian federal election coverage was aired on radio. Hockey broadcasts started in 1922, and in 1923 Foster Hewitt launched his long and memorable career as the voice of hockey in English Canada and the inventor of the phrase "He shoots! He scores!" Mystery series became a staple of radio programming as of the mid-1920s.

As with crashes on today's computer networks, the technical reliability of the first radio transmissions was questionable. "Dead air" was part of one's connection with the new medium, and the phrase "There will now be an intermission of 10 minutes" was just part of the listening experience. Then, as now, people tended to be forgiving because the benefits of the innovation far outweighed its inconveniences.

In Canada, the prevalence of radio as a mass medium was conclusively demonstrated during the festivities surrounding Canada's Diamond Jubilee on July 1st, 1927. Prompted by a suggestion made by Graham Spry (a figure who played an important role in promoting public broadcasting[2]), the government of the day, under Mackenzie King, orchestrated a grandiose affair that would allow Canadians, for the first time, to celebrate a national event together. For the occasion, the telephone and telegraph lines that made up CNR's extensive network were interconnected so that orchestras located in its 23 stations from east to west could simultaneously play the national anthem. As they played, the network switched seamlessly from orchestra to orchestra. Originating from Ottawa, an estimated five million Canadians and Americans tuned in that day to the various Diamond Jubilee broadcasts. Never before had a mass medium played such a spirited role in building the national consciousness of Canadians. The Toronto *Globe* called the role radio played in the event "a democratic science, ready to instruct and entertain all manner and conditions of humankind who prepare to receive its blessings" (Nash, 1995, p. 49).

'CANADIANIZING' THE AIRWAVES

To say that American programming caught the fancy of Canadian listeners in the early days of radio would be an understatement. Approximately 80 percent of the time Canadians spent listening to radio went to programs originating from south of the border. This worried many. Indeed, governments were only beginning to assess the cultural and economic ramifications of American domination of the film industry. It was felt that if nothing were done, a similar predicament would soon befall the radio industry. Clearly, the fact that Canadians showed a preference for American programming unnerved the federal government. An overabundance of American artists, stories, ways of perceiving events, and values was the last thing any government preoccupied with nation-building wanted. The stakes were such that, in 1928, the federal government struck the first of many royal commissions, the Aird Commission, chaired by Sir John Aird. Its mandate was to study the state of Canadian broadcasting; to make recommendations on the way it should be administered, managed, and monitored; and to provide an informed assessment of its financial needs if it was to prosper and respond to the expectations of the Canadian audience. Predictably, the commission's final report offered a rather bleak analysis by confirming that, indeed, American networks did pose a threat to both our airwaves and our culture.

The Aird Commission did more than simply state what everybody already suspected. It recommended the creation of a distinctive feature of today's Canadian radio environment—namely, a public broadcasting network that would be supervised by an independent federal agency. The fundamental mandate of the public network would be highly nationalistic: to produce and air Canadian programs for and by Canadians. Such a novel idea had quite an impact on the private radio station owners who had been living quite comfortably under the existing situation. They suddenly found themselves on the defensive, called on to justify why a national publicly funded radio network, a *Crown corporation*, might not be required after all. After three years of public debate, the federal government finally acted. It determined that Canada was to have a *mixed* broadcasting system, composed of both public and private radio stations. Graham Spry's dream of having radio "make the home not merely a billboard, but a theatre, a concert hall, a club, a public meeting, a school, a university" (Nash, 1995, p. 69) was about to come true.

The Canadian Radio Broadcasting Act, passed in 1932, provided the required impetus for the creation of the Canadian Radio Broadcasting Commission (CRBC), which began its broadcasts in 1933. The CRBC's mandate was twofold: (1) to regulate and control all broadcasting activities in the country; and (2) to provide a national broadcasting service. In 1936, the Canadian Radio Broadcasting Act was amended and the CRBC was replaced by a new Crown corporation, the Canadian Broadcasting Corporation (CBC). The CBC took over the CRBC's staff and facilities. From the outset, the CBC assumed the responsibility for providing the much sought-after *national* radio service, which was able to reach about half the population of the time.

Significantly, the CBC was not only a broadcaster in competition with private stations. Indeed, the Broadcasting Act also gave it the authority to regulate the entire system, and therefore to grant or deny licences to its private competitors. This fact—that the CBC was both competitor and regulator—provoked much criticism from a broad range of industry players and analysts. As a result, in 1958, the federal government revisited the functions of the CBC and created a new independent regulatory body, the Board of Broadcast Governors (BBG), whose role was to regulate *both* the private broadcasters *and* the CBC. From that date on, the CBC was restricted to being solely a broadcasting network. In 1968, the BBG was replaced by the Canadian Radio-Television Commission (CRTC), which had the power to regulate radio and televisions stations in Canada.

THE RADIO REGULATORY ENVIRONMENT

The CRTC (whose name was changed in 1975 to the Canadian Radio-television and Telecommunications Commission) plays the key role in awarding and renewing broadcasting licences, as well as in setting standards and quotas by which the radio and television industries must abide. The CRTC is an independent public agency that reports to Parliament through the Minister of Canadian Heritage and that is governed by both the Broadcasting Act of 1991 and the Telecommunications Act of 1993. Its role is to maintain a balance between the cultural, social, and economic goals of the legislation on broadcasting and telecommunications in the public interest. It does this by ensuring that programming in the Canadian broadcasting system reflects Canada's linguistic duality and multicultural diversity, and the special place of Aboriginal people in Canadian society.

Perhaps the most definitive aspect of Canadian broadcasting regulation has to do with Canadian content requirements, or *CanCon* as it is known. Although specific CanCon requirements change as the CRTC adapts its policy to reflect the constantly evolving media environment, they nevertheless always adhere to the same basic objectives of the Broadcasting Act. As a whole, the CanCon regulations consist of a series of quantitative measures intended first and foremost to "ensure that the work of Canadian recording artists and program producers is available to Canadians"; furthermore, as the CRTC itself argues, the regulations "have led to the development of a healthy Canadian recording and program production industry" (CRTC, 2001).

There are more than 400 English-language radio stations in Canada, all of which must respect the following CRTC requirements as a fundamental condition of licence:

1. At least 35 percent[3] of popular music selections played by commercial AM and FM radio stations each broadcast week must be Canadian.

2. To ensure that the Canadian music selections are broadcast during periods of high listening, a minimum of 35 percent of popular music selections aired between 6:00 a.m. and 6:00 p.m., Monday through Friday, must qualify as Canadian.

The only exception to these quotas applies to stations whose playlists consist of at least 35 percent instrumental music. These licence holders are permitted to broadcast a lower percentage of Canadian content because the pool of music they can draw from is much more limited in that specific category.

The CBC must abide by slightly more stringent conditions. On a weekly basis, at least 50 percent of general popular music and 20 percent of traditional and special interest selections aired by CBC during the broadcast day (6:00 a.m. to midnight) must be Canadian. Nowhere is the contribution of public broadcasting to the promotion of Canadian talent more apparent than in the number and diversity of music styles played on its regional stations and national networks. For example, CBC Radio 1 and Radio 2 air a weekly average of 4800 different musical selections. Of these 4800 selections, approximately 60 percent (roughly 2300 different musical selections) qualify on a weekly basis as CanCon, thereby exceeding the CRTC requirement of 50 percent. Moreover, the CBC exceeds the CRTC's 20 percent quota for special interest and classical music, since 40 percent of its 2500 average weekly musical selections also qualify as CanCon.

It is worth noting that the approximately 100 French-language private stations are subjected to even more demanding requirements. For them, the obligation to promote French-speaking artists translates into an expectation that at least of 65 percent of the popular vocal music selections they broadcast each week be in French. If taken literally, however, this requirement could result in a radio station playing only artists from France, Belgium, or another French-speaking country, since the Canadian market could not supply the demand. In order to avoid that outcome, the CRTC also requires that at least 35 percent of popular music selections aired weekly by French-language commercial AM and FM stations be Canadian. In addition, at least 55 percent of the popular French vocal music selections aired weekly must be played between 6:00 a.m. and 6:00 p.m., Monday through Friday.

The requirements for French-language public broadcasting are stricter than for French-language private broadcasting, and this mirrors the relationship of the CBC to the English-language private radio stations. Radio-Canada's generalist La Première chaîne (the equivalent of CBC Radio 1) is required to air 95 percent French-language content, of which 50 percent must be by Canadian artists. A maximum of 5 percent of its playlist can be devoted to English-Canadian vocal selections. La chaîne culturelle (the equivalent of CBC Radio 2) must guarantee a minimum 20 percent airplay to Canadian traditional and special-interest music. Finally, every song must be played in its entirety in order to be counted toward the CanCon quota.

As one might expect, the CRTC goes to great lengths to define just what qualifies as a "Canadian selection." The definition is so critical to the entire radio industry that it has given rise to a typically Canadian designation, the MAPL system, a subset of the overall Canadian content regulations. It was conceived with two goals in mind: (1) a cultural goal intended to encourage increased audience exposure to Canadian performers, lyricists, and composers: and (2) an industrial goal intended to support the Canadian music and recording industry.

The MAPL system consists of four elements that resulted from an extensive round of public hearings during which the CRTC consulted informed opinion on how radio regulations could support the development of every sector of the Canadian music industry. Under the MAPL system, a musical selection must meet *at least two* of the following criteria in order to qualify as Canadian:

M, for music: is the music composed entirely by a Canadian?

A, for artist: is the music, or are the lyrics, performed principally by a Canadian?

P, for production: does the musical selection consist of a live performance that is

   (i) recorded entirely in Canada, or

   (ii) performed entirely in Canada and broadcast live in Canada?

L, for lyrics: are the lyrics written entirely by a Canadian?

In addition, exceptions can be made for special situations. For instance, if the musical selection was recorded before 1972, or if the selection is an instrumental performance of a musical composition written or composed by a Canadian, it need not conform to the MAPL system.

Despite the fact that the MAPL system appears to be a fairly efficient incentive to optimize exposure to and stimulate the careers of many musical talents in the country, it nonetheless falls victims to very harsh criticism. The criticism almost always occurs every year at the same time, typically just when the Juno[4] nominations are announced. Every March since 1970, Canada has celebrated its worthiest talents by handing them the emblem of what is considered by many the regulatory quota that saved an industry some 30 years ago when it was in dire need of both protection and promotion. The Canadian Academy of Recording Arts and Sciences (CARAS) and CBC Television have been longstanding partners in the festivities.

Critics argue that the problem with CanCon is actually a problem of the music industry. For example, the public tends to develop a strong personal or emotional attachment to a rather limited number of artists. Indeed, such artists as Alanis Morissette, Shania Twain, the Tragically Hip, Céline Dion, Amanda Marshall, Brian Adams, the Barenaked Ladies, Roch Voisine, and Sarah McLachlan have been able to generate very strong followings over the last few years. As a result, they are icons of not just the national music scene but also the international music scene. That so many Canadians artists have garnered international acclaim may be a cause for celebration, but we should be equally concerned about the impact of so few big names on the entire music industry.

From the perspective of CanCon's critics, the real impact of the quotas is to intensify the dominance of a small group of stars to the detriment of promising new artists who simply cannot generate the same kind of bonding with audiences as the big names. Larry LeBlanc, Canadian editor of *Billboard* magazine sums it up succinctly: "The negative impact of Cancon regulation is very simple. If you're releasing a record today at the same time as Shania Twain or Nelly Furtado, you're going to have a lot of trouble" (cited in Everett-Green, 2001). Critics do not hesitate to point an accusing finger at radio stations that have become part of a sophisticated marketing system in which only those artists capable of producing and promoting a CD and a video receive airtime. Furthermore, many accuse commercial stations of not giving fair consideration to artists who are not distributed by one of the four major multinational conglomerates that dominate the entire music industry. Should the current regulations be amended, then, in order to force radio stations to increase the diversity of the artists who make up their daily playlists?

THE PROMOTION OF CANADIAN MUSIC

Regulations impose conditions on licence holders in order to expand the variety and number of ways through which the music industry can be assisted. At the same time, some of the major stakeholders have proposed their own voluntary commitments in order to ensure that the Canadian music scene continues to grow while cultivating the next generation.

The Canadian Association of Broadcasters (CAB) ranks among the most active and determined of these stakeholders in terms of promoting Canadian music. Among the host of initiatives the CAB has launched over the last few years is the Annual Canadian Radio Music Awards. Established in 1998 to celebrate and promote first-time top-charted artists in different radio formats, these awards constitute the highlight of a series of activities that take place during Canadian Music Week (www.cmw.net). Another CAB initiative is Canadian Radio Music Month, which precedes the Canadian Music Awards each year, serving as a teaser to get the public acquainted with the nominees. Also, in 2001 and in cooperation with the Canadian Independent Record Production Association (CIRPA) and the Canadian Recording Industry Association (CRIA), the CAB created the $26-million Radio Starmaker Fund (and its French-language counterpart, Le Fonds RadioStar), which will provide free promotion to new artists and new recordings over the next decade or so. Finally, the CAB established the Canadian Music Marketing and Promotion Fund, which provides marketing and promotional events for both the music industry and emerging talent.

In the eyes of the CAB, such initiatives are essential if the Canadian music scene is to sustain the level of success it has attained over the last couple of decades. Unquestionably, Canada must put in place a set of conditions that will foster the blossoming not only of a few major international superstars but also of a rich spectrum of musical talent. At present, the Canadian music industry is far from having enough stars, and it is unlikely that current regulations can fill the void. According to the CAB's figures, and despite CanCon quotas that oblige radio stations to air at least 35 percent Canadian selections, sales of Canadian music hover around 12 percent of all music sales. The gap between airplay (35 percent) and market share (12 percent) cannot be closed by regulation alone. Indeed, since 1970, the regulations have demonstrated their inability to close this gap. Creative alternatives are needed to heighten the visibility and relevance of Canada's musical talent.

In addition to the CAB-initiated events, private radio stations spend an estimated $1.8 million annually on talent development organizations such as FACTOR (www.factor.ca), MusicAction (www.musicaction.ca), and other locally based endeavours. Furthermore, the CAB claims that its radio members spend some $20 million annually in voluntary assistance to promote and market Canadian artists. In June 2001, Canadian Heritage Minister Sheila Copps announced the establishment of a much-awaited new national program that will inject some $28 million into the Canadian sound recording industry over the 2001–04 period. An umbrella organization called the Canada Music Fund will set the guidelines for accessing the new funds and will integrate the various policy strands that currently exist for the music industry. More specifically, the Canadian Music Fund is expected to oversee Canadian Sound Recording Policy's objectives and funding procedures through no less than seven programs: the Creators Assistance Program, the Canadian Musical Diversity Program, the New Musical Works Program, the Musical Entrepreneur Program (to help entrepreneurs make the transition to the digital economy), the Support to National Sector Association Program, the Collective Infrastructure Initiatives Program, and the Canadian Music Memories Program. Behind all these initiatives lies one common goal: to seek out and identify the most promising musical artists and then back them up with the required marketing and promotional support.

Today's music environment is significantly different from the one Paul Anka, Joni Mitchell, The Band, and Neil Young knew in the 1950s through 1970s. In the era of global culture, Canadian artists must learn to live with competition from all over the world. The newest marvels of digital technology, such as Napster, Gnutella, and MP3, can divert local audiences from traditional sources of entertainment. In such a multifaceted environment, how can Canada's radio stations develop any semblance of competitive advantage? Some argue that the solution depends on finding ways, incentives, and mechanisms that show a clear bias toward showcasing Canadian talent. For example, some favour Web sites and search engines that automatically steer users to Canadian selections.

CANADIAN PUBLIC RADIO

As indicated earlier, CBC/Société Radio-Canada was one of the prime architects of the development of a viable radio industry in Canada, and it continues to be the object of a very singular attachment for the majority of the Canadian public. In December 1999, when the CRTC renewed the network radio licences of CBC/Radio-Canada, it reiterated some of the defining characteristics of public radio. It provides a unique style of radio within the industry and its noncommercial nature allows it to explore unorthodox programming styles and hence reach constituencies that are not currently being targeted by mainstream stations.

To most listeners, CBC Radio is easily identifiable. It has a very distinct sound and mode of delivery and, above all, is commercial-free. What is less apparent is its deep presence in every province of the country, with a regional representation in both official languages, which makes it a unique organization in the international broadcasting community. Statistics Canada estimates that more than 50 percent of Canadians use at least one of the four CBC radio services weekly. This translates to average weekly audience reach of some 3.5 million Canadians for English-language radio and over 800,000 for French-language radio.

Over the next few years, CBC Radio intends to explore opportunities to offer radio content on new delivery platforms, including digital radio, Internet applications, external syndication, and after-market distribution. Already the CBC's news headlines are distributed to wireless telephone users by most major Canadian cellular service providers. CBC and Radio-Canada have also recently launched an Internet-only, Canadian alternative-type music multimedia service called Radio 3 (www.120seconds.com, www.justconcerts.com and www.newmusiccanada.com) and Bande A Part (www.bandeapart.fm).

The CBC plays a vital role in promoting local talent across the musical spectrum (popular music, jazz, contemporary, rap/hip hop, country/folk, children's, classical). Over the last 20 years, CBC has become the largest manufacturer and distributor of classical music in Canada, certainly one of the best-kept secrets in the industry.

RADIO TYPES AND FORMATS

From a regulatory standpoint, there are four main types of licence: (1) an AM licence, of which there are some 300 across the country; (2) an FM licence, of which there are more than 550 currently; (3) a digital radio service, of which there are currently 55 in Montreal, Toronto, Windsor, and Vancouver; (4) a pay-audio digital (two currently exist), offered nationwide via local satellite, cable, or wireless systems.

The categorization extends further. As a licence holder, one can possess a permit to operate one of the following types of stations (in one of the four above-named categories):

(a) commercial station (e.g., CHUM-FM in Toronto or Z95.3 in Vancouver, with over 500 in total) with a mandate to generate profits;

(b) public-service station (e.g., CBC and Radio-Canada, 74 stations) owned and operated by a public enterprise;

(c) campus station (37);

(d) community station (61);

(e) ethnic station (13);

(f) Native station (121 mostly low-power radio stations).

In addition, the CRTC uses over two-dozen different content categories to describe the various programming styles available on radio. Whereas radio was a unifying force in its early days, the proliferation of niche stations has seen a fragmentation of audiences that cuts radically into the common experience listeners once shared. The original mass media nature of radio has given way to a form of localized "walled garden" programming that caters to highly specialized tastes and preferences.

The vast majority of Canadian radio listening falls into eight main formats. According to the Spring 2000 BBM Bureau of Measurement ratings, which surveyed Canada's 12 largest radio markets, adult contemporary (AC) music, also known as light or adult rock, is by far the most popular format, capturing a 27 percent listening share. Although still the favourite radio format, AC is not nearly as dominant as it once was. Its 27 percent rating is down 1.6 percent from 1999 and a full 5 percent from its 1998 results. Between 1999 and 2000, four stations stopped programming AC, with one station in Toronto and one in Vancouver electing to move to modern rock (Bohn, 2000).

AC is followed by news/talk radio with a 22 percent listening share. Of Canada's 31 news/talk stations, 19 are concentrated in the four largest markets. Montreal appears to be the most news-hungry market with six such stations, including two recently licensed all-news stations (one each for the French and English markets). Contemporary hit radio, or top 40, gets a 19 percent listening share or 55 million hours annually; from 1998 to 2000, this category has experienced a substantial 6.5 percent growth. Album-oriented rock (AOR) and classical music stations both get a 7 percent share. The latter category proved to be one of the big gainers in the Spring 2000 survey, with its 7 percent score being its all-time high. Toronto and Montreal have the most classical music aficionados, as indicated by the three stations in each market. Country, classic rock, gold, and an aggregate of alternative, sports, adult standards, and other such stations round out the list of the most listened-to formats.

Of all the formats, country appears to be hurting the most, with its share of hours dropping from 18 percent in 1993 to below 6 percent in 2000. Nowhere in Canada does country succeed in winning a market. In the two largest radio markets, Toronto and Montreal, there is no country music to be heard at all.

COMMERCIAL RADIO STATION OWNERS

The role of the CRTC is not limited to allocating broadcasting licences and setting content quotas. From an economic standpoint, recent changes in the CRTC's commercial radio policy have significantly modified the Canadian radio landscape.

The change that received the most media attention concerned ownership. Since spring 1998, in markets with eight commercial radio stations or more broadcasting in a given language—the operative word is *commercial*, which excludes any public, community, campus, or ethnic stations from the calculation—the CRTC has allowed a person or company to own or control as many as two AM and two FM stations in that language. For those markets with fewer than eight commercial stations operating in a given language, the ownership can go as high as three stations, with a maximum of two stations in any one frequency band (AM or FM). Those hoping to acquire more than one AM and one FM station in a given language in the same market are asked to assess the likely impact of their ownership on the following issues: (1) the diversity of news voices, (2) the level of competition in the market, (3) the benefit to the local community and the furtherance of the objectives of the Broadcasting Act as a result of the programming they will typically broadcast, and (4) any other issues that may arise in the case of applicants who already own other media or have an interest in other radio stations in the same market.

Why did the CRTC introduce this change? In the mid-1990s, the financial situation of many commercial stations became so bleak that their survival was seriously threatened. Pressures for relaxation of ownership rules also mounted as consolidation along the lines of what was happening in the United States became the economically sensible thing to do. Balancing both cultural and economic objectives became a challenge the CRTC had to resolve. Although by definition never perfect, the regulation that the CRTC tabled was perceived as an acceptable compromise by most interested parties.

Not only does the CRTC now allow consolidation to occur, but in its desire to foster competition and choice for consumers, it has also abandoned the criteria that were traditionally applied in its commercial radio policy. This allows current radio station owners to solidify their financial situation, to attract much-needed new investment, and—of particular importance in this era of convergence—to compete more effectively with other media.

As in any negotiation, the softening of ownership issues involved some give and take on the part of the industry. The CRTC expected two key concessions: (1) that private radio stations raise the CanCon percentage from 30 to 35 percent; and (2) that the purchasers of profitable stations make a financial contribution equivalent to at least 6 percent of the value of the transaction to help support the development and visibility of Canadian music talent. The 6 percent contributions are to be distributed as follows:

(a)   2 percent to either FACTOR in English Canada or MusicAction in French, at the discretion of the purchaser, to support the record industry and artists;

(b) 3 percent to the newly created Radio Starmaker Fund and its French-language counterpart, Le Fonds RadioStar;

(c) 1 percent, at the discretion of the purchaser, to either (a) or (b) above or to any other eligible third party directly involved in the development of Canadian musical and artistic talent.

The CRTC's new policy is intended to encourage a closer collaboration between the radio and music industries. It would indeed be irresponsible for any national policy regulator to tolerate a situation in which one party focuses strictly on ratings, while another tries to promote both the emergence and development of new talent.

Taken as a whole, the recent wave of mergers, acquisitions, and consolidations among private radio stations represents transactions worth roughly half a billion dollars, with roughly $85 million in the French-language market and $400 million in the English-language market. The changes to the ownership rules will also result in an injection of approximately $26 million into the radio broadcasting system with initiatives such as Le Fonds RadioStar and the Radio Starmaker Fund getting the lion's share or 48 percent of that amount, FACTOR and MusicAction receiving a third, and various discretionary projects receiving the remaining 20 percent.

The Canadian radio industry comprises well over 500 stations. As with most other media and telecommunications sectors nowadays, the total number and ownership of these stations is subject to change as key players regularly revisit their strategic priorities, partnerships, and posture. We can nevertheless identify the top five groups that, in spring 2001, dominated the radio business. CBC/Radio-Canada possesses a combined network of 74 stations across the country. Standard Broadcasting Corp. Ltd., with 73 stations from Montreal to Vancouver, is the single largest private radio group. Corus Entertainment Inc. (a division of Shaw Communications Inc.) possesses 49 stations. Rogers and Astral Radio Group each own 31 stations and CHUM owns 28. Until Spring 2001, Telemedia Corporation, with 81 stations, had been Canada's largest radio station owner. However, in two blockbuster deals, Astral Media acquired 19 Telemedia stations in Quebec, New Brunswick, and Nova Scotia, while Standard Broadcasting Corp. Ltd. acquired some 60 Telemedia stations in Ontario and Western Canada.

The province with the largest number of commercial stations is Ontario (76), followed by British Columbia (39), Alberta (32), Quebec (28), Nova Scotia (8), New Brunswick (6), and Manitoba (6). (The station ownership situation remains fluid because of ongoing transactions and an unstable marketplace.) Following many years of losses in the 1990s, the collective revenues of private radio broadcasters surpassed $1 billion for the first time in 2000, up 5 percent from 1999. Much of the gain was attributable to FM stations, which experienced overall revenue growth of 8 percent. Only New Brunswick, Quebec, Manitoba, and British Columbia grew at a rate below the national average (Statistics Canada, 2001).

THE ADVENT OF RADIO-ON-DEMAND

Like most other industrialized countries, Canada has recently witnessed an explosive growth of Internet usage and streaming audio. In this context, it may seem paradoxical that the CRTC elected in June 1999 not to regulate any Internet activities. The CRTC was concerned that any attempt to control Canadian new media might jeopardize Canada's competitive advantage in the global marketplace. In its view, new media in general, and the Internet in particular, are to be seen as a novel means to distribute Canadian content and, as such, constitute a valid complement to the Canadian broadcasting system.

However, the "customizing" of content on the Internet runs counter to the fundamental definition of broadcasting as the transmission of programs to the general public. New media radically transform the notion of what an audience is and how it should behave. Since 1997, Canadians have had the option of subscribing to digital audio services either through satellite, cable, or MMDS (multipoint microwave distribution system). These pay services offer some 30 commercial-free, uninterrupted, no-talk channels of music that cover a range of styles including rock, urban, contemporary, jazz, classical, nostalgia, and various niche genres that receive only limited airplay on conventional channels.[5]

Some 2.5 million homes pay to receive this type of multi-format audio service. Despite this substantial subscriber base, most radio operators see digital pay services as competing directly with the CD or audiocassette player, not local radio. The confidence of radio operators in the power of traditional radio may not be entirely misplaced, but what will happen when people discover the added value of getting their favourite music in a streamlined, seamless fashion? Might they then do to radio what they have already done to traditional television by turning to specialized channels? Already, 52 percent of pay audio subscribers listen to their pay channel at least once a week, a figure higher than that relating to many TV specialty services (Hyatt, 2001). The main limitation on mass adoption of pay audio services appears to be the fact that they are still fixed appliances (i.e., they plug into a home television or stereo and are therefore nonportable). And portable radio, whether it be in the car or a Walkman, is still a strongly ingrained listening environment that is not about to change.

Another much-heralded technology that may affect the status of radio is digital audio broadcasting (DAB). DAB is a digital radio system that operates on a new frequency—the L-Band—and that includes AM and FM services. Both AM and FM will continue to be offered alongside the new digital services for at least a decade or so, at which point they will be gradually phased out. DAB offers CD-quality sound, interference-free reception, program-associated data, graphics and text (including lyrics) either at home or in the car. A display window or screen attached to the receiver provides users with dynamic labels describing the artists, song title, serial number of the album, and so on. Traffic and news briefs scroll in a text format while listeners enjoy their music. As DAB matures, services such as maps, visual traffic reports, pictures, and real-time stock market information will be made available in both free and subscription formats. Furthermore, as they drive across Canada, listeners will be able to stay tuned to the same station with no signal fade and without changing frequency.

Already launched in Toronto (18 private and 4 CBC services), Montreal (8 private and 4 CBC stations), Windsor (4 private and 2 CBC services), and Vancouver (11 private and 4 CBC services), DAB currently reaches about 35 percent of the Canadian population. At the same time, DAB is an innovation that has generated far more sceptics than supporters. Although there are some 250 million people around the world capable of receiving over 400 DAB services, the technology faces a major roadblock: in order to enjoy the benefits of DAB, listeners must purchase a special receiver. The price tag, in the $1000 range, predictably prevents DAB from quickly reaching a critical mass of users. In order to accelerate the release of affordable receivers, the WorldDAB association is pledging a $100-million global radio ad campaign to give DAB receiver manufacturers free airtime in exchange for dropping the price to a more palatable level. Until DAB enters the car market, its prospects remain uncertain. General Motors of Canada is reported to be working with DAB receiver manufacturers to develop a model that would be put in GM vehicles. The fact that no date has been set for the release of GM's DAB-equipped models has done little to quell scepticism toward the new technology.

Of all the new technologies, none has had a greater impact on conventional radio than the Internet. By the end of 2001, home Internet connections are expected to be as common as cable television, a take-up rate in the neighbourhood of 80 percent of Canadian homes (POLLARA, 2001). Since 1999, the growth curve of Internet usage, and of streaming media in particular, has been nothing short of explosive. The future looks even brighter when one considers that the adoption of broadband typically provokes a significant surge in both time spent on-line and with streaming media.

Clearly, Internet users develop habits, preferences, and expectations toward on-line content that are significantly different from the ones they manifest vis-à-vis traditional media. The "my content when I want it" mantra is creating a mindset that many conventional media are forced to catch up to. The interactive, multi-task, free-time-rich Generation Y is discovering the virtue of being its own music and entertainment programmer and even its own webcaster. Within this context, media content becomes dissociated from its traditional mode of distribution. As a result, niche content takes on a much larger role in the media diet of Internet users. With streaming audio, MP3 players, peer-to-peer file transfers (e.g., Napster, DG2fx, Gnutella), our former mass-media consumption becomes characterized by a behavioural triad that is based on (1) asynchronous listening (i.e., "I" pick the time that best suits me to listen to any given music selection or program element), (2) personalization of content, and (3) the mobility of my surrounding when I choose to consume, which is brought about by such technologies as MP3 players, personal digital assistants, portable PCs, digital cameras, and DVDs.

A spring 2001 study indicated that "streamies"—those who watch or listen to webcasts on-line—represent 44 percent of all Internet users and 27 percent of the general American population overall, a figure likely to be even higher as you read this chapter (Arbitron/Edison, 2001). The same study reveals that the most regularly listened-to Internet ratio stations are "over-the-air" stations with strong core audiences. It would appear that the more one appreciates a station off-line, the more likely one is to be a faithful listener on-line, and vice versa. Interestingly, it is precisely this finding that resonates with those who advocate free sharing of music over the Web. They argue that free access to music on the Net, far from cannibalizing CD sales, actually promotes them. Much like free play on radio and TV, music specialty channels help drive the market. In a May 2000 survey of some 3000 on-line users, 75 percent reported buying about the same number of CDs since they began listening to music on-line, 12 percent reported buying more CDs, and 13 percent said they had bought fewer (Forrester, 2000).

Regardless of the true impact of free or pay music distribution over the Internet, there is no question that the many legal sagas unfolding in the courts over peer-to-peer file sharing will modify the way in which music is distributed in the years to come. The proposed or existing joint ventures involving media heavyweights, such as AOL and Time Warner, Bertelsmann AG and the EMI Group or Yahoo, and Vivendi Universal and Sony Music Entertainment, signal the imminent launch of personalized playlists over the Internet. Broadband connection has all the ingredients to form the basis of a new product format in the commercial music and entertainment industry. Digital music providers can now combine technology and content around their core library of songs. Over the next five years, the volume of music transfers and sales over the Internet is expected to grow at unprecedented rates.

The popularity of music on the Internet becomes more obvious when compared with all other on-line activities. Following e-mail (83 percent) and chatting on-line (26 percent), 23 percent of respondents identify listening to and downloading music from the Internet as their third most frequent on-line activity (POLLARA, 2001). The salience of radio and/or audio-related activity on-line is further illustrated by another finding: 34 percent of those surveyed plan to spend more time listening to radio over the next 12 months, while 30 percent expect to increase their use of the Internet (only 20 percent anticipate heavier consumption of television) (Arbitron/Edison, 2001).

If Internet audio providers are to continue webcasting their musical content, they will have to find a way to get credit for their efforts. Indeed, more than three out of four people who have listened to audio on-line could not name even one audio provider. This brings to the fore the critical issue of brand recognition. Like their conventional radio counterparts, Internet audio providers must find revenue-generating strategies in order to remain in business. Audio providers are unlikely to attract advertising dollars if their listeners do not pay any attention to where their favourite music is coming from.

THE FUTURE OF RADIO

One would be hard-pressed to describe what tomorrow's radio will be. In spite of all the recent technological advancements that have modified many aspects of our relationship with audio content, the fact remains that traditional radio listening still outweighs Internet audio listening by a ratio of ten to one (Forrester, 2000). Rather than replacing radio, new technologies seem to be acting more like "enrichers" of the audio experience, allowing for a host of personalized, customized activities that solidify the relationship users have established over the years.

In an era marked by technological euphoria and uncertainty over the future, it is radio's ability to connect with the listener that sets it apart from more flamboyant electronic media. Although radio is a medium that is undeniably dominated by music, it cannot be reduced to the sole function of music provider. Radio is the grandfather of virtual space as it has always existed in that "unseen" dimension. Radio is a meeting place where we gather to find out what happened in our village today. Radio is the medium of speech, a place where words flow and generate a sea of images. Radio is a voice speaking to us as a special person who deserves to be told meaningful stories and to hear beautiful music. It is a place where public debates are held, where people sing, where emotions run high.

Specialized audio channels, which will undoubtedly proliferate on the Internet, present a formidable challenge to traditional radio stations as more and more "streamies" discover the advantages of customized playlists that can be accessed anywhere, anytime. However, despite their initial appeal, those 5000-odd self-service on-line stations[6] offer a product that is radically different from what one generally finds on any traditional station. Internet radio, for all it has to offer, is a predominantly utilitarian and highly fragmenting medium. This is mainly due to the absence of any human voice in its mode of presentation. Internet audio services offer sterilized, compartmentalized, dehumanized, and largely soulless content—in short, the epitome of a mechanized cultural industry.

Audio content today, whether distributed via traditional radio stations or Internet niche services, is akin to a huge archipelago—a collection of some one thousand islands, open to all and each with its own idiosyncrasies. On most of those little gems in the middle of this beautiful ocean, people can party late at night, go to fiestas, ride their Sea-Doos and motorcycles and yachts, and play upbeat music all day. Conversely, a tiny minority of those islands is protected, and a totally different code of conduct is enforced. There people elect to spend some quiet time, reading their books and magazines, sailboarding, snorkelling, and bicycling. Not that these islands are any better; they just cater to different needs.

What this metaphor attempts to convey is both the disparity and the complementarity that exist between commercial and Internet audio services, which draw the bulk of audio listeners, and the objectives and priorities of public-service radio, which, free from market imperatives, focuses on being a distinct and innovative radio service resolutely centred on furthering the notion of citizenry and the common good. If the wave of media mergers is to continue unabated, the need for an independent, impartial, unbiased public "infomediary" might be greater than ever. Public radio in Canada and the rest of the world may be one of the last lines of defence against the complete privatization of the collective imagination.

QUESTIONS

1. What is meant by CanCon and what are some of the arguments for and against it?
2. What is MAPL?
3. "CBC Radio plays an important role in solidifying Canadian identity." Discuss.
4. Should the amount of Canadian music played on radio be linked to the sales of Canadian music?
5. Is the success of radio bound up with the intimacy of the human voice or is it the result of some other factor(s)?
6. In what ways should we be worried about transformations in the way radio is delivered and consumed?

WEB SITES

Canadian Music Week: **http://www.cmw.net/**
Canadian Recording Industry Association: **http://www.cria.ca/**
CBC: **http://www.cbc.ca/**
Digital audio broadcasting: **http://www.digitalradio.ca/** *and*
    http://www.worlddab.org/dab/
Canadian Association of Broadcasters: **http://www.cab-acr.ca/**
Radio Starmaker Fund: **http://www.radiostarmakerfund.com/**
Society of Composers, Authors and Music Publishers of Canada:
    http://www.socan.ca/
Web radio: **http://www.120seconds.com** *and* **http://newmusiccanada.com/**

NOTES

1. The author wishes to acknowledge the dedicated assistance provided by Philippe Andrecheck during the research phases of this chapter.
2. Graham Spry (1900–1983) was a journalist, diplomat, and activist who campaigned tirelessly on behalf of public broadcasting in Canada. In 1930, he cofounded the Canadian Radio League, which was instrumental in orchestrating public support for national broadcasting.

3.   Prior to the spring of 1998, the requirement stood at 30 percent.
4.   The Juno Awards ceremony, originally called the Gold Leaf Awards, is the Canadian equivalent of the American Grammy Awards. The Junos were named in honour of CRTC chairman Pierre Juneau, who in 1971 decreed the first CanCon quota (set then at 20 percent). The name was changed to "Juno" when it was discovered that this was also the name of the Chief Goddess of the Roman Pantheon (visit http://www.juno-awards.ca).
5.   Due to a regulatory quirk at the time operating licences were granted, subscribers to Bell ExpressVu satellite service and Vidéotron cable service receive only Galaxie, CBC's continuous music network. However, subscribers to StarChoice satellite service and Rogers, Shaw, and Cogeco cable services receive Galaxie as well as DMX Music, a division of Corus Entertainment Inc.
6.   An extensive list of on-line channels (including a good sample of Canadian channels) can be found at http://www.kickinthehead.com.

REFERENCES

Arbitron/Edison Media Research. (2001). *Internet VI: Streaming at a Crossroads.* Retrieved from http://www.edisonresearch.com/Internetvisum.htm

Bohn, Patrick. (2000, October 16). Radio, radio. *Marketing Magazine*, 50.

CRTC (Canadian Radio-television and Telecommunications Commission). (2001). *Fact sheet: Canadian content on radio and on TV.* Retrieved from http://www.crtc.gc.ca/Eng/INFO-SHT/G11.HTM

Everett-Green, Robert. (2001, March 1). Why Nelly became a radio star. *Globe and Mail*, p. R1.

Forrester Research Inc. (2000, May). The self-serve audio revolution. Retrieved from http://www.forrester.com/

Hyatt, Laurel. (2001, February 1). *The digital dance.* Retrieved from http://www.broadcastermagazine.com/issues/2001/Feb01/page16.asp

Nash, Knowlton. (1995). *Microphone wars: A history of triumph and betrayal at the CBC.* Toronto: McClelland and Stewart.

POLLARA Inc. (2001). *New media perspectives: Connected Canadians—What they think, what they do.* Retrieved from http://www.pollara.com/

Statistics Canada (2001, August). *Broadcasting and telecommunications bulletin, 31(2).* Document No. 56-001-XIE.

10

Canadian Film

Gary Evans
University of Ottawa

THE EARLY YEARS: 1896–1914

On June 28, 1896, film arrived in Canada. The venue was a former shooting gallery in Montreal, and the program was from France: the Lumière brothers' extraordinary moving pictures of workers leaving their factory, along with a series of "actualities" that lasted less than a minute each. Viewers paid five cents of a typical dollar-a-day pay to see them. In July, Ottawa audiences shared a similar experience when they saw Thomas Edison's 30-second Vitascope film, *The Kiss*, and several actualities. Until television arrived after World War II, movies as entertainment and education enjoyed the prestige of being the century's most popular cultural attraction.

As in the United States, entrepreneurs built permanent theatres called nickelodeons in major Canadian cities and charged five cents a ticket. Most films in these early years originated in the United States, Britain, or France, and a show usually consisted of a group of ten one- to five-minute spectacles of actuality footage—horses pulling firewagons, the visit of royalty, the departure of soldiers to the Boer War, brief items of comedy or drama. In Montreal in 1906, Ernest Ouimet built the opulent 1200-seat Ouimetoscope to attract a more refined paying audience, but he was unable to compete with the cheaper nickelodeons that the lower classes could afford.

Film could also be used to lure prospective immigrants to Canada. In 1898, the Canadian Pacific Railway (CPR) hired James S. Freer to tour Britain to show realistic films of life in his Canadian west. In 1902–03, the CPR engaged Charles Urban's Bioscope Company of Canada to shoot promotional films for a series called *Living Canada*. These "scenics" were set against a backdrop of beckoning Canadian landscape and the promise of opportunity. The Grand Trunk Railway tried its hand at Canadian promotional films too, as did other American producers. Their first film commercials promoted lumbering, fishing, mining, and agricultural machinery.

What was obvious about the new medium was its great potential for narrative. Edwin S. Porter's *The Great Train Robbery* (1905) became the archetypal action film (the term "western" entered the vernacular years later), and it was not long before American producers were shooting melodramatic story films in Canada. These films became the mainstay of what was later called Hollywood's Canada, and did much to give the world an incorrect impression of Canadians. Ironically, Canadian talent hardly ever contributed to this distortion. There was none to be found. The population was too small, and there was no substantial theatrical or music-hall tradition. When talents emerged, they almost always went south. This exodus helped block formation of an indigenous Canadian film industry. An American company filming Canadian stories on sets in Canada, or on location in the United States, became the pattern—a pattern that persists to this day, although a Canadian film industry (backed by government grants since the 1960s) tries to give Canadian stories a greater chance of actualization.

The main reason for the failure of a homegrown film industry was simple economics. In order to be financially successful, a film shot in Canada had to be exhibited in either Britain or the United States, where there was a large enough audience and the means of reaching it. Thus, foreign distributors became the rule. To be sure, there were occasional competent local productions, but their failure to find distribution abroad spelled box-office failure. For Canadians, the business end of films lay more in exhibition. Entrepreneurs like the Allen brothers opened movie theatres across Canada, featuring American, British, and European films, although the supply of films to be exhibited was usually controlled by foreign distributors who practised block booking.[1]

It is easy to assume that direct government involvement in film production might have averted this rather dismal beginning. In fact, Ottawa was interested in film, more from the actuality (later called documentary) perspective than the entertainment one. In 1902, the federal government supported CPR-funded films that were shown in Britain to promote immigration and trade, thereby balancing the veritable flood of largely American settlers pouring into Canada's "Last Best West." A few similar endeavours followed over the next decade as Ottawa funded "scenics" to attract tourists while also encouraging "industrials" to increase trade and commerce. Film advertisements praised Canadian farm implements and grain, as well as water resources. The entertainment film was left to the private sector and foreign distributors.

PROPAGANDA NEWSREELS: CANADA AT WAR (1914–1918)

Against the backdrop of World War I (1914–1918), Canada's first newsreel was the privately produced *Canadian Animated Weekly*, which featured troops training and some mock battles. For the next four years, the Allies allowed no cinematographers on the active European front, fearing that real images of war might discourage enlistment. There are virtually no filmed wartime battles, only re-creations and actuality images of post-battle craters, ruins, and trenches. In 1916, the flamboyant Canadian press baron, Max Aitken (later Lord Beaverbrook), became chair of Britain's War Office Cinematograph Committee and supervised the production of a flood of pro-Canada propaganda newsreels from the front. Regular newsreels started to appear in 1917. Three- to five-minute patriotic "trailers" became familiar propaganda items in Allied cinemas; produced by private companies for government, they urged civilians to save, plant, recycle, or enlist.

While there were plenty of skilled Canadian newsreel cinematographers, Ottawa preferred to hire experienced American firms such as Pathescope of Canada to make its commercial films. In 1918, the federal government centralized film work in order to avoid duplication and, where possible, to coordinate the work of provinces such as Ontario that were making tourist, immigration, and educational films. Hence, the Exhibits and Publicity Bureau was created, primarily to make 10- to 20-minute travelogues. Ben Norrish became the architect of the Bureau's principal series, *Seeing Canada*, a biweekly film release catering to audiences at home and abroad. The titles released in the series' first year say it all: *Most Picturesque Spot in North America*, *Lake Louise*, *Wooden Shipbuilding in Canada*, *Harvest of the Sugar Maple Tree*, and *A Fish and Bear Tale*. Audiences grew accustomed to tourist films extolling Canadian scenic wonders, and to campy plays on words such as *Where the Moose Run Loose* and *Fishing Gamely for Game Fish*.

WHY NO CANADIAN FILM INDUSTRY?

In the 1920s, there was little chance to establish a viable commercial Canadian feature-film industry. After absorbing Canada's largest chain, Allen Theatres, Hollywood film mogul Adolph Zukor of Paramount Pictures won control of most first-run Canadian cinemas through Famous Players Canadian Corporation. American distributors First National and Fox were also beginning to dominate the industry, and as the majors moved closer to a vertical monopoly of production, distribution, and exhibition, the prospects of Canadian feature films obtaining foreign distribution dimmed.

A few businessmen-promoters like "ten-percent" Ernest Shipman (who took his percentage from the actors' salaries) had some success. He achieved authenticity by using location shooting for Canadian stories. In *Back to God's Country* (1920), his wife, Nell, became famous for posing nude behind a distant waterfall, a daring indiscretion (at the time) that helped the film earn a profit. Another Canadian company backed the 1928 feature film, *Carry On, Sergeant*, a World War I melodrama that fell flat and for years had the dubious distinction of being Canada's most expensive film failure. It found no foreign distribution because its seduction scene offended the British and because Hollywood had numerous look-alike projects. Canada was a bad place to invest in film: half the projects never materialized, or promoters robbed the till, or there was no distribution abroad.

If most Canadian-made productions never made the cut, three Americans shooting in Canada produced exceptional work. Robert Flaherty, Douglas Burden, and Varick Frissell found in Canada genuine stories that they parlayed into separate feature films. Ironically, each film served to confirm popular belief that Canada was a frozen wasteland, whose inhabitants, Native or white, spent much time struggling for food or pelts. Robert Flaherty became best known for his 1922 ethnographic documentary film *Nanook of the North*. Most of the "authenticity," from igloo building to walrus harpooning, was staged. (John Grierson introduced the word "documentary" in referring to the Flaherty style of revealing and dramatizing a people's culture.) In *The Silent Enemy*, a 1930 silent film set in Northern Ontario, Douglas Burden used 150 Native nonprofessionals to portray a 15th-century story of Ojibway Indians searching for caribou. In *The Viking* (1930), Varick Frissell accompanied Newfoundlanders on an annual seal hunt. The remarkable footage of heaving ice floes that he captured was far more interesting than the hopelessly trite love story Hollywood insisted on including in the film. Frissell and 25 crew members died in a shipboard explosion while shooting supplementary footage. Even though it had the distinction of being Canada's first sound feature, *The Viking* failed at the box office.

Other Americans manufactured Canadian "reality" in dozens of synthetic features shot in California. The favourite subject was the North-West Mounted Police, whose image of law and order provided a "good versus evil" story line combined with a "love versus duty" tension. This was Hollywood's Canada. However, while Ernest Shipman used authentic locations for his 1922 Mountie film, *Cameron of the Royal Mounted*, Hollywood managed to produce 23 similar films that same year and another 41 Mountie features by 1926. It is hardly surprising, then, that Canadians were unable to vault over the distribution barrier in the United States.

What Americans *were* willing to distribute theatrically were Canadian trade and tourism shorts. Ottawa's Exhibits and Publicity Bureau became the Canadian Government Motion Picture Bureau in April 1923, and its scenic travelogues became regular items on the American theatrical circuit. In 1927, sound came to film, but the Bureau failed to adopt the new technology until 1934 and lost its international theatrical market. From 1929 to 1934, the agency's films were exhibited on nontheatrical circuits. The Motion Picture Bureau failed to acknowledge the Depression, avoided industrial themes and the urban landscape, and depended too much on scenics; it quietly folded in 1941. A parallel body, the Ontario Government Motion Picture Bureau, began producing its own films from 1923 to 1934. Some uninspired titles tell all: *Someone at Home*, *Making Butter*, *A New Era of Agriculture*, and *Cinderella of the Farms*.

Lest this depressing overview seem too negative, government filmmaking did not always mean death by boredom. A remarkable cinematographer, Bill Oliver, worked for the National Parks Bureau and shot a series of conservation films. The titles sounded too cute (*Beaver Family*, *Beaver People*, *Strange Doings in Beaverland*, *Pilgrims of the Wild*, and *Grey Owl's Neighbours*), yet audiences could not miss Oliver's sincerity and sympathy for wildlife. His *Home of the Buffalo* (1930) remains a breathtaking observation of Canada's largest buffalo herd, at one point seen from a camera positioned in a pit as the stampeding herd thunders above. Sadly, Ottawa's Motion Picture Bureau dismissed these great pieces of cinematic art as "unprofessional."

FIGHTING HOLLYWOOD: THE BRITISH QUOTA AND A CANADIAN COURT CASE

In 1927, Britain's Parliament tried to stem the American tide by passing legislation calling for a sliding 5–20 percent British film quota. From 1928 to 1938, Hollywood entrepreneurs circumvented the law by sending British-born personnel to Canada to produce "British" films. Because Canada was part of the British quota, these American-produced "quota quickies" could be exported to Britain and thereby earn a profit. Depression-era Victoria, British Columbia, was grateful for the work, but Britain was peeved. Not surprisingly, when it renewed the Cinematograph Films Act in 1938, Britain excluded Canadian productions. The companies producing the quickies collapsed and the crews retreated south.

In 1930, the Government of Canada initiated a lawsuit intended to halt Hollywood's predatory and monopolistic activities. An investigation launched under the Combines Investigation Act resulted in a failure to convict Famous Players, most likely because the law was not specific or inclusive enough. (Nor was the legislation sufficient to successfully prosecute other industries whose operations were also deleterious to the national interest.[2]) Ottawa did not introduce legislation to close the loopholes. For Americans, Canada remained a land of opportunity. After the dust settled, eight Hollywood majors came to control film distribution so effectively that Canada was considered part of their "domestic" market, an attitude that persists to this day.

INTO CANADA'S FILM VOID: JOHN GRIERSON

The Canadian Government Motion Picture Bureau films, impersonal, silent, and inanimate, were obsolete on release. Depression or no, Canadian film needed a fix. Britain had slammed the door on "quota quickie" features, and it was universally understood that a tonic was needed. It was serendipitous that the British documentary movement's founder, John Grierson, who had been leading Britain's documentary film training centre, was available to help; in 1938, he was commissioned to survey the Dominion's film needs.

Grierson began his report with a simple truth: the Canadian Government Motion Picture Bureau suffered from a complacency that robbed it of dynamism. He recommended that Ottawa establish a central body to coordinate government film work. The government asked Grierson to establish a strong coordinating policy, so in March 1939 he helped draft the legislation that created the National Film Board (NFB). By the fall of 1939, World War II had begun and because no one in Canada had more experience, Grierson became first head or commissioner of the NFB. By the end of the war, the number of NFB employees had ballooned from 8 to 787.

THE NFB AT WAR: PROPAGANDA WAS NOT A FOUR-LETTER WORD

As commissioner, Grierson used propaganda to develop national unity and show the reality of a country at war. He persuaded Famous Players Canada to make its 800 commercial cinemas available nationally (and for free) to show NFB propaganda films. He also persuaded Louis de Rochemont, producer of the popular American screen journal series *The March of Time*, to undertake a joint production in Canada to be called *Canada at War*. In Grierson's view, propaganda was all about educating citizens to accept their "public duty" to contribute to and secure the democratic idea. His propaganda sharpened a sense of responsibility to the community at a time when many were flirting with totalitarian ideologies.

In 1941, Grierson amalgamated the Canadian Government Motion Picture Bureau with the NFB. The Bureau effectively ceased to exist, though its staff remained civil servants who worked under civil service rules of employment alongside the NFB's contract employees, who, as part of an evolving bureaucracy, had renewable short-term contracts. Grierson believed that a creative institution needs a revolving-door policy whereby artists are free to come and go, and he feared that a civil service mentality might develop. His fears were justified; by 1967, the NFB found itself crushed by overhead costs brought on, in part, by the unionization of Canada's public service.

Grierson also became head of the Wartime Information Board, a new government body responsible for print and radio information. He stayed until January 1944, overseeing what he called a gigantic ministry of education. His political masters approved, as the "Propaganda Maestro" reinforced a solidly liberal theme: after the war, there would be a brave new world of reconstruction that would lessen poverty and assure general prosperity.

Not surprisingly, given the history of film production in Canada, commercial film companies specialized in short films. Grierson commissioned a number of projects from Associated Screen News, Crawley Films, and other film companies across the country. While encouraging the private sector, he was also building a veritable film school at the National Film Board. There he established a cadre of talented young English Canadians, led by Tom Daly, who were taught by top documentary filmmakers like Raymond Spottiswoode, Stanley Hawes, Irving Jacoby, and Joris Ivens. Scotsman Norman McLaren, one of the century's geniuses of animation art, formed the first animation studio in 1941 and began training young Canadians, too.

It was widely recognized that film was the best way to reach the less literate and the young; the challenge was to explain why things were happening and what was likely to happen after the war. The confluence of visuals, music, and narration created a dynamic resonance. Many films used voice-over narration, often employing the services of actor Lorne Greene; his style was to enunciate an authoritative, crisp, concise English with a reassuring tone that provided viewers with consistency and a sense of hope.

At the same time, the Quebec filmmaking scene had been characterized by the domination of priests Albert Tessier and Maurice Proulx in the 1930s. Their documentary work had emphasized rural colonization and religion. Grierson was always sensitive to the fact that the NFB was also the ONF (l'Office national du film). Consequently, most films were dubbed into French. The first original French-language script, *Un du 22ième*, was shot in November 1940 as part of the *Canada Carries On* series. Nonetheless, Grierson and Quebec's clerical and political elite remained suspicious of each other.

A second theatrical series, *The World in Action*, began in April 1942. The series was internationalist, stressing national interdependency and the imminence of a better postwar world. Grierson believed that NFB propaganda complemented government policy, yet not everyone interpreted his efforts in the same way. *The World in Action* reached a larger market than *Canada Carries On*. Estimates run from as high as 30–40 million to as low as several million. When the films touched the controversial subject of the Soviet Union, U.S. and British distribution figures plunged. Films like *Inside Fighting Russia* (1942) and *Our Northern Neighbour* (1944) were careful to ignore political differences and never mentioned the word "communism," but they cost Grierson political friends nonetheless. Films on the USSR were political dynamite that would eventually explode in Grierson's face.

HOW FILM REACHED ACROSS CANADA

The 800 theatres Famous Players Canada made available to the NFB provided solid audiences, but it was harder to reach rural people. The NFB therefore expanded a pre-existing nontheatrical film circuit. Every month, a travelling projectionist equipped with 16mm equipment would visit 20 rural communities. (There were 85 of these circuits.) The projectionist would show a 70- to 90-minute program that typically consisted of a retired theatrical film, a short such as *Four New Apple Dishes for Homemakers* or *Wings of Youth* (about Canada's role in training fliers), and a sing-along animation by Norman McLaren (or perhaps a two-minute Hollywood-style musical encouraging female enlistment, such as *The Proudest Girl in the World*). The English-language offerings attracted an audience of about one-half million each month, while the French-language versions drew some 133,000 viewers.

Further reinforcement came from creation of a system of industrial film circuits and the series *Front Line Reports*, whereby workers at lunch or between shifts saw informational films. To complement these, a system of trade union circuits was implemented in mid-1942. In addition, by 1944 there were NFB libraries and 20 other libraries across the country. The men in uniform also saw monthly newsreels; material shot by the Canadian Army Film Unit appeared in *Eyes Front*, *Canada Communiqué*, and *Pictorial Home Town News*—all short items that the NFB edited for the troops from retired theatrical releases. Besides the wartime propaganda, one might find NFB ethnographic films on Inuit and Native life, such as *Arctic Hunter* and

People of the Potlatch, or a short on cultural pluralism like *Peoples of Canada*. In sum, nontheatrical distribution linked rural and working-class Canada to global events, encouraged schoolchildren to think in national terms, and informed citizens in other countries that Canada and its diverse population were active partners in the war.

At war's end, Grierson wrote *A Film Policy for Canada*, in which he presented strategies for bringing Canadian theatrical shorts to American screens. He recommended that Hollywood make feature films in Canada and Canadians occasionally do the same in Hollywood. But Canada could not conjure features out of the local sky; a few references to Canada in Hollywood film scripts could not hurt tourism, Grierson suggested. Hollywood responded with the Canadian Cooperation Project (CCP)—a promise to film a few features in Canada annually, to insert references to Canada into scripts, and to encourage more distribution of tourist and NFB shorts in the United States. The CCP was ultimately ineffective.

POSTWAR TO THE 1950S: A NEW BEGINNING FOR THE NFB AND CBC

The industry problem emerging in the postwar world was twofold: (1) the independent Canadian film companies wanted more of the work that the NFB was doing (especially the sponsored films for government departments); and (2) some private companies were feeding the Conservative opposition negative information. Echoing the Cold War rhetoric coming from the United States, an anti-NFB campaign based on the spectre of communism began to gather steam. Although Grierson had resigned by 1946, he was tainted by the Gouzenko spy scandal: a secretary he had once employed had been named in evidence presented to the Royal Commission on Espionage in Government Service.

The NFB's mandate was eventually revised. Its new purpose was to produce and distribute films "in the national interest" and to make films "to interpret Canada to Canadians and to other nations," words that became the NFB's lifeline. In 1952, the Royal Commission on National Development in the Arts, Letters and Sciences, popularly known as the Massey Commission, helped even more. It pointed the federal government toward assuming a direct role in underwriting culture, thereby offering the NFB a new lease on life.

In 1952, television screens lit up in Canada. The Canadian Broadcasting Corporation/Radio-Canada intended to do most of its own film programming, without recourse to the NFB. With a tenfold increase in telecasts from 1952 to 1954, television was transforming Canada. Many at the NFB were hostile to the "bastard" medium, with its deadline pressures and demand for economy of statement. But the CBC needed to fill the vacuum, and the NFB eventually produced the *Window on Canada (Regards sur le Canada)* series, 26 weeks of half-hour films edited for television, followed by *On the Spot (Sur le vif)*, 26 weeks of 15-minute newsreel-style content. By 1957, half of the NFB's annual production of 68 original films was television-bound.

CANADIAN FEATURES A NONSTARTER; THEATRICAL SHORTS OKAY

English-Canadian feature films remained insignificant flotsam in an American sea. A few postwar productions like *Bush Pilot*, a one-hour mediocrity, and the crime thriller *Whispering City/La Forteresse* went virtually nowhere. The latter was notable for its astronomical $1-million budget, having been shot in English and French, with different actors. A typical French feature cost only $100,000, and if it had a famous name attached, such as Gratien Gélinas, who wrote and starred in *Tit-Coq* (1953), it might turn a small profit. Slowly, French-language features developed over the next two decades at Radio-Canada, at the NFB/ONF (after 1964), and eventually in the Quebec private sector.

The flops aside, many NFB theatrical shorts had panache. *Canada Carries On* (*En avant Canada*) and *Eye Witness* (*Coup d'oeil*) were highly polished items that, once retired, went to television. An NFB documentary, *Royal Journey*, was an unexpected blockbuster emerging from Princess Elizabeth's royal visit in 1951. The next year, animation genius Norman McLaren directed the Oscar-winning *Neighbours*, which became the most popular NFB film of all time. This experiment in pixilation animation is a moral parable of two neighbours who destroy each other in a squabble over a flower that grows on their property line. From the early 1950s, Canadian animation enjoyed worldwide renown.

Two of the very best NFB theatrical shorts were *Paul Tomkowicz: Street-Railway Switchman* (1953) and *Corral* (1954). The latter, a salute to the craft of horsemanship, is a wordless romantic portrait of a cowboy who rounds up wild horses and plunges into a glorious ride across the spectacular Rocky Mountain foothills. *Paul Tomkowicz* turns Winnipeg's night streets into an arena of near-fantasy as an immigrant streetcar tender plods through his inconsequential routine. The man's humorous commentary lifts the entire opus from potential existential bleakness to lyrical heights. Another theatrical short, *City of Gold* (1957), features animated historical photos taken during the famous 1900 Yukon gold rush.

The NFB also made highly polished children's films whose costliness generally placed them beyond the means of private industry. Almost five million children annually enjoyed these positive infusions of Canadian culture. Favourites included *Ti-Jean Goes Lumbering* (1953), the story of a boy with superhuman powers, and *One Little Indian* (1954), a puppet film about a boy who learns urban traffic safety rules. Other children's classics included *Teeth Are to Keep* (1949), *How to Build an Igloo* (1950), *The Longhouse People* (1951), *Age of the Beaver* (1952), *The Story of Peter and the Potter* (1953), *Angotee: Story of an Eskimo Boy* (1953), and *The Pony* (1955).

DIRECT CINEMA/CINÉMA VÉRITÉ AND CANDID EYE

In 1958, a small French production group, influenced by the "decisive moment" idea in the still photography of Henri Cartier-Bresson, began to experiment with new lightweight equipment in a style they called Candid Eye, which became known as cinéma vérité, or direct cinema, after 1963. Michel Brault and Gilles Groulx co-directed *Les Racquetteurs*, the seminal film of the new documentary style. Ostensibly about a snowshoe congress in Sherbrooke, Quebec, it was an ethnographic short capturing the immediacy of the common people. Television audiences loved Quebec humour, music, and dance, as spontaneous language was used to cultivate an aura of innocence. The filmmakers of the new équipe française used this genre from 1958 to 1964 in the television series *Temps présent*. Some key films of the series were *Normétal* (1959), *La Lutte* (1961), *A Saint-Henri le 5 septembre* (1962), *Les Bûcherons de la Manouane* (1962), *Jour après jour* (1962), *60 Cycles* (1965), and *Huit témoins* (1965). Another film in the series, *Pour la suite du monde* (1964), was notable for being Quebec's first feature documentary.

In English film, the most highly regarded expression of the Candid Eye approach is *Lonely Boy* (1961), a behind-the-scenes look at teenage pop star Paul Anka. The hand-held camera captured a number of spontaneously "candid," if innocent, moments. But the young crooner was fully in control of his image, unlike nonprofessionals who in other documentary films might inadvertently pillory themselves or allow themselves to be exploited.[3] The filmmakers generally agreed that it was unethical to steal the cinematic moment and run away. Critics have called this approach to documentary the "innocent eye" technique, but it was more than that. One notices in these films of moderate expectations qualities of compromise and self-effacement. Their lack of hypocrisy and pretence gives them a certain cultivated innocence.

During this period, Donald Brittain, who was not part of the NFB's Unit B, emerged as one documentary filmmaker who avoided cultivated innocence. He developed what some called the "golden hinge," an ability to use images and words to carry the viewer through time and space to enlightenment. He and John Spotton addressed the painful and difficult subject of the Holocaust in *Memorandum* (1965), a documentary that gives substance to Hannah Arendt's phrase "the banality of evil." The narration identifies perpetrators of genocide as those who "murdered by memorandum . . . filing and typing from nine to five, with an hour off for lunch." Brittain conveys the magnitude of the Nazis' crimes without using grisly photographs. He lets words paint the grim picture, as when a former teacher describes being forced to sort the clothes of victims—including his own class of Jewish children—prior to their gassing. As they enter the gas chamber, the man helplessly tries to comfort them with the words, "There's nothing to worry about." The viewer is left contemplating the grim fact that their last human refuge was hope, when there was no hope. Adding to the film's bitter irony is its coverage of a 1965 trial of Nazi criminals, most of whom were found not guilty due to lack of evidence.

FEATURES AT THE NFB/ONF

The NFB's first English-language feature, *Drylanders* (1963), a dust bowl drama about the opening of the Canadian West in 1900, was produced with close attention to the historical record. This film spurred many Quebec documentary filmmakers (and especially those who believed that cinéma vérité had exhausted itself stylistically) to make features. These years marked what has been called the "Quebec New Wave," a period dominated by four key auteurs—Claude Jutra, Gilles Groulx, Gilles Carle, and Jean-Pierre Lefebvre—who displayed personal vision and a commitment to the new Quebec. Jutra's feature *À tout prendre* (1963), a self-financed autobiographical love story, was a catalyst for the new era of cinema in that it was both intellectually stimulating and noncommercial. Yet it was NFB/ONF films, not those stemming from the private sector, that reflected cultural ferment in the 1960s.

Gilles Groulx's seminal film about the torment of restless teenagers, *Le Chat dans le sac* (1964), provoked a debate over Quebec's identity and aspirations. Gilles Carle's *La vie heureuse de Léopold Z* (1965) was a funny saga of a harried Montreal snowplow driver who satisfies everyone's impossible demands one snowy Christmas Eve. Jean-Pierre Lefebvre, who had made five low-budget features in the private sector, shot two features at the NFB in 1967–68. *Mon amie Pierrette* used a surrealist approach to tell the story of two adolescents who experience a generational battle at a parental country home. *Jusqu'au coeur*, stylistically similar to the films of Jean-Luc Godard and influenced by contemporary antiwar fever, dealt with the question of personal freedom versus societal demands and state power. The outstanding French-language feature of the era was the ONF's *Mon oncle Antoine* (1971) directed by Claude Jutra. In this original and brilliant tale of youth and innocence (some have called it the best film ever made in Canada), an adolescent boy sees the veil of childhood fall away as he confronts human frailty, sexuality, humour, depression, and death.

English production jumped on the features bandwagon when Donald Owen directed *Nobody Waved Goodbye* (1964). This film about the conflict between youth and middle-class parental authority dramatizes Oedipal rebellion rather than sociopolitical upheaval. The young protagonist falls into delinquency and crime and, having abandoned his pregnant girlfriend, finds himself walking aimlessly down the highway.

THE BIRTH OF THE CANADIAN FILM DEVELOPMENT CORPORATION

In 1967, spurred by private-sector lobbying and recommendations emanating from the NFB, the federal government established the Canadian Film Development Corporation (CFDC), a $10-million features fund on which the NFB itself could not draw. The plans was for the CFDC to vet scripts, provide production and distribution assistance, and loan up to half of a film's budget. A decade later, the "bank" aspect of the organization was undermined by the fact that the CFDC had been paid back only several hundred thousand dollars of the $10 million "loaned." On the other hand, the CFDC did underwrite a few stellar items, and Canadian-made features employed scriptwriters, actors, and crew. For example, the CFDC gave David Cronenberg seed money for his second feature, *Crimes of the Future* (1970), and launched his career by backing *Shivers* (1975). It later supported *Rabid* (1976), *Fast Company* (1979), *The Brood* (1979), *Scanners* (1980), and *Videodrome* (1982). Perhaps the best CFDC-supported English feature of this period was Don Shebib's *Goin' Down the Road* (1970), which told the story of two Maritimers who seek their fortunes in Toronto but end up broke, unemployed, and in trouble.

A number of Québécois directors also benefited from CFDC support during the 1970s. Between 1968 and 1974, the agency backed a dozen low-budget soft-core films (sometimes called "maple syrup porno"), most of which were directed by Denis Héroux and Claude Fournier. While such cash infusions did not result in film art, they did help create an infrastructure for a Canadian feature industry. Some of the better-known films and directors of the period include *Isabel, Act of the Heart, Journey* (Paul Almond, 1967, 1970 and 1971), *The Rowdyman* (Peter Carter, 1971), *Fortune and Men's Eyes* (Harvey Hart, 1971) *Wedding in White* (William Fruet, 1972), *Paperback Hero* (Peter Pearson, 1972), *U-Turn* (George Kaczender, 1972), *Réjeanne Padovani* (Denys Arcand, 1972), *Lies My Father Told Me* (Jan Kadar, 1972), *The Man Who Skied Down Everest* (Judith Crawley, 1973, an Oscar winner), *Bingo* (Jean-Claude Lord, 1973), *Les Ordres* (Michel Brault, 1974, winner of Grand Prize at Cannes Film Festival), *Skip Tracer* (Zale Dalen, 1976), *The Disappearance* (Stuart Cooper, 1977), *The Silent Partner* (Darryl Duke, 1977), *Murder by Decree* (Bob Clark, 1978), *La cuisine rouge* (Paule Baillargeon, 1979), and *Ticket to Heaven* (Ralph Thomas, 1980).

The English-language features were not spotlighted as being particularly Canadian since the object was to attract distributors and audiences in the United States. The results were indifferent. The CFDC also underwrote adaptations of well-known Canadian novels, including *Kamouraska* (1972), *The Apprenticeship of Duddy Kravitz* (1974), *Who Has Seen the Wind* (1976), *Why Shoot the Teacher?* (1976), *Jacob Two-Two Meets the Hooded Fang* (1976), *Two Solitudes* (1977), *In Praise of Older Women* (1977), *The Grey Fox* (1982), *Les Plouffe* (1981), *The Tin Flute* (1982), and *Joshua Then and Now* (1985). Yet because distributors devoted only 3 percent of annual screen time to Canadian productions, these films were more likely to earn cultural prestige than profits.

The CFDC's attempt to co-produce features with other countries led to mixed results. Such titles as *Full Circle, Leopard in the Snow, Blood and Guts, New York Blackout, Search and Destroy, Caro Papa, Death Ship, Haute Surveillance, Au Nom de tous les miens*, and *For Those I Loved* were quickly forgotten. Co-productions that had artistic merit included *Sweet Movie* (Dusan Makavejev, 1974), *The Disappearance* (Stuart Cooper, 1977), *Una Giornata Particolare/A Special Day* (Ettore Scola, 1977), *Les liens de sang* (Claude Chabrol, 1977), *Violette Nozière* (Claude Chabrol, 1977), *A Man Called Intrepid* (Peter Carter, 1978), *À Nous Deux* (Claude Lelouch, 1979), *Bear Island* (Don Sharp, 1979), *Middle Age Crazy* (John Trent, 1979), *Circle of Two* (Jules Dassin, 1979), *Fantastica* (Gilles Carle, 1979), *Atlantic City, U.S.A.* (Louis Malle, 1980), *Hotel New Hampshire* (Tony Richardson, 1983), *Louisiane* (Philippe de Broca, 1983), and *The Bay Boy* (Daniel Petrie, 1987). Two films that brought adolescent mayhem to the screen—*Meatballs* (Ivan Reitman, 1979) and *Porky's* (Bob Clark, 1981)—were commercial hits. *Porky's* was the largest-grossing Canadian film in history, and *Meatballs* gave Reitman his ticket to Hollywood.

In 1974, Ottawa introduced a capital cost allowance scheme whereby Canadian film investments could be used as a 100 percent tax shelter. The scheme encouraged a boom, but many unscrupulous investors profited from films that went unseen. (For some observers, the lesson of the CFDC years is that the government trough is a poor place to teach the unscrupulous to honour Canadian culture.) A decade later, chastened and much smarter, the CFDC introduced the Broadcast Fund, which included video and made-for-television programs in its mandate. It changed its name to Telefilm Canada in 1983 and tightened up its rules by making loans contingent on distribution guarantees. Still the principal agency behind Canadian commercial (theatrical and television) production, Telefilm has a respectable track record for television-bound material at home and abroad, generating considerable economic activity in the audiovisual sector of the economy. If Canadian television production is a relative success story, Canadian feature films remain largely unseen.

NFB/ONF: RELEVANCE?

While the CFDC was struggling to create a viable film industry from the 1960s, the NFB went through internal upheaval. The filmmakers, reflecting the open protest of the decade and the prominence of cinema auteurs, took over programming initiatives. They also followed Canada's civil servants and unionized; many in the private sector responded by calling them "pensionable anarchists," even though escalating salaries and fringe benefits were becoming commonplace throughout the public sector. To make matters worse, two 1967 co-productions with the CBC, *The Ernie Game* and *Waiting for Caroline*, were savaged by critics. Then, following the spending spree of the centennial celebrations in 1967, the CBC terminated its expensive contract with the NFB. From that point on, only 15–20 percent of NFB production would be television-bound. On the eve of its 30th birthday, the NFB found itself without an apparent mission.

The birthday was glum. Back in Canada after a 22-year absence, John Grierson opposed the whole idea of NFB features, which he felt were expensive pursuits of personal rather than national interests. He was intrigued, however, by Ottawa's recommendation that the NFB consider films exposing national poverty. The Challenge for Change/Société Nouvelle program emerged after the nationwide broadcast of *The Things I Cannot Change* (Tanya Ballantyne, 1966), a direct cinema exploration of an insolvent family's struggle with daily life. In 1967, eight federal departments formed a committee to generate film ideas with the NFB. The experiment, which continued until 1980, was dismissed by some as "government-sponsored subversion." Others called the effort a sham for perpetuating the myth that the forgotten elements of Canadian society could escape poverty by finding their own voices. Nonetheless, the program's spinoff served to justify the NFB's continued existence from the 1980s to the present. The NFB claims that it gives voice to minority groups and other specialized audiences; it also makes literary and intellectual film essays.

The desire to empower minority voices led to the creation of Studio D, a women's studio, in 1974, and its French counterpart, Studio B, in 1986. Both studios energetically imposed "integrative feminism" on a host of social issues. Among the most provocative NFB films that came from Studio D were *Not a Love Story* (1981), a journey through the world of pornography, and the Oscar-winning anti–nuclear war film *If You Love This Planet* (1982).

ACCLAIM AND LOSS OF MOMENTUM

On the English-language side, feature films did not flourish—perhaps because they were noncommercial or were poor competitors next to the private-sector features funded by the CFDC. Several features received short commercial runs, including *One Man* (1977), *Why Rock the Boat?* (1974), and *The Company of Strangers* (1988). A few others, such as *The King Chronicles* (1988), *Sitting in Limbo* (1986), and *The Boys of St. Vincent* (1993), found television outlets. Other NFB talents left for the private sector.

A number of Québécois artists sharpened their feature filmmaking skills at the ONF during this time. But there was also turmoil in the early 1970s as several Québécois directors produced political documentaries. Film Commissioner Sydney Newman was dogged by controversy around such films as *On est au coton* (1970), *24 heures ou plus* (1973), and *Québec, Duplessis et après* (1972). He suppressed the films in question in order, as he put it, "to protect the agency from itself." Many in French production railed against NFB censorship.

By the 1980s, some feared the NFB was careening toward oblivion. It was perceived both as a hotbed of separatists and as not producing enough to justify its $70-million annual budget. While it is true that NFB films won numerous Academy Awards,[4] stories of filmmakers being paid but having no resources to work were also true. The civil service nature of the organization had sealed its doom, yet Ottawa forbade layoffs, fearing that they would lend ammunition to the critics of federalism.

Some thought that the NFB should make more advocacy films as it had done through the Challenge for Change program. The NFB appeared to lose even more ground when, in 1982, the Applebaum-Hébert Committee urged Ottawa to support the private sector and the government responded by launching a new National Film and Video Policy the following year. NFB filmmaker Jacques Godbout predicted that the policy would guarantee cultural underdevelopment as Canadian talent assembled American-style television drama ("tv disco"). He was, however, swimming against a worldwide tide. After the free trade election of 1988, federal policy favouring the private sector intensified and public-sector spending dropped precipitously. The CBC/Radio-Canada and the NFB endured severe funding and job cuts; they survived, but only as shadows of their once-corpulent selves.

During the 1990s, Telefilm Canada became the major governmental player in the production of film and video. After creating the Canadian Television Fund in 1996, it supported more than 1500 productions in its first four years. Telefilm's efforts have had a cultural benefit in that two-thirds of its budget went to original drama programs featuring Canadian themes and contexts; nearly half of these programs were destined for CBC/Radio-Canada. Made-for-television Canadian products seem to fall into one of two camps: they have little or no Canadian flavour (especially if destined for export); or they are very Canadian in content, and reach limited Canadian and American audiences.

As for theatrical features, by 2000 Telefilm's Feature Film Fund hovered around $16 million annually, with additional help being given to Canadian producers though the Production Sharing Revenue Program. Yet the old distribution inequities remain, and few taxpayers ever see the films in cinemas. Statistics explain why: with Telefilm loans, a typical Canadian feature costs around $3 million; a typical American company shooting in Canada has a budget of $26 million. Production in Canada has been good for business, as Canadian crews work (for less) on largely American projects, to the tune of a yearly average of nearly $1 billion generated per province; thus, it is argued, globalization has been good for the feature-film business. There may be a small silver lining. A few directors who persevere and are lucky and brilliant enough may establish themselves internationally, as did David Cronenberg, Atom Egoyan, Denys Arcand, Don McKellar, and Bruce Macdonald.

THE FUTURE: A GLASS HALF EMPTY OR HALF FULL?

To summarize the last two decades, Canada has done much to help its filmmakers through Telefilm support of private-sector filmmaking. As for the long-range cultural impact of Canadian features, the old distribution and economic problems remain. Home audiences are too small to support the significant investment that features require, and distribution into the United States is rare. Even with U.S. distribution, there are difficulties. There are cases in which U.S. distributors pocketed millions and promptly declared bankruptcy. Or consider the fate of *Decline of the American Empire* (1986). Denys Arcand's biting satire won a prize at Cannes and was nominated for an Oscar. Hollywood bought the rights to make an English-language version of the film—and then promptly forgot about it. In addition, while directors such as Patricia Rozema (*I Heard the Mermaids Singing*, 1987), David Wellington (*I Love a Man in a Uniform*, 1993, *Long Day's Journey Into Night*, 1995), Mort Ransen (*Margaret's Museum*, 1996) and François Girard (*32 Short Films About Glenn Gould*, 1993, *The Red Violin*, 1998) may make their mark in Canada, they also remain largely unknown to the American public.

There may be room for optimism on the grounds that computer-based technologies are promising to change and widen distribution options. Rather than the commercial theatres to which Hollywood distributors still dictate, the 500-channel television universe and personal computer monitors might be the source of future audiences. The question to be asked in the new millennium is not "Will there be a Canadian feature industry?" Rather, it is "Will Canadian and Quebec stories find a niche in the new world of homogenized film and video culture?"

Film and television production in Canada makes good economic sense. In 2000, some $4.4 billion worth of film and video was shot. While $1.5 billion of that amount came from foreign companies shooting in Canada, two-thirds of the activity occurred in Ontario and Quebec—due in no small part to the existence of federal and provincial tax credits, co-production treaties, and funding from Telefilm Canada and the Canadian Television Fund. Thus, the financial side looks bright even if most in the industry would admit that most Canadian programs make good cultural sense and little commercial profit. There are plans afoot by the new owner of CTV, Bell Canada Enterprises, to underwrite an independent production fund for mid-range programming that currently comes from the United States, and to replace that programming with Canadian product. Will the Canadian public support such programs, and will markets in the global economy be willing to buy them?

In short, if the industrial base seems secure, the optimist might argue that Canada's is a multibillion-dollar annual industry that is part of a worldwide audio-visual market. Yet, one is left to ponder whether there will be resources and artists available to make films that articulate Canada's authentic national interest. Instead of propagating unbridled consumerism and trash television, will there be visual media to promote Canadian traditions of tolerance, progressivism, and humanism? Once this was the function of the National Film Board, whose work stands in opposition to the alienating forces of consumerism that dominate film culture. But the NFB/ONF today is just one among many bodies producing film and video images, and the audience for its documentary and artistic records of Canadian life is painfully small. Could the global economy end up being the Trojan horse that obliterates a century of Canadian national imagery?

QUESTIONS

1. How do recent Hollywood movies depict Canada?
2. Hollywood succeeds by making blockbuster films that attract huge audiences. Given Canada's small population relative to that of the United States, should Canadian films be supported through various forms of government intervention?
3. Does it matter if Canadians make their films in Hollywood rather than in Canada? Give reasons for your answer.

4. In what ways has globalization affected Canadian film and filmmakers?
5. Why is it difficult for Canadians films to find an audience? What are the best ways to overcome the difficulties?
6. Are there genuinely national character traits that different film industries can capture and convey to audiences? Give reasons for your answer. If you think such traits do exist, what would they be for Canada? For the United States? For another country?

WEB SITES

Alliance Atlantis Motion Picture Production Group:
   http://www.allianceatlantis.com/MotionPictures/index.html
Canadian Film Centre: **http://cdnfilmcentre.com/index1.html**
National Film Board of Canada: **http://www.nfb.ca/**
Telefilm Canada: **http://www.telefilm.gc.ca/**

NOTES

1. Block booking is the practice of requiring theatre owners to reserve in advance an entire slate of films, usually sight unseen. One of those films will be a major success, but in order to acquire it the exhibitor must agree to take all the films of the slate, most of which will not be successes.
2. See Peter White, *Investigation into an Alleged Combine in the Motion Picture Industry in Canada* (Ottawa: King's Printer, 1931). See also Peter Morris, *Embattled Shadows: A History of Canadian Cinema, 1895–1939* (Montreal: McGill-Queen's University Press, 1978, chap. 6).
3. See Peter Harcourt, "The Innocent Eye," *Sight and Sound, 34*(1), Winter 1964–65; reprinted in Seth Feldman and Joyce Nelson (Eds.), *Canadian Film Reader* (Toronto: Peter Martin, 1977).
4. For example, the Oscars for best documentary short went to *I'll Find a Way* (1977) and *Flamenco at 5:15* (1983). Oscars for animation were won by *The Sand Castle/Le Château de sable* (1977), *Special Delivery* (1978), and *Every Child* (1980).

SELECTED BIBLIOGRAPHY

Berton, Pierre. (1974). *Hollywood's Canada: The Americanization of our national image*. Toronto: McClelland and Stewart.
Canadian Heritage. (1998). *A review of Canadian feature film policy*. Ottawa: Department of Canadian Heritage.
Clandfield, David. (1987). *Canadian film*. Toronto: Oxford University.

Evans, Gary. (1991). *In the national interest: A chronicle of the National Film Board of Canada from 1949 to 1989*. Toronto: University of Toronto Press.

Evans, Gary. (1984). *John Grierson and the National Film Board: The politics of wartime propaganda*. Toronto: University of Toronto Press.

Fetherling, Douglas. (1988). *Documents in Canadian film*. Peterborough, ON: Broadview Press.

Knelman, Martin. (1977). *This is where we came in: The career and character of Canadian film*. Toronto: McClelland and Stewart.

Marsolais, Gilles. (1968). *Le cinéma canadien*. Montreal: Editions du jour.

Morris, Peter. (1978). *Embattled shadows: A history of Canadian Cinema, 1895–1939*. Montreal: McGill-Queen's University Press.

———. (1984). *The film companion*. Toronto: Irwin.

National Film Board of Canada. (1991). *NFB film guide: The productions of the National Film Board of Canada from 1939 to 1989 / Le répertoire des films de l'ONF de 1939 à 1989*. Montreal: National Film Board.

Pendakur, Manjunath. (1990). *Canadian dreams and American control: The political economy of the Canadian film industry*. Toronto: Garamond Press.

Turner, D. John. (1987). *Canadian feature film index, 1913–1985*. Ottawa: Public Archives Canada, National Film, Television and Sound Archives.

Veronneau, Pierre, and Piers Handling (Eds.). (1980). *Self-Portrait: Essays on the Canadian and Quebec cinemas*. Ottawa: Canadian Film Institute.

11

A Brief History of the Recording Industry

Don Wallace[1]
Carleton University

INTRODUCTION

In December 1999, several record companies with the backing of the Recording Industry Association of American (RIAA) filed suit against a relatively small Web company called Napster. The plaintiffs claimed that the exchange of music between Napster's users constituted copyright infringement; that is, Napster and its clients were using music without paying for it. The dispute is complex, but in very important ways it is a replay of another confrontation over copyright almost a century earlier. In fact, many of the issues that were central to the music industry even before the advent of recorded sound have remained central after almost a century of technological change and global expansion. This chapter will present a brief history of the music industry with reference to three of the most important of these issues: technological innovation and its control; control of intellectual property and copyright; and growth within and between cultural industries.

TECHNOLOGY

Technological innovation within the music industry has not been directed simply toward the improvement of sound quality, nor were the changes that did emerge somehow inevitable. On the contrary, most technological change that has occurred since the arrival of recorded sound has been concerned primarily with the commodification of music,[2] and with control over the manufacturing and distribution of music commodities. Furthermore, technological innovation was (and remains) a source of conflict as different interests sought to control technology as a means of gaining competitive advantage in the consumer marketplace. Finally, a great deal of technological innovation in all of the cultural industries has been linked to the rise of a consumer culture and thus is inextricably linked to the idea of individualized consumption.

INTELLECTUAL PROPERTY

In the music industry, "intellectual property" refers to a song's actual words and music, not to physical recordings of the song (e.g., in CD or tape format). A song can be recorded by a variety of artists, but in each case the owner of the song (usually the composer or record company) receives payment (royalties). While recording artists receive income from the sale of records and from live performances, the single most important source of revenue within the recording industry comes from *copyright*, which is the ownership and control of the intellectual property. Control over copyright and the establishment of related rights was crucial to the formation and development of the music industry and, as demonstrated by the Napster dispute, it continues to be a central issue.

MUSIC AND OTHER CULTURAL INDUSTRIES

Throughout the history of the cultural industries, firms have sought to expand markets and control different sectors through mergers, alliances, and so on, and music corporations have been key elements in this process. The music industry is one of the oldest of the modern cultural industries, predating radio, film, and television. It is also one of the most extensive cultural industries in that it is implicated in almost all other entertainment media. Both live and recorded music were an essential part of radio since the first commercial broadcasts, and music is at the centre of most modern radio programming. Film and later television were equally crucial to the establishment of broad audiences for many popular singers. More recently, the Internet is emerging as a significant medium for the promotion and distribution of music products. For these reasons, it is virtually impossible to understand the music industry in isolation from the broader context of other media and other forms of cultural production in general.

THE MUSIC INDUSTRY BEFORE RECORDED SOUND

In the late 19th and early 20th centuries, before the advent of modern recording and broadcast technologies, there was already an extensive music industry in North America. The principal commodity of this industry was printed sheet music. Unlike modern recordings, sheet music was used in private live performance. One would sing the song, usually accompanied on the piano—as essential an item in many middle-class homes as is the sound system or television of today.

Although commercially produced songs had been widely popular in Europe and North America for at least a century, the music industry in the United States experienced a period of extremely rapid growth in the late 19th century. There were two primary reasons for this. First, there was an increasing concentration of population in urban centres, which allowed for the development of mass markets for a wide range of new consumer goods such as household appliances, cooking and cleaning products, patent medicines, and entertainments (including sheet music). Second, a growing percentage of the population enjoyed greater disposable income in combination with more leisure time; together, these could be devoted to entertainment commodities such as music.

By the end of the 19th century, the music publishing business in North America was increasingly concentrated in New York City, particularly around West 28th Street between Fifth Avenue and Broadway. This area, as well as the industry itself and the style of music that it produced, became known as "Tin Pan Alley."[3] Tin Pan Alley relied almost exclusively on live performance to promote its product, and the most important venue was a type of theatre known as "vaudeville," which featured a variety of acts such as jugglers, comedians, and singers. Vaudeville and Tin Pan Alley were very much dependent on each other. Vaudeville singers relied on songwriters to supply them with new material, and Tin Pan Alley required the extensive vaudeville theatre chains to popularize its music in an expanding entertainment market. Although vaudeville was the most important form of family entertainment in the early 20th century, with the rise of radio and particularly film, it went into decline and by the mid-1920s had virtually disappeared.

THE ADVENT OF RECORDED SOUND

The most significant single change in the early music industry was in the principal commodity—the transition from printed to recorded music. The invention of a means of recording sound was not only a significant technological development in an age of many such developments (electric light, motor cars, telegraph, telephone, motion pictures), but like these others, it heralded profound social change. In terms of music, recording separated an individual performance from an audience in space and time, allowing it to be commodified and reproduced for private listening. It also opened enormous potential for social exchange between groups, regions, and even entire cultures that previously might have had little contact but that could now encounter each other through recorded sound. At the same time (and this would be of growing concern as cultural industries became national and later global), it increased the possibility of the assimilation of smaller cultures into the mainstream.

The first successful sound recording process was developed by Thomas Edison in 1877. Edison imagined his invention—the "phonograph"—being used for a variety of purposes, with music reproduction being only one among many (e.g., dictation, language preservation, recorded books); but the sound was crude, the recordings were not permanent, and after some initial curiosity, public interest waned. Others continued to pursue the idea, and in the 1880s there were two important technical developments that led to the establishment of a record industry: permanent recordings and the capability of mass production.

The first major improvement was the use of wax-coated cylinders on a new device called the "graphophone." Although this machine was very much like Edison's, its recordings were permanent. The possibility of mass production had not yet been a significant consideration because the primary business applications for which the process had been originally intended (e.g., dictation) did not require it. Multiple copies had to be made by using multiple machines (i.e., a performance would be recorded on several machines simultaneously). However, a German inventor, Emile Berliner, recorded onto a flat disc rather than a cylinder; although the sound quality was as poor as that of cylinders, the method produced a master disc that could be used to stamp copies.

Over the next few years, there was a very complex series of legal battles and manoeuvres over the patents for these different methods of recording and reproduction. By the early 20th century, two major firms—Victor and Columbia—dominated the industry. They manufactured mainly discs and agreed to share patents with each other, an arrangement that allowed them to dominate the North American market without any serious competition until after 1914. Although Edison continued to produce cylinders, their popularity declined and the flat disc became the industry standard.

Although it is difficult to establish reliable statistics from this early period, it has been estimated that, by about 1910, worldwide record sales were approaching 50 million units. The largest market was the United States, but other countries such as Germany, Russia, and Great Britain were significant consumers of records (at about 10 million each), and there had been large recording companies operating in Europe since 1900 (e.g., Pathé in France, Lindstrom in Germany). The primary market for recorded music was home entertainment; manufacturers of record-playing machines sought to enclose their equipment in attractive cabinets that could also be part of the household furniture, just as the piano had been in the past. Recorded music also became quite common in a wide range of public places; coin-operated machines could be found anywhere people might gather, such as hotel lobbies, train stations, and entertainment establishments.

The music that the public heard in this early period covered a wide range of tastes. Early catalogues of recordings included a variety of instrumental ensembles such as small orchestras and marching bands. There were also vocal recordings of the popular Tin Pan Alley songs of the day. These early recordings were for the most part regarded as novelties, but many artists, such as the opera singer Enrico Caruso, began to emerge as genuine recording stars. Caruso's recordings, first produced in Milan in 1902, were issued on a prestige label and sold very well (even though they were much more expensive than the average recording). Caruso's success gave an aura of cultural legitimacy to the new recording industry. Perhaps more important, for singers and performers of all kinds of music, it established an important connection between recording and a successful career.

Many of the issues that were to remain central to the music industry emerged in nascent form during this early period. Technological innovations were not simply scientific advancements in a social vacuum; they were directed toward the commodification of music and the establishment of industrial practices that could exploit this commodification in a rapidly growing market for a variety of consumer goods. Not surprisingly, technology was the source of considerable legal disputation between firms, many of which attempted to establish control through legal agreements, as well as mergers or acquisitions.

In this early period, many companies not only recorded music but also manufactured and distributed the recordings as well as the equipment on which they were played. This type of organizational structure, known as "vertical integration," is found in most large entertainment corporations today (e.g., AOL Time Warner has extensive holdings in music, publishing, film, television, and so on). Although debates over international versus national interests had not yet emerged, it is interesting to note that by the early 20th century each of the major firms had established either distribution or actual recording companies in Canada. Such moves would later become a source of great concern to the Canadian state in terms of the domination of Canadian industry by foreign interests, as well as from the standpoint of cultural identity and sovereignty.

THE STRUGGLE FOR COPYRIGHT

Early copyright law in the music industry attempted to establish legal rights over the use of music in three basic contexts: live performance, mechanical reproduction, and public use. The first type (*performing rights*) applies to the actual live performance of a piece of music and not, for example, to the playing of a record on radio. Rights over reproduction (*mechanical rights*) pertain to music in a physical format, such as an actual recording or music in printed form. Finally, *public performance rights* (the name is confusing because these rights do not refer to actual live performance by the composer) pertain to the broadcasting or public use of an actual recording. The owner of the intellectual property—whether the composer or a publishing company— is paid each time a song is performed by others or reproduced in some physical form, or when recordings of the songs are broadcast.[4] Thus, the owners of these rights have the potential to earn far more than the performers (who are paid only to play the song) or the recording company (which is paid for the sale of the record).

The establishment of these different forms of rights was crucial to the formation of the music industry and its later development because it enshrined in law the degree of financial control over musical property (a fourth and more recent form of copyright, "neigbouring rights," will be discussed later). The strong resistance of the contemporary music industry to Web-based music distribution and exchange is a measure of the significance of copyright control.

By the early 20th century, recorded music was becoming a significant business. However, composers of the music and publishers who promoted it were unable to profit from the use of their music because copyright law did not cover the new recording technology. They did have the right to collect revenues from the live performance of music (in vaudeville, for example), but in practice this was not often done since live performance was considered primarily as a means of promotion of the main commodity, printed music. With the growing popularity of recordings, however, composers and publishers began to demand a share of the profits. The record industry responded by arguing that it should be able to use any music without paying fees because (1) it was actually promoting the music, and (2) this form of reproduction was not covered under the copyright act. The publishing industry countered with an argument that was to be used many times throughout the 20th century. It claimed that while the recording technology did not exist when the copyright act was passed, and was therefore not covered by the *letter* of the act, the *spirit* of the act should nonetheless enforce copyright. The United States Supreme Court decided in favour of the composers and publishers: record companies were legally obliged to pay royalties for each record sold.

The live performance of music was also growing rapidly because of the proliferation of places of public entertainment, such as dance halls, nightclubs, restaurants, and theatres. In 1914, a group of American publishers and composers set up an organization based on European models that was to be responsible for the collection of fees paid for the live performance of their music. The new organization, the American Society for Composers, Authors, and Publishers (ASCAP), did not propose to collect fees for every performance of every piece of music (this would have been a tedious and onerous task). Rather, ASCAP would sell licenses to establishments that used music as part of their entertainment, and the fees collected would be distributed among ASCAP members. By the early 1920s, ASCAP was firmly established as one of the most powerful forces in the music industry. Within a decade both the film industry and radio, having put up quite furious resistance, were paying fees to ASCAP. Although there have been important changes since then, control over copyright and other rights associated with music has remained absolutely central to the modern music industry.

A MATURING INDUSTRY

In spite of the early success of records, sales began to decline dramatically in the early 1920s because of the impact of commercial radio. Radio was cheaper than records because further music purchases were not necessary. Furthermore, the sound quality of radio, while unsophisticated by contemporary standards, was vastly superior to that of records. The method of recording sound (acoustic recording) was still quite primitive. Performers had to position themselves near a large horn that picked up the sound, an arrangement that made it impossible to record large groups effectively. Furthermore, both the frequency and dynamic range were very narrow (i.e., sounds of low or high pitch or that were either very soft or very loud were not reproduced well).

Radio, on the other hand, used electric microphones (which were much more sensitive to sound) and electric amplifiers (which boosted the original sound level). Although this technology had been applied successfully to sound recording,[5] the recording industry was reluctant to change because of the large amount of acoustically recorded music already in stock. By the mid-1920s, however, competition from radio encouraged the recording industry to switch to electrical recording, precipitating a worldwide boom in record sales that lasted until the Crash of 1929. Although sheet music sales were still significant, recordings had begun to replace printed music as the primary commodity of the music industry.

The important symbiotic relationship that still exists between radio and the music industry developed very quickly in the early 1920s. Within a very short time, music became an essential part of radio programming as recording artists recognized that regular exposure on radio was essential to a successful career. Both local radio stations and the national networks began to broadcast live performances of dance bands, which assisted in making dance music one of the most popular forms of recorded music in this period. With the advent of sound film in the late 1920s, the interdependence of entertainment media grew, and many stars aggressively pursued careers that spanned records, radio, and film. Al Jolson, a popular vaudeville singer, was also a successful recording star but is most remembered for his appearance in the 1927 film *The Jazz Singer*, usually considered the first film with synchronized sound and music. The importance of the relationship between the music industry and radio was underlined in 1929, when the radio equipment manufacturer Radio Corporation of America (RCA) purchased the Victor recording company to become RCA Victor, one of the earliest and most significant mergers of major firms in different media.

It was also during the 1920s that the different styles (or genres) of music on record became more varied and distinct. Most recording companies already had subsidiary "labels" that produced music directed at a specific market, but in the 1920s clearly defined genres (e.g., country music, blues, and jazz) catering to distinct tastes began to take shape. Frequently, these new styles were established by small, independent companies looking for niche markets in order to establish themselves in the industry. Since they had considerably less capital than the large firms (the "majors"), they were forced to take greater risks, which often resulted in the recording of music that was outside of the mainstream.

Perhaps the most important example of the role of independent record companies and the emergence of distinct genres is that of African-American music (both blues and jazz) and country music. Although the music of African Americans had been an important part of the popular music industry since the turn of the century, black performers were rarely recorded. In 1921, a small record company, Okeh, had an enormous hit with a blues song performed by a black female vaudeville singer named Mamie Smith. Over the next few years, many black female vaudeville singers were recorded as record companies (both independents and the majors) sent teams of engineers with portable recording equipment to the rural south, where they searched for potential blues stars. It was during one of these so-called field trips in 1925 that Okeh Records recorded a group of white musicians from the rural south playing traditional folk music. This genre also proved very successful, and by the late 1920s blues and country (or "race" and "hillbilly" as they were called originally) were, together with jazz, important genres for many independent record companies, as well as for the majors (usually via subsidiary labels such as Victor's "Bluebird" label).

After a brief period of spectacular growth in the late 1920s, the industry was in trouble again by the early years of the Great Depression. Record sales in the United States, which had peaked at about 150 million, plummeted to only 10 million by 1933. While large companies such as Victor and Columbia had serious financial problems, many of the smaller American independents that had established themselves by filling niche markets in the 1920s either disappeared overnight or were bought at bargain prices by larger firms. The record companies that remained standing cut back dramatically on production, quickly dropping artists who were not consistent sellers.

In the Depression years, the star system within the music industry became even more important, as did exposure through other media. Perhaps the most important star of the period was Bing Crosby, whose career exemplified the growing interdependence of entertainment media. Crosby and other singers, known as "crooners," exploited the possibilities of the new electrical technology and sang in a much softer and more intimate style than was possible in live performance in unamplified vaudeville theatres. By the mid-1930s, Crosby was an extremely popular figure on radio, on records, and in Hollywood films.

The most popular musical genre to develop in the 1930s was undoubtedly that arising out of the "big bands." Since the 1920s, the music of many big bands had been broadcast live over the radio from either the network studios or the hotels where the bands performed; because of their popularity on radio, they were able to sell records consistently. From the big bands emerged "swing," a jazz-based dance music that virtually saved the record industry in the late 1930s and remained the most popular genre of music until the end of World War II.

ASCAP VERSUS RADIO

In the early 1940s, there was a confrontation between ASCAP and radio that not only changed the structure of the industry but also had a long-term impact on the sound of popular music in general. Since the 1920s, ASCAP had received fees from radio stations for the use of music it controlled. In 1940, ASCAP informed the radio industry that it was going to demand a substantial increase when the current contract expired. In 1939, the radio industry, in anticipation of such a problem, had formed a rival copyright organization, Broadcast Music Incorporated (BMI). Unfortunately, ASCAP controlled an enormous amount of music, including

virtually all material produced by the
radio industry would soon find itself

Forced to look elsewhere, B?
American, blues, and swing—styl?
relied on established Tin Pan Alle
method of determining copyrigh
songs played on radio. The disp
forbade the use of any of its m?
force concessions on the part of
be very popular, and in 1941 it v

This dispute tended to incre
mainstream, such as country musi
important industry newspaper, be?
black music, which it eventually name?
role as a popular form of urban dance music. ?
enjoyed large audiences, now entered the pop mainstr?
artists as Frank Sinatra and Louis Armstrong. BMI's method ?
radio encouraged music that was current and fresh and thus ac?
turnover rate of hits on radio. These changes in tandem hastened the shift ??
reliance on a centralized songwriting industry (Tin Pan Alley) to a new emphasis
on vernacular music—a shift that would have a profound impact on the music
industry in the postwar years.

YOUTH AND ADULT MUSIC

The post–World War II economic boom in North America allowed for the consolidation and expansion of a consumer culture that had been developing since the early
part of the century. One of the most important consumer markets to develop during
this period was the youth market. With increasing urbanization and the concomitant
expansion of public education, the period of adolescence had been lengthened. The
modern concept of the "teenager" as a distinct social group developed in the mid-
20th century. In the postwar years, young people had more disposable income and
there began to appear distinct products aimed exclusively at a youth market.

Significantly, popular music had usually been directed at all age groups, with
young people tending to listen to the same music as their parents. During the
1920s, jazz was sometimes associated with youth culture, and in the 1930s Frank
Sinatra began to attract a large and obviously young following. The identification
of different performers and musical styles with youth culture continued. By the
mid-1950s, there was a clear division between adult and youth music. "Rock and
roll," as youth music became known, was less a distinct genre than a collection of
styles that originated in rhythm and blues, country music, black vocal groups, or a
combination of these. Many of the earliest rock and roll records were aimed initially

...try music audiences but achieved unanticipated success
... the pop mainstream), becoming "crossover hits." The
...esley, for example, were intended for country audiences but
...pular on both rhythm and blues and pop charts.

...the general development of a youth market within consumer
...ors specific to popular music also contributed to the rise of youth
...ecline of network radio and the rise of the disc jockey; (2) inde-
...d labels; and (3) film and television exposure. By the late 1940s, net-
...began to lose its advertising revenues to television, which was making
...ads into home entertainment. The main product of network radio in the
...tates had been half-hour programs such as dramas, soap operas, comedies,
...uiz shows (much like the product of contemporary television). This kind of
...ramming was expensive, so many radio stations not affiliated with a network
...gan to broadcast recorded music. The announcers or "disc jockeys" who hosted
these shows used specific forms of music to define themselves and their programs;
many began to feature a great deal of music by black rhythm and blues artists, consciously cultivating an audience composed mainly of white teenagers. By the end of
the 1950s, the diversity of music on radio been drawn together in a format that
became known as "Top 40." In this format, songs that proved to be most popular
with listeners were played on a highly repetitive basis known as "tight rotation."

Almost none of the earliest rock-and-roll stars were from the mainstream of
popular music. Rather, most had recorded with small, independent record companies specializing in rhythm and blues or country music. Like the independents of
the 1920s, these small companies had less to lose and more to gain by adopting a
strategy of experimentation and risk, and thus were able to take chances on
unproven performers. Up to the late 1940s, most independent firms were local in
orientation and without extensive distribution, mainly because of the cost of shipping records. The industry standard was the 78-rpm (revolutions per minute) disc,
which was relatively heavy and very fragile. Most major companies had their own
national distribution or relied on well-established distribution firms. In the late
1940s, the development of a light and almost unbreakable 45-rpm vinyl record
allowed smaller firms to distribute their own records more easily and thus reach
broader geographical markets. Another technological innovation instituted by the
majors but of great importance to smaller companies was tape recording. In contrast to the expensive process of recording directly to permanent master discs, tape
could be reused and edited, giving companies greater control over the recording
process and the final results.

The disc jockeys who played rock and roll reached mainly local markets. Rock
and roll was given national exposure on a number of popular variety shows in the
mid-1950s. Of particular note were Elvis Presley's 1956 appearances on *The Ed
Sullivan Show* (a hugely popular family-oriented variety program), which captured
over 80 percent of the television audience. Within a few years, youth music achieved
more regular television exposure through local and national teenager-oriented

dance programs such as *American Bandstand*, which began in 1957 and inspired the production of similar shows in Canada and Europe by the early 1960s. The movie industry had been cultivating an association with youth culture since the 1940s. This tendency was accelerated by the arrival of rock and roll. By the late 1950s, there were innumerable full-length films directed at teenagers. Many of these films featured popular rock and roll stars and relatively benign plots based on generational misunderstandings; many more linked youth music and culture with juvenile delinquency, crime, or moral decay.

During the period in which youth culture was emerging, there was a corresponding effort on the part of the record industry to cultivate a mass market for specifically adult music. Until the late 1940s, records contained only about two to three minutes of music per side. The development of a 33 $1/3$-rpm record increased the playing time to 23 minutes. The "LP" (i.e., "long-playing" record), also known as an "album," contained a collection of tracks on each side and was marketed as a more serious form of entertainment than the smaller and shorter 45-rpm record, which had only a single song per side. Mail-order record clubs began to pursue white, middle-class record buyers, offering packaged sets of music that were intended to appeal to more adult tastes. Some of these sets were sold in elaborately decorated boxes (often with fake leather binding) designed to give an aura of sophistication. Packaging that had been associated with classical music in the past was now applied to collections of jazz, Broadway songs, and other forms of popular music. Another important aspect of the adult market was the development of high-fidelity playback equipment (including stereophonic sound) aimed primarily at adult males for whom the idea of record collecting and buying, or even of building exotic playback equipment, became (and remains to this day) a popular and expensive hobby.

ECONOMIC EXPANSION

The economic prosperity of the postwar period continued to drive an expanding consumer culture. With the maturation of the baby boom into adolescence during the 1960s, youth music expanded dramatically and became the most important market for record companies. Youth music also spread internationally, and for a period the American dominance of popular music was challenged by groups from the United Kingdom such as the Beatles and the Rolling Stones.

There was also a gradual shift in attitudes toward popular music and popular culture in general. By the late 1960s, some forms of rock music had emerged as serious forms of artistic expression. This trend was accompanied by the rise of music journalism (the "rock press"), an emphasis on the album (formerly associated with serious adult music) rather than the single, and the exploitation of new recording technologies (in particular, multi-track recording). Earlier technology required that all elements of a record be recorded live in real time (i.e., all performers were recorded simultaneously). With multi-track recording, individual elements could be recorded one at a time and any mistakes could be redone without affecting the other tracks. While initially intended as a means of exercising greater industrial control over the recording process, this technology became the basis for considerable aesthetic exploration. An early example, the Beatles album *Sgt. Pepper's Lonely Hearts Club Band* (1967), was recorded on two four-track machines; by the early 1970s, most major recording studios were using 16- and 24-track machines.

With the huge postwar generation serving as its primary market, the music industry was becoming extremely profitable. It began to attract major capital investment, which in turn sparked a period of rapid and extensive expansion. As in the 1920s and 1930s, there were moves toward both vertical integration and new alliances between firms in different media. There was also a significant move toward conglomeration. *Conglomerates* are large firms that have interests, all under one management umbrella, in a variety of financial and industrial sectors. During the 1960s, many of the large corporations that dominate the international industry today began to take shape. Warner Records, for example, was in the early 1960s the relatively small and unprofitable record division of the large film corporation, Warner Bros. In 1967, Warner Records was purchased by Seven Arts, an independent film production and distribution company. The acquisition instantly increased the record company's power within the entertainment industry. By the early 1970s, having acquired several smaller record labels, Warner Records emerged as a major firm under the control of Warner Communications International, a parent company formed to manage film, television, and music interests. The story of Warner Records during this period is not unusual, and the trend toward conglomeration on such a large scale has continued. Today the contemporary music industry is dominated by a few giants that are themselves mere parts of huge entertainment and business empires.

With increased capital spending in the music industry came the demand for a faster and greater return on investment. As the stakes grew higher, so did the cost of record production in an increasingly competitive environment. A much greater volume of sales was required for a record to become profitable. Accordingly, record companies began to focus on established stars such as Paul McCartney, Elton John, and the Bee Gees, who did not require long-term development. Accompanying the emphasis on the superstar was the rise of live performances that were both visually and aurally spectacular. Artists whose records were technically and artistically complex went to enormous lengths both to reproduce their material in live performance and to develop forms of visual expression that were as sophisticated as the music. Tours of bands such as Pink Floyd or Genesis were extremely expensive, involving extensive road crews to transport and assemble huge sound and light systems. As in earlier periods, the emphasis on the superstar prompted independent record companies to explore niche markets that did not require enormous levels of investment or profit. Disco, punk, rockabilly, and some forms of heavy metal that developed completely outside the rock mainstream were indicative of an increasing fragmentation of consumer markets in general.

In spite of this boom in music sales, the Canadian recording industry was still dominated by the Anglo-American majors and the musical content of Canadian radio was almost exclusively foreign. Since the earliest days of the recording industry, Canadian artists had migrated to the United States, drawn by its much larger market and greater opportunities for financial success. In 1970, the Canadian Radio-television and Telecommunications Commission (CRTC), which regulates broadcasting in Canada, implemented a policy requiring that the musical programming of AM radio stations be at least 20 percent Canadian throughout the day (a similar policy for FM radio was introduced in 1975). The levels of Canadian content required rose to 30 percent and eventually 35 percent. Radio stations were also required to help promote and develop Canadian artists at the local and regional level. The main intent of the Canadian content policy (also known as "CanCon") was to cultivate and encourage a greater sense of Canadian cultural identity, although it was also hoped that the policy would produce financial benefits for the Canadian recording industry.

By the mid-1970s, most radio stations had complied with CanCon (although its long-term effects remain a subject of debate to this day). Canadian recording artists were receiving much greater radio exposure as well as increased revenues from copyright, both of which were beneficial to the growth of the recording industry in Canada. More recently, Canadian recording artists such as Céline Dion, Alanis Morrissette, Shania Twain, and Sarah McLachlan have become international stars, and Canadian policy on music has served as a model to other countries seeking to protect and promote local music cultures and a national recording industry.

Ironically, the rapid growth of the Canadian recording industry during this period was assisted to a large extent by the infrastructure of manufacturing and distribution that had been established by multinationals. Since the earliest days of the recording industry, the Canadian state had imposed tariffs on the importation of records, thereby encouraging foreign firms to locate branch plants in Canada rather than simply import recorded product. By the early 20th century, major foreign firms had established subsidiaries in Toronto (Edison and Columbia) and Montreal (Berliner). Unlike the other major firms, Berliner showed considerable interest in Canadian artists, both anglophone and francophone, and recorded in Montreal as early as 1904. By the late 1920s, Berliner had issued over 1800 recordings of Canadian artists. Almost half of these were French-language recordings. Although small, the market for these recordings was relatively dense (Quebec, New Brunswick, and parts of the northeastern United States), and Berliner was able to develop this niche. Other firms with branches in Canada, including Victor, Columbia, and Brunswick, also recorded Canadian artists during this period (although not on the scale of Berliner); with the exception of Victor, these firms were not particularly interested in the francophone audience.

Most of the new Canadian firms that developed in the CanCon environment attached themselves to multinational firms for distribution. Some of these companies, such as Attic and Anthem, changed affiliations frequently in search of more advantageous contracts. The distribution network established by multinationals provided access to national markets and allowed the smaller Canadian firms to concentrate primarily on the development of Canadian talent.

MUSIC VIDEO AND THE CD

The baby boom, which had brought about the massive expansion of the market for recorded music, had the opposite effect as it aged and its music consumption declined. The first response of the record industry was simply to raise prices in an attempt to recoup in dollars what had been lost in unit sales. There were two other developments that not only helped to save the music industry but also had significant long-term effects: music video and the CD.

The relationship between music television and the music industry paralleled that which had developed between music and radio. With the advent of MTV in 1981, music programming became, as with radio, a 24-hour format and an extremely important promotional outlet for the music industry. Initially, MTV was believed to have little or no impact on record sales. Within a few years, however, artists whose videos appeared on MTV increased their sales by as much as 15 percent. Stars such as Michael Jackson and Madonna not only promoted their music through video but, with relatively long and expensive videos, exploited the capabilities of the new medium much like film stars.

MTV was not broadcast in Canada until 2001 because of federal legislation regulating competition in Canadian specialty cable channels. A Canadian version, MuchMusic, was launched in 1984 and was followed a few years later by a French-language equivalent, MusiquePlus. Like the radio stations that had implemented Canadian content policy before them, MuchMusic and MusiquePlus provided greater exposure to Canadian artists, which in turn helped to strengthen the Canadian recording industry. In essence, music video became an important new marketing tool.

The compact disc, which was introduced in 1983, also helped to rescue the music industry, although for different reasons. At first, the CD simply allowed the recording industry to raise the dollar value of sales without increasing the actual number of units sold. Eventually, the CD also helped to re-establish an older audience whose declining music consumption had precipitated the crisis in sales in the first place. Many of these record buyers, attracted by the improved sound quality and archival potential of the CD, began to replace their vinyl record collections, and most recording companies responded by reissuing older material. This was quite a windfall for the music industry because the only major costs involved were copyright (which they frequently owned anyway), manufacturing, and distribution.

By the late 1980s, CDs had replaced vinyl records as the industry standard. More important than the actual physical format was the digital technology of which the CD was a product. Digital technology, which originated in the computer industry, records sound as a set of numbers, a process that has two extremely important advantages. First, when digital recordings are reproduced or transmitted, there is no loss in the quality of the sound because a copy contains the same set of numbers as the original. Second, digital technology applies not only to sound but to all sorts of media (including print, image, film, and video)—a characteristic that has allowed for the development of a global media infrastructure.

MODERN DEVELOPMENTS

Over the last two decades, there have been two broad and seemingly contradictory tendencies in the music industry and in other cultural industries in general: (1) a move toward concentration and merger, which had been fundamental to the music industry since its earliest days; and (2) an increasing fragmentation of audiences and genres, as well as a general decentralization of the large corporations. In the late 1970s, the music industry was dominated by five firms. Four of these firms were Anglo-American: EMI (U.K.); Warner, Columbia, and RCA (U.S.). The other firm, Polygram, was owned by the Dutch electronics giant, Philips.

Within a decade, after a series of large acquisitions and mergers, the music industry had become internationalized in terms of ownership and had also become more integrated into larger entertainment conglomerates. EMI was bought by Thorn, a U.K.-based electronics and television company, and Columbia, one of the oldest record companies, was bought by Sony, a large Japanese electronics firm that manufactured home audio and video equipment. The record division of RCA, another of the oldest American record companies, became part of the West German publishing firm Bertelsmann AG. Warner remained in American hands but merged with the huge news corporation Time.

The pattern of mergers and acquisitions was counterbalanced by a movement toward more decentralized forms of management, as firms in all industries sought to control the increased risks associated with an emerging global business environment. Rather than directing all aspects of the business from the top of a corporate pyramid, record companies devolved into relatively autonomous management units that could respond to changing tastes more rapidly and with a greater degree of flexibility. While pop superstars (such as Michael Jackson in the 1980s and Céline Dion more recently) continued to dominate record sales, there were increasingly finer gradations of musical genres that required record companies to be more responsive to subtle and rapid shifts in audiences. In the 1980s, the major record companies began to depend more and more on formalized and mutually beneficial arrangements with the independent companies—arrangements in which the latter acted more or less as scouts for new talent and new markets.

As the major record companies moved toward larger conglomerates, the shift to fragmentation in terms of musical genres and audience niches continued. On one level, this was simply part of a broader tendency within consumer culture in general.

But it was also the result of two other factors: FM radio and the development of inexpensive multi-track recording. Top 40 radio, which had been the dominant form of programming since the 1950s, had gone into decline with the proliferation of specialized FM radio stations. By the 1980s, these stations had become the dominant form in the United States, targeting increasingly narrow segments of the total music audience. This trend developed later in Canada because of a federal FM radio policy that encouraged a greater diversity of programming, with less emphasis on only hit music. (Whereas American FM fragmented the audience for popular music into ever finer segments—urban, alternative, rap, etc.—Canadian FM, whose markets were defined partly by the CRTC, could not define its audience so narrowly and tended to offer all types of popular music.) Top 40 remained, as contemporary hit radio or CHR (mainly pop and rock with some alternative and rap), but became only one format among many formats, which included adult contemporary (oldies and softer rock); oldies ('60s and '70s rock); urban contemporary (African-American rhythm and blues, rap, and dance); and country (now of several different types ranging from traditional to rock-oriented).

The development of inexpensive recording technologies lowered considerably the cost of record production. Early multi-track recording had been largely confined to expensive studios, but by the late 1970s more affordable eight-track machines were becoming quite common, giving rise to the proliferation of smaller recording facilities. By the mid-1990s, high-quality digital audio tape (DAT) recorders were also available to these smaller operations. Only a few years later, it became possible to edit music on home computers. With these digital technologies, small operations could record music, edit and mix, produce the artwork and packaging, and promote and distribute the final product in digital format over the Internet. This new environment gave audiences access to artists who were not of interest to major companies. It also encouraged considerable experimentation, a luxury previously available only to a select few who had the financial resources. The result was the international growth of a wide variety of local musical cultures and the cross-fertilization of different types of music, producing new genres and audiences.

The merger trend of the 1980s accelerated in the last decade of the 20th century. Record companies today are part of huge media conglomerates. The largest of these conglomerates is AOL Time Warner, created early in 2000 by a merger between America Online, the Internet service, and Time Warner. A list of AOL Time Warner's various interests illustrates the extent of the interconnections among media under one corporate umbrella; the company has holdings in the Internet (AOL), print publishing (Time-Life Books, *Time Magazine*, DC Comics, *Mad Magazine*, and several other publishing firms), cable and television (HBO, CNN, WB Television Network, Turner Entertainment), news (CNN), film (Warner Bros. Studios, Hanna-Barbera Cartoons, Warner Bros. International Theaters, New Line Cinema, First Line Features), music (Warner Music Group, which includes Atlantic, Elektra, Warner Bros. Records, Reprise, 47 smaller record labels, and the large music publishing firm Warner/Chappell Music), merchandising (Warner Bros. Studio Stores), theme parks, and sports (Atlanta Braves, Atlanta Hawks).

The largest single music corporation, with a 22 percent share of the world market, is the Universal Music Group (which now includes Polygram), owned by the European-based conglomerate Vivendi, whose main interest is in privatized water supplies. Like AOL Time Warner, Vivendi has extensive holdings in other media and entertainment areas. The other members of the "Big Five" record companies are, as of the turn of the century, Sony Music, EMI, and Bertelsmann Music Group (BMG). In this new corporate context, music has become only one point in a larger constellation of entertainment products. For example, one firm can produce and distribute a film made from a book it owns and distributes; the film has a soundtrack CD and associated music videos, both of which are promoted through the firm's radio and television networks; spinoff merchandise is sold through a variety of the firm's retail outlets; and copyright revenue is generated from all of these related activities because the firm also has publishing interests.

In Canada, the most significant move toward vertical integration occurred in 1999, when Alan Gregg, a well-known Tory Party pollster, media talent, and rock artist manager, established the Song Corporation. In the context of continental free trade agreements and an industry marked by increasing concentration, Gregg believed that Canadian firms could survive only if they developed the vertically integrated structure typical of large multinational firms. Accordingly, the Song Corporation absorbed Attic Records, one of Canada's most important independent record companies, and bought various other recording, publishing, and music distribution entities. Early in 2001, the Song Corporation went out of business. The company's failure may well be the first of further significant problems for the Canadian record industry. With the disappearance of tariffs on the importation of recordings, multinational firms may no longer find it necessary or profitable to maintain subsidiaries in Canada, calling into question the distribution infrastructure that served the Canadian recording industry so well in the past.

While music publishing still holds the most significant position in terms of revenues, there have been important recent changes in copyright protection with regard to performers' rights. For most of the history of the music industries, composers and music publishing companies alone benefited from the distribution of music through media such as radio or television. Performers (and the record companies to whom they were signed) regarded radio and television as effective channels for the promotion of their recordings, but they were not reimbursed for the use of their music in these media. In 1996, Bill C-32 introduced radical revisions to Canada's copyright regimes. Through the principle of "neighbouring rights," performers and recording companies will now be paid each time their music is used in electronic media. As an example, say that Leonard Cohen composes a song. As the copyright holder, he receives a royalty whenever that song is performed. In the past, if Jennifer Warnes did a cover version of the song, and if her version was played on the radio, she did not get paid (but Leonard Cohen did). Under neighbouring rights, Warnes now also receives a royalty. Neighbouring rights allow record companies to profit from the introduction of new means of delivering music, from digital radio through Internet-based music services. In this respect, the Canadian context more closely resembles that of Europe, where neighbouring rights have existed for some time, than that of the United States, where such rights have been only partially recognized.

In addition to the intermedia marketing of the new music and entertainment giants, digital communications hardware and software have made possible the convergence of a wide range of mass media on a global scale. Although the Internet is not yet a major source of music, it presents the possibility of simple worldwide mass distribution. It is clear that the way in which entertainment is delivered will change considerably in the not too distant future. For record companies, it will no longer be a question of simply manufacturing concrete entities such as CDs and distributing them to retail outlets. Just as Tin Pan Alley and vaudeville depended on each other, so too will there be increased integration between different forms of the electronic packaging of sound and image. With the proliferation of Web sites featuring music with live action video, the idea of recorded sound alone is already becoming dated.

The integration of different media will, in fact, present music as it was originally intended—a combination of sound and image. The music video of the early 1980s, while intended mainly as a promotional vehicle for record companies, was the start of a move toward a reintegration that will probably be realized on a more widespread basis with the next generation of digital technology. The reach of these new technologies is truly staggering, and there will be few aspects of modern life that will lie outside the realm of entertainment media. At the dawn of the modern music industry in the late 19th century, the motto of Procter's vaudeville theatre in New York City was: "After breakfast, go to Procter's, after Procter's, go to bed." More recently, Rupert Murdoch expressed a similar sentiment with global implications: "Our reach is unmatched. We're reaching people from the moment they wake up until they fall asleep."

QUESTIONS

1. What is the process of concentration and fragmentation in the music industry?
2. What are ASCAP and BMI?
3. What industrial circumstances favoured the rise of alternative or nonmainstream music in the 1940s and 1950s?
4. How did CDs help the sound recording industry in the 1980s?
5. How is sound recording implicated across the range of cultural industries?
6. Name a type of music or performer whose success is tied to the use of a particular technology. Can that music or performer break out to a larger audience? If so, how?

WEB SITES

MediaChannel (media ownership page): **http://www.mediachannel.org/ownership/**
Recording Technology History: **http://history.acusd.edu/gen/recording/notes.html**
Virtual Gramophone: Canadian Historical Sound Recordings (National Library of
    Canada): **http://www2.nlc-bnc.ca/gramophone/**

NOTES

1. The author wishes to thank the following people for their assistance in
    researching this chapter: Professor William Straw, Department of Art History
    and Communication Studies, McGill University; John Feihl, Canadian
    Radio-television Telecommunications Commission; and Richard Green,
    National Library of Canada.
2. Commodification of music refers to the process by which the experience of lis-
    tening to music, which is traditionally freely and universally available, is trans-
    formed into a market exchange. For example, when music is pressed into CDs
    and can be heard only when the CDs are purchased, it has been commodified.
3. The origin of the term "Tin Pan Alley" is unknown, but the most common
    explanation is that it refers to the tinny sound of a piano in the office of Harry
    Von Tilzer, one of the most famous and prolific songwriters of the period.
4. A public performance right also attaches to the live performance (in a stadium,
    bar, nightclub, etc.) of a musical piece not written by the performer. So, when
    bands perform cover versions of songs written by others, a public performance
    right must be paid. Since it is impossible to police the multitude of such per-
    formances, the venue in which the performance occurs pays a general royalty
    covering all its performance to a royalty collection agency, which in turn redis-
    tributes all the royalties collected from all the venues to the copyright holders.
5. The first commercial electrical recording was made by two Canadians, Lionel
    Guest and Horace O. Merriman, in 1919.

FURTHER READING

Ennis, Philip H. (1992). *The seventh stream: The emergence of rock and roll in American
    popular music*. London: Wesleyan University Press.
Gronow, Pekka, and Saunio, Ilpo. (1998). *An international history of the recording
    industry* (Christopher Moseley, Trans.). New York: Cassell.
Negus, Keith. (1992). *Producing pop: Culture and conflict in the popular music industry*.
    London: Edward Arnold.
Sanjek, Russel. (1988). *American popular music and its business: The first four hundred
    years*. New York: Oxford University Press.

12

Television in Canada

Paul Attallah and Derek Foster
Carleton University

Canadian television was officially launched on September 6, 1952, when station CBMT went on the air in Montreal, broadcasting in both English and French. On September 8, station CBT went on the air in Toronto; its opening image consisted of a map of Canada over which were superimposed the words "Canadian Broadcasting Corporation, Société Radio-Canada"—unfortunately, the map appeared upside down. A year earlier, *before* the arrival of Canadian television, there were already some 150,000 television sets in Canada. Clearly, many people were already watching American television. The tension between observable audience preferences, the availability of American television, and the existence of Canadian television virtually defines the story of television in Canada.

It is useful to begin that story by considering the success of U.S. television, against which the relative failure of Canadian television is easier to understand. Television in the United States was launched in 1946 with the full backing of the radio networks NBC, CBS, and ABC. The launch was so successful that television became the fastest-growing home technology ever introduced to the North American market. Television set ownership jumped from less than 1 percent of the population in 1946 to 70 percent in 1955 to virtual saturation by 1960. The forms and genres of American television—sitcoms, police dramas, westerns, talk and game shows, among others—quickly established themselves, and the stars and personalities of American television soon became worldwide icons.

Plainly, American television was repeating the success of the media that had preceded it, radio and film. It was a success that extended north of the Canada–U.S. border. Indeed, that specific fact—the love of Canadian audiences for American television—greatly exercised the Canadian cultural elite and led directly to the creation of Canadian television. While Canadians had long enjoyed American culture (film, magazines, radio, music, etc.), television was perceived as an especially dangerous threat because it was thought to be more seductive, more constant, and more intimate.

The federal government tried to address these concerns in 1949, when it struck a Royal Commission on National Development in the Arts, Letters and Sciences (better known as the Massey Commission after its distinguished chairman, the Honourable Vincent Massey). The commission, whose purpose was to formulate policy recommendations, delivered its final report in 1951. Its view of television was sharp and succinct. To begin, television was "becoming an important and even dangerous rival of the other mass media" (Canada, 1951, p. 42). The commission noted that the "combined influences of sight, sound and motion are intensified when received in the quiet of a home" (p. 42), and warned of "the danger of encouraging passivity in the viewer, especially in children" (p. 49).

In addition, the commission argued that American programming would serve commercial interests rather than "our national needs" (p. 47):

> [American programming] is essentially a commercial enterprise, an advertising industry. Thus sponsors, endeavouring to "give the majority of the people what they want," frequently choose programmes of inferior cultural standards [and] appeal to material instincts of various kinds. (p. 47)

Nonetheless, while the commission expressed "generally unfavourable observations on American programmes" (p. 42), it also conceded the existence of some good U.S. programming, including:

> [i]mportant news events, such as the sessions of the Security Council of the United Nations ... superb programmes of operas and of other music and of drama; group discussions ... interesting and imaginative demonstrations of scientific research and of technical training ... [and] well-planned children's programmes. (p. 47)

The commission recommended that Canadian television depart from the American model by eschewing its commercial orientation. Rather than appealing to the lowest common denominator, the "men and women who devote themselves to [broadcasting] ... must do not what noisy uninformed clamour tells them to do, but what they believe to be right" (p. 48). If American television was commercial and devoted to fun and entertainment, Canadian television would be public and "a valuable instrument of national unity, of education, and of entertainment" (p. 301).

Canadian television was thus born into a paternalistic atmosphere that distrusted popular culture (especially American culture) and presumed to instruct the population in what it should and should not enjoy. Reality failed to match the attitude, and Canadian television grew as a mixture of both good and bad. However, one of Canadian television's enduring difficulties has been in achieving sustained popular contact, in establishing itself as a permanent source of entertainment, in breeding the habit of regular tuning. This difficulty may be the legacy of the patrician disdain for popular taste that the Massey Commission imparted to Canadian television.

1952–1960: DOMINANCE OF THE CBC

In 1952, television fell under the exclusive authority of the Canadian Broadcasting Corporation (CBC). There were no private television stations (though there were private radio stations), and the context of Canadian television was very different from that of American television. First, there were no powerful radio networks in Canada (besides the CBC itself) to lend financial support to the nascent television industry. Second, whereas American television could turn to the huge technical, managerial, and financial resources of Hollywood, there was no Canadian equivalent to Hollywood. Television in Canada thus began without a film centre comparable to Hollywood, without a backlog of filmed stories to draw on, without a star system, without a promotional infrastructure, without huge teams of writers, producers, technicians, and directors.

CBC television naturally drew on its acquired internal radio expertise. The CBC radio network reached its maturity during World War II, addressing an audience eager for information about the Canadian war effort. CBC television soon also developed an expertise in news, documentary, and public affairs; sports programming (which, in its generally objective and documentary presentational form, shares many characteristics with news); and children's programming (*The Friendly Giant*, *Chez Hélène*, *Razzle Dazzle*). Indeed, up to the present day, these three areas—news, sports, children—have remained strengths of the CBC in particular and all Canadian television in general.

In the 1950s and 1960s, the CBC also developed some variety programming (*Wayne and Shuster*, *Don Messer's Jubilee*, *Cross-Canada Hit Parade*, *Juliette*) and some drama (one-off plays, *Seaway*, *Quentin Durgen, M.P.*, *Wojeck*, *Adventures in Cariboo Country*). An especially important year was 1953: the coronation of Queen Elizabeth II in June of that year prompted many Canadians to buy their first television set. In December 1953, many of those sets were tuned to an episode of the hugely popular *I Love Lucy*, in which Lucille Ball's character gave birth—an event that itself served as yet another spur in the explosion of television set sales on both sides of the border.

Structural and regulatory factors were just as important to the CBC's development. Although the government had originally intended the CBC to have sole responsibility for broadcasting, it soon became apparent that the cost of television production and distribution was so great that the CBC could not bear it alone. As part of its public mandate, the CBC was required to deliver its signal to all parts of the country. This undertaking proved to be colossally expensive given the sheer landmass of the country. As more and more of the CBC's operating budget was absorbed by the construction and maintenance of one of the world's largest terrestrial (and later satellite) delivery systems, funds were diverted from program production. To rectify the situation, in 1953 private stations were authorized in various locations to act as "rebroadcasters" of the CBC's signal (as well as other content they might acquire or produce). By showing that private television stations *could* operate in Canada, these private rebroadcasters laid the groundwork for a future private network.

Significantly, because the CBC was the dominant television producer, there were almost no independent production houses in Canada. (The situation was very different in the United States, where the Hollywood studios themselves became major suppliers of professional filmed content for television, and where a large industry of smaller, independent companies competed for the right to manufacture television content.) The lack of an independent production centre meant that virtually all Canadian content was produced in-house by CBC employees (producers, writers, etc.). As the same crews worked on all television genres, from variety to hockey, the CBC rapidly developed a recognizable network style: clear, expository, deliberate, with an emphasis on the didactic and the documentary. This style was consistent with the CBC's mandate to be a public broadcaster devoted to *national unity* and *education* rather than to entertainment, and with the corporation's accumulated expertise in news and public affairs.

Why, we might ask, was the CBC given sole responsibility for broadcasting in the first place? There was enormous suspicion of private broadcasting in the early days. Many feared that private television would lack the financial resources to produce Canadian programming and would therefore be unable to resist the pull of American content, as had happened in radio. More important was the fact that CBC was *already* the broadcast regulator. Indeed, when the CBC was created as a radio network in 1936, it was given the power to grant and deny licences to private radio stations. Years later, this power was simply extended to television.

Private radio broadcasters accused the CBC of gross unfairness (since it was both a competitor and the regulator), and vigorously lobbied the federal government to transfer the CBC's regulatory power to some neutral, third-party body. In defending itself, the CBC would argue that the airwaves belonged to the public and that the private broadcasters used them only with the public's permission. In 1958, the newly elected Conservative government of John Diefenbaker gave the private broadcasters what they wanted. It transferred the CBC's regulatory authority to a new body called the Board of Broadcast Governors (BBG). In 1961, the BBG authorized the creation of the first private television network, CTV, whose directors were perceived as friendly to the Conservative Party.

1961–1968: FROM THE BBG TO THE CRTC

CTV was neither the boon nor the bust that many had predicted. It did effectively expand television choice, but it also confirmed the laws of television economics: Canadian content is expensive to produce, and the market to which it can appeal is, in terms of its size, dwarfed by markets such as that in the United States. The end result is that Canadian content is often produced at a loss.

The same cannot be said of American content. Although a U.S. television show can easily cost $1 million per hour to produce, an American network can afford that cost because it can sell advertising spots within the program worth $5 to $15 million per hour. Consequently, against an expenditure of $1 million per hour, a U.S. network can turn a potential profit of several million dollars. For a Canadian network that attempts to produce a show costing $1 million per hour, the situation is very different. In Canada, it is usually impossible to sell enough advertising time within a show to cover that kind of expense—hence the program is produced at a loss.

A way for Canadian broadcasters to avoid bankruptcy is to purchase U.S. programs. These programs can be purchased at a fraction of their initial cost because their producers have already recouped their expenses from the U.S. networks. In this way, a U.S. show worth $1 million can be purchased in Canada for approximately $100,000. (Fortunately, it is entirely possible to sell more than $100,000 worth of advertising per hour in this country.) A potential loss thus turns into a net gain, generating for the Canadian network a profit that can be invested in further production. What Canadian networks have done historically is import popular U.S. programs and use some of the resulting profits to produce Canadian programs, which are considerably less popular and often result in a loss. Since Canadian content tends to be costly, there is a parallel tendency to produce the least expensive types of Canadian content and to schedule Canadian programs at times when they will least damage the Canadian network's profitability (i.e., outside prime time, which is reserved for the most successful U.S. shows).

Even with this accusation levelled against it, CTV slowly increased in popularity until it rivalled, and then surpassed, the CBC. The lack of independent production houses in Canada prompted CTV to follow the CBC in producing content in-house. And like the CBC, it soon developed an expertise in the traditional Canadian genres of news and public affairs (*CTV News, Canada AM, W5*), sports (*Wide World of Sports*, Olympic coverage), and children's programming (*Romper Room*). The main difference between CTV and CBC was that whereas the CBC was a highly centralized body, CTV had no strong central authority. Instead, its affiliates, located from Halifax to Vancouver, participated equally in the management of the network, frequently lending it a weak or chaotic structure.

In 1968, the BBG was replaced by the Canadian Radio-Television Commission (CRTC). The CRTC, which had the authority to license individual stations, networks, cable companies, and eventually specialty channels and satellite operators, was a much more activist regulatory body than the BBG, and its chairman, Pierre Juneau, possessed a strong vision for the future of Canadian broadcasting. Among the CRTC's most important decisions were (1) the 1970 imposition of Canadian content quotas on both radio and television, and (2) the creation of a framework for the development of cable television.

The content quotas required all private television broadcasters to show a minimum of 50 percent Canadian content per day and for the CBC to show at least 60 percent per day. From the very beginning, these quotas proved to be a bone of contention as private broadcasters were accused of failing to meet them or of systematically evading them, and as the broadcasters themselves pleaded for economic relief. The CBC, however, has traditionally met or exceeded its quotas. Roughly coinciding with the imposition of these quotas was a huge expansion of Canadian cable television. Under CRTC rules, cable operators must ensure a preponderance of Canadian content by guaranteeing that there are always more Canadian services than American, that the Canadian services are located in the first (and least expensive) tiers, and that there are no American channels that duplicate Canadian services.

CANADIAN CONTENT: SOLUTION OR PROBLEM?

The question of Canadian content is a serious one that deserves serious consideration. No country in the world would abandon its own broadcasting or let another country supply all of its television. But are content quotas the best way to ensure a Canadian television industry?

Audience measurements consistently show that Canadian audiences prefer U.S. prime-time drama to the Canadian equivalent. Content quotas, however, restrict the supply of programming Canadians most enjoy and increase the supply of programs they least enjoy. By making the most enjoyable programming harder to watch, content quotas may actually make that programming more desirable and provide incentives to Canadians to seek it out, even when a good Canadian alternative is available. More significantly, though, content quotas set aside certain hours that *must* be filled with Canadian content. Since that content must be shown, it hardly matters whether it is very popular or very good. After all, it's less trouble to make something quick and cheap that must be shown than it is to lavish time and effort on it. Indeed, it may in fact be more rational to satisfy quota requirements as inexpensively as possible.

If content quotas are problematic, might there be a better way? Some of the factors that have made American television successful include a massive promotional infrastructure and a star system. Unfortunately, both of those tend to be in short supply in Canada. The promotional infrastructure—the talk and game shows on which celebrities can make guest appearances, the magazines and books that celebrate them and their programs, the fan clubs, the gossip columns, the specialty publications (such as *People* magazine)—tends not to have a strong presence in Canada. Likewise, the Canadian star system is merely embryonic. There are very few "bankable" Canadian stars, and those who are have gone to the United States (along with many talented writers, directors, designers, producers, etc.). While there's plenty of first-rate Canadian television, it tends to be made in Hollywood!

1968–1983: CONSOLIDATION

The regime instituted by the CRTC in the early 1970s continued unabated into the early 1980s. In the United States, too, the 1970s effectively marked the last time that traditional broadcast television would dominate popular culture. Specifically, cable became the delivery medium of choice for an overwhelming majority of Canadians, with the result that Canada became one of the world's most heavily cabled countries. The expansion of cable was matched by the rise of large-scale cable operators, most notably Shaw, Vidéotron, and Rogers. In 1975, the CRTC, having acquired responsibility for the management of telecommunications, was renamed the Canadian Radio-television and Telecommunications Commission.

The expansion of cable greatly increased the number of television signals available to the average Canadian. Indeed, cable virtually eliminated *spectrum scarcity*. The era of *channel abundance* ushered in by cable generated unanticipated pressures. Consumers began to demand more and more American channels, especially as the justification based on spectrum scarcity no longer existed. In addition, cable operators wanted to distribute new channels in order to maintain their rates of profit. Indeed, the cable television was fast becoming a *mature industry*—that is, an industry in which all likely subscribers have already subscribed, and in which revenue growth can come only from the selling of new services.

The cable operators' desire for increased profits and consumer demand for increased choice placed the CRTC in a conundrum. The most-requested new services were American; however, the CRTC did not want to license *American* choices because it harboured the fear, first expressed by the Massey Commission, that American television was base and vulgar (despite persistent and reliable evidence that audiences preferred it). The CRTC's solution was to encourage the creation of *Canadian specialty channels* that could serve as alternatives to the U.S. channels. In short, the CRTC introduced *managed choice*, in which the services it deemed appropriate were distributed by cable operators (1) in order to satisfy the operators' desire for new services, and (2) in the hope of meeting consumer demand.

In fact, the explosion of specialty channels had already begun in the United States. HBO, which had been launched in 1973, was followed by MTV, CNN, superstations such as WTBS, and eventually a plethora of services ranging from The Romance Channel to the Game Show Network. Quite unexpectedly, the U.S. specialty (or pay-cable) channels had such a great appetite for programming material that they began to acquire Canadian content.

The CRTC's first foray into specialty channels occurred in the early 1980s when it mandated the launch of a raft of movie channels (First Choice, Alberta Superchannel, Ontario Superchannel, Star Channel, TVEC) and a lively arts channel (C-Channel). In short order, all of these collapsed or significantly altered their business plans. In the 1970s, a new private broadcaster—CanWest Global— was licensed, and the number of independent stations multiplied. The most significant of these stations was Toronto's Citytv under the stewardship of Moses Znaimer.

1983–1993: THE RISE OF INDEPENDENT PRODUCTION

Canadian television was historically characterized by an absence of independent producers. As noted earlier, Canada had no equivalent to Hollywood, with its major studios or small suppliers who could compete for the right to manufacture television programming. All that changed in 1983, when the federal government created Telefilm Canada and altered the mandate of the CBC. Telefilm Canada provides funding for both Canadian film and television productions. However, only independent producers are eligible to receive financial assistance (CBC and CTV, as broadcasters, are not eligible). In addition to assisting production, distribution, and exports, the funding encourages international co-productions (i.e., film or television programs undertaken by a Canadian producer and an international partner).

The creation of Telefilm coincided with a shift in the CBC's mandate. The CBC was now required to obtain 50 percent of its entertainment programming from independent producers. In this way, through Telefilm and the new mandate, the government transferred funds from the CBC to Telefilm, and from Telefilm to independent producers. In essence, it transformed the CBC from an in-house producer into a purchaser of outside content, thereby supporting Telefilm Canada's goal of building an independent television production sector in Canada.

Several companies emerged, most notably Alliance Atlantis Communications, Nelvana, Cinar, and Corus Entertainment. By the end of the 1990s, Canadian television resembled American television more than ever. It was dominated by three major broadcasters (CBC, CTV, CanWest Global) who not only produced in-house but also acquired product both on the international market and from the nascent Canadian production industry. The independent producers competed against each other by "pitching" stories to networks in the hope they would be picked up and developed. Whereas their U.S. counterparts could generally recoup all of their production costs in the U.S. market alone, Canadian producers could not recover their costs in Canada alone. To make up for the absent market, they could call on Telefilm, seek out international partners through a co-production, or obtain assistance in the form of tax credits by conforming to the point system (discussed below). Often, they would use all three strategies (Telefilm, co-production, tax credit) in tandem.

Examples of *co-productions* include the television shows *Katts and Dog* and *Bordertown*. Both were co-productions between companies located in Canada and France, and both were sold to U.S. pay-cable channels. Both shows presented their creators with the problem of designing a story that could appeal to audiences in all three countries and still qualify for Canadian funding. Both shows solved the problem by featuring prominent French characters as well as locations that could be either Canada or the United States. Thus, *Katts and Dog* is a police story set in a generic "North American" city, while *Bordertown* is a western set on the border between Canada and the United States. Whatever the merits of these productions, Canada is among the world's leading co-producers. The government incentives lower everyone's costs and result in content with high production values. Furthermore, the most desirable market to enter is the United States, and U.S. pay-cable channels are among the most reliable purchasers of Canadian content. A sale to a U.S. network can be extremely lucrative, so it is not surprising that a U.S. broadcaster frequently features as an element in current Canadian production strategies.

Of course, throwing the American market into the mix can result in programs that many in Canada do not even consider Canadian. Programs such as *RoboCop*, *Traders*, and *Psi Factor* have been dismissed by critics as "inauthentic" or "industrial Canadian" and therefore as unworthy of public support. Others maintain that such shows are worthy of support precisely because they connect with a popular audience and thus help lay the foundation for a stronger industry. Indeed, we should be careful of defining *Canadian* in such a way that it cuts out the full range of things on which Canadians may wish to express themselves, thereby restricting creative endeavour to a narrow segment of stereotypically Canadian topics. It should be pointed out, as well, that production incentives have resulted in a number of critically acclaimed programs, including *DaVinci's Inquest*, *The Boys of St. Vincent*, *Wind at My Back*, and *Nuremberg*.

One final strategy producers use to compensate for the absent market is to earn tax credits by adhering to a point system. The television point system is similar to the MAPL system used in the recording industry. Points are given for observable "Canadian" features: two points if the lead performer is Canadian, one point if the director, writer, camera operator, etc., is Canadian. If a production achieves at least ten points, it becomes eligible for tax credits.

As the independent production sector thrived, the 1980s and 1990s were also marked by the continued expansion of Canadian specialty channels and the arrival of new delivery systems (especially satellite TV and the Internet). The CRTC licensed new rafts of specialty channels in 1984, 1988, and 1995; in late 2000, it licensed more than 260 specialty *digital* channels. The second, third, and fourth waves of specialty channels were considerably more successful than the first, introducing such mainstays as MuchMusic, TSN, Newsworld, and YTV, as well as Vision, Bravo!, Space, and TalkTV, among others. While the new specialty channels helped to consolidate the position of the major cable companies, they did not in all instances satisfy consumer demand for access to the most desired American channels.

More significant than the consolidation of cable was the introduction of satellite TV and the Internet. Both of these delivery systems are, by their very nature, international in scope and fail to respect existing political boundaries. Furthermore, they virtually eliminate any lingering doubts over spectrum scarcity by using *digital compression* to make the promise of the 500- or 5000-channel universe both achievable and affordable. Both delivery systems have caused profound concern among the existing broadcasters, who fear that they will be left behind in the new universe of choice. Of course, it is possible that consumers, when faced with 5000 channels, will be drawn to recognizably Canadian content as something distinctive and desirable. Nonetheless, the existing players have been hedging their bets, initiating a frenzy of mergers and convergence intended to guarantee their presence on the new platforms—and hence their economic survival.

1993–2001: THE IMPACT OF DIGITAL TECHNOLOGY

The period since 1993 has been characterized by the introduction of digital technology and media mergers. In addition to providing both higher quality and a far greater number of television signals, digitization makes it feasible for viewers to watch what they want, when they want, thereby disrupting traditional delivery mechanisms and entrenched media habits.

Digital technology can be transmitted over the air, via the Internet, on cable, via microwave, and, perhaps most significantly, by *direct broadcast satellite* (DBS). In the 1990s, when terms such as "information superhighway" were still fresh and the Internet was an exciting new technology, it was DBS that was of greatest concern to the Canadian television industry. Cable companies dubbed digital satellites "Deathstars" and claimed that they threatened Canadian culture.

The CRTC more or less concurred: it fashioned a satellite or *direct-to-home* (DTH) policy that would block U.S. satellite companies. Despite the fact that satellites are a *digital* platform with all the advantages mentioned above, the CRTC also determined that the *made-in-Canada* satellite industry would broadcast only what was already available on cable. In essence, the CRTC restricted satellites to existing cable carriage in order to protect the existing cable industry, thereby defeating the whole purpose of DBS.

Nonetheless, the U.S.-based DirecTV went to air in 1994, and, as had happened at the dawn of television, attracted many Canadian subscribers who wanted to watch U.S. television. The so-called grey market—Canadians who want satellite-delivered television and are not waiting for the government to act—naturally revived longstanding fears about the threat of American television. However, many observers noted that the real threat posed by DBS was to the monopoly enjoyed by cable companies. DBS represented the first real competition the cable companies had ever known.

Moreover, if consumers could unplug from the regulated universe of cable TV and plug into the relatively unregulated and international universe of satellite TV, then the rationale for the CRTC itself would be called into question. The CRTC, for its part, set about creating a made-in-Canada DBS policy whose outcome, by 1997, was the dominance of the market by two satellite providers: Bell ExpressVu, owned and controlled by BCE, and StarChoice, owned and controlled by Shaw Communications; rather than bringing new entrants into the television market, the CRTC actually helped to consolidate the power of existing giants.

Another important feature of the 1990s was the trend to convergence. *Convergence* refers to the integration not only of technologies (broadcast, cable, satellite, computer) but also of the corporations that intend to use the technologies. In addition, as technologies and corporations converge, they tend to produce *fragmentation* of the audience. In a world of digitization that delivers a multiplicity of options to viewers, almost every conceivable interest can be targeted with specific programming. Media owners, producers, and advertisers are thus able to splinter audiences into narrower segments and distinct niches.

CONVERGENCE IN CANADIAN TELEVISION

In 1995, the CRTC opened up the media playing field by allowing carriers—cable, telephone, and satellite—to acquire a significant financial interest in *content* through the acquisition of digital and broadcast licenses. This new policy laid the foundation for subsequent mergers. In 2000, Canada's two largest private broadcasters both engaged in mergers. In a deal worth $3.5 billion, CanWest Global took over Western International Communications and the Southam newspaper chain, formerly owned by Conrad Black's Hollinger Inc. Similarly, CTV was acquired by telephone giant Bell Canada Enterprises (BCE), which also acquired the *Globe and Mail*. Rogers Communications, Canada's largest cable distributor, aligned itself with American giants Microsoft and AT&T. Also in 2000, Quebecor Inc. (owner of the Sun Media newspaper group, the Quebec-based TQS television network, and the Internet portal canoe.ca), acquired Groupe Vidéotron, Quebec's largest cable company, for $4.9 billion.

In all these mergers, those who own the *means of delivery* are acquiring *content* and *content providers*. BCE, for example, owns the largest and richest wired network in Canada, telephone lines. It launched the Bell ExpressVu satellite system and the Internet portal Sympatico in 1995 and 1997 respectively. In 2000, it acquired CTV and the *Globe and Mail*, creating BellGlobeMedia, a monolith that produces content in-house (*Globe and Mail*, CTV) and distributes it via satellite and Internet.

Smaller operators have also been involved in mergers. For example, Shaw Communications, Canada's second-largest cable operator, acquired the production house Nelvana (the premier creator of animated programs in Canada) through its subsidiary Corus Entertainment. The independent production companies Alliance Communication and Atlantis Television Ventures became Alliance Atlantis Communications following a merger in 1998. Alliance Atlantis has significant stakes in a number of specialty channels, including History Television, Showcase, Life Network, Home & Garden Television, Headline Sports/The Score, and Food Network Canada). It also recently acquired Great North Productions (*Jake and the Kid*) and Salter Street Films (which holds the licence for Independent Film Channel Canada and produces *This Hour Has 22 Minutes*, *Made in Canada*, *The Awful Truth with Michael Moore*, *Blackfly*, *Emily of New Moon*, and *LEXX*).

Instead of "new" media (such as the Internet and DBS) cannibalizing "old" media (such as TV), it appears that the established media players are using the new media to reach and target the diverse audiences that they themselves fragmented. Old media do not disappear in the wake of the new: they adapt to changing circumstances and are transformed into something different that meets new demands and attracts new audiences and niches. The impetus for content providers (independent production houses, television networks, etc.) and content suppliers (satellite undertakings of specialty channels, etc.) to merge is clear. Regardless of the specific players involved, the goal is always to control not just the pipeline but also the source of content that fills the pipeline.

CONVERGENCE: TECHNOLOGY IN THE SERVICE OF PROFIT

One major factor driving corporate mergers is the expectation that in the near future, the Internet will be able to deliver reliable, high-quality television images into the home. At present, most people connect to the Internet via phone lines. The challenge for service providers is to connect users to high-speed Internet, which is capable of delivering movies, television programs, and other content that is most likely to be desired by consumers. When BCE acquired CTV for $2.3 billion, it did so in order to gain access to CTV's programming, which it hoped to webcast via its high-speed Sympatico service. Indeed, reflecting the "bigger is better" mantra and the hope that more synergies will present themselves, the deal's subsequent value grew to $4 billion with the addition of the *Globe and Mail*.

However, while digital technology makes convergence possible and even desirable, it does not mean that old media will simply be replaced by new media or that the new merged entities will form happy unions. An example of old media fighting back occurred in November 1999 when William R. Craig established the Canadian Web site iCraveTV.com. Its purpose was to make 17 Toronto-area television channels available on-line, without seeking the broadcasters' approval. Cable television had started in a similar fashion 40 years earlier, but iCraveTV.com proposed a very different business model: the site, a kind of "Internet superstation," would be free to visitors and supported solely by banner advertising.

The iCraveTV.com start-up was made possible by the CRTC's ruling, in May 1999, that it would not attempt to regulate Internet content. For all intents and purposes, then, iCraveTV.com was a perfectly legal undertaking. Yet, it drew the ire of a powerful array of "old media" representatives, including the Motion Picture Association of America (MPAA), the National Football League (NFL), and the Canadian Association of Broadcasters (CAB). They accused iCraveTV.com of "cyberspace stealing," and eventually the start-up was forced to shut down. In this way, the terms of convergence are being dictated by the media industry's largest, most established players.

When it comes to assessing the prospects for webcasting deriving from cross-media partnerships, the signals are decidedly mixed. In May 2000, more than one million people saw the webcast of a Victoria's Secret fashion show. However, as standard network fare declines in popularity, a measure of scepticism about Internet TV is warranted. It is not at all clear that a majority of viewers will want to watch television on a computer monitor, especially as new television technologies such as HDTV are launched.

Nonetheless, in a further attempt to realize media synergies, Rogers Communications bought the Toronto Blue Jays baseball team for $110 million. By owning the content (sporting events) that people want to watch, Rogers hopes to attract more subscribers to the service that offers that content. The Rogers strategy reflects a profit-driven view of the role of Canadian content. According to this model, the value of Canadian content lies not in "telling our stories to ourselves." Rather, it lies in increasing the customer base—and hence the revenues—of large corporations. Evidence for this view is found in the fate of the Montreal Canadiens. When that team was put up for sale in 2000, not a single Canadian bidder came forward, and the franchise was eventually sold to an American company. It would appear that potential bidders like BCE and Quebecor decided that the Canadiens were unlikely to increase their viewership enough to make a takeover worthwhile.

Convergence strategies must also be considered in light of the precipitous decline in technology stocks (including those of media companies such as Rogers) that began in early 2000, and in light of the fact that media conglomerates such as Quebecor are being forced to sell assets in order to pay down the crushing debt that resulted from their convergence-driven acquisitions.

FRAGMENTATION

Large corporations try to position themselves across multiple media outlets (newspapers, television, the Internet). In so doing, they implicitly recognize that the audience is *already* fragmented. Different people have different media habits, and it is increasingly difficult to assemble truly large audiences around a single medium or media event. Indeed, the new media environment is characterized by an abundance of content and of channels to deliver it. Confronted with this abundance, Canadians are choosing to watch not just more content of international origin but also more specialty services. For example, the percentage of viewing time devoted to specialty channels rose from 14 percent in 1990 to 19 percent in 1995 to 22 percent in 1998. French-language specialty channels went from 17 percent of all viewing time to almost 30 percent (Taras, 1999, p. 97). These figures indicate not just an increase in channel availability but also a demand for products that speak to increasingly specialized and sophisticated viewer interests.

Fragmentation is also promoted by the increasing *personalization* of media. For instance, MP3 players plug users into a private world of music enjoyment but also unplug them from the broader world of shared musical experience. The introduction of a new tier of cable services in the late 1990s was marketed by Rogers Communications as "Me TV." Satellite providers likewise promise to let subscribers build personalized menus. While the VCR lets people watch what they want, when they want, *personal video recorders* such as TiVo and Replay TV *learn* the viewer's preferences and program themselves to record all programs matching the PVR's record of the viewer's favourites.

The mere fact of digitization does not mean that fragmentation is a fait accompli or a bad outcome. The civic rituals that tie a country do not vanish simply because there is more choice. Even with the cable and specialty channel explosion and the alternative of Internet programming, "close to two and a half million people still assemble at ten and eleven o'clock each night to watch *The National* on CBC and *The CTV Evening News*" (Taras, 1999, p. 9). In addition, the digital satellite initiative has not lived up to its earlier promise. Today's most successful service, Bell ExpressVU, boasts about 650,000 subscribers. Digital cable has experienced similar growing pains. Despite the effort by the cable industry to upgrade its infrastructure and to convert analog subscribers to the more expensive digital option, between 1988 and 2001 only 500,000 cable subscribers converted to digital. (Indeed, only an estimated two million cable and satellite subscribers have the capability to receive digital signals.) There may be a tendency on the part of audiences to seek out common experiences, at least at certain times or around certain events, and to resist total fragmentation. At any rate, the current state of television does not allow us to draw any definitive conclusions either way.

CANADIAN CONTENT ISSUES

Recent developments in the television industry have reignited the perennial debate over Canadian culture and its protection and promotion. It is certainly reasonable to expect that Canadian media should present Canadians with a reflection of the country itself. No one would deny that American media achieve this goal for American viewers. And, of course, the CBC's mandate includes the requirement to tell "Canadian stories." But what counts as a Canadian story? And do our regulatory structures favour or hinder such an enterprise?

Canada shares a border with the largest economic, military, and entertainment power on the planet. It is hardly surprising, then, that Canadians share at least some of the interests and values of their American neighbours. Indeed, in 2000 approximately 5.3 million Canadians—the biggest television audience of the year—watched the Academy Awards on CTV (by contrast, some Canadian award shows are not even televised). As well as demonstrating a strong liking for much American television, Canada is divided into highly distinct regional and linguistic markets; the same shows are rarely hits across all regions and rarely enjoy the same degree of popularity everywhere.

Nonetheless, Canada continues to produce—and to export—a surprising amount of television. According to some estimates, Canada is the second-largest exporter of television programs in the world, after the United States (Keller, 1997, p. C3). Still, as noted earlier, there is some question as to the "Canadianness" of some domestic products. Successful "Canadian" productions such as *Nikita* or *Earth: Final Conflict* may provide useful content to networks starved for a constant flow of material, but they also bear little resemblance to their country of origin.

Throughout the 1990s, partly in the hope of appealing to an increasingly fragmented audience, Canadian networks experimented with so-called fringe genres. These included dramas about cowboys (*Lonesome Dove*), Natives (*North of 60*, *The Rez*), aliens (*Psi Factor*), investment bankers (*Traders*), and even park rangers (*Destiny Ridge*). Traditionally, the most successful Canadian series have been based on television's most common genres, such as cop shows (*Due South*, *DaVinci's Inquest*), lawyer shows (*Street Legal*), and mysteries (*Wojeck*). In the modern media environment in which too many shows call out for attention, it may be that a more conventional show with built-in familiarity will appeal to the most people most quickly. Furthermore, familiar forms may also help international sales, which are increasingly important to Canadian producers. An immediately recognizable product may be more easily exportable than something that is heavily marked as "Canadian," though the danger exists that so-called Canadian programming will be indistinguishable from the American programming it emulates.

The recent television phenomenon known as "reality TV"—part documentary drama and part contest—underlines the complicated relationship between audience appeal and mandated Canadian messages. The best-known example of reality TV is *Survivor* (CBS). Ratings throughout 2000 and 2001 indicate a sustained demand for this type of programming. At first glance, reality TV would seem tailor-made for Canadian television because it is far cheaper to produce than standard prime-time dramas.

Canadian public policy and financing regulations, however, limit what is possible. It is difficult for new genres such as reality TV to be recognized by existing bureaucratic structures that determine which programs are eligible for funding. As a result, at the beginning of 2001, Global's *Popstars* was the only domestic reality series carried by a private broadcast network. It averaged more than 600,000 viewers per week in Ontario alone, which made it the top-rated Canadian show. *Popstars* draws three times as many viewers as *Making the Band*, a similar American series that was broadcast on Global the previous year (Atherton, 2001, p. D1). However, because *Popstars* is so "ordinary" and replicable (any production company anywhere in the world could produce the same thing), it is a less attractive candidate for exportation to other countries than previously successful programs such as *Night Heat*, *Road to Avonlea*, and *Street Legal*. *Popstars* meets the requirement to tell "stories about ourselves to ourselves," but its inability to attract meaningful foreign revenue confines its producer to the relatively small Canadian market. Thus, even relatively inexpensive shows with potential audience appeal can become financially unattractive.

WHAT CONSTITUTES CANADIAN CONTENT?

The problems with financing, viewer taste, and regulatory measures invariably return us to the question of what really constitutes Canadian television. To a large extent, the answer is *sports*. The purchase of the Toronto Blue Jays by Rogers

Communications, and the protracted struggle between CTV and Rogers for control of the leading sports specialty channels (SportsNet and TSN). underscore the importance of sports in corporate strategies. Equally significant is the fact that over 35 percent of the CBC's prime-time audience is tuned to sports. Indeed, sports has been called "the cornerstone of the English schedule" (Mandate Review Committee, 1996, p. 67). Not only is the CBC a perennial serious bidder for the right to broadcast the Olympic games, but *Hockey Night in Canada* is one of only two CBC shows that can be depended on regularly to pull in more than a million viewers per broadcast. Furthermore, the most successful Canadian specialty channel is TSN, an all-sports network.

Successful Canadian television is not limited to sports or (reflecting the traditional Canadian expertise) news, current affairs, and documentary. Increasingly, successful Canadian programming also includes *music*. MuchMusic, the flagship channel of the CHUM media empire, is the most visible specialty station in CHUM's stable and has come to represent the company's production aesthetic. In the words of one pundit, "for young Canadians, MuchMusic has become the new CBC—cultural glue with a Technicolor sniff" (Roberts, 1995, p. B2).

CHUM Limited, which originated with the purchase of the Toronto-based AM radio station 1050 CHUM in 1954, owns and operates 24 radio stations. It is also the owner of Citytv, Canada's largest independent television station. Originally owned by Moses Znaimer, a former CBC producer, Citytv debuted in 1972 with a low-budget, high-concept style distinguished by a frenetic pace, open studios, and hand-held cameras. Seeking to replicate this style but narrowing its entertainment-based content even further, Znaimer introduced MuchMusic as one of the first Canadian specialty channels in 1984.

Since its debut, the "nation's music station" has been a breakout success. In its first year, it made a profit two years ahead of projection. Spinoffs include MuchMoreMusic, a sister channel in Canada for those who like their music a little older, and MusiquePlus, a music channel launched in 1986 for the French-language market. The success of the formula is also evident internationally. MuchUSA reaches 12 million households via DirecTV and is also received in Bermuda, the Barbados, Grenada, and Trinidad. MuchMusic Argentina was started in 1992, and took just six years to surpass MTV Latin America to become the most-watched cable music station in the country. It is also seen in Bolivia, Chile, Paraguay, and Uruguay.

CITYTV: A NEW CULTURAL SENSIBILITY?

Domestically, CHUM owns a number of local television stations, including CKVR in Barrie, Ontario, and CHRO in Ottawa. With its established channels and its application for digital services, CHUM/Citytv illustrates the fragmented nature of the contemporary television environment. Its strategy is to start with a show and then create first a channel and then a series of specialized channels. Thus, it would not be surprising to see Citytv programs such as *FashionTV* and *QueerTV* morph into specialty channels. CHUM/Citytv grows its business by narrowcasting to niche audiences, rather than creating one homogenized signal that attempts to appeal to all.

Perhaps even more important to the question of *Canadian* television is the success of ChumCity International in marketing Citytv and MuchMusic programming worldwide. In fact, Citytv became Canada's first broadcaster to export itself when the leading private broadcasters in Brazil and Finland sought to copy its logo, urban focus, and local programming via licensing arrangements. Since 1996, Citytv's format has been tested in Helsinki, where the top private broadcaster duplicated some City/MuchMusic programs daily in a 90-minute late-afternoon time slot that drew good ratings and became Finland's highest-rated youth programming block. This led to an application for Citytv Helsinki, a round-the-clock cable channel. Similarly, in Brazil, a São Paulo channel was transformed into a Citytv look-alike, with both countries sending annual franchise fees back to Canada. In 1999, a station in Bogota, Columbia, practically cloned Citytv.

Licensing the original model has meant the local production of shows such as *Mujeras en Linea* (*Women on the Line*); a version of the morning talk show *CityLine*; *Circo Electrico*, a dance program adapted from CHUM's *Electric Circus*; and *CityNoticias*, an evening newscast modelled after *CityPulse*. Other shows that run on Citytv are not just copied but see their original content franchised internationally. *FashionTelevision* is seen in 120 countries. Even fringe shows such as *Ed's Night Party* (starring Ed the Sock, MuchMusic's irascible sock-puppet video jockey) have found a home on the College Broadcast Network in the United States.

CONCLUSION

The fact that Canadians can play a role in the era of increasingly powerful global media corporations need not mean the death of the local. Instead, a decidedly Canadian invention—the street-front, studio-less television "environment"—has been successfully exported to other countries in order to provide other broadcasters with distinctive local programming. Unlike CBC and CTV, which Znaimer accuses of merely aping British and American models of broadcasting, Citytv claims to be a novel Canadian formula that is known worldwide. Yet, the defining feature of Citytv programming is its *originality*, not the fact that it is Canadian. Citytv does not try to make *Canadian* television, but to make successful television for Canadians *and* for a worldwide audience. Its Canadianness lies not principally in its content, but in the conditions of its production and in its cultural sensibility.

Unique, interesting, and groundbreaking content can certainly be produced in Canada. This material can resonate with Canadian audiences. But it should not be imposed on them. Canadian television can be unique fare, but it need not be stereotypically Canadian. Though there are undoubtedly Canadian stories that many

Canadians wish to see, Canadian television is more than a product made for the domestic market; it is also a product that is willingly bought by international audiences.

Convergence is both a challenge and an opportunity for those who produce television in Canada. Along with bigger corporations go increasingly sophisticated audiences for whom traditional strategies of content production and distribution seem increasingly irrelevant. In the 500- or 5000-channel universe, Canadian programming will almost certainly be distinctive by definition. But the truly successful programming will also likely be as sophisticated as its intended audience.

QUESTIONS

1. Is there a specific feel or sensibility to Canadian television? Give reasons for your answer.
2. There is no real difference between the Canadian television audience and the American television audience. Discuss.
3. Are content quotas the best way to ensure a Canadian television industry? Give reasons for your answer.
4. What is the impact of digital technologies on Canadian television?

WEB SITES

Canadian Audio-Visual Certification Office:
   http://www.pch.gc.ca/culture/cult_ind/cavco_bcpac/english.htm
CRTC (Broadcasting Act) **http://www.crtc.gc.ca/**
Massey Commission (Royal Commission on National Development in the Arts, Letters and Sciences 1949–1951): **http://www.nlc-bnc.ca/2/5/**
Watching TV: The MZTV Museum:
   http://www.civilization.ca/hist/tv/tv04eng.html

REFERENCES

Atherton, Tony. (2001, March 1). Zoo TV won't be made in Canada. *Ottawa Citizen*, p. D1.

Canada. Royal Commission on National Development in the Arts, Letters and Sciences (Massey Commission). (1951). *Report of the Royal Commission on National Development in the Arts, Letters and Sciences*. Ottawa: King's Printer. Retrieved from http://www.nlc-bnc.ca/2/5/

Keller, Anthony. (1997, September 13). Have Can-con, will travel. *Globe and Mail*, p. C14.

Mandate Review Committee CBC, NFB and Telefilm. (1996). *Making our voices heard: Canadian broadcasting and film for the 21st century*. Ottawa: Ministry of Supply and Services Canada.

Roberts, Mike. (1995, January 6). Much ado about music. *Vancouver Province*, p. B2.

Taras, David. (1999). *Power and betrayal in the Canadian media*. Peterborough, ON: Broadview Press.

FURTHER READING

Attallah, Paul. (1996). Canadian television exports: Into the mainstream. In J. Sinclair, E. Jacka, and S. Cunningham (Eds.), *New patterns in global television* (pp. 161–191). Oxford: Oxford University Press.

———. (2000). Public broadcasting in Canada. *Gazette, 62*(3–4), 177–203.

Bird, Roger. (1988). *Documents of Canadian broadcasting*. Toronto: Oxford University Press.

Canadian Film and Television Production Association. (1998). *The Canadian film and television production industry: A 1998 profile*. Ottawa.

Collins, Richard. (1990). *Culture, communication, and national identity: The case of Canadian television*. Toronto: University of Toronto Press.

Fraser, Matthew. (1999). *Free-for-all: The struggle for dominance on the digital frontier*. Toronto: Stoddart.

McKinsey and Company. (1999, January). *Public-service broadcasters around the world: A McKinsey report for the BBC*. London: McKinsey and Company.

Raboy, Marc. (1990). *Missed opportunities: The story of Canada's broadcasting policy*. Kingston, ON: McGill-Queen's University Press.

Weir, E.A. (1965). *The struggle for national broadcasting in Canada*. Toronto: McClelland and Stewart.

13

Computers and the Internet

Susan Bryant
University of Windsor

and

Richard Smith
Simon Fraser University

This chapter discusses the computer industry and the industry that has grown up around the global networking of computers (the Internet). The computer industry in Canada originated in the 1940s when Canadian universities and research labs participated with their U.S. counterparts in designing devices to assist in the war effort. The Internet industry in Canada is much younger, dating from the 1990s (although Canadian universities and research institutes were involved in the precommercial era, almost to the very beginning of the Internet).

The chapter is divided into six sections that examine: (1) the technological and social history of the computer and Internet industries, and how they are merging in the 21st century; (2) the organization of these industries, including concentration of ownership, major players, and potential challenges to organizational patterns; (3) regulation issues and policy initiatives around the industries; (4) the social uses of computers and the Internet; (5) traditional and emerging computer and Internet applications; (6) ethical issues around these technologies (specifically, pornography on the Internet and electronic surveillance in the workplace); (7) the relationship between traditional media and Web-based media; and (8) areas for future research.

TECHNOLOGICAL AND SOCIAL HISTORY

Nowadays, computers and the Internet are inextricably linked. This was not always the case. Computers have a long history, dating from the 1840s or even earlier. At one time, the word "computer" referred to a person who had special training and did a special job, namely calculating complicated equations by hand. As electronic programmable devices, such as those familiar to users today, computers date back to the 1940s.

The basic design of the computer has not changed since the 1940s, although the speed, capacity, and connections have changed dramatically. This design, called a *von Neumann* architecture after the computer pioneer John von Neumann, refers to the way in which the computer is organized and constructed. Computer scientists working in university and government laboratories established these designs.

In the last two decades, as the computer industry has become a major force in the economy, the focus of computer design has shifted from public institutions to private-sector research and development facilities.

Modern computers are conceptually simple. They are binary logic devices—that is, they do their work by evaluating instructions with "yes" and "no" answers. To choose between "yes" and "no," computers use logic "gates." The power of computers depends on the number of gates (allowing complex combinations) and the speed with which they operate (into the trillions of operations per second when working in parallel in supercomputers). These two aspects of computers—numbers of internal connections and speed of operation—have been the markers by which computer evolution has been charted since the 1970s.

Prior to the 1970s, two other significant events occurred that shaped the computer and the computer industry. The first event, which derived from the work of Walter Brattain, John Bardeen, and William Shockley at AT&T Bell Labs in the 1950s, was the development of the *transistor*. Smaller, less expensive, cooler, and more reliable than the vacuum tube, the transistor allowed computer manufacturers to shift away from the vacuum tube (or "valve") type of computers. Vacuum tubes were not the first attempt at mechanical and electromechanical computers. The "difference engine" of Sir Charles Babbage, made famous by William Gibson and Bruce Sterling in the novel *The Difference Engine*, was an early attempt at using mechanical devices to perform computational tasks. Before the difference engine, there were knitting machines that ran on punch cards and calculators that used ratcheting wheels and rods to perform complex calculations. In fact, at the beginning of the 20th century, International Business Machines (IBM) Corporation specialized in building mechanical adding machines that were used to process U.S. census data.

The second major change occurred when transistors were "etched" onto silicon wafers (often called a "chip") and then packed, in increasing numbers, onto a single chip—the birth of the integrated circuit. This development stemmed from the work of Robert Noyce at Fairchild Semiconductors and Jack Kilby at Texas Instruments in the late 1950s. From then on, the race was on to pack more transistors ("circuits") onto a chip and run them at a faster pace.[1]

Computer networks or connections are what enable two or more computers to "talk" to one another. These networks were initially "overlaid" on existing telecommunications networks. Some of the first computer connections were made through telegraph lines, using a remote keypunch to transmit data and instructions to a distant computer. Later the telephone network was used to carry computer instructions and data, using a device that converted the digital signals of the computer into the analog signals of the voice network. These devices, which modulated and demodulated pulse (on/off) signals into wave (sound) signals, were called "modems." Modems are still widely employed for that purpose, despite growing use of network systems designed specifically for computers.

In the 1970s, Bob Metcalfe, as part of his Ph.D. thesis at MIT, developed a computer networking technique called *Ethernet*. This technology was implemented by Metcalfe on the experimental "Alto" computer at Xerox's Palo Alto Research Center (PARC). In a move that was emblematic of the era, Dr. Metcalfe relinquished the commercial rights to his invention, releasing them to the public as a standard that anyone could use. Today, Ethernet is the most widely used networking standard in the world.

Computer networks are built in layers, with the concrete physical layer (the wires or fibres) at the bottom to the abstract (software) layers at the top. This networking model is broken into seven layers known collectively as the OSI (Open Standards for Interconnection) networking model. Much of the excitement around "convergence" stems from the fact that the Internet has established widely accepted, open standards for several of these layers. The existence of open standards at the lower levels allows computer programmers to work more quickly, as well as with confidence that their efforts will work in a variety of situations. There are clear benefits for computer users as well. For example, when you upgrade from a modem connection to a high-speed cable or ADSL (asynchronous digital subscriber line) connection at home, all of your Internet software (e-mail, Web browser, chat software) continues to work as before.

Convergence is also occurring because the underlying technologies (networks and computers) are being built to run at much higher speeds. Faster computers and networks allow for a delivery of converged services and content (e.g., voice or video) that matches or betters that provided by television and telephones. Typically, computer users have little tolerance for delays in receiving voice or video. Television and telephone are the respective standards by which they tend to judge the performance of computers in delivering video and voice.

There are two ways to send a representation of something (voice or video) through a network. You can create a special network that is designed to carry an analog signal directly from one place to another. Taking care not to introduce interference or distortions into that signal is very important because they are impossible to remove. (The scratches you hear on an old vinyl record are an example of analog signals that have been damaged.) The alternative is to send a signal through a *digital network*. The benefit of a digital network is that the bits (of your image, for example) can be re-sent if they do not arrive, compressed if there are a lot of them, and checked for accuracy and consistency. An image or sound that is cut up into tiny pieces has been "digitized" or "sampled." In the past, the limitations of computers were such that the process was too expensive for home use. In recent years, however, general-purpose computers have become fast and cheap enough to make the sampling process possible, while special computer chips known as "digital signal processors" have facilitated that process by increasing speed.

Just as computers are getting better at dealing with the conversions of analog to digital and back again, networks are getting faster and faster. For the home-computer user ten years ago, a connection to a computer network ran at just over 1000 bits per second. Today, 56,000 bits per second is the norm, and many homes have an Internet connection capable of running more than 1,000,000 bits per second. This vast increase in speed is completing the convergence process and leading to an ever-broadening set of options delivered by computers and computer networks, including video entertainment, interactive voice communication, and games.

THE COMPUTER AND NETWORK INDUSTRY IN CANADA

The computer industry in Canada dates back to the 1950s. Computers in Canada were first used at universities, most notably the University of Toronto, where an early computer was assembled from parts imported from the United States. These computers were large, expensive, noisy, hot, and unreliable. As noted earlier, they were constructed not from transistors or integrated circuits, but from vacuum tubes and mechanical relays.

In the early days, people went to the computer—or, rather, the computer operator—in order to submit computation requests and receive results. Researchers at the University of Toronto and University of Saskatchewan, tired of sending boxes of instructions and reports back and forth via the post, pioneered the use of a telegraph system to send instructions from Saskatoon to Toronto. Using a directly connected line and modified paper tape machines, operators in Saskatchewan were able to make the first "remote" computing operations in Canada in the early 1950s.

Computer manufacturing has never been a significant business in Canada, despite some notable attempts by governments to promote the activity. One initiative, the IKON computer designed for the Ontario school system, saw only limited use in schools and never became the commercial success that its promoters hoped for. Other notable computer manufacturing operations in Canada include various "branch plants" for major American corporations such as IBM and Digital Equipment Corporation (DEC, now owned by Compaq). More recently, Canadian entrepreneurs have also done well in niche parts of the computer business, designing and assembling clone computers for local and regional markets. Some of these businesses have grown from small garage or warehouse operations to truly national competitors, although not on the scale of the major international manufacturers. Most of these companies do little research and development, focusing instead on the production of copies of dominant designs.

Canadian firms have carved out more of a place for themselves in computer services, particularly in the era of "service bureau" computing in the 1960s and 1970s. At that time, computers were generally too expensive and specialized for most organizations to be able to justify owning one of their own. Most computer software was custom designed, as there was little in the way of general-purpose software. As a result, computing was done as a full service that included software design, data entry, and report production. Canadian firms like IP Sharp flourished in this business until the era of the desktop and minicomputer, with its packaged software and cheaper prices. Today, computer consulting firms that provide advice and support to organizations continue to make up a Canadian contribution to the overall industry.

Like their counterparts in the United States, Canadian hobbyists built the first desktop and home computers, typically from a kit. Small retail stores grew up to service this market and to provide accessories and spare parts. Some of the first significant orders of desktop computers came from the school systems and universities. Computers like the Apple II were deemed unsuitable for business use, but pioneering teachers and students created software and developed applications for them. The Internet had similar hobby and education roots in Canada, as elsewhere. One of the earliest uses of computers was remote computing applications (exemplified by the University of Toronto/University of Saskatchewan initiative noted above). Unfortunately, no record exists of the noncomputational messages that may have traversed that link. What we do know is that sending messages, the precursors of e-mail, was one of the earliest applications of the connections between American university and military computing installations.

In Canada, as elsewhere, hobbyists pursued a parallel development, using a modem to connect their computers to each other via telephone lines. Soon clusters of hobbyists began to share messages back and forth in a local area on what became known as a *bulletin board system* (BBS). These messages were "posted" on the bulletin board and left there for the next visitor. Refinements to this model came quickly. Private mailboxes were established, groups and subgroups were set up for the public messages, and, most notably, messages for other clusters were shared (often at night to save long-distance charges) with other clusters in other cities. The hobbyist version of these early networks were called *PCBoard* and *FidoNet*, after the software used to manage them. A somewhat more formalized set of networks grew up in (mainly) universities and research and development organizations, called UUNet, named after the software UUCP (unix to unix copy) that ran it.

Canadians were very active in both FidoNet and UUNet, contributing time, expertise, and equipment. A researcher at the University of Toronto developed a foundational program that provided a mechanism for the exchange of *newsgroups*. Canadians also established and supported a national network of FidoNet and Alternet (a spinoff using the same technology) hosts. It is important to remember that virtually all of this early effort was produced on a nonprofit, voluntary basis or as part of research projects at universities. The ethos of the time was such that the notion of charging for computer networking services was thought to be inappropriate, in part because these services were built from volunteer labour or government support, and in part because there was a sense that the free exchange of information could lead to a better world. While this perspective may seem naive in the context of today's commercial, advertising-driven Internet, it did reflect the spirit of the time. In fact, in the early 1990s one of the authors of this chapter was a participant in an on-line discussion group that debated the *possibility* that commercial speech might be permitted on the Internet!

From a technical perspective, the Canadian Internet evolution followed international developments. Among those who contributed to the evolution were researchers at the major Canadian universities, including University of Toronto,

University of Alberta, and University of British Columbia. A precursor of the World Wide Web, *Hytelnet* was developed by Peter Scott at the University of Saskatchewan. The hypertext connection system included information from institutions around the world, but it was restricted mainly to libraries and was soon eclipsed by *gopher*, a program developed at the University of Minnesota, and the *World Wide Web*, developed at The Conseil Européen pour la Recherche Nucléaire (CERN) and popularized by Mosaic, a browser created at the University of Illinois. Another Canadian initiative from the pre-Web era was *Archie*, a protocol developed at McGill University that allows users to search archives of computer files located in file transfer protocol (FTP) sites around the world.

Although the Canadian government did not initially support national networking initiatives to the same degree as the U.S. government, in the last decade it has undertaken major Internet initiatives. Through its CANARIE initiatives, the federal government has built successive research and teaching networks (including CA*net 2 and CA*net 3) that carry ever-increasing amounts of data across the country. The Canadian government is a world leader in initiatives aimed at deploying dark fibre, which allows communities and regions to build telecommunication infrastructure in the same way they build roads and sewers. In this context, dark fibre is seen as a platform for innovation and as a public utility to be shared by all, not as a scarce resource to be marketed by a select few as an end in itself.

POLICY AND REGULATION

Both the computer and the Internet industries remain largely unregulated in Canada. Canadian policy has generally supported the rapid growth and development of high technology production and use as a means of remaining competitive in an era of globalization. The Canadian government's Internet policy is detailed in a report by the Information Highway Advisory Council (IHAC). In commissioning IHAC to do the report, the federal government identified three strategic objectives for the information highway: to create jobs through innovation and investment in Canada, to reinforce Canadian cultural identity and sovereignty, and to ensure universal access at a reasonable cost (Government of Canada, 1997).

IHAC's final report stresses the importance of developing electronic commerce based on an infrastructure that maintains Canada's place as a world leader in communication and information technology. Legislation such as the Bell Canada Act and the Radiocommunication Act has been amended to allow for increased competition and convergence, and to facilitate the introduction of new types of technologies. Amid all the competition and convergence in the television, cable, and telecommunications industries, the Canadian Radio-television and Telecommunications Commission (CRTC) has been shifting away from a policy of intervention. Determining which technologies are appropriate for delivering a given service is seen as a function of market forces.

The benefits to business—in particular, small and medium-sized businesses—have been a key focus of Canada's policies on the information highway. Using the Internet can lower the costs of doing business with suppliers. The Internet also presents opportunities in the form of networking and online sales. As Diebert (1998) points out, the Internet has made possible the shift from national to transnational production and the emergence of global finance. In its final report, the IHAC suggested that the federal government encourage Internet use among Canadian businesses by becoming a "model user" of the Internet in the delivery of its own services. Indeed, the government is providing more and more of its information and services on-line.

A key policy concern related to the information highway is the question of access. In spite of Canada's vast geography, Canadians have enjoyed virtually universal access to broadcasting and telephone services. The information highway must be equally accessible—and accessible to all Canadians, including those with low incomes, those with disabilities, and those living in remote or rural areas. In addition, a distinction must be made between low-speed and high-speed access. High-speed access, which is needed for real-time video and other sophisticated uses, requires that a costly infrastructure be put in place. Is this infrastructure something that can be made available to all Canadians? The issue of access may well be the greatest challenge policymakers will face in the coming years of Internet history.

SOCIAL USES

The social uses of computers and the Internet are perhaps one of the most interesting aspects of this set of technologies. The communication potential of such uses as e-mail and chat rooms is diverse and far-reaching, and is becoming more and more a part of the fabric of our everyday experience. Whether we are maintaining existing relationships with family and friends, meeting new people, playing games, or participating in a community, the on-line social world is exciting and ever-changing.

Electronic mail, or e-mail, has transformed the lives of countless users. The asynchronous character of e-mail means that both parties in an e-mail exchange are free to send or respond to a message at their convenience. Moreover, the ability to communicate with e-mail users around the world contributes to our sense of living in a global village. Closer to home, we exchange e-mails on a daily basis with friends, family, colleagues, teachers, students, and a host of others. Testimonials abound as to the salutary effects of e-mail on family relationships (e.g., parents and grown children in difficult relationships report that they have been brought closer together by the opportunity to communicate in this mediated form). On a less positive note, e-mail has also brought us the *flame*, an inflammatory e-mail that an individual sends to a person in anger or haste and without thinking of the potential consequences.

E-mail has dramatically changed the workplace as well. It was recognized early on that electronic communication, by making it easier for all workers in an organization to communicate with management, had the potential to make workplaces more democratic. It was also predicted that the ways in which individuals navigate the formal structure of their organization might change once the gatekeepers to middle and senior managers were eliminated on-line, thereby making workplace hierarchies less rigid (Sproull and Kiesler, 1991). Both of these developments have been borne out to some extent, but they have also been shown to have limitations. For example, the formal organizational structure has tended to remain intact in terms of how much communicational bypassing an employee can actually get away with.

As a vehicle for increasing workplace efficiency, e-mail has had decidedly mixed results. On the one hand, its convenience and ease of use has facilitated communication in the workplace. On the other hand, those very features encourage indiscriminate e-mail use, creating obvious inefficiencies for workers who must spend a substantial part of their workday reviewing and responding to e-mail messages, many of which may not even be work-related. According to Bertman (1998), e-mail and other technologies introduced into the workplace have produced an "acceleration of expectations." These expectations, which include the implicit requirement that we respond almost immediately to e-mail messages, may insidiously lead to higher stress levels for many types of workers.

In addition to the one-to-one communication offered by e-mail, computer and Internet technologies make it possible for individuals to participate in a variety of groups and communities, including mailing lists, newsgroups, and chat rooms. An Internet *mailing list* is a group of people who have chosen to belong to a particular group based on a common interest or experience. The messages for the group "arrive" in one's e-mail inbox and are therefore asynchronous in nature. Discussions on mailing lists tend to wax and wane over time according to outside events, season, availability of members, and so on.

Newsgroups (also called message boards, bulletin boards, conferences, or forums) are much like mailing lists in that the discussion is via e-mail (and is therefore asynchronous), and a "conversation" may extend from a few days to several months. Newsgroups are typically used for larger communities and are more amenable to in-depth discussions. They may be "threaded" or "linear," terms that refer to two different ways of branching off from the main discussion (i.e., into subtopics or into questions that are pursued by only some of the members). Newsgroups may also provide a sense of place by requiring that members access their messages via a Web site that establishes a common interface—and possibly therefore a common experience—for its members.

Chat rooms are synchronous—that is, unlike newsgroups, they operate in real time. They are used for formal community and organizational events such as scheduled meetings and discussions, but are best known for giving their users purely social opportunities to relax, converse, flirt, and gossip with friends new and old. Some chat rooms are text-based, such as IRC (Internet Relay Chat), while others are graphical and/or voice-based. In such venues, individuals can take on another identity if they choose. Although some users are uncomfortable with the idea of impersonation within chat rooms, it can be a harmless and often useful means of working through identity issues. Supporters of chat rooms also point out that the synchronicity of the communication in a chat room fosters a greater sense of immediacy and therefore a sense of *connection* to the other participants. In addition, the wide range of subjects and interests available for discussion creates exciting opportunities to meet like-minded others.

One of the questions that arises regularly in both scholarly and popular discussions of the Internet is the degree to which connections formed on-line constitute genuine communities. Howard Rheingold, an early advocate of community-building on the Internet, has argued that individuals find on the Net companionship, friendship, emotional support, laughter, debate, and discussion, and that these characteristics form the basis for communities (Rheingold, 1993). Critics of the notion that on-line, or virtual, communities constitute actual communities point to the isolation of individual participants, the lack of physical commitment involved, and the potentially transient nature of on-line groupings. Such analysis tends to be based on comparisons between virtual communities and an *ideal* of face-to-face community experience, rather than on comparisons between virtual communities and face-to-face communities as they actually are. Wellman and Gulia (1999), among others, have concluded that virtual communities are genuine and meaningful, and may even interact with and enhance face-to-face communities in important ways. This set of discussions and analysis is likely to be an ongoing part of analyses of the social uses of the Internet.

ESTABLISHED AND EMERGING APPLICATIONS

The early years of computer networks were characterized by a preoccupation with social and political causes. One pioneering group on the Net was the Whole Earth 'Lectronic Link, or the Well, a bulletin board system based in San Francisco (1985). This community of computer-using social activists, whose early participants and enthusiasts included Howard Rheingold, was a model for numerous other networks, including *freenets*. The first Freenet, based in Cleveland, Ohio (1986), provided wide access to the Internet, as well as a place for individuals to share local experience and interests. Freenets, or community networks as they are called in Canada, operate on a nonprofit basis and are committed to being locally based, locally controlled, and locally owned. Initiatives similar to the Cleveland-based Freenet sprang up in Ottawa, Toronto, and Vancouver in the 1990s. The Vancouver Community Network (http://www.vcn.bc.ca/) is a good example of this kind of site.

A model for the use of on-line communication as a tool for social activism is the Association for Progressive Communications (APC). The APC provides an on-line forum for a wide range of activist groups concerned with social and environmental issues (major forums include PeaceNet, LaborNet, WomensNet, and EcoNet). APC services can be accessed in Canada through Web Networks, a service provider and access point for over 3500 Canadian activists, artists, and nonprofit groups. Other examples of on-line services and communities related to social and environmental justice include Electronic Frontier Canada (the Canadian equivalent to Electronic Frontier Foundation, an organization that focuses on issues related to electronic privacy rights); the National Action Committee on the Status of Women (Canada's largest coalition of feminist groups); and ALTERNATIVES, a Canadian on-line journal devoted to environmental issues.

In the last decade, computers and networks have been widely used in education. In Canada, the federal and provincial governments, as well as numerous private corporations, have supported a wide variety of practical and theoretical investigations into how to use computers for teaching. With the growing popularity of global networks (especially the World Wide Web), Canadian schools and universities are moving rapidly to integrate networked computer technology into teaching and learning at all levels. At the national level, Canada's two most significant programs involve applications of computer and network technologies (e.g., SchoolNet) and research on the use of networked computers in education (e.g., TeleLearning Network of Centres of Excellence). Other federal initiatives include the work done by and for the Office of Learning Technologies, a division of Human Resources Development Canada; a research project on the social impact of computers in schools, sponsored by the Social Sciences and Humanities Research Council; various programs that support community and research networks (e.g., SchoolNet GrassRoots Program); and programs devoted to upgrading the research network used by universities (e.g., CANARIE, CA*net 3).

Historically, technology in education has been an initiative with many isolated applications but few general initiatives, in large part because of the cost and the relatively low return on investment. Public schools in Canada are not well funded, so until recently computers were simply too expensive for widespread use. Networking those computers was almost unthinkably expensive except on a trial basis. The cost of computing has dropped precipitously in the last few years, and technological and policy initiatives have made networking much more possible. At the same time, the increasing use of computers and Internet in homes and offices made parents wonder why their children lacked access to computers in their schools.

All of these factors have led to a tremendous growth not just in the number of computers in schools, but in the introduction of new computer applications into the curriculum. The old "drill and practice" mode of computer use, in which the computer acts as an infinitely patient questioner for simple skills-based tasks such as times tables and spelling, is not disappearing. However, computers are increasingly being used as research and presentation tools in the classroom as software becomes more sophisticated and as students become more adept at using computers not just as a calculator or a word processor, but as a communication device. The nature of computer use is also changing in Canadian universities. In the past, computers were mainly used for the purposes of instruction and research. Today, a growing number of students receive some or all of their course materials through Web pages. In addition, many students interact with their professors and each other via chat rooms and e-mail.

In Canada, as in the rest of the world, a key emerging application of computers in education is *coordination*. Students, administrators, and teachers are using the tools provided by computer software to coordinate schedules, meetings, classes, and presentations. Some schools are using Web-based technology to bridge the gap between school and home. Homework assignments, curricula materials, current topics, and even marks and attendance records are being posted on Web sites that can be accessed by interested parents.

The use of computers in schools and universities is often promoted as a means of controlling both costs and content. Some administrators argue that computers are more cost-effective than other modes of delivery, especially in Canada where there are relatively small numbers of students spread over large distances. In addition, there is the desire on the part of some administrators to "standardize" the curriculum: making it available in the form of downloadable Web page ensures that teachers are all working from the same material. Finally, computer and network vendors have an obvious financial interest in tapping into the enormous education market for equipment and connectivity.

Most teachers and principals, however, support the use of computers out of a genuine desire to improve the teaching and learning experience for themselves and their students. For these individuals, some significant challenges lie ahead. Perhaps the most important of these is training teachers to make effective use of computers and network connections, and to respond appropriately in the event of a computer or network breakdown. At present, such training programs are offered mainly at the school and district levels, although a few regional programs (such as the T-LITE program in British Columbia) are also available. University-based teacher education programs that emphasize teaching with technology have started to emerge, but they are by no means universal.

ETHICAL ISSUES

In Canada and elsewhere, the use of computers and the Internet has given rise to a number of ethical concerns and questions. Two particularly contentious issues are pornography on the Internet and the electronic surveillance of people in the workplace.

Pornographic images are widely available on the Web. One study estimates that six million people around the globe spend at least 11 hours a week visiting Internet porn sites (Cheney, 2000). This situation has prompted calls for censorship or regulation of content on the Internet. However, while possession of pornography is a criminal offence under the Criminal Code of Canada, applying this standard to content on the Internet is problematic. First, the fluid, borderless nature of the Internet makes enforcing antipornography legislation on-line extremely difficult, since producers of pornography can simply post to a site outside Canada and thus beyond the reach of such legislation. Second, and perhaps more important, it has proven extremely difficult (if not impossible) at a practical level to effectively police the Internet's vast and rapidly expanding terrain (it is not uncommon for porn producers to fill their sites with keywords that are typically used in searches for nonsexual topics). Third, the commitment to free speech in both Canada and the United States has led to the relaxing of restrictions on the creation and distribution of certain types of pornography over the past 50 years. The contemporary social consensus seems to be that there should be few restrictions on sexually explicit material that cannot be shown to be harmful to women or children.

However, at the time of writing, the Canadian government has introduced amendments to the Criminal Code that are designed to better protect *children* from becoming the victims of crimes committed via the Internet. Under the proposed legislation, it would be a crime (punishable by a maximum penalty of ten years' imprisonment) to (1) transmit child pornography, (2) make child pornography available either on a Web site or by providing the Web site address of such a site, or (3) export child pornography. In addition, the amendments would make the intentional accessing of child pornography over the Internet an offence punishable by a maximum of five years' imprisonment. Individuals who communicate with children via the Internet in order to lure them to a face-to-face meeting for the purpose of committing a sexual offence would receive a maximum penalty of five years' imprisonment. This proposed legislation represents a noteworthy step in the establishment of legal boundaries around virtual behaviour.

Another ethical concern arising from the use of computers and the Internet involves the electronic surveillance of people in the workplace. While the formal monitoring of workers' behaviour dates back at least a century, electronic technologies have opened up opportunities for more far-reaching and intrusive forms of individual-level surveillance (see Bryant, 1995). Listening to and recording phone calls, installing visible or hidden video cameras, and monitoring voice mail and fax messages are some of the general monitoring techniques used by employers today. Computer-related surveillance techniques include reading employees' e-mail or using software that either signals when games are being played on a computer or tracks the Web sites an employee visits. Screen and keystroke capture software can produce either a "freeze-frame" of a particular moment in a worker's day or a detailed account of every key he or she hit on a keyboard (even if the file was not saved or the backspace key was used to erase what was input).

In Canada, there are few legal restrictions on employee surveillance. While the Criminal Code of Canada makes it an offence to intercept a private conversation, the notable exception to this rule is those circumstances in which there is no reasonable expectation that the conversation will be private (as is typically deemed to be the case when an employee is conducting tasks on behalf of an employer).

Employers justify the snooping by citing the lost productivity that results when employees spend time on personal e-mails and Web surfing; one study estimates that as many as half of those who visit sex-related sites do so from a workplace computer (Cheney, 2000). To date, the argument that whatever takes place on a company's computer network is the property of that company has generally been upheld in law when employees raise questions about their right to privacy.

Especially contentious are recent technologies that enable employers to capture the history of keystrokes an employee makes even when the file is not saved. Employee monitoring has its roots in industrial work, and it has long been thought that intellectual work was to some extent beyond the scope of truly intrusive surveillance techniques. However, when screen and keystroke software is used, a highly detailed picture of the intellectual/creative process emerges. While reviewing this output might be instructive for the employee (i.e., as an indicator of his or her strengths and weaknesses), it seems to offer the employer a form of intrusion far more pervasive than that associated with merely quantifying outputs of individual workers. Clearly, the monitoring of employees' computer and Internet use will be a subject of ongoing ethical debate.

IS NEW MEDIA 'NEW'?

The relationship between traditional media (newspapers, television, radio, etc.) and Web-based media has changed over time. Initially, as might have been expected, people in traditional media viewed the Web and streaming Internet services as a competitive threat. However, it soon became apparent that mere technology did not give those newcomers an insuperable advantage. The traditional media, it turned out, had something the newcomers needed—content.

The need for content prompted the establishment of numerous "hybrid" or "blend" sites that make use of "repurposed" content from traditional media. Among the first to take advantage of the repurposing trend were newspapers, which have been working to computerize and automate their own production systems over the past two decades in order to reduce labour and material costs. The leaders in the field, such as globeandmail.com, quickly found that some parts of their product actually work much better on the Web. For classified ads, job listings, and similar material, features like a search engine make a lot of sense and add value for readers.

The same sort of repurposing has been taking place in audio and visual media. CNN.com, BBC.com, and CBC.com are among those organizations that have made significant—and largely successful—forays into new media applications for their existing content. BBC.com's recent decision to reduce shortwave service in favour of using streaming audio raises the possibility that, in some sectors, traditional media will be displaced by new media (although direct delivery via digital media is far more expensive than delivery via the two broadcast models (i.e., satellite and ground-based antenna).

AREAS FOR FUTURE RESEARCH

While it is perhaps too early to identify clearly any genuine blindspots in the research on computers and the Internet, there are several areas that need to be analyzed more fully. As we noted earlier, there are many questions of a technological nature that must be addressed in order to ensure that all Canadians have access to the Internet and its related services. The issue of access, however, encompasses more than the technical minutiae of hardware, software, and service providers. Accessing the wide array of information on the Internet requires literacy, both conventional and technological. That is, before a person can even begin to make meaningful use of computers and the Internet, he or she must be able to read reasonably well. Reading and writing skills are the foundation of what might be called *technological literacy*, the ability to use a computer and to navigate the Internet (see Alexander and Pal, 1998). The interrelationship of these two factors—conventional and technological literacy—clearly points to a potential reinforcement of disadvantages already faced by those of low socioeconomic status in Canadian society. Further research on the issue of access must include attention to the relationship between conventional literacy and computer/Internet access. This research should also include a recognition of the special issues faced by those Canadians for whom English (still the dominant language of the Internet) is not the first language.

Another area for further research relates to the potential for democratic and political uses for the Internet. In addition to the community-based uses already discussed in this chapter, there have been some efforts by political parties to begin using the Internet as a means of encouraging more Canadians to participate in the political process. Such efforts have thus far involved using the Internet as a tool for disseminating information (e.g., federal and provincial party Web sites), rather than actually fostering dramatic increases in public participation in the democratic process (see Cross, 1998).

Yet another area that requires further consideration and research is the use of computers and the Internet by women and girls. While there are many examples of women's groups that use on-line communication to inform, communicate, and organize, there is reason to be concerned about the socialization of girls and young women with respect to the use of these technologies. This broad topic encompasses such issues as access to computer/Internet hardware and software, the relationship between leisure time and computer use, and the marketing of preteen/teen computer games. Regarding the latter subject, while the number of females playing computer games appears to be growing, the market remains heavily dominated by games targeted at boys. Researchers interested in gender equity with respect to quantitative questions (such as how many women use computers and the Internet), as well as qualitative issues (such as how competently women use these technologies, and what they use them for), will continue to follow contemporary developments.

The question of which model the ongoing development of these technologies will follow—that of the Internet or that of the information highway—is also an area for further research, analysis, and indeed public involvement and activism (see Menzies, 1996). The distinction that may be made between the Internet and the information highway relates to their respective histories. The Internet began life as a tool for communication and collaboration among researchers. As we have shown, the Internet's roots are at least partially based on a model of freely shared information and resources, on a tradition of debate and discussion, and on openness to and respect for divergent perspectives. This model is evident in the history of the research uses of the Internet, as well as in the multitude of formal and informal groups of individuals involved in bulletin boards, newsgroups, and mailing lists of all kinds. The information highway, on the other hand, is a communication network whose purpose is the transmission of information. As such, it is concerned less with the free flow of information than with the dissemination of information in a *commodified form*—that is, a business model of the treatment of information and the use of the technologies themselves. While there is no denying the enormous value of computer and Internet technologies for business purposes, researchers and activists interested in social justice will continue to be concerned about, at the very least, the degree of balance between these two communication models in the development of computers and the Internet.

QUESTIONS

1. Is it possible to regulate the Internet? Give reasons for your answer.
2. The Internet contributes to the formation of a global culture. Discuss.
3. What is meant by the digital divide? Why should public policy address—or not address—this issue?
4. What was IHAC? What were its recommendations?
5. How is the Internet being used for educational purposes?

WEB SITES

Canadian Advanced Network History: **http://www.canarie.ca/advnet/history.html**
CANARIE: **http://www.canarie.ca/**
History of Computing: **http://ie.cs.vt.edu/~history/**
History of Networks and the Internet: **http://ie.cs.vt.edu/~history/networks.html**
Hobbes' Internet Timeline: **http://zakon.org/robert/internet/timeline/**
Web Networks: **http://www.community.web.net/**

NOTE

1. It is a race that persists to this day. The prediction—made by Gordon Moore, cofounder of Intel Corporation—that the "power" of these chips would double every 18 months has been proven true for over 20 years. Popularly known as

Moore's Law, this prediction is not a law of nature, but rather the outcome of investment by corporations and governments around the world. Such conflations of social action into a technological imperative is typical of some of the hyperbole and fuzzy thinking that pervades discussions of technology.

REFERENCES

Alexander, Cynthia J., and Leslie A. Pal. (1998). Introduction: New currents in politics and policy. In Cynthia J. Alexander and Leslie A. Pal (Eds.), *Digital democracy: Policy and politics in the wired world* (pp. 2–22). Toronto: Oxford University Press.

Bertman, Stephen. (1998). *Hyperculture: The cost of human speed*. Westport, CT: Praeger.

Bryant, Susan. (1995). Electronic surveillance in the workplace. *Canadian Journal of Communication*, *20*(4), 505–521.

Cheney, Peter. (2000, December 5). A solitary obsession that can ruin a life. *Globe and Mail*, pp. A8–9.

Cross, Bill. (1998). Teledemocracy: Canadian political parties listening to their constituents. In Cynthia J. Alexander and Leslie A. Pal (Eds.), *Digital democracy: Policy and politics in the wired world* (pp. 132–148). Toronto: Oxford University Press.

Diebert, Ronald J. (1998) Altered worlds: Social forces in the hypermedia environment. In Cynthia J. Alexander and Leslie A. Pal (Eds.), *Digital democracy: Policy and politics in the wired world* (pp. 23–45). Toronto: Oxford University Press.

Government of Canada. (1997). *Preparing Canada for a digital world: Final report of the information highway advisory council*. Ottawa: Industry Canada.

Menzies, Heather. (1996). *Whose brave new world: The information highway and the new economy*. Toronto: Between the Lines.

Rheingold, Howard. (1993). *The virtual community: Homesteading on the electronic frontier*. Reading, MA: Addison-Wesley.

Sproull, Lee, and Sara Kiesler. (1991). *Connections: New ways of working in the networked organization*. Cambridge, MA: MIT Press.

Wellman, Barry, and Milena Gulia. (1999). Virtual communities as communities: Net surfers don't ride alone. In Marc A. Smith and Peter Kollock (Eds.), *Communities in cyberspace* (pp. 23–45). London: Routledge.

FURTHER READING

Alexander, Cynthia J., and Leslie A. Pal (Eds.). (1998). *Digital democracy: Policy and politics in the wired world*. Toronto: Oxford University Press.

Carroll, Jim. (1999). *Canadian Internet handbook: Tools, tips and techniques for enhancing your Internet activities.* Scarborough, ON: Prentice Hall.

Gutstein, Donald. (1999). *E.con: How the Internet undermines democracy.* Toronto: Stoddart.

Kim, Amy Jo. (2000). *Community building on the Web: Secret strategies for successful online communities.* Berkeley, CA: Peachpit Press.

Lewis, Brian, Richard Smith, and Christine Massey. (2001). *A tower under siege: Education and technology policy in Canada.* Montreal: McGill-Queen's University Press.

Lyon, David. (2001). *Surveillance society: Monitoring everyday life.* Philadelphia, PA: Open University.

14

On-line Journalism

Mike Gasher
Concordia University

Networked computers have become so commonplace in the Canadian education system, the workplace, and government that it is tempting to conclude that *everyone* has a World Wide Web site. The news media, too, have leapt on the Internet bandwagon. For news organizations such as newspapers, magazines, radio and television stations, the Internet is a particularly attractive medium of news-gathering and diffusion. First of all, it has a potential global reach; the Internet is available wherever people have access to a computer and a telephone line. An estimated 391 million people around the world were "wired" as of December, 2000 (Global Reach, 2001). Second, it is a relatively inexpensive delivery system, especially for newspapers and magazines, which stand to save the significant costs involved in printing and transporting bulky hard-copy editions. Third, the Internet does not have the time or space constraints of the conventional news media. A news organization can update its Web site whenever news occurs, without having to wait for the normal production cycle and without having to conform to rigid radio and television schedules. Further, there is no limit to *how much* information can be provided through the Web site, either contained within the site itself, or via external hypertext links. Finally, the Internet provides the opportunity for direct interaction with news audiences, bringing journalists and the general public into much closer contact.

There are literally thousands of news sites on the World Wide Web. Some are run by brand-name news organizations like the *New York Times*, the *Globe and Mail*, the CBC, the BBC, and CNN. Others are operated by people who have used the Internet as their entrée into journalism and hope to employ the particular applications the technology affords to redefine how journalism is practised. Perhaps the best-known of these cyberjournalists is Matt Drudge, whose Drudge Report (www.drudgereport.com) is produced single-handedly out of his small Hollywood apartment. Drudge prides himself on beating the high-powered U.S. news organizations to major stories, such as the Monica Lewinsky scandal (see Drudge, 2000). In March 2001, the Internet portal Tehelka (www.tehelka.com) made a name for itself when it released video footage of Indian government officials accepting bribes. This prompted the resignation of Bangaru Laxman, president of India's

Bharatiya Janata Party, and put significant pressure on Indian Prime Minister Atal Bihari Vajpayee to resign (Associated Press, 2001; Sahi, 2001).

In the face of the Internet's potential as a news medium, however, there remain many questions about precisely *how* these Web sites will be used by news organizations themselves, by audiences, and by advertisers. To what extent, for example, will newspapers merely reproduce their standard content in electronic form? Will newspapers and magazines take advantage of the audiovisual capacity of the Internet to use sound and moving images on their Web sites? What will radio and TV news operations do to render their Web sites distinct from their regular broadcasts? What are visitors to these sites looking for that they cannot already find in existing news publications and broadcasts? And how will advertisers use these news sites as venues to promote their products and services?

All of these questions remain to be answered as news organizations continue to experiment with the World Wide Web. While there is no shortage of people willing to gaze into their crystal balls to engage in fantastic speculation—some predicting the death of newspapers, others the rebirth of news reporting—it is important to understand two things about on-line journalism. First, it is a very new development, barely a decade old. Historically speaking, the Internet is still very much an embryonic news medium, and no one knows exactly how this ongoing experiment will turn out. Second, news organizations are no longer simply interested in nifty computer applications, but in on-line applications that can deliver both audiences and revenues. The Internet is being increasingly exposed to the economic demands of the news-production business.

HISTORY

The history of on-line journalism is closely tied to the history of the Internet itself. Some would argue that the origins of the Internet can be traced as far back as 1843, when English mathematician Ada Lovelace outlined the fundamentals of computer programming in her analysis of Charles Babbage's Analytical Engine (see Moschovitis, Poole, Schuyler, and Senft, 1999). But a more conventional starting point is 1958, when, in response to the Soviet Union's launching of two Sputnik satellites a year earlier, the U.S. government founded the Advanced Research Projects Agency (ARPA) within the Department of Defense to try to establish a lead in military-related science and technology. Throughout the 1960s, ARPA researchers worked toward the development of ARPAnet, a "cooperative network of time-sharing computers" that went on-line in December 1969, with nodes at the University of California (Los Angeles), the Stanford Research Institute, the University of California (Santa Barbara), and the University of Utah (Zakon, 2000).

While ARPAnet itself was restricted to affiliated scientists, computer networking and the exchange of digitized information quickly found other, more accessible applications in the 1970s. Some of the earliest included the exchange of news via bulletin board systems (BBS) and Usenet news and discussion groups. The *New York Times*, for example, introduced in 1973 an information service that offered on-line searches of six databases via telephone access (Carlson, 2001). In Canada, the Southam and Torstar newspaper companies together created Infomart in 1975, initially as a Canadian sales agency for commercial U.S. databases. In November 1977, the on-line database InfoGlobe was established to give subscribers full-text access to the *Globe and Mail*, the *Financial Times*, and the *Canadian Parliamentary Guidebook*, and to provide a gateway to a number of Dow Jones publications. As Desbarats (1996) notes: "Almost as soon as newspapers began to store journalism in computers as bits of electronic data, there was speculation about the possibility of creating a 'paperless' newspaper" (pp. 249–252).

It was by no means certain that electronic news services would be delivered by computer-to-computer systems. Alternative teletext and videotex systems were developed in the 1970s and early 1980s to provide news and information services to household television sets. Teletext allowed conventional TV stations to broadcast screens full of static printed information and graphics, which could be received like any other TV station. One of the earliest teletext applications was the BBC's 1974 introduction of Ceefax, which offered two teletext channels featuring news, information, and TV programming schedules (Singleton, 1983, pp. 127–131). In Canada, the CBC experimented briefly with teletext on the Telidon system in 1983 (Desbarats, 1996, pp. 251–254).

Videotex provided a two-way link via telephone and/or cable lines between central computers and specially equipped TV sets, permitting the reception of news and information in text form, as well as early versions of on-line shopping, banking, and bill-paying. Early videotex systems were developed in Britain (Prestel), France (Télétel, better known as Minitel), Canada (Telidon), Japan (Captain), the Netherlands (Viditel), and West Germany (Bildschirmtext) (Gibb, 1982). Britain's Prestel "home information retrieval system," which became available to the public in 1979 and operated until the spring of 1994, linked a central British Post Office computer to the TV sets of subscribers who could call up a table of contents offering such things as news, horse-racing results, restaurant menus, and theatre schedules (Carlson, 2001). Other videotex applications provided real-estate listings (with line drawings of homes for sale), weather forecasts, movie listings, transportation schedules and games, as well as electronic banking and home shopping (Singleton, 1983, pp. 115–121). In what later became a familiar refrain applied to Internet usage, Gibb (1982) writes:

> The great advantages of videotex are the possibilities of making up-dated information available at all times of the day, of shopping by catalogue, of making travel and hotel reservations etc., with payments being made by charging a credit card account. Future scenarios include the delivery of a personalized newspaper, holding opinion polls and even voting over local administrative issues. (p. 1)

West German newspaper companies were involved in Bildschirmtext trials from the beginning (Goetz, 1982). French regional newspapers *Le Courrier de l'Ouest* (Angers), *Le Maine Libre* (Le Mans), and *Le Parisien Libéré* (Nantes) participated in the early Minitel trials (Tournier, 1982), while a group of daily newspapers founded the Dutch videotex organization Krantel in 1980 (Swets, 1982). Knight Ridder, the second-largest newspaper chain in the United States, spent $55 million (U.S.) on its videotex trials before shutting down its Viewtron system in March 1986 (Brown, 1999, pp. 61–62).

Both teletext and videotex had a number of disadvantages. These included their prohibitive costs to subscribers, their technical complexity, and the poor quality of the content they offered. Their timing was also bad; at about the same time they were being introduced to the public, personal computers were increasing in popularity as a rival information retrieval system (Desbarats, 1996, pp. 257–258). Apple, to cite the best-known example, released the first affordable and easy-to-use personal computer—the Macintosh—in January 1984. Featuring windows and icons, the Macintosh introduced the notion of computer "user friendliness" to the general public (Moschovitis et al., 1999, p. 100).

Other early ideas for the electronic transmission of news included multimedia "tablets" and "fax newspapers." Newspaper companies such as Knight Ridder in the United States and Southam in Canada experimented with computerized tablets on which subscribers could download their daily newspaper through telephone lines or cable. The Montreal *Gazette*, for example, developed a tablet with a 21-inch computer screen, capable of downloading both text and audiovisual clips ("Interactive Gazette," 1994). Some companies continue to pursue the idea of the fax newspaper, combining the advantages of printed newspapers' convenience, legibility, and disposability with the global reach of electronic news. The Vancouver-based company NewspaperDirect, for example, allows clients to order a printed facsimile of their preferred newspaper through distribution outlets in North American, Europe, and Asia. Catering primarily to business travellers, NewspaperDirect (www.newspaperdirect.com) has distribution contracts with luxury hotels, airlines, libraries, research institutions, corporate offices, and even cruise ships (Perkin, 2001).

As the 1980s progressed, more and more people became linked to what came to be called the Internet. If the vast majority of these people gained Internet access through universities or the workplace, the establishment of the Cleveland Free-Net Community Computer System in July 1986 marked the first time *anyone* with access to a computer and a modem could tap into the Internet. Commercial Internet service providers (ISPs) like AOL and The World came on-line in the early 1990s to satisfy increasing demand (Moschovitis et al., 1999, p. 126; Zakon, 2000).

But it was the creation of the World Wide Web in 1991, and the subsequent introduction of the user-friendly Web browser Mosaic in 1993, that really allowed the Internet to become a mass news medium. Almost instantly, news organizations began to establish World Wide Web sites, even if they were initially cautious about giving away too much content for free. As Brown (1999) writes: "Different papers took different electronic paths, but in the mid-1990s, like tributaries in a vast watershed, they all began to converge, drawn together by developments in technology" (p. 59).

The University of Florida established what is believed to be the first journalism site on the Web in October 1993, and the Palo Alto (California) *Weekly* became the first newspaper to publish regularly on the Web, with twice-weekly (and free) postings of its full content. By August 1995, there were an estimated 350 newspapers on-line—some operating as bulletin board systems with their own dial-up numbers; others affiliated with AOL, Prodigy, or CompuServe; and 230 on the World Wide Web. Sixteen of these newspapers were Canadian. When the *New York Times* launched its Web site on January 21, 1996, it required visitors to register but provided free access to U.S. residents; in July 1998, the site became free to all registered users (Carlson, 2001). Some of the earliest news sites offered little more than highlights of their current content along with information about how to subscribe and how to place an advertisement. Others offered their full content on-line but charged a subscription fee.

News events such as the Karla Homolka trial, the O.J. Simpson trial, the death of Princess Diana, and the Mars Pathfinder mission made the potential of on-line news readily apparent. Because a publication ban on the 1993 Homolka trial gagged the conventional Canadian news media, the Internet became the forum for a combination of news, rumour, speculation, and gossip:

> On two newsgroups—ont.general, and a special forum morbidly called alt.fan.karla-homolka—information concerning the St. Catharine's [sic] murders was presented in a mix of plausible hearsay and outlandish rumour ... but much of it, gathered in an FAQ (a "Frequently Asked Questions" document) at the end of August, was consistent with the few facts in general circulation. (Friedman, 1997, p. 167)

Internet users could follow the twists and turns of the 1995 O.J. Simpson trial by reading trial transcripts, perusing photographic evidence, downloading news stories, and engaging in newsgroup discussions (Friedman, 1997, p. 170). The Mars Pathfinder team set up 21 "mirrored" Web sites to provide video coverage of the July 1997 mission, and recorded between 40 and 50 million visits daily (Toporek, 1997). Similarly, the death of Princess Diana in August 1997 prompted millions of postings to on-line bulletin boards, tens of millions of visits to news organizations' Web sites, and the creation of hundreds of sites devoted to the princess's memory.

APPLICATIONS

News organizations today use the Internet in two main ways: as a news-gathering tool in what is called computer-assisted reporting (CAR); and as a means of dissemination through their World Wide Web sites. Computer-assisted reporting is the use of networked computers to seek information, to conduct interviews, and to file stories. Early forms of CAR were applied in the 1970s when the introduction of video display terminals in Canadian newsrooms allowed reporters and editors to access news wires and exchange simple messages with colleagues within the same news organization. By the late 1970s, the first generation of portable computers—too heavy and bulky to be called "laptops"—allowed reporters to file stories from remote locations. At the 1984 Los Angeles Olympics, with competition venues scattered all over Southern California, a private network known as an *intranet* allowed accredited officials, coaches, athletes, and journalists to access schedules and results, and to exchange e-mail messages using special terminals located at the Games' numerous media centres.[1]

Broadcast journalists initially used the Internet in the 1980s to vet their scripts with producers prior to reading them over telephone lines. Today, thanks to sophisticated and user-friendly software programs, radio reporters in the field can put together a multi-element sound mix and then file the final copy of their report over a phone line. David McLauchlin, a national reporter for CBC Radio News, recalls first being able to send a fully mixed audio report as early as 1995, when he was filing stories from Cuba and Oklahoma City. Covering the Florida vote recount in the aftermath of the November 2000 U.S. election, McLauchlin filed studio-quality reports by connecting his laptop to a telephone at a West Palm Beach ice-cream parlour (David McLauchlin, personal communication, March 9, 2001).

If the earliest portable computers enabled reporters to file text-based stories from home or the road through telephone lines, subsequent generations of laptop computers with their greatly increased memory allowed journalists to carry with them an archive of previously filed stories, as well as any other reference data they required. Today, whether working from their newsroom workstations, home, or a remote location, journalists can access through the Internet a wide variety of increasingly sophisticated databases and news archives to help them prepare their stories. E-mail has also become a more convenient and less costly means by which to conduct interviews, even if face-to-face or telephone interviews remain the preferred methods in a conservative industry.[2]

It is the rare news organization today that does *not* have a World Wide Web site. Not surprisingly, the quality of these sites varies dramatically. Most newspaper and magazine sites offer at least a selection of full-text articles and illustrations from their current editions; e-mail access to news, advertising, and subscription departments; and a searchable archive of previously published stories. Similarly, most radio and television news sites offer current programming schedules, some program playback capability, and e-mail access to program production and advertising departments. The best Web sites are those that combine a comprehensive store of news and information with the kind of applications that distinguish the Internet from the conventional print and broadcast media. Such applications include e-mail interaction with reporters, editors, and producers; the presentation of stories in both textual and audiovisual forms; keyword search capability; an extensive archive of past editions and previous broadcasts; hypertext links to related Web sites; and discussion forums.

The *Globe and Mail* Web site (www. globeandmail.com), for example, is a "breaking news" site, which means it updates its site whenever newsworthy stories in the areas of business, technology, and sports occur. The *Globe* site also makes extensive use of audiovisual materials with links to a generous selection of top stories from CNN.com, ROBTv, and CTVnews.com, all of which feature segments available in Real audio and/or video format. The *Globe*'s business-travel section has searchable databases offering flight information from Canada's major airports, government travel advisories and visa information, and restaurant guides for 11 Canadian cities. In 2001, *Editor and Publisher Online* named the *Washington Post* Web site (www.washingtonpost.com) the best overall U.S. on-line news service, citing its extensive news coverage in text-based and audiovisual form; its Live Online feature of computer-mediated chats with *Post* reporters and columnists; and its Camera Works exhibition of news photographs. Similarly, The *New York Times* (www.nytimes.com) provides constant updates, some stories in audiovisual form, and an archive of articles dating back to 1996.

The CBC Web site (www.cbc.ca), with links to all of its radio and television services in French and English, is a cornucopia of frequently updated news stories in textual and/or audiovisual form, special columns, diaries and notebooks, galleries of still photographs, archived programming and, of course, a current guide to all CBC broadcast offerings. The CNN site (www.cnn.com) provides stories in text and/or audiovisual form, as well as links to CNN Asia (asia.cnn.com), CNN Europe (europe.cnn.com), CNN financial network (cnnfn.cnn.com), and the CNN/Sports Illustrated site (sportsillustrated.cnn.com).

Even small community weekly newspapers can be on-line innovators. The Moosomin (Saskatchewan) *World-Spectator* site (www.world-spectator.com) has a directory of e-mail addresses and home page URLs of current and former Moosomin residents and hypertext links to literary sites, other newspapers, and the *World-Spectator*'s news archives. Fort McMurray (Alberta) *Today* (www.today.ab.ca) features an Our Community link with articles about the history of the town, the region, its people, and the Athabasca oilsands.

It does not require very much browsing on the Web to realize that it is not just "old media" people who are getting into the on-line news business. Besides providing links to thousands of news organizations' home pages, Internet portals such as Yahoo (www.yahoo.com) and AltaVista (www.altavista.com) assemble news packages at their own home pages, tapping into major U.S. and British news organizations. The Web has also given birth to stand-alone news sites such as *Salon* and *Slate*. Founded in 1995 by David Talbot, *Salon* is an Internet media company that produces ten original Web sites, including a very literate daily "web newspaper" devoted to political and cultural coverage (http://salon.com). *Slate* was founded in 1996 by Microsoft Corp. under the direction of former *New Republic* editor Michael Kinsley; like *Salon*, it strives for quality journalism in the areas of politics, culture, leisure, economics, and sports, posting new articles and features on a daily basis (http://slate.msn.com).

Other news sites are the products of joint ventures between companies. The best known of these sites is MSNBC.com, a multimedia site founded by Microsoft and NBC News in 1996; this site has "content partnerships" with a number of other news organizations, including the *Washington Post*, *Newsweek*, the *Wall Street Journal*, *ZDNet*, and *The Sporting News* (www.msnbc.com). A number of other news organizations have established collaborations between their newsrooms. The Canadian Broadcasting Corporation, for example, announced a news partnership with the *Toronto Star* in March 2001 ("Star Out of Alignment," 2001). Radio-Canada, the French-language service of the CBC, has partnerships on special projects with the Montreal newspaper *La Presse* (http://cbc.radio-canada.ca), while the Radio-Canada Web site's "zone éducation" (http://radio-canada.ca/education) has 20 partners, including the Quebec newspaper *Le Devoir*. CanWest Global Communications, an international media company with television, radio, news-paper, and magazine holdings in five countries, operates the portal Canada.com, which presents a package of stories from more than 50 Southam and Hollinger newspapers, breaking news from the Canadian Press wire service, and links to both the individual home pages of its major daily newspapers and its Global TV affiliates (www.canada.com).

INTERACTIVITY

The characteristic that is most likely to distinguish news on the Internet from news on traditional media is *interactivity*, which refers to all the ways in which readers can participate in the production and consumption of news texts. Internet users who contribute to on-line discussion groups or chat rooms, e-mail letters to the editor, or navigate through news stories and news sites are all engaged in various forms of interactivity.

Elmer (1997) refers to the *indexicality* of the World Wide Web, by which he means the way in which on-line texts incorporate hypertext links that point to other possible destinations or paths:

> The link thus not only signifies the possibility of other spaces, its very purpose is, moreover, one of enabling us—by the movement of the on-screen cursor (first arrow and then index finger) and click of a mouse—to move to other spaces. (pp. 184–185)

Elmer notes that some of the most popular sites on the Web are portals (Yahoo, Webcrawler, Lycos, AltaVista, Infoseek), which serve precisely as indexes to information that can be found elsewhere (pp. 184–185).

A particularly vibrant area of Internet research is devoted to understanding *how* Web surfers use news sites—which sites they frequent, which features interest them, how long they stay, which internal and external links they follow, and so on. While the precise answers to these questions remain elusive, it is clear that Web surfers create their own unique and composite news packages—or *hypertexts*—as they click from site to site, from news item to news item, follow a link, backtrack, then follow another link, and on and on (see Purves, 1998). Hilliard (2000) compares the Internet experience with the relatively linear fashion in which people read a newspaper or view a television newscast (moving, that is, in an A to Z sequence):

> [T]he Internet does for aural-visual-print communication what Picasso's cubism did for painting. As Picasso interpreters have stated, the early 20th century developments in communication and transportation no longer restricted the view of an object to a single plane, but the transcending of time and space made it possible to see an object from many viewpoints virtually at the same time. This is what the Internet has done for communication: Hypertext interactivity enables the receptor to receive and also to originate many varied stimuli from a virtually unrestricted space-time continuum with many varied sources virtually at the same time. (p. 416)

What this suggests is that journalists working on-line need to recognize that they are producing not texts, but hypertexts. This means building into their presentation of a news story opportunities for audiences to link to other parts of the story, sidebars, audio and video segments, graphs, charts or maps, and primary document sites.

News organizations are beginning to show signs of awareness that interactivity is an inherent feature of on-line storytelling, making the interaction between journalists and audiences much more integral to news reporting itself. A step in this direction was taken in December 1999 when the Quebecor portal Canoe.ca released what it described as "the first piece of investigative journalism in Canada written specifically for the Internet" (see Benedetti and MacPhail, 1999). A two-month investigation by Paul Benedetti and Wayne MacPhail into the proposed merger between the Canadian Memorial Chiropractic College and York University in Toronto resulted in a "hyperjournalism" package that included a series of stories by the authors, primary documents, sound clips of interviews, and links to other pertinent Web sites. Besides being advised to navigate through the site as they saw fit, readers were invited to e-mail the authors, vote in opinion polls, and express their views in a discussion forum.

In February 2001, *Slate* introduced a series of stories based on what it called "transparent journalism" (Kinsley, 2001). Instead of first researching and then presenting his finished article about a California sperm bank devoted to the collection of semen from Nobel Prize winners, reporter David Plotz instead filed regular dispatches *as* he investigated the story, inviting readers to participate in the writing of "Seed" by suggesting story angles, research sources, and interview subjects. "[O]ne interesting, if not alarming, aspect of the experiment," commented *Slate* editor

Michael Kinsley, "is that it will be transparent to the very people David will need to interview and gather information from. His sources will be able to read his mind." *Slate* plans to publish the finished product as an e-book.

Interactivity has both spatial and temporal dimensions. If the World Wide Web's "indexicality" invites audiences to move from site to site, it also offers Web surfers a new geographical mobility. We are no longer restricted to our local newspaper or television station for news from abroad; we can just as easily visit the Web sites of international news organizations for reportage on distant events. For example, for varying perspectives and more in-depth coverage of the April 2001 collision between a U.S. spy plane and a Chinese F-8 fighter over the South China Sea, we could have visited China's Xinhua news agency (www.xinhua.org) and major American newspapers like the *New York Times* and the *Washington Post*. For information on events in the Middle East, we can visit the *Jerusalem Post* (www.jpost.com), the *Jordan Times* (www.jordantimes.com), or the Lebanon *Daily Star* (www.dailystar.com.lb). In this respect, the Web is the world's largest newsstand. At the same time, the Web produces news 24 hours a day; we don't have to wait for the six o'clock news or the delivery of our daily newspaper. As noted above, a number of news organizations provide frequently updated "breaking news" at their Web sites. On-line newspapers and news magazines are thus able to "publish" constantly, while radio and television sites enjoy even greater immediacy than their conventional broadcasting arms.

Stanford University and the Poynter Institute for Media Studies have developed an annual "eyetrack study" to record Web viewers' eye movements in order to understand how Web surfers navigate on-line news sites (Poynter Institute, 2000). Attaching special eyetracking headgear to 67 subjects (30 women, 37 men) in Chicago and St. Petersburg, Florida, researchers analyzed 24,530 mouse clicks and 608,063 eye "fixations." They discovered that eyes are initially attracted to text when a Web page is opened; the average viewing session lasts 34 minutes; viewers call up three times as many brief items as longer articles; and an average of six news providers are viewed in each viewing session. Mainstream general news sites like the *New York Times*, the *Washington Post*, ABC News, and MSN.com were the most active news sites, accounting for 54 percent of the 211 total news providers called up and 79 percent of the first sites that viewers visited. Forty percent of the subjects started a session with their local news provider before moving on. Studies like this are essential if we are to understand how people use the World Wide Web as a news medium. News organizations, too, are no doubt watching carefully in order to see how visitors navigate their sites and to determine which news applications they favour.

BUSINESS AND ECONOMICS

To date, the World Wide Web has been a losing proposition for most news organizations, who have invested millions in their Web sites and have little to show for it in return. Unfortunately, precise financial information for Canadian on-line news operations is not available. While news organizations such as the Canadian Broadcasting Corp. (www.cbc.ca) and the Gesca newspaper group (www.cyber-presse.ca) continue to expand their on-line offerings, Quebecor Inc. shut down the Web sites at two of its biggest newspapers, *Le Journal de Montréal* and *Le Journal de Québec*, in July 2000, claiming that the simple on-line reproduction of the two newspapers "with no value added" was a fruitless exercise (Partridge, 2000). Despite having reported a second-quarter loss of $11 million on its new media operations in 2000, Quebecor continues to maintain Canoe.ca, a multilingual news and information portal (Leger, 2000).

In the United States, there are clear signs that on-line journalism has been a commercial bust as profits remain elusive. Between October 2000 and February 2001, industry giants such as the *Los Angeles Times*, the *New York Times*, CNN, NBC, News Corp., Dow Jones, and Knight Ridder scaled back their Internet operations. Disappointing advertising revenues were repeatedly blamed and the profit horizon was pushed back once again, this time to mid-2002 (Lasica, 2001; Reuters, 2001; White, 2001). As Barringer (2001) wrote in the *New York Times*:

> The first era of newspaper experiments on the Internet, fueled in part by the fear that the Web would devour profits, is over. A new era of newspaper experiments on the Internet, fueled in part by the fear that the Web will not generate profits, has begun.

A number of exclusive on-line news operations shut down altogether in 2000, including PressPoint, a New York–based print-on-demand delivery service ("PressPoint," 2000), and Newswire.com.au, an Australian news subscription service ("Online Newswire," 2000). Others sites, such as the on-line magazines *Industry Standard*, *Salon*, and *Red Herring*, dramatically reduced staff (White, 2001).

The commercial news media have typically relied on two principal sources of revenue: subscription sales and advertising.[3] But as the preceding paragraphs indicate, news organizations are still seeking the magic formula for on-line profitability. If initially an "acceptable use" policy prohibited Internet commerce, the medium has increasingly become commercialized since the U.S. National Science Foundation decided in 1992 to permit commercial Internet traffic (see Goggin, 2000, p. 104). Nonetheless, a vast amount of Internet content remains free, reflecting the failure of news organizations' early attempts to charge subscription fees for access to their Web pages. The *Wall Street Journal* (www.wsj.com) is one of the few mainstream on-line daily newspapers that has been able to maintain access fees (US$59 per year), but it has yet to make a profit (Arnold, 2001; Kumar, 2001). The *New York Times* site and *Slate* initially charged for access, but quickly abandoned that strategy. With the poor returns of on-line advertising to date, sites such as *TheStreet.com* and *Salon* are revisiting the idea of subscription fees (Kumar, 2001). *Salon*, in fact, introduced in April 2001 a pay service called Salon Premium, which permits subscribers to view the site without intrusive banner or "pop-up" advertisements (Talbot, 2001).

Some news and information providers believe that the increasing numbers of people who access content via wireless technology (mobile phones, Palm Pilots, etc.) will be more inclined to pay access or subscription fees. On-line news analyst Steve Outing (2000) argues that there are two main reasons for this. First, such personal communication devices require personalized content because "browsing is not something done as easily or quickly—mostly due to the small screen sizes of the devices." The fact that wireless browsing comes with toll charges means that consumers may be prepared to pay for tailored content that is of value to them if it can be delivered conveniently and quickly. Second, Outing believes that wireless content should be cheaper than Web content because the infrastructure already exists to add low per-item fees to the wireless customer's telecommunications bill. "With wireless content, the billing is already in place between consumer and wireless service provider (the mobile phone company, typically). There's no need to register for payment, so there's no friction for the consumer to make a purchase." Web content purchases are usually made by credit card, where a fee for each transaction is added to what may be the minimal value of the content purchased. FT.com, the Web service of the *Financial Times*, already provides a wireless headline service to mobile-phone subscribers, charging about 50 cents for each message received.

While Internet advertising has to date been a disappointing revenue source for news sites, spending continues to increase and advertisers continue to experiment with different formats. The Internet Advertising Bureau predicted Canadian spending of $125.1 million for the year 2000, up 92.2 percent from the $65.1 million spent in 1999 (Diekmeyer, 2000). But this still represents only 1.29 percent of the money Canadian advertisers were expected to spend on newspapers, television, and radio in 2000. Even in relative terms, the Canadian Internet advertising market lags far behind the $5.3-billion (U.S.) American market.

Banner ads, which invite viewers to link to the advertiser's own Web site, are becoming less and less popular because they "hijack" viewers away from the originating news site. Much more endearing to both advertisers and their host sites are "skyscrapers" (ads that run the length of the Web page, usually along the right-hand side) and advertising "windows," which occupy a large central space on the site's home page. Both formats give viewers the information they need without luring them away from the news page (see Mostafa, 2001).

Like its "old media" predecessors—newspapers, magazines, radio, television—the Internet operates in what has been called an "attention economy." As Gauntlett (2000) explains: "To triumph on the Web is to have lots of people giving attention to your site, instead of giving it to someone else's. Attention is what everyone wants. So it's an *attention economy*" (p. 9). As with the old media, there is a belief that if you can attract the attention of audiences, you should be able to sell those audiences to advertisers. Dan Finnigan, president of KnightRidder.com, remains confident that on-line advertising will work: "For anyone to suggest that the Internet cannot be a successful advertising medium is, to me, on its face, silly. If you have people's attention, you can sell advertising" (cited in Quinn, 2000).

Nevertheless, news organizations continue to explore nonconventional revenue sources, such as royalties on e-commerce transactions originating from news sites, syndication fees from the use of their content by other on-line publishers, and user-pay access to archives and searchable classified advertising. Vancouver's two daily newspapers, for example, teamed up to establish the classified advertising Web site ClassifiedsBC.com. But until on-line news sites begin to realize their commercial potential, news organizations will be reluctant to invest the kinds of human and material resources on-line journalism requires to truly distinguish itself as a new news medium.

CONCLUSION

On-line journalism holds out considerable promise for expanding the ways in which news organizations provide news and information, and in which audiences access the latest intelligence from around the world. The development of the Internet as a news medium has increased the number of news sources available to us, given us greater geographical mobility, and enabled us to scan several news sites at a sitting. We have access to both textual and audiovisual reports at the same news sites, and we are freed from the production cycles of the conventional news media.

But each of these apparent improvements carries with it important qualifiers. Not everyone has access to the Internet, raising concerns about a "digital divide" between the information rich and the information poor. This divide undermines the notion of the Internet as a *mass* medium, and it may encourage news organizations to develop highly specialized sites catering exclusively to the segments of society and the parts of the world that are wired, privileging the kinds of content those people seek.

Perhaps the most extreme example of tailoring news is an application called the Daily Me, in which news providers use sophisticated filtering software to send subscribers a package of "personalized news" chosen from a preselected menu of topics and keywords. A number of portals offer this service. The subscriber receives only items from those news topics in which he or she has expressed an interest. A service that allows its subscribers to screen out much of the world's affairs represents a radical change from today's general-interest newspapers and news broadcasts. University of Chicago law professor Cass R. Sunstein goes so far as to suggest that personalized news could have negative implications for the health of democracy. "Democracy requires at least two things: that people have common spaces where they can share experiences some of the time, and that people have unanticipated, un-chosen exposures to ideas and other people" (cited in Kaplan, 2001).

Of course, the Internet could also act as a bridge between people. Carey (1998), for instance, maintains that the Internet should be understood as "the first instance of a global communication system," replacing the largely national communication systems of radio and television (pp. 30–34). The Internet could be the gateway to increased international news flows and thus to increased awareness of events beyond our borders, places beyond our experiences, and people beyond our understanding. But that is not certain. International news-flow research, which examines the origin, content, and destination of news stories, has drawn attention to the unequal coverage historically afforded the various regions of the world—an inequality owing to the heavy concentration of journalists in some areas (e.g., Western capitals such as Washington, New York, and London) and their virtual absence in others (e.g., sub-Saharan Africa) (van Ginneken, 1998).

There is no indication, however, that communications technology has been a factor in this unbalanced coverage (see Wu, 2000). In fact, Canadian journalist Jonathan Manthorpe (1998) writes: "It is a paradox of modern journalism that as the revolution in information technology has made the corners of the world more and more accessible, the presentation of news has become increasingly parochial" (p. 131). He cites the example of Southam News, a news agency run by Canada's largest chain of daily newspapers, which as recently as 1988 had foreign correspondents in seven cities around the world but by 1997 had closed all of its bureaus except those in Washington and London: "The relative lack of interest in international affairs in Canadian newspapers merely mirrors the attitude of society as a whole. Canada has only one vital international relationship and that is with the United States" (p. 131).

The immediacy of on-line news raises questions as well. For instance, what impact will the ability of news organizations to update news sites whenever news occurs have on the accuracy and depths of those reports? As Outing (2000) notes: "The biggest issue with instant Web news publishing is, of course, accuracy to go along with the speed. The worst thing that a newspaper site can do is post news so quickly that mistakes creep in." Will the rush to publish lead to more errors in fact and judgment, or will on-line journalists be more prudent, given viewers' ability to double-check facts and compare news stories at one site with those posted elsewhere on the Web (see Hilliard, 2000, p. 413). Rheingold (2000), for whom the Internet represents "the world's greatest source of information, misinformation and disinformation," believes the first role for on-line journalism "is to try to maintain some kind of gold standard for truth-seeking" (pp. 174–176).

Another credibility issue concerns news sites' practice of embedding commercial hypertext links within their news packages, especially as e-commerce is seen as a potential revenue stream. For example, it has become common practice for news sites to provide links to book and music retailers next to their book and CD reviews. This "linkalism" is a particular concern at sites that offer news items simply as complements to other types of content (see McNamara, 2000). Is the book being reviewed as a service to readers, or is it simply partly of a sales pitch?

Finally, the quantity of news sites available on the World Wide Web does not necessarily equate with a greater variety of news coverage or a broader range of voices. The struggle for dot-com survival is leading more and more independent sites into the arms of media conglomerates, which have long profit horizons and deep pockets with which to ride out this early period of commercial uncertainty. According to McChesney (1999), by May 1998 more than three-quarters of the 31 most-visited news and entertainment sites on the Web were affiliated with large media conglomerates. These conglomerates have large holdings of digital programming, enjoy cross-promotional opportunities through their other media properties and name-brand visibility, and are well positioned to grab the lion's share of advertising revenues (McChesney, 1999, pp. 170–172). As McChesney notes:

> [T]he most striking feature of digital communication may well be not that it has opened up competition in communication markets, but that it has made it vastly easier, more attractive, and more necessary for firms to consolidate and strike alliances across media, telecommunications, and computer sectors. (p. 163)

The biggest qualifier of all is the fact the no one knows precisely what on-line journalism will become. That will depend on how news organizations, advertisers, working journalists, and audiences use the Internet in the years to come. This uncertainty presents students of communication with a tantalizing opportunity; like the generations before us who witnessed the birth of radio and television news, we have the chance to participate in the emergence of the Internet as a new medium and as a news medium.

QUESTIONS

1. Why did videotex systems such as Telidon fail?
2. How would you describe the interactivity of on-line news sites?
3. What are the disadvantages of the Daily Me?
4. Is on-line news a democratic medium? Give reasons for your answer.
5. What are the advantages of on-line news?

WEB SITES

Drudge Report: **http://www.drudgereport.com/**
Interactive Advertising Bureau: **http://www.iab.net/**
OnlineNewspapers.com: **http://www.onlinenewspapers.com/**
Pierre Bourque's NewsWatch: **http://www.bourque.com/**
Salon: **http://www.salon.com/**
Statistics Canada Internet Use Survey:
   http://www.statcan.ca/Daily/English/010326/d010326a.htm

NOTES

1. The author covered the Los Angeles Olympics for the Vancouver *Province* and used the Games' intranet system to exchange information with other reporters, to search for results from other venues, and to conduct interviews with the American and Canadian judges following the duet competition in synchronized swimming.

2. A certain amount of caution about e-mail interviews is warranted. How can a journalist be certain of the authorship of an e-mail message? Of course, the same question can be asked with regard to telephone interviews, which are standard journalism practice. In March 2001, in fact, Matthew Johnson, executive assistant to Edmonton-Strathcona MP Rahim Jaffer, impersonated Jaffer during a live interview with Vancouver radio station CKNW (see Naumetz, 2001). The Montreal *Gazette*'s coverage leading up to the April 2001 Summit of the Americas in Quebec City featured regular e-mail interviews with leaders of protest groups (see, for example, Dougherty, 2001).

3. There are, of course, many exceptions to this rule. As a public broadcaster, the CBC receives a large annual subsidy from the federal government, and its radio services do not carry advertising. Community radio stations generate revenues from government grants and fund-raising activities. Until the late 19th century, many daily newspapers were closely affiliated with political parties and funded themselves through party funds and government printing contracts (see Lorimer and Gasher, 2001, pp. 203–233).

REFERENCES

Arnold, Martin. (2001, March 30). Dow Jones to cut WSJ.com staff in online rethink. *Financial Times*. Retrieved from http://www.ft.com

Associated Press. (2001, March 15). India's PM weathers storm. *Gazette* (Montreal), p. A16.

Barringer, Felicity. (2001, January 22). Rethinking Internet news as a business proposition. *The New York Times on the Web*. Retrieved from http://www.ntyimes.com/2001/01/22/technology

Benedetti, Paul, and Wayne MacPhail. (1999, December). Spin doctors: Deaths, deceptions and dubious claims haunt chiropractors' bid for academic acceptance. Retrieved from http://www.canoe.ca/ChiroYork

Brown, Chip. (1999, June). Fear.com. *American Journalism Review*, 50–71.

Carey, James W. (1998, Spring). The Internet and the end of the national communication system: Uncertain predictions of an uncertain future. *Journalism and Mass Communication Quarterly*, 75(1), 28–34.

Carlson, David. (2001, March 1). David Carlson's online timeline. Retrieved from http://iml.jou.edu/carlson/professional/new_media/timeline.htm

Desbarats, Peter. (1996). *Guide to Canadian news media* (2nd ed.). Toronto: Harcourt Brace.

Diekmeyer, Peter. (2000, November 7). Canada lags US in online ads. *Gazette* (Montreal), p. D6.

Dougherty, Kevin. (2001, March 20). Quebec summit to feature more than one agenda. *Gazette* (Montreal), p. A13.

Drudge, Matt. (2000). *Drudge manifesto*. New York: New American Library.

Elmer, Greg. (1997). Spaces of surveillance: Indexicality and solicitation on the Internet. *Critical Studies in Mass Communication, 14,* 182–191.

Friedman, Matthew. (1997). *Fuzzy logic: Dispatches from the information revolution.* Montreal: Véhicule Press.

Gauntlett, David (Ed.). (2000). *Web.studies: Rewiring media studies for the digital age.* London: Arnold.

Gibb, J.M. (1982). Opening Address. In R. Rapparini and R. Sabatelli (Eds.), *Videotex and the press*. Oxford: Learned Information.

Global Reach. (2001). Global internet statistics. Retrieved from http://www.glreach.com/globstats/index.php3

Goetz, G. (1982). A new mass medium for newspaper information? In R. Rapparini and R. Sabatelli (Eds.), *Videotex and the press*. Oxford: Learned Information.

Goggin, Gerard. (2000). Pay per browse? The Web's commercial futures. In David Gauntlett (Ed.), *Web.studies: Rewiring media studies for the digital age*. London: Arnold.

Hilliard, Robert L. (2000). *Writing for television, radio, and new media*. Belmont, CA: Wadsworth/Thomson Learning.

Interactive Gazette offers glimpse of future. (1994, December/January). [Newsletter]. Canadian Daily Newspaper Association.

Kaplan, Carl S. (2001, April 13). Law professor sees hazard in personalized news. *The New York Times on the Web*. Retrieved from http://www.nytimes.com

Kinsley, Michael. (2001, February 6). An experiment in long-form journalism. *Slate*. Retrieved from http://slate.msn.com

Kumar, Aparna. (2001, March 30). Are the days of free over? *Wired News*. Retrieved from http://www.wired.com

Lasica, J.D. (2001, January 25). Soul-searching time at online news units. *Online Journalism Review*. Retrieved from http://ojr.usc.edu/content

Leger, Kathryn. (2000, August 2). Quebecor targets new media losses. *Financial Post*. Retrieved from http:// www.nationalpost.com/financialpost

Lorimer, Rowland, and Mike Gasher. (2001). *Mass communication in Canada* (4th ed.). Toronto: Oxford University Press.

Manthorpe, Jonathan. (1998). The decline of foreign news in Canada's media. In Donna Logan (Ed.), *Journalism in the new millennium*. Vancouver: Sing Tao School of Journalism.

McChesney. Robert W. (1999). *Rich media, poor democracy: Communication policy in dubious times*. Urbana and Chicago: University of Illinois Press.

McNamara, Tracy. (2000, July/August). Defining the blurry line between commerce and content. *Columbia Journalism Review*, 31, 35.

Moschovitis, Christos J.P., Hilar Poole, Tami Schuyler, and Theresa M. Senft. (1999). *History of the Internet: A chronology, 1843 to the present.* Santa Barbara, CA: ABC-CLIO.

Mostafa, Karim. (2001, February 2). News sites experiment with larger ads. *Editor and Publisher Online*. Retrieved from http://www.editorandpublisher.com

Naumetz, Tim. (2001, March 20). MPs forgiving of Jaffer gaffe. *Gazette* (Montreal), p. A12.

Online newswire forced offline. (2000, November 23). *ZDNet*. Retrieved from http://www.zdnet.com.au

Outing, Steve. (2000, November 29). Will consumers pay for wireless content? *Editor and Publisher Online*. Retrieved from http://www.editorandpublisher.com

Partridge, John. (2000, July 18). Quebecor pulls plug on Web sites. *Globe and Mail*. Retrieved from http://www.globeandmail.com

Perkin, Julian. (2001, April 4). Quest for digital "paper" and "ink": Electronic newspapers. *Financial Times*. Retrieved from http://www.ft.com

Poynter Institute. (2000). Stanford Poynter Project. Retrieved from http://www.poynter.org/eyetrack2000/index.htm

PressPoint to go out of business. (2000, September 19). *Editor and Publisher Online*. Retrieved from http://www.editorandpublisher.com

Purves, Alan C. (1998). *The web of text and the web of God: An essay on the third information transformation*. New York: Guilford Press.

Quinn, Kathleen. (2000, November 19). *News alert!* Retrieved from http://www.zdnet.com

Reuters. (2001, January 17). CNN tightens belt, slashes jobs. *Wired.com*. Retrieved from http://www.wired.com

Rheingold, Howard. (2000). Community development in the cybersociety of the future. In David Gauntlett (Ed.), *Web.studies: Rewiring media studies for the digital age*. London: Arnold.

Sahi, Ajit. (2001, March 15). Tehelka reporter exults in trailblazer journalism. *India abroad*. Retrieved from http://www.indiaabroaddaily.com

Singleton, Loy A. (1983). *Telecommunications in the information age: A nontechnical primer on the new technologies*. Cambridge, MA: Ballinger.

Star out of alignment. (2001, March 24). *National Post*, p. A15.

Swets, R.A.G. (1982). Krantel, the viewdata organisation of the Dutch newspapers: Experiences, trends and the future. In R. Rapparini and R. Sabatelli (Eds.), *Videotex and the press*. Oxford: Learned Information.

Talbot, David. (2001, March 20). Announcing Salon Premium. *Salon*. Retrieved from http://salon.com

Toporek, Chuck. (1997, July 18). Webmastering Mars. *Web Review*. Retrieved from http://www.webreview.com/1997/07_18

Tournier, M. (1982). Vélizy Télétel experiment. In R. Rapparini and R. Sabatelli (Eds.), *Videotex and the press*. Oxford: Learned Information.

van Ginneken, Jaap. (1998). *Understanding global news: A critical introduction*. London: Sage.

White, Erin. (2001, January 8). New York Times web unit to cut staff by 17% amid slow ad market. *Wall Street Journal*. Retrieved from http://interactive.wsj.com/archive

Wu, H. Dennis. (2000, Spring). Systemic determinants of international news coverage: A comparison of 38 countries. *Journal of Communication, 50*(2), 110–130.

Zakon, Robert Hobbes. (2000, November 19). *Hobbes' internet timeline v 5.2*. Retrieved from http:// www.zakon.org/robert/internet/timeline/

FURTHER READING

Herman, Andrew, and Thomas Swiss (Eds). (2000). *The World Wide Web and contemporary cultural theory*. New York: Routledge.

Rowland, Wade. (1997). *Spirit of the Web: The age of information from telegraph to Internet*. Toronto: Somerville House.

Part IV
Social and Policy Issues

Introduction

The chapters in this section deal with various social, policy, and ethical issues around communication media. Many of these issues have involved a variety of stakeholders, and many are contested and ongoing.

The section begins with an introduction to globalization, a concept that has been widely used in the last decade. Chapter 15 examines the various dimensions of globalization (with an emphasis on cultural globalization), international "right to communicate" movements, and communication among diasporic communities and transnational ethnic media. Chapter 16 presents a case study of the Aboriginal Peoples Television Network, a success story that has been emulated in several countries. The oft-contested arena of media convergence is explored in Chapters 17 and 18.

As chapters in previous sections have demonstrated, new media present salient and challenging policy issues. The issues of intellectual property/copyright and privacy are examined in Chapters 19 and 20 respectively. Both of these chapters highlight the struggles over control and who should benefit from this control—corporate interests or citizens?

Another crucial policy issue is that of Internet access. Access must be considered as access not only to the technical infrastructure—the hardware and software—but also to the social infrastructure, which encompasses literacy, diverse content, vibrant communities, and the ability of Internet users to create and communicate rather than simply act as passive recipients of streaming video, flashy graphics, and branded stickiness. Access also includes geographic availability in rural, remote, and Northern communities; the establishment of public access sites for Canadians who don't have residential Internet services (or even a residence); and universal usability—innovative designs that can accommodate a diverse citizenry.

Several chapters address the issue of media ownership in Canada. Canada has one of the most concentrated systems of media ownership and conglomerization in the world. Chapter 21 examines the consequences for political reporting and identifies venues for alternative expression. Chapter 22 looks at culture and trade debates and discusses cultural sovereignty, a theme addressed in previous chapters.

The details of the media landscape—particularly patterns of ownership—are in flux, so by the time you read this book new developments in the form of acquisitions, mergers, and the like will undoubtedly have occurred. It is important to keep in mind the range of groups—policymakers, corporations, consumers, and public-interest advocates—that have a stake in debates about the media.

15

Globalization, Communication, and Diaspora

Karim H. Karim
Carleton University

THE DIMENSIONS AND DIRECTIONS OF GLOBALIZATION

Globalization has several dimensions including the economic, political, migratory, and communicative.[1] The economic dimension of globalization is generally reflected in the increased flow of goods and services across borders. Various treaties such as the North American Free Trade Agreement (NAFTA) have facilitated the growth of trade. The World Trade Organization (WTO) plays a major role in lowering the tariffs and duties paid at borders and in reducing the control that governments have over their own economies and the environment. Economic globalization is further characterized by changes in regulations for many industries (especially telecommunications), and by an increased pace of mergers between corporations, both within countries and transnationally. Politically, globalization has been closely intertwined with various trade liberalization initiatives, changes in industry regulations, privatization of state-owned corporations, and the transfer of some powers to international organizations such as the WTO. The European Union has gone the furthest among regional and international organizations in politically integrating its member states. However, it is a mistake to assume that the power of national governments has been completely eroded or that borders have become completely insignificant. Governments continue to maintain substantial control over most areas of life—including various aspects of media and communication—in the respective countries where they have sovereignty.

Apart from the expansion in the global movement of goods, the transnational migration of people has grown exponentially in recent decades. The increasing ease and speed of transportation has facilitated the migration of people over large distances. Business travellers, migrant workers, students, tourists, and immigrants regularly cross continents. This has led to the growth of diasporas[2] of different ethnic groups who live around the world. Globalization depends on the growth of communicative capacity. The ease with which people can be in touch with other parts of the world has promoted economic, political, and migratory activities on a transnational basis. Indeed, the transnational flow of information includes mail; print materials (newspapers, magazines, books, technical and scientific journals);

news agency content; film and sound/video products; advertising; telecommunications (telephone, telegraph, telex, fax, etc.); broadcasting (radio, television, digital broadcasting); computer-mediated data flows (Internet, World Wide Web, chat lines); the physical movement of people in tourism, travel, and migration, and government; and educational, artistic, and cultural exchanges (conferences, exhibitions, sports events) (Mowlana, 1996).

Richard Falk has distinguished between "globalization-from-above" and "globalization-from-below." He identifies globalization-from-above as reflecting the "collaboration between leading states and the main agents of capital formation" (Falk, 1993, p. 39). At the intergovernmental tier, international policy and legislation that governs other forms of transnational communication is shaped and policed. Bodies such as the World Trade Organization, the International Telecommunications Union, the World Intellectual Property Organization, United Nations Educational Scientific and Cultural Organization, and Intelsat operate at this level. Transnational corporations are also major players in the globalization of communication. They include giant communications companies (AOL Time Warner, News Corp., CNN, Disney, MTV, Bertelsmann, etc.), telecommunications companies (AT&T, Microsoft, Nortel, Cisco), and noncommunications global corporations (Coca Cola, Nike, Exxon) that are engaged in massive transnational information flows. The latter carry out large amounts of advertising around the world and transfer significant amounts of data through computers and other means.

Globalization-from-below is carried out mainly by organizations that do not have strong links with governments or large corporations. Organizations such as Amnesty International and Greenpeace are transnational civil society groups that monitor the performance of governments on human rights and environmental protection respectively. Other organizations such as the International Committee for the Red Cross and Médecins Sans Frontières act as relief agencies around the world. Academic and professional associations, religious organizations, and diasporic groups also participate in globalization-from-below by developing lateral communication links between members in various parts of the world. They may not necessarily challenge international governmental activities or transnational corporations, but they are nevertheless distinct from them.[3]

THE HISTORICAL ROOTS OF TRANSNATIONAL COMMUNICATION

Globalization as we know it today has origins in history. People have been trading and communicating with distant lands for thousands of years. The present form of globalization represents the intensification and acceleration of transnational contacts. Ancient and medieval civilizations had developed relatively sophisticated systems of transportation and communication. In medieval times, the Silk Road efficiently connected the lands of China, Central Asia, Iran, and Eastern Europe, and even served as the route for a rudimentary postal system. The Chinese, Indians,

Persians, and Arabs regularly communicated with each other, sharing knowledge and innovations. Sea trade routes across the Indian Ocean linked South Asia, Iran, Arab lands, and Africa. Middle Eastern civilizations passed on their scientific discoveries to Europe, enabling it to emerge from its Dark Ages into the Renaissance. European colonization of other continents represented a significant step on the road to contemporary globalization.

The eventual result of colonization has been to bring all countries of the world into a political system of nation-states that originated in Europe. European names were transplanted around the globe as the northern continent remade the world in its own image. Systems of transportation and communication linked colonies with "mother countries" in Europe like umbilical cords, laying the groundwork for the telecommunications infrastructures and communications patterns that are in place today.

The invention of the telegraph in the 1830s ushered in a new era of telecommunications, in which a message need not be delivered *physically* over long distances. For the first time in human history, people separated by barriers such as mountains, deserts, and oceans could communicate almost instantly using the Morse code. Telegraph lines were first installed along railway tracks in Britain. By 1862, 240,000 kilometres of telegraph lines had been built around the world. This new form of communication tended to diminish somewhat the power of political centres in the 19th century. It enabled southern American states to fight the Civil War. It also accelerated the disintegration of the Habsburg Empire (which had dominated European affairs for several centuries), precipitating the growth of nationalism and eventually the First World War in the early 20th century. On the other hand, the telegraph strengthened the control of European colonial powers over their colonies.

The telegraph also enabled the growth of "wire services." In 1835, Charles-Louis Havas created the Havas news agency in Paris. The agency, which provided information from around France and translations of foreign newspapers, collected and disseminated news by using the newly invented telegraph. Paul Julius Reuter, a German immigrant living in London, expanded his telegraph company, which was serving business with stock quotations, to establish a news agency. It grew to have correspondents in various continents. In 1869, Havas, Reuters and Wolff (the German news agency), signed a treaty of alliance to carve up the world into news zones: Reuters received the British Empire and East Asia; Havas the French, Spanish, Italian, and Portuguese empires; and Wolff the territories controlled by Germany, Austria, Netherlands, Scandinavia, and Russia. These first transnational companies thus created a cartel that globally controlled their product—news—by generally operating in their respective government's spheres of influence.

The invention of the telephone in 1876, allowing for voice communication between individuals, also helped to overcome the limitations of distance. People separated by large distances could communicate without needing to know the Morse code or even how to write. Companies like AT&T, which realized the enormous benefits of this new invention, were able to amass huge fortunes. This saw the emergence of telecommunications corporations, which are key players in the process of globalization. Guglielmo Marconi developed wireless telegraphy or radio, and in 1901 he successfully transmitted a message across the Atlantic from Cornwall, England, to Signal Hill, Newfoundland. Military demands provided strong impetus for the development of these technologies in World War I. The advent of radio broadcasting saw the birth of mass audiences. Radio became a powerful medium for the consolidation of nation-states and, conversely, for cross-border propaganda. There emerged a number of government-run transnational broadcasters that disseminated information in many languages in order to influence other countries and populations.

Television became feasible in 1931, and was launched by the BBC in 1936. This represented a major step in human communication because not only did television transmit sound like radio, but it also had the advantage over film of broadcasting live pictures. However, this technology is dependent on capital-intensive production and centralized transmission facilities. Its limited free-to-air broadcast range has been extended through cable technology. However, it was satellite transmission that really expanded the reach of simultaneous TV broadcasts. Television pictures were first broadcast via satellite in the early 1960s. This is especially important for large countries like Canada, where it enables simultaneous live coverage of nationally significant events. Satellite broadcasts also enable live intercontinental coverage of occurrences considered to be of transnational importance (e.g., international summits, the Olympic Games, and royal weddings).

New satellite technologies have spurred the growth of mass intercontinental audiences, which are integral to globalization. The arrival of Ku band satellites and digital compression technology has enabled a vast increase in the amount of information that can be beamed over large distances directly to sites equipped with pizza-sized (generally between 45 and 60 centimetres) satellite dishes. Previously, only the largest broadcasting networks could afford to utilize satellites; but the increased transponder capacity of direct broadcast satellite (DBS) has lowered the costs and has resulted in the proliferation of specialty channels. This technology makes it possible to narrowcast to specific audiences that have similar interests but are separated by vast distances. The availability of direct-to-home television services has also led to the fragmentation of mass national audiences that previously had a limited choice of national networks to watch. Commentators ask whether such developments are leading to the collapse of a national public sphere or to a democratization of media that were previously controlled by dominant groups in society (e.g. Gitlin, 1998). New satellite technologies have also permitted the growth of transnational broadcasting, not only by the giant media corporations but also by television networks serving diasporic audiences.

Another set of new communication technologies that have had an impact on globalization are on-line media. The origins of on-line systems are to be found in the U.S. military's development of ARPAnet in 1969. This communications system was designed during the Cold War to withstand nuclear bombardment. In the event that several parts of the network were destroyed, its decentralized structure was expected to enable surviving American decision-makers to continue communicating. This technology was used in the 1980s to establish a network linking American researchers and academics; it expanded to Canada and then to other countries. The early 1990s saw the emergence of a more widely available system called the Internet, which allows for intercontinental communication between connected institutions or individuals around the world, and has thus become one of the major symbols of globalization. Based on the design of the decentralized structure of ARPAnet, the Internet has generally proved resistant even to government control. It allows information to flow easily across borders, enabling closer communicative links between individuals and groups in various parts of the world. To date, the Internet remains largely unregulated in most countries. However, major corporations have been attempting to commercialize the use of this technology.

THE EMERGENCE OF INTERNATIONAL REGULATION

International organizations did not exist 150 years ago because nation-states generally dealt with each other in a bilateral (i.e., involving only two governments) rather than multilateral fashion. The 19th century witnessed several important developments in international relations. National governments began to come together and initiate the process of multilateral policymaking for sovereign states, specifically in the area of communications. Some of the earliest European conferences, held in the second half of 19th century, dealt with postal and telegraph services and intellectual property. The International Telegraph Convention, the first treaty to address international communication, was signed in 1865; it established the International Telegraph Union (ITU), headquartered in Switzerland. A number of basic norms were stipulated, including the universal right to use international telegraphy, and the state's right to stop transmissions considered dangerous for state security or in violation of national laws, public order, or morals. The apparent contradiction between these two norms underlined the dilemma that contemporary telecommunications still pose for governments in enabling citizens to use such technologies while seeking to control their applications.

The 1883 Paris Convention for the Protection of Industrial Property signed by European governments was designed to help the people of one country obtain protection in other countries for their intellectual creations in the form of industrial property rights (patents and trademarks). Copyright entered the broader international arena in 1886 with the Berne Convention for the Protection of Literary and Artistic Works. The aim of this treaty was to help nationals of its member states obtain international protection of their right to control and receive payment for the use of their creative works, including written, musical, and artistic materials. The United International Bureaux for the Protection of Intellectual Property (known by its French acronym BIRPI) was established to administer the international treaties.

With the growth of newer media, the regulation of telephony and radio-telegraphy was incorporated into the ITU's work in 1903. The Berlin Radio Convention of 1906 was aimed at managing the radio frequency spectrum, which was a limited natural resource. ITU was to administer the allocation of frequency bands to applicants in various countries in order to avoid overlap on the spectrum. In 1927, the Radio Convention and Radio Regulations were signed at a conference in Washington, and the Radio Union was established. European governments tended to favour state authority, while the United States argued for private-sector control. American communications companies, a dominant presence at the Washington conference, "practically wrote the Radio Convention" (Hamelink, 1994, p. 20). Corporations lobbied against public control of their operations and promoted the "first come, first served" approach to finite communications resources such as the electromagnetic (radio) spectrum. In 1932, the International Telecommunication Convention was signed; it merged the Radio Union and the International Telegraph Union into the International Telecommunications Union, also known by the acronym ITU.

THE NWICO DEBATE

Following World War II, American cultural industries gained a strong position globally because most European countries were preoccupied with rebuilding the infrastructures that had been destroyed during the long conflict. The United States also became a key player in the newly established United Nations organization. In 1946, it managed to gain the agreement of European powers for the Declaration on Freedom of Information, which promoted the American concept of the free flow of information "within countries and across frontiers" (Gunter, 1978, p. 143). The United Nations Educational, Scientific, and Cultural Organization (UNESCO) began studying the role of communication in development in the 1960s. It identified certain minimum levels of communication capacity necessary for development, and concluded from its research that this minimum was unavailable to 70 percent of the world's population. Consequently, the UN shifted some of its development activities to address communication needs more directly.

In the early 1970s, several developing countries began to question Western (especially American) dominance over global communication. They argued that technical assistance did not alter their dependency status on the North, and stated that *cultural imperialism* had become the successor of territorial colonialism following the political independence of many countries in the Southern continents. They said that continued Northern hegemony served as a barrier to their cultural and economic development. Developing countries pointed to the overwhelming influence that the North had over the South in terms of news flows, which were largely controlled by news agencies such as Reuters, Associated Press, United Press

International, Agence France Presse, and TASS. They also saw as a threat to their national sovereignty the ability of the satellite-owning countries to scan their territories for commercial, political, and military purposes.

Developing countries could participate in international bodies, such as the UN and ITU, upon gaining independence. As colonies, most African and Asian states did not have a seat at the UN when the Declaration on Freedom of Information was passed in 1946. By the 1960s, however, developing countries were gaining the ability to voice in international forums their concerns over such issues as the lack of equal access to telecommunications. Twenty European states had established the ITU in 1865; by 1970, 100 of its 154 members were developing countries. They complained vigorously that ITU's "first come, first served" principle gave the advantage to the more technologically advanced Northern countries in staking claims to the radio spectrum and geostationary satellite orbits. Developing countries also proposed that states which owned satellites should obtain "prior consent" before scanning their territories or beaming in broadcasts.

These concerns and demands became part of the celebrated New World Information and Communication Order (NWICO) debate. This long, drawn-out international discussion took place in the context of the Cold War between the NATO and Warsaw Pact countries. To facilitate their continued independence from this standoff between NATO (led by the United States) and the Warsaw Pact countries (led by the USSR), a number of African, Asian, and Latin American states formed the Non-Aligned Movement (NAM). NAM was the initial forum for the airing of issues related to NWICO, which were later taken into other organizations such as UNESCO and ITU. These issues included the imbalance in transnational news flows, the overwhelming influence of Western culture, the lack of technology transfer to developing countries, the threat posed to national sovereignty by satellites, and the identification of human communication as a basic right.

Following intense rounds of debate between certain developing and developed countries at UNESCO meetings, the former gained the upper hand and were able to obtain support for a Mass Media Declaration, which was passed in 1978. The declaration expressed the concept of a "free flow and wider and better balanced dissemination of information," which reformulated the earlier notion of the "freedom of information" (Hamelink, 1994, p. 156). The latter concept was criticized as working in favour of those who had the more advanced means of communication. UNESCO also established the International Commission for the Study of Communication Problems to explore four issues: the current state of world communication, the problems surrounding a free and balanced flow of information, how a NWICO could be established, and how the media could become vehicles for educating public opinion about global problems (MacBride, 1980). Chaired by Sean MacBride, the commission proposed the democratization of communications, while acknowledging that democracy was impeded in many countries by the systems in place, by corruption, and by the lack of access to means of communication. The report adhered to UNESCO's Mass Media Declaration and recontextualized the freedom of press to the right to communicate by everyone. It criticized the censorship of media, as well as the self-censorship carried out by journalists. The commission also assailed the one-way flows of information from North to South and the constraints on communication imposed by commercialism, advertisers, and media concentration.

Western countries were not pleased with the report. The American government and media were especially critical, placing NWICO-related issues (such as the social responsibility of the press and the right to communicate) within the framework of government control of the media. They attacked UNESCO for engaging in the political arena, which was supposed to be reserved for the General Assembly of the UN. Opponents of NWICO suggested that the disparity in communications development could be resolved by technical support from the West. However, following the tabling of the MacBride report, the General Conference Session of UNESCO passed a resolution for the attainment of a NWICO. Subsequently, attacks against the body from the United States under President Ronald Reagan and the United Kingdom under Prime Minister Margaret Thatcher became more intense; both governments withdrew from UNESCO, taking with them a significant proportion of its budget.

GLOBALIZATION FROM ABOVE AND BELOW

The New World Information and Communication Order, as envisioned by NAM and UNESCO, did not materialize because Northern countries (including the USSR) did not support it. NWICO ceased to be on the UNESCO agenda in the 1990s and lost its profile in international discussions on communications. At present, UNESCO's communication and information section focuses on communication research, information flows and exchange, the development of communications systems, and communications means and infrastructures. It seeks to promote freedom of information by supporting international agreements aimed at removing customs duties on educational, cultural, and scientific materials; decreasing postal charges for publications; and lowering rates for certain telecommunications services. It sponsors the training of journalists and communications specialists, and helps to organize regional news exchanges and to set up press or information agencies in developing countries.

UNESCO's *World Culture Report 2000* indicates that there were remarkable changes in communication capacities around the world in the last two decades of the 20th century. The number of radios in developing countries grew by 42 percent from 1980 to 1997. However, even though most of the planet's population lives in the South, industrialized countries had four-fifths of the radios. Developing countries' average annual rate of growth in television sets between 1980 and 1997 was a phenomenal 92 percent, but more than three-quarters of the televisions are to be found in industrialized countries.

Following the Second World War, the ITU became a specialized UN agency responsible for harmonizing and coordinating the use of telecommunications among countries. It plays a major role in setting standards for most new communications technologies. By 2001, 189 member countries had signed the International Telecommunication Convention. However, the power of the ITU in the political economy of global telecommunications has been much diminished since the establishment of the World Trade Organization in 1995. The WTO has become a key player in determining the parameters of the telecommunications policies that individual states can adopt.

There were also major developments on the intellectual property front in the late 20th century. As the importance of intellectual property grew, the structure and form of the United International Bureau for the Protection of Intellectual Property changed, and it was replaced by the World Intellectual Property Organization (WIPO). In 1974, WIPO became a specialized agency of the United Nations, with a mandate to administer intellectual property matters recognized by the UN. It expanded its role in the 1990s by incorporating intellectual property rights in the management of globalized trade. This new focus was solidified by WIPO's cooperation agreement with WTO in 1996. WIPO is also preoccupied with the problems that the new media pose for intellectual property.

Unlike telecommunications and intellectual property, the transnational administration of satellites has *not* come to be associated with the United Nations system. The United States launched the first communications satellite in 1958, and the USSR soon followed suit. Canada became the third country in space; it designed Alouette I, which was launched into orbit by NASA in 1962. In 1964, 11 Western countries agreed to establish the International Satellite Organization (INTELSAT), with the United States playing the dominant role. Membership in INTELSAT was open to all ITU members. INTELSAT's guiding principle was to provide equal access to all countries on an equal basis; to that end, members and nonmembers were charged the same rates.

The early INTELSAT satellites and ground stations were concentrated over and at the Northern Hemisphere, but they soon spread to cover the planet. Satellites are placed in geostationary orbit (around 35,900 kilometres above the earth) over the Atlantic, Indian, and Pacific Ocean regions, providing audio, video, and data facilities. The rapidly increasing demand for international satellite services by users such as financial networks, transnational corporations, and international news organizations has caused INTELSAT services to undergo a remarkable period of growth since the 1980s. The organization carries a large proportion of transnational television broadcasts and telephone calls.

The liberalization of telecommunications regulations in the 1980s had a major impact on the operations of INTELSAT. Reflecting its commitment to ensure that services are provided around the world on a nondiscriminatory basis, the organization's tariff policies allowed for cross-subsidization (i.e., revenues from dense routes, such as those between North America and Europe, subsidized rates in the thin routes connecting developing countries). INTELSAT's system of price averaging ensured affordable communication on a worldwide basis. However, the technological merging of telecommunications with computer technology, optical fibre cable, and the fax machine, together with the erosion of distinctions between voice and data, contributed to the growth of telecommunications and, conse-quently, pressure from largest users in the West to reduce tariffs. "The more serious threat came with open skies policy of the Reagan administration (in 1984) which claimed that new private entrants on the transatlantic satellite market would be in the national interest" (Hamelink, 1994, p. 70). The U.S. government ended INTELSAT's national monopoly arrangement; it thus has to compete with other satellite operators who tend to "cream skim" the dense routes. This shift from cross-subsidization to a practice based on market principles was followed by similar developments in the United Kingdom and Japan. INTELSAT was further inte-grated into the global market economy in 2001, when it was transformed from an intergovernmental agency into a private corporation.

The ITU's (1998) research shows that whereas the profits of the top 50 telecommunications operators in the world grew from under $40 billion (U.S.) in 1990 to almost $60 billion in 1996, large parts of the world had very little access to basic telephone services. Around a quarter of the world's countries have a tele-density of below one phone line per 100 households, compared with that of 71 in the Americas.[4] Data from Latin America and the Caribbean shows that the privati-zation of telecommunications structures has led to rapid increases in the number of telephone lines (ITU, 1997). However, in 1997 the average cost in developing countries of making an international telephone call was twice as much as that in industrialized countries; it was cheapest (US$1.20) in North America and the most expensive (US$9.50) in sub-Saharan Africa, the poorest region of the world (UNESCO, 2000, p. 367).

With the growth of new technologies, there have emerged other disparities between "information haves" and "have-nots." Despite the visions expressed by Western countries of establishing a "global information society," the primarily North American and European countries of the Organization for Economic Cooperation and Development, which have only 19 percent of the world's popula-tion, accounted for 91 percent of Internet users in 1998 (UNDP, 1999). However, the global digital divide does not necessarily run horizontally between the North and the South. Winseck (in press) indicates that the world's communications grid is marked by certain nodal points that include São Paulo, Hong Kong, Shanghai, Singapore, and Johannesburg. The more affluent residents of such urban areas in developing countries are better connected with Western cities than with most of their own compatriots.

The global debate on the NWICO that had raged in previous decades revolved around the imbalance in communication flows between the North and the South. A key complaint of developing countries was that while the West argued in support of the free flow of information, most of the traffic was from North to South, and that it was impossible for Asians, Africans, and Latin Americans to compete with the technological superiority and established cultural industries of the North.

In the area of news dissemination, the infrastructures established in the colonial period continued to maintain the advantage in the North's favour. This continued Northern hegemony was viewed in the context of a cultural imperialism. The UNESCO discussions failed to resolve the problem. Indeed, the ensuing period of communications deregulation, trade liberalization, privatization, and technological innovation has made it even more difficult for governments in developing states to have a say in managing transborder information flows (Herman and McChesney, 1997).

However, there have been in the South a number of success stories that are contributing to "globalization-from-below." The commercial performance of the popular-film industry in Mumbai, India (Bollywood), is comparable to that of its American counterpart in Hollywood. Whereas the Indian cinema does not have the enormous budgets or digital special effects of Hollywood blockbusters, it annually produces the largest number of films in the world. And since the vast majority of these films are musicals, there has grown over the last nine decades a massive recording industry centred on Bollywood. The late introduction of television in India has resulted in this medium using Bollywood film, reviews, retrospectives, music, and gossip as fodder for entertainment programming. Whereas the extent of Indian film's transnational distribution is much smaller than that of Hollywood, it has significant penetration in South Asia, Southeast Asia, the Middle East, Africa, and the Caribbean. India is the main source of film imports in many developing countries (UNESCO, 2000, pp. 304–307). The Indian diaspora remains the mainstay of audiences and of distribution networks in some of these countries, as well as in the West, where cinemas exclusively showing popular Indian films flourish in cities with significant populations of South Asian origins.

Similarly, the Cairo film and television industry exports to Arabic-speaking countries and to the larger Arab diaspora. Whereas Hong Kong action movies have had some success among non-Chinese audiences around the world, it is the Mexican and Brazilian television networks Televisa and TV Globo respectively that have been able to capture major cross-cultural markets beyond their borders. Televisa and TV Globo capitalized on the advantages of their own large domestic audiences and their "geolinguistic regions" (Sinclair, 1997)—Spanish-speaking Latin America in the case of Televisa and the string of former Portuguese colonies scattered around the planet that receive TV Globo's programming. Of increasing importance for Televisa is the Spanish-speaking population of the United States, which is growing rapidly and is relatively affluent. Televisa and TV Globo are also exporting products to former colonial powers such as Spain, Portugal, and Italy, and even dubbed versions to Russia and developing countries. Going against the arguments put forward by cultural imperialism theorists, these networks, which are the largest in the non-English world, have used the technological, organizational, artistic, and programming models of U.S. television to produce their own success stories. American television's soap opera genre, adopted by the Latin American networks in the "telenovela," has provided a workable formula for worldwide cross-cultural exports. The cultural imperialism perspective failed to realize the ability of the media entrepreneurs in Southern countries to use and adapt new technologies for their own innovations.

WHAT ARE DIASPORAS?

Whereas the term "diaspora" has traditionally referred primarily to the existence of Jewish communities around the world, it is increasingly being used to denote communities with similar dispersion (Cohen, 1997). The identities of individuals and groups within specific diasporas are formed by complex historical, social, and cultural dynamics within the group and with other groups. Retention of ancestral customs, language, and religion; the marriage patterns of its members; and the ease of communication between various parts of the transnational group help determine its characteristics.

The mass migrations of the 1700s and 1800s led to accelerated economic growth in the New World (while at the same time displacing indigenous economies and communities). These migrations included movements of slaves from Africa, indentured labourers from Asia, and settlers from Europe. Following the lifting of restrictions on race-based immigration in the 1950s and 1960s, Asians and Africans began to migrate in larger numbers to North America, Australasia, and Europe. There has also been substantial migration from Latin America into the United States. These movements of people of various origins to different parts of the world have created diasporas that are layered by periods of migration, the extent of integration into receiving societies, and the maintenance of links with the land of origin as well as with other parts of the transnational group. This layering has resulted in wide variations in the connections and attachments among such worldwide communities.

It is important to locate the diasporic phenomenon within the context of globalization processes of the last few centuries, which have intensified in recent times owing to vastly improved transportation and communication technologies. Human migration patterns have been determined by colonization and by trading connections. Northern economic activity, such as moving production of goods to developing countries, investing in the South's export-oriented agriculture, and the power of multinationals in the consumer markets of developing states, has contributed indirectly to the mass movement of people from South to North (Sassen, 1996, p. 77). Organized recruitment of workers by governments or employers has also stimulated migration.

In many instances, diasporas are themselves participants in transnational economic activity. From the banking network of the Rothschilds, originating in 18th-century Europe, to more recent global businesses like the Hinduja Group, diasporic families have been leading players in global transactions. At $450 billion (U.S.), the annual economic output in the early 1990s of the 55 million overseas Chinese was estimated to be roughly equal to that of the 1.2 billion people in China itself

(Seagrave, 1995). Commentators writing from cultural studies and postcolonial perspectives, on the other hand, tend to view diasporas as ranged against global and national structures of dominance—of "the empire striking back." The diasporic site becomes the cultural border between the country of origin and the country of residence—Homi Bhabha's "third space" (Bhabha, 1994). This is the zone of intense, cutting-edge creativity born out of the existential angst of the immigrant who is neither completely attached to the homeland nor fully accepted in his or her adopted country.

While the globally dominant Eurocentric cultural structures (particularly media conglomerates) are being vastly strengthened (Herman and McChesney, 1997), there have emerged over the last few decades a variety of voices from the South and from diasporas that attempt to present other worldviews. Shohat and Stam (1994) explore a "constellation of oppositional strategies, which taken together have the potential of revolutionizing audio-visual production and pedagogy" p. 10). They refer to the aesthetics of resistance in the New Cinemas of Cuba, Brazil, Senegal, and India, as well as to diasporic films made in Canada, the United States, and the United Kingdom. Just within the South Asian diaspora, one can cite a list of accomplished authors that includes Michael Ondaatje, Shyam Selvadurai (Sri Lanka/Canada), Anita Rau Badami, Rohinton Mistry, Anita Desai (India/Canada), Bharati Mukerjee (India/Canada/United States), M.G. Vassanji (Kenya/Tanzania/Canada), Cyril Dabydeen (Guyana/Canada), Salman Rushdie (India/United Kingdom), V.S. Naipaul (Trinidad/United Kingdom), and Hanif Kureishi (United Kingdom). Diasporic artists are viewed by the likes of Bhabha and Shohat and Stam to be at the cutting edge of modernity.

ETHNIC MEDIA AS TRANSNATIONAL MEDIA

The role of ethnic media in global communication flows is steadily growing in importance. Transnational ethnic-based commercial broadcasting infrastructure is integral to the increasingly global ethnic economy. Advertising on ethnic radio and television is viewed by niche marketers as a way to reach growing minority populations in a time of fragmenting audiences. Univisión, the largest Spanish-language U.S. network, which "owns 11 stations and has 19 affiliates, is also carried on 740 cable systems and is seen by 92 percent of Hispanic households in 162 markets across the United States" (Collins, 1996, p. C6). Sociologists and communication scholars have viewed ethnic media as serving two primary purposes: (1) to contribute to ethnic cohesion and cultural maintenance, and (2) to help members of minorities integrate into the larger society (Riggins, 1992, p. 4). Husband (1994) asserts that "we need autonomous ethnic minority media which can speak for, and to, their own community; ethnic minority media which can generate a dialogue between ethnic minority communities; and between these and dominant ethnic community audiences" (p. 15).

However, obtaining sufficient space for the ethnic broadcast media on the electromagnetic spectrum has involved a continual struggle with national regulators.[5] For example, France's main broadcast authority, the Conseil Supérieur de l'audiovisuel, was actively encouraged by the centre-right government to exclude Arabic stations from licensed cable networks. The response of a significant number of Maghrebi immigrant families was to subscribe to DBS services that provide them with programming from Arab countries from across the Mediterranean Sea. In the autumn of 1995, a survey conducted for the European satellite company Eutelsat indicated that 21 percent of Arabic-speaking households in France had invested in satellite receivers, compared with 4 percent of the general population. A year later, the number of Arabic-speaking households with satellite dishes was believed to have doubled (Hargreaves and Mahdjoub, 1997, p. 461). With the availability of new communication technologies, diasporas are able to obtain cultural materials with growing ease from other parts of the world. Governments are finding it increasingly difficult to assimilate minorities into the dominant national culture in the face of globalization-from-below.

A number of ethnic television broadcasters export their programming to other parts of the diaspora; for example, the weekly Vision TV program *West Indians United*, produced by a group of South Asian diasporics in Toronto, is being regularly rebroadcast in Guyana and the United States. On a much broader scale, either Univisión or Telemundo—the two largest Spanish-language networks in the United States—is available on almost every cable system in Latin America. "And in smaller, poorer countries, local television stations often simply tape stories from Univisión or Telemundo's nightly newscasts for their own use, which gives these American networks a degree of credibility and visibility unusual in the region" (Rohter, 1996 p. 6). The picture that Latin Americans see of American society in these North–South news flows is very different from that presented by mainstream U.S. television (e.g., CNN) or by global TV news agencies such as the World Television Network and Reuters Television. Univisión and Telemundo adhere to Latin American news values that favour greater analysis than that offered by mainstream American television. The Spanish-language networks also seek out Hispanic perspectives on national news stories.

The relatively small and widely scattered nature of communities they serve have encouraged diasporic media to seek out the most efficient and cost-effective means of communication. Technologies that have generally been favoured are those that allow for *narrowcasting* (i.e., the targeting of specific audiences), rather than those that provide the means for mass communication. Ethnic media have frequently been at the leading edge of technology adoption owing to the particular challenges they face in reaching their audiences. In discussing the Indian community in Southhall, England, Gillespie (1995) notes that many families obtained VCRs as early as 1978, "well before most households in Britain" (p. 79). Television program exports in Mexico were vastly enhanced through the use of videotape. Later, satellite technology was used to interconnect the various Spanish-language

TV stations that Televisa controlled for many years throughout the United States, thus establishing a national network for Mexican-originated programs and creating a national audience of "Hispanics."

Whereas governments in developing and developed countries have expressed fears that DBS would erode their sovereignty by transmitting foreign programming to their populations in an unregulated fashion, this technology is providing remarkable opportunities for diasporic communities. Ethnic broadcasters, who previously had limited access to space on the electromagnetic spectrum in Northern countries, are finding that DBS presents much greater opportunities. Diasporic programming that uses DBS has grown exponentially in the last few years, well ahead of many mainstream broadcasters. Even as mainstream networks in Europe were making plans to introduce digital broadcasting, the Arab-owned and -operated Orbit TV in Rome had by 1994 begun to provide extensive programming via DBS to Arab communities both in Europe and the Middle East. Arab Radio and Television (ART) has several channels that are broadcast to Arab countries, and one each to Europe and North America. One of the most fascinating uses of DBS technology in the Middle Eastern context is MED-TV, a Kurdish satellite television station (Hassanpour, 1998). This is a case of a diaspora within and without the divided homeland attempting to sustain itself and to counter forceful suppression with the use of communications technology. MED-TV has faced resistance not only from governments of the various states straddling Kurdistan, but also from antiterrorist police forces in the United Kingdom, Belgium, and Germany.

Quite apart from the DBS television offered by global conglomerates like Rupert Murdoch's Star TV, which beams programming to several Asian countries, there have emerged several diasporic DBS-based networks that serve Asian diasporas. The Chinese Television Network, headquartered in Hong Kong, has been broadcasting to East Asia, Australia, the Pacific Islands, and the United States since 1994. Hong Kong's Television Broadcasts International "reaches into several Asian markets and to Chinese communities just about everywhere" (Berfield, 1997, p. 31). The London-based Chinese Channel's programs are received in the United Kingdom and continental Europe. India's state-run network Doordarshan has taken its International Channel to over 40 countries, while Zee TV has emerged as a very popular global Indian network in recent years (Thussu, 2000, pp. 197–199).

Satellite networks in the United States have realized the viability of ethnic channels and are making them an integral part of their services. DirecTV and DISH Network provide a wide variety of these channels. WMNB (Russian), Network Asia (India-oriented), Ukrainian Broadcasting Network, CiaoTV–The Italian Superchannel, Egyptian Satellite Channel, and Nile TV appear on DirectTV. The DISH Network's offerings include Fox Sports Americas, MTV Latino, and Telemundo, all in Spanish; Antenna in Greek and Croatian; ART in Arabic; TV5 and RFI in French; RTPi in Portuguese; and RAI in Italian. In January 1998, California-based Space TV launched five Chinese video channels, ten Chinese audio channels, one Thai video channel, one Filipino video channel, and an Asian Business News channel for North American subscribers. The company has also announced plans to launch Korean, Japanese, and Vietnamese offerings.

Diasporic groups are also making extensive use of on-line services such as the Internet, Usenet, Listserv, and the World Wide Web. For members of communities residing in various continents, these worldwide networks allow for relatively easy connections. Whereas the broadcast model of communication is linear, hierarchical, and capital-intensive, on-line media are nonlinear, largely nonhierarchical, and relatively cheap (Karim, Smeltzer, and Loucheur, 1998). The ability to exchange messages with individuals on the other side of the planet and to have access to community information almost instantaneously changes the dynamics of diaspora, allowing for qualitatively and quantitatively enhanced linkages. As the number of language scripts and translation capabilities of on-line software grow, an increasing number of non-English speakers are drawn to the medium.

Diasporic Web sites are already creating global directories of individuals, community institutions, and businesses owned by members of diasporas. Some sites have hypertext links to sites of alumni associations. Listings of forthcoming festivals and cultural events are also provided for those travelling to other parts of the diaspora. The availability of on-line versions of newspapers from countries of origin further enhances intercontinental connections. Global on-line technologies also offer some unique advantages for diasporic groups. For example, a worldwide registry would be extremely useful for the medical purposes of locating matches for human marrow donors, who are generally limited to one's own ethnic group. Similar databanks would facilitate global genealogical searches and searches for adopted children's biological families. Members of endogamous groups are already using the medium to register themselves in matrimonial sections of diasporic Web sites.

Many Web sites catering to transnational communities have chat rooms where users can carry out a discussion by posting messages. Usenet also allows for ongoing discussions between individuals with common origins through newsgroups such as soc.culture.germany and soc.culture.pakistan. Topics for discussion include culture, literature, entertainment, politics, and current events in the countries of origin and settlement. Newsgroups allow for the participation of users with common interests, located around the world (Mitra, 1997). Indeed, the electronic chat room becomes the "place" where some members of these global communities come together electronically to reconstitute the relationships that existed before migration.

By participating in creating content, Usenet users are able to circumvent the hierarchical mass media as well as to counter the material from dominant government and commercial sources. We need to keep in mind that, even though the use of on-line media and DBS is increasing steadily around the world, there are wide differences in use of these technologies. Whereas Canadian surveys have indicated high levels of use among ethnic minorities like the Chinese (Environics, 1997) and South Asians (Chow, 1998, p. D1), the lowest levels in the United States are among the African-American and Latino communities (Chabran, 1996). As we move beyond North America, Europe, and Australia, the ownership of computer hardware and subscription to Internet services falls dramatically. Ethnic-based programming on DBS uses a market model and is targeted at fairly affluent members of various diasporas. Mainstream companies are showing increasing interest in ethnic media, with Shaw Communications buying a stake in the Telelatino network in Canada, CBS in the United States acquiring TeleNoticias, and Rupert Murdoch's interests expanding their operations to reach South Asian audiences in the United Kingdom. As ethnic broadcasters become successful on the national and global stages, they will likely become targets for takeovers by global media conglomerations, to the detriment of local community content.

ETHNIC MEDIA IN CANADA

Ethnic media in this country remain connected to diasporic communication flows as they simultaneously operate within a uniquely Canadian context. The last decade has seen a significant growth in this sector, which ranges from small newspapers run from home basements to well-established and professionally run broadcast stations. Most third-language media in Canada not only have substantial diasporic content, but they are also the only source of information on such matters as public health, education, training, job-seeking, and business opportunities for many recent Canadian newcomers who have not yet obtained proficiency in an official language.

There are hundreds of ethnic newspapers across the country, most of which publish on a weekly or monthly basis. The larger dailies include the Chinese-language *Ming Pao*, *Sing Tao*, and *World Journal* and the Italian *Corriere Canadese* (which publishes Montreal and Toronto editions). Ethnic print organs, many of which also publish in English and French, are becoming increasingly sophisticated in terms of operation and content, and in some cases compete directly with mainstream newspapers. The total circulation of the 46 ethnic papers in Vancouver, where around half the population belongs to ethnic minorities, is reportedly larger than the combined figure of its two major English-language dailies (Grescoe, 1994/95, p. 82).

A unique approach to ethnic broadcasting has developed under official multiculturalism. The Multiculturalism Act proclaims the federal government's policy of recognizing the diverse cultures of Canadian society. In the same vein, the Broadcasting Act asserts that the country's broadcasting system should reflect the diversity of the country's cultures. The Canadian Radio-television and Telecommunications Commission (CRTC), which introduced an Ethnic Broadcasting Policy in 1985 and updated it in 1999, specifies the conditions under which the dissemination of ethnic and multilingual programming can be carried out.

Ethnic radio programming, which is present in most Canadian cities of significant size, ranges from time slots acquired on mainstream stations, community radio, and campus radio to 24-hour multilingual broadcasters. The CRTC has granted 13 ethnic radio licences to AM and FM frequencies in six metropolitan areas, as well as to a number of Aboriginal stations. Subsidiary Communications Multiplex Operation (SCMO) technology has allowed the emergence of several third-language stations operating on subcarrier frequencies to emerge in various cities across the country. However, subscribers need to acquire specialized radio equipment to access programming carried on these frequencies.

Apart from two multicultural channels serving Southern Ontario (CFMT) and Montreal (CJNT), ethnic and multilingual television programming in Canada is to be found in various time slots on community cable, commercial stations, and a national network (Vision TV). Italian/Spanish (Telelatino), Chinese (Fairchild), South Asian (ATN), and Greek (Odyssey) services are variously available on a national basis via DBS, Look Television, and cable. These Canadian channels carry a blend of programming produced in this country and in other parts of the respective diaspora. Two foreign services, Black Entertainment Network (BET) from the United States and Deutsche Welle from Germany, are offered on some specialty cable packages.[6] The Aboriginal Peoples Television Network (APTN) was established in 1999. Recipients of new digital licences in 2000 have included a number of ethnic broadcasters.

Ben Viccari, a prominent Canadian ethnic media journalist, asserts that through the ethnic media the newcomer can learn about Canadian culture, history, social services and a multitude of other things that can help him or her understand the privileges and the responsibilities inherent in Canadian citizenship (Viccari, 1995, p. 6). Some ethnic media provide extensive coverage of Canadian current affairs to help members of minorities remain informed about the larger Canadian society (Karim, in press).[7] However, not all ethnic media offer such information to readers or audiences. The smaller the print media publication or broadcast production, the less likely it is that civic discourse relating to Canada will be carried in it. A primary goal of most ethnic media is to provide cultural and informational programming related to the respective community, which is generally unavailable in Canadian mass media. Once this goal is met, the medium is able to devote any additional available time or space to discussions about Canada-related public affairs. Programming in radio stations such as CHIN, as well as in some 24-hour SCMO stations (e.g., CHIN in Toronto and Rhim Jhim in Vancouver), offers information on Canadian public affairs through news bulletins, feature programs, and talk shows. The Toronto ethnic television station CFMT also provides time for Canadian issues on its news programming. In this way, ethnic media in Canada participate in globalization-from-below while at the same time responding to the needs of their readers and audiences in this country.

CONCLUSION

Transnational communication, a key aspect of globalization, is carried out not only by international bodies and large corporations but also by smaller organizations and groups. Diasporas may be strung out in small settlements in various countries, but together they form communicative and other links that contribute to globalizing tendencies. Nevertheless, they are dependent to a large extent on the global infrastructures built and operated by states and corporations. They are also subject to the international and national regulations that control the operations of these networks.

Diasporas innovatively use the transnational communications systems that are in place, and are often early adopters of new technologies. In some cases, diasporas participate in global capitalist structures. Immigrant engineers and entrepreneurs from India and China are integral to the success of the high-technology industries of various Western countries, including that in the Silicon Valley of California and Canadian technopolises such as Ottawa. But even though some diasporic cultural products have been able to make cross-cultural breakthroughs, they largely follow transnational routes that are distinct from those starting from Hollywood, London, Paris, and Toronto. Frequently, they run in counter-parallel directions (i.e., from developing to developed countries), but they also run from one Southern continent to another, and from one Northern continent to another. Globalization-from-below of this form is genuinely creating alternative networks to those that were created under European colonialism.

The NWICO debate brought to the fore some of the fundamental problems that underlie general disparities between North and South. It helped to uncover the basic inequalities perpetuated by the global communications structures. Some of these inequities have become worse over the last decade even though the availability of telephones and televisions has grown in many developing countries. The widespread communications facilities enjoyed by the West continue to provide it with economic advantages over the rest of the world. However, the supporters of NWICO largely failed to recognize the internal divide *within* developing countries where rich, urban individuals had a level of access to communications generally comparable to that in industrialized states.

The development of the concept of cultural imperialism provided a popular framework for analyzing the relative communications positions of countries. But in presenting the idea in terms of a hypodermic model, its proponents did not account for differing interpretations that people bring to cultural products such as films and television programs; recent research has provided more nuanced expositions of the concept. NWICO supporters also failed to see the ingenuity of those Southern communicators who have successfully countered North–South flows with their own cultural productions. Diasporas have given us a world with multilateral flows of communication, although the volume and intensity of the traffic from developed countries remains the highest. We also need to acknowledge that, despite the many advances over the last few decades, there remain deep divides in the access to and use of communication technologies in the world.

QUESTIONS

1. What is the difference between economic and cultural globalization? How are they related?
2. What are diasporas and how are they layered over time and space?
3. What are globalization-from-above and globalization-from-below? Give some examples of each.
4. What were the principal claims of (a) supporters of NWICO and (b) opponents of NWICO?
5. In light of recent technological developments, increased media concentration, and globalization, do you think that we need to revisit NWICO today? Give reasons for your answer.

WEB SITES

Diasporas: **http://www.diaspora-net.org/**
Intelsat: **http://www.intelsat.com/**
International Telecommunication Union: **http://www.itu.int/home/index.html**
MacBride Round Table on Communication:
   http://www2.hawaii.edu/~rvincent/macbride.htm
World Intellectual Property Organization: **http://www.wipo.org/**
World Trade Organization: **http://www.wto.org/**

NOTES

1. The views of some of the major theorists on globalization are presented in Sreberny-Mohammadi, Winseck, McKenna, and Boyd-Barrett (1997).
2. Diasporas comprise members of ethnic groups who reside in the homeland and in a number of other countries where they or their ancestors arrived as immigrants.
3. Falk tends to limit his conception of globalization-from-below to groups actively involved in countering the influence of governments and large corporations.
4. The telephone penetration rate in Canada is one of the highest in the world, at 98.5 per 100 households (Dickson, 1996, p. 16).
5. The major exception to this trend occurred in 1980 when the Australian government established Special Broadcasting Services. This national multicultural network shared features of both public service and community broadcasting (Patterson, 1990, pp. 93–99).
6. Canadian audiences also watch many externally based DBS networks that are not licensed in Canada by the CRTC.

7. In their study of the viewing patterns of residents of Maghrebi origins in France, Hargreaves and Mahdjoub (1997) found that whereas older, first-generation immigrants tended not to desire channels other than those received from Arab countries via DBS, younger viewers also wanted access to American services such as MTV and CNN and their French counterparts (p. 474). Gillespie (1995) noted similar viewing patterns among the Indian community in Southhall.

REFERENCES

Berfield, Susan. (1997, February). "Global TV: Still local after all." *World Press Review*, 31.

Bhabha, Homi. (1994). *The location of culture*. London: Routledge.

Chabran, Richard. (1996). Local communities in global society: Reflections on the California SB 600 Task Force. Retrieved from http://www.laplaza.org/about-lap/archives/cn96/collar.html

Chow, Wyng. (1998, January 2). B.C.'s South Asians ready market. *Vancouver Sun*, p. D1.

Cohen, Robin. (1997). *Global diasporas: An introduction*. Seattle: University of Washington Press.

Collins, Glenn. (1996, May 14). Advertising: Information Resources takes aim at the ethnic market, and Nielsen. *New York Times*, 3/3.

Dickson, Paul. (1996). *Access to the information highway: Canadian households*. Ottawa: Industry Canada.

Environics Research Group. (1997, February). *The Chinese-Canadian Technology Report*. Toronto: Environics Research Group.

Falk, Richard. (1993). The making of global citizenship. In Jeremy Brecher, John Brown Childs, and Jill Cutler (Eds.), *Global visions: Beyond the new world order* (pp. 39–50). Boston: South End Press.

Gillespie, Marie. (1995). *Television, ethnicity, and cultural change*. London: Routledge.

Gitlin, Todd. (1998). Public sphere or public sphericules? In Tamar Liebes and James Curran (Eds.), *Media, ritual and identity* (pp. 168–174). London: Routledge.

Grescoe, Taras. (1994/95, Winter). Hot type. *Vancouver*, 81–84, 114–118.

Gunter, Jonathan F. (1978, Autumn). An introduction to the great debate. *Journal of Communication*, 142–156.

Hamelink, Cees J. (1994). *The politics of world communication*. Thousand Oaks, CA: Sage.

Hargreaves, Alec G., and Dalila Mahdjoub. (1997, December). Satellite television viewing among ethnic minorities in France. *European Journal of Communication*, 459–477.

Hassanpour, Amit. (1998, April). Satellite footprints as national borders: MED-TV and the extraterritoriality of state sovereignty. *Journal of Muslim Minority Affairs, 18*(1), 53–72.

Herman, Edward, and Robert McChesney. (1997). *The global media: The new missionaries of corporate capitalism*. London: Cassell.

Husband, Charles (1994). General introduction: Ethnicity and media democratization within the nation-state. In Charles Husband (Ed.). *A richer vision: The development of ethnic minority media in western democracies* (pp. 1–19). Paris: UNESCO.

ITU. (1997). *World telecommunication development report: Trade in telecommunications—world telecommunications indicators*. Geneva: ITU.

———. (1998). *World telecommunication development report: Universal access—World telecommunications indicators*. Geneva: ITU.

Karim, Karim H. (2000). Diasporic networks in cyberspace. *World Culture Report* (p. 188). Paris: UNESCO.

———. (in press). Public sphere and public sphericules: Civic discourse in ethnic media. In Sherry Ferguson and Leslie Regan Shade (Eds.), *Civic discourse and cultural politics in Canada: A cacophony of voices*. Westport, CT: Ablex, 2002.

Karim, Karim H., Sandy Smeltzer, and Yohanna Loucheur. (1998). On-line access and participation in Canadian Society. *SRA reports*. Ottawa: Canadian Heritage.

MacBride, Sean. (1980). *Many voices, one world: Communication and society today and tomorrow*. Paris: UNESCO.

Mitra, Ananda. (1997). Virtual commonality: Looking for India on the Internet. In Steven G. Jones (Ed.), *Virtual culture: Identity and communication in cybersociety* (pp. 55–79). London: Thousand Oaks.

Mowlana, Hamid. (1996). *Global information and world communication: New frontiers in international relations*. Thousand Oaks, CA: Sage.

Patterson, Rose. (1990). Development of ethnic and multicultural media in Australia. *International Migration, 29*(1), 89–104.

Riggins, Stephen Harold, (1992). The media imperative: Ethnic minority survival in the age of mass communication. In Stephen Harold Riggins, *Ethnic minority media: An international perspective* (pp. 1–20). Newbury Park, CA: Sage.

Rohter, Larry. (1996, December 15). Broadcast news: In Spanish, it's another story. *New York Times*, 4/1, 6.

Sassen, Saskia. (1996). *Losing Control: Sovereignty in an age of globalization*. New York: Columbia University Press.

Seagrave, Sterling. (1995). *Lords of the Rim*. New York: Putnam.

Shohat, Ella, and Robert Stam. (1994). *Unthinking eurocentrism: Multiculturalism and the media*. London: Routledge.

Sinclair, John. (1997). The decentring of cultural imperialism: Televisa-tion and Globo-ization in the Latin World. In Kenneth Thompson (Ed.), *Media and cultural regulation*. London: Sage.

Sreberny-Mohammadi, Annabelle, Dwayne Winseck, Jim McKenna, and Oliver Boyd-Barrett. (1997). *Media in global context: A reader*. London: Arnold.

Thussu, Daya Kishan. (2000). *International communication: Continuity and change*. London: Arnold.

UNDP. (1999). *Human development report 1999*. New York: UNDP.

UNESCO. (2000). *World culture report 2000*. Paris: UNESCO.

Viccari, Ben. (1995). *Canada's ethnic media*. Paper presented at the Media and Ethnicity Conference, Mississauga, Ontario.

Winseck, Dwayne. (in press). Wired cities and transnational communications: New forms of governance for telecommunications and the new media. In Leah Leivrouw (Ed.), *New media handbook*. Thousand Oaks, CA: Sage.

16

First Peoples' Television in Canada's North: A Case Study of the Aboriginal Peoples Television Network

Lorna Roth[1]
Concordia University

Among all the First Peoples around the world, those in Canada have led the way in establishing legislatively based, nationwide television services that reflect their diverse cultural perspectives and multiple languages. The negotiation of an infrastructure for First Peoples' television in Canada occurred between 1970 and 1999. During that time, the federal government shifted from attempting to assimilate First Peoples (Government of Canada, 1969) to recognizing First Peoples as a national constituency group with collective broadcasting rights and a special status.

For most of the 1970–99 period, federally funded broadcasting undertakings were located north of the 55th latitude. This region, which includes one-third of Canada's land mass, encompasses the Northwest Territories, Nunavut, Yukon Territory, Labrador, and the northern parts of all of the central and western provinces. After consistent successes with pilot experiments and more permanent undertakings, northern broadcasters seeking to integrate southern First Peoples into their established services convinced the federal government of the viability of a national indigenous service. They subsequently gained federal, territorial, provincial, and a broad range of institutional support through legislation, regulation, and financial assistance to operate an Aboriginal Peoples Television Network (APTN).

In 1991, the federal government passed a new Broadcasting Act enshrining multiculturalism, multiracialism, and Aboriginal broadcasting. The broadcasting system is composed of public, private, and community-based network sources. Section 3 of the act states:

> [T]hrough its programming and the employment opportunities arising out of its operation, [the Canadian broadcasting system should] serve the needs and interests, and reflect the circumstances and aspirations of Canadian men, women and children, including equal rights, the linguistic duality and multicultural and multiracial nature of Canadian society and the special place of aboriginal peoples within that society. (Broadcasting Act, 1991, s. 3 [d][iii])

Getting APTN on the air on September 1, 1999, was the result of First Peoples' broadcasting initiatives, pilot projects, satellite-access negotiations, national infrastructural changes, regulatory openings, and governmental will downloaded onto resistant cable operators.

AN OVERVIEW OF KEY PHASES IN NORTHERN TELEVISION HISTORY

The history of northern television can be divided into six phases separated by shifts in representational practices, improved technological infrastructures, and corresponding expansions of target audiences (Roth, 1994, 1998).

Phases I and II: Pre-Northern TV Context and (de)Romancing the North

Phase 1 is well documented in the literature (see, for example, Alia, 1999; Roth, 1994) and consists of the period in which southern-produced imagery of First Peoples was characterized by stereotypical misrepresentations, when and if they were presented at all. This period precedes the entry of television into the Canadian North, but provides important background information. When television was parachuted into the North, its initial impact was to reinforce the absence of First Peoples and their lands from media texts.

It was in Phase II that First Peoples became aware of the potential of televisual media to record themselves and their concerns. This phase witnessed the passage of the Telesat Act (1969), whose purpose was to introduce the first domestic satellite in the world. Discussions on Aboriginal northern television also began. In the wake of a federal policy initiative advocating First Peoples' assimilation (Government of Canada, 1969), First Peoples began to realize the power of the media to erode their cultural strength; at the same time, they saw the media as a potential tool for self-development/empowerment in their struggles against pressures to conform to mainstream values of Canadian society, and as a vehicle for mediating social and race relations.

By 1975, all northern communities with populations over 500 were equipped with receiving dishes. From First Peoples' perspectives, the main activity of this period was their use of television as an experimental medium through which to explore interactive communications and community development practices. At the same time, the federal government wanted First Peoples to "modernize" and to become familiar with new technologies as a possible substitute for travel (expenses were prohibitive at the time), especially in relation to education and health matters. They also wanted First Peoples' feedback on alternative uses of satellite technology for community development, and on viable forms of intercommunity communications. In other words, there emerged a convergence of interests and objectives to make it worthwhile for the government to invest money in field tests and for First Peoples to undertake the project work.

Between 1978 and 1981, the Department of Communications set up a competition for field groups in Nunavut and Northern Quebec to gain access to the Anik B satellite. Among the several groups receiving the monies, the most prominent was Inuit Tapirisat of Canada (the Eskimo Brotherhood), which was given over $1 million with which to conduct interactive experiments in exchange for provision of relevant data. On the basis of their demonstrated successes with Projects "Inukshuk" in the Northwest Territories and "Naalakvik" (run by the Northern Quebec Inuit Association) in Northern Quebec, the Inuit were able to negotiate the network licensing of the Inuit Broadcasting Corporation in 1981. At the same time, the CRTC decided to license Cancom (Canadian Satellite Communications) to deliver a range of southern programming into northern and remote communities, as well as to provide carriage for northern-produced broadcasts. The CRTC expected CBC Northern Service to carry Native-language programming as a social cost of public-service broadcasting.

Phase III: Policy-ing the North

Phase III consists of a critical and continuous period between 1981 and 1991 when the current Broadcasting Act was introduced and passed. The 1991 act did indeed enshrine Aboriginal broadcasting, but the path that led to this parliamentary decision was rough and winding. At this historical conjuncture, policy was recognized as being an essential tool for putting in place a new technical infrastructure and legal discourse.

Essentially, what was happening in the field was carefully monitored and documented as data, and shaped into an argument to grant constituency groups access rights and to provide fairer and more equitable distribution services for the North. Lobbyists from the North and the South began critically surveying each other. First Peoples and their allies began to search for openings in the 1968 Broadcasting Act to enable the enshrinement of their own constituency groups as having a special status with accompanying rights to both receive and transmit broadcasting materials. Academics and historians witnessing the process often used data from pilot field experiments and projects to mediate relations between First Peoples and federal government representatives.

Phase IV: Consolidation and Expansion of Broadcasting Infrastructures

Phase IV began around 1983. By this time, 13 regional Native communications societies had developed north of 60 and had organized a lobby campaign directed toward the establishment of an explicit Native Broadcasting Policy. They considered this to be a critical step toward the enshrinement of their communication rights in legislation.

On March 10, 1983, the Government of Canada announced a Northern Broadcasting Policy that recognized the importance of Native participation in both media programming and the regulatory process (Government of Canada, 1983, p. 2). The Northern Broadcasting Policy consisted of the following five principles:

1. Northern residents should be offered access to an increasing range of programming choices through the exploitation of technological opportunities.

2. Northern native people should have the opportunity to participate actively in the determination by the CRTC of the character, quantity, and priority of programming broadcast in predominantly native communities.

3. Northern native people should have fair access to northern broadcasting distribution systems to maintain and develop their cultures and languages.

4. Programming relevant to native concerns, including content originated by native people, should be produced for distribution on northern broadcasting services wherever native people form a significant proportion of the population in the service area.

5. Northern native representatives should be consulted regularly by government agencies engaged in establishing broadcasting policies which would affect their cultures. (Government of Canada, 1983, p. 2)

An accompanying program called the Northern Native Broadcast Access Program (NNBAP) was established at the same time, and $40.3 million was earmarked as a budget for the long-term production goal of twenty hours of Native-language radio programming and five hours of Native-perspective television per week. The initial funding was for four years, but the program has continued to exist under considerable financial strain.

Back in 1983, there was cause for celebration, but it soon became apparent that the CRTC's expectations for CBC and Cancom to deliver indigenous programming as a social cost for their licences would become problematic. Both broadcasters technically fulfilled their obligations, but they did so at unpopular hours. For example, the CBC Northern Service carried Inuit Broadcasting Corporation (IBC) programming for five hours per week, but the programs were broadcast in the wee hours of the morning, such as 3 a.m. Furthermore, national programming often pre-empted Native programming on the CBC.

An "expectation" is based on good will and amiable negotiations; it has no weight other than in the moral realm. First Peoples' broadcasters recognized that more authority had to be invested in the demand for carriage of their programming than mere "expectations." In 1985, interested parties began to discuss a policy framework for a dedicated northern transponder as a corrective response to the challenges identified around the distribution of native programming. In January 1987, Aboriginal and northern broadcasters met in Yellowknife, Northwest Territories, to form a consortium with the goal of establishing a Pan-Northern distribution service. In 1988, the federal government's Department of Communications approved research and development monies to explore the feasibility of a separate northern channel.

Satisfied that a dedicated northern transponder would fulfill Aboriginal distribution needs, the Department of Communications approved $10 million in 1990 to prepare an application for a Pan-Northern distribution service.

Meanwhile, there were severe budgetary cutbacks in NNBAP program funding as the federal government responded to pressures to privatize the cultural industries in Canada. First Peoples were receiving distribution money, but they could not afford to produce programs to distribute. To diversify their funding sources, some engaged in fundraisers, while others increased efforts to find a stronger advertising base. This brings us to the next period.

Phase V: Crossing Cultural, Racial, and Territorial Borderlines

During the early part of the fifth period, beginning around 1990, several Native communications societies initiated contracts to produce programming for southern viewers (Inuit Broadcasting Corporation, Northern Native Broadcasting, Yukon [NNBY], Wawatay Native Communications Society). This initiative was organized partly in response to the cutbacks, partly as an effort to reach a broader audience and see how they would be perceived, and partly to overcome the dependency into which the federal government and First Peoples had historically positioned themselves. In the case of NNBY, they negotiated a weekly program, *Nedaa* (*Your Eye on the Yukon*), with CBC Newsworld. The deal, which marked the first ongoing national channel commitment to broadcast First Nations programming to a nationwide audience, prompted both celebration and minor criticisms around the issue of regional versus national audiences within the Native communications societies and federal government circles.

In programming for a national audience, NNBY had to develop a culturally hybrid approach targeting at least two distinct audiences (Native and non-Native) within which there was already a diversity of communities. Given that federal funding was disseminated for the purpose of developing regional media, the secondary, non-Native audience was considered somewhat outside federal criteria for the Northern Native Broadcast Access Program. NNBY's contractual arrangement was very significant in that it crossed over social, racial, territorial, and cultural borders and opened a position for Aboriginal broadcasting within the mainstream of Canadian media—albeit a very small one. It led the way South. NNBY programming had a loyal following in the South, which provoked some interesting discussions in the North about how one goes about building cross-cultural alignments for political ends. Though a bold initiative, NNBY's national project did little to solve the Pan-Northern challenges of distribution.

The passage of the current Broadcasting Act in June 1991 was followed by a public hearing in Hull, Quebec, on October 28, 1991. At the hearing, the CRTC approved the Television Northern Canada (TVNC) application for a Native television network established "for the purpose of broadcasting cultural, social, political and educational programming for the primary benefit of aboriginal people in the North" (CRTC, 1991). By granting the licence to TVNC, the CRTC recognized the importance of northern-based control over the distribution of Native and northern programming. TVNC was to become the vehicle through which First Peoples would represent themselves and their concerns to the entire North. They would no longer be restricted by geography or technology to local or regional self-representation and identity-building. In this sense, TVNC constituted a de facto recognition of the communication rights of First Peoples in the North.

TVNC began broadcasting at a primary level of service on January 21, 1992. Spanning five time-zones and covering an area of over 4.3 million kilometres, TVNC network members broadcast approximately 100 hours per week to 96 communities (in English and multiple Native languages).[2] TVNC was not a programmer, but a distributor of its members' programming, which consisted of

- 38 hours per week of Aboriginal language and cultural programming;
- 23 hours per week of formal and informal educational programming; and
- 12 hours per week of produced and acquired children's programming, over half of which is in Aboriginal languages. (TVNC, 1993, p. 4)[3]

At the time, TVNC was the only Aboriginal television network in the world that broadcast such a high volume of programming from indigenous sources. CAAMA (Central Australian Aboriginal Media Association) was awarded a remote commercial television service licence in 1987; its service, "Imparja," broadcasts to mostly non-Aboriginal viewers, so its programming tends to be more European-oriented (Browne, 1996, p. 38).[4] TVNC and CAAMA programming have little in common other than the fact that they were both Aboriginal-controlled.

As a Pan-Northern distribution undertaking, TVNC was theoretically in a position to forge—through program exchanges and uplink/downlink satellite arrangements—connections with Inuit and Aboriginal groups in other countries, such as Greenland, Alaska, Finland, and Siberia, as well as Australia, New Zealand, Brazil, and Bolivia. In reality, TVNC did not do much of this because of both technical and financial barriers. What it did offer to northern viewers was limited access to programming about the "activities of indigenous people from around the globe" (TVNC, 1993, p. 4). For example, the network aired a half-hour weekly current-affairs program called *Heartbeat Alaska*. This program originated in Anchorage, Alaska, and was supplied to TVNC for the cost of one-way shipping.

The CRTC permitted TVNC to be listed as an eligible service for cable companies in the South to distribute; few availed themselves of the opportunity. At any rate, the TVNC administration did not consider piecemeal distribution an appropriate route for extension of service to the South. The challenge was to become a Canada-wide national network. In achieving that goal, how would they deal with cross-culturally sensitive questions? For example, what kinds of cultural programming would meet the information and entertainment needs of Native/non-Native northerners *and* Native/non-Native southerners? What considerations and constraints would be imposed on, or voluntarily assumed by, programmers in order to please a hybrid audience? Of even greater concern were program subjects that might generate controversy when removed from their original context. For example, there were fears that animal-rights groups might object to programs from the Eastern Arctic that touched on the hunt (seal, fox, walrus, etc.).

Finally, the cost of acquiring rights for broadcasting in the South would also multiply due to the expansion of target audiences. Northern acquisition rights were extremely economical because TVNC was a nonprofit, public broadcasting distribution organization. Indeed, program distributors, who recognized that TVNC's special financial conditions prohibited the purchase of expensive programming, virtually subsidized the rights. These are just a few of the programming considerations TVNC would have to address if and when it negotiated a broadcasting arrangement with the South.

Phase VI: The Aboriginal Peoples Television Network—Going National

> There are some 600 First Nations. We are always fighting for this right or that right. But we are one people. This [channel] would bring us together. (Focus-group participant)

> I am very excited by the opportunity the aboriginal people of Canada have been given. This historic decision will be a major step in building bridges of understanding between aboriginal and non-aboriginal people in Canada. (Abraham Tagalik, former APTN chairman, quoted in TVNC, 1999, p. 1)

TVNC's Pan-Northern successes encouraged its board of directors and staff to pursue the establishment of a nationwide network, and so, after a vote in June 1997, steps were initiated to make this dream into a reality (APTN, 1999a). At its Annual General Assembly, the Assembly of First Nations (AFN) passed a resolution supporting TVNC's attempts to develop a national service (APTN, 1999a). TVNC presentations to national Aboriginal organizations and submissions to the CRTC became a regular occurrence.

In January 1998, TVNC hired Angus Reid (a public-opinion consulting firm) to conduct an audience survey of a representative cross-section of 1510 adult Canadians in order to measure support for a national Aboriginal broadcasting undertaking. Results indicated that 79 percent or "two out of three Canadians supported the idea of a national aboriginal TV network, even if it would mean displacing a currently offered service" (APTN, 1999a). In February 1998, the CRTC responded with Public Notice 1998-8, which stated:

> The Commission recognizes that TVNC is a unique and significant undertaking serving the public interest and the objectives of the Broadcasting Act, especially those objectives that relate to the

special place of aboriginal peoples within Canadian society. Such a service should be widely available throughout Canada in order to serve the diverse needs of the various Aboriginal communities, as well as other Canadians. The Commission will consider any application by TVNC designed to achieve these objectives.

The Commission expects any application by TVNC to demonstrate how it will adapt its programming service to reflect the diversity of the needs and interest of aboriginal peoples throughout Canada. (cited in TVNC, 1998b, p. 1)

In June 1998, TVNC submitted to the CRTC an application for a broadcast licence for the Aboriginal Peoples Television Network. To be economically viable, APTN was to be a mandatory service, available to nearly eight million households with cable in Canada, as well as to those with direct-to-home and wireless service providers, including ExpressVu, Star Choice, and Look TV (APTN, 1999b, p. 1). To ensure consistent and secure funding over the long term, TVNC requested that the CRTC require the cable operators to charge $0.15 per month to each subscriber household. This would make up the anticipated revenue of $15 million for the first years, although APTN administration expected that in the future the budget would increase as a result of advertising revenues (APTN, 1999b, p. 1). In exchange for the small charge of $0.15, subscribers would receive programming aimed at both Aboriginal and non-Aboriginal audiences: children's animation, youth shows, cultural and traditional programming, music, drama, dance, news and current affairs, live coverage of special events, and interactive programming (APTN, 1999b, p. 1). APTN promised 90 percent Canadian content with the remaining 10 percent consisting of indigenous programming from, among other places, the United States, Australia, New Zealand, and Central and South America (APTN, 1999b, p. 2).

The CRTC received approximately 300 letters from the general public urging it to license the channel. Support for the network was fairly consistent among the existing Native communications societies in the North. However, during the transition from a northern to a national network, there were some expected challenges around issues of organization and control, which indicated a need for a period of negotiation, clarification, and resolution. The primary challenge, raised by Northern Native Broadcasting, Yukon, centred on the question of guaranteed northern representation on the board of directors. Specifically, NNBY was concerned with shifting power relations and the possible "systemic changes that might undermine the interests of the Aboriginal peoples of the North" (NNBY, 1998, p. 5). It demanded guarantees for the "unrestricted right of continued distribution of their programs to support their languages, dialects, and cultures" (NNBY, 1998, p. 6). TVNC responded in writing that it would give NNBY's concerns serious attention and that it was planning a professional workshop focused on board structure and selection (TVNC, 1998a, p. 11). Eventually, issues of contention were worked out, and a 21-member Native board of directors was selected from all regions of Canada.

Strong and organized resistance to APTN came from the cable operators and from several existing broadcasters who regarded as undemocratic the idea of a mandatory, national channel to be carried on all cable services. Although there were some dissenters (including Cancom and WETV), most cable operators thought that APTN should be licensed "on the same optional distribution basis as all other fee-based Canadian services have been licensed" (Canadian Broadcasting Corporation, 1998); in other words, TVNC/APTN should be a specialty service targeted to a particular audience. As far as TVNC/APTN were concerned, they were *not* a specialty service, but one with a special status based on First Peoples being one of Canada's three founding nations. This, of course, is a very contentious issue in Canada and Quebec, both of which operate on the assumption that there are only two founding nations, namely their own. That APTN should be carried on a mandatory basis as a service parallel to that of the Canadian Broadcasting Corporation and Radio-Canada raised the political/historical stakes in Canada's national debate about Confederation.

The Canadian Cable Television Association (CCTA), Canada's largest cable industry lobby group, complained that the signal would, in effect, be forced on cable subscribers if they had to pay $0.15 for a service they had not requested. Their argument, which was framed in terms of economic competition and customer choice, grew out of the view that APTN should be a specialty service. In addition, the CCTA protested the "one time costs associated with forcing a service on basic. These include expenses related to informing customers of the change in the line-up through channel line-up stickers and explanatory letters, and in order to receive the signal, additions to headend equipment" (CCTA, 1998, p. 3). The estimated cost would be nearly "$4.8 million dollars with line-up sticker costs at 40 cents per subscriber and headend expenses at $3,500 each, for 500 headends" (CCTA, 1998, pp. 3–4). Finally, the CCTA pointed out that it would be expensive to shift channel allocations; in some cases, as with the Weather Channel in Winnipeg, an existing channel would no longer be offered or would be bumped up from one of the basic tiers to a more expensive premium package (Cobb, 1999, p. F5).

The cable industry's prevailing concern was cost recovery for its investments. Most cable operators did not accept the argument that First Peoples, who represented only 3 percent of the national population, should have either a special status or a mandatory national channel in Canada. The CCTA said that it "supported the concept of the network but not the insistence that it be offered as part of the basic cable service" (Cobb, 1999, p. F5). Thus, the CCTA regarded APTN as it would any other specialty channel. For the most part, it is difficult to disentangle the cable operators' economic perspectives from their politics. Could it be that their political opposition to the acknowledgment of First Peoples as having a special and unique national status, and therefore access to facilitative conditions to mark this symbolically via the airwaves, was conveniently masked by economic rationales? What is clear is that cross-cultural sensitivity and a political will based on the fair distribution of resources to minority peoples was not a concern for most cable operators, although it clearly was for members of the CRTC.

On February 22, 1999, the CRTC approved TVNC's application and granted mandatory carriage on basic cable throughout Canada with a $0.15 cost per subscriber per month in the South. In the North, residents of the 96 communities would continue to receive the service free of charge (TVNC, 1999, p. 1). To provide continuity of service to northerners, a separate northern feed was established, thereby ensuring that "special northern programming, including legislative coverage and special events will be broadcast in the North on an on-going basis" (TVNC, 1999, p. 1).

The time between the date on which the licence was granted and APTN's actual launch was a mere six months. This was highly unusual (and no doubt stressful for the organization) but necessary, according to representatives at APTN, because they wanted to launch at the same time several specialty services licensed in 1996 were to go on air. Doing this would mean that APTN expenses could be included within the one-time costs for publicity and head-end equipment incurred by the other service launches (Personal interviews, n.d.). APTN began broadcasting, as planned, on September 1, 1999. Until programming surpluses can be created, there are three programming cycles per day (i.e., each day programs are repeated three times—once every six hours).[5] Broadcast languages break down into 60 percent English and 15 percent French, with 25 percent being a variety of Aboriginal languages. Carriage of international programming and the possibility of being broadcast internationally puts APTN on the edge of Phase VI: An International Turn.

INITIAL IMPACT OF THE ABORIGINAL PEOPLES TELEVISION NETWORK

First Peoples' television did not go through the hearing/licensing process and launch without generating some controversy within the Canadian press. There was a fair amount of editorial commentary about APTN's status as "the first in the world," and about the political context for the CRTC decision.

There was also apparent criticism. On the day after the CRTC decision was announced, the *National Post* published an article with the headline/byline: "Coming Soon to Your Living Room—the CRTC is forcing a new aboriginal TV channel—and its cost—on most Canadian cable viewers." The article proceeded to lay out the arguments of both the cable industry and APTN (Chwialkowska, 1999, p. A3). However, despite its attempt to appear objective, the piece gave the overall impression of supporting the cable operators.

The *Globe and Mail* expressed a decidedly more sympathetic view in an editorial:

> Just to be seen on TV makes people genuine. . . . This is the psychological underpinning for the CRTC's recent decision to grant a license for an aboriginal television network. Not only will the . . . [n]etwork be a place for native people . . . it will be an electronic arena in which many Canadians will encounter aboriginals. . . . Aboriginal television will be inescapable. And that inescapability will express something that the isolation and marginality of many native people's lives often obscures. Their relation to other Canadians isn't tangential; it is inevitable. (*Globe and Mail*, 1999, p. A16)

The *Globe and Mail* editorial raises a very important question about the relationship between the absence and presence, (in)visibility, and (in)audibility of an important national community in Canada. It is easy to express liberal tolerance when the subject/person/community in question is absent from our visible and conscious world. But when a formerly invisible constituency group becomes a mandatory new presence on the airwaves, a more fundamental intolerance becomes harder to mask.

On its launch date of September 1, 1999, APTN presented a live broadcast that wove together commentators, members of native communications societies that had been involved in television production since at least 1983, entertainers (singers, dancers, drummers, and other musicians), clips of key events in First Peoples' history, and landscape images. The program was a celebration of the opening up of mainstream Canada to the lives of First Peoples. Since the launch, APTN's regularly scheduled programming has been a source of information and entertainment for First Peoples and for those interested in acquainting themselves with Native perspectives on the world.

Not everyone welcomed the launch. A Vancouver *Province* editorial titled "Consumers Should Decide What They Want to Watch" illustrates a common perspective that circulated after APTN's first night of programming:

> The CRTC decision was another in a long line of loopy broadcast regulations that amounts to political correctness disguised as social engineering. We wish APTN the best of luck. But, while Ottawa can make consumers pay for the new channel, it can't make them watch it. It's a good job APTN won't have to rely on Vancouver ratings to pay its way. (*Province*, 1999, p. A36)

Arts commentator Morley Walker expressed a more thoughtful view in a *Winnipeg Free Press* article titled "Aboriginal TV Deserves Better Spot on Dial." In the article, he characterizes "the tenor of commentary in the white man's press surrounding the fledgling aboriginal cable TV channel" as "skeptical, if not outright hostile" (Walker, 1999, p. B7). He goes on to assert that

> [f]ifteen cents a month today is a small price to pay as a cable sub-
> scriber to support a voice that is both indigenous to our country
> and vital to offering role models for a dispossessed minority. It
> seems to me that a first nations TV channel is an excellent addi-
> tion to the Canadian television landscape. (Walker, 1999, p. B7)

Besides expressing disappointment with those elements of the press that framed APTN as an exercise in social engineering, Walker also raised the issue of APTN's remote location on the channel grid. This topic symbolizes, in a most concrete way, First Peoples' social placement—slightly outside of the centre of things.

APTN: ON THE MARGINS OF MAINSTREAM TELEVISION

APTN is competing with a sophisticated technological and broadcasting infra-structure put in place in Canada in the 1950s. Although it benefits from these tech-nologies, APTN's underfunding, its difficulties in finding sponsors for programming, and its lack of national experience all underline its need for a transi-tional period in which to build human resource capacity, program surpluses, finan-cial stability, and broad public support from cross-cultural audiences.

A key technical issue that contributes to APTN's marginalization is its location on the majority of cable systems' channel grids. Due to considerations of existing industry tier structures, as well as cable operators' expressed concerns in regard to the shifting of current channel configurations, APTN has been allocated to the high end of the channel grid in most communities. In Montreal, for example, it is received on channels 67 and 58. In most other places, too, it is well beyond the fre-quent stops of channel grazers.[6] A bad location on the dial will not deter committed viewers, but it very likely *will* deter the new audiences APTN needs to recruit.

The configuration of Canada's airwaves may be perceived as reflecting the actual political arrangements and social networks into which multicultural and mul-tiracial constituency groups have been placed within mainstream society by domi-nant governing bodies. Given their current disadvantaged location on the margins of the mainstream, it is clear that APTN still has a way to go before it can effec-tively compete for cross-cultural audiences with central and powerful networks such as those of the Québécois and the English/American broadcasting services.

APTN AS A PUBLIC MEDIUM IN CANADA

Despite its complex place in Canada's overall broadcasting system, the case of APTN is a prototype for other states within which there are diverse constituency groups competing for service access to permit them to address and construct align-ments across race, social, economic, and territorial lines. Over the years, First Peoples have been granted political opportunities to build a nationwide media space to heal the historical communication ruptures within their societies and between their communities and others living within Canada. These community-building opportunities have been the result of First Peoples' persistence in overcoming challenges and demonstrating skills to develop and manage new broadcasting infrastructures.

With the convergence of a strong political will on the part of the federal cabinet and the CRTC, amiable negotiations among all key parties, and the policy savvy that First Peoples have demonstrated publicly, APTN has evolved from an idea to a fully operational television broadcasting undertaking. The network is moderately secure in terms of funding and distribution and, most important, its existence is enshrined in national legislation. This regulatory support is a highly significant and symbolic demonstration of the collective will on the part of the Canadian government to include First Peoples' media/voices/images as integral to the national broadcasting system's infrastructure. Furthermore, their being among the key nationally mandated services represents a consolidation of new power relationships among Canadian media institutions, policy bodies, and audiences.

APTN has enabled indigenous messages to be heard by constituency groups that might never have had access to a live person of Aboriginal descent. It provides an opportunity to share imagery and histories, as well as to build bridges of understanding and to bridge cultural borders. An equally important point is that APTN is on the air, is one of many services competing for audience attention, is now a performer on the electronic power grid, and has transformed the roles that were anticipated for public media since its early theorizations. This is important to recognize. APTN provides access only for cable subscribers. It attracts niche, not mass audiences. It is not free. In trying to figure out how to maintain secure funding over long periods of time, the CRTC has introduced a social cost to cable operators that carry APTN.[7] Subscriber costs of $0.15 per month are paid to cable operators who then transfer the money to APTN to be used for television production in communities that are not economically viable enough to sustain their media economies. This, perhaps, is an emergent model by which states can assure the sponsorship and sustenance of public-service programming that might be otherwise unaffordable.

APTN lies somewhere between what has traditionally been defined as public and private broadcasting. It carries advertising, yet addresses public issues to Canada's national publics, modelling itself after public-service television. It is multilinguistic, multicultural, and multiracial in content and production staff and management. It attempts to be both local and global. It does very little original production on its own; it distributes locally and regionally produced cultural programming to a national audience. The point that APTN is already integrating international programming and is considering the possibility of expanding to become an international First Peoples' television network, comparable to CNN and BBC World Service, tells us of its global objective of international constituency-group-building across national borders. It does not easily fit into existing categories of public-service broadcasting.

The look of APTN's national programming is much like the look of public access television in the United States or like that of community television in Canada. Its quality is uneven and inconsistent. It replays each program three times in a 24-hour period because of budgetary constraints. Its mandate to serve all Aboriginal communities, North and South, as well as the rest of the Canadian population, is extremely complex and difficult to manage.

Despite all of its challenges, APTN—even at the immature stage in which it finds itself—has served its constituency groups well. It has northernized and indigenized Canadian programming. It has delivered distinct imagery from coast to coast to coast with perspectives that express what it is like to "live the difference" that is so extensively discussed in the cultural studies literature. And in the age of the 500-channel universe and the World Wide Web, APTN offers another kind of lurking opportunity for non-Native peoples—a way to quietly reflect on First Peoples' cultures and issues that they will inevitably have to acknowledge over time.

QUESTIONS

1.   What are the six phases of Native broadcasting discussed in this chapter?
2.   Do you think it is important to have a service such as APTN? Give reasons for your answer.
3.   Are there other populations in Canada that you feel should have their own broadcasting system?
4.   How does APTN serve as a model for other indigenous communities?
5.   Do you feel it is important that Natives in Canada have a presence on the Internet?

WEB SITES

Aboriginal Voices: **http://www.aboriginalvoices.com/**
APTN: **http://www.aptn.ca/**
Cancom (Native Broadcasting): **http://www.cancom.ca/english/natives/**
First Nations Broadcasting: **http://www.palmsradio.com/upnorth.html**
Wawatay Native Communications Society: **http://www.wawatay.on.ca/**

NOTES

1.   This chapter was adapted from Lorna Roth (2000), "Bypassing of Borders and the Building of Bridges: Steps in the Construction of the Aboriginal Peoples Television Network in Canada," *Gazette: International Journal of Communication Studies*, *62*(3/4), pp. 251–269; and Lorna Roth (in press), "(Re)Colouring the Public Broadcasting System in Canada: A Case Study of

the Aboriginal Peoples Television Network," in Linda K. Fuller (Ed.), *Community Media: International Perspectives (Aboriginal/Indigenous Experiences, Current Case Studies, Virtual Community Visions* (London: Sage).

2. TVNC's network members consisted of the Inuit Broadcasting Corporation (Ottawa, Iqaluit), the Inuvialuit Communications Society (Inuvik), Northern Native Broadcasting, Yukon (Whitehorse), the OkalaKatiget Society (Labrador), Taqramiut Nipingat Incorporated (Northern Quebec), the Native Communications Society of the Western N.W.T. (Yellowknife), the Government of the Northwest Territories, Yukon College, and the National Aboriginal Communications Society. Associate Members included CBC Northern Service, Kativik School Board (Quebec), Labrador Community College, Northern Native Broadcasting, Terrace, Telesat Canada, and Wawatay Native Communications Society (Sioux Lookout).

3. These figures total only 73 hours per week. The remainder of the 100 hours per week consisted of reruns, wraparound programming by Broadcast News, and Environment Canada forecasts.

4. For further information on the Aboriginal broadcasting in Australia, see Meadows (1993) and Ginsburg (1992, 1993).

5. To view a current APTN program schedule, visit http://www.aptn.ca/

6. For a list of APTN channel locations in Canada, visit http://www.aptn.ca/

7. For example, as part of a social benefits package offered in exchange for taking over CTV, a national private network, Bell Canada Enterprises has agreed to give $3 million to APTN to establish several news offices across the country.

REFERENCES

Alia, Valerie. (1999). *Un/Covering the north: News, media, and Aboriginal people.* Vancouver: UBC Press.

APTN (Aboriginal Peoples Television Network). (1999a) *About APTN.* Retrieved from http://www.aptn.ca/

———. (1999b). *APTN fact sheet.* Retrieved from http://www.aptn.ca/

Browne, Donald R. (1996). *Electronic media and indigenous peoples: A voice of our own?* Iowa: Iowa State University Press.

Canadian Broadcasting Corporation. (1998, October 19). Intervention Letter to CRTC. Ottawa.

CCTA (Canadian Cable Television Association). (1998, November 12). Intervention Letter to CRTC. Ottawa.

———. (1999, February 22). Decision CRTC 99-42. Ottawa.

Chwialkowska, Luiza. (1999, February 23). Coming soon to your living room. *National Post*, p. A3.

Cobb, Chris. (1999, February 23). Aboriginal TV goes Canada-wide. *Gazette* (Montreal), p. F5.

CRTC. (1991, October 28). Decision CRTC 91-826. Television Northern Canada Incorporated. Ottawa.

Ginsburg, Faye. (1992). Indigenous media: Faustian contract or global village? In George E. Marcus (Ed.), *Rereading cultural anthropology* (pp. 356–376). Durham, NC: Duke University Press.

———. (1993, Spring). Aboriginal media and the Australian imaginary. *Public Culture, 5*, 20.

Globe and Mail. (1999, February 24). The native media (p. A16). Editorial.

Government of Canada. (1969). Statement of the Government of Canada on Indian Policy Presented to the First Session of the Twenty-Eighth Parliament by the Honourable Jean Chrétien, Minister of Indian Affairs and Northern Development. Ottawa.

———. (1983, March 10). *The northern broadcasting policy.* Federal Government News Release.

Meadows, Michael. (1993). Voice blo mipla all ilan man: Torres Strait Islanders' struggle for television access. In J. Craik, J. James Bailey, and A. Moran (Eds.), *Public voices, private interests: Australia's media.* Sydney: Allen and Unwin.

NNBY (Northern Native Broadcasting, Yukon). (1998, October 19). An Intervention of Conditional Support of Application 199804068 to the CRTC. Whitehorse, Yukon.

Personal interviews (n.d.) of APTN staff: Patrick Tourigny, Director, Regulatory Affairs and Industry Relations; Jennifer David, Director of Communications; Abe Tagalik, Chairman of the Board of Directors; Gerry Giberson, Operations Manager; Dan David, News Dire.

Province (Vancouver). (1999, September 2). Consumers should decide what they want to watch (p. A36).

Roth, Lorna. (1994). *Northern voices and mediating structures: The emergence and development of First Peoples' television broadcasting in the Canadian North.* Doctoral dissertation. Montreal: Concordia University.

———. (1998). Television broadcasting north of 60. In L. d'Haenens (Ed.), *Images of Canadianness: Visions on Canada's politics, culture, economics* (pp. 147–166). Ottawa: University of Ottawa Press.

TVNC (Television Northern Canada). (1993, March 1). Response to CRTC Public Notice 1992-13, p. 4.

———. (1998a, October 30). Replies to interventions submitted with respect to an application by TVNC Inc. for a national aboriginal television network (Application #199804068). TVNC Letter to the CRTC. Ottawa.

———. (1998b, March). *North Link.* Ottawa: TVNC Newsletter.

———. (1999, March). *North Link.* Ottawa: TVNC Newsletter.

Walker, Morley. (1999, September 40). Aboriginal TV deserves better spot on dial. *Winnipeg Free Press*, p. B7.

17

Convergence

Matthew Fraser
Ryerson University

The term "convergence" has indisputably been the most fashionable buzzword in the media industries over the past decade. And yet, paradoxically, there remains a great deal of confusion about what convergence actually means. The term has suffered a semantic slippage that has rendered the concept fluid, imprecise, and often self-serving. Even top executives at major media groups admit they aren't certain where convergence, whatever the term means, is leading the industry. They invariably add, however, that they can't afford not to join the convergence juggernaut. No one, it seems, wants to get stranded on the shoulder of the information superhighway.

While many media companies boasted "convergence" strategies throughout the 1990s, the term exploded into the popular imagination at the outset of the new decade—in January 2000—when America Online announced its megamedia takeover of conglomerate Time Warner. It seemed fitting that a new millennium was being baptized with a corporate merger heralding the information age. The AOL–Time Warner fusion, which saw an upstart Internet-based company swallow an established media giant for more than $160 billion (U.S.), was the biggest media merger ever. The logic of the corporate combination was simple: America Online would commercially exploit Time Warner's vast stable of brands—from Bugs Bunny, CNN, Madonna, and Warner Bros. to *Time*, *Sports Illustrated*, and *People* magazines—to drive proprietary content via the Internet to AOL's global community of Web-based subscribers. Heralded as the ultimate "convergence" merger in the dawning Internet century, the AOL–Time Warner marriage was seen as the triumph of "new" media over "old" media.

The AOL–Time Warner union immediately triggered a series of similar, albeit less colossal, media mergers in Canada. In February 2000, Bell Canada Enterprises (BCE) announced it was buying the CTV television network and affiliated media properties for $2.3 billion; several months later, BCE acquired control of the *Globe and Mail*. In July 2000, Winnipeg-based media mogul Izzy Asper expanded his Global TV empire in Canada and, a month later, purchased Conrad Black's Southam newspaper chain plus a 50 percent stake in the *National Post*. Cable baron Ted Rogers, for his part, bought the Toronto Blue Jays sports franchise and made an unsuccessful bid for the Montreal-based cable group, Vidéotron. The Montreal-based publishing group, Quebecor, succeeded in grabbing control of Vidéotron and its wholly owned television network, TVA, to forge a Canadian media giant. Meanwhile, Calgary-based Shaw Communications had made a bold foray into content through subsidiary Corus Entertainment, which soon purchased the children's TV production house, Nelvana. By the end of 2000, five corporate giants dominated the Canadian media landscape: BCE, CanWest Global, Rogers, Quebecor, and Shaw. Besides the similar scale and scope of their corporate interests, all five groups claimed to be pursuing a "convergence" strategy. And yet, on closer examination, the corporate strategies of these Canadian media giants revealed as many differences as similarities.

So, what is convergence? Let's start with a simple definition. Like parallel lines that suddenly meet, convergence is the integration of separate streams of communication—television, telephony, data—through a single distribution system. A generation ago, most people received television signals through coaxial cable or through antennas that captured over-the-air frequencies. They received telephone service through copper phone wires, and their home electricity came through yet another wired system. All of these services, which were often regulated as monopoly utilities, functioned distinctly and providers maintained a separate billing relationship with consumers. Convergence, in a word, brings together these formerly separate functions. Convergence makes it possible for consumers to receive all these, and other, services from a single provider. Convergence also describes the technological connection between commercial applications and personal behaviour (e.g., using a television set as a telephone or personal computer connected to the Internet). In theory at least, convergence is synonymous with competition because consumers are no longer captive to one monopoly service provider.

Distinguishing between different types of convergence is another way of conceptualizing the term. *Technological* convergence describes the capacity, through integrated broadband networks, to transmit video, voice, data, and other services through the same distribution system; technological convergence, in other words, is an achievement of engineering. *Commercial* convergence occurs when market players exploit these technological innovations to offer "bundled" services combining video, voice, and data; commercial convergence thus shifts the emphasis from pure technology to marketplace laws of supply and demand for services. *Corporate* convergence describes the industry consolidation, through mergers and acquisitions, that occurs as media companies attempt to compete in a marketplace where video, voice, data, and other services can be provided by single distribution systems. From the perspective of competition law, this third form of convergence has raised concerns about the reassertion of oligopoly power in the media industries.

The trend toward convergence in the 1990s was actually not new. As far back as the 19th century, telegraph wires were used to transmit not only messages but also newspaper copy. In the 1920s, telephone companies such as AT&T in the United States were active in radio broadcasting and played an instrumental role in developing early prototypes of television. By the mid-20th century, the telephone and broadcasting sectors had evolved as separate commercial activities. Governments allocated scarce broadcasting frequency to either state-owned entities or a limited number of competing commercial stations, while telephone systems were generally monopoly "common carriers" subject to rate regulation. In many countries, cross-ownership rules banned the integration of television and telephony. In Canada, the Canadian Radio-television and Telecommunications Commission (CRTC) imposed a cable/telephone cross-ownership ban in 1968, when it ruled that it would not be in the public interest for telephone companies to offer television service. Also in 1968, Parliament revised Bell Canada's charter to prohibit the telephone company from applying for a cable television licence.

The technological optimism of the 1960s nonetheless provided the stimulus to harness the potential of convergence. The first satellites had been launched in geostationary orbit, computer power was increasingly recognized, cable television was taking off, and there was much futuristic talk about the advent of a wired "smart home." In a country like Canada, whose tradition of technological nationalism stretched back to the 19th-century railway—popularly called Canada's "national dream"—the prospect of a new technological revolution triggered both enthusiasm about harnessing the potential of new technologies and concern about possible negative consequences for Canada's cultural sovereignty.

In this context, the federal government decided to play a key role in guiding the development of new technologies. In 1968, Ottawa created the Department of Communications (DOC) as the institutional expression of Canada's embrace of the communications revolution. The department's first minister, Eric Kierans, declared that "communications has moved to the forefront of our national affairs." The DOC immediately announced three major initiatives. First, the government created Telesat Canada to launch and operate communications satellites. Second, a Canadian Computer/Communications Agency was created to build a national computer network. Third, a "Telecommission" of experts was established to develop a national communications strategy. In 1971, the Telecommission produced more than 40 studies, including a final report called *Instant World*. Foreseeing the marriage of computers and communications, *Instant World* called for the merging of broadcasting and telecom regulation and predicted the transition from passive one-way television viewing to interactive TV (Government of Canada, 1971).

Despite the prescience of *Instant World*, very little policy attention was given to the promise of convergence for nearly two decades. In the late 1970s, it is true, business pressures began mounting for the liberalization of telecommunications to lower the costs of telephone service; but there was little discussion of competition across sectoral boundaries (i.e., cable competing with telephones). In the early 1980s, Ottawa backed heroic technological projects such as the state-sponsored teletext system, Telidon, but it failed embarrassingly because—unlike France's Minitel—it wasn't fully interactive. In the United States, interactive TV experiments were producing mixed results. In the late 1970s, Warner Cable launched a "QUBE" experiment in 38,000 households in Columbus, Ohio, that allowed subscribers to request programs among ten pay-TV channels. But while the trial produced some interesting results, consumers showed little interest in interactive video features. Later experiments with so-called full-service networks offering home shopping, television, banking, movies on demand, and other services likewise produced disappointing results.

By the early 1990s, convergence was back on the policy agenda in both the United States and Canada (though the Canadian approach consisted mainly of following U.S. trends). Bill Clinton's electoral victory in 1992 marked a shift in U.S. policy in favour of high-tech sectors such as telecoms and computers. Clinton's vice-president, Al Gore, was particularly interested in communications issues. As a senator, Gore had established a reputation for sponsoring important U.S. legislation in the communications sector, including the 1992 Information Infrastructure and Technology Act. In the White House, Gore immediately struck an Information Infrastructure Task Force to develop an "information superhighway" policy to assert America's global leadership in the burgeoning "new economy," which had been the main platform of the Clinton-Gore election campaign.

Ottawa, meanwhile, was under mounting pressure from powerful industry interests to liberalize the communications industries to allow cross-sectoral competition. After a 1992 regulatory decision, the major Canadian telephone companies were facing competition in the long-distance market, and it was obvious that infrastructure provision would soon be a commodity business generating lower profits. Canada's big telephone companies were eager to put an end to restrictions prohibiting their entry into broadcasting. In mid-1993, the Stentor lobby group representing an alliance of Canada's major telephone companies outlined its industry vision as a "network of networks" integrating small facilities with the main infrastructure owned by the phone companies themselves.

When the Liberals returned to power in October 1993, the newly elected government of Jean Chrétien tore a page from the Clinton-Gore policy by announcing an "information highway" initiative. In April 1994, the Liberals set up an Information Highway Advisory Council (IHAC) modelled largely on Al Gore's Information Infrastructure Task Force. The IHAC was split into five working groups that reflected a mixture of social and industrial objectives: access and social impacts, competition and job creation, learning and training, research and development, and Canadian content and culture.

Major industry interests immediately understood that Ottawa's information highway was a perfect opportunity to consolidate and seek further deregulation. In February 1994, cable baron Ted Rogers made a $3.1-billion takeover of media giant Maclean Hunter, which owned a vast collection of media assets, including Ontario cable TV systems, *Maclean's*, and the Sun Media newspaper chain. To win regulatory approval for the takeover, Ted Rogers told the CRTC that Maclean Hunter would offer his cable wires strategic "synergies" by providing Rogers with valuable content to pump through its coaxial wires. A merged Rogers-Maclean Hunter would "tell Canadian stories and paint national dreams." The Rogers takeover bid struck the right chord at a time of tremendous hype about digital technology, media megadeals, a 500-channel universe, and globalization.

Not to be outdone by Ted Rogers, on April 5, 1994, Stentor announced a $10-billion "Beacon Initiative" aimed at upgrading and digitizing Canada's copper telephone wires so that telephone companies could carry TV signals, data, and multimedia services to Canadian homes and schools. The Beacon Initiative included five main components: (1) about $8 billion directed to network upgrades; (2) $500 million earmarked for regional infrastructure investments; (3) the creation of a new multimedia company to produce content for the information highway; (4) a venture capital fund to finance the development of new services for the information highway; and (5) investments to ensure that schools, hospitals, and cultural institutions benefited from interactive and multimedia services.

In the mid-1990s, digital television and high-speed electronic highways were appealing themes for political leaders, especially since these visions held out the promise of technological innovation, job creation, and economic growth. But in Canada, as elsewhere, the government focused its convergence and information highway policies on the two sectors—telephone and cable TV—that were longstanding monopolies profoundly hostile to change. As policymakers would soon realize, the "two titans" they had designed to build the information highway were more interested in protecting their monopoly turf than charging boldly into the highly competitive information age. Convergence was a useful buzzword that could be evoked to lobby for industry deregulation, but convergence policies didn't necessarily inspire commercial actors to embrace convergence in the marketplace.

CONVERGENCE AND POLICY MUDDLE

In the 1980s, Ottawa had initiated a long, arduous process of redrafting federal broadcasting and telecommunications legislation. The new Broadcasting Act was finally passed in 1991, followed by the Telecommunications Act in 1993. In the late 1980s, technological convergence clearly had not been foremost in the minds of policymakers, for Ottawa enacted two separate statutes and not a single piece of legislation. The timing also turned out to be unfortunate, because the World Wide Web was emerging at precisely the time these statutes were being drafted in complete ignorance of the imminent impact of the Internet explosion. In the United States, a single piece of legislation, the Telecommunications Act, was passed into law in 1996; but that statute, too, had been drafted before the importance of the Internet was fully understood.

The Internet blind spot of Ottawa policymakers persisted well into the 1990s. In 1996, the federal government released its information highway policy, which confined itself to general principles and vague policy jargon. It was more of a non-policy than a policy. Disagreement among the industry interests that composed the Information Highway Advisory Council appeared to have been the cause of the indecision and muddle. And yet the IHAC continued through another phase of protracted deliberations, and produced yet another report in 1997. The IHAC's work was regarded, for the most part, as a policy sideshow that may have created the positive optics of "consultation" with industry players, but had little impact on policy decisions.

More serious consideration of convergence was taking place in Ottawa ministries and at the CRTC. Still, the government fell into the same trap of conceiving convergence issues as a "two titans" policy matter involving the cable TV and telephone industries. The reason for this was as much institutional as conceptual. In 1993, the short-lived Conservative government of Kim Campbell had split the Department of Communications into two separate ministries. The result, ironically, was that at the very moment technological convergence was merging industry segments, Ottawa's policy apparatus was diverging into separate, and often quarrelsome, ministries. The Department of Canadian Heritage, which had responsibility for arts policy and broadcasting, tended to take a cultural approach to communications issues, often through protectionist policy tools. Industry Canada, on the other hand, was responsible for telecommunications and tended to favour deregulation and market liberalization. Throughout 1994, differences between the two ministries made it impossible to agree on a coherent policy approach to convergence. The government thus called on the CRTC to hold public hearings into the matter. In May 1995, following its regulatory hearings, the CRTC submitted to Cabinet its convergence report, *Culture and Competition on Canada's Information Highway: Managing the Realities of Transition.*

The CRTC report evoked many familiar themes inspired by Canada's long-standing technological nationalism:

> The information highway is more than cable and copper wire. It is a metaphor for the promise and uncertainty surrounding the emergence of a world-wide communications network driven by innovation, competition and technology. The highway links past achievements in communications to future aspirations, binds economy and culture in ways that harness the creative energies of Canadians, and opens gateways to global trade in information products and services. Throughout Canada's history, policy makers have seen the importance of communications to economic and cultural sovereignty, and have fought to build roadways that link all parts of this country. (CRTC, 1995)

Beyond affirming high-minded principles, however, the CRTC's approach to concrete issues was unmistakably cautious. The ball was now in the government's court to take policy decisions.

With the CRTC report in hand, Ottawa issued its convergence policy on August 6, 1996, six months after passage of the U.S. Telecommunications Act. The convergence policy dealt with three broad areas that revealed a familiar tension between market competition and cultural protectionism: (1) interconnection and interoperability of network facilities; (2) competition in facilities, products, and services; and (3) continued support for Canadian content. The convergence policy's chief preoccupation, however, was fixing rules for competition between cable TV and telephone companies. This was made explicit in a government statement accompanying the convergence policy: "Getting cable service from your phone company or telephone services from the local cable company moved closer to reality today."

That statement turned out to be a naive exaggeration. Indeed, press reports following the release of the convergence policy didn't share Ottawa's optimism. The *Globe and Mail*, for example, reported that "Canadians hoping to buy cable television from their telephone companies or phone service from their cable operator will have to wait a while—probably into the next millennium" (cited in Fraser, 1999, p. 86). As industry expert Eamon Hoey put it:

> If you listen to the voice in the woods, the telephone companies are now becoming less enamoured of being in the cable business than they were four years ago, and the cable entities are now having a real close look at the telephone business and slowly concluding that it's not as simple as they thought it was. These policy statements may open up markets, but that doesn't mean there will be market entrants. (cited in Fraser, 1999, p. 86)

Indeed, by the mid-1990s, the cable TV industry was no longer interested in using its coaxial wires to provide competitive local telephone service. Most major cable groups, in both Canada and the United States, were focused on protecting their monopoly franchise against the threat of "death star" satellite TV services such as DirecTV. Capital spending therefore was needed to digitize cable networks to compete in the heralded 500-channel universe, not to diversify into costly ventures like telephone service. Major telephone companies, for their part, were more preoccupied by competition from other telecom rivals, including wireless operators, in the long-distance and local phone markets. Making a bold foray into the video-delivery business was put on the backburner.

Industry foot-dragging must have been vexing for the policymakers, who had been liberalizing and deregulating in a tacit tradeoff for convergence competition. In Canada, the CRTC had opened up the residential market to full competition between cable and the telephone companies. The regulator also had allowed Canada's two biggest telephone companies, Bell Canada and Telus, to offer their subscribers interactive multimedia services on a trial basis. Bell chose two prosperous towns—London, Ontario, and Repentigny, Quebec—and in each place hooked up 3500 homes to high-speed digital networks. Telus chose suburbs of Calgary and Edmonton for its trial. In both market trials, Bell and Telus laid high-capacity fibre-coaxial wires and installed digital hardware to store and deliver video and data. These were similar to "video dialtone" trials in the United States, in which telephone companies acted as common carriers for video delivery. In June 1998, the

CRTC went even further by awarding a broadcasting licence to NB Tel, the New Brunswick telephone company. And Bell Canada's statute was finally amended to allow the telephone giant to enter broadcasting.

But Ottawa policymakers learned that convergence is little more than an abstraction if market players don't follow through by implementing their boldly announced plans. In July 1998, Jean Monty, the CEO of Bell Canada Enterprises, announced that Bell Canada was pulling out of its fibre-optic experiments in London and Repentigny. Moreover, Bell was withdrawing completely from its wireline broadband strategy to compete against cable TV. Bell would offer television service via ExpressVu's satellite service. In other words, Bell Canada wasn't interested in technological convergence at all: its telephone business would continue to depend mainly on Bell's wired infrastructure, and its television service would be delivered via satellite. Bell customers could buy both services, but separately. Cable companies such as Rogers and Shaw, for their part, didn't offer local telephone service at all (the exception being Rogers' mobile service, Rogers AT&T).

With lacklustre competition between Ottawa's "two titans," there remained some hope that wireless operators would fill the competitive void after Ottawa issued licences to companies seeking to compete with cable and telephone companies. Two promising wireless firms were SkyCable, owned by Manitoba's Craig family, and Look TV, which was backed by telecom entrepreneur Charles Sirois. But neither turned out to be significant competitors in a market dominated by monopoly giants. Perhaps the most overlooked players in the convergence wars were public utilities. Some believed that lazy monopoly providers of electricity were poised to become major players in telecommunications. They were unquestionably well positioned thanks to their installed network of wires running into households, networks of underground conduits, and rights of way. But while ambitious plans were announced by utilities, no significant market belligerents actually stepped forward to compete with cable and telephone companies.

In fact, while government policy initiatives were focused on competition between cable and telephone systems, the electronic highways of the future were being built elsewhere on the World Wide Web. As *The Economist* observed:

> For the past few years the titans of media and communications have waged a war for the digital future. With great fanfare, telephone and cable TV companies have launched dozens of trials to demonstrate their vision of speedy electronic networks. . . . Shambling towards their distant goal of a wired world, they have been too busy to notice the unruly bunch of computer hackers, engineers and students scurrying about at their feet. They should have paid more attention. For while the giants have just been talking about an Information Superhighway, the ants have actually been building one: the Internet. ("Accidental Superhighway," 1995)

In Canada, policymakers had completely missed the Internet explosion in the early 1990s. Yet two separate statutes—the 1991 Broadcasting Act and 1993 Telecommunications Act—were carved in policy stone. This lack of foresight forced Ottawa into a muddled, improvised approach toward convergence that would drag on for several years.

IT'S THE INTERNET, STUPID

It wasn't until the late 1990s that former monopoly players like cable TV and telephone companies began taking the Internet seriously; when they did, the Internet became the focus of revitalized business plans. At first, cable and telephone companies began offering access to the Web for a monthly fee, thus generating additional subscription revenues. Big Canadian cable companies such as Rogers and Shaw, which owned vast networks of thick coaxial wires that could provide broadband connections, took an early lead in the high-speed Web access business. Bell Canada and other telephone monopolies soon began catching up with their own high-speed services, notably Sympatico. But providing access to the Web was a commodity business, for in the broadband world infrastructure had no scarcity value. Media giants quickly realized that consumers would find more value in content developed for the Internet. Millions of teenagers were already downloading music from the Internet via peer-to-peer file-swapping services like MP3 and Napster, and some were even watching full-motion video on the Web.

Against this backdrop, it soon became apparent that convergence wasn't necessarily competition between cable TV and telephone companies in the video and voice business. Thanks to the Web, another form of convergence was emerging that could serve as a delivery system for music, video, and even telephony. Web-friendly interactive TV services and Internet-protocol telephone services were soon available. WebTV, for example, was owned by Microsoft, which later developed a more sophisticated product, UltimateTV. While these services didn't immediately take off as mass-market products, Web-based convergence seemed to hold out more commercial promise than the "two titans" competition for television and telephone service.

Today, as the Internet increasingly becomes a major distribution network for the sale of cultural products, a number of key policy matters have remained unresolved. For example, should regulators impose any rules on the Internet at all? Interestingly, while the Web is borderless and hence nonterritorial (much like satellite communications), tremendous pressures have been exerted on courts and national regulators to assert territorial borders on cyberspace. In some cases, these demands have been contradictory. Canadian broadcasters strenuously lobbied the CRTC to refrain from regulating the Internet, hoping that a deregulatory approach would spill over into broadcasting. In 1999, the CRTC announced that it would *not* regulate the Internet, although it would re-examine that position five years later. But when Web-based broadcasters ("webcasters") such as iCraveTV and JumpTV began streaming television signals on the Internet, Canadian broadcasters reversed their position and called on the CRTC to intervene to protect their intellectual property rights. These kinds of tensions remain. Libertarians believe cyberspace should be a free-for-all Wild West, while others call on states to crack down on pornography, hate literature, and other forms of Internet content and transactions.

Despite these tensions, cultural products are being delivered via broadband Web-based delivery systems. In the past few years, Hollywood studios, major record companies, and other players in the entertainment industries have established "new media" divisions and have tested consumer habits with Web sites. But as the hostile reaction to Napster demonstrated, global media giants like Disney, Vivendi Universal, Time Warner, and News Corp. are exceedingly reluctant to sell or rent their intellectual property as digital products on the Internet without exercising commercial control. There are two reasons for this conservatism. First, owners of intellectual property are concerned that their products will be copied, at no marginal cost, by individuals and distributed via the Web to millions of users worldwide. Only fail-safe encryption systems will solve this problem. Second, since downloading video and music takes a long time on narrowband Web connections, a global mass market for Internet-delivered products will not be fully exploited until broadband networks are universally deployed. It is only a matter of time, however, before both these problems are resolved—the copyright issue by international treaty and the market adoption of reliable encryption systems, and the technical issues by the build-out of digitized broadband networks. Indeed, in mid-2001 the biggest global music labels and Hollywood studios announced plans to sell on-demand music and movies directly via the Web.

Policymakers, meanwhile, seem uncertain about how digital cultural products should be regulated, if at all. In the United States, antitrust officials have expressed concern that music giants and Hollywood studios may exploit their dominant market position to control Web-based sales of their products. In Canada, a patchwork of contradictory policies remains in place. The CRTC, for example, does not regulate Web-based radio stations and video delivery, but had decided to regulate video-on-demand (VOD) even though VOD products will soon be delivered via the Web to millions of households. The CRTC nonetheless defined video-on-demand as "broadcasting," an assertion that remains highly contentious. In Europe, for example, video-on-demand is defined as "telecommunications," not broadcasting. In its "Television Without Frontiers" directive, the European Commission stated: "VOD services, like all genuinely interactive services, are classed as telecommunications in that transmission is in response to individual demand." In other words, VOD is considered to be switched, point-to-point communications, not point-to-multipoint broadcasting. Or to put it differently, VOD is "pull" technology (individuals order movies that they "pull" down from servers), whereas broadcasting is "push" technology (the same signals are sent out to all TV sets indiscriminately).

The CRTC appears to have rejected that definition of video-on-demand, opting instead to assert its own jurisdiction over VOD services. The CRTC has issued video-on-demand licences on two separate occasions (first in 1997, then in 2000) to several established Canadian broadcasters. The CRTC, it is true, took a light-touch approach when granting these VOD licences, insisting only on guaranteed "shelf space" for Canadian products and financial contributions for Canadian content production. But by issuing VOD licences, the CRTC followed the same approach it had adopted in the past: facilitating the market entry of a limited number of large-scale Canadian players so they could "occupy the field" before an incursion of foreign-based operators. There is no reason to believe, however, that the market logic of VOD will, in the long term, respect national territories and obey national regulations. A computer server from which on-demand movies are retrieved does not have to be located on Canadian soil. Consequently, there is no reason why those who control foreign-based digital retrieval systems will feel compelled to gain access to the Canadian market through CRTC-approved agents. Why, for example, would Disney or AOL Time Warner–controlled Home Box Office (HBO) wish to operate through a CRTC-licensed Canadian middleman to sell movies in Canada via the Internet?

The debate in Canada about video-on-demand and multimedia services has been part of the ongoing battle between the broadcasters and telephone companies. Broadcasters generally prefer an expansive definition of "broadcasting" that captures video-on-demand services, because it would limit competition through regulatory barriers to entry. The telephone companies and computer industry, on the other hand, prefer a more restrictive definition of "broadcasting" that would permit them to commercially exploit video-on-demand and other multimedia services with no fear of onerous regulations and market-entry barriers.

Video-on-demand is likely to evolve from pay-per-view services available on cable and satellite TV. The first litmus test for the CRTC's hand's-off approach to the Internet will come when video-on-demand services are offered on the Web by significant non-Canadian players with global market power—namely, Disney, AOL Time Warner, Viacom, Vivendi Universal, Sony, News Corp., and Bertelsmann. It will be interesting to see whether the CRTC is forced into the awkward position of admitting that, while it cannot regulate some forms of content on the Web, it wishes to assert its authority over video-on-demand to protect the licences of Canadian companies offering video-on-demand via traditional broadcasting systems.

CONCLUSION: CONVERGENCE, DIVERGENCE

A decade after excitement about "convergence" triggered a trend toward megamergers in the media industries, there still is little agreement on what the term actually means. Jean Monty, chairman and CEO of BCE, admitted as much in April 2001 when he noted in a speech:

> Convergence is one of those words in the lexicon that seems to be constantly evolving. Ten years or so ago, telecom convergence meant simply the marriage of computers and telephones. A few years later ... it was meant to represent the blending of voice, data and video in a single stream where before they were separate. It was a technological view where video was added to the bundle. And the concept has now evolved further. Convergence now refers to the melding of what is often referred to as "content"—newspapers, television and the Internet—with carriage or distribution. (Monty, 2001)

So, the debate about convergence continues. For some media giants, convergence has been a convenient buzzword to describe what can more properly be described as *vertical integration*. When AOL and Time Warner merged, for example, the result was a global media powerhouse that promised to exploit synergies between Time Warner's content and AOL's Web-based subscription service. But a more strategically crucial aspect of the deal was accorded less hoopla: AOL now had privileged access to Time Warner's 13 million cable TV subscribers in the United States. In other words, the fusion was based on vertically integrating content and distribution. In Canada, BCE's takeover of CTV was, in like manner, a move toward vertical integration of content and delivery. Other media megamergers, such as CanWest Global's buyout of Conrad Black's Southam newspaper chain, can better be described as horizontal integration. And yet, whatever their precise configuration, most of these deals invoke "convergence" to rationalize their commercial logic.

If we stick to the formal definition of convergence established at the outset—that is, the provision of previously separate services like video, voice, and data through a single distribution system—it can be said that very few media companies are actually engaged in genuine convergence strategies. As noted, BCE offers video and voice telephony on entirely separate platforms (i.e., satellites for television, wires for phone service). No cable company can yet boast of competing head-on with telephone giants in the local phone market. The unavoidable conclusion, therefore, is that the "two titans" vision of convergence promoted by policymakers has largely failed to materialize. One of the main reasons for this failure, as noted, was a lack of foresight and inability to understand the importance of the Internet.

At the same time, convergence has not achieved its promised benefits of breaking up monopolies, promoting competition, and favouring consumer empowerment. Those benefits may come one day, but the short-term result of convergence has been massive industry consolidation. Convergence has been a bonanza for Wall Street and Bay Street investment bankers who have earned huge fees from the frenzy of corporate combinations. But consumers have often found their expectations frustrated by technological hype that fails to materialize in the form of new services in the marketplace.

In the recent past, however, major market players have been aggressively shifting their convergence strategies towards the Web (despite the high-tech stock market meltdown of early 2000). Cable companies like Rogers and Shaw are offering "bundled" services that include television channel, high-speed Internet access, and interactive TV. Big telephone companies are adopting a similar strategy. In early 2001, Bell Canada announced a "ComboBox" product that offered customers an Internet gateway via Bell ExpressVu satellite TV and Bell Sympatico. And both cable and satellite TV services are already offering digital television, interactive TV, personal video recorders, and other enhanced services that will create an incentive for consumers to convert to high-speed digital broadband delivery.

In the final analysis, convergence appears to be less revolutionary, and more evolutionary, than many of its more ardent advocates had predicted in the 1990s. The slowness of the convergence revolution can be explained on a number of levels. First, technological change usually occurs not as a sudden rupture, but as an extended process in successive stages (i.e., invention, commercial implementation, and consumer acceptance). Second, incumbent industry interests—in this case, cable and telephone monopolies—are by nature stubborn adversaries of change because their economic interests are threatened by disruptive technologies. Finally, the law of unintended consequences often reveals that consumers use technology in different ways from those that had originally been predicted. It is still not certain, for example, how consumers will use interactive TV and the Internet as an "entertainment" medium. In a climate of uncertainty about these issues, investing billions of dollars in infrastructure and content is a precarious enterprise.

Still, the day will come when the notion of "television" and "computer" are interchangeable—multiple apparatuses in separate rooms of a house serving different functions, but essentially the same type of equipment. The day will also likely come when making telephone calls via the Internet will be a banal experience. Already, it is possible to retrieve and send e-mails on portable wireless devices that also serve as telephones and video screens. What we have seen in the short term, however, is corporate convergence in the form of consolidation through large-scale combinations. Mass-market commercial convergence for global consumers is still several years in the future.

QUESTIONS

1. What is convergence?
2. What are the tensions between market competition and cultural protectionism?
3. What are the challenges in digital delivery of cultural products?
4. What does the author mean by the "two titans" view of convergence promoted by Canadian policymakers?
5. Do you think that media convergence will be successful? Give reasons for your answer.

WEB SITES

AOL Time Warner: **http://www.aoltimewarner.com/index_flash.adp**
CRTC (Canadian Radio-television Telecommunications Commission):
   http://www.crtc.gc.ca/
Industry Canada: **http://strategis.ic.gc.ca/**
National Broadband Task Force (Industry Canada): **http://broadband.gc.ca**

REFERENCES

Accidental superhighway: A survey of the Internet. (1995, July 1). *The Economist.*

CRTC (Canadian Radio-television and Telecommunications Commission). (1995). *Culture and competition on Canada's information highway: Managing the realities of transition.* Ottawa: Government of Canada. Retrieved from http://www.crtc.gc.ca/ENG/publications/reports.htm

Fraser, Matthew. (1999). *Free-for-all: The struggle for dominance on the digital frontier.* Toronto: Stoddart.

Government of Canada. (1971). *Instant world: A report on telecommunications in Canada.* Ottawa: Information Canada.

Monty, Jean C. (2001). *"Made-in-Canada convergence": Maintaining Canadian leadership in a converging world.* Speech delivered at the Speakers Forum, Toronto, May 14, 2001.

FURTHER READING

Baldwin, Thomas F., D. Stevens McVoy, and Charles Steinfield. (1996). *Convergence: Integrating media, information and communications.* Thousand Oaks, CA: Sage.

Cairncross, Frances. (1997). *The death of distance: How the communications revolution will change our lives.* Cambridge, MA: Harvard Business School Press.

Government of Canada. (1996). *Building the information society: Moving Canada into the 21st century.* Ottawa: Information Highway Advisory Council.

———. (1997). *Preparing Canada for a digital world.* Ottawa: Information Highway Advisory Council.

Lessig, Lawrence. (1999). *Code and other laws of cyberspace.* New York: Basic Books.

Owen, Bruce. (1999). *The Internet challenge to television.* Cambridge, MA: Harvard University Press.

Winseck, Dwayne. (1998). *Reconvergence: A political economy of telecommunications in Canada.* Cresskill, NJ: Hampton Press.

18

Lost in Cyberspace

Dwayne Winseck
Carleton University

This is a story of media convergence, ownership concentration, netscapes of power, and walled gardens. It begins with the observation that, in the last few years, the Canadian and global mediascape has been turned upside down by mergers, the Internet, and the prospect of media convergence. The information revolution and its progeny—digitization, the Internet, and globalization—are exploding the distinctions between telecommunications, the press, broadcasting, and computing as well as governments' capacity to regulate the media. A new vista of experience—cyberspace—is opening up and access to a cornucopia of information promises a renaissance of culture and of democracy.

Of course, this fantasy obscures as much as it reveals. Convergence is neither new nor a consequence of changing technology or mysterious forces of globalization. It has been part and parcel of the modern media since the mid-19th century when the telegraph, mass press, and global news agencies (Reuters, Associated Press) were born together. Indeed, convergence ebbed and waned throughout the 20th century as Bell Canada and AT&T shaped the advent of broadcasting in the 1920s and AT&T became the second-largest financier of Hollywood films until being chased out by the U.S. government for antitrust reasons in the mid-1930s.

In 1971, Canada's Department of Communications resurrected the idea of media convergence in a prescient report entitled *Instant World*. The melding of telecommunications, broadcasting, publishing and computing, and the goal of wiring Canadian households, government, and businesses to broadband networks, was seen as inevitable and likely to be completed by the mid-1980s. These visions, however, turned out to be premature and economically unviable. Moreover, the concept of "wired cities" did not mesh with people's needs and lent itself too easily to fears of Big Brother, surveillance, and information control. Finally, the fantasy was also undermined by the view that it was really only a way for the telephone companies to extend their monopolies to all electronic media. Consequently, even telecommunications companies originally shunned convergence for fear that promoting it would draw new competitors into their existing "natural monopolies" (Winseck, 1998, chap. 5).

However, there has been a revival of talk about media reconvergence. This has been brought about by changes in both government and corporate policies that used to *prevent* convergence but now actively *promote* it. The new goal is to turn information/communication into the driving force of the "new economy" and "information societies." The shift from prevention to promotion was clearly signalled in a key document published by the federal government in 1996, *Building the Information Society*, and in a host of other reports by Cabinet, the Canadian Radio-television Communications Commission (CRTC), and the Information Highway Advisory Council. The shift also required greater tolerance of ownership concentration as well as the popularization of a worldview that placed the expansion of information and media markets over questions of free speech and democratic society. Indeed, the new worldview believes that the Internet is such a creative force and will create so much information abundance that concerns over media ownership are simply anachronistic.

The shape of things to come was first signalled in 1998 and 1999 in the United States when AT&T took over the cable company TCI and the TV station group MediaOne. AT&T had decided that it wanted to own the networks that allowed American households to watch television and use high-speed Internet access. Shortly afterwards, AOL merged with the world's largest "old media" conglomerate, Time Warner, in a bid to gain access to Time Warner's cable networks, film studios and archives, specialty cable channels, music catalogues, and magazines.

Canadian communication companies saw in what was happening a model for their own "convergence dreams." Consequently, in rapid succession, CanWest Global took over broadcaster Western International Communications as well as the Southam newspaper chain, which stretched from Vancouver to Halifax and had previously been owned by Conrad Black. Quebecor absorbed cable giant Vidéotron. Rogers Communications formed a partnership with Microsoft and AT&T, as well as an alliance with Shaw Communications to divide the cable industry between East and West. Shaw Communications bought the production house Corus Entertainment, which in turn took over the leading creator of animated programs, Nelvana. Finally, Bell Canada Enterprises (BCE) parlayed its dominance in telecommunications by launching the satellite television service ExpressVu (and its Internet portal Sympatico) in 1994 and 1995, and by acquiring the television network CTV and Toronto's *Globe and Mail* newspaper in 2000.

These sweeping changes raise two crucial questions: (1) what are the impacts of these changes on the existing media?; and (2) should those who control the medium also control the message? The answer to the first question is broad and can emerge only through the course of this paper. But we can give a very quick outline of the standard answer to the second question. Usually, the answer is yes. Indeed, the argument is increasingly made that vertically integrated multimedia companies that control both the medium and the message are not only necessary to compete internationally but also desirable. Convergence, runs the argument, actually creates *new* media channels, all clamouring for content; the proliferation of channels thus eliminates the need to control media ownership. Indeed, it is also claimed that the *information abundance* which characterizes our times effectively means that no single outlet can exert an inordinate influence over citizens' access to information; this is especially true given the arrival of the Internet, which provides too much information rather than too little. Proponents of media convergence also claim that concentrated ownership will build up "national champions" capable of competing internationally and of building the complex information infrastructure that will catapult Canada into the future, guarantee access to Canadian content, and even ensure our cultural survival in a "global information age." This view is shared not only by the media conglomerates themselves but also by such regulatory agencies as the CRTC.

As a result of convergence, Canada now has one of the most consolidated media systems in the world and an unrivalled degree of cross-media ownership. This is perhaps best exemplified by the fact that the two major English-language dailies, the *Globe and Mail* and the *National Post*, are owned by the respective parent companies (BCE and CanWest Global) of the two largest private television networks, CTV and Global. Indeed, cross-media ownership is a defining feature of the Canadian media system. Over 60 percent of Canadians now receive their local daily newspaper from the same company that owns one or more of their local/regional television stations. Furthermore, the same companies also own cable systems, specialty channels, satellite delivery systems, and so on.

To date there has been little focus on the potential impact of cross-media ownership on freedom of the press or the role of the media in a democratic society. This is surprising because changes in ownership *do* have far-reaching affects. For example, media ownership changes are sometimes followed by the closure of news bureaus, layoffs, and a greater emphasis on regional and national news and entertainment programs to the detriment of other types of content. Indeed, in Canada, many local television stations no longer produce their own programs or news. These patterns became particularly prominent following the spate of acquisitions in 1999 and 2000. For example, after it acquired the Sun Media newspaper chain as well as cable giant Vidéotron in 2000, Quebecor instituted massive cuts across its operations in television, newspapers, cable, and the Internet (Marotte, 2000a, p. B3; 2000b, p. B3). Likewise, because of debts incurred by its takeover of the Southam newspaper chain and Western International Communication, CanWest Global is now yoked to the short-term and hypersensitive rhythms of the stock market and to the need for "synergies" and efficiencies. As a result, it is striving to eliminate $150 million in costs through hiring freezes and resource amalgamations (Damsell, 2001, p. M1; Dixon, 2001, p. B7).

Similar trends occurred in the U.S. television networks over the last 15 years and led to the elimination of foreign news bureaus, a one-third reduction in news staffs, and an overall reduction in news (Aufderheide, 1990, p. 51). The cutbacks in international news were especially severe, a disturbing phenomenon in light of the trend to globalization. While media convergence might make good business sense, it is not good for journalism or democracy, where citizens continue to look to the media to reflect, extend, and amplify public life.

The media convergence trend mirrors trends at the CBC over the last decade in response to government cutbacks. Indeed, the formation of multimedia conglomerates has occurred in tandem with the elimination of local broadcasting in favour of tighter integration into a more regional, national, and global media economy, while the ensuing scramble for synergies and "brand identity" has further eroded diversity and helped to foster a star system among the few media professionals endlessly circulated through the self-referential image machinery of BCE/CTV/*Globe and Mail* and CanWest/*National Post*.

All of these trends also reflect the new stress placed by media policy on the need to foster large multimedia conglomerates that can build information infrastructures and produce the type of Hollywood-style programs that will appeal to domestic and global audiences. This aim has underwritten the CRTC's increasingly permissive view of mergers. Since the mid-1990s, the CRTC has stressed its belief that consolidation is good for Canadians and for Canadian content. For example, in commenting on the BCE/CTV transaction, it pointed to

> tangible benefits consisting of $230 million in expenditures over seven years that will be directed to the development, production and promotion of new priority programming.... This will include drama, ... documentaries and a major annual variety program [as well as] incremental enhancements to news and current affairs programming. (CRTC, 2000, p. 6)

BCE also promised to open five new foreign news bureaus in Berlin, Hong Kong, Johannesburg, New Delhi, and New York; to provide funding for journalism schools across the country (whose directors duly lined up to support the deal); and to earmark 95 percent of all new funding for dramatic and entertainment programs to independent production companies. The CRTC (2000) endorsed the plans as "significant, *unequivocal* [italics added] and commensurate with the size ... of the transaction" (p. 6).

Unfortunately, the pledges made by BCE/CTV and CanWest are not unequivocal. BCE's takeover of CTV will not increase funding for program creation at the network. Instead, it will merely stop the loss of funds that has occurred over the last few years. CanWest has increased investment in content production, though only marginally, and the scale of its investment pales alongside that of CTV and other broadcasters. However, BCE only plans to return to 1997 funding levels (in current dollars) by 2002 and to stabilize investment relative to revenues at the historically low level set by the network in 2001. The hope is that stable funding for network news and Hollywood-style productions will stave off an even worse fate while contributing to BCE's broader ambitions for the Internet.

These developments reveal far-reaching changes in the spatial and cultural orientation of the evolving mediascape. The emerging mediascape is being disembedded from local communities and integrated into the dynamics and rhythms of a national and global media economy, the nodal points of which intersect in a handful of Canadian cities: Vancouver, Calgary, Halifax, Montreal, Ottawa, and Toronto.

In turn, the nascent media economy is organized around a cluster of vertically integrated multimedia conglomerates capable of creating and distributing block-buster-style entertainment programs, and based on the following four pillars: (1) convergence, (2) consolidation of ownership, (3) concentration of production resources in a few cities, and (4) centralized information flows. The effects are significant as the potential of new technologies to decentralize and democratize cultural production and information flows is subverted and yoked ever more closely to a media economy that is spatially and institutionally clustered, and oriented strictly according to the ability to pay rather than the need to know.

These are not the conditions of an industry threatened by new technologies. While new technologies generate much uncertainty, the Internet and other new media are not so much disruptive technologies as vehicles that allow multimedia firms to reinforce their existing positions and to colonize new mediaspaces with their well-honed "brands." In the United States and Canada, the most visited Web sites and portals belong to telecommunications companies, broadcasters, newspapers, and Hollywood. The crucial exceptions, of course, are AOL, one of the "new media" stars, and Microsoft, whose operations are swiftly moving from the desktop to the network by way of investments in cable systems, set-top boxes, high-speed Internet access, and its Internet portal, MSN. In short, there is a certain resilience in the "old media" that will not simply yield in the face of new technologies (Brethour, 2001a, p. B1; McChesney, 2000).

These realities are also deeply rooted in other facets of the media culture. As a recent Pew Foundation study (2000) indicates, newspapers and television are by a considerable margin still the main sources of news and entertainment for most people (even those who use the Internet). This is simply because most people do not have Internet access and also because conventional media—in both their "real space" and "on-line" versions—outstrip the Internet in terms of perceived quality, credibility, and trustworthiness. Even though there is room for improvement, quality journalism plays a vital role in public life and people continue to turn to it for insight and understanding. The claim of *information abundance* mistakes the sheer quantity of sources for the quality of content. It also ignores the fact that most people still use "old media," and it eliminates from its notion of *journalism* such crit-ical factors as interpretation and analysis in favour of the mere abundance of data.

Consequently, media ownership concentration still *does* matter despite the availability of alternative information sources of information. As we saw above, the Internet serves just as much to conserve and extend existing sources of information as to provide alternatives. Furthermore, the Internet-as-alternative-to-media-power argument neglects the fact that Internet access is far from universal and is stubbornly skewed by income, education, and age. Even though Canadians are among the most enthusiastic users of the Internet in the world, and despite the con-stant hyperbole about the growth of the Internet, only about 30 percent of Canadian households had access to the Internet at the end of 1999 (Statistics Canada, 2000); worldwide access stands at a mere 3 percent (Netwizards, 1999).

The Internet is not universal and cyberspace is a class-divided space. The link between access and class is direct and unequivocal. In Canada, families in the top income quartile are more than 3.5 times as likely to have access to a computer and five times more likely to be connected to the Internet at home as those in the bottom quartile. In fact, more than 80 percent of households in the bottom half of the income curve do not have access to the Internet from home, a fact that obviously undercuts the image of the Internet as an alternative to conventional media. Of course, one can argue that this will change over time. However, the gap between "information rich" and "information poor" is expanding, and trends in computer ownership, even among high-income households, suggest that access to cyberspace will never be universal, at least for a long time to come (Statistics Canada, 1999, 2000). Even more interesting is the finding that many people (around 25 percent in Canada) *do not want* to use the Internet—not because they are Luddites, but because of cost, lack of trust, and the perception that going on-line is a waste of time (Katz and Aspden, 1999; Reddick, 2000, 3; Statistics Canada, 1999). Clearly, policies governing media evolution should deal with realities—and people—as they *are* rather than as they *might be* in the distant future.

FROM TECHNOLOGIES OF FREEDOM TO NETSCAPES OF POWER

Significant consequences flow from decisions to allow those who control the medium to own the message. While broadcasters, the press, and cable barons have always been able to do so, in telecommunications (such as telephone and satellite distribution) those who owned the "wires" were specifically prevented from influencing or owning the messages flowing through them. This created an open media system that encouraged those who controlled the pipes to seek profit by attracting as many content providers and users as possible, rather than by controlling content. As Abbatte (1999) and Lessig (1999) observe, the success of the Internet is due to the fact that it was explicitly designed as an open system in which network links between users were kept simple, intelligence and computing power were pushed to the ends of the network and onto users' desktops, and interfaces between users, content, and networks were kept open and relatively transparent. Media convergence threatens this model as more and more functions and intelligence are sucked back into the network and as those who own the medium become, through ownership and strategic alliances, tightly bound to those who control the content. As this occurs, there is a shift in the evolution of new media from the open systems model of telecommunications and the Internet toward a closed model in which in-house content is favoured over other sources—either in a heavy-handed manner, such as by refusing access to networks altogether (the history of the cable industry and specialty channels), or subtly through network design, acceptable use policies, user menus, search engines, portals, and so on in ways that give priority access to some sources of content and deny it to others.

This is not a problem if there are multiple gateways to cyberspace and an unconstrained range of information sources. However, such is not the case. The Internet is not immune from the forces of consolidation. Consolidation already exists in ownership of the Internet backbone that links cities worldwide. In Canada, there are hundreds of Internet service providers (ISPs), but the vast majority are scrambling for survival while the top five—Sympatico, Telus, AOL, the cable companies' @Home, and AT&T—accounted for 75–80% of all Internet subscribers in 2000. This trend is widely expected to continue (and, indeed, to be intensified by the collapse of the dot-com bubble), especially among those providing high-speed access (Brethour, 2001b, pp. B1, B10; Convergence Consulting Group, 2000, p. 12).

These trends would be unremarkable if networks were open and transparent gateways to cyberspace. They are not. Networks are powerful entities that both include and exclude. Those who control them can exercise a great deal of influence over who has access to users and over users' access to content. These features are rapidly being bolstered as telecommunications and cable companies seek to augment their influence over the development of the Internet. After coming late to the Internet, both groups are striving to remedy their early years of neglect by implementing strategies that will help them "attain mind and market share" as well as greater control over their own networks and, more broadly, the evolution of the Internet as a whole (Cisco, 1999a, p. 6).

Nortel and Cisco, among others, have recognized these needs by creating network architectures that put intelligence, resources, and capabilities back in the network and under the control of those who own them. Consequently, open network architectures are yielding to network designs that enhance network providers' ability to allocate resources, bandwidth, and speed to varying types of information and services based on their relation to the network owner, revenue potential, class of user served, and judgments regarding the quality of content (i.e., "objectionable content" such as pornography, hate literature, and so on, but also political dissent where that is objectionable). According to Cisco (1999b), the company's networks put "absolute control, down to the packet, in your hands. . . . You can identify each traffic type—Web, email, voice, video . . . [and] isolate . . . the type of application, even down to *specific brands*, by the *interface used*, by the *user type and individual user identification* or by the *site address* [italics added]" (p. 3).

While this strategy is marketed as a boon to media companies seeking to cultivate markets, the potential to squelch competition, diversity, dissent, and freedom of expression is considerable. The impact of the strategy on the contours of the Internet and media markets is made remarkably clear in the following passage from Cisco's marketing material:

> The [network's capabilities] allow you to specify the user access speed of any packet by allocating the bandwidth it receives, depending on its IP address, application, precedence, port or even Media Access Control (MAC) address. For example, if a

> "push" information service that delivers frequent broadcasts to
> its subscribers is seen as causing a high amount of undesirable
> network traffic, you can . . . limit subscriber access speed to this
> service . . . to discourage its use. At the same time, you could
> promote and offer your own or partners' services with full-speed
> features to encourage adoption of your services. . . . Further you
> could specify that video coming from internal servers receive
> precedence and broader bandwidth over video sourced from
> external servers. (Cisco, 1999b, p. 5)

This describes a netscape of power. Far from being transparent means of channelling information from one point to another, the networks Cisco describes are
technologies of discrimination that regulate information flows according to fine-
grained criteria set by network owners, whether this entails creating different
classes of users based on technical needs or perceived economic value, regulating
competitors' access to audiences, or suppressing undesirable forms of speech based
on source, the prerogatives of authority, type of content, or destination. In essence,
gatekeeping functions have been hardwired into network architectures as part of
the communications industries' strategies to cultivate and control markets.

These are not abstract potentials. They are the networks used by AOL Time
Warner, AT&T, Bell Canada, Cable & Wireless, Cogeco, Comcast, Microsoft,
Rogers, Shaw, Vidéotron, and "160 of the most successful service providers around
the world" (Cisco, 2000a, p. 2; Cisco, 2000b; Nortel, 2000). These companies now
have the unprecedented ability to regulate the Internet, endowed as they are with the
technical capabilities and the incentive to stifle threats to their own services (such as
alternative sources of video programming and competing Web-based services) and to
integrate users into a more dependent relationship with networks and services. The
extent to which these capabilities will be used is unclear, but, as AT&T's Internet
Services CEO Daniel Somers exclaimed in his defence of the company's refusal to
adopt open network policies: "AT&T didn't spend $56 billion to get into the cable
business to have the blood sucked out of our veins" (cited in Lessig, 2000, p. 995).

THE PRIVATIZATION OF CYBERLAW

As the Canadian government and many others abandon their traditional attempts
to regulate the media, conglomerates are stepping into the breach. They are doing
so through three strategies: (1) network design (as discussed above), (2) acceptable
use policies, and (3) "walled gardens." These strategies are most evident with respect
to high-speed Internet services. Even though such services are used by only about
5–10 percent of households in the United States and Canada respectively
(Convergence Consulting Group, 2000, p. 12; GAO, 2000, p. 6), they constitute the
pillars of the conglomerates' visions of convergence and the future of cyberspace.

From the perspective of users, communication networks are literally part of the woodwork and thus the kinds of design features that enable and constrain use tend to fall beneath the threshold of awareness. But users nonetheless confront the realities of a privately regulated on-line world through "acceptable use" policies created and enforced by on-line services. It is, therefore, interesting to examine acceptable use policies in order to understand the vision of users and appropriate use that they contain. While telecommunications companies are less restrictive than cable companies, both providers see users as mere appendages who should use the Internet in a "read-only" manner and access additional network functions on a pay-per-use basis.

In fact, this view is hardwired into the architecture of the networks. Both are asymmetrical, which means that they allow information and images to flood into the home while allowing only a narrowband stream of data to trickle out. Of course, this accurately reflects the usage patterns of most users. However, networks span cities, regions, countries, and even the globe. Thus, constraints that may be insignificant for separate individuals in their own homes can have unintended social consequences if thousands of users are deprived of the *potential* to *become* creators of media culture in an autonomous, disorganized, and spontaneous way. Why saddle those who wish to do more than read the Internet with the additional barriers of cost, ability, and so on? Furthermore, these possibilities are not simply the outcropping of a deluded imagination, they are an integral aspect of "cyberculture" wherein unforeseen uses and unanticipated cultural forms literally drive innovation. People *can* have a dramatic impact on the Internet, *despite* attempts to commercialize it and to turn users into simple appendages. This is a distinguishing feature of the new media that separates them from the "old" media, and one that needs to be preserved and amplified. Give users symmetrical bandwidth!

For some, the power of people to affect the evolution of cyberspace is dangerous. Excite@Home sees users as a threat to network security, to viable markets, and to shareholders. Consequently, it places numerous restrictions on what people can and cannot do. This is made abundantly clear in reports filed with the United States Securities and Exchange Commission, in which the company refers to its practice of "limiting users' upstream bandwidth in order to prevent abuse . . . by users, and [its expectation to] continue to limit upstream bandwidth" (@Home, 2000a, p. 13). The company also sees its economic viability as being jeopardized by users who "employ new technology to . . . filter online advertising, . . . prevent cookies from being stored on [their] hard drive . . . and shielding e-mail addresses . . . and other electronic means of identification" (pp. 22–23). In essence, @Home's view of cyberspace as a thoroughly commercialized, read-only medium clashes with users' expectations, although the latter must yield because, in cyberspace, those who own the networks make the rules.[1]

As already mentioned, there are differences between the telecom companies and the cable companies. However, there are also parallels. Both establish policies that involve editorial rules, reserved rights of the network owner, prohibited uses, surveillance, and enforcement. Both reserve considerable discretion with respect to monitoring and blocking access to content that contravenes their acceptable use policies or the laws of society. The kinds of content targeted—libellous material, child pornography, copyrighted material, and so on—are usually already covered by existing laws with the result that the use policies are not particularly troubling. A bigger problem, though, is the unbound editorial right that service providers have assumed over other types of content. As @Home (2000b) states, the company "reserves the right to remove or refuse to post *any* information ... that they, in *their sole discretion, deem to be offensive, indecent, or otherwise inappropriate regardless of whether such material ... is unlawful* [italics added]" (p. 5). This makes service providers powerful gatekeepers who can establish detailed and arbitrary distinctions between kinds of content that would otherwise be tolerated under freedom of expression rights in North America.

DSL (telephone) and cable-based high-speed ISPs also prohibit hacking, bulk emailing, and cross-posting of messages to multiple newsgroups or lists. While such limits are not onerous, the roster of proscribed uses is lengthy and troublesome. Key restrictions include a ten-minute limit on the amount of streaming video users can download in a day and another that prevents subscribers from using services that compete with those offered by cable system owners (e.g., Internet telephony) (@Home, 2000a, p. 33). The list of proscribed uses includes

- bulk mailing of messages, including information announcements, charity requests, petitions for signatures and political or religious messages;
- maintaining more than two chat connections at the same time;
- downloading Usenet articles in bulk;
- the operation of a news service or e-mail distribution service, or the sending of a news feed; and
- connecting a server to the network or using a server to operate multiuser interactive forums. (@Home, 2000b)

Those who disobey can be banished. At the very least, these restrictions strive to neuter the Internet as a competitive threat as well as to narrow the overall role of users vis-à-vis the network. In the face of information abundance and the devolution of media power to users' desktops, the communication industries are trying to pull these powers back into the network, and under their control, where they think they belong. The result is an attempt to turn cyberspace back into a model that resembles "old media."

After spending hundreds of billions of dollars to acquire networks and content, it was inevitable that multimedia goliaths would design mediaspaces that enhance their investments rather than promote open and transparent communication. Attempts to manage people's relationship to and uses of the Internet reflect these attempts *as well as* the push to turn the Internet into an entertainment-driven medium based on advertising, pay-per-use services, and e-commerce. The media conglomerates *have* to go that route in order to recoup their investments. A key problem, however, is that the use of *entertainment-oriented* content (especially their own) to turn the Internet into a *commercially viable* medium clashes with people's perceptions and uses of the Internet. Yet, because of their investments, media conglomerates cling to the belief that without content the Internet is—as Edgar Bronfman, CEO of Seagram Universal, said before the company was bought by France-based multimedia firm Vivendi—"a valueless collection of silent machines with grey screens" (cited in *Economist*, 2000a, p. 24).

The world is awash in information, though most of it is neither owned/controlled nor in conformity with the views of the media conglomerates. The notion that we need their content in order to make the Internet meaningful is highly questionable. The interest of the conglomerates is to *own* specific kinds of content that they believe will generate revenues sufficient to finance acquisition binges and bring about a commercially viable Internet (video-on-demand, subscriber-based services, television, etc.). However, it is not really necessary for BCE to own CTV or the *Globe and Mail* simply in order to distribute their content. Moreover, if it really wants to *own* content, BCE could go into the content-production business rather than buying out the content already produced by others. Indeed, to do so could actually *add* to the stock of information available to citizens. The conceit of such companies is the attempt to impose the entertainment-based model in opposition to the lengthy list of other activities actually preferred by users. There is a chasm between views of the Internet as an entertainment-driven medium versus the reality in which most people continue to use it as a means of communication, research, access to personally relevant information, and game play. It is clear that e-commerce, entertainment-oriented uses, and pay-per-use services play a rather marginal role. Nonetheless, the major multimedia players are seeking to change people's behaviour by bringing it into line with their preferred model.

The strategy of *walled gardens* was developed by AOL Time Warner but has subsequently been embraced by many of the media players (Marotte, 2000b, p. B3; Marotte and Damsell, 2000, p. B4). In the walled garden, content, journalism, and all organizational resources are organized in such a way as to keep users within designated zones for as long as possible through the creation of content and service menus, the organization of hyperlinks, the bias of search engines, network architecture, content synergies, elimination of alternative paths to somewhere else, and so on. The creation of enclosed spaces alters the orientation and role of users, media content (whether journalism or entertainment), and cyberspace altogether, as some potentials are amputated and others amplified. Instead of being driven by quality journalism, creativity, autonomy, or just pleasure, content and the organization of network capabilities and space are turned in on themselves and thus distort the experience of mediated communication in order to preserve the stock value of highly leveraged multimedia conglomerates. The drive to "repurpose content" and to extend "brand identity" across media platforms—which is the essence of the walled garden—requires that information, content, and news be subordinated to the maintenance of the organization as a whole. In an *information economy*, where information is the new wealth of nations, words/messages/content are double-edged swords: the anticipated source of great profits and human creativity, *as well as* threats to the market valuations of firms on which national, even global, information economies depend.

The role of content, images, and language in creating cybernetically enclosed worlds is plainly illustrated in the agreement between AOL Time Warner and Disney. The agreement requires Disney to deter users from using Disney's site and related hyperlinks as departure points for larger forays into cyberspace in order to be granted entry to AOL's "walled garden." Indeed, AOL can cancel the agreement if more than 25 percent of users visiting Disney's site subsequently leave the AOL "space" (Klein, 2000, p. E1). In essence, Disney assumes the role of an immigration officer, policing people's movement in and out of AOL space, rather than serving as a neutral inhabitant of cyberspace. These are subtle influences, layered in ways that imperceptibly encourage people to abandon a nomadic approach to cyberspace in favour of a more organized, structured, and confined approach. Of course, users *do* have choices, but the spaces in which such choices are made are explicitly designed to discourage them. As a result, approximately one-third of *all time* spent by Americans on the Internet is spent at AOL Time Warner–related sites (Walker, 2001, p. E1).

As media merge, organizational cultures collide. This has become particularly evident within AOL Time Warner as journalists from *Time* magazine or CNN, for example, are confronted with a management that appears to know a great deal more about Web page design than journalism. This has translated into pressures for journalists to give more thought to how their role fits into the larger organization, to learn a broader range of skills that can be used across the organization, and to consider ways to help AOL meet its aggressive financial goals. The impact on journalism has been detrimental in other ways as well. Staff and resources at CNN, for instance, were cut 10 percent, while the rest of AOL Time Warner suffered cutbacks that were about one-third that size (Anwin and Rose, 2001, p. B1; Beatty, 2001, p. B9). If nothing else, such actions reveal the declining priority of news within the overall organization.

These issues are not unknown in Canada. BCE's emergence as a dominant force across the Canadian mediascape must be considered in a light similar to AOL's role in the United States. BCE not only modelled its acquisitions of CTV and the *Globe and Mail* on the AOL Time Warner deal, but it also had no experience in journalism, news, or entertainment (despite taking over Canada's leading players in these fields). Moreover, BCE's history and organizational culture—again, like the fit between AOL and Time Warner—may pose threats to quality journalism and media freedoms. Throughout its history, Bell has demonstrated a rigid and bureaucratic approach to management, resisted the formation of labour unions, strictly supervised its labour force through intensive surveillance, and provided little autonomy to its employees.

The threat posed by BCE to journalism is unlikely to be expressed directly, though. It will more likely be filtered through screens of corporate culture and things left unsaid. Of course, BCE rejects such claims and it recently defended before the CRTC the ability of CTV and the *Globe and Mail* to operate autonomously and even to report critically on all aspects of BCE itself. BCE also proposed to create an elaborate set of internal corporate divisions meant to preserve editorial autonomy within its units (CTV, 2001, p. 9). CanWest Global makes a similar argument, especially in defence of its extensive cross-media ownership holdings in cities across the country (CanWest, 2000a, p. 13). Yet, both organizations also rejected the CRTC's proposal to adopt a code of ethics that would guarantee editorial autonomy within their organizations. CanWest had no choice but to reject such a proposal in light of its agreement with Hollinger, the company that owned the other 50 percent of the *National Post* at that time. The agreement stipulated that Hollinger inform CanWest of any stories or changes in editorial policies at the *National Post* that *could materially affect its interests* (CanWest, 2000b, p. 19).

The Machiavellian approach to language, power, and news evinced by BCE and CanWest reappears time and again in their responses to the CRTC's request to place information on the public record. At virtually every turn, they proclaim through the front door that they do not wish to control information and that media concentration is good for journalism but smuggle that same control back in through the back door by claiming that *certain* information is competitively sensitive and could harm *perceptions* of the companies and therefore their market valuations (CanWest, 2000a, p. 13; CTV, 2001, p. 9). In the face of such hypocrisy, it is unlikely that journalists in either organization will be either able or willing to engage in the kind of autonomous and critical journalism that CanWest and BCE insist is still possible.

NETSCAPES OF POWER AND BANDWIDTH KINGS

There is great irony in the fact that BCE's attempt to consolidate its influence across the Canadian mediascape occurred precisely around the time that its U.S. counterparts were abandoning key aspects of BCE's convergence policy. Throughout the last year or so, U.S. telecommunications firms abandoned their content- and television-centric view of the Internet in favour of another view that, while still marked by many of the same characteristics discussed above, tends instead to focus on data storage, the creation of Web-server farms, bandwidth, and *corporate* users.

This shift has been driven by a reassessment of broadband trials conducted in the United States, Canada, Europe, and elsewhere, and of the investments made by Microsoft, Rogers, and Aliant (the Maritime-based telephone conglomerate), among others, in Web-based television services. These trials revealed a distinct lack of demand and reluctance to pay for content, especially for video-type services. As a result, the American telecommunication companies jettisoned their plans to match up with Hollywood and the television industries. Whereas in the mid-1990s all the U.S.-based telephone companies formed alliances with Hollywood studios and announced plans to hardwire households to the information superhighway, by 2000 these initiatives had been junked in favour of more modest projects, such as high-speed Internet or DSL (Borland, 2000; FCC, 2001).

Perhaps this was not surprising. As stated at the outset of this chapter, telephone companies have been experimenting with visions of wired cities and full-scale convergence since the 1970s, but none of these efforts has borne fruit. The reasons for the failure have remained remarkably constant: uncertain demand; the fact that many people do not want the new media; and the economic reality that, in a media economy based on the finite resources of time, money, and attention, new media often simply cannibalize old media (e.g., if telephone companies enter the video-distribution market, rather than expand the total video market, they actually only divert people away from the corner video store) (Baldwin, McVoy, and Steinfield, 1996). This is worth considering in light of the fact that, in Canada over the last 15 years, the greatest area of expenditure growth has been telecommunications and computers, while the slowest area has been cable, video-on-demand, and pay-per-view (Statistics Canada, 1999). In other words, growth has been concentrated in bandwidth, connectivity, and computers, not in the areas on which the proponents of full convergence have pinned their hopes.

These trends suggest that connectivity and bandwidth, not content, might be king (Odlyzko, 2000). Other trends support this view, including the inability of most content-based Web sites (with the notable exceptions of the *Wall Street Journal* and a few porn sites) to sustain a pay structure, and the declining prospects for advertising as a mechanism to generate value in cyberspace as clickthrough rates (the number of times users click on advertising banners) plunge below 1 percent (*Economist*, 2000b, p. 54). The failure of many portals constructed by major conglomerates (e.g., Time Warner's Pathfinder, Disney's Go, Dreamworks' Den), as well as massive cutbacks, layoffs, advertising losses, and stock devaluations at other portals (e.g., Altavista, AOL, Canoe, Excite@Home, NBCInternet, Yahoo), all point in the same direction (CNET, 2001; *Economist*, 2000c, pp. 5–27; Marotte, 2000a, p. B3).

The Machiavellian view of the media is symptomatic of the larger role that has been placed on information and media in the so-called information society. In this view, media titans Jean Monty (head of BCE), Ted Rogers (CEO of Rogers Communications, the Aspers (heads of CanWest Global), and Pierre Karl Péladeau (head of Quebecor) claim a grand vision—a "projet de société," as Quebecor's Péladeau recently asserted. Yet, this is pure conceit, although one that derives from a fertile context in which the idea of the "information society" functions as a giant ruse that conceals the exercise of power while cloaking it in noble purposes.

Communication and information media are vital to a society, but they should *never* be thought of in terms of a "grand social project." To do so is to put them on the path of domination by those arrogant enough to believe that they can play such a transformative role in *building* the information society. From this vantage point, the transition to a "new economy" or an "information society" becomes a mere technical, or resource, problem. A much more viable—and modest—approach is to recognize that a democratic society rests upon democratically organized communications media. Starting from there, the principles of organization are relatively straightforward and stripped of the "will to power." They are (at least for starters) openness, transparency, the decentralization and distribution of power and resources to the ends of all networks, and, crucially, a nonmanipulative view of information and individuals.

QUESTIONS

1. Should people have symmetrical broadband connections to and from their homes? Why or why not?
2. Discuss some of the past and present barriers to media convergence and consider the prospects for convergence today and in the near future.
3. What would be necessary in order for the Internet to develop as a democratic means of communication?
4. Explain the impact of media ownership on the evolution of new media as a whole.
5. Why should the analysis of communication networks become a more central focus of communication research? Why has such analysis been neglected in the past?

WEB SITES

BCE: **http://www.bce.ca/**
Cisco Connection Online: **http://www.cisco.com/**
CRTC Index of Multiple Ownerships:
  http://www.crtc.gc.ca/Ownership/title_org.htm
National Broadband Task Force (Industry Canada): **http://broadband.gc.ca**
Nortel Networks: **http://www.nortelnetworks.com/index.html**
OneWorld Guides to Media Democracy:
  http://www.oneworld.org/guides/media_democracy/front.shtml/

NOTE

1. At the time of writing, @Home was on the verge of bankruptcy. Its financial troubles do not alter the fact that the kinds of policies it has adopted continue to serve as a model for the industry as a whole. Moreover, it is unlikely that a change in ownership would alter these policies in a material way.

REFERENCES

Abbatte, Janet. (1999). *Inventing the Internet*. Boston, MA: MIT.

Anwin, J., and Rose, M. (2001). Frays, both small and big, emerge after AOL, Time Warner merger. *Wall Street Journal*, p. B1.

Aufderheide, Patricia. (1990). After the Fairness Doctrine: Controversial broadcast programming and the public interest. *Journal of Communication, 40(3)*, 47–72.

Baldwin, Thomas F., D. Stephens McVoy, and Charles Steinfield. (1996). *Convergence*. London: Sage.

Beatty, S. (2001, January 18). 400 job cuts at CNN units. *Globe and Mail*, p. B9.

Borland, John. (2000, August 30). Phone companies' TV ambitions on the chopping block. Retrieved from http://news.cnet.com/

Brethour, Patrick. (2001a, March 21), PsiNet crisis seen as first shake-out. *Globe and Mail*, p. B1.

———. (2001b, March 23) Bill comes due for Web freebies. *Globe and Mail*, p. B1.

CanWest Global. (2000a). *Station group license renewal: Supplementary brief (schedule 5A) (Dec. 4)*. On file with CRTC Public Examination Room, Hull, Quebec.

———. (2000b). *Amended and restated partnership agreement between Global communications and NP Holdings Company and 3048510 Nova Scotia Company (Nov. 15)*. On file with CRTC Public Examination Room, Ottawa, Canada.

Cisco Systems. (1999a). *New revenue opportunities for cable operators from streaming media technology*. San Jose, CA: Author.

———. (1999b). *Controlling your network: A must for cable operators*. San Jose, CA: Author.

———. (2000a). *Cisco new world ecosystem for cable*. San Jose, CA: Author.

———. (2000b). *Company profiles—@Home*. San Jose, CA: Author.

CNET News.com. (2001). Write-offs point to content sector struggles. Retrieved from http://news.cnet.com/news/0-1005-202-4653582.html

Convergence Consulting Group. (2000). *Strategies and trends in the Canadian Internet/ISP market*. Toronto: Author.

CRTC (Canadian Radio-television and Telecommunications Commission). (2000). Transfer of effective control of CTV Inc. to BCE Inc. (December 2000-747). Retrieved from http://www.crtc.gc.ca/archive/Decisions/2000/DB2000-747e.htm

CTV. (2001). *Station group license renewal: Response to Commission's correspondence of Feb. 8*. On file with CRTC Public Examination Room, Hull, Quebec.

Damsell, Keith. (2001, January 12). CanWest needs a debt diet. *Globe and Mail*, p. M1.

Dixon, Guy. (2001, January 25). CanWest touts unit cross-promotion. *Globe and Mail*, p. B7.

Economist, The. (2000a, October 7), New media, old message (p. 24).

———. (2000b, August 19). The failure of new media (pp. 53–54).

————. (2000c, October 7). E-entertainment survey.

FCC (Federal Communications Commission). (2001). *Competition in the market for the delivery of video programming (7th annual report)*. Washington, DC: Author.

GAO (General Accounting Office, United States). (2000). *Telecommunications: Technological and regulatory factors affecting consumer choice of Internet providers* (Gao-O1-93). Retrieved from http://www.gao.gov/

@Home. (2000a). *1999 10K report filed with U.S. Securities and Exchange Commission*. retrieved from http://www.home.com/

————. (2000b). *Acceptable use* policy. Retrieved from http://www.home.com/sgppport/aup

Katz, J.E., and Philip Aspden. (1998). Internet dropouts in the USA: The invisible group. *Telecommunications Policy, 22*(4/5), 327–339.

Klein, Alec. (2000, November 3). Merger puts AOL's methods on trial. *Washington Post*, p. E1.

Lessig, Lawrence. (1999). *Code and other laws of cyberspace*. New York: Basic Books.

————. (2000). Forward to symposium on cyberspace and privacy. *Stanford Law Review, 52(5)*, 987–1003.

Marotte, Bertrand. (2000a, September 16). BCE raises bet on Web content. *Globe and Mail*, p. B3.

————. (2000b, November 25). Vidéotron CEO resigns post. *Globe and Mail*, p. B3.

Marotte, Bertrand, and Damsell, Keith. (2000, September 12). Content key to Monty's plan: BCE strategy aimed at being major player in multimedia world. *Globe and Mail*, p. B4.

McChesney, Robert. (2000). The Titanic sails on: Why the Internet won't sink the media giants. *Extra*! Retrieved from http://www.fair.org/extra/0003/aol-mcchesney.html

Netwizards. (1999). *Internet user survey*. Retrieved from http//:www.netwizards.org

Nortel Networks. (2000). *A policy-based approach to application optimized networking*. Cambridge, ON: Author.

Odlyzko, Andrew. (2000). Content is not king. *First Monday, 6*(2). Retrieved from http://firstmonday.dk/issues/issue6_2/odlyzko.index.html

Pew Research Center (2000). *Media report: Internet sapping broadcast news audience*. Retrieved from http://www.people-press.org/mediaOOrpt.htm

Reddick, Andrew. (2000). *The dual digital divide: The information highway in Canada*. Ottawa: Public Interest Advocacy Centre and Human Resources Development Canada. Retrieved from http://olt-bta.hrdc-drhc.gc.ca/download/oltdualdivideen.pdf

Statistics Canada. (1999). *Household Internet use survey*. Ottawa: Ministry of Supply and Services.

————. (2000). *Plugging in: The increase of household Internet use continues into 1999*. Retrieved from http://www.statcan.ca:80/english/research/56F0004MIE/56F0004MIE00001.pdf

Walker, Leslie. (2001, February 26). AOL Time Warner sites dominate Web traffic data. *Washington Post*, p. E1.

Winseck, Dwayne. (1998). *Reconvergence: A political economy of telecommunications in Canada*. Cresskill, NJ: Hampton Press.

19

Intellectual Property and Copyright Issues in the Global Economy

Daniel M. Downes
University of New Brunswick, St. John

INTRODUCTION

The word "convergence" is used a great deal these days in the context of globalization, international trade, and technological developments such as the Internet. As other chapters have pointed out, there are several related though distinct areas in which convergence is an important concept.

Convergence applied to technology and business creates a new environment. *Technological convergence* refers to the application of computers to a variety of processes that were once managed using other means; for example, the telephone was once a mechanical and analog device, but it is now both electronic and digital. *Business convergence* refers to such phenomena as phone companies, print media, and broadcasters merging with each other and with software companies and Internet service providers.

As information crosses borders and forms the basis of a new global economy, nations are compelled to adapt to rapid changes and to harmonize their domestic policies both to meet the requirements of global trade and to protect domestic interests abroad. This new environment fosters a third type of convergence, *regulatory convergence*. For example, Internet TV is regulated not by the Broadcasting Act but by certain aspects of the Copyright Act. Consequently, separate pieces of legislation are brought to bear on the same phenomenon. Regulatory convergence also indicates that the concepts of *intellectual property* and *copyright* are increasingly important.

A fourth dimension of convergence concerns the globalization of culture made possible by technological advances in travel, the migration of workers, and the spread of media. In this sense, formerly distinct activities belonging to different social groups are converging. From these different arenas of convergence, we can make two important observations: (1) convergence highlights the extent to which things we once considered distinct are increasingly interconnected, making it difficult to think about technologies, industries, and regulatory institutions without considering their global implications; (2) communication becomes increasingly important since cultural products—creative works—are the goods that drive the new media economy.

The global media scene raises a number of questions about the operation of the media in the new economy. Who owns the creative works we see, hear, or read? How are the rights of authors and other creators protected such that they will continue to inform, enlighten, and entertain us? Conversely, how do we guarantee that everyone has reasonable access to new information and new ideas? To what extent can we ensure that innovations will not be controlled by a few at the expense of the rest of society? Questions such as these are addressed in law and regulation by the concepts of intellectual property and copyright.

WHAT IS INTELLECTUAL PROPERTY?

Intellectual property is the result of intellectual or creative work that can be owned by an individual, institution, or company. A variety of creative products, including works of art, film, written texts, or even computer software, can be created and owned by individuals or companies. The main methods used to protect intellectual property are trademarks, patents, and copyright.

Trademarks ensure that a person or business is able to take advantage of commercial symbols. In particular, trademark holders protect a brand name, a company logo, or an advertising slogan. Trademarks are territorial and depend on local trademark use or reputation. A trademark does not protect a word (apple, for instance) unless that word is a symbol for a business or enterprise (Apple Computers). Such words can be used in different circumstances (the same name can be used for Atlas Van Lines and Atlas Catering) as well as in different places. A trademark must be registered in order to be protected; a trademark holder can lose his or her rights if the trademark is not used.

In contrast, *patents* give exclusive rights to inventors to demand payment in the form of royalties regarding the manufacture, use, or sale of their inventions. Rather than names or symbols, a patent applies to inventions—processes, machines, and combinations of matter. Patents protect an invention for up to 20 years.

Finally, *copyright* applies to creative rather than industrial or commercial forms of intellectual property. As soon as a person creates a work, it can be copyrighted without formal registration or payment. Copyright protects the rights of a creator for up to 75 years after the creator dies. One copyrights an original work of authorship, including writings, music, drawings, computer programs, dances, or movies. One cannot copyright ideas, concepts, facts, or knowledge. Ideas are not copyrightable. Only the expression of ideas such as the particular words on a page can be protected by copyright.

Why is the distinction between trademark, patent, and copyright important to media studies? Take computer applications as an example. In the United States, it was considered impossible to patent a computer program until 1990. Before that time, computer programs were considered devices that merely executed mathematical formulas. Such formulas are the product of mental processes and thus fall outside the range of patent-protected devices. A computer program is more like a document than a patentable device. As a particular kind of document, computer programs *could* benefit from a different form of protection. Since they are particular expressions of mathematical ideas, software has been, since 1976, subject to copyright protection. One might think that patents would be the most desirable form of protection for computer software. However, while patent protection is more specific, it does not provide the long period of protection available through copyright. In the United States, patents give an inventor 17 years of exclusive rights to benefit from the use, manufacture, or sale of an invention; in Canada, the period of exclusive rights is 22 years.

In addition, patents protect an invention from *reverse engineering*—the process of copying an innovation that performs the same function as an inventor's with a different underlying structure of computer instructions. In contrast, copyright does not prevent reverse engineering and affords protection only against duplication of those instructions (the computer code), the screen display, and the command sequence. Copyright does, however, protect software for up to a century, since protection lasts the lifetime of the youngest member of the development team plus 50 years.

It is important to realize that the extension of copyright protection to new expressions of creative work such as computer programs raises important questions about what constitutes intellectual property—that is, what kinds of creative work can be owned and exploited by private interests.

WHAT IS COPYRIGHT?

Canadian copyright law gives copyright owners the exclusive right to reproduce, distribute copies of, publicly perform, or display the original work of authorship—or create derivative works based on that original—for the duration of the author's life plus 50 years (70 years in the European Union and 75 in the United States). These rights have some important exceptions. In Canada, legislation and court decisions are not copyrightable, though other government documents can be copyrighted. In the United States, government works are not copyrightable, which means that anyone can use them. In Great Britain, government documents can be copyrighted. The American *fair use* provision, like Canadian *fair dealing*, gives researchers, educators, and libraries special privileges to use copyrighted material. The goal of copyright law is to encourage authors to invest effort in creating new works of art and literature, not to deny others legitimate access to those works.

To qualify for copyright protection, a work must be both *fixed* and *original*. There are many ways to fix a work in permanent form. It can be written down on paper or stored in a computer file. It can be recorded on audio- or videotape. It can be cast in bronze, built from cement, steel, and glass, or carved in wood. A professor's comments to a student or a colleague are not subject to copyright, but the same professor's written lectures are. In effect, all I have to do is write something on a piece of paper and it is protected by copyright. The originality of a work is more difficult to determine. The work must display a certain amount of creativity (a vague requirement that is hard to define), and it must be more than a copy of previously existing material.

For media students, copyright is an important concept. Copyright is the primary method for protecting ownership rights in a number of communication and information industries such as publishing, radio, television and film production, advertising, the music industry, and, since the 1970s, the computer software and video game industries. As all of these industries move toward integration as a result of their increasing reliance on computers, copyright legislation in many countries has had to adapt to rapid technological and industrial change.

Within the context of an emerging *new media economy*, large, hybrid organizations produce, distribute, and exhibit copyrighted material in a global information market. Copyright thus becomes a key issue as it becomes ever more difficult to control who copies and circulates images, texts, sound, and visual information over the Internet. The control and monitoring of legitimate and illegal copies of copyrighted material is important to those who create information and media content that might be redistributed in digital form. It is also an important issue for people who design and maintain Web pages whose content is often adapted or digitized from existing sources. Further, copyright is important to traditional copyright holders (e.g., publishers, record companies, or film studios) who want to protect their ability to exploit their copyrights when faced with new distribution systems such as the Internet. Such issues are not unique to the digital era. With the introduction of new technologies (e.g., radio, the VCR, and the personal computer), tensions have often arisen as the rights of copyright owners and creators are weighed against the rights of users to have fair access to information.

HISTORICAL CONTEXT OF COPYRIGHT

As a form of regulation, copyright is linked to the rise of a particular development in the history of media—the printing press. Before the invention of the printing press, books were difficult and expensive to produce. Further, literacy was not sufficiently widespread to support more than a limited market for books. As printing presses were established throughout 15th-century Europe, books became cheaper and more widely available. Consequently, there was a need to protect the right of authors and printers to profit from their written works.

Copyright was a reaction to the fact that the new print technology allowed the fixing of literary works in a tangible medium—books—that could be mass-produced on an unprecedented scale and then sold in the marketplace. Bettig (1996) compares the creation of a market for intellectual property like books to the actions of private owners who consolidated tangible property, such as the common lands in England: when governments decided what printing privileges to grant to whom, the literary "common" became subject to enclosure movements (pp. 6–17). Bettig's point is that, through copyright, intellectual works (the products of human creativity) were turned into commodities. Copyright transforms creative acts into exchangeable property or commodities.

To control the spread of politically dangerous material, the government of England granted a printing monopoly to a group of publishers. In 1557, Philip and Mary granted a charter for the incorporation of the Stationers' Company, thereby creating a monopoly over printing and publishing in Britain that lasted 150 years. Only members of the Stationers' Company could secure government licences to operate printing presses. Members policed themselves, as well as pirate operations, and received exclusive rights to titles or classes of books in exchange for loyalty to the Crown. As Bettig (1996) puts it, "Copyright laws emerged simultaneously with censorship out of the trade practices of this monopoly" (p. 18).

Intense lobbying and pressure from printers and authors, including the philosopher John Locke, prompted in the late 17th and early 18th centuries a series of reforms affecting the printing of books and pamphlets. The British Statute of Anne (1710)—the first real copyright law in the modern sense—granted authors the exclusive right to authorize the printing or reprinting of books for a limited number of years. This act established the main aspect of copyright protection we recognize today: authors and publishers should benefit from their published works by retaining the exclusive right to print and reprint books for a limited number of years, after which time the works pass into the public domain where all can benefit from them.

CANADIAN COPYRIGHT

Canada's Copyright Act, originally enacted in 1924, was not sufficiently broad to deal with subsequent technological advances in the media industries—advances that throughout the century affected all aspects of media production, distribution, storage, and exhibition. It was not until 1988, however, that the act was amended in a first phase of copyright reform.

When the Free Trade Agreement (FTA) came into effect in 1989, copyright in Canada was extended to works communicated to the public by means of telecommunication. Prior to this, the retransmission of television and radio signals by cable systems to private subscribers did not require copyright licensing or royalty payments. Following the extension of copyright to transmission via telecommunication, the nature of cable distribution changed to accommodate payment of royalty fees to copyright holders. In particular, Canadian cable operators became liable for the retransmission of U.S. broadcast, satellite, and cable signals and were incorporated into a compulsory licence system similar to that established in the United States a decade earlier.

A second phase of copyright reform was completed in 1997 when Bill C-32, an act to amend the Copyright Act, received royal assent and was proclaimed law. Still in progress is a third phase of copyright reform that began in the fall of 2001. This phase deals with issues relating to new media and digital technology, and with such questions as whether compulsory licence should apply to Internet-based transmissions.

As new trade agreements and new technologies indicate, copyright is a form of regulation that increasingly depends on international cooperation and coordination. Canadian copyright is therefore influenced by our trading relationships with other countries such as the United States.

AMERICAN COPYRIGHT

The United States Constitution recognized the importance of copyright and included authorization for a national copyright system. Thus, in 1790 the United States passed its first Copyright Act. U.S. copyright law has been amended frequently, often in reaction to new inventions such as photography and motion pictures. A major revision was the Copyright Act of 1909, which remained in effect until it was replaced by the Copyright Act of 1976. The 1976 statute continues to be the legal basis for copyright protection in the United States.

The 1976 Copyright Act extends copyright protection to all "works of authorship fixed in a tangible medium of expression," including computer programs, literature, music, drama, pantomimes, choreography, pictures, graphics, sculpture, motion pictures, audio-visual productions, and sound recordings. One major exemption to copyright protection is the body of work prepared by government employees, including court opinions, acts of Congress, and other government documents. Anyone may reproduce such government documents without obtaining permission.

The Digital Millennium Copyright Act (1998) addresses Internet issues. The act gives legal support to copy-protection systems, making it a crime to disable or circumvent antipiracy measures built into commercial software. It also reduces the liability of Internet service providers (ISPs) for copyright infringement in cases where they are simply transmitting other peoples' information over the Internet. In addition, the act limits some aspects of fair use by (1) raising the possibility that providing links from one Web site to another without prior permission may violate copyright, and (2) requiring ISPs to monitor user Web sites for compliance with copyright laws. Finally, webcasters are required to pay licence fees to record companies for disseminating recorded music on the Internet.

INTERNATIONAL ASPECTS OF COPYRIGHT

There are two international copyright conventions: the Universal Copyright Convention (signed by more than 50 countries), which protects works for the life of the author plus 25 years; and the Berne Convention, which protects works for life plus 50 years. These conventions provide minimum standards for protection and guidelines for enforcement because, in the end, copyright practices are the responsibility of each member state. They depend on national laws and enforcement (Bettig, 1996, p. 204).

The Berne Convention was the first and perhaps the most important international treaty concerning copyright law. First adopted in 1886, it has been revised several times since. Most countries of the world are members of the Berne Convention, including Canada (which joined in 1928) and the United States. The Berne Convention states that an author who is not a national of the country of origin of the work for which he or she is protected under the convention shall enjoy in that country the same rights as national authors. In short, an Italian author whose work is published in Canada enjoys the same protection as a Canadian author in Canada. The same holds true for protection of Canadian works in other countries.

Other international agreements have had an impact on copyright practices. In the Uruguay Round of the General Agreement on Tariffs and Trade (GATT) (1986–94), 123 countries agreed to reduce trade barriers in goods, services, and intellectual property. Trade liberalization was boosted further in the 1990s by the creation of a number of global institutions. The World Trade Organization (WTO), established in 1994 after the successful completion of the GATT's Uruguay Round, has two broad roles: (1) it serves as a kind of watchdog over the liberalized global trading order, and (2) it mediates in trade disputes between member states. Multilateral agreements sponsored by the WTO have furthered global integration by creating a new framework for international trade.

Led by the United States, the WTO moved to liberalize trade in services. In 1994, many countries of the world signed an important treaty dealing with copyright law. The Agreement on Trade-Related Aspects of Intellectual Property Rights (TRIPS) clarified several aspects of copyright law and strengthened copyright protections internationally. However, through its protection of intellectual property rights, the TRIPS has been critically evaluated as strengthening the dominance of transnational corporations and dominant economies (such as the U.S. economy) in the international trade of services, particularly business services (Castells, 2000, pp. 114–120). Further, in 1994 the governance forum of the Berne Convention—the World Intellectual Property Organization (WIPO)—extended copyright protection to digital formats, including the Internet and digital storage of music and film. The Digital Millennium Copyright Act was, in part, the product of U.S. compliance with the WIPO Copyright Treaty of 1996. Computer programs are protected as literary works under both the Berne Convention and the 1996 WIPO treaty.

Canada's current phase of copyright reform is, to a great degree, a response to the commitments made in signing the WIPO treaty. Canada is considering how to incorporate several WIPO provisions, including the establishment of exclusive rights to copyright owners who provide their works on-line and the prosecution of people who circumvent software protection. Canada is also considering whether to follow the United States and the European Union in extending the duration of copyright protection to life plus 75 years.

Compliance with international agreements has been a source of particular tension between the United States and countries in which copyright violation continues to be a serious problem (as in China even after the Chinese government signed agreements to combat copyright piracy). International agreements like the TRIPS and international organizations like WIPO and the WTO provide places where countries can lobby other governments to fight piracy more vigorously.

The justification for copyright protection is that some form of protection is needed to encourage the creation of new creative works. If there is no guarantee that creators will benefit financially from their labour, there is little incentive to create. On the other hand, copyright legislation is designed to place reasonable limits so that outdated works can be incorporated into new works.

HOW DOES COPYRIGHT WORK?

In Canada, when an individual creates an original work, it is automatically protected by copyright. The creator has neither to pay a fee nor to formally register the work for copyright protection to apply. Copyright owners generally mark their works with their name, the year in which the work was first published, and the copyright symbol ©. The copyright symbol, which is not obligatory in Canada or the United States for works published after 1989, indicates that a work is copyright protected.

A work that is created by an employee or a contractor generally belongs to the employer who commissioned the work (a magazine, for example), unless a written agreement states otherwise. However, even when a creator gives or sells copyright to someone else, the creator still retains *moral rights* to the work unless the creator waives these rights. Moral rights refer to a creator's right to have the integrity of a work respected. Consequently, while a creator may sell or transfer the copyright (the right to benefit materially) to another person, he or she still maintains the moral right to prevent anyone—even the new copyright holder—from changing the work without permission. In addition, the copyright owner cannot use the work in ways that might damage the creator's reputation. Canadian artist Michael Snow prevented the Toronto Eaton Centre from decorating one of his sculptures for Christmas even though the centre owned the work.

A creator cannot transfer his or her moral rights to another individual but can waive these rights when transferring copyright. Moral rights exist for the lifetime of the creator, plus 50 years, and pass on to a creator's heirs even if they do not inherit the copyright itself.

Extent of Copyright Protection

Rights established by the Canadian Copyright Act give copyright owners control over who can copy their creations as well as over the manner in which the works are used. Creators are entitled to benefit from their works financially, whether their work is reprinted (as in a short story or an academic article republished in a new collection) or even photocopied (as in a page from a novel).

Copyright owners may not want to use all their rights themselves; indeed, they may not be able to manage all aspects of copyright. So, copyright law permits a copyright owner to enter into agreements that allow others to use some or all of the owner's rights in return for payment. These transactions are called *copyright licences*. Licensing greatly increases the ability of the copyright owner to make money from the work. An author or creator can license different aspects of the work; for example, one publisher can hold the hardcover rights to a book, another publisher the softcover rights, and a production company the film rights. Licensing also binds the copyright owner to the licensee for a defined period after which the copyright owner can terminate the licence.

The copyright owner can also sell the copyright entirely. This is called an *assignment*. Writer Edward Lear sold the rights to his work for £125 and lived to see his publisher profit from 19 editions of his work without receiving another penny in royalties. Similarly, Paul McCartney tried to buy the publishing rights to the early Beatles song catalogue but was outbid by Michael Jackson, who now enjoys the material benefit whenever the songs are reproduced. Recently, recording artists such as David Bowie and Rod Stewart sold the rights to their song catalogues as public offerings, creating the opportunity for people to buy shares in the artists' royalties.

As noted, a copyright owner may not be able to manage all aspects of licensing. There are times when people can use copyrighted works without having to negotiate a licence with the copyright owner, provided they pay a set fee, called a royalty, determined by the government. This is known as a *compulsory licence*. The U.S. Copyright Act of 1976 gives cable television systems and satellite television systems this type of compulsory licence. It also grants a compulsory licence to record companies to collect royalties once the copyright owner has authorized someone to make a recording of his or her music. The determination of fair royalty rates is one of the functions of the Canadian Copyright Board. In the United States, royalty amounts are set by Copyright Arbitration Royalty Panels set up by the U.S. Copyright Office.

In general, anyone who wants to make a copy of a written or visual work must still ask the permission of the copyright owner and pay royalties as requested. Since 1988, the Canadian Copyright Act has allowed collectives such as SOCAN (Society of Composers, Authors and Music Publishers of Canada) and CANCOPY (Canadian Copyright Licensing Agency/Canadian Reprography Collective) to collect royalties and licensing fees that are distributed among copyright holders. Recently, the Copyright Board has extended the right of SOCAN to collect royalties for music delivered over the Internet as long as the music is stored on a server in Canada. The Department of Canadian Heritage, Public Works and Government Services Canada, and Industry Canada created an Electronic Copyright Fund ($3 million over three years) to help copyright collectives streamline the management of rights for Internet transmissions.

Duration of Copyright Protection

In Canada, copyright generally exists for the life of a creator plus 50 years after the end of the calendar year of the creator's death. In the United States, the Sonny Bono Copyright Extension Act of 1998 extended the duration of copyright protection to 75 years from the previous 50-year limit established in the 1976 Copyright Act. The Bono Act was the result of intense lobbying from film companies (including Disney, which was about to lose its copyright on Mickey Mouse).

INFRINGEMENT OF COPYRIGHT

An infringement of a copyright is the reproduction, distribution, performance, or display of any copyrighted work without permission of the copyright owner or without a compulsory licence. Infringement includes plagiarism (unauthorized reproduction). The test for this form of infringement is subjective: would an ordinary observer consider the second version "substantially similar" to the copyrighted work? Copyright violation cases more often involve the unauthorized distribution of copyrighted material.

Fair Use and Fair Dealing as Exceptions to Infringement

It can be argued that copyright serves a dual purpose. While it is necessary to protect the rights of creators, it is also necessary to establish principles of use so that people have reasonable access to copyrighted materials. In some cases, copying does not damage the interests of a copyright owner. For example, a passage from a novel quoted in a book review can benefit the copyright holder.

Recent copyright legislation in both the United States and Canada makes it possible for users to copy parts of works for study in the classroom, for inclusion in academic publications, or for incorporation in artistic works as long as these are not resold. As noted earlier, this important exception to the rule of copyright infringement is known as fair use in the United States and fair dealing in Canada and the United Kingdom. It is through these concepts that broader social interests are protected against unfair or unreasonable control of creative works. Remember, one of the purposes of copyright is to encourage continued production of creative works for the benefit of society. An overly stringent application of copyright protection would deny society the benefit of the creative works.

Fair dealing allows copying of portions of copyrighted material for such purposes as private study, research, criticism, comment, and teaching, even without permission of the copyright owner. The U.S. Supreme Court has ruled that it is also fair use to use a home videocassette recorder to make copies of television programs and movies for later viewing. An example of fair use that is of particular relevance to university students involves copying. A student who copies a limited amount of published materials is not in violation of copyright, whereas a copy shop violates the law if it copies a textbook without paying royalties. In the United States, this principle was established in 1991 when Kinko's lost a legal challenge launched by the publishing industry. The result was that it now costs more for a university to prepare selections of readings for use in its courses because the copy shop must obtain the rights to copy.

MASS MEDIA AND COPYRIGHT PROTECTION

The main issue concerning media and copyright involves the question of who owns a creative work and can thus control its production, reproduction, sale, and use. One of the main arguments for copyright is that such protection provides an incentive for the promotion of creative work. As works are adapted from one medium to another (a filmed version of a stage play or a novel), two issues arise: unlawful copying of a work (plagiarism) and unlawful distribution of a work (piracy). These issues are played out in the distinction between the creator's right to profit from his or her creations and the public's right to have access to creative works.

Originality is a cornerstone of copyright law. So too is the concept of public domain, which comprises elements that are ineligible for private ownership. In media, the tension between originality and public domain appears often. For example, with the advent of motion pictures, a number of authors of plays, stories, and magazine articles attempted to sue film studios and production companies for making movies that were conspicuously close to the source material. By the early 1940s, courts decided that many of the broad outlines and ideas expressed in dramatic works were what Judge Leon Yankwich called "*scènes à faire*—the common stock of literary composition—cliches [*sic*]—to which no one can claim literary ownership" (cited in Litman, 1990, pp. 987–988). A far different outcome was seen in a famous case involving former Beatle George Harrison, who was successfully sued for unconsciously plagiarizing the Chiffons' hit "He's So Fine" in his 1970 song "My Sweet Lord."

Throughout the history of copyright, protection has been extended to new forms of authorship. In the United States after 1976, it became possible for computer companies to sue each other on the basis of copyright infringement, since protection was extended to computer applications as expressions of authorship in tangible form. These cases tended to centre on the *look and feel* of a computer application or the user interfaces it employs. During this period, we see cases that illustrate how copyright is the backbone of the media industries.

A watershed case is *Sony Corp. of America v. Universal Studios Inc.* (otherwise known as the Betamax case). This case hinged on the question of whether viewers infringed on copyright by videotaping programs for later viewing. While representatives of Universal Studios argued that home taping would open the doors for further loss of control of copyright (a situation that would arise through continued technological development), the U.S. Supreme Court ruled that home taping fell within the conditions of fair use (Major, 1998, p. 95). While Canada has no equivalent to the Betamax case, tacit acceptance of the practice of home taping would make it difficult, if not impossible, for a copyright holder to launch a successful case in Canada (Vaver, 1996, p. 76). Indeed, Canada eventually placed a tax on blank video cassettes so that a fund could be created to compensate copyright holders in case home taping occurred. No such tax dedicated exists in the United States. Bettig (1996) argues that it is an inevitable consequence of the copyright system that copyright owners will seek to impede innovation: "The general logic of the copyright system drives copyright owners to seek compensation *from all new forms of use* [italics added]. The logic of copyright also determines that intellectual property owners consistently realize such compensations" (p. 160). In the next section, we will look at two recent examples of how copyright holders use their power to either forestall or gain compensation from new forms of media use.

DIGITAL MEDIA AND COPYRIGHT PROTECTION

One of the most common forms of copyright infringement is the creation of unauthorized copies of an original work. As we have seen, the traditional media industries have been quick to challenge technological innovations on the grounds that new methods of copying and distributing information pose a threat to revenues earned through the exercise of copyright privileges. Computers have added some recent complications, such as the temporary copies in packet buffers or on screens, and copies left on backup tape. It is often assumed that transfer of information via e-mail or the Internet is another form of the kind of fair use described in the Betamax case. Copyright holders take issue with that assumption. As technological developments such as tape recorders, VCRs, photocopiers, and computers have made it easier for people to copy information without paying for it, policymakers have responded with policy and legal solutions that include making unauthorized copying a crime, making copying more difficult, and appealing to people not to take advantage of creators by denying them money or recognition for their creative work.

The illegal copying and distribution of works is called *piracy*. In the 1990s, in the United States commercial copyright violation involving more than ten copies and a value of over $2500 (U.S.) was made a crime. In one case, an operator of a pirate bulletin board system (BBS) was acquitted because he did not charge users; however, Congress amended the law to tighten restrictions applying to Internet service providers (Digital Millennium Copyright Act). Industry players and copyright holders have also lobbied to protect their rights to exploit the creative works under their control. The Motion Picture Association of America (MPAA) fought the manufacture and sale of VCRs for commercial use as well as the practice of home taping of music. However, their attempts to block the technology were unsuccessful. Home copying of television broadcasts is not prohibited under both the Canadian and U.S. Copyright Acts; copying copyrighted material from one VCR to another is prohibited.

U.S. media companies are particularly concerned about countries that do not acknowledge international copyright agreements. Unauthorized recordings of music on compact discs, copies of computer software, and videocassettes of movies are often available at very low prices in these countries. The result is a black market in which American copyright owners, who receive royalty payments only from authorized copies, lose billions of dollars annually in sales and royalties. The U.S. film industry has responded by pressuring law-enforcement agencies to enforce copyright infringements by commercial pirates.

New media in Canada are confronting copyright issues of their own. In 1999, the Canadian Radio-television and Telecommunications Commission (CRTC) issued an order that

> exempts from regulation, without terms or conditions, all new media broadcasting undertakings that operate in whole or in part in Canada. New media broadcasting undertakings are those undertakings that provide broadcasting services delivered and accessed over the Internet. (CRTC, 1999)

The CRTC has refrained from regulating the Internet as a broadcasting technology on the grounds that new media complement rather than replace traditional media services. More specifically, the Internet elaborates on, rather than duplicates, the information provided by television programming.

While the Internet may not be considered a threat to traditional broadcasting within Canada, the global nature of the Internet creates jurisdiction issues. The Copyright Act applies to copyright protection in Canada, but it does not have power to deal with infringements that occur outside our borders. However, where broadcasting regulation fails to protect the interests of the traditional copyright holders in the new media economy, copyright steps in. This point is illustrated by the case of the Internet company iCraveTV.com, which streamed (i.e., broadcast over a Web site) 17 television signals without paying royalties or licensing fees to the copyright holders of the programs. The company collected over-the-air signals with an antenna and broadcast the signals over the Internet. Not only is the practice of retransmission allowed under Canada's Copyright Act, but it is the very foundation of the cable industry in Canada. Signals that are piped to private subscribers are not considered *public broadcasts*. Although cable operators are subject to compulsory licence, iCravetv.com argued that it was exempt from compulsory licence under the CRTC's 1999 order on Internet broadcasting. Even so, it offered to pay a tariff to be administered by a copyright collective. The offer was rejected.

The problem was that iCraveTV.com's Web site could be accessed by users outside Canada even though the Web site had a sign-in mechanism that was supposed to limit access to Canadian users. U.S. copyright holders (including Twentieth Century Fox Film Corporation, the Disney Corporation, ABC, CBS, NBC, and the National Football League), as well as the CBC in Canada, sued iCraveTV.com. The basis of the suits was that iCraveTV.com was guilty of copyright infringement and posed a real threat to their ability as content owners to exploit their copyrights (Stern, 2000).

The Internet company's lawful activities in Canada could offer no protection against charges of copyright infringement made by U.S. copyright holders. The case was settled when iCraveTV.com agreed to shut down operations should the plaintiffs drop their suits. The Canadian Association of Broadcasters has since lobbied for amendments to the Copyright Act specifically banning Internet streaming of television signals. At the same time, BCE is planning to use its Sympatico Internet service to stream content from its recently acquired television network, CTV. The tensions between Internet-based media and other media industries are thus not likely to be resolved soon.

On another front, the Recording Industry Association of America, representing Sony, Universal, BMG, Warner, and EMI, launched a $6.8-billion (U.S.) lawsuit against MP3.com—an AOL subsidiary—for selling digitized music over the Internet without paying royalties to the record companies (Anderson 2000). In another lawsuit, the same assembly of dominant players used the courts to shut down Napster.com, a company that facilitates the trading of music files across the Internet. Napster provides users with free software for exchanging MP3 files and acts as a hub for users to connect with each other in a point-to-point transfer of music files. To use the example of home taping, Napster would be the digital equivalent of two friends meeting somewhere to trade cassette tapes of their favourite music. Because there was no sale involved, Napster hoped to invoke the fair use concept in its defence. Napster is experiencing a temporary reprieve while the case is in appeal, but it seems unlikely that the company will survive the legal attacks from the big players.

According to the Canadian Copyright Board, however, Napster does not violate Canadian copyright law because its server is located outside Canada. Further, because Canadian copyright legislation has a provision whereby copyright collectives (e.g., the Canadian Private Copying Collective) collect fees on audio recording material on behalf of Canadian copyright holders, Napster's activity does not give rise to the problem of noncompensation. In the U.S. case, Napster agreed to charge for downloads, even though the basis of its case was that the site simply facilitated the trading of music files between individuals and was thus innocent of copyright violation. Charging for downloads meant that Napster now had something it could give to the big record companies—a percentage of the download fee. The response of musical artists to the Napster case run the gamut from heavy metal rock group Metallica, which sued Napster for copyright violation, to Canadian recording star Alanis Morissette, who was a major shareholder in MP3.com.

COPYRIGHT—GOOD OR BAD?

What are the benefits and dangers associated with copyright protection in the global economy? To answer this question, we must evaluate the three main arguments invoked to justify strong copyright legislation and enforcement: (1) copyright protects the rights of individual creators by ensuring some compensation for them and for their heirs; (2) copyright provides the necessary incentives for creators to continue to produce works of art; and (3) copyright benefits all of society by ensuring the continued creation of creative works.

From this perspective, copyright protects individual creators from those who would deprive them of the fruits of their work. In the digital age, copying becomes easier and policing more difficult. Jack Valenti, president of the MPAA, has responded to this reality by arguing that stronger intellectual property laws are needed to protect media against challenges posed by the Internet. Underpinning Valenti's aggressive attempts to prosecute copyright violation cases is the notion that piracy threatens the incentive structure on which the creative arts depend and thus has the potential to destroy the market.

Let's deal with each of these claims separately. First, does copyright actually protect the rights of individual creators? It *can* but the fact of the matter is that, ever since the first copyright act became law, protection has been more likely to benefit those who publish and distribute creative works than those who create them. This is because individual creators, in order to make their work widely available, frequently assign or licence that work to large enterprises. As a result, the most powerful copyright owners are large corporations whose employees are paid to produce works whose copyrights the corporations own. Such companies lobby for strong protections. So, while copyright *could* protect starving artists and their families, it frequently protects corporate profits.

If copyright protects business interests, does it actually promote new creative work? Again, the answer is not really. Indeed, because copyright protection is so extensive and broad, it can actually impede new work. Copyright vests within its holders, often large corporations, the right to be protected against infringement by others. This means that the disposition of ideas contained within *commercial activities* is afforded the same protection as the disposition of ideas contained in an *individual creative work*. For example, the Visa symbol is not only a trademark, it is also a copyrighted work of art. As a result, Visa is not merely protected against the use of its name by other companies operating in the same field, it is also protected against any company—competitor or not—from using the same *disposition of ideas* at all. The corporate interest in the form of expression allows the largest rights holders to police the activities of others, thereby limiting creativity.

This leads us to the third argument for strong copyright, namely that it benefits society. As already mentioned, those who argue for strong copyright protections talk about protecting starving artists from plagiarists and pirates. However, once we realize that copyright actually protects the interests of copyright owners (who are as likely to be big businesses as individual artists or authors), we can think of the debate over copyright as a tension between private interests (copyright owners) and society (the public domain). The problem is that the concept of protection for life plus 50 years provides almost perpetual protection to commercial rather than artistic work. Further, since such work is frequently produced by employees, copyright belongs to the employer and no benefit goes to the creator's heirs. In the end, copyright protection does not provide incentive to produce. Indeed, it is absurd to think that computer software needs protection for up to a century or that industry needs to amortize profits over a long period of time in order to innovate (Vaver, 1996, pp. 69–76). The lengthy protection period actually makes it easy for the corporation to avoid innovation and to prevent others from innovating in the same area.

It can be argued that copyright is not about creativity. In fact, it restricts the public sphere, which is the true source of innovation. Intellectual property jeopardizes the public domain as well as the principle of an "intellectual commons" or sphere of exchange of ideas in which we all share equally. Of course, the situation is not entirely bleak. It can and frequently does happen that when too many similar works appear (as in the case of narrative elements in films), the courts can assign the raw materials of authorship to the "commons" of the public domain, thereby leaving them for all to use (Litman, 1990, pp. 1022–1023). But the very fact that ideas and forms of expression can become so common that no one can claim ownership of them indicates precisely the extent to which copyright is an attempt to impose control over the public sphere.

CONCLUSION

The concepts of intellectual property and copyright help us to understand how media operate in the context of technological, business, and regulatory convergence. Copyright balances the need to compensate creators so that they will create new works with the rights of the rest of society to benefit from works that have been created in the past. Technological advances affect copyright in a number of ways. As new forms of expression emerge, copyright protection is extended to new media. At the same time, copyright holders who operate in older media contexts are often quick to launch court challenges in order to impede technological innovation. When such tactics fail, copyright holders develop means to exploit their copyright in new contexts.

As industries, technologies, and regulations converge, it might seem that information and creative work will inevitably be controlled by a few private interests at the expense of the rest of society. However, in the Canadian and British traditions at least, copyright has always tried to balance the rights of creators and owners with the broader needs of society.

QUESTIONS

1. In what ways do new technologies of communication challenge existing intellectual property protections?

2. To what extent is it possible to protect against copyright violations on the Internet?

3. Whose interests are served by the extension of copyright protection to new forms of creative expression?

4. What are the copyright implications of trade liberalization and globalization?

5. Is copyright a good thing? Give reasons for your answer.

WEB SITES

Canadian Intellectual Property Office: **http://cipo.gc.ca/**
CANCOPY: **http://www.cancopy.com/**
Copyright Board of Canada: **http://www.cb-cda.gc.ca/**
United States Copyright Office: **http://www.lcweb.loc.gov/copyright/**
World Intellectual Property Organization: **http://www.wipo.org/**

REFERENCES

Anderson, Lessley. (2000, January 31). To beam or not to beam: MP3.com is being sued by the major record labels—does the digital download site stand a chance? *Industry Standard*. Retrieved from http://www.thestandard.com/

Bettig, Ronald. (1996). *Copyrighting culture: The political economy of intellectual property*. Boulder, CO: Westview Press.

Castells, Manuel. (2000). *The rise of the networked society* (2nd ed.). Oxford: Blackwell.

CRTC. (1999, May 17). *CRTC won't regulate the Internet* [News release]. Retrieved from http://www.crtc.gc.ca/ENG/NEWS/RELEASES/1999/R990517e.htm

Litman, Jessica. (1990, Fall). The public domain. *Emory Law Journal, 39*(4), 965–1023.

Major, April M. (1998). Copyright law tackles yet another challenge: The electronic frontier of the World Wide Web. *Rutgers Computer and Technology Law Journal, 24*, 75–105.

Stern, Christopher. (2000, March 6). Court ruling shuts down iCraveTV.com. *Variety*.

Vaver, David. (1996). Rejuvenating copyright. *Canadian Bar Review, 75*, 69–76.

20

Privacy and New Media

Valerie Steeves
Carleton University

> *Conceal your life.*
> —*attributed to Neocles, father of Epicure, 3rd century B.C.*

In her novel *The Fountainhead*, author Ayn Rand wrote:

> Civilization is the progress toward a society of privacy. The savage's whole existence is public, ruled by the laws of his tribe. Civilization is the process of setting man free from man. (Rand, 1943)

A short 56 years later, a much-read article in *The Economist* argued that privacy is dead. New communication technologies, and the surveillance society that flows from them, mean that individuals' commercial transactions, travel arrangements, academic grades, health information, financial records, and personal preferences will all be recorded and accessed by a growing legion of bureaucrats, employers, spouses, insurance companies, marketers, and researchers. *The Economist*'s best advice? "Get used to it" ("End of Privacy," 1999).

And yet we have a long history of rejecting surveillance. In 1763, after Englishman John Wilkes criticized a speech given by King George III, the king ordered his agents to break into Wilkes' home and seize his private diaries from his desk drawer. Professor Jeffrey Rosen points out that the king's actions directly influenced the leaders of the American Revolution: "The writers of the US constitution drafted the Fourth Amendment banning unreasonable searches and seizures of persons, houses, papers and effects, with Wilkes' house and Wilkes' papers in mind" (cited in McDougall, 1999, p. 9).

The balance between the individual's right to a private life and the ability of others to invade that privacy is an old and established one. Why is our privacy so beset, therefore, at the beginning of the new millennium? Part of the answer lies in the enabling effects of new technologies. When Oregon police wanted to investigate whether or not Danny Kyllo was growing marijuana in his triplex apartment, for example, they didn't have to break down Kyllo's door. Instead, they sat in a car and pointed a thermal radiation imager at the Kyllo residence. The scanner, which detects heat radiation and projects an image based on it, was able to "see" growing lights located in the apartment. Unfortunately, the same scanner could also "see" people sitting at the kitchen table, sleeping in bed, or taking a shower in any of the three apartments in the triplex.

Ordinarily, police are required to obtain a warrant before they enter and search private property. A search warrant is given only if a justice is convinced that the officers have reasonable and probable grounds to support their suspicions that a crime has occurred. In the Kyllo case, however, the Ninth Circuit Court of Appeals decided that no warrant was necessary. The court argued that the emissions were "waste heat" and, as with any garbage Kyllo may have left at the side of the curb on garbage day, others were free to sift through it if they wanted (*USA v. Kyllo*).[1]

The privacy balance has changed because new technologies like thermal imaging allow others to watch us without physically intruding in our lives. Your local electronics store sells, for less than $100, miniature cameras that can be placed on the shoes of young boys so they can look up women's dresses.[2] The prankish nature of this practice becomes much more unsettling when it is used by pornographers, as it has been in Toronto, to create pornographic movies featuring images of real Catholic schoolgirls who unwittingly have had their pictures taken in the same manner.[3]

Stories about Web tracking are legion. In 2001, Privacy Council CEO Gary Clayton demonstrated how, once a visitor logs onto a Web site, Web bugs can be used to surreptitiously download information from his or her hard drive within minutes. During Clayton's demonstration, a bug extracted all 1800 telephone numbers in his electronic address book and copied a file containing a congressional memorandum (U.S. Congressional Privacy Caucus, 2001). In the off-line world, advertisers scan passing cars to see which radio station drivers are listening to, and people attending the Super Bowl have their faces scanned, digitized, and cross-matched against a database of "criminals."[4] With all due respect to *The Economist*, it's a lot to get used to.

NOTHING TO HIDE

Proponents of this new wave of surveillance argue that the loss of privacy is justified because these practices reduce crime, cut costs, and fuel the information economy. When the Employment Insurance Commission routinely crossmatches its database against the customs database, for example, it is doing so in order to catch "cheaters" who collect unemployment insurance benefits when they are out of the country. Although the federal privacy commissioner argued that the practice should not be allowed because it treats all the people in the database like criminals (Privacy Commissioner of Canada, 1999), the government has continued crossmatching because it is cost-effective and efficient. After all, the argument goes, travellers do not have to worry if they have nothing to hide.

The argument that citizens do not need privacy if they have nothing to hide warrants close examination. To that end, let's look at the hypothetical case of Jo, a middle-aged mother of three who is surfing the Net. Jo has heard that her on-line actions are not private and that her virtual travels can be tracked and recorded. Since she has nothing to hide, she doesn't worry about it. The first Web site she visits is a children's site. Her oldest child is turning ten in a few weeks, and she is looking for ideas for his birthday party. The Web site asks her to reveal her child's age, city of residence, and hobbies. The information is innocuous enough, so she provides it and gets a list of games to consider.

Since the advent of the World Wide Web, marketers have become aggressive collectors of children's personal information, offering "prizes", audio files, and video clips to children who fill out on-line surveys. Marketers have consistently argued that the practice does not harm children. However, in 1996, television journalist Kyra Phillips contacted Donnelly & Sons, the largest consumer data firm in North America. Donnelly & Sons tracks the consumer patterns of over 90 percent of North American households, and its huge databases store electronic information about, among other things, children. For $277, Phillips was able to buy a list of the names and addresses of over 5000 children in the Los Angeles area, even though she used the name of a notorious child killer when she placed the order.

Jo's next visit is to a site with information on weight loss. She figures no one else would be interested in the fact that she has 40 pounds to lose. Once again, she is wrong—marketers are very interested. In 1999, a Canadian candy manufacturer obtained a membership list from a weight-loss organization. They used the list to mail candy samples to the dieters at times when they thought they were most likely to go off their diets.

Jo follows a link from the weight-loss site to a site containing sexual advice for larger women. It might be embarrassing if her children were to walk in, but, really, it's no one's business. In 1999, a man was being treated for diminished sexual potency at a medical clinic. When he arrived home from work one day, he found his mailbox stuffed with direct mail from drug companies advertising remedies for impotence. He felt more than embarrassed; he felt exposed and humiliated.

Jo clicks on a discussion forum for women experiencing sexual problems after a mastectomy. She posts a message about her experiences with cancer and shares her fear that her illness might return. When she applies for a job a few weeks later, her prospective employer does a standard Web search and pulls up her message. Web searches on employees are becoming standard practice. More than half of the *Fortune* 500 companies surveyed in 1999 admitted that they use medical information (often without the employee's knowledge) to help them decide whom to hire, fire, and promote.

Jo's story tells us that when we are watched, we become vulnerable to embarrassment, humiliation, manipulation, and discrimination. The right to privacy is not about secrecy; it's about autonomy. The right to a private life enables us to enter into relationships of trust and to enjoy a sense of freedom. In the words of Justice La Forest of the Supreme Court of Canada, "[privacy] is at the heart of liberty in a modern state. Grounded in man's physical and moral autonomy, privacy is essential for the well-being of the individual" (*R. v. Dyment*, 1988).

This chapter will examine different definitions of the right to privacy and explore ways in which Canada and other countries are regulating invasive practices. Throughout the chapter, we will examine how the digital environment has changed our experience of privacy and identify the major stakeholders in the emerging privacy debate.

DEFINITIONS OF PRIVACY

The most oft-quoted definition of privacy was popularized in 1890 by Samuel Warren and Louis Brandeis. Warren and Brandeis were concerned about the ways in which new technologies and business practices were changing the modern experience of a private life. They were specifically concerned that journalists were using recently invented photographic equipment to take pictures of private persons and publish them:

> Recent inventions and business methods call attention to the next step which must be taken for the protection of the person, and for securing to the individual what Judge Cooley calls the right "to be let alone." Instantaneous photographs and newspaper enterprise have invaded the sacred precincts of private and domestic life, and numerous mechanical devices threaten to make good the prediction that "what is whispered in the closet shall be proclaimed from the housetops." For years, there has been a feeling that the law must afford some remedy for the unauthorized circulation of portraits of private persons; and the evil of the invasion of privacy by the newspapers, long keenly felt, has been but recently discussed. (Warren and Brandeis, 1890)

Warren and Brandeis's definition of privacy as the "right to be let alone" was not a legalistic one. Their concerns grew from their own experience of personal and social relationships. Like many today, they worried that new technologies were invading established social boundaries and that these invasions were fuelled by the commercial value of the information obtained. Underpinning their argument that commerce should not be allowed to overrun the right to privacy was their strong belief in the "inviolate personality" of the individual.

As new communication technologies continued to develop, others built on Warren and Brandeis's vision. During its seminal public consultation on privacy rights and new technologies, the House of Commons Standing Committee on Human Rights and the Status of Persons with Disabilities concluded:

> Classically understood as "the right to be let alone," privacy in today's high-tech world has taken on a multitude of dimensions. According to certain privacy experts, it is the right to enjoy private space, to conduct private communications, to be free from surveillance, and to respect the sanctity of one's body. To the ordinary Canadian, it is about control—the right to control one's personal information and the right to choose to remain anonymous. (Canada, 1997, appendix I, p. 1)

Choosing between these definitions is not a neutral process. As the Standing Committee noted, "experience has shown us that the way you ask the question will often determine the type of response you get" (Canada, 1997, p. 33). The current ways to "ask the question" reflect four different ways of looking at privacy:

- privacy as a human right;
- privacy as an essential part of the democratic process;
- privacy as a social value; and
- privacy as data protection.

1. Privacy as a Human Right

The dangers inherent in the modern nation-state's ability to seize information about citizens and use it to invade their private lives was exemplified by the Nazi government. When German forces took towns during World War II, the first buildings they seized were often the town halls; Gestapo officers would then search through records to identify the whereabouts of Jewish residents so they could be deported to extermination camps.

The postwar international community responded in 1948. Denouncing the "disregard and contempt for human rights" that resulted in the "barbarous acts" of the 1930s and 1940s, the General Council of the United Nations adopted the Universal Declaration of Human Rights in 1948. Article 12 of the Declaration proclaims that no one "shall be subjected to arbitrary interference with his privacy, family, home or correspondence." This right to privacy, and the other human rights proclaimed in the Declaration, reflected the United Nations' belief that "the inherent dignity ... of all members of the human family is the foundation of freedom, justice and peace in the world" (United Nations, 1948).

In the international arena, Canada took a leadership role in establishing privacy as a fundamental human right. Canadian John Humphrey was one of the authors of the 1948 Declaration; in 1976, Canada ratified the International Covenant on Civil and Political Rights (United Nations, 1966), which contains the same guarantee of privacy that is set out in the Declaration. However, within Canada, the protection of privacy as a human right is patchy at best. The Canadian Charter of Rights and Freedoms does not include an express right to privacy, in spite of the fact the federal government suggested to first ministers that it be included as early as 1979. The Supreme Court of Canada has written a limited right to privacy into the Charter,[5] but the tests it has developed make it unlikely that this limited right will be able to deal with new invasive technologies.

For example, the Supreme Court has ruled that section 8 of the Charter, which protects everyone from unreasonable search and seizure, includes the right to be secure from such a search when the individual has a "reasonable expectation of privacy" (*Hunter v. Southam*, 1984). Under this test, it is unreasonable to surreptitiously videotape what happens in a private hotel room (*R. v. Wong*, 1990), but the police are free to videotape acts of gross indecency in a public washroom because there is no reasonable expectation of privacy in that location (*R. v. LeBeau*, 1988).

"Reasonable expectation" has been defined as follows:

> A person's privacy is intruded on in an unreasonable manner whenever the state, without a prior showing of just cause before a neutral judicial officer, arrogates to itself the right surreptitiously to record communications *that the originator expects will not be intercepted* [italics added] by anyone other than the person intended by its originator to receive them. (*R. v. Duarte*, 1990)

The trouble with this test is that, in a wired environment, the technologies we use to communicate make it extremely easy for others to intercept our communications, and we all know it. Open communications networks are just that—open. Any user can use the technology to capture and read the unencrypted communications of any other user. It is difficult to argue that we have a reasonable expectation of privacy when we send e-mail, participate in an on-line discussion, or visit a Web site that collects cookies, because the technology itself gives us *no* expectation of privacy.

The law has been slow to understand the extent to which new technologies are changing our experience of privacy. When the police received a "crime stoppers" tip that Mr. Plant was growing marijuana in the basement of his house, they had no evidence to justify a search warrant. However, they reasoned that growing plants indoors must consume a large amount of electricity. They then used their own computer system to log onto the local utility's computer and pull up Mr. Plant's electricity bills. The Supreme Court of Canada applied the reasonable expectation test, and concluded that

> Section 8 of the Charter should seek to protect a *biographical core of personal information* [italics added] which individuals in a free and democratic society would wish to maintain and control from dissemination to the state. This would include *information which tends to reveal intimate details of the lifestyle and personal choices of the individual* [italics added]. (*R. v. Plant*, 1993)

Mr. Plant's electricity bills, they argued, did not reveal intimate details of his personal life; they just showed how much electricity he consumed. This may not be an accurate conclusion in a nonwired environment. As Justice McLachlin, who disagreed with her fellow judges' conclusions, argued:

> The records are capable of telling much about one's personal lifestyle, such as how many people lived in the house and what sort of activities were probably taking place there. The records tell a story about what is happening inside a private dwelling, the most private of places. I think that a reasonable person looking at these facts would conclude that the records should be used only for the purpose for which they were made—the delivery and billing of electricity—and not divulged to strangers without proper legal authorization. (*R. v. Plant*, 1993, p. 213)

The test is even more invasive in a wired world where each little detail, such as a utility bill, does not exist in isolation. Data-matching software can locate and connect a multitude of personal details: purchases recorded on our "preferred customer" cards at the local grocery; the kinds of books we like to buy at amazon.com; the comments we post in newsgroups on baking or politics. When all these details are linked together, they create an accurate picture of our private lives. As former privacy commissioner Bruce Phillips warns, "The technology is making it possible to introduce more and more forms of intrusive surveillance of people conducting their lives in ordinary ways. And unless we're prepared to see ourselves being looked at, spied upon, probed and tested, we had better get a grip on this" ("Ottawa Vows to Protect Privacy," 1996).

Privacy, the right to be free from being watched, spied upon, and tested, is a human right because it is an essential part of human dignity and autonomy. World War I prisoners of war felt that the worst part of their internment was the lack of privacy they experienced in POW camps. Observers concluded that the POWs' irritable and resentful behaviour, "revealed in excessive fault-finding and boasting about themselves[,] . . . was an attempt to maintain personal identity in the face of a complete lack of privacy in their day-to-day existence" (McDougall, 1999, p. 4). Philosopher Lubor Velecky argues that "a person's human right to privacy is a right to be the captain of his soul without any evil-minded interference by others" (cited in McDougall, 1999, p. 11). Life without privacy makes it impossible to enjoy the dignity and freedom that human rights seek to protect.

2. Privacy as a Democratic Value

Because it is so connected to individual freedom, privacy is also an important element of a healthy democracy. As Justice La Forest notes, "[privacy] has profound significance for the public order. The restraints imposed on government to pry into the lives of the citizen go to the essence of a democratic state" (*R. v. Dyment*, 1988). In many ways, privacy is a "preconditional right" that enables us to enjoy all our democratic freedoms.

This is not surprising. At its core, any political system describes three important relationships or interactions: between individuals, between the individual and government, and between government and the individual. In a healthy democracy, individuals freely relate to each other as fellow citizens and place special value on the personal autonomy that makes that citizenship possible. Individuals see government as the legitimate servant of the public will and government, for its part, relates to individuals as free citizens from whom it derives its power and legitimacy. By contrast, individuals in an authoritarian state relate to each other as competitors, view their government as oppressor or political master, and are themselves viewed by their government as security threats or risks to state authority. In a fundamental sense, privacy is the value that allows citizens to communicate freely with each other and with their government. It is also a very human value that continually requires the state to relate to individuals as citizens and human beings.

Western governments readily accept that privacy is an important democratic value when invasive practices are being used to suppress political dissidents in authoritarian states such as North Korea or China.[6] They recognize that such practices as mounting on street corners video cameras that scan, record, and identify individuals by name make it much less likely that people will choose to participate in a political demonstration (exercising their right to assemble) or even say what they think (exercising their right to free expression). However, when those same practices are used to watch Canadians, officials often justify them because they are efficient and help to reduce risks.

Communication technologies enable the state to collect and process vast amounts of information about citizens; by looking for "patterns" in the "data stream," officials seek to identify those people who pose some "risk." For example, research indicates that there are certain "types" of people who are more likely to commit acts of violence. People filling out a firearms registration form are therefore required to reveal whether or not, in the past five years, they have been treated for depression, substance abuse, or emotional problems; considered suicide; been through a divorce or the dissolution of a significant relationship; lost their jobs; or gone bankrupt. Any of these "factors" indicates the person is "at risk" because she fits the profile of a person who is more likely to commit acts of violence. The trouble is, the profile catches a much larger number of people who are *not* at risk of doing anything violent, but the state has no way of distinguishing them from the potential criminal.

Following the logic of "risk reduction," anyone who checks off one of these boxes must be investigated because they pose a potential "risk." The applicant is asked for full written details—highly personal details of their depressed mental state, divorce, or drug problem—and a regional firearms officer then begins an investigation. The officer may speak to anyone associated with the applicant, including neighbours, bosses, and ex-spouses, to decide whether or not that person is a risk to herself or others. If the officer is not satisfied, he can ask the local police to act as the firearms centre's agent and conduct a full investigation into whether or not the person is dangerous.

Many public interest groups and privacy advocates argue that this foray into the private lives of applicants puts the innocent citizen in a position in which she is forced to defend her actions to the state or face the consequences. This process may or may not catch a potentially violent offender, but it will easily catch a bankrupt, depressed, or divorced farmer who, in need of a gun for his livelihood, is forced to reveal intimate details of his life to the state and, even worse, have the state call and discuss his life with his neighbours, boss, and ex-spouse. This willingness to invade privacy in the name of risk reduction means that the state is dealing with individuals not as citizens, but as suspects, safety risks, or threats to "efficient" and "cost-effective" government. In such a situation, the relationships that are essential to our understanding of democracy are undermined.

The risk reduction imperative is facilitated by communication technologies in subtle ways. Theorists like Ursula Franklin argue that new technologies have changed our experience of community and therefore of democracy. Verbal communications between people encourage intimacy because they occur when people are together in the present tense. They create a sense of *synchronicity*, encouraging members of a community to live together in the same rhythms of time and space. By contrast, networked communication technologies like voice mail or e-mail are *asynchronous* because they "decouple" activities from the patterns that naturally develop in real time and space. As Franklin (1996) writes:

> The ping-pong pattern of verbal communications is no longer tied to space or time. You can send your ping to someone before going to lunch; she may pick it up when and where she can and, at some point, send back her pong—and there goes the joy of intimate contact, and with it the heart of what verbal communication was thought to be: an exchange of messages between people in the present tense. (p. 151)

Franklin argues that asynchronous communications encourage governments and corporations to communicate with other governments and corporations, rather than with the citizens in their own local communities. These "horizontal" patterns of communication encourage globalization and break down local democratic interactions as governments become increasingly unresponsive to citizen concerns. This, in turn, weakens the state's commitment to civil and human rights, including the right to privacy.

As former privacy commissioner Bruce Phillips noted in his 1998–99 *Annual Report*, the danger—and allure—of the emerging model of risk reduction is that

> we participate voluntarily, seeing only the obvious advantages— convenience, speed and personal safety—not the less tangible and more complex disadvantages. The most chilling of these is that we will conform because we assume that we are all being watched at all times. Put more starkly: freedom is diminished and, in some cases, disappears. (Privacy Commissioner of Canada, 1999)

3. Privacy as a Social Value

Privacy has a strong effect on our social behaviour and organization. Historians suggest that Elizabethan homes, with their kitchens, parlours, and bedrooms, replaced the single medieval common hall because people wanted to enjoy a level of privacy that had before been available only to the rich. W.G. Hoskins writes that "one can see this desire for withdrawal [from the common life] reflected, even in farmhouses, in the increasing use of the chair instead of the bench" (cited in McDougall, 1999, p. 8). In a 1956 landmark study of a Canadian suburb called Crestwood Heights, researchers concluded that

> increased space, a reason why people buy houses in Crestwood, means increased privacy. . . . Privacy for each member of the family is the ideal—but not the isolation of anonymous shelter as offered by a hotel. The essence of the desired privacy is its very presence within the family unit. (McDougall, 1999, p. 8)

Privacy, then, is not the same as withdrawal from social relationships. Rather, it is the power to control and define those relationships.

Contemporary discussions of privacy often focus on this aspect of individual control. We establish social relationships based on different degrees of intimacy; the closer the relationship, the more we share with the other person. When entry into our private lives occurs without our knowledge or consent, this sense of control is lost and we feel violated. Indeed, the very act of surveillance changes the behaviour of the people being watched. As we know from the experience of Communist East Germany and the Soviet Union, the first casualty of that surveillance is trust.

Privacy, as such, encompasses our social understanding of intimacy. The argument that technology determines the level of privacy we enjoy is dissatisfying because it fails to account for the fact that technological developments themselves are also the result of our social understanding and choices. Emerging forms of invasion redistribute social power. In the proverbial small town, everyone knows what everyone else is up to. This means that everyone is also called to account for socially harmful actions. A banker in a small town in the 1940s would face the social censure of the members of his community if he refused to give someone a loan because the borrower came from a family with a history of cancer. In the modern information society, however, the watchers are invisible. When banks, marketers, drug companies, and insurance companies invade our private lives, we are not even aware of it, and we cannot see what they are doing with their knowledge of us. This lack of reciprocity means that it will become increasingly difficult to hold others accountable for decisions that harm us or discriminate against us in some way. And those who have access to the information gain a significant amount of control over us.

Ironically, new technologies are often the justification for increasing that social control further. Individual privacy, the argument goes, must give way to society's need to deal with new waves of cyberterrorists, on-line pedophiles, and high-tech organized crime. Illustrating this dynamic is the draft *Council of Europe Convention on Cyber-Crime*, which sidesteps many of the freedoms normally enjoyed in an open society by giving states broad powers to seize and share data in order to facilitate investigations of "new" cybercrimes, such as data interference, on-line copyright infringements, cyberfraud, and on-line child pornography. Although these are old and established crimes, the fact that they now occur on-line is used to justify more invasive forms of social control.

Ultimately, the level of openness and privacy we enjoy is a social choice. Privacy is not a function of our technological environment. In the words of privacy advocate Darrell Evans:

> I think the vanishing of privacy would be a victory of materialism over the human spirit. I find it very hard to picture what kind of room there would be for creativity on the part of human beings in such a world. . . . We are constantly told it is a more secure world, of course, a more efficient world, a world that catches fraud much better, but to me, that is the victory of bureaucracy over human creativity. . . . We want to put individuals in a place of causation rather than being a complete effect of technologies and of a gradual erosion of our privacy. If we are to maintain human freedom, I think that's what we have to do. (cited in Canada, 1997, p. 21)

4. Privacy as Data Protection

Concerns about technology and freedom are not new. However, the advent of the computing age has brought with it its own unique set of problems. Information technologies enable organizations to collect, manipulate, and use vast amounts of information about individuals. The need to place some limits on the electronic manipulation of personal information was recognized by the Council of Europe in the 1970s. Europeans, remembering the lessons of World War II, were sensitive to the fact that large organizations like governments and banks were using mainframe computers to collect and process information about citizens.

Recognizing that this data made individuals vulnerable to human-rights abuses, the Council of Europe passed the *Convention for the Protection of Individuals with Regard to Automatic Processing of Personal Data* in 1980. The *Convention* set out a framework for the collection, use, access, accuracy, and disposal of personal information. Concerned that national legislation based on the *Convention* might block the international flow of data, the OECD released its *Guidelines Governing the Protection of Privacy and Transborder Flows of Personal Data* in the same year. The *Guidelines* contained the following eight fair information practices (FIPs):

1. When data is collected, the purpose for the collection must be disclosed.

2. The data collected must be relevant to the purpose for which it is collected.

3. The data must be accurate and of high quality.

4. Security safeguards must be established to prevent unauthorized access to the data.

5. The data must only be used for the purpose for which it was collected, unless the consent of the individual has been obtained.

6. The collector of the data must establish open policies regarding the nature of the data and the manner of its storage.

7. The individual must have knowledge of and access to the data.

8. The collector of the data must be accountable for its collection and use of the data. (OECD, 1980)

The OECD principles sought to ensure that the information collected would be accurate and kept confidential. This approach, which concentrates on protecting the integrity of the data itself rather than the individual who is the subject of the data, is called "data protection."

Data protection made a certain amount of sense in the 1980s, when computing was dominated by mainframe computers. In the mainframe environment, data processing was centralized, so all the data about a particular individual could be easily located and its use regulated. In addition, mainframes were extremely expensive and required constant technical supervision. Accordingly, only large organizations, such as governments, banks, and universities, were able to afford them. This meant that regulation had to apply only to a few, large, easily located organizations. However, as the nature of computing changed in the late 1980s and we migrated from mainframes to distributed networks, data storage and processing became highly decentralized. By 1990, the power to collect and manipulate personal information was no longer in the hands of the few. Because of this, the data itself became an extremely valuable commodity.

This fact—that personal information is now worth a great deal of money in the electronic marketplace—is one of the most complicating features of the new privacy landscape. The sale of personal information is indeed big business. For example, the *New York Times* reports that the American Medical Association alone generates $20 million (U.S.) per year by selling doctors' biographies to drug companies. The biographies are crossmatched with electronic records of pharmaceuticals sales so that drug companies can better identify which doctors are selling which drugs. The drug companies then spend $12 billion (U.S.) a year encouraging the doctors to sell more of their drugs by treating them to dinner, theatre, and expensive conferences (Gay Stolberg and Gerth, 2000). As former privacy commissioner Bruce Phillips writes:

> We are in fact buying and selling large elements of our human personae. The traffic in human information now is immense. There is almost nothing the commercial and governmental world is not anxious to find out about us as individuals. (Canada, 1996, pp. 12–13)

By the mid 1990s, stories of cookies, Web tracking, and data matching began to make people nervous. Some commercial sectors feared that public concerns about privacy would erode consumer confidence in the information economy; accordingly, they set out to create voluntary codes and practices. However, the voluntary nature of these codes gave an unfair competitive advantage to businesses that failed to comply with minimum data protection standards. The Canadian Standards Association (CSA) responded by creating a national standard. In 1996, the CSA released the *Model Code for the Protection of Personal Information*. The *Model Code* was the result of negotiations between industry, consumer representatives, and government. In May 1996, the International Organization for Standardization Consumer Policy Group passed a unanimous, 25-country resolution to develop an international standard based on the CSA standard.

The *Model Code* sets out ten principles of fair information practices:

1. Accountability: An organization is responsible for personal information under its control, and shall designate an individual or individuals who are accountable for the organization's compliance with the Code's principles.

2. Identifying Purposes: The purposes for which personal information is collected shall be identified by the organization at or before the time the information is collection.

3. Consent: The knowledge and consent of the individual are required for the collection, use or disclosure of personal information, except where appropriate.

4. Limiting Collection: The collection of personal information shall be limited to what is necessary for the purposes identified by the organization. Information shall be collected by fair and lawful means.

5. Limiting Use, Disclosure and Retention: Personal information shall not be used or disclosed for purposes other than those for which it was collected, except with the consent of the individual or as required by law. Personal information shall be retained only as long as necessary for the fulfilment of those purposes.

6. Accuracy: Personal information shall be as accurate, complete and up-to-date as is necessary for the purposes for which it is to be used.

7. Safeguards: Personal information shall be protected by security safeguards appropriate to the sensitivity of the information.

8. Openness: An organization shall make readily available to individuals specific information about its policies and practices relating to the management of personal information.

9. Individual Access: Upon request, an individual shall be informed of the existence, use and disclosure of his or her personal information, and shall be given access to that information. An individual shall be able to challenge the accuracy and completeness of the information and have it amended as appropriate.

10. Challenging Compliance: An individual shall be able to address a challenge concerning compliance with the above principles to the designated individual or individuals accountable for the organization's compliance. (Canadian Standards Association, 1996)

The CSA built on the principles developed by the OECD, and added two new ones: (1) information must be collected, used, and disclosed with the knowledge of the data subject, "except where appropriate"; and (2) the data subject should be able to challenge how an organization complies with all of the fair information practices.

TENSIONS IN THE PRIVACY DEBATE

Many experts argue that fair information practices will ensure that privacy is protected in the new millennium. For example, former British Columbia privacy commissioner David Flaherty writes, "I have never met a privacy issue that could not be satisfactorily addressed by the application of fair information practices" (Bennett and Grant, 1999, p. 35). There is, however, a fundamental tension between privacy as a human right and access to information as a tool to enhance competitiveness and control. Fair information practices do not capture the "rights" side of the equation because they were designed by stakeholders to ensure that data will continue to flow into the information marketplace. They create a form of "consensual invasion" whereby the consent process is designed to protect the interests of everyone except the individual who is revealing the information.

In effect, consent is an agreement between the individual disclosing the information and the organization collecting the information. In order for consent to adequately protect the individual's autonomy and freedom of choice, there has to be an equality of bargaining power between the parties to the transaction. But that equality of bargaining power is often absent. If my employer, bank, or insurance company asks me to consent to the release of my personal information, what happens if I refuse to give it? I may find I will lose access to employment, financial services, or insurance coverage.

Consent is also easily sidestepped by legislation and government practices. The United Kingdom has passed a law giving insurance companies the "right" to demand a genetic sample from prospective clients. Iceland sold the genetic records of its entire population to a drug company without asking its citizens first. It is estimated that you will have your image captured by 300 surveillance cameras on your way to work in the morning, all of which have been installed and operated without your consent and often without your knowledge. Statistics Canada releases your tax records to epidemiologists conducting medical research because they have decided "it's good for you."

These practices are all justified because they are efficient and reduce risk. Marketplace efficiency, public safety, and the development of new medical treatments are important goals, but not if they are accomplished in ways that sacrifice our individual rights. We have learned this lesson before. In 1939, for example, the Supreme Court of Canada decided that tavern owners must have the freedom to transact their business as they see fit. If customers don't like it, they can always go to another bar. The Court argued that individual rights must be balanced in a way that does not unduly hamper commerce. This use of marketplace language will be very familiar to anyone who has followed the privacy debate since 1990. But in this case, the needs of the marketplace meant that the Montreal Forum Tavern was acting lawfully when it refused to serve a Mr. Christie a drink after a Canadiens game just because he was black (*Christie v. York*, 1940).

The dynamics of the marketplace could not help Mr. Christie and others like him. To do that, we had to develop a language of human rights. Our choice of language is equally important in the context of the privacy debate. As Franklin (1996) has said:

> When human rights informs the language in which the discussion among you and the general public and Parliament takes place, you speak, then, rightfully about citizens and all that comes with that. On the other hand, if the emphasis is primarily on the protection of data, one does look at a market model, one does look at an economic model, and all the things you've heard about the new economy. Then it is the language of the market that informs your discourse.... When those who primarily locate themselves in the human rights climate speak about citizens, about the relationship between groups and power, those who are in the market language speak primarily about stakeholders. And when one speaks about rights and obligations, others speak about binding contracts.

PRIVACY LEGISLATION

To date, Canadian privacy legislation has been firmly rooted in the language of the marketplace. When Canada drafted its Privacy Act in 1982, it applied the OECD guidelines to the ways in which the federal government collects, uses, and discloses personal information about citizens and federal employees. The Privacy Act was limited in a number of ways. For example, the "exceptions" to the rules were extremely broad, and although the privacy commissioner was given the power to investigate complaints, he or she lacks any real enforcement powers. The Privacy Act's greatest limitation was that it focused solely on the public sector, leaving private-sector data collection completely unregulated.

However, as the commercial imperatives of the information economy grew and consumer confidence in the electronic marketplace wavered, the private sector began to lobby for legislation that would encourage consumers to take part in e-commerce by assuaging concerns about privacy. These commercial imperatives were made even more pressing by the European Union in October of 1995. Under a European Parliament directive designed to harmonize data protection standards within Europe, member states are required to pass legislation blocking the transfer of information to nonmember states that do not provide an adequate level of data protection (Council of Europe, 1995).

In January 1998, Industry Canada and the Department of Justice released a discussion paper suggesting that legislation should be modelled on the CSA standard. However, the discussion paper made it quite clear that the government was defining privacy solely as a trade issue:

> Legislation that strikes the right balance between the business need to gather, store, and use personal information and the consumer need to be informed about how that information will be used . . . is an important element of building the consumer trust and the market certainty needed to make Canada a world leader in electronic commerce.

> The ability to provide effective protection for personal information may be crucial to Canada's ability to remain competitive internationally in the global information economy. . . . This [European Union] Directive has the potential to make the protection of personal information a major non-tariff trade barrier with Canada. . . . Canadian businesses may be forced to undertake individual comprehensive negotiations to show compliance with the European Union rules. This process will be fraught with uncertainty and could become lengthy and expensive. (Industry Canada, 1998)

It is also worth noting that the discussion paper used the word "citizen" ten times, compared with a collective 78 occurrences of "consumer," "business," and "industry."

The legislation that grew out of this discussion paper was aptly named Personal Information Protection and Electronic Documents Act (PIPEDA). As stated in section 3, the purpose of the legislation is to establish, "in an era in which technology increasingly facilitates the circulation and exchange of information," rules that recognize the individual's right of privacy and "the need of organizations to collect, use or disclose personal information for purposes that a reasonable person would consider appropriate in the circumstances."

PIPEDA represents an uneasy compromise on the parts of industry, government, and privacy advocates, the latter of whom hoped some protection would be better than none. That compromise began to unravel even before the act was passed on April 13, 2000. Drug companies, pharmacists, and the Ontario Ministry of Health argued before the Senate Committee on Social Affairs that PIPEDA should not apply to personal health information, because it would unduly hamper the efficiency of health-care delivery and research. In spite of the fact that opinion polls and public consultations have consistently indicated Canadians want more, not less, protection for their health information, the Senate Committee exempted health data for one year so as to give health-sector "stakeholders" an opportunity to come up with a compromise of their own.

Similar problems occurred when U.S. President Bill Clinton passed health privacy legislation near the end of his term. One of President George W. Bush's first actions was to delay implementation of the law, thereby affording health companies time to lobby for lower standards of protection. Although American legislators have been unwilling to interfere with the private sector in general, relying instead on voluntary standards and privacy policies, there has been a great deal of interest in health privacy and the protection of children.

Early attempts at regulation of electronic data in the United States were draconian. The Communications Decency Act, for example, made it a criminal offence to use a telecommunications device to "knowingly make, create, or solicit . . . any comment, request, proposal, image, or other communication which is obscene, lewd, lascivious, filthy, or indecent." In June 1996, a three-judge panel in a Philadelphia court struck down the Communications Decency Act for contravening constitutional guarantees of freedom of speech (*Reno v. ACLU*, 1996); a year later, the United States Supreme Court affirmed the lower court decision (*Reno v. ACLU*, 1997). More narrowly drafted was the subsequent Children's Online Protection Act (COPA), which made it unlawful to communicate, on the World Wide Web and for commercial purposes, material that is "harmful to minors" unless good faith efforts are made to prevent children from obtaining access to such materials. On June 22, 2000, COPA was also struck down for unduly restricting freedom of speech (*ACLU v. Reno II*).[7]

The United States continues to follow the privacy debate, although the major concern appears to be the need to avoid trade sanctions because of noncompliance with the 1995 European Union directive. Now that most of the members of the European Union have passed data protection legislation, pressure is mounting for the Americans to act as well. The Federal Trade Commission has set out voluntary standards for on-line commercial privacy, and the Department of Commerce has developed a "safe harbour" framework under which American firms can "certify" that they comply with a minimum set of fair information standards acceptable to the European Union. In Canada, there is still pressure to move beyond the data protection framework and entrench a quasi-constitutional right to privacy. On March 13, 2001, Senator Sheila Finestone introduced a Privacy Rights Charter (Bill S-21) that

(1) seeks to make it clear that every individual in Canada has a right to privacy in the broad sense, and (2) expressly acknowledges the importance of privacy as a human right, an essential element of democracy, and a social value. Dead or alive, privacy is emerging as one of the most contentious political issues of the early 21st century.

QUESTIONS

1. Is privacy a fundamental human right? Give reasons for your answer.
2. According to the author, what are the four different ways of understanding privacy?
3. Which do you feel poses the greater threat to privacy—the public sector or the private sector? Give reasons for your answer.
4. In what sense do privacy codes adopt the point of view of business and neglect the rights of citizens?
5. What is a reasonable expectation of privacy in a digital age?

WEB SITES

Electronic Frontier Foundation: **http://www.eff.org/**
Electronic Frontier Canada: **http://www.efc.ca/**
Electronic Privacy Information Center: **http://www.epic.org/**
Media Awareness Network: **http://www.media-awareness.ca/**
Privacy International: **http://www.privacyinternational.org/**
Public Interest Advocacy Centre: **http://www.piac.ca/**

NOTES

1. The Court of Appeal decision was overturned by the United States Supreme Court in *Kyllo v. US* (2001) 121 S. Ct. 2038. The Court held that where the government uses a device that is not in general public use to explore the details of a private home, the surveillance is a "search" and is presumptively unreasonable without a warrant.
2. Forty-four-year-old Bruce Kreifels was convicted under Texas law for secretly videotaping people in their bedrooms and bathrooms. Kreifels also admitted that he had used a miniature camera on his shoe to videotape up women's skirts when they stopped to give him directions in a shopping mall (Reuters, 2001).
3. The Catholic Civil Rights League first reported this practice to the police in the fall of 2000.

4. The City of Tampa was awarded Privacy International's Third Annual Big Brother Award for Worst Public Official for scanning Super Bowl attendees in 2001 (Privacy International, 2001).
5. The major constitutional protection is afforded under section 8, as discussed below. Recent case law suggests that the Court is also willing to interpret section 7 ("the right to life, liberty and security of the person") in ways that will protect privacy (see *Blencoe v. British Columbia*; *Godbout v. Longueuil*). However, section 7 rights have also been limited to reasonable expectations of privacy.
6. For a review of China's response to the Internet, see Neumann (2001).
7. Further information on *ACLU v. Reno*, *Reno v. ACLU*, and *ACLU v. Reno II* can be accessed through the Electronic Privacy Information Center Web site (http://www.epic.org/).

REFERENCES

ACLU v. Reno (1996, June 12). United States District Court for the Eastern District of Pennsylvania, No. 96-963.

ACLU v. Reno II. (1999). United States Court of Appeal for the Third Circuit, No. 99-1324.

Bennett, Colin J., and Rebecca Grant. (1999). *Visions of privacy: Policy choices for the digital age.* Toronto: University of Toronto Press.

Blencoe v. British Columbia (Human Rights Commission) [2000] S.C.J. No. 43.

Canada. House of Commons Standing Committee on Human Rights and the Status of Persons with Disabilities, 35th Parliament, 1st Session. (1996). *Evidence.* Meeting No. 15.

———. House of Commons Standing Committee on Human Rights and the Status of Persons with Disabilities. 35th Parliament, 2nd Session. (1997). *Privacy: Where do we draw the line?* Ottawa: Public Works and Government Services Canada.

Canadian Standards Association. (1996). *Model code for the protection of personal information.* CAN/CSA-Q830-96.

Christie v. York Corporation, (1940) S.C.R. 139.

Council of Europe. (1980). *Convention for the protection of individuals with regard to automatic processing of personal data.* ETS No. 108.

———. (1995, October 24). *Directive on the protection of the individual with respect to the processing of personal data and on the free movement of such data.* 95/46/EC.

End of privacy. (1999, April 29). *The Economist.*

Franklin, Ursula. (1996, September 19). *Stormy weather: Conflicting forces in the information society.* Closing address at the 18th International Privacy and Data Protection Conference, Ottawa.

———. (1999). *The real world of technology* (Rev. ed.). Toronto: Anansi.

Gay Stolberg, Sheryl, and Jeff Gerth. (2000, November 16). Medicine merchants: Tracking the doctors. *New York Times*.

Godbout v. Longueuil (Ville). (1997). 152 D.L.R. (4th) 577 (S.C.C.).

Hunter v. Southam. (1984). 11 D.L.R. (4th) 641.

Industry Canada and Department of Justice Canada. Task Force on Electronic Commerce. (1998). *Building Canada's information economy and society: The protection of personal information*. Ottawa: Public Works and Government Services Canada.

Lin Neumann, A. (2001). *The great firewall*. Committee to Protect Journalists. Retrieved from http://www.cpj.org/Briefings/2001/China_jan01/China_jan01.html

McDougall, Bruce (Ed.). (1999). *Perspectives on privacy*. Toronto: Zaxis Publishing.

OECD (Organisation for Economic Co-operation and Development). (1980, October 1). *OECD recommendation concerning and guidelines governing the protection of privacy and transborder flows of personal data*, OECD Doc. C(80)58 (Final).

Ottawa vows to protect privacy on info highway. (1996, May 24). *Toronto Star*.

Privacy Commissioner of Canada. (1999). *Annual report, 1998-1999*. Ottawa: Public Works and Government Services Canada.

Privacy International. (2001). *Third annual big brother awards*. Retrieved from http://www.privacyinternational.org/bigbrother/us2001/

Rand, Ayn. (1943). *The fountainhead*. Indianapolis, IN: Bobbs-Merrill.

Reno v. ACLU. (1997, June 26). United States Supreme Court, No. 96-511.

Reuters. (2001, March 7). *Caught! Voyeur faces up to ten years in jail*. Retrieved from http://www.dailynews.yahoo.com/hnm/20010307/od/voyeur_dc_1.html

R. v. Duarte, (1990) 1 S.C.R. 30 at 46.

R. v. Dyment (1988), 45 C.C.C. (3d) 244.

R. v. LeBeau (1988), 41 C.C.C. (3d) 163 (Ont. C.A.).

R. v. Plant (1993), 84 C.C.C. (3d) 203 at 213.

R. v. Wong, (1990) 3 S.C.R. 36 (S.C.C.).

United Nations. (1948, December 10). *Universal declaration of human rights*. Resolution 217 A (III).

United Nations. (1966). *International covenant on civil and political rights*. U.N. Doc. A/6316, 999 U.N.T.S. 302.

US Congressional Privacy Caucus. (2001, March 2). Briefing.

USA v. Kyllo, 96-3033 (CA9 1999).

Warren, Samuel, and Louis Brandeis. (1890). The right to privacy. *Harvard Law Review, 4*, 193–220.

21

Media and Politics

Anne McGrath
University of Calgary

Canadians tend to think of the news media as an objective, neutral reporting of significant events in our community and world. Rarely is there much consideration given to the issues of ownership, the bias inherent in the backgrounds and formation of journalists, the filtering processes of production, or the diversity of audiences. There is an accepted role for the media in presenting news about society and politics that will keep us informed and point out areas where we need to be vigilant. We like to be assured that the best interests of democracy are being served by an effective news media dedicated to professional standards of objectivity, fairness, balance, and investigative reporting. We rarely question the events and ideas that do not make it into the pages of our newspapers, the hourly radio news, or the nightly television broadcasts. Nor do we, for the most part, question the underlying values that dominate news coverage. Those who adamantly question and challenge the status quo are usually presented as anomalous and ineffective.

Communication scholars have queried the organization of the news media and the validity of the journalistic assumptions about fairness, balance, objectivity, and investigation. In addition, important questions have been raised about the ways in which audiences incorporate and make sense of the news that is presented to them. In particular, there is increasing concern among media scholars and others about recent trends in media ownership in Canada. The dominance of corporate interests in Canadian media is connected to limited ownership by corporations run by influential and powerful media barons who have a direct interest in the politics of the country and the development of particular forms of media. Coverage of elections, community issues, and federal/provincial/municipal government reflect the particular ways in which the world is seen by those in power and by those who report on those in power. Students interested in the media and its role in the political life of the country need to consider ways in which the trends toward increased privatization, monopoly ownership, convergence, and sensationalism can be countered to provide Canadians with critical information and opinion on important social and economic policy issues facing the country.

This chapter is about politics and media. Politics is about power, specifically the exercise of public power. Political reporting concerns itself principally with the

motivations and the actions of political elites and with aspects of government institutions. This doesn't mean that the coverage is monolithic and undifferentiated.
There are significant differences between certain journalists and columnists,
although differences between particular outlets are less apparent.

The interaction between the media and political life in Canada is complex and
multifaceted. Media formations, style, and activity change over time. Some have
argued that there is a rapid disintegration in the value and content of political journalism. The rise of "tabloid journalism" and its application to political reporting is
widely lamented. Taras (1999) suggests that

> the quality of journalism has deteriorated. Our local newscasts
> and front pages are dominated by blood-and-gore crime stories,
> celebrity news, sports hype, and the latest tidbits from the world
> of entertainment, while reports about political and social poli-
> cies rarely grab the spotlight unless they feature high-octane
> confrontation or pathetic victims. (p. 1)

POLITICS IN CANADA

Popular perceptions about politics in Canada usually relate to the comings and
goings of federal and provincial politicians. In recent years, a great deal of attention
has been paid to the status of right-wing parties and their relative health. The dominant news frame has been to lament the misfortunes of right-wing parties as they
struggle to unify their forces in order to defeat the Liberal Party. However, the
right-wing policies and practices of the Liberal Party are rarely highlighted in this
frame. In reporting that closely mirrors the coverage of the two-party system in the
United States, the Liberal Party is portrayed as a centrist/left party whose right-
wing approach is the only logical alternative. The predilections of media owners
and the homogeneity of reporters and columnists are rarely called into question.

Although the left of the political spectrum has also been in disarray, major
media outlets seem less concerned with the trials and tribulations of those seeking
to reinvent and unify left-wing forces under a common banner. News media offer
distant advice to the left about the necessity of abandoning left-wing ideas, but that
advice is rarely seen as more than a passing interest in a curiosity. Advice for the
right, however, is doled out as a matter of national importance because the existence
of a solid and viable right-wing party is deemed essential to a functioning democracy and an important counterweight to the governing Liberals. Rarely is a stable,
coherent, and articulate left-wing party viewed as an essential and valuable element
of democratic society.

The 2000 federal election was particularly interesting for students of politics
and the media as the political landscape shifted significantly in Canada. The current parliamentary configuration is highly regionalized and is further characterized

by a fairly weak opposition and a remarkable majority for the federal Liberals under the leadership of Jean Chrétien. The election campaign itself featured a campaign by the ruling Liberals that portrayed the Canadian Alliance Party as a scary threat to Canadian values that could be beaten only by returning the Liberals to power with a solid majority. This construction of two opposing choices with no other possibilities was successful. It convinced voters that the Canadian Alliance was operating from a hidden agenda that would alter basic Canadian programs, and that the Liberal Party was the only legitimate alternative since it was the only party capable of forming a majority government.

The threat emanating from the Canadian Alliance was the pretext for calling an early election well in advance of the need to seek a new mandate. The Canadian Alliance emerged on the federal scene as an attempt to combine elements of the Progressive Conservative Party with the Reform Party. Since the Reform Party was the only party to the merger that agreed to be merged, it was a rather halfhearted combination of forces and the Conservative Party stayed on in a somewhat weakened state. The Canadian Alliance, which was presented as a major threat to the country and thus a force to rally against by voting for the Liberals, was only a few months old when the federal election was held in the fall of 2000. Although the Canadian Alliance was a new party, with a new name and a new leader, it was presented as somehow without history, despite its deep roots in the right-wing fundamentalism of its previous incarnation, the Reform Party of Canada.

The overwhelming majority achieved by the Liberals was a surprise to many, including many Liberals, and certainly many members of the media. There had been intense speculation leading up to the actual vote that a minority government was highly likely. The absence of a cohesive opposition and the relatively small numbers of seats achieved by every opposition party, with the Conservatives and the New Democratic Party barely hanging on to official party status, created an unlikely Parliament by usual Canadian standards.

Voter turnout for the federal election was at its lowest in 75 years, a fact that led many observers to conclude that politics has little relevance to Canadians. The weak mandates afforded to elected governments in the first-past-the-post electoral system can mean that a very small minority of voters actually determine the shape of a government and a Parliament. The sense that the outcome of the 2000 federal election had been predetermined renewed demands, in its aftermath, for different voting mechanisms such as proportional representation.

The shift to the right in Canadian politics was formally initiated with the arrival of the Reform Party on the federal scene. The evolution of the Reform Party into the Canadian Alliance was documented in breathtaking detail by radio, television, and print media. Indeed, the permutations and gyrations of the right wing in general have been a source of media fascination. Rebick and Roach (1996) provide an illustration of the media's preoccupation with right-wing organizing when they compare the coverage of the Women's March Against Violence and Poverty (organized by the Canadian Labour Congress and the

Reform party
↓
Canadian Alliance

National Action Committee on the Status of Women) with the coverage of the Winds of Change conference:

> [T]he national media did not cover the march at all until it arrived in Toronto, where it was greeted by a large demonstration. At the same time, when a small group of New Right old boys—and young boys—had a private meeting in Calgary called Winds of Change (or as I prefer to call it, Windbags of Change), they got massive coverage. Their meeting was supposed to plot out a strategy to unify the Right, but it accomplished absolutely nothing. The women's march, on the other hand, culminated in a demonstration in Ottawa that turned out to be the largest women's protest in Canadian history. (p. 34)

The introduction of the organized New Right, represented by the provincial Progressive Conservative parties in Alberta and Ontario, and the Canadian Alliance federally, has alarmed many conservatives, including Dalton Camp, Hugh Segal, Don Getty, and Peter Lougheed. As Taras (1996) notes:

> Even veteran conservatives such as Hugh Segal believe that hatred of government, the blaming of government for all of society's evils, has reached outrageous proportions in certain quarters. He contends that private greed is the prime motivation for those who want to save tax dollars by privatizing, downsizing, and discrediting any activity that involves the use of public funds. (pp. 178–179)

The relentless mantra of the right for less government and more private ownership has become an accepted part of the public discourse. Criticism of social movements as "special-interest groups" and support for business as part of the "public interest" have become the primary construction of news stories, commentaries, and popular discourse.

RELATIONSHIP BETWEEN MEDIA AND POLITICS

Early accounts of the relationship between the media and political institutions focused on the media's role in presenting information to the public and keeping a watchful eye on the excesses and predilections of government leaders and bureaucrats. More contemporary discourse centres on the complexity of the relationship between the media and the political establishment, with a view to determining the appropriate levels of interaction and the presence (or absence) of distance. Concerns about media concentration and ownership, and about their impact on democracy, have intensified in recent years. As media converge and ownership of major channels of public information are increasingly held by fewer and fewer individuals, it has become clear that there are serious dangers inherent in the narrowness of the mass media in Canada.

In any examination of the media's relationship to business and government, it is important to differentiate between private and public media outlets in Canada. The mainstream private media is characterized by ownership in limited hands, the dominance of media barons, an attachment to notions of professional objectivity, and an allegiance to the norms of society and to dominant ideas promoted by business interests. By contrast, public broadcasting in Canada—despite constant reductions in capacity and a difficulty in maintaining ratings and programming quality—has been remarkable for its ability to reach deeper into the political infrastructure than privately run media. In addition to the CBC, there are a variety of alternative news publications that tend to be nonprofit, precariously financed, and critical of both the political establishment and the established media.

Critical theorists used the term _hegemony_ to describe the media's ability to shape and inform public opinion. The theory of media hegemony is part of a political economy approach to news production that defines the media as a corporation involved in producing a commodity for the purpose of generating profit. Issues of ownership, control, advertising income, technology, production routines, and profit are central to these discussions. According to this view of the news media, the social system privileges dominant groups and dominant institutions. Moreover, the media and the state are interrelated in the sense that their objectives are the same: both work to maintain existing power relations.

Gitlin (1980) uses the term _ideological reproduction_ to describe the process whereby the media make the ideas of the dominant forces in society the ideas of the mass of people. The ideology promoted by the state and the media, according to Gitlin, is "private property relations which honor the prerogatives of capital; committed to reform of selected violations of the moral code through selective action by State agencies; and committed to approving individual success within corporate and bureaucratic structures" (p. 258). The processes by which people take on the central and controlling ideology of the system are complex and nuanced. The sense of control that journalists have over their work operates as part of that hegemonic system: "Indeed the hegemonic ideology of bourgeois culture is extremely complex and absorptive; only by absorbing and domesticating conflicting values, definitions of reality, and demands on it, in fact, does it remain hegemonic" (p. 256).

Political economists argue that the media should be viewed as a commodity or product to be bought and sold, and that the process of news production must be analyzed from that perspective. Clarke (1990) suggests that the study of news media must "integrate study of production and product to disclose and discuss all the ways in which the ideological construction of production creates the product" (p. 67). The relationship between the news media and politics embodies mutuality. The two are interwoven. References to the media as the "fourth estate" highlight the idea that the media is one of the pillars that works with the government to underpin the liberal democratic state. The notion of hegemony incorporates the tensions and conflicts that arise in the relationship between the media and political institutions and figures.

The reporting of two recent stories—"Shawinigate" and "Peppergate"—illustrates how apparent tensions between media and government serve to heighten liberal notions of democracy while leaving unquestioned the basic values of the liberal democratic state. The Shawinigate controversy erupted in the media following the post-election discovery that Prime Minister Jean Chrétien had some financial involvement in a golf club in his home riding that has since benefited from government decisions. The media, together with all the opposition parties, attempted to uncover shady activities. Especially intense in its pursuit of the story was the *National Post*, then owned by Conrad Black's Hollinger. With the merger of Hollinger and CanWest Global, the pro-Liberal Aspers became co-owners of the *National Post*. In an editorial, new co-owner David Asper charged that journalists were too enthusiastic and even unfair in their search for a smoking gun in the Shawinigate story.

The "Peppergate" scandal concerns the use of excessive force against protesters. At the APEC (Asia Pacific Economic Cooperation) meetings held in Vancouver in November 1997, the RCMP used pepper spray to quell student protesters. The police action was disturbing to many Canadians, and the media covered the story—and in particular the controversy over the use of pepper spray—in some detail. A central question involved the role of the Prime Minister's Office in the decision to use such aggressive and violent actions to stop what were essentially peaceful student protesters. The intensive media coverage of the controversy put considerable pressure on the prime minister and the government. Unexpectedly, the role of the media was brought into question with the discovery of an e-mail correspondence between CBC reporter Terry Milewski and protester Craig Jones, in which Milewski referred to the government as the "forces of darkness." Questions about journalistic integrity, objectivity, and fairness were raised by other media and members of the prime minister's entourage. The Prime Minister's Office demanded action, and the CBC moved Milewski to another assignment, away from the burgeoning avalanche of stories pointing to prime ministerial involvement in the decision to pepper-spray peaceful protesters. Although the prime minister's actions have been attacked, the focus has been on his character and conduct.

Both these controversies deliberately use terms evocative of the infamous American Watergate scandal. The actions of the media in exposing the corruption in the Republican Party reached into the highest offices in the country and led to the resignation of U.S. President Richard Nixon. These terms, in the Canadian context, are deliberately designed to call into question the values, ethics, and behaviour of the highest-ranking elected official in Canada.

CONVERGENCE

Disputes between the government and the media are common, which would seem to suggest that the media are playing the role of watchdog and, in some cases, are even an actively hostile opponent of government. However, in none of the recent cases of aggravated conflict between the media and government (including

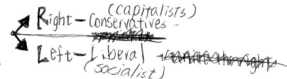

Shawinigate and Peppergate) has there been a suggestion of media opposition to the basic values and operations of government. Similarly, mainstream media reports on the intensive security at the APEC meetings and Quebec Summit adopted varying positions on the protesters and the rights of citizens to dissent, but few if any questioned the validity of liberalized world trade and economic globalization. The underlying values and activities of the state are safe from media scrutiny.

Current trends entrench this media acquiescence even more deeply as media ownership becomes concentrated in fewer and fewer hands and profit motivation becomes more and more explicit and controlling. Larger and larger "news/entertainment" corporations are being created in buyout after buyout, merger after merger. The dizzying pace of mergers and acquisitions makes almost every description of the current state of media ownership quickly outdated. The most spectacular case of convergence in recent history was the 2000 CanWest Global $3.5-billion acquisition of the Hollinger newspaper chain and all of its Internet properties. Concerns about the crossover between the different forms of media in the newly merged company focus on the issues of editorial control, diversity of voices, and the promotion of corporate interests. When one company includes several different forms of media, the potential for crossover is enormous. The ability of the newly merged CanWest Global/Hollinger company to draw stories together and present the same version through television, newspaper, radio, and Internet has been the subject of considerable discomfort on the part of media scholars, journalists, and regulators. Barlow and Winter (1997) suggests that

> the increasing concentration of media ownership in fewer and fewer hands, the underfunding of public service broadcasting, the rising commercialization of news and information, and the commercial exploitation of the new communications technology all threaten to limit the accountability of the media, the diversity of views given public expression, and the ability of citizens to access the news and information we need to participate in and make informed decisions about our social, economic, and political affairs. (p. 208)

Responses to the threats posed by convergence and the overlapping of media outlets under the umbrella of large single conglomerates have been halting and disjointed. The federal government has announced several different possible task forces and commissions along the lines of the 1970 Davey Senate Committee on the Mass Media, which investigated the concentration of media ownership in Canada. There has been a startling lack of clarity about the formation of such a body or its ability to actually function. In addition, there has been pressure for the CRTC to prevent the worst aspects of convergence through regulation. However, calls for the introduction of a code of principles separating editorial and journalistic functions were met with immediate and vociferous opposition by both CanWest Global and CTV, who argued that a voluntary self-monitored code would suffice.

From their perspective, the full benefits of convergence can be realized only if journalists and editors have access to all of a conglomerate's resources. Critics maintain that such crossovers compromise journalistic integrity and stifle diversity.

The emergence of new technologies and the possibilities they present have been a major argument and impetus for convergence. Many have argued that the Internet has the capacity to revolutionize news reporting. Certainly, many social movements have relied extensively on the Internet in organizing efforts against globalized trade. The major media companies have been equally enthusiastic about the emerging possibilities of new technology. In the news release announcing the merger between CanWest Global and Hollinger, Leonard Asper, president and CEO of CanWest, stated: "This merger is the ultimate convergence transaction. It unites the powerful conventional media of print and electronic content with the 21st century online, interactive and immediate technology of the Internet" (Asper, 2000, p. 2).

Despite urgent calls for action by important media thinkers and citizens' groups, the trend toward increased corporatization of the media continues. As Taras (1999) points, it is a trend with serious implications:

> My worry is that the growth of huge media conglomerates, the lack of support for public broadcasting, and the failures of contemporary journalism are creating a narrower and more limited media world. The Canadian media system and the Canadian political system with which it is so deeply enmeshed are risking the democratic equivalent of heart disease—the arteries that carry the flow of democratic discussion are hardening and clogging up. The beginning of wisdom and action is to recognize that a crisis exists. (p. 27)

NEWS COVERAGE OF CANADIAN POLITICS

Canadian journalists were somewhat smug in their reaction to the U.S. media's massive reversal during the Fall 2000 presidential campaign. At a crucial point on the first night of counting, every major U.S. media outlet declared George W. Bush the winner. They were forced to reverse their stories the next morning when it became clear that there was no declared winner in the crucial Florida vote and that Al Gore was still in the running. On November 9, the *Globe and Mail*, which a day earlier had run the headline "Bush Wins a Squeaker" only to subsequently retract it, focused its attention on the same blunder made by U.S. media outlets.

In Canada, the public sees media portrayals of government on television that reinforces the impression that politicians are negative, self-interested, and arrogant. Only the powerful could get away with the immature, boorish behaviour that most Canadians see on television screens when scenes from Question Period are aired.

This behaviour has clear implications for the public perception of politicians. According to Taras (1999), politicians "have sunk to the point where they rank not much above car thieves, leaders of crackpot religious cults, and members of bike gangs" (p. 39).

Media in Canada portray a limited political landscape, one preoccupied almost entirely with the trials and tribulations of some members of the government and the opposition. Narrow definitions of politics prevail in Canadian mainstream media. The preoccupation with capital "P" politics and the almost complete marginalization of alternative political formations reveals a very shallow understanding of social and political processes. In addition, this narrow focus prevents serious debate over important policy questions. Process and personality becomes the story and the machinations of government and opposition politicians and bureaucrats take precedence.

In the 2000 federal election campaign, for instance, the leader of the Canadian Alliance, Stockwell Day, was presented in the media as a leading contender for the office of prime minister in the short space of six months leading up to the voting day. Although Day was a recent arrival on the federal scene, the media granted him the role of "contender" upon his election as leader of a new party formation. Little attention was paid to Day's background. Instead, the media focused on the many photo opportunities presented to them—the Canadian Alliance leader posing on a Sea-Doo, running with his campaign team, playing touch football. Thus, until Day's political fortunes turned, his media image was that of contender and athlete. Conversely, Joe Clark, leader of the Progressive Conservatives was treated as a loser throughout the federal election campaign, only to be transformed into the "unofficial" official opposition after the vote.

But politics in Canada is about much more than federal, provincial, and municipal elections and governments. Many political theorists have been critical of the tendency to view politics in such restricted terms. The activity of groups in civil society to challenge dominant systems is very political even though it doesn't often fall easily into the domain of partisan politics. Feminists, for instance, have argued forcefully that "the personal is political" and have rejected the division of the world into a public domain for men and a private domain for women. For feminist theorists and activists, the activities of the private sphere are intensely political, as are campaigns for child care, equal pay, and racial equality. The inability or unwillingness of media and political leaders to envision a realm of politics outside the halls of elected partisan political institutions has been a source of great frustration.

Many groups in civil society would argue that the media doesn't cover politics at all since there is such reluctance to broaden the political to reflect social and popular movements. It has been pointed out, for instance, that homelessness is a political issue that should be tackled by all sectors of society. Yet it is only treated as a political issue when a federal, provincial, or municipal politician makes a statement or announcement, opens a homeless shelter, or meets with an antipoverty group. The deaths of homeless people on the streets of major Canadian cities are rarely part of political coverage and certainly receive less attention than a political party leadership convention. Groups that challenge this domination are given little space in the domain of politics or the media. For example, in a *Globe and Mail* article on Canadian think tanks, "the Fraser Institute was cited 139 times . . . and the left wing Centre for Policy Alternatives was cited 18 times" (Rebick and Roach, 1996, p. 46).

Organizers of the World March of Women, which culminated in a march of 50,000 women, men, and children on Parliament Hill in October 2000, were horrified at the media coverage they received. The World March developed out of successful marches organized in previous years by the Quebec Federation of Women in 1995 and the National Action Committee on the Status of Women and the Canadian Labour Congress in 1996. Both these marches attracted thousands of participants and presented concrete proposals to governments to end women's poverty. Discussion in Beijing at the World Conference of Women in September 1995 launched the idea of a world march to draw international attention to these issues and mobilize women globally. The participation was spectacular and marches were held in several regions around the world. In some European cities, the marches attracted hundreds of thousands of women. The Canadian media consistently underreported attendance, with estimates of the numbers of participants ranging from hundreds to about 5000. (The police and RCMP, hardly boosters of feminist campaigns, estimated attendance at somewhere between 30,000 and 50,000.) Months of sustained activity, negotiated demands, and worldwide efforts to raise issues of violence and women's poverty were thus reduced to a minor event. Organizations like Fairness and Accuracy in Reporting (FAIR) in the United States report regularly on the political stories that don't make the news. In an annual report, FAIR documents the interference from political and corporate interests that prevent stories from receiving fair, accurate, or balanced coverage (Fairness and Accuracy, 2000).

The processes by which news stories about popular movements are constructed to minimize and marginalize has been described very effectively by political media theorist Todd Gitlin in his 1980 book *The Whole World Is Watching*. Gitlin's study traces the news coverage of the anti–Vietnam War protestors and illustrates the tools used by the media to undermine and manage the opposition to the war and the New Left politic that arose from, and coexisted with, the protest movement. The framing devices that Gitlin describes can be applied to the coverage of most political protest groups in contemporary Canadian society. They minimize the potential and filter the message and impact of popular movements. Gitlin (1980) identifies the following framing devices:

- trivialization (making light of movement language, dress, age, style, and goals);
- polarization (emphasizing counterdemonstrations and balancing the antiwar movement against ultra-Right and neo-Nazi groups as equivalent "extremists");

- emphasis on internal dissension;
- marginalization (showing demonstrators to be deviant or unrepresentative);
- disparagement by numbers (undercounting); and
- disparagement of the movement's effectiveness.

There is little doubt that framing devices are operative, whether consciously or unconsciously, in the media reporting of unions, feminism, environmentalism, antiracism, lesbian and gay activism, and most certainly antiglobalization protests.

The degree to which motivation and malevolence on the part of the media is attributed depends on political perspective. The minimal, negative, or condescending coverage of extraparliamentary political protest, as well as the positive or benign coverage given to corporate and government stories, is explained by Noam Chomsky and Edward Herman in their influential book *Manufacturing Consent*. As the title implies, Chomsky and Herman believe that the mass media are a propaganda tool whose main purpose is to manipulate people into supporting corporate and government interests. Their political economy approach "traces the routes by which money and power are able to filter out the news fit to print, marginalize dissent, and allow the government and dominant private interests to get their messages across to the public" (Chomsky and Herman, 1988, p. 13). They describe in detail a series of news filters that accomplish these goals, including the size, ownership, and profit orientation of the mass media; the role of advertising as the primary source of income, rendering the audience irrelevant; the use of financial and political elites as the main sources for stories and opinion; the influence of right-wing pressure groups; and fear of left-wing politics.

This "propaganda model" tends to be somewhat crude and reductionist in its explanatory potential. Many critical scholars are alert to nuances, fair-minded and sympathetic reporters, publicly owned media outlets, smaller stations, public influence, community input, limited but nonetheless important diversity among reporters, and a myriad of other factors that influence news reporting. John Fiske, Stuart Hall, Robert Hackett, and Todd Gitlin are among those critical media theorists who place significant emphasis on other factors and, most important, give credit to the ability of audiences to reshape and reinterpret the news that is presented to them. Hackett (1986) suggests that a socialist perspective "requires moving beyond an instrumentalist approach on media ownership, to include an adequate understanding of ideology and audience–media relations" (p. 141). He argues forcefully against the view that audiences are mere vessels taking in media messages: "Viewing the audience as passive dupes carries at least two political dangers. First, it leads us to underestimate the possibilities for audience resistance. Second, it implies contempt towards "the masses," reinforcing a tendency towards elitist-vanguardist politics" (p. 146).

Like the reporting of sports events, media coverage of electoral campaigns, campaign shuffles, and political pronouncements is suffused with references to "winners" and "losers." Fox (1999) suggests that the media's "strict adherence to the 'game schema' has … led to a reliance on 'horse race'-style reporting, both in the United States and in Canada. Campaign reporting [has] evolved to coverage of politics as a strategic game" (p. 50). Accordingly, the focus of such reporting is not the position a given politician takes, but rather his or her skill at outmanoeuvring an opponent.

The insider nature of political reporting is also apparent. Reporters and the politicians move in the same circles, share similar experiences, and swap insider jokes. "Too often," says Bill Fox, "politicians and reporters engage in what is the equivalent of insider baseball—a dialogue that excludes the very public both are dependent upon" (p. 15). For example, pundit panels consisting of politicians and reporters exchange barbs and small jabs, but it is "all in good fun." The emphasis on camaraderie and "entertainment" can be at the expense of an honest airing of sharp, serious disagreements.

The phenomenon of journalists talking to journalists about politics has increased markedly in recent years. The elevation of certain journalists to the status of expert commentator with the "inside scoop" has changed political reporting. Rarely are the views and opinions of politicians reported directly to the public. There are always journalists available to explain and interpret the political scene to viewers, listeners, and readers. Sound bites, which used to be substantial clips from a media source, have been reduced to what Taras (1999) calls "sound nibbles." Taras notes that research from the Fraser Institute, a right-wing think tank, indicates that sound bites for federal politicians during the 1997 federal election were on average between 7.1 and 8.2 seconds. It is, of course, impossible for a politician to encapsulate in a sound bite a position of any substance on complex issues such as trade liberalization and globalization.

Another feature of the political scene in Canada is the emergence of the media adviser. Some media advisers are celebrities in their own right. Alberta Premier Ralph Klein's campaign manager, spin doctor Rod Love, was a key player on the Alberta political scene. The public relations career of Ezra Levant, a self-confessed "Stockaholic" and former Director of Communications for the Canadian Alliance, was as colourful as it was short-lived. Fox (1999) sums up the spin doctor phenomenon:

> In recent years, spin doctors have positioned themselves as the stage managers of politics. Carefully coifed, nattily attired in Armani or Brooks Brothers, they often appear on current-affairs programs to share their insights, crowding their clients for face-time. They are the self-declared masters of the universe of the pseudo-event, and their days are numbered. (p. 260)

Yet another prominent feature of current news reporting is the use of polling. Government and opposition officials of all stripes make regular use of polls to assess their positions, gauge their publics, and test new ideas. Premiers like Ralph Klein are well known for sending out "trial balloons" and then using polls to check the results. The use of polling by the media, particularly during elections, has been under intense scrutiny. The American election fiasco of 2000 is largely attributed to network reliance on exit polling as a mechanism for determining a winner and declaring a race lost or won. Some have argued that the publication of polls during election campaigns has undue influence and can serve, often for the benefit of the status quo, as a powerful campaign tool.

REPRESENTATION OF FEMALE POLITICIANS

Feminists have consistently criticized mainstream media for being sexist in their reporting and commentary on female politicians. Early female politicians, at a time when women were rarely seen in public life, remarked that they were viewed either as decorative or as unwomanly in their aggression. When Canada's first and only woman prime minister, Kim Campbell, described her life as a federal politician as "unspeakably lonely," she echoed the comments of the women who had come before her. The derision heaped on many female politicians has often been related to their gender rather than their politics: when they are meek and mild-mannered, they are ridiculed for being too much like a woman; when they are forthright and sharp, they are attacked for being too masculine. Judy LaMarsh, in her memoir, lamented:

> Wherever and whenever I say something, my words, coming from the mouth of a woman, suddenly look larger than life, sound harsher and less reasonable, too colourful, too *partisan*. Maybe the trouble is that the reports of me filter through male reporters with their layers of unacknowledged prejudice that a woman doesn't talk like that, she doesn't fight like that, she doesn't act like that! (1969, p. 38)

The special treatment reserved for female politicians includes a particular level of scorn for any errors. When Heritage Minister Sheila Copps was alleged to have behaved badly on a plane trip (by refusing to give up her seat for a passenger with a disability), most of the media took up the story with relish. When the gaps in the story were later revealed, some attributed the glee with which the story had been first reported to the dissonance between Copps's "aggressive" style and "proper" female behaviour.

The rules, habits, and customs of the parliamentary press gallery have often been exclusive in their application. Many female politicians and journalists would argue that, despite the appearance of inclusivity, the invisible barriers still exist. The press gallery dinner, an insider affair, did not open its doors to women until 1967. Judy LaMarsh, who couldn't understand why women had been excluded, found it "a very staid affair, neither as drunken as repute has it nor as hilarious" (LaMarsh, 1969, p. 302).

A final feature of political reporting on women has been a focus on wardrobe. Until recent years, it was not unusual for the media to consider the cut and colour of a female politician's clothes as newsworthy as a statement of policy. Nor is the pre-occupation with personal appearance entirely a thing of the past. In the 1997 federal election, the Liberal campaign offered the following advice to its female candidates:

> Your wardrobe is a reflection of you; therefore it should be planned with the same care that you define your policy, develop your strat-egy, and plan the organization of your campaign team. Remember that during the campaign, there will be no time to do things like laundry, cleaning the house, cooking, picking up the children or the dry cleaning. Complete as much as you can before the writ is dropped. Campaigns are a series of ups and downs—be prepared for mood swings. (Abu-Laban and McDaniel, 1998, p. 95)

This advice is not new. In 1960, Judy LaMarsh, as one of the first women par-liamentarians, was advised to wear an evening dress to her first session of Parliament.

CONCLUSION

Anyone watching the media coverage of the 2001 Summit of the Americas in Quebec City saw a powerful and unitary media message. Despite the apparent diversity of media opinion, an overarching message was conveyed concerning the inevitable and inherent violence of protest politics, the bewilderment of staid and well-meaning world leaders, and the benign and fruitless negotiations between countries of the Americas. The role of the mainstream media in presenting the pro-testers as alternately scary and ineffective was matched by the portrayal of the leaders' perplexity at the reaction to their gathering. Media critics have been atten-tive to the role of mass media in perpetuating the idea that opponents of corporate globalization are at best incomprehensible and misguided, and at worst violent thugs dedicated to shutting down free speech.

Although there was some coverage critical of the excessive security and the violence directed at protesters, none of the major media outlets questioned the underlying tenets of capitalist globalization. Nor was there any extensive or deep coverage of the issues raised by the thousands of participants in the People's Summit or the 50,000 demonstrators in the World March of Women. While the CBC and some *Globe and Mail* columnists questioned the role of the security forces, the overwhelming message from all commercial media outlets was that free trade between the countries of the Americas was positive, benign, and inevitable. Glossed over was the fact that many journalists reporting from the streets of Quebec City wore gas masks as they filed their reports. The fact that the thousand or more journalists inside the Summit were locked in and had to lobby organizers to allow them to watch the outside scenes on closed-circuit monitors was presented as an interesting bit of trivia rather than an outrageous violation of journalistic freedom.

Media theorists and practitioners concerned about journalistic freedom in Canada and ability to report the news with integrity and safety have proposed the following strategies:

- Support for the CBC and increased pressure on it to fulfill its mandate. Public pressure groups like the Friends of Canadian Broadcasting monitor the CBC and pressure the management structures to maintain commitment to its mission. The Friends group also lobbies the federal government and the CRTC to continue support for public broadcasting. They offer practical suggestions and criticize actions that contribute to the deterioration of support.

- Increased regulation of private media outlets. The CRTC should use its power to strictly enforce codes of conduct for private media. Canadian content and division of functions in converged media companies should be strictly monitored and enforced. Pressure to accept voluntary codes and self-regulation is unacceptable.

- A federal investigation into the concentration of media ownership and the state of journalism in Canada. Special attention must be paid to the issue of diversity, in terms not only of the number of outlets but also of the diversity within newsrooms.

- Support for alternative publications with a critique of the increased corporate control in the mainstream media and an opposition to increased corporate control over democratic structures. There are several significant alternative publications on the Internet and in print that challenge dominant discourse and suggest actions for citizen participation. Community and campus radio stations can also be effective alternatives to mainstream corporate media.

- Continued pressure on the mainstream corporate media to take up their responsibility to represent public interests fairly and report dissent in a more balanced manner. Opposition to media convergence should be kept on the front burner and companies like CanWest Global should be kept under the microscope of critical media analysis.

Most Canadians get their news from the CBC radio or television, CTV, American television networks, private radio broadcasters, a Southam newspaper, a Sun newspaper, the *Globe and Mail*, or the *Toronto Star*. Those searching out alternative sources can look to such publications as *This Magazine*, *Canadian Dimension*, *Briarpatch*, a handful of community and campus radio stations, and on-line sources such as straightgoods.ca, rabble.ca, and mediachannel.org. For students of political media, it is important to follow both mainstream sources and alternative sources in order to arrive at a more complete picture. It is important to evaluate the state of mainstream media in this country and press for change, and also to actively support the alternative sources that provide a needed and critical counterweight to the business-driven agendas of the mainstream.

QUESTIONS

1. Are Canadian media biased toward a certain political viewpoint? Give reasons for your answer.
2. What framing devices do the media use to minimize popular movements?
3. What is the propaganda model of media?
4. What is "horse race"-style reporting?
5. What are the main criticisms of polling?

WEB SITES

Corporate Watch: **http://www.corporatewatch.org.uk/**
Council of Canadians: **http://www.canadians.org/**
Fairness and Accuracy in Reporting: **http://www.fair.org/**
NewsWatch Canada: **http://newswatch.cprost.sfu.ca**
PoliticsWatch: **http://www.politicswatch.com/**
Rabble: **http://www.rabble.ca/**

REFERENCES

Abu-Laban, Sharon, and Susan McDaniel. (1998). Beauty, status, and aging. In Nancy Mandell (Ed.), *Feminist issues: Race, class and sexuality* (2nd ed.). Scarborough, ON: Prentice Hall.

Asper, David. (2000, July 31). Canadian media giants announce landmark convergence deal. Retrieved from http://www.newswire.ca/releases/July2000/31/c7304.html

Barlow, Maude, and James Winter. (1997). *The big black book: The essential views of Conrad Black and Barbara Amiel*. Toronto: Stoddart.

Chomsky, Noam, and Edward Herman. (1988). *Manufacturing consent*. New York: Pantheon Books.

Clarke, Debra. (1990, February). Constraints of television news production: The example of story geography. *Canadian Journal of Communication, 15*(1).

Fairness and Accuracy in Reporting. *Fear and favor 2000: How power shapes the news*. Retrieved from http://www.fair.org/ff2000.html

Fox, Bill. (1999). *Spinwars: Politics and new media*. Toronto: Key Porter Books.

Gitlin, Todd. (1980). *The whole world is watching: The making and unmaking of the new left*. Berkeley: University of California Press.

Hackett, Robert. (1986, Spring). For a socialist perspective on the news media. *Studies in Political Economy: A Socialist Review, 19*.

LaMarsh, Judy. (1969). *Memoirs of a bird in a gilded cage*. Toronto: McClelland and Stewart.

Rebick, Judy, and Kiké Roach. (1996). *Politically speaking*. Vancouver/Toronto: Douglas & McIntyre.

Taras, David. (1999). *Power and betrayal in the Canadian media*. Peterborough, ON: Broadview Press.

O Canada: What Happens When the Mouse Meets the Mounties?

Leslie Regan Shade
University of Ottawa

This concluding chapter will revisit some of the themes and trends discussed in earlier chapters, particularly as they relate to the issue of Canadian "identity" and culture. It will consider the notion of cultural sovereignty and its importance for Canada. It will describe some of the issues arising from the culture and trade debates, and the role of Canadian culture within the global context. Finally, it will look at media ownership and related issues such as the role of the CRTC, the future of the CBC, and the impact of new media.

WHAT IS 'CULTURAL SOVEREIGNTY'?

Cultural sovereignty can be defined as the ability of a country to enact laws and policies that protect and promote its culture and cultural industries. In Canada, cultural policies on heritage, film, television, and now multimedia policy are instituted through legislation, regulation, program support, or taxation measures. Legislation enacted by the federal government has created or modified cultural institutions such as the CBC. Cultural rights were established through the Copyright Act, and regulations have also established the governance of Canada's broadcasting, cable, and telecommunications sectors. For instance, the Broadcasting Act requires that television and radio stations play or air a predominant amount of Canadian content, and the CRTC reinforces this regulation. Program support includes a variety of grants and contributions for Canada's cultural industries; agencies such as the Canada Council, Telefilm Canada, and the National Film Board administer many of these programs. Specific programs for targeted cultural industries include the Feature Film Fund and the Book Publishing Industry Development Program. Taxation measures include tax credits for corporations that support Canadian cultural industries. The Income Tax Act, for instance, allows Canadian advertisers to claim expenses on advertising placed in periodicals and on television stations that are Canadian owned (75 and 80 percent, respectively).

Why is there such a concern about making sure that Canadian content is allowed to thrive? Many feel that these various measures are needed to protect us from American culture (or "monoculture," as some would say). For almost a century,

Canadian nationalists have attempted to assert Canadian cultural sovereignty in order to counterbalance the American newspapers, films, television, magazines, comic books, videotapes, and music flooding across the border. Although American cultural products flow continually into other countries (both First World and Third World) as well, Canada's situation is somewhat unique in that its exposure is mediated by its geographical proximity to the U.S. border (about 80 percent of the Canadian population resides within 100 kilometres of the U.S. border) and the considerable distances between communities (Thompson, 1992, p. 189).

As early as the 1920s, Graham Spry and members of the Canadian Radio League recognized and advocated the importance of establishing a public broadcasting system distinct from its commercial counterpart to the south. "It is a choice between the State and the United States," Spry said, calling for government support of a communications policy that would foster "Canada as a nation, as a community, as a social organism" (cited in Babe, 2000, p. 41). This sense of broadcasting as a social and noncommercial utility (related to and encompassing the concerns of the community) is, as communication scholar Marc Raboy has shown, one of the strengths of the Canadian "identity" (Raboy, 1990), and it has been discussed in this book with particular reference to radio (Chapter 9), film (Chapter 10), television (Chapter 12), and Native communications (Chapter 16). Whereas U.S. public broadcasting depends on a mix of foundational, corporate, and individual donor support, public broadcasting in Canada—in the form of the CBC—has been and remains a stalwart institution since it is still dependent on state funding (although increasingly it is becoming dependent on advertising) (Ledbetter, 1998).

Debates over Canadian content have centred on the cultural imperialism thesis: Are Canadians swamped by an intrusion of American monoculture? Will the Canadian identity be eroded if Canadians are not able to consume and produce their own media products? For instance, many Canadians were upset when the Walt Disney Company signed an agreement with the Mounted Police Foundation—which is affiliated with the Royal Canadian Mounted Police (RCMP)—to license and control the promotion of Mounties merchandise. How could such a revered Canadian icon join hands with the Mouse? The Police Foundation contended that the move was designed to stop the production of "tasteless merchandise ... everything from Mountie swizzle sticks to porn flicks ... and to raise funds for some of the Mounties' community projects" (Wasko, 2001, p. 65). Although the licensing agreement with Disney has expired, critics fear that similar agreements will be struck with other Canadian cultural icons.

International sales of U.S. software and entertainment products were estimated at $60.2 billion (U.S.) in 1996 alone, "more than any other U.S. industry" (Farhi and Rosenfeld, 1998, p. 6). American media critics such as Benjamin Barber, Robert McChesney, and Herbert Schiller have documented the strength and power of the American cultural and media industries. All are concerned with the erosion of democracy in light of huge media consolidation, technological convergence, and the decline of public broadcasting. Schiller (2000) critiques the American "free flow of information" doctrine as an attempt to establish a new world information and communication order. Barber (1998) discusses the "McWorld" phenomenon, which he contends "represents an American push into the future animated by onrushing economic, technological, and ecological forces that demand integration and uniformity and that mesmerize people everywhere with fast music, fast computers, and fast food, MTV, Macintosh, and McDonalds" (1998, p. 1). McChesney (2000) examines the connections between the global media system and the global capitalist political economy, and concludes that neoliberalism is the culprit: "The centrepiece of neoliberal policies is invariably a call for commercial media and communication markets to be deregulated. What this means in practice is that they are 're-regulated' to serve corporate interests" (p. 2).

Some Canadian critics who take issue with the notion that American culture is a threat to Canadian sovereignty deride the establishment of Canadian content requirements for radio and television broadcasting:

> [The regulations] have become intolerable. They restrict the choices of viewers/listeners and raise the price of cable TV services. Worst of all, the Cancon policy involves the coercion of the many (including taxation) to provide benefits to a few, notably the producers of Cancon and the few people who enjoy consuming it. (Stanbury, 1996)

Taras (1999), on the other hand, makes a case for *stronger* CanCon regulation: "The result of an unregulated market would be even greater control by the Hollywood entertainment conglomerates. Ted Turner and Rupert Murdoch have no interest in telling Canadian stories or reflecting Canadian realities" (p. 223).

Minister of Canadian Heritage Sheila Copps has taken an international role in the debates on cultural globalization. Arguing that "world institutions must see culture as more than merely entertainment or merely an afterthought of decision-making" (Copps, 1998, p. 17), she has enlisted the support of other ministers of culture to form the International Network on Cultural Policy. Forty-six countries are members of this network, which builds on the work initiated at the UNESCO Intergovernmental Conference on Cultural Policies for Development in Stockholm and has a mandate "to build increased awareness and support for cultural diversity in an era of globalization and technological change" (www.incd.net/). Other network objectives include strengthening cultural and linguistic diversity, supporting local and national cultures, and ensuring that culture is accounted for in international negotiations. The network has two working groups: one is involved with cultural diversity and globalization, and the other is concerned with cultural diversity and broadcasting. Jean-Louis Roux, chair of the Canada Council for the Arts, has this to say about the relationship between culture and trade:

> [Culture] cannot be treated like just another thing to be bought and sold, subject to the vagaries of market demand. American pop culture is so pervasive. . . . Obviously, we can't prevent that, but we need to make certain our own culture has a chance. (cited in Gauthier, 2000, p. E4)

CULTURE AND TRADE DEBATES[1]

Many Canadians fear that the global sweep of networked technologies, coupled with a climate of growing open competition, could result in the commercialization and Americanization of Canada (Menzies, 1996; Raboy, 1997). Will Canadians have the same access to the channels of production and distribution as their southern neighbours? Culture and trade debates have exacerbated these concerns. The MAI (Multilateral Agreement on Investment) debate in 1997 raised new questions about cultural rights. The MAI followed in the wake of other global agreements such as the North American Free Trade Agreement (NAFTA), which gave a cultural exemption for Canada; the General Agreement on Tariffs and Trade (GATT); and the World Trade Organization (WTO) (Clarke and Barlow, 1997).

With the introduction of the Free Trade of the Americas (FTAA) and General Agreement on Trade in Services (GATS) deliberations, the debates over trade and culture have become even murkier and more controversial. According to Magder (1999), Canada's cultural industries suffered "a devastating blow" (p. 12) when the World Trade Organization overturned legislation designed to block the sale in Canada of U.S. split-run magazines through the imposition of an 80 percent excise tax on the accrual of Canadian advertising revenues.

Split-run magazines are Canadian editions of magazines originally published in another country. These magazines contain the basic content of the original, but advertisements targeted at Canadians replace more than 5 percent of the original ads. Sales and advertising in Canada cover the cost of producing split-run magazines. Split-run magazines and Canadian-produced magazines compete for advertising revenue needed to cover production costs.

The dispute over split-run magazines arose in the 1990s, when *Sports Illustrated* (owned by Time Warner) began to electronically transmit the magazine in order to evade physical borders. The Canadian government's response was to impose an 80 percent excise tax on advertising in split-run magazines and to provide lower postal rates and subsidies to Canadian magazines. The WTO ruling, settled through the WTO Dispute Settlement Body (DSB), made clear that Canadian cultural policies are not sacrosanct. *Canada—Certain Measures Concerning Periodicals* challenged the cultural aspect of a "good" and failed to acknowledge the cultural distinction of "goods." A clear victory for the United States, this ruling exemplifies how the free flow doctrine of information—first enunciated in the New World Information and Communication Order (NWICO) debates of the 1970s (see Chapter 15)—has become "the doctrine of free trade" (Magder, 1999, p. 14).

The role of the WTO has raised many concerns about the future of global democracy. The WTO was established in 1995 as part of the Uruguay Round of the General Agreement on Tariffs and Trade that was designed to formulate a set of rules governing international trade. The WTO consists of 137 member countries committed to pursuing a free trade agenda (Ellwood, 2001). Carmody (1999) contends that the "dominant gaze of WTO decision-making is so fixedly economic that it is in some ways blind to context" (p. 25). In the case of the split-run magazine decision, the WTO did not recognize or accept cultural justifications for regulation and legislation. A cultural waiver under WTO agreements is one remedy that could ameliorate future cultural disputes. In the meantime, as a result of the WTO ruling, the Canadian government has opened its market to U.S. split-run magazines, relaxed foreign ownership controls in the Canadian publishing industry, and abolished the postal subsidy. In compensation, the government has promised more subsidies to the Canadian publishing industry.

Will current negotiations of the Free Trade of the Americas further undermine the role of cultural sovereignty? The FTAA, considered by government leaders at the Summit of the Americas in Quebec City in April 2001, had as its goal the integration of the General Agreement on Trade in Services with the powers of the defunct Multilateral Agreement on Investment (Lee, 2001). Critics fear that such integration would "create a new trade powerhouse with sweeping new authority over every aspect of life in Canada and the Americas" (Barlow, 2001).

How would this agreement affect culture? Barlow (2001), speaking for the Council of Canadians, believes that culture will be either fully included in the pact or exempted using language similar to that used in NAFTA Annex 2106. There, articles dealing with the cultural industry (Art. 2005:2) give the United States "the right to retaliate against Canada with measures 'of equivalent commercial effect' and to do so using sectors unrelated to culture" (Barlow, 2001, p. 36). In effect, this agreement allows the United States to decide if Canadian cultural measures are "inconsistent" with NAFTA and to retaliate against Canada, which would have no legal recourse in the event of an unfavourable ruling.

The fear is that cultural services will be included in the definition of "services" under the General Agreement on Trade in Services. GATS is "a multilateral agreement that restricts government actions affecting services through legally enforceable constraints backed up by trade sanctions" (Sinclair, 2000, p. 29). Services commercialized and regulated could include broadcasting (even public broadcasting) and telecommunications. If GATS is put into place, then the principles of national treatment and most-favoured nation will apply to cultural services. The national treatment principle accords the same status to imported goods and foreign services as to locally produced goods, domestic services, local trademarks, copyrights, and patents. The most-favoured nation principle states that countries are to grant equal treatment (neither favourable nor discriminatory) to goods and services produced by all WTO members (UNESCO, 2000).

These principles challenge government subsidies to cultural industries, including those to the CBC and Canadian book publishers. The principles also call into question legislation limiting foreign investment in broadcasting, telecommunications, and cable companies, as well as regulations governing Canadian content. The Canadian government would not be able to restrict its arts and culture subsidies and grants to Canadian individuals and organizations; moreover, it would have to award funds to American and other corporations within the FTAA hemisphere.

The threat here is that "Canada's domination by the U.S. entertainment industry would be written into international law" (Council of Canadians, 2001).

THE FUTURE OF CANADIAN MEDIA INDUSTRIES

Culture and trade issues are just one among many challenges facing the Canadian communication industry as we enter the 21st century. This section provides a brief review of five trends in world communication: (1) convergence; (2) demassification; (3) conglomeration and consolidation; (4) globalization; and (5) deregulation.

Convergence refers to the manner in which digital technology alters the traditional distinctions between media such as radio, television, and cable broadcasting systems. As documented in Chapter 17, convergence has been a contested arena for policymakers and for media industries themselves; the "two titans" view of convergence promoted by Canadian policymakers is reflected in the operations of Rogers Communications, with its @Home Internet service, and Thomson/BCE, with its *Globe and Mail* family of Web sites and Sympatico Internet portal.

Demassification refers to the sheer plethora of media products that are available in diverse forms (particularly magazines, cable television, and the Internet) and cater to a wide range of tastes. For instance, in Canadian television, there is not only mainstream French- and English-language programming but also specialty channels ranging from the Women's Television Network to the Comedy Network. Our magazines run the gamut from *Owl Magazine* to *Chatelaine* to *Queen's Quarterly*, with similar fare offered in Quebec.

Conglomeration and *concentration* are structural features of the global media system whereby a small number of media firms own the lion's share of media products. There are basically two forms of concentration: horizontal concentration of ownership and vertical concentration of ownership. Horizontal concentration of ownership occurs when a firm in one line of media buys a major interest in another media operation not directly related to the original business; or when it takes a major stake in a nonmedia company. Conglomerate ownership, in which the subsidiary firms are in different lines of business, is exemplified by the merger of ABC and Disney, which gave Disney control over ten television stations and 29 radio stations in the United States. Vertical concentration of ownership is characterized by a concentration of firms within a line of business that extends a company's control over the process of production and/or distribution. This form of ownership is illustrated by Disney's TV production and distribution through Touchstone, Miramax Films, and Buena Vista.

Globalization (the subject of Chapter 15) refers to the transformation of communication spaces and social relations occurring across national borders. It is characterized by (1) economic globalization, or the integration of the global economy through free trade mechanisms and international bodies such as the WTO; and (2) cultural globalization, or the absorption and integration of global cultural forms into other cultural products and services.

Finally, *deregulation* occurs when governments and international trade bodies try to foster a more competitive environment by not regulating the media. As noted in Chapters 13 and 18, governments are particularly loath to impose restrictions (relating, for example, to content and foreign ownership) on the Internet.

CONCENTRATION OF MEDIA OWNERSHIP

Ben Bagdikian, former dean of the Graduate School of Journalism at the University of California at Berkeley, was one of the first media critics to write a full-length study of media ownership concentration. In the first edition of *The Media Monopoly*, published in 1983, he documented 50 major corporations that controlled the media; by the time the sixth edition of this book came out (Bagdikian, 2000), there were only six major media corporations.

The six major transnational corporations that make up the current global media-entertainment complex are Disney, Bertelsmann AG, AOL Time Warner, Vivendi Universal, Viacom, and News Corp. Each is characterized by concentration and conglomerization. The power and reach of these companies is illustrated by the following chart, which delineates some of Disney's ownership holdings. Of particular interest are the cross-licensing agreements between Disney and McDonald's: the California Adventure Park, which opened in 2001, features a McDonald's restaurant on its site; Disney licenses its "classic" characters (Mickey Mouse, Snow White) for use as toys in McDonald's Happy Meals; and the two companies are "developing a promotion based on the television game show, 'Who Wants to Be a Millionaire?'" (Williams, 2001).

THE WALT DISNEY COMPANY

Chairman and CEO: Michael D. Eisner
Employees: 120,000
Revenues: $23.4 billion (U.S.)

Television Holdings

ABC TV and radio networks; 10 television stations; 29 radio stations (U.S.)
International holdings include The Disney Channel in the U.K.; France, Italy, and Spain; ESPN Inc. International; Eurosport; Sportsvision Australia; ESPN Brazil; ESPN STAR; and sports channels globally.

Television Production and Distribution

Buena Vista Television; Touchstone Television; Walt Disney Television; Walt Disney Television Animation (including production facilities in Canada).

Film Production and Distribution

Walt Disney Pictures; Touchstone Pictures; Hollywood Pictures; Caravan Pictures; Miramax Films; Buena Vista Home Video; Buena Vista Home Entertainment; Buena Vista International

Magazines and Newspapers

ABC Publishing Imprints; Disney Publishing Inc.; Diversified Publications Group; Miller Publishing Group; four daily U.S. newspapers

Internet and Electronic Services

Buena Vista Internet Group; ABC Internet Group; ABC.com; ABCNEWS.com; Oscar.com; Mr. Showbiz; Disney's Daily Blast; Disney.com; Family.com; ESPN Internet Group; ESPN.sportszone.com; Soccernet.com (60 percent); NFL.com; NBA.com; NASCAR.com; Go Network; Infoseek (43 percent); Toysmart.com; Disney Interactive

Music

Buena Vista Music Group; Hollywood Records; Lyric Street Records; Mammoth Records; Walt Disney Records

Theatre

Walt Disney Theatrical Productions (including stage versions of *The Lion King* and *Beauty and the Beast*)

Sports

Franchises in Anaheim Sports Inc.; Mighty Ducks of Anaheim; Anaheim Angels

Theme Parks

Disneyland: Anaheim Disney; MGM Studios; Disneyland Paris; Walt Disney World; Disney's Animal Kingdom (Orlando, Florida); Walt Disney's World Sports Complex; California Adventure Park

Other Properties

Disney Cruise Line; The Disney Institute; The Disney Store (720); Celebration, a planned community in Orlando, Florida
Adapted from http://www.mediachannel.org/ownership/

As noted in Chapter 18, "Canada now has one of the most consolidated media systems in the world and an unrivalled degree of cross-media ownership." The following chart outlines the holdings of the major corporations that controlled the media in Canada as of May 2001. This media landscape, it should be noted, will invariably change with future buyouts and mergers.

CANADIAN MEDIA COMPANIES

Hollinger Inc. (www.hollinger.com)

Owned by the flamboyant Conrad Black, Hollinger is the leading publisher of English-language newspapers in Canada, the United States, the United Kingdom, and Israel. Hollinger owns 60 regional and community newspapers in Canada, and is the former owner of the *National Post*, a national daily that Conrad Black founded in 1998 to compete with the *Globe and Mail*.

Bell Canada Enterprises Inc. (www.bce.ca)

BCE is best known for Bell Canada, which boasts 21 million points of contact. Other holdings include:
- *Globe and Mail*—national daily newspaper with a weekly circulation of about 2,000,000
- Sympatico-Lycos—Internet service provider with one million subscribers
- Teleglobe—international Internet backbone

- Bell ExpressVu—satellite TV service with 722,000 subscribers
- CTV—private TV network that reaches 99 percent of Canadians
- The Sports Network, ROBTv
- BCE Emergis—e-commerce applications

CanWest Global Communications Corp. (www.canwestglobal.com)

Owned by the Asper family, CanWest Global Communications is best known for the private TV broadcaster Global Television Network, CanWest Entertainment, and CanWest Interactive. CanWest is the largest daily newspaper provider in Canada. In 2000, it acquired from Hollinger 14 daily newspapers, 126 community newspapers, and a 50 percent stake in the *National Post.* (Hollinger sold its remaining stake in the *Post* to CanWest in 2001.) CanWest controls broadcasters in New Zealand, Australia, Northern Ireland, and the Republic of Ireland. Other holdings include the Canada.com Internet portal and Toronto-based Fireworks Entertainment, which finances, develops, and produces film and TV projects.

Quebecor Inc. (www.quebecor.com)

In 1999, Quebecor became the second-largest newspaper group in Canada when it purchased Sun Media Corporation, with 8 metropolitan dailies, 181 local newspapers, and other publications in Canada and Florida. Other holdings include:
- Groupe Vidéotron, with many cable and broadcasting holdings
- magazines, entertainment weeklies, and alternative newspapers
- 12 publishing houses
- Internet portals CANOE and NetGraphe
- TQS—Quebec television network
- Archambault music chain (12 megastores in Eastern Canada)
- Le SuperClub Vidéotron (160 stores)

Torstar Corporation (www.torstar.ca)

Torstar publishes the *Toronto Star,* the *Hamilton Spectator,* the *Kitchener-Waterloo Record,* and 70 community newspapers. Other holdings include Metroland Printing, Publishing and Distributing and Harlequin Enterprises, the world's largest publisher of romance novels.

Concerns about media ownership concentration in Canada are not new. In 1970, the Davey Senate Committee on the Mass Media warned that daily newspapers were owned by fewer and fewer owners. The Royal Commission on Newspapers (Kent Commission) reiterated this concern ten years later, at which time the three largest chains controlled 57 percent of the daily circulation. Today, the three biggest chains—Hollinger, Quebecor, and CanWest Global—control more than 72 percent of the daily circulation. In New Brunswick, all of the daily newspapers are owned by the Irving family. In Saskatchewan, Prince Edward Island, and Newfoundland, all but one of the dailies are owned by Conrad Black's Hollinger chain. In television, five Canadian corporations account for more than 60 percent of all viewers, while three cable TV companies account for 68 percent of Canada's cable subscribers. Radio is dominated by ten companies that account for 55 percent of the revenues (an increase of 50 percent since 1990).

What is new about today's media ownership concentration is the dramatic increase in cross-media ownership that has resulted from frenzied takeover activity.

Rogers Communications, for example, has over five million cable subscribers and a one-third share of AT&T Canada. It owns the Canadian Home Shopping Network, 20 retail video stores, ten radio stations, the YTV network, the Rogers Cantel cellular phone network, Viewer's Choice cable TV service, and several magazines, including *Chatelaine*, *Maclean's*, *Flare*, and *Canadian Business*. This is convergence in the brave new world, as detailed in Chapters 17 and 18.

The media industry has come up with all sorts of rationales as to why such concentration is good for Canadians. For instance, Quebecor CEO Pierre Karl Péladeau argued before the Canadian Radio-television and Telecommunications Commission (CRTC) that Quebecor's takeover bid for cable and broadcast giant Groupe Vidéotron went beyond economic imperatives: "[The proposed takeover] is a project of considerable interest to the greater collectivity because its success will secure a preponderant place for French-speaking Canada in the digital and multi-media universe" (cited in Marotte, 2001). BCE Chairman Jean Monty exulted that the $4-billion merger between BCE and Thomson Corp. would create "a true gem in the Canadian content field," and that "the Internet facilitates the possibility of cross-selling, cross-promotion and repurposing" (cited in Damsell, 2000, B1).

Others are appropriately concerned about the decline of public interest imperatives amid such rampant media ownership concentration and privatization (Hackett, 2000). The Campaign for Press and Broadcasting Freedom, consisting of academics, activists, and labour/community groups, has been active in raising awareness about Canadian media ownership and promoting the need for a greater diversity of media ownership. They are pressuring the government to enact legislation aimed at addressing the problem of media ownership concentration through three broad goals: (1) limiting and eventually reversing the current level of media ownership concentration; (2) providing measures that will promote a diversity of media ownership; and (3) encouraging the media to more effectively "live up" to their social responsibility and provide a more diverse range of coverage and content.

Journalistic freedom is one of the areas threatened by media ownership concentration. The choice and quality of news can be undermined, as controversial topics are deemed too sensitive to explore. As detailed in Chapter 21, coverage of labour, environmental, and women's issues in mainstream dailies has become negligible. *Globe and Mail* columnist Naomi Klein discusses the ethical implications of journalistic self-censorship:

> As the conglomerates that own newspapers and TV channels dramatically expand their holdings, the zones where journalists are expected to tread cautiously are also stretching. It becomes awkward to cover not only one's parent company, for fear of being accused of boosterism, but all of their holdings, and their competitors' as well, for fear that it will seem like sour grapes. (Klein, 2000, p. A15)

Media ownership concentration also poses a threat to public-service broadcasting. The recent CRTC call for public comments on the ownership of specialty channels calls into question diversity in our broadcasting system. Bill Roberts, president and CEO of Vision TV, argued in a *Globe and Mail* opinion piece that "the independent, distinctive voices and public-service channels risk becoming orphans. They are being marginalized as communications conglomerates that own the content and the delivery systems begin to exercise their power" (Roberts, 2001, p. A11). McChesney (1997) stresses the need for a reconceptualization of public-service broadcasting, which he regards as "a necessary democratic agency."

In 2001, the federal government announced the establishment of a House of Commons heritage committee that will review broadcast policy; a separate panel will assess the role of the CRTC (Scoffield, 2001a). The challenge is to maintain cultural diversity in Canada within a context of globalization and national media ownership concentration. Responding to the recent wave of media mergers in Canada, the CRTC announced in August 2001 that television networks and newspapers owned by the same corporate parent "can work together closely, as long as both media keep separate management structures" (Scoffield, 2001b, p. B1). At the same time, the CRTC struck a cautionary note:

> [We] are concerned that cross-ownership of television stations and newspapers . . . could potentially lead to the complete integration of the owner's television and news operations . . . leading to a reduction of the diversity of the information presented to the public and of the diversity of distinct editorial content. (Scoffield, 2001b, p. B2)

CONCLUSION

Some might argue that concerns about culture and trade debates, and about the concentration of media ownership in Canada, are overblown. After all, if we don't like what we see in the mainstream media, we can always turn to the Internet, which accommodates a wide range of alternative voices. The problem with this solution is that the Internet is no longer a commercial-free bastion. Traditional media behemoths are becoming an increasingly dominant presence on the Internet, and governments are reluctant to institute any controls on governance.

Communication studies in Canada has never been more exciting. There are great opportunities for engaging the public with the salient issues concerning the fate of Canadian media, culture, and identity in a globalized world. The development of new technologies, rapid convergence, and the porous nature of national boundaries are also creating stimulating challenges. One of the more endearing and lasting traits of Canadian communication scholarship is the notion of communication as a common good. We hope that this book will inspire you to continue to engage with these pressing issues.

QUESTIONS

1. Explain why cultural sovereignty does, or does not, matter in the Canadian context.
2. "In a globalized world, the regulation of culture and trade is not feasible." Discuss.
3. Should Canadians fear "American monoculture"? Give reasons for your answer.
4. In what ways could regulators and citizens respond to the increasing concentration of media ownership?
5. Should we be concerned about threats to public-service broadcasting? Give reasons for your answer.

WEB SITES

Campaign for Press and Broadcasting Freedom (Canada):
http://www.presscampaign.org/
Columbia Journalism Review (Who Owns What): **http://www.cjr.org/owners/**
Media Awareness Network: **http://www.media-awareness.ca/**
MediaChannel (media ownership page): **http://www.mediachannel.org/ownership/**
UNESCO: Culture, Trade and Globalization (Questions and Answers):
http://www.unesco.org/culture/industries/trade/

NOTE

1. This section is adapted from Leslie Regan Shade, "Who's Afraid of Canadian Culture?" in Sherry Devereaux Ferguson and Leslie Regan Shade (Eds.), *Civic Discourse and Cultural Politics in Canada: A Cacophony of Voices* (Westport, CT: Ablex Books, 2002).

REFERENCES

Babe, Robert. (2000). *Canadian communication thought: Ten foundational writers.* Toronto: University of Toronto Press.

Bagdikian, Ben. (2001). *The media monopoly* (6th ed.). Boston: Beacon Press.

Barber, Benjamin. (1998). Democracy at risk: American culture in a global world. *World Policy Journal, 29*(13), 1–9.

Barlow, Maude. (2001). *The Free Trade Area of the Americas and the threat to social programs, environmental sustainability and social justice in Canada and the Americas.* Ottawa: Council of Canadians.

Carmody, C.C. (1999). When 'cultural identity was not an issue': Thinking about Canada—certain measures concerning periodicals. *Law and Policy in International Business, 231*(1), 1–62.

Clarke, Tony, and Barlow, Maude. (1997). *The Multilateral Agreement on Investment (MAI) and the threat to Canadian sovereignty.* Toronto: Stoddart.

Copps, Sheila. (1998). Céline Dion: Made in Canada. *New Perspectives Quarterly, 15*(5), 17–18.

Council of Canadians. (2001). *Stop the FTAA!: Democracy before trade/Non à la ZLEA—La démocratie d'abord!* [Pamphlet].

Damsell, Keith. (2000, September 16). BCE, Thomson converge into titan. *Globe and Mail*, p. B1.

Ellwood, Wayne. (2001). *The no-nonsense guide to globalization.* Toronto: New Internationalist and Between the Lines.

Farhi, Paul, and Rosenfeld, Megan. (1998, November 30). Exporting America. *Washington Post* (National Weekly Edition), pp. 6–7.

Gauthier, Natasha. (2000, November 30). Ottawa, the world's cultural stage. *Ottawa Citizen*, p. E1.

Hackett, Robert. (2000, Autumn). Taking back the media: Notes on the potential for a communicative democracy movement. *Studies in Political Economy, 63*, 61–86.

Klein, Naomi. (2000, September 13). One person's synergy is a columnist's nightmare. *Globe and Mail*, p. A15.

Ledbetter, James. (1998). *Made possible by . . . : The death of public broadcasting in the United States.* London: Verso.

Lee, Marc. (2001, April). *Inside the fortress: What's going on at the FTAA negotiations.* Ottawa: Canadian Centre for Policy Alternatives.

Magder, Ted. (1999, August). Going global. *Canadian Forum*, 11–16.

Marotte, Bertrand. (2001, March 27). Quebecor pitches to CRTC. *Globe and Mail*, p. B11.

McChesney, Robert W. (1997). Graham Spry and the future of public broadcasting: The 1997 Spry Memorial Lecture. *Canadian Journal of Communication, 24*(1). Retrieved from http://www.cjc-online.ca/

———. (2000). *Rich media, poor democracy: Communication politics in dubious times.* New York: New Press.

Menzies, Heather. (1996). *Whose brave new world? The information highway and the new economy.* Toronto: Between the Lines.

Raboy, Marc. (1990). *Missed opportunities: The story of Canada's broadcasting policy.* Toronto: University of Toronto Press.

———. (1997). Cultural sovereignty, public participation, and democratization of the public sphere: The Canadian debate on the new information infrastructure. In Brian Kahin and Ernest Wilson (Eds.), *National information infrastructure initiatives: Vision and policy design* (pp. 190–216). Cambridge, MA: MIT Press.

Roberts, Bill. (2001, January 15). Media mergers: More is less. *Globe and Mail*, p. A11.

Schiller, Herbert. I. (2000). *Living in the number one country: Reflections from a critic of American empire*. New York: Seven Stories Press.

Scoffield, Heather. (2001a, March 26). Ottawa and the Goliaths. *Globe and Mail*, p. R1.

———. (2001b, August 3). CRTC okays newsroom convergence. *Globe and Mail*, p. B1.

Sinclair, Scott. (2000). *GATS: How the World Trade Organization's new "services" negotiations threaten democracy*. Ottawa: Canadian Centre for Policy Alternatives.

Stanbury, William T. (1996, October). Cancon rules should be canned. *Policy Options*. Retrieved from http://www.media-awareness.ca/

Taras, David. (1999). *Power and betrayal in the Canadian media*. Peterborough, ON: Broadview Press.

Thompson, J.H. (1992). Canada's quest for cultural sovereignty: Protection, promotion, and popular culture. In Helen Holmes and David Taras (Eds.), *Seeing ourselves: Media power and policy in Canada* (pp. 188–201). Toronto: Harcourt Brace Jovanovich Canada.

UNESCO. (2000). *Culture, trade and globalization: Questions and answers*. Retrieved from http://www.unesco.org/culture/industries/trade/

Wasko, Janet. (2001). *Understanding Disney: The manufacture of fantasy*. Cambridge, U.K.: Polity.

Williams, Granville. (2001). Global media giants. Retrieved from http://www.mediachannel.org/ownership/granville.shtml#aol

CONTRIBUTORS

Paul Attallah is president of the Canadian Communication Association and an associate director of the School of Journalism and Communication at Carleton University. He is the author of two books on communication theory and numerous publications on the media and culture.

Pierre Bélanger is an associate professor in the Department of Communication at the University of Ottawa and the author of numerous articles dealing with various aspects of both traditional and new media in home and learning contexts. During a three-year leave of absence, he worked for the Canadian Broadcasting Corporation, first as director of new media for the French-language radio services for two years and then as chief national adviser of new media development.

Susan Bryant, who holds a Ph.D. in Communication from Simon Fraser University, teaches communication studies at the University of Windsor. Her research focuses on the social implications of new technologies and the relationship between contemporary culture(s) and outcomes for the natural environment.

Roger de la Garde is a professor in the Department of Information and Communication at Université Laval. He is the founding editor of *La Revue Communication*, a former president of the Canadian Communication Association, and the author of numerous publications dealing with communication and culture.

Michael Dorland is a professor in the School of Journalism and Communication at Carleton University. He is the editor of *Canada's Cultural Industries: Policies, Problems and Prospects* (1996), the author of *So Close to The States: The Emergence of Canadian Feature Film Policy* (1998), and co-author of *Peace, Order and Good Government: Law, Rhetoric and Irony in Canadian Civil Culture* (2001).

Daniel M. Downes, who holds a Ph.D. in Communications from McGill University, is coordinator of the Information and Communication Studies Program at the University of New Brunswick (Saint John). He is the author of *The Poetics of Cyberspace* (2002) and researches issues pertaining to cultural diversity, communication technologies, and the regulation of the new media economy.

Charlene Elliott is a doctoral candidate in the Communication Program at Carleton University. Her research interests include cultural politics, intellectual property, and the branding of colour.

Gary Evans has taught widely on film and image-based media. His extensive writings on Canadian film include *In the National Interest: A Chronicle of the National Film Board of Canada from 1949 to 1989* (1991) and *John Grierson and the National Film Board: The Politics of Wartime Propaganda, 1939–1945* (1984).

Derek Foster is a doctoral candidate in the Communication Program at Carleton University. He lectures on the subject of communication and has published articles on the Internet, Marshall McLuhan, and popular culture.

Matthew Fraser is a professor of communications at Ryerson University's School of Radio and Television Arts. He is the author of *Free-for-All: The Struggle for Dominance on the Digital Frontier* (1999) and writes a regular column on media industries for the *National Post*.

Mike Gasher teaches journalism at Concordia University. His research interests include the feature-film industry in British Columbia. He was a journalist in Ontario and British Columbia for 20 years, and is co-author (along with Rowland Lorimer) of *Mass Communication in Canada*.

Sheryl N. Hamilton is an assistant professor in the Department of Art History and Communication Studies at McGill University. She teaches gender and technology, qualitative methodology, cultural policy, and law and culture, and has published numerous articles in journals and anthologies.

Karim H. Karim, the author of *Islamic Peril: Media and Global Violence* (2000), is an assistant professor in the School of Journalism and Communication at Carleton University. He has also worked as a researcher for the federal government in the departments of Multiculturalism and Canadian Heritage. His research focuses on media, communication, and ethnicity issues.

Anne-Marie Kinahan is a doctoral candidate in the Communication Program at Carleton University. Her research interests include communication and the public sphere; the history of the women's movement in Canada; and feminism and popular culture.

Gord Lucke is a management consultant for both the private and the public sectors, specializing in marketing and communications, change management, strategic and operational planning, human resources, technology development and implementation, and program evaluation. He lectures on research methods, public opinion, and organizational communication in the Department of Communication at the University of Ottawa.

Anne McGrath, a doctoral candidate at the University of Calgary, is a researcher with the Canadian Union of Public Employees (CUPE) and teaches part-time in the Department of Communications at the University of Ottawa. She was a long-time regular guest on the CBC Radio program and has taught women's studies and social work at the University of Calgary and Mount Royal College.

Lorna Roth, an associate professor in the Communication Studies Department at Concordia University, has been involved in broadcasting policy development/analysis and consulting with First Peoples and multicultural/multiracial groups since the late 1970s. She is the author of numerous articles on First Peoples, television, technology, access, and communication rights.

Eileen Saunders is director of the Arthur Kroeger College of Public Affairs at Carleton University and associate dean of the Faculty of Public Affairs and Management. She is the author of numerous publications on regulatory guidelines concerning gender representation in the media, the role of violence in the media, public opinion and social inequality, and access of visible-minority groups to new media.

Leslie Regan Shade is an assistant professor in the Department of Communication at the University of Ottawa. Her research and teaching focuses on the social, ethical, and policy aspects of information and communication technologies. She is the author of *Gender and Community in the Social Construction of the Internet* (2002) and co-editor of *E-Commerce vs E-Commons: Communications in the Public Interest* (2001) and *Civic Discourse in Canada: A Cacophony of Voices* (2002).

Richard Smith is an associate professor of communication in the Faculty of Applied Science at Simon Fraser University. He is also director of the Centre for Policy Research on Science and Technology (CPROST) at Simon Fraser University.

Valerie Steeves is an adjunct professor in the Department of Law at Carleton University. Her main area of research is the impact of new technologies on human-rights issues. She has spoken and written extensively on privacy in a networked environment.

Don Wallace is a computer archivist at the National Library of Canada, a musician of long standing, and a doctoral candidate in the Department of Sociology at Carleton University. His research is concerned with the history of consumer culture.

Dwayne Winseck is an associate professor in the School of Journalism and Communication at Carleton University. He is the author of *Reconvergence: A Political Economy of Telecommunications in Canada* (1998); co-editor of *Democratizing Communication: Comparative Perspectives on Information and Power* (1997) and *Media in Global Context* (1997); and the author or co-author of numerous articles.

François Yelle, a doctoral candidate in the Department of Communication at Université de Montréal, teaches communication in Quebec. His research is concentrated on the history of media research in Quebec.

COPYRIGHT ACKNOWLEDGMENTS

"First People's Television in Canada's North: A Case Study of the Aboriginal Peoples Television Network," by Lorna Roth, is adapted from her paper "Bypassing of Borders and the Building of Bridges: Network Canada," published in *Gazette: International Journal of Communication Studies 62*(3–4), pp. 251–269. Copyright © Sage Publications Ltd. Reprinted by permission of Sage Publications Ltd.

"Sipping Starbucks: (Re)Considering Communicative Media," by Charlene Elliott, is adapted from her article "Consuming Caffeine: The Discourse of Starbucks and Coffee," which appeared in *Consumption, Markets & Culture 4*(4). The adaptation appears here by permission of CMC.

INDEX

Aboriginal peoples
   broadcasting and, 164
   films and, 182, 185–86
   television and, 295–308
Aboriginal Peoples Television
      Network (APTN), 295–96, 301–8
ACNeilson Canada, 129, 130
administrative research, 4–8
   Canadian, 48
   critical research and, 4–8, 10–12
advertising, 88, 92
   children and, 137, 140–47
   coffee (*see* coffee)
   film and, 180
   Internet and, 130–33, 262–64,
      333–37, 338
   magazines and, 400
   market share and, 128–30
   radio and, 169
   regulations, 142–43, 145
   research and, 120–33
   social role of, 110
   television and, 128–29, 219–20
Alliance/Reform Party, 382
ARPA (Advanced Research Projects
      Agency), 253, 275, 276
ASCAP (American Society for
      Composers, Authors, and
      Publishers), 202, 204–5
audience, 31–33, 87–104
   Aboriginal programs and, 299, 302,
      303, 306
   AOL, 132
   attracting an, 101, 108, 111–12,
      299, 319
   behaviour, 95–100
   Canadian, 41–42
   characteristics of, 95–98

competence of, 96–97, 103, 112–13
defined, 102–4
ethnicity and, 284–89
films and, 96–99, 179, 185–86, 193
fragmentation of, 97–98, 211,
   225–26, 228–29, 275
interactivity and, 259–61
Internet, 131–33, 174, 175, 252,
   319–21
mass, 90, 97–98, 104, 275
music and, 99, 100, 198, 200,
   203–7, 211–12
pornography and, 245
radio, 169, 170, 212
research, 120–33 (*see also* polls)
role of, 31–33
specialty channels and, 228, 285–89
swapping, 101–2
television, 87, 97–100, 128–30,
   206–7, 216, 221, 229–30
type of media and, 98–101

Beatles, the, 207, 208
behaviourism, 91–93, 147–51
Berne Convention, 348–49
Board of Broadcast Governors, 164,
   219. *See also* CRTC
brand names, 107–8, 311, 329. *See also*
   copyright; intellectual property
   children and, 140, 142, 144
   coffee, 112–17
Brittain, Donald, 188
broadcasting. *See also* radio; rights;
   television
   Aboriginal peoples' (*see* Aboriginal
      peoples)
   digital-audio, 173
   journalism and, 128–30, 252–66

media, 128–30, 319–21
telecommunications *vs.*, 320–21
Broadcasting Act, 163, 164, 288, 295, 297, 299, 315
Broadcast Music Incorporated, 204–5
bulletin boards, 239, 243, 253–54
Bureau of Measurement, 129, 170

cable television, 220, 221–23, 225, 229
  Aboriginal programs and, 303–4, 306, 307
  convergence and (*see* convergence)
  copyright and, 347
Campbell, Kim, 392
Canadian Academy of Recording Arts and Sciences, 166
Canadian Alliance Party, 382
Canadian Association of Broadcasters, 167–68
Canadian Broadcasting Corporation. *See* CBC
Canadian Cable Television Association, 303
Canadian Film Development Corporation, 189–91, 192
Canadian Journal of Communication, 17, 55
Canadian Radio-television and Telecommunications Commission. *See* CRTC
Canadian Satellite Communications. *See* Cancom
Cancom, 297, 298
CanCon, 164–68, 171, 209, 219–21, 397–99
CanWest Global, 222, 226, 405
Caruso, Enrico, 200
CBC, 41, 394
  Aboriginal programs and, 298, 299, 303
  films and, 186, 191, 193

Internet and, 258
  radio and, 163–65, 169, 172
  television and, 217–19, 223
CDs, 167, 175, 210
censorship, 192, 245, 256, 279, 347
census, 122–23, 236
Charter of Rights and Freedoms, 364–65
chat rooms, 241, 242–43, 287
Chicago School, 13
children, 136–53
  advertising and, 140–47
  as consumers, 140–47, 205–7
  films and, 138–39, 144, 147–48, 187
  Internet and, 246
  media and, 137–41, 376
  music and, 139
  television and, 217, 218
  violence and, 136–40, 147–52
chip, 236
  V-, 151
Chomsky, Noam, 390
CHUM, 172, 231–32
Citytv, 222, 231–32
codes, 31–33, 88
  industry conduct and, 150–51, 372–73, 375, 386
coffee, 109–17
colour, 107–8
commissions. *See* CRTC; royal commissions
commodity
  coffee as, 109–13
  as exotic, 114, 115, 116
  media as, 384
  Mounties as, 398
  music as, 198–201
communication, 1–3
  audience and (*see* audience)
  codes and, 31–33, 88

culture and, 3, 35, 36–37, 39, 52–53, 68
developing countries and, 277–79
as a discipline, 54
experience and, 117
human migrations and (*see* diasporas)
industries (*see* industries)
privacy and, 368
satellites (*see* satellites)
science of, 50–51
social power and, 9, 10, 14, 16, 22
technologies (*see* technology)
theory of, 9
transnational, 273–89
communication studies
American, 48
Canadian, 15–22, 46–61
critical, 4–14
emergence of, 50–51
"founding fathers" of, 5
government and, 21, 48, 51, 54
in Quebec (*see* Quebec)
universities and (*see* universities)
communicators, 107
computers, 159, 235–49. *See also* Internet
applications and, 243–45, 256–59, 344–45
children and, 151
design of, 235–36
education and, 244–45
ethical issues and, 245–47, 354–56
history of, 253–56
journalism and, 252–66
laptop, 257
music and, 212
networks and, 236–40, 243–44
news gathering/dissemination and, 256–59
personal, 255

service and, 238–39
social uses of, 241–43
speed and, 237
voice and, 237
workplace and, 241–42, 246–47
conglomeration, 402
consumerism, 103
children and, 140–44, 205–7
coffee and (*see* coffee)
music and, 197, 205–8
control/ownership, 9, 41, 47, 226, 266, 280–82, 313, 326–32, 380–84, 402–7. *See also* convergence; globalization
communication, 201, 211, 273, 277–78
films and, 179–83, 186
music and, 198, 200, 206–13
radio and, 171–72
television and, 222, 223, 225, 231, 282, 284
convergence, 211, 256, 311–23, 325–28, 337–38, 402. *See also* globalization
cable television and, 317–21, 405–6
Canadian television and, 225–28
computers and, 237
CRTC and, 314, 316–18, 325–26, 328, 337, 407
government policy and, 385–87
journalism and, 335–37, 380–91, 406
media, 201
newspapers and, 254–56
radio and, 171
regulatory, 343
Copps, Sheila, 168, 392, 399
copyright, 197, 198, 201–5, 209, 213–14, 343–58
American, 348
Canadian, 347–48

defined, 344, 345–46
digital media and, 354–56
duration of, 352
fees and, 205
history of, 346–47
infringement of, 352–53
international, 276–77, 320, 348–50
licensing, 351, 352
mass media and, 353
royalties and, 198, 202, 351
crime
children and, 136, 138–40, 147
technology and, 139, 354–56,
369–70, 376
critical research, 4–8, 12–22
administrative research and, 4–8,
10–12
defining, 8–14
Crosby, Bing, 204
CRTC, 41, 164–66, 169, 170, 394
Aboriginal people and, 297–302,
304–5
commercial radio and, 171–72
convergence and (*see* convergence)
ethnic programming and, 288–89
Internet and, 173, 227, 240,
319–21, 355
television and, 220–22, 225, 226, 227
CTV, 219–20, 226, 227
cultural imperialism, 277–79, 398
cultural studies
British, 27–36
Canadian, 27, 36–43, 48
diasporas and, 284
sub-, 34–35
culture. *See also* coffee; diasporas;
hockey; toys
Aboriginal, 38, 295–301
American, 38–42, 46–47, 163,
216–17, 229, 398 (*see also*
globalization; *various media*)

brands and, 113
Canadian, 27, 36–43, 52–53,
397–407 (*see also* national
identity/sovereignty; Quebec)
children and, 136–39, 145–46
communication and, 3, 35, 36–37,
52–53
critical theory and, 13
government and, 37, 38, 39, 186,
397–401
industrialization of, 5, 145 (*see also*
industries)
information as, 53
Internet and, 333
mass, 90
music and, 139, 198–214
policy and (*see* government policy)
popular, 30–31, 40–42, 141, 207
popular *vs.* "high," 27, 28
radio and, 163, 164
regional, 40–41
society and, 36–37
television and, 216–17, 221–22
violence and, 149
Western, 111, 117, 278–79, 281–82
working-class, 28
cyberspace, 325–39. *See also* Internet

Daily Me, 264
databases
on-line, 254, 258
privacy and, 370–73, 375
Day, Stockwell, 388
DBS (direct broadcast satellite). *See*
satellites
demassification, 402
democracy, 264, 278, 326, 380, 398
privacy and, 366–68
dependency, 47, 54
Diana, Princess, 98, 256
diasporas, 272, 282–89

digital divide, 264, 281–82, 329–30
digital networks, 173, 237, 317–21
disc jockeys, 206
dominance/subordination, 32–33, 34
Drudge, Matt, 252

Edison, Thomas, 179, 199–200
elections, 381–82, 386, 390–91
Electronic Frontier Canada, 244
e-mail, 239, 241–42, 257
empirical approach, 11, 120–33
encoding/decoding, 31–33
entertainment, 329, 334–35
    children and, 141–46
    crime and, 139–40
    film as, 179–80
    music as, 198–201
entertainment experience, 102–3
environmentalism, 111
Ethernet, 236–37
ethics, 245–47, 337
European critical theory. *See* Frankfurt
    School
experience
    entertainment as, 102–3
    social, 110–13
eyetracking, 261

fair dealing/use, 345, 352–53, 354
Fairness and Accuracy in Reporting,
    389
Famous Players Canada, 181, 183, 185
Ferment in the Field, 7–8
Fessenden, Reginald, 161
films, 96–99
    Aboriginal people and, 182, 185–86
    audience and, 99, 101, 179, 185–86,
       193
    budgets and, 193
    Canadian, 179–94
    Candid Eye, 187–88

children and, 138–39, 144,
    147–48, 187
control of (*see* control/ownership)
diasporas and, 282
distribution of, 180–83, 185, 193,
    194
documentary, 180, 182–88
government and, 182, 191
India and, 282
"Mountie," 182
music and, 207
private-sector, 192–94
propoganda and, 180–81
Quebec and, 185, 187–92
quotas and, 183
sound and, 203
technology and, 194
television and, 186, 191, 193–94
flame, 241
Frankfurt School, 5, 6, 7, 13
freedom of information. *See* informa-
    tion, freedom of
Freenets, 243, 255
Frye, Northrop, 4, 15, 20
functionalism, 91, 93–95

globalization, 39–40, 199, 201,
    211–13, 272–83. *See also*
    convergence
copyright and, 343–58
diasporas and, 283–89
government policy and (*see* govern-
    ment policy)
government policy. *See also* CRTC
communication and, 37, 41, 54,
    55–56, 163–64, 185 (*see also*
    CRTC; regulations)
communication studies and, 21,
    48, 51, 54
culture and, 37–39, 38, 39, 47, 54–56,
    186, 240, 397–401, 399–401

film and, 180, 182, 183, 192–93
globalization and, 240–41, 272–73, 313–21 (*see also* convergence)
Internet and, 240–41, 315–21
media and, 380–95
northern television and, 296–300
privacy and, 367–68, 374–77
trade agreements and, 40, 272, 347, 349, 399–401
violence and, 150
welfare state and, 67, 68
Gramsci, Antonio, 7, 13, 34
Gregg, Alan, 213
Grierson, John, 15, 182, 183–86, 191

hegemony, 30–31, 384
ideology and, 34
Herman, Edward, 390
hockey, 120–28, 162
homelessness, 388–89
Homolka, Karla, 256
hypertext, 260, 265

iCraveTV.com, 227, 319, 355–56
identity
Canadian, 17–22, 40–41, 201, 209, 397–407
culture and, 35, 38, 39
ideological state apparatus, 30
ideology
culture and, 29–30, 33
hegemony and, 34
research and, 12, 13
indexicality, 259, 261
industries, 159–266, 314–23
coffee (*see* coffee)
computer, 235–49
conduct codes and, 150–51, 372–373, 375, 386
control/ownership (*see* control/ownership)

corporate interests and, 4, 21
cultural, 38–42, 198, 277, 397–407 (*see also various media*)
dot-com, 159
global (*see* convergence; globalization)
Internet, 235–49
licensing agreements and, 143–44, 403
monopolies and, 314, 316, 318, 322, 325
profits/revenues (*see* profits/revenues)
structure of, 201, 208, 211–14, 322, 326, 329, 402
information, 54, 380
copyright and (*see* copyright)
culture as, 53
freedom of, 277–79, 326–27, 334–37
globalization and, 272–73, 281–82, 398–99
Internet and, 252–66, 325, 326, 334–37
privacy and (*see* privacy)
Information Highway Advisory Council, 240, 314, 315–16, 326
Innis, Harold, 4, 15–16, 20, 46, 47
Instant World, 313, 325
intellectual property, 198, 201, 276, 280, 320, 343–47, 349
INTELSAT, 280–81
interactivity, 259–61
International Telegraph Union, 276–80, 281
Internet, 130–33, 235–49, 329–39. *See also* computers; globalization
advertising and, 130–33, 262–64
age and, 131
business/economics and, 241, 261–64
copyright and, 348, 354–56

diasporas and, 287–88
education/income and, 131 (*see also* digital divide)
ethical issues and, 245–47, 326
evolution of, 239–40, 255, 275–76
gender and, 131, 248
information highway and, 248–49
interactivity and, 259–61
joint ventures and, 259
journalism and, 252–66
literacy and, 248
mailing lists and, 242
music and, 197, 212, 214
news sites, 254–62
political process and, 248, 315–21
radio and, 169, 173–76
social uses of, 241–43
television and, 224, 225, 227, 229
Internet service providers, 331, 348, 354
intranet, 257

journalism, 329
audience research and, 128–30
broadcast, 257
convergence and (*see* convergence)
female politicians and, 392–93
Internet and, 252–66, 335–37
privacy and, 363
transparent, 260
Journal of Communication, 5, 7
Juno awards, 166

knowledge, 60–61
claims, 14
formation, 51
media and, 57, 113
as social construct, 46

labels. *See* brand names
LaMarsh, Judy, 392, 393
language

children and, 136–37
communication studies and, 54
meaning and, 1, 31–33, 87–89
media and, 31
Lazarsfeld, Paul, 5–7, 93–94
Liberal Party, 381–82

magazines, 128–29, 400
mailing lists, 242
Manufacturing Consent, 390
MAPL system, 166
Marconi, Guglielmo, 161, 275
marginality, 19–20
margin of error, 123–25
marketing, 107–8, 120–33.
See also advertising; commodity; consumerism
children, 140–47
coffee, 109–17
Internet and, 130–33, 331, 362
music, 213
technology and, 116–17, 213, 362
toys, 143–46
market share, 128–30, 331
Marxism, 5, 7, 13
construction of meaning and, 33
cultural studies and, 29–30, 34
mass, defined, 104
mass media, 1, 3, 107
codes and, 31–33
culture and, 27, 30–31, 39–42
institutions, 2–3, 48–50, 51, 56
(*see also* industries)
in Quebec, 66, 76–77
social power of, 30–31, 51
McLaren, Norman, 184, 185, 187
McLuhan, Marshall, 4, 15, 16, 20, 46, 47, 55
media. *See also various media*
advisers, 391
alternate, 394–95

audience and (*see* audience)

behaviour and, 5, 91–93, 98–101, 147–51

broadcast (*see* broadcasting)

Canadian, companies, 404–5

children and, 138–52

conglomeration, 402

content and, 3, 39, 40, 247, 330–37 (*see also* CanCon; radio; television)

control/ownership and (*see* control/ownership)

convergence (*see* convergence)

crime and, 137

cross-, 101–2, 212–13, 221, 225–26, 228

culture and, 27, 37–41, 70, 75–78, 145–46, 199, 211–13

ethnic/transnational, 284–89

industries (*see* globalization; industries)

integration of, 212–14, 225–26 (*see also* convergence)

mass (*see* mass media)

news coverage and, 387–92

new *vs.* old, 162, 226, 227, 247, 258, 311, 326

on-line (*see* Internet)

politics and, 380–95

polls, 120–30, 150, 301, 391–92

print (*see* magazines; newspapers)

protesters and, 385, 386, 389–90, 393

royal commissions and (*see* royal commissions)

social issues and, 382–83, 389–91

systems *vs.* effects, 52

technology and (*see* technology)

violence and, 93, 147–52

Media Monopoly, 403

MED-TV, 286

membership groups, 94

Memorandum, 188

messages, 94
  codes and, 31–33
  meaning and, 1, 87–89

methodologies and methods, 10–12

Milewski, Terry, 385

modernity, 2
  diasporas and, 284
  in Quebec, 65–67

Motion Picture Bureau, 182, 183, 184

movies. *See* films

MTV, 210

MuchMusic, 210, 224, 231, 232

music. *See also* sound recordings
  albums and, 207–8
  audience and (*see* audience)
  Canadian, 164–68, 170, 201, 209–10, 213–14 (*see also* CanCon)
  children and, 139
  control/ownership and (*see* control/ownership)
  distribution and, 206
  films and, 207
  genres/labels, 139, 203–7, 211–12
  Internet and, 173–75, 197, 212, 214
  live performance and, 208
  mass production and, 199–201
  packaging of, 207
  promotion of, 167–68, 171–72
  radio and, 161–62, 164–68, 170–76, 202–6, 209, 212
  recording (*see* sound recordings)
  research and, 5–6
  rights and (*see* copyright; rights)
  sales and, 208, 211
  technology and, 197–201, 205–14
  television and, 206–7, 212, 231
  trademarks and, 108
  videos, 210, 214

MusiquePlus, 210, 231

Napster, 97, 197, 198, 319, 320, 356
National Film Board, 183–89, 191–94
national identity/sovereignty, 17–22,
     40–41, 201, 209, 397–407
nationalism. *See* national identity/
     sovereignty
networks, 331–32
     computer, 236–40, 243–44, 252–55
     full-service, 314, 326
     radio, 206, 216, 218
news agencies, 274, 277–78, 285
newsgroups, 239, 242
newspapers, 95, 128–29, 329. *See also*
     journalism
     Aboriginal television and, 304–5
     ethnic, 288
     Internet and, 229, 247, 252,
          254–59, 264–66
     television and, 227
New World Information and
     Communication Order. *See*
     NWICO
Northern Broadcasting Policy,
     297–98
NWICO, 277–79, 281

objectivity, 11, 12
Office national du film, 185, 187, 189,
     191
Okeh Records, 203–4
Oliver, Bill, 182
opinion leaders, 94
organizational communication, 78

patents, 344
Pavlov, Ivan, 91
Payne Fund Studies, 147–48
"Peppergate," 385
piracy, 353, 354–56
plagiarism, 353
policy. *See* government policy

politics
     left-/right-wing, 381
     media and, 380–95
     news coverage and, 387–92
     women in, 392–93
polls, 120–30, 301, 391–92
     violence and, 150
pornography, 192, 245–46, 334, 361
positivist methods, 11
power. *See* social power
pragmatism, 13
privacy, 244, 246–47, 360–77
     definitions, 363–73
     democracy and, 366–68
     health care and, 376
     human rights and, 364–66, 370, 373
     information collection and, 370–73
     legislation, 374–77
     social values and, 369–70
profits/revenues
     children's market and, 142–44
     copyright and, 357–58
     entertainment products and, 398
     film and, 193
     hegemony and, 384
     music and, 202
     radio and, 172
     telecommunications and, 281
     television and, 219–20, 227–28
propoganda, 92, 390
     film and, 180–81, 184–85
protesters, 385, 386, 389–90, 393
public, 103–4
public opinion. *See* polls
public policy. *See* government policy

Quebec
     communication studies in, 47–50,
          54–56, 65–81
     culture and, 38
     films and, 185, 187–92

media in, 76–77
research in, 77–81
sociology courses in, 48

radio, 159, 161–77, 275, 405
    American, 163
    developing countries and, 279
    digital, 169, 173–74
    ethnic/transnational, 284, 288–89
    French-language, 165
    frequencies, 277
    future of, 176–77
    Internet and, 169, 173–76
    licensing, 161, 164–65, 169–70
    music and, 161–62, 164–68,
        170–76, 202–6, 209, 212
    newspapers and, 162
    pay-audio digital, 169, 173–74
    private/commercial, 163, 164, 169–72
    public, 163–65, 169, 177, 398
        (see also CBC)
    regulations and, 163–66, 169–72, 209
    station ownership, 171, 172
    types and formats, 169–70
Radio-Canada, 165, 169
railways
    film and, 179, 180
    radio and, 161–62
raves, 139
recordings. See sound recordings
regulations, 399. See also CRTC
    computer/Internet and, 240–41,
        332–37
    international, 276–79
    music (see CanCon)
    radio, 163–66, 169–72
    television, 142–43, 145, 219–23
religion, 18, 47–48, 66
research. See also theory
    administrative (see administrative
        research)

agendas, 56
apparatus, 65–66
children and, 136–44, 147–52
communication, 4–22
critical (see critical research)
effects, 147–52
ideological, 12
Internet use, 130–33, 175
market, 120–33
methodology/methods, 10–12
        (see also polls)
problems in, 9
propaganda and, 390
in Quebec (see Quebec)
scholarship, 17, 48, 73, 78–79
technology and, 248–49
rights, 373–74. See also copyright;
        intellectual property
    children's, 146
    communication and, 278–79
    human (see privacy)
    moral, 350
    music and, 201–2, 213–14
    property, 276–79
Royal Canadian Mounted Police,
        182, 398
royal commissions, 21, 48
    film and, 186, 192
    newspapers and, 405
    radio and, 163
    television and, 216–17
royalties. See copyright

Salon, 258, 262
satellites, 224–26, 253, 275, 280–81,
        286, 313, 326
    Aboriginal peoples and, 296–97
scientific method, 11
semiotics, 32
"Shawinigate," 385
signifier/signified, 32

Simpson, O.J., 98, 256

Slate, 258, 260–61, 262

social issues

    media coverage and, 382–83, 389–91

social power. *See also* dominance/
    subordination

    communication and, 9, 10, 14, 16,
      50–51

    cultural studies and, 36

    Internet and, 241–44

    mass media and, 30–31, 51

social researchers, 121

society

    culture, media, and, 36–37

    mass, 91–92

    organization of, 2, 50–51

sound recordings, 168, 197–214.
      See also music

    Canadian, 209–10

    copyright and, 353, 354, 355, 356

    digital, 210–12

    history of, 199–211

    technology and, 197–203, 206–7,
      210–14

specialty channels, 222, 224, 226,
      228–29, 231, 407

    Aboriginal programs and, 303–4,
      306

    diasporas and, 275, 285–89

speech, freedom of, 246, 326

speech programs, 59

Spry, Graham, 15, 162, 398

Starbucks, 107–17

"streamies," 175

surveillance, 246–47, 333, 336, 361–68

surveys. *See* polls

technology, 159–60, 329. *See also*
    various media

    broadband, 175, 312, 318–20, 323,
      337–38

convergence and (*see* convergence)

crime and, 139, 197, 354–56,
    369–70, 376

cultural imperialism and, 277–79

diasporas and, 284–89

digital, 169, 173–74, 210–12, 225,
    237, 286

education and, 244–45

information, 53

literacy and, 248

marketing and, 116–17, 213, 362

modernization and, 16

privacy and, 361–66

in Quebec, 76, 78, 210, 228

research and, 130–33, 248–49

satellite (*see* satellites)

surveillance and (*see* surveillance)

wireless, 263, 274–75

telecommunications, 275–77, 314–15,
    337–38

    broadcasting *vs.*, 320–21

    international, 279–83

Telecommunications Act, 164

Telefilm Canada, 191, 193–94, 223

telegraph, 274, 312

telephones/telephony, 274–75, 281,
    312, 315, 318

teletext, 254–55, 313

television, 93, 96–97, 275

    Aboriginal peoples and, 295–308

    advertising and (*see* advertising)

    American, 216–22, 229

    audience and (*see* audience)

    cable (*see* cable television)

    Canadian, 186, 216–33

    children and, 141–44

    content quotas, 219–21

    developing countries and, 279

    diasporas and, 282

    digital channels and, 224, 225, 229,
      286, 287–88

ethnic/transnational, 284–87, 289
exports, 229, 230, 285–87
films and, 186, 191, 193–94
genres, 230
Hollywood and, 218, 221
independent productions and,
    222–24, 226
Internet and, 224, 227, 247, 252,
    254, 256, 258
music and, 206–7, 210, 231
private stations and, 217, 218–21
production, 218–20, 222–24, 226
programming and, 100, 217–18,
    228, 328
in Quebec, 76–77
ratings systems, 150–51
reality, 230
regulations, 142–43, 145, 218–21,
    223
revenues and, 227–28
satellite (*see* satellites)
specialty channels and (*see* specialty
    channels)
sports and, 230–31
tax credits and, 223, 224, 397
violence on (*see* violence)
Television Northern Canada
    (TVNC), 299–304
theory. *See also* Chicago School;
    Frankfurt School; research
behaviourist, 91–93, 147–51
communication, 9
critical, and culture, 13, 37
critical research and, 6, 13–14, 22
feminist, 388
functionalist, 91, 93–95
linguistic, 32
Marxist (*see* Marxism)
political economy, 48, 52, 57, 58,
    141–44, 152, 384, 390
social, 6, 14

stimulus-response, 91–93, 148
strong media/weak minds, 93
think tanks, 389
Tin Pan Alley, 199, 200, 205
toys, 143–46
trade agreements. *See under* government
    policy
trademarks, 107–8, 344. *See also* brand
    names
transistor, 236

Understanding Media, 55
UNESCO. *See* United Nations
Unique Selling Proposition, 114
United Nations, 277–79, 282, 364
Universal Copyright Convention,
    348
Universal Declaration of Human
    Rights, 364
universities, 47–49, 51, 54, 59, 60,
    67–68
    Quebec, 67–68, 71–75

values, 380
    American (*see* culture, American)
    Canadian scholarship and, 18
    privacy and, 369–70
    research and, 12–13
    television and, 100
vaudeville, 199
V-chips, 151
VCRs, 96, 228, 285
videos
    computers and, 237
    music, 210
    on-demand, 320–21
    personal recorders and, 228
    surveillance and, 246
videotex, 254–55
violence, 93
    children and, 136–40, 147–52

culture and, 149
   government policy and, 150
   measuring, 148–50, 367

walled garden, 335–36
Web sites. *See* Internet
wire services, 274
World Intellectual Property
   Organization, 280

World Trade Organization, 272, 273,
   280, 400–1

youth. *See* children

Znaimer, Moses, 231, 232